COMPUTERIZED PSYCHOLOGICAL ASSESSMENT

COMPUTERIZED PSYCHOLOGICAL ASSESSMENT

A PRACTITIONER'S GUIDE

JAMES N. BUTCHER

EDITOR

BASIC BOOKS, INC., PUBLISHERS

NEW YORK

Library of Congress Cataloging-in-Publication Data

Computerized psychological assessment.

Includes bibliographies and index.
1. Psychological tests—Data processing.
2. Psychodiagnostics—Data processing. 3. Microcomputers.
I. Butcher, James Neal, 1933- . [DNLM: 1. Computers.
2. Diagnosis, Computer Assisted. 3. Personality Assessment—instrumentation. 4. Psychological Tests—instrumentation. BF 176 C738]
BF176.2.C66 1987 150'.28'7 86-47735
ISBN 0-465-01348-1

Printed in the United States of America
Designed by Vincent Torre
87 88 89 90 RRD 9 8 7 6 5 4 3 2 1

In memory of

Neal Glynne Butcher

(1965–1985)

CONTENTS

CONTRIBUTORS

KENNETH M. ADAMS, PH.D.
Chief Psychologist, Henry Ford Hospital; and Clinical Professor, Department of Psychiatry, University of Michigan, Detroit, Michigan.

BARBARA A. ALLEN, M.A.
Research Associate, Addiction Research Foundation, Toronto, Ontario, Canada.

WILLIAM E. BELL, M.S.
Mental Health Applications Coordinator, Veterans Administration Medical Center; and Programmer Analyst, University of Texas Health Science Center, Dallas, Texas.

MASSIMO BIONDI, M.D.
Associate Professor, Psychiatric Clinic, University of Rome, Rome, Italy.

JAMES N. BUTCHER, PH.D.
Professor, Department of Psychology, University of Minnesota, Minneapolis, Minnesota.

JOHN E. EXNER, JR., PH.D.
Executive Director, Rorschach Workshops, Asheville, North Carolina.

ALLAN S. FINKELSTEIN, PH.D.
Clinical Psychologist, Psychology Service, and Clinical Instructor, Department of Psychology, Veterans Administration Medical Center, Albany, New York.

D. ROBERT FOWLER, M.D.
Chief, Psychiatry Service, Veterans Administration Medical Center; and Professor, Department of Psychiatry, University of Texas Health Science Center, Dallas, Texas.

RAYMOND D. FOWLER, PH.D.
Professor Emeritus, Department of Psychology, University of Alabama, Tuscaloosa, Alabama; and Senior Consultant, National Computer Systems, Washington, D.C.

RONALD A. GIANNETTI, PH.D.
Professor, Department of Psychiatry and Behavioral Sciences, Eastern Virginia Medical School; and Chairman, Virginia Consortium for Professional Psychology, Norfolk, Virginia.

CHARLES J. GOLDEN, PH.D.
Professor, Medical Psychology, University of Nebraska Medical Center, Omaha, Nebraska.

JO-IDA C. HANSEN, PH.D.
Professor, Department of Psychology, and Director, Center for Interest Measurement Research, University of Minnesota, Minneapolis, Minnesota.

ROBERT K. HEATON, PH.D.
Associate Professor, Department of Psychiatry, University of Colorado, Denver, Colorado.

BONNIE ITZIG, M.S.
Research Associate, University of Texas Health Sciences Center, Dallas, Texas.

SAMUEL KARSON, PH.D.
School of Psychology, Florida Institute of Technology, Melbourne, Florida.

LAURA S. KELLER, B.A.
Research Associate, Assessment Systems Corporation, St. Paul, Minnesota.

SAMUEL E. KRUG, PH.D.
President and Chairman, MetriTech, Inc., Champaign, Illinois.

DAVID LACHAR, PH.D.
Director, Psychology and Clinical Psychology Residency Program, Institute of Behavioral Medicine, Good Samaritan Medical Center, Phoenix, Arizona; and Adjunct Professor, Arizona State University, Tempe, Arizona.

KEVIN L. MORELAND, PH.D.
Product Development Manager, National Computer Systems, Professional Assessment Services Division; and Clinical Assistant Professor, Department of Psychology, University of Minnesota, Minneapolis, Minnesota.

JERRY W. O'DELL, PH.D.
Department of Psychology, Eastern Michigan University, Ypsilanti, Michigan.

PAOLO PANCHERI, PH.D.
Full Professor of Psychiatry, Medical Faculty, Psychiatric Clinic, University of Rome, Rome, Italy.

WALTER E. PENK, PH.D.
Associate Professor, Department of Psychiatry, Tufts University School of Medicine; and Research Psychologist, Veterans Administration Medical Center, Boston, Massachusetts.

HARVEY A. SKINNER, PH.D.
Senior Scientist, Addiction Research Foundation; and Professor, Department of Preventive Medicine and Biostatistics, University of Toronto, Toronto, Ontario, Canada.

STEVEN J. STEIN, PH.D.
Coordinator of Research, Thistletown Regional Centre for Children and Adolescents; and Assistant Professor, Department of Psychiatry, University of Toronto, Toronto, Ontario, Canada.

C. DAVID VALE, PH.D.
President, Assessment Systems Corporation, St. Paul, Minnesota.

DAVID J. WEISS, PH.D.
Professor of Psychology and Director, Psychometric Methods Program, University of Minnesota, Minneapolis, Minnesota.

FOREWORD

My colleague Jim Butcher, in a recent "get-acquainted" session of faculty and new clinical students, alluded to this excellent volume as giving them advance notice of what psychological assessment will look like in the year 2000. To say that confidently, like editing this book, takes not only foresight and cognitive flexibility but considerable courage. (Being an unreconstructed believer in traits, I conjecture this relates to Jim's being a flier and a therapist interested in crisis intervention.) One may anticipate resistance to some of the book's ideas, partly ideological and partly Luddite; but no clinical psychologist or psychiatrist, whether mainly a teacher or practitioner, can afford to remain ignorant of the matters here explained. It would be strange, and embarrassing, if clinical psychologists, supposedly sophisticated methodologically and quantitatively trained, were to lag behind internal medicine, investment analysis, and factory operations control in accepting the computer revolution.

The authors invited to contribute are of the highest competence in their areas of expertise, which range widely over such diverse domains as adaptive testing of abilities, Rorschach interpretation, lifestyle assessment using microcomputers, and the automated problem-rating interview. (It is rash to dogmatize about "what computers can't do," and no clinician who reads this volume openmindedly will be caught making that mistake.) The expositions are scrupulously fair-minded, the disadvantages honestly faced, problems awaiting solutions are mentioned, and costs and benefits are weighed. As would be expected (traits again!) from psychologists knowledgeable in this domain, the writing is concise, rationally sequenced, and beautifully *clear*. These are not tendentious, woolgathering, or muddle-headed scholars. A useful appendix lists commercially available computerized psychological services, with addresses and telephone numbers.

Inviting me to write this foreword, Dr. Butcher said, "After all, it seems appropriate that the fellow who started all this should do the honors." He did not mean, of course, that Paul Meehl "started" computerization of psychological tests, ratings, or life history data—a technology in which I claim no expertise. Setting aside the use of computers in administering, storing, retrieving, norming, and communicating psychometric or historical data, the point of his remark was my modest contribution, for better or worse, to the *psychological interpretation* of multivariate data to diagnosis and prediction in psychopathology. The first validity study of MMPI profile patterns, as contrasted with research presenting significance tests of single scales against the named diagnostic rubrics, was my article in Paterson's *Journal of Applied Psychology* (1946). Rough, semi-objective ("clerical") pattern criteria were employed, and subsequently improved by my doctoral candidate Donald R. Peterson. My Midwestern Psychological Association Presidential address, "Wanted—a good cookbook" (1956), showing the superiority of actuarially-derived Q-sort personality descriptions to the conventional "clinical eyeballing" of profiles, inspired Marks and Seeman, Gilberstadt and Duker, Caldwell, and others to work along these lines. This computerization (adumbrated theoretically in my book *Clinical vs. statistical prediction* [1954]) remains today the subject of intense controversy, going beyond statistical-empirical questions to deep issues of inductive logic, epistemology, welfare economics, and ethics. The clinical psychologist's professional self-image is also involved in several ways (*e.g.*, Am I merely an inaccurate computer? Was my theoretical education irrelevant? How about technological unemployment?).

The only disappointing thing about this book reflects the present state of the art rather than deficiencies in editor or authors. We need to know more than we do about the concurrent, predictive, and construct validity of actuarial interpretations; the relative merits of the available competitors; validity generalization over describable clinical populations (demographic, diagnostic, criterial); feasible procedures for integrating (including amending?) "the best actuarial interpretation of Test T" with other data; the comparative efficacy of linear and configural systems; and—a question I discuss in Dr. Butcher's *Objective personality assessment* (1972)—how to identify individual current cases where the "statistically best" description is almost certainly wrong (*e.g.*, a Marks-Seeman curve type whose trait characterization simply does not "fit" the individual before us). One hopes that this volume will stimulate investigators to give these difficult matters the high priority they deserve, both for their theoretical interest and their importance in patient care.

—PAUL E. MEEHL
Minneapolis, September 29, 1986

PREFACE

Clinical practice in the mental health field is currently undergoing a dramatic revolution as computer technology is being incorporated in all phases of activity at an ever-increasing rate. Computers are being widely used not only in the business operation of clinical practice, such as in keeping patient records or billing, but in many areas of patient care as well. Many mental health facilities and independent practitioners are finding more practical applications for computers in their clinical service, ranging from computer-assisted data collection; administration, scoring, and interpretation of psychological tests; computer-assisted interview and computer-derived report generation; and even in heretofore "sacred" areas of clinical practice of clinical intervention such as cognitive retraining, stress management, and psychotherapy.

The rate at which computers are being adopted to clinical settings is astounding and stands as one of the most significant developments to appear in clinical practice over the past quarter century.

This volume is devoted to one of the earliest and most active computer applications in the mental health field—psychological assessment. Personality assessment, beginning with the pioneering effort at the Mayo Clinic in the early 1960s with the Minnesota Multiphasic Personality Inventory, has continued to be the center of computerized assessment, although, as the scope of this volume attests, a broad range of other assessment techniques are now being automated.

In the past ten years the advent and ready availability of microcomputers has led to a great increase in computerization of psychological assessment procedures. The broad acceptance of computers in clinical settings and the accelerating pace of technological development has set the stage for even more pervasive changes in the future. It is likely that by the turn of the twenty-first century, practitioners in mental health centers and in independent practice will rely even more heavily on computers.

The stimulus for this volume was threefold: We wanted to develop a "handbook" on computerized psychological assessment that addressed several timely issues concerning the introduction of computer technology into direct patient services. Several chapters address important issues related to the new technology: the chapters by Samuel E. Krug, Kevin Moreland, Raymond D. Fowler, C. David Vale and Laura S. Keller, and my own provide timely discussions on issues surrounding computerized assessment. Our second major goal in selecting contributors to this book was to review a broad range of assessment techniques. For breadth, we sought chapters from individuals who have made substantial contributions to the computer assessment field. Paolo Pancheri and Massimo Biondi describe the fifteen-year program involving clinical application of computers at the Institute of Psychiatry at the University of Rome; and a number of authors of widely used or promising new interpretation programs are represented: D. Robert Fowler, Allan Finkelstein, Walter Penk, William Bell, and Bonnie Itzig describe the DPRI; Barbara Allen and Harvey A. Skinner discuss the Lifestyle Assessment; Ronald A. Gianetti describes his GOLPH; Steven J. Stein discusses the DICA; Samuel Karson and Jerry W. O'Dell describe the 16 PF; John E. Exner, Jr. details the Rorschach; David Lachar provides information on the Personality Inventory for Children; Jo-Ida C. Hansen describes work with the SVIB; David J. Weiss and C. David Vale describe the Adaptive Ability Test; Charles J. Golden provides details on the Luria-Nebraska; and Kenneth M. Adams and Robert K. Heaton describe recent work in the area of cognitive and ability assessment.

A final goal was to include two sources of information about computerized assessment that would be of value to interested practitioners: an alphabetized listing and description of a number of available computer systems and a reprint of the American Psychological Association's newly adopted Guidelines of Computerized Psychological Assessment.

I wish to thank Karen Gayda for her assistance in cataloging and indexing the information on computer assessment services.

—James N. Butcher

PART I

INTRODUCTION TO COMPUTER APPLICATIONS IN CLINICAL SETTINGS

The test results in this book are factually accurate, but all names and identifying characteristics in the case presentations have been changed. Many of the cases represent common sets of symptoms, rather than the story of any specific individual.

1

The Use of Computers in Psychological Assessment: An Overview of Practices and Issues

James N. Butcher

Computer applications in psychology have been rapidly increasing over the past ten years. Almost every area finds itself immersed in important, novel computer applications, such as monitoring physiological measures, retraining stroke patients, developing information retrieval systems, psychological test scoring and interpretation, and even interviewing and psychological treatment, which are altering the way psychologists function.

The field of psychological assessment, the focus of this volume, was a proving ground for automated technology and computer applications in psychology. It was here that the electronic computer was first welcomed in applied psychology, and here lie the most rapidly developing applications and the greatest progress toward bringing the psychologist into contact with this expanding technology.

Psychological Assessment as an Activity That Can Be Automated

Computerized psychological testing began with the routine scoring of item responses. The early simple use of machine scoring procedures soon gave way to more ambitious efforts at automating interpretive activities. The computerized interpretation of psychological tests has been in existence for almost twenty-five years. The procedures currently being automated, such as the Rorschach and the Halstead-Reitan Battery, far exceed in technical complexity the early computer applications involving true-false personality inventories.

The following scenario may have seemed at one time like a vision of the twenty-first century:

The patient is ushered into a well-lighted, comfortable cubicle, seated in front of a video screen, and given brief instruction on the procedures that are to be followed. Left alone, the patient begins to interact with the machine—viewing questions and other visual stimuli on the screen, making decisions, providing judgments, answering questions, and so on, as the machine, from its own memory bank, determines what questions to ask and how to evaluate the patient's responses. After the testing session is complete and as the patient is ushered into the next phase of hospitalization, the testing machine quietly and efficiently prints out a thorough objective evaluation and provides some tentative guidelines as to the nature, extent, and likely course of the patient's problems and the most potentially effective treatment approaches that might be taken to remedy them.

This is not a scene from the year 2001 but rather one from a contemporary clinical facility. At present, a number of sophisticated computer-assisted psychological testing programs are available, covering a wide range of psychological procedures, to evaluate patients over a range of psychological attributes. The future is actually here as far as computer-based testing goes.

This volume provides a state-of-the-art summary of this rapidly growing field of computerized clinical assessment methods. The contributors were chosen for their extensive work in the areas represented, or because of their special expertise and perspective in evaluating the field of automated assessment. The volume introduces the reader to the most widely used and promising psychological assessment approaches, and provides some historical perspective on computer applications in the assessment field. In addition, it provides an overview of some contemporary developments in several fields of computerized assessment, including diagnostic interviewing, behavior rating, neuropsychological measurement, adaptive ability measurement, and personality assessment. It presents issues and problems involved in the use of computer-based assessment programs. It discusses the appropriateness of using computer-based psychological testing for assessing complex human behavior and explores problems and limitations of this measurement approach. Finally, it evaluates future directions computer-based psychological assessment is likely to take.

Predictions about the form and content of clinical psychological assessment typically underestimate the changes that are occurring. Clinical practitioners today are incorporating computer technology into their practice with such rapidity and ease that it is impossible to predict what clinical practice will be like in ten years. It is clear, however, that we are only beginning to view the possibilities in store for the clinical practitioner in automating his or her psychological practice in the future.

Advantages and Disadvantages of Computerized Psychological Assessment

The electronic computer, as an aid to psychological assessment, is here to stay. It is no longer a novel toy or a curiosity. Computerized assessment results and reports are working tools for the clinician to use to advantage when making clinical decisions.

There are some clear advantages, and some disadvantages, in using computerized tests in addition to our clinically administered or interpreted procedures.

ADVANTAGES

Objectivity. Computer-based reports are not subject to interpreter bias as are clinically generated conclusions. Once the test rules are programmed, they are automatically applied to specified cases regardless of extraneous circumstances.

Use as an "Outside Opinion." Computerized psychological reports can serve as objective opinion in forensic settings. Automated reports can have special significance in court hearings since they can be viewed as "untouched by human hands" and generally free of subjective bias.

Rapid Turnaround. Computerized reports can be turned around quickly, eliminating the delays that frequently occur in a busy clinical practice.

Cost Effectiveness. Computer-scored and interpreted psychological procedures cost considerably less than those produced by human effort.

Reliability. The computer seldom has an off day as human test interpreters do. Consequently, the product is the same no matter how many times the answer sheets are processed by the machine.

DISADVANTAGES

The Question of Excessive Generality. Computer reports have been criticized as being *too general* and not tailored specifically enough to the individual patient. One of the major criticisms raised by Matarazzo (1986) in his critique of computerized psychological assessment involved its reliance upon "modal" descriptions. The use of well-established empirical correlates as *prototypes* for describing clinical cases is a common approach in personality assessment (Fowler and Butcher, 1986; Meehl, 1954; see also chapter 10). The actuarial approach is truly at the heart of most automated personality assessment systems and may be viewed as a strength rather than as a flaw. The most valid computerized reports are those that most closely match the researched prototype. The criticism of "excessive generality," or what has been described as the "Aunt Fanny" type of psychological report (a report that says everything that could be true about anyone), is more pertinent to procedures in which the patient descriptions are based on insufficient empirical research. That is, the excessively general report is most often found when a computer-based interpretive report is marketed prior to an accumulation of valid descriptors for the instrument on which it is based. The narrative reports consequently tend to include numerous highly general statements that could apply to anyone. Psychological interpretation procedures vary in the amount of actual research data that support them. Practitioners should be aware of the "data vacuum" for some tests and should insist on documentation of empirical validity prior to subscribing to a test-interpretation service.

Potential for Misuse. The potential for misuse of computerized psychological reports is possibly greater than for clinically derived reports. The greater abuse potential may come, in part, from the computerized reports' wide availability and mass production. Human beings also tend to uncritically accept statements coming from a computer as more factual than statements coming from reports written by people. As with any clinical data on patients, access control of computerized reports needs to be carefully maintained.

Form Equivalence. Computer system developers need to ensure that sufficient research has been completed to establish that the computer-administered tests are equivalent to paper-and-pencil tests and produce essentially the same results. A clinician needs to evaluate this factor before adopting computer-administered psychological tests.

Clinician Start-up Time. Some computerized psychological testing applications may require the clinician to take time away from practice initially in order to become familiar with computer utilization. However, this initial time investment will pay off in the long run.

Confusing Abundance of Packages. The myriad of computers and computer software packages available is mind boggling, making it hard for clinicians to decide which system or software package is best for their setting. Fortunately, there are already some excellent workshops to introduce the clinician to computer utilization. Readers interested in the wide range of clinical assessment techniques available should consult the alphabetized listing and description of computerized psychological tests in appendix A of this volume, or the more extensive descriptions of "psychware" described by Krug (1984).

Issues Specific to the Use of Automated Technology in Psychological Assessment

A number of issues recur throughout this book that affect or at least visibly bear on each topic in some way. Some have lingered since the early days of psychological assessment by computer. Others, perhaps no less intransigent, have become more prominent in the last few years as computer applications have increased and the technology has advanced.

LINGERING ISSUES

Several issues persist even though they were addressed, with recommendations for dealing with them, in the 1966 American Psychological Association (APA) Guidelines on Computerized Testing. These issues are ennumerated in the following pages. They are problems that continue to haunt us as we approach the second quarter century of automated psychological assessment. In any case, new guidelines now exist: *Guidelines for Computer-Based Tests and Interpretations,* developed by the Committee on Professional Standards (COPS) and the Committee on Psychological Tests and Assessment and accepted by the APA Council of Representatives in 1986. (These guidelines are reproduced in appendix B of this volume.)

WHO SHALL HAVE ACCESS TO AUTOMATED REPORTS?

There is great potential for abuse when psychological tests are placed in the hands of individuals untrained or uninformed about their appropriate use—for example, if untrained people are given access to psychological testing services. Although most computerized testing services are advertised as professional-to-professional consultation services, some reporting services target audiences, such as personnel managers or clients themselves, that do not have the requisite background to interpret the tests adequately. The potential for abuse is also great when psychological test results are provided without supervision to other professionals, such as attorneys, chiropractors, and social workers who are untrained in psychological testing theory and test applications.* It appears that, in practice, the targeted audience for psychological testing services may have broadened considerably in recent years without the APA changing its stated policy about test usership. This problem of nonprofessionals having access to psychological test results is compounded when commercial organizations market and provide psychological testing services without sufficient professional consultation to commercial customers. For example, after the death of one psychologist who had developed a computer assessment system, his interpretation programs were taken over by computer analysts who continued to provide services without professional psychological consultation. Where no psychologists are involved in monitoring the testing service, APA ethical guidelines are of no practical value in controlling test abuses.

Another problem that occurs, and may be considered "out of the hands" of

* A frequent question about test access is whether psychiatrists should have direct access to computerized reports. It should be remembered that many psychiatrists have substantial knowledge about psychological testing. In fact, several major assessment procedures were developed (in part) by medical doctors, including the Rorschach, the Thematic Apperception Test, the Bender-Gestalt test, the Beck Depression Inventory, the Zung scale, the Diagnostic Interview Schedule, and the Minnesota Multiphasic Personality Inventory (MMPI), to mention only a few.

psychologists, is that of psychological test reports and test material being placed in the patient's file and subsequently read and utilized by "unqualified" professionals. Many professionals untrained in psychological testing or even nonprofessionals have access to patient charts. In such instances any psychological report with its "interesting" descriptions may be dwelt upon. Computerized reports are often of particular interest because they may appear to the reader to be more "scientific" and objective than traditional psychological reports. Psychologists working in settings where general access to patient charts is the rule might consider alternative filing methods to prevent this problem from occurring.

CONTINUING QUESTIONS ABOUT TEST VALIDATION

What are acceptable criteria of validity for automated reports? Actually this problem has two parts: validation of the test itself and validation of the automated reports from which the protocols are derived. With regard to the first point, some test publishers market psychological tests without sufficient developmental research. Test publishers who follow APA standards for psychological testing assume some responsibility for ensuring that only valid tests are marketed and made commercially available through a test-scoring service. However, these standards appear to have been eroded in recent years. With more psychological tests being computerized, there is a greater demand for new and specialized measures of psychological attributes. To meet this demand some publishers have rushed to make available various computer versions of tests, sometimes without sufficient test validation studies. The unwary test-scoring service customer may well find that the new, flashy test to measure trait *y* or psychological characteristic *x* may not have been cross-validated or even initially validated sufficiently to meet minimum test publication standards. This problem has increased in recent years and may, in the long run, prove detrimental to the psychological testing field.

Why do some professional psychologists continue to use tests or computer reports of poorly crafted tests in spite of their lack of demonstrated validity? Perhaps they have fallen victim to a false belief that "anything that comes out of a computer is scientific and must be believed"! It is important for the clinician to review the test manual, documentation, and the computerized report *before* using computerized psychological tests.

With regard to validation of automated reports, can validity of a computer-based report be assumed simply because the computer-generated reports are based on test scores or indices that have been shown to be valid? Most computerized systems based on the MMPI or Sixteen Personality Factor Questionnaire (16 PF) are predicated on this assumption. There may be sufficient "generalization validity" from established psychological tests to warrant their being considered "valid" when acceptable interpretations are automated. For example, an IQ score of 105 on the Wechsler Adult Intelligence Scale-Revised means the same thing (intellectual functioning within the average range of intelligence) when interpreted by a computer as when interpreted by an individual tester. The important question to be asked in this instance is how closely the interpretive reports match the established test correlates that have been previously validated. The potential report user should sample the outputs from the prospective computerized testing service before placing great reliance on the products. One way of ensuring adequacy is to run through several known cases and contrast the output provided by the computer with what is known about the case from a clinical interpretation of the test.

WHO SHALL PROVIDE THE STANDARDS FOR COMPUTER TEST APPLICATIONS?

Should it be the test publishers, the test users, the APA? At present, there are few uniform standards guiding computer test use. The original guidelines accepted by the APA Council in 1966 have gotten buried to some extent, and some current users may actually be unaware of their existence. Recently the APA established new guidelines for computer-based tests and interpretations (see appendix B) aimed at providing standards for test manufacturers and scoring services. These guidelines, if followed, should go a long way toward ensuring quality control over computerized psychological testing.

Who has the clinical and legal responsibility for a diagnostic study? What role does an automated report play in a diagnostic study? As previously noted, the acceptable standard for computer-based reports is that they are professional-to-professional consultations. The computer service or microdisk library contains the relevant test inferences, correlates, and so forth, for the test scores and indices. The specific information provided by the service on the individual case is a summary of the "most likely" test correlates for the individual in question. In this way the computer service simply serves as a memory or a "look-up table" for the clinician. The final arbiter of the accuracy and adequacy of the computer-based report (according to APA Guidelines) is the psychologist who receives the report. It is he or she who must decide if the report is acceptable in the individual patient's case.

Increasingly, however, computer-based reports are being viewed as an objective, outside opinion for some purposes. For example, they are being more accepted in forensic cases as valuable diagnostic testimony (Ziskin, 1980) since they may be viewed as "unbiased" sources of interpretive information and therefore a potentially more credible witness than reports generated by clinicians, who are considered to be more subjective. Such use of computerized reports assumes, however, that a trained clinician verifies the appropriateness of the computer-based report and testifies as to its validity.

NEW ISSUES

In addition to the lingering issues just mentioned, some new and unresolved issues have emerged as computer technology has increased the range of administration and scoring formats and as computer-clinical applications have proliferated.

CAN COMPUTERS BE PROGRAMMED TO TAILOR-MAKE PERSONALITY TESTS?

An article by Weiss (1985) documents the use of adaptive, or branched, ability testing. A technical issue that is likely to become the focus of computer-based personality testing involves computer-adapted item administration of personality test items (Butcher, Keller, and Bacon, 1985). At present, most personality test administration done by computer involves the presentation of *all* items to all subjects. This rigid format is required because of the paucity of psychological test data on *how* to branch personality items so that a particular person is given only those items necessary for his or her evaluation. An article by Butcher, Keller, and Bacon (1985) concludes that progress in this direction must be made if personality assessment by electronic computer is to realize its maximum potential.

LIMITS OF PSYCHOTECHNOLOGY

One problem facing assessment psychology in the computer age involves the disparity between computer technology and the available psychological technology. Recent electronic computer advances have made it possible for us to have numerous response formats, highly complex scoring patterns, and integrated interpretive programs in psychological assessment. For example, technically speaking, with existing computers we could administer virtually any psychological test stimuli to our patient, monitor and record a large number of physiological states, score and interpret interviews and test data, and prepare an integrated psychological and physiological report on the patient. Unfortunately, there is a paucity of psychological information available to program into computer systems. Very few psychological tests have enough substantial foundation of valid empirical information on which to base generalizable test inferences. There have been several instances in which scoring and interpretation services have been made available to the public without a single validation study. Such marketing of unvalidated psychological tests is, of course, questionable and reflects a commercialism that appears to substitute for sound psychology. This problem of premature computer system development will probably increase in the future as the demand for clinical products runs high and as computer software developers generate more sophisticated test packages. Even unproven test interpretations can look attractive when they are generated by a computer. It is hoped that the guidelines for computerized psychological tests (see appendix B) will reduce the problems discussed here.

Of course, some psychological assessment procedures may not require as extensive validation research as do psychological tests. Procedures such as diagnostic interviewing, patient information systems, history, bio-data, and so forth, are typically interpreted on the basis of face validity. These sources of personal data are summarized as content themes or, in the case of a diagnostic interviewing schedule, follow a sequence of questions to arrive at a particular classification.

CAN COMPUTERS PRODUCE TOTALLY INTEGRATED PSYCHOLOGICAL REPORTS?

If so, what impact will this development have on psychological diagnosis in the future? Will the computer effectively replace the integrating function of the psychological diagnostician?

Computer test specialists have frequently noted the desire on the part of some computer services and consumers for a fully computerized diagnostic report. The idea is to have a computer program that will combine the results of diverse psychological tests, such as interview information, intelligence tests, and specific personality measures, and synthesize them into a full diagnostic report on the patient. Currently available computer technology clearly would make this sort of integrating task feasible. However, the relative lag in psychotechnology probably does not permit very sophisticated syntheses of psychological test results at this time. The development of valid psychological measures has lagged behind the rapid innovations in computer technology, and research on combining various psychological measures is rudimentary at best. Yet there is a great demand for new or expanded test applications involving combined psychological measures. (This demand appears to come more from professionals, such as psychiatrists, social workers, and psychologists, who are not trained in testing but who are interested in obtaining diagnostic information from psychological testing.) The automated "integrated report," of course, is a direct threat to clinicians who perform assessment activities because it has the potential of making the human diagnostician unnecessary. As interest in developing integrated clinical diagnostic reports broadens, more research on system adequacy will be stimulated, and, no doubt, more intense dialogue will be generated on the appropriateness of machines to perform what is believed by some to be an essentially human activity.

QUALITY CONTROL OF COMPUTERIZED SYSTEMS

Since computer programming skills have become rather commonplace, it is relatively easy for a clinical institution to obtain, or for an individual clinician to write, a program that will score or interpret some psychological tests to run on a microcomputer. However, many of the "home-built" interpretive packages suffer from problems of limited perspective, lack of sufficient review of available literature, use of inappropriate norms, failure to note particular psychometric problems inherent in some test procedures, programming of inaccurate or out-of-date information, and so forth, that result in quality-control problems. How can potential test users become acquainted with the characteristics of a particular piece of software or interpretive program before investing money and time and jeopardizing clinical patient information? Clearer standards for developing and marketing computer assessment software to score and interpret psychological tests need to be established if the quality of computer-based psychological assessment is to be ensured.

CONTROL OF ACCESS TO TEST SCORING CAPABILITY

The policy of ensuring the qualifications of test users has been eroded in recent years. It has been possible, for example, for anyone (even nonpsychologists) to purchase test-interpretation software directly from the advertiser whose ads are placed in the APA *Monitor*. Neither the professional qualifications nor the licensure status of the software developer (as a representative of the test copyright holder) has been verified by the advertising staff of the magazine. Nor has the adequacy of the advertiser's products been checked by the magazine staff prior to running the ads. It is indeed a situation where the admonition BUYER BEWARE applies. Many unsuspecting individuals have acquired programs only to find that they were defective, inadequate, or constituted a copyright infringement.

COPYRIGHT INFRINGEMENT

Related to the widespread diffusion of home-built computer scoring and interpretation systems is the fact that most psychological tests are owned by someone and protected under copyright laws. Developing unauthorized computer-based interpretation systems for existing tests may infringe on a copyright. When developing or acquiring computer software or purchasing scoring services from a test-scoring service, copyright issues are important to consider. These issues of test ownership may become increasingly important as more and more test publishers begin to automate tests from their storehouses and growing numbers of computer-literate clinicians apply their programming skills to their practices.

Goals of This Volume

Where will all this computerization end for the psychologist? Will nearly all diagnostic tasks eventually be relegated to the computer? What role will the psychologist play in future clinical practice? We hope that this volume will focus discussion on important and relevant developments that will take place over the next few years. With the rapid innovations in computer-based psychological applications comes an "overturning" of clinical psychological practice and new ways of approaching old tasks.

This volume was constructed to explore some of the issues central to computerized psychological assessment, to highlight some of the proven methods we have available, and to introduce the clinical practitioner to the wide range of computer-based assessment techniques available.

In part one we highlight some of the advances in computerized psychological assessment methods and discuss some of the lingering issues and contemporary problems with automated psychological assessment approaches. Chapter 2, by

Samuel E. Krug, provides an overview and discussion of the values of automated assessment in clinical practice. In chapter 3 Kevin Moreland presents a valuable introduction to the various computerized test options and procedures available to the practitioner. This is followed by chapter 4 by Raymond D. Fowler, an informative chapter detailing what it takes to develop a computerized psychological assessment program. This chapter serves as an introduction to the requirements and difficulties of developing a computer interpretation system for individuals who wish to develop their own interpretive software or simply want to know the issues commercial test developers face when new products are contemplated. C. David Vale and Laura S. Keller, in chapter 5, discuss steps involved in developing "expert" systems in psychological interpretation.

Part two explores several approaches to collecting and organizing clinically valuable information from clients. In chapter 6 D. Robert Fowler and his colleagues describe the development and validation of a clinically useful problem-oriented interview that is administered by computer to the adult patient. A somewhat different approach, one that seeks clinical information in the area of personality and lifestyle factors, is described in chapter 7 by Barbara Allen and Harvey A. Skinner. Yet a different, somewhat more general approach is described in chapter 8 by Ronald A. Giannetti. In this chapter he presents the revised version of his extensive social history questionnaire, the GOLPH, along with an illustration of the type of information it presents to the clinician. In chapter 9 Steven J. Stein describes the use of the computer in giving a diagnostic interview (the DICA) to children and adolescents.

Computer-based interpretation of standardized measures of personality are covered in part three. In chapter 10, I describe the extensive data base and rationale for computerized interpretation of the most widely used personality inventory, the MMPI. Computer interpretation of the MMPI is described and illustrated with examples of the Minnesota Report, published by the University of Minnesota Press and National Computer Systems. In chapter 11 Samuel Karson and Jerry W. O'Dell provide an informative description of the computerized 16 PF Report, which Karson authored; the chapter includes an illustration of its use. In chapter 12 John E. Exner describes his well-known work on the computerized Rorschach and its use in clinical psychological assessment. It provides an interesting view of how even highly clinical and traditionally subjective instruments can be interpreted by electronic computer. Paolo Pancheri and Massimo Biondi, in chapter 13, follow with an interesting update on the extensive computer-based psychological interpretation program at the Institute of Psychiatry at the University of Rome, which was one of the earliest and most broadly based assessment programs incorporating computers. In chapter 14 David Lachar describes computer-based personality assessment using the Personality Inventory for Children. Chapter 15, on the Strong Interest Inventory, presents Jo-Ida C. Hansen's up-to-date description and survey of the most widely used interest inventory.

Part four contains several chapters dealing with the use of computers in the cognitive ability assessment area. In chapter 16 David Weiss, a pioneer in adaptive ability testing, and C. David Vale, of Assessment Systems Corporation, describe the use of computers to select and administer relevant ability items to subjects contingent upon their previous responses to ability items. In chapter 17 Charles J. Golden provides an overview of the use of computers in neuropsychology with special emphasis on neuropsychological assessment using the Luria-Nebraska Battery. Finally, Kenneth M. Adams and Robert K. Heaton provide an overview of the use of computers in neuropsychological assessment in chapter 18.

Two appendixes are included to provide the reader with additional specialized information on computerized psychological assessment. Appendix A provides a survey of computerized tests that are currently available, along with the information on publishers and vendors. Appendix B reprints the *Guidelines for Computer-Based Tests and Interpretations* recently adopted by the APA.

REFERENCES

Adams, K. M., and Heaton, R. K. (1985). Automation of neuropsychological reports. *Journal of Consulting and Clinical Psychology*, 53, 790–802.

Butcher, J. N., Keller, L., and Bacon, S. (1985). Current developments and future directions in computerized personality assessment. *Journal of Consulting and Clinical Psychology*, 53, 803–815.

Erdman, H. P., Klein, M., and Greist, J. H. (1985). Directed patient computer interviewing. *Journal of Consulting and Clinical Psychology*, 53, 760–773.

Fowler, R. D. (1985). Landmarks in computer-assisted psychological assessment. *Journal of Consulting and Clinical Psychology*, 53, 748–759.

Fowler, R. D., and Butcher, J. N. (1986). Critique of Matarazzo's views on computerized testing: All sigma and no meaning. *American Psychologist*, 41, 94–95.

Hofer, P., and Green, B. F. (1985). The challenge of competent creativity in computerized psychological assessment. *Journal of Consulting and Clinical Psychology*, 53, 826–838.

Krug, S. E. (1984). *Psycheware: A reference guide to computer-based products for behavioral assessment in psychology, education, and business*. Kansas City, Mo.: Test Corporation of America.

Matarazzo, J. D. (1986). Computerized clinical psychological test interpretations: Unvalidated plus all mean and no sigma. *American Psychologist*, 41, 14–24.

Moreland, K. (1985). Problems in validating computerized reports. *Journal of Consulting and Clinical Psychology*, 53, 816–825.

Weiss, D. J. (1985). Adaptive testing by computer. *Journal of Consulting and Clinical Psychology*, 53, 774–789.

Ziskin, J. (1980). Use of the MMPI in forensic settings. *Clinical Notes on the MMPI*. Minneapolis: National Computer Systems.

2

Microtrends: An Orientation to Computerized Assessment

Samuel E. Krug

I often wonder if Professor Harold Hill would be any less concerned about the presence of a microcomputer in a testing office than he was about a pool table in River City. Just as surely as this pool table transformed the vocabulary, attitude, and minds of the residents of a sleepy Iowa town (at least as Professor Hill saw it), computer technology has transformed the face of psychological assessment.

For example, there was a time when terminal meant "the end." In the 1980s "terminal" is more likely to be associated with the beginning of a new era in assessment and evaluation for mental health practitioners. An increasing number of journals have software reviewers working alongside book reviewers (who may soon find themselves on the endangered species list as publishing becomes increasingly electronic).

New articles regularly appear in the *Wall Street Journal*, the *New York Times*, or the *EAP Digest* commenting on the growth, impact, and profitability of the computer testing industry. And, recently, various regulatory boards and professional associations have begun to issue guidelines relating to computerized assessment.

There's no denying that after little more than a quarter century, computer testing has become an overnight sensation.

Some people view computer assessment as an impersonal, sometimes frightening technology and, like the legendary golem, a soulless, imperfect imitation of humanity. They are concerned about the impersonal nature of computer test administration, problems with the validity of computerized reports, and the potential for misuse of computer-based psychological test products.

Others have vigorously embraced the new era of solid-state psychology by acquiring sophisticated systems, scanners, modems, and extensive software libraries.

What does this perplexing new technology really offer the practitioner? Is computerized testing an electronic fad that only substitutes keyboard and screen for paper and pencil? Or does the technology really broaden and enhance the science and practice of human assessment?

The Role of the Computer in Psychological Assessment

Many people tend to think of the role of the computer in assessment solely in terms of convenience or speed. Others see it as a device for playing a game of psychological Pac Man. Both groups fail to grasp the real significance of what the computer offers.

With advances in technology and research over the years, an increasing number of instruments that began life as paper-and-pencil devices have grown far beyond their original design concepts. For example, hundreds of scales have been developed from the original Minnesota Multiphasic Personality Inventory (MMPI) item pool. The time involved just in scoring so many scales for a single answer sheet—if done by hand—far exceeds the time available to most assessors. That does not include, of course, the additional time required to organize and interpret the pattern of scale elevations and the significance of various score deviations.

Instead of thinking of the role of computers in psychological assessment solely as "scoring machines" or toys, we need to think of them in terms of the broader potential they offer for improving and expanding the practice of human assessment.

THE COMPUTER AS PSYCHOMETRIC ASSISTANT

Judging from the products that are currently available, new offerings that regularly appear in the marketplace, and research trends that are evident, computerized test administration is likely to become more and more popular.

Test administration by computer offers a number of significant benefits over conventional test administration, even for instruments that were originally developed in a paper-and-pencil format or are easily administered in that format.

The first and perhaps most significant benefit is the increased control over the testing process that computerized administration offers. Over the years, the sheer simplicity of many paper-and-pencil instruments has led to a number of questionable practices. Clients are sometimes asked to work under poor environmental conditions, which include inadequate lighting, poor ventilation, insufficient desk or work space, or under uncontrolled conditions, as happens when assessment takes place by mail. The use of an answer sheet, an accepted tradition in human assessment, in itself adds significant potential for error as clients lose track of their place on the sheet, fill in the wrong blank, fail to darken a response grid sufficiently, or commit any one of a large number of potential errors.

Scoring, even for an objective test with a carefully developed scoring stencil, is a process fraught with potential for errors of measurement. Gorsuch (in press) has estimated that errors involving a difference of one or more points in the final score are made in 10 percent of cases involving hand scoring of objective tests. These and similar "errors of measurement" may have more impact on the reliability of scores obtained in practice than some of the better analyzed sources of error in measurement theory.

Although the conditions under which data used to develop and standardize a test are usually carefully controlled, the conditions under which many instruments are routinely used are not. Consequently, it seems likely that computer administration and scoring could lead to achieving in practice the levels of reliabilities routinely reported in test manuals, but probably rarely obtained in practice.

THE COMPUTER AS CONSULTANT

One of the most significant contributions the computer makes to psychological assessment is its ability to organize and systematically access massive data bases. In that context, consider the extensive body of empirical research findings that relate to many tests in use today. The *Mental Measurements Yearbooks* have catalogued in excess of seventy thousand references involving more than a thousand different tests.

Access to this information is vital if the assessor is to make the most informed interpretation of the assessment data. Yet its sheer size makes it increasingly difficult for the unassisted test user to access even a small portion of this data base. Gone from our midst are the ancient priests, poets, and storytellers who could commit vast sagas to memory and, on demand, recall vivid details of Odysseus' return to Penelope or complex genealogies stretching centuries into the past.

The computer is, of course, ideally suited to the indexing, storage, and information retrieval tasks that challenge the most enthusiastic, unassisted test user. Scale correlates that have been identified and replicated can be easily stored and reliably recalled when a particular configuration of test scores or certain scale elevations appear in a particular protocol. That is true whether the pattern is one that occurs frequently or whether the pattern is rarely encountered within the professional experience of a single test user.

At their best, computerized test reports produced by various systems provide the individual test user with expert consultation in interpreting individual test results for a wide variety of purposes.

A recent review of available computer-based interpretive systems (Krug, 1984b) showed that 47 percent of the entries were aimed primarily at clinical assessment. An additional 17 percent of the entries listed clinical assessment as one of several application areas. Personal counseling was the second most popular area. Although only 9 percent of the entries listed this as the primary application area, 38 percent of the nearly two hundred entries listed it as one of several product applications. Vocational guidance was the primary or secondary application area for 35 percent, personnel selection for 29 percent, educational evaluation for 26 percent, training and development for 8 percent, and behavioral medicine for 6 percent.

With improvements in both hardware and software, the concept of a "computer report" has expanded considerably as products have been tailored to particular applications and needs. For example, in one case (Henry, Henry, and Krug, 1984) the "computer report" is actually one element of a comprehensive relationship training program. Pages of interpretive material are interspersed with instructional material to provide participant couples with a balanced presentation of insight into personal resources and practice in developing skills such as decision making and communications.

Recent Trends in Computer Applications

For many years the computer primarily served testing needs from a remote location. Answer sheets were sent to a distant site for processing. Reports were received in a few days or a few weeks, depending on just how remote the computer was. This necessarily imposed some limitations on application areas. For example, when tests are used to assist in job selection decisions, it is not always possible to wait for even a few hours. Decisions need to be made promptly.

This situation improved somewhat in the 1970s as several of the major service providers began to offer teleprocessing options. Some of these were designed, at least initially, as electronic mail services. Test data were transmitted by phone line to a central computer, which subsequently processed the data and returned results by phone line within twenty-four hours of the original call.

Other systems were truly interactive and provided reports instantly. These interactive teleprocessing systems did much to meet the need for immediate feedback. However, the approach was not entirely satisfactory, at least from the user's standpoint. Connection or line charges often became a significant part of the total testing costs. Sometimes the quality of the transmission equipment or network was poor. Under these circumstances, "line noise" could cause garbage to be inserted in the reports that were returned or, more critically, in the test data that were sent.

Recent improvements in the architecture of computer systems, especially in regard to microcomputers, has opened the door to a new era in computerized assessment. These new systems are capable of fully supporting the vast majority of interpretive systems currently in operation on the larger computers used by central scoring services. The hardware is generally sufficiently reliable so that the costs of maintaining a system locally are negligible. And these new systems are affordable. Systems that cost $100,000 in the mid-1970s can be replaced in the mid-1980s with equally powerful (or, in some cases, more powerful) and more reliable systems for one-tenth of the investment.

Although automobiles were around for several decades before Henry Ford's assembly line began operation, it was his low-cost, reliable Model T that revolutionized transportation and, subsequently, altered the face of American culture. In a similar way, while the introduction of computers into the psychological assessment process in the late 1950s had a significant impact on the nature of human evaluation, the introduction of low-cost reliable microsystems seems likely to alter the assessment process even more profoundly.

IMPROVEMENTS IN TEST ADMINISTRATION

With the increasing availability of low-cost terminals, measurement experts have really begun to develop the test-administration capability of the computer (Johnson and Johnson, 1981) in addition to its use for scoring and interpretation. The benefits of on-line testing at first appeared to be simply greater control of reaction time and immediate availability of scored output. But within a very short time new and perhaps unintended benefits began to emerge. For example, the computer may be a particularly powerful administrator of tests for neurological deficits that require shape or symbol manipulation.

A second benefit of computerized testing is that testing time is usually shorter compared to administration of the same instrument in paper-and-pencil format. The discrepancy becomes even more significant when a separate answer sheet is used. Clinical experience suggests that the savings may range from 15 percent to 50 percent of total testing time. This may allow us to collect greater amounts of information with the computer as test administrator in the same or even less time than was formerly required.

Improvements in computer graphics and displays permit the development of entirely new kinds of tests (to examine spatial ability, for example) using stimuli that simply were not possible in paper-and-pencil format.

Measurement error arising from administration procedures in the case of tests that require complex presentation of stimuli, tightly controlled time limits, and so forth, can be dramatically reduced. And the ability of the computer to accommodate a variety of input-output modes makes it easier to adapt tests to people with handicaps. The electronic capabilities provided by microcomputer systems open an entirely new horizon with respect to the assessment dimensions that can be explored and the measurement process itself.

ADAPTIVE TESTING

Although theoretical developments in adaptive or tailored testing have proceeded rapidly for more than a decade now, the practical application of this approach had been stalled by the prohibitive cost of terminals and work stations.

In adaptive testing each person receives only those items that are relevant. Items that are too easy or too difficult, in the case of ability measures, or those that lie outside the person's range of functioning, in the case of noncognitive measures, are omitted. Few skilled interviewers would ever ask a man how many times he has been pregnant. In the same way, computer adaptive software selects from a bank of precalibrated items only those that will provide useful information about each individual tested. Consequently, assessment can be completed in a shorter time with equal or better reliability and validity. Because of the obvious savings in testing time, adaptive testing opens the possibility for measurement of a broader range of characteristics than can normally be assessed in the limited amounts of time available for real-world applications.

DECISION SUPPORT SYSTEMS

Microcomputers have provided substantial impetus for large-scale applications of psychological decision support systems. These systems use the expert systems component of artificial intelligence to provide a data base and a fixed set of decision rules with which the computer can offer advice regarding psychological decisions (Eyde and Kowal, 1985).

One new microcomputer software system, TEST PLUS (Krug, 1985), offers some exciting new possibilities for the integration of assessment and artificial intelligence. At one level of operation, TEST PLUS provides controlled administration and immediate scoring and reporting of results on the Adult Personality Inventory (Krug, 1984a). However, the inclusion of an on-line process for structuring the decision process introduces a new facet in the application of expert systems.

Through a series of paired-comparison judgments, TEST PLUS allows the user to define assessment objectives prior to the assessment process itself and to build a measurement model, or "ideal" profile, based on the test user's familiarity with the assessment-setting and decision needs.

This process serves several functions. First, it allows the test user to determine the applicability of the test scales to any particular assessment objective. For example, if the resulting decision model shows an ideal profile in which all test scales fall within essentially normal limits, this suggests that the decision is likely to rest on characteristics that lie outside the test space of the Adult Personality Inventory and that some other instrument may provide more useful information for this decision.

Second, it provides the test user with a convenient method of considering assessment objectives before the testing process begins. Few people would consider initiating any new activity without the development of a plan or budget model. But it is amazing how many test users routinely administer tests without first considering some "standard of performance" (Wiggins, 1973) against which results can be evaluated.

Finally, the discrepancy between an ideal profile and an individual's obtained profile can serve an important developmental function by identifying areas for growth and change.

This on-line integration of decision theory and psychological assessment opens the door for other applications of expert systems and artificial intelligence models in psychological assessment.

The Other Side of the Story (or the *Real* Problem in River City)

If Father Flanagan had been a reviewer of computerized test systems instead of the founder of Boys' Town, it is probably a safe bet that we would never have heard the immortal line "There's no such thing as a bad system."

So far we have looked only at the best the computer offers test users. If this were the whole story, there would be little need for the increasing attention focused on regulation of such services and products. States like Kansas would not enact laws that specifically regulate the use of "computers in any aspect of psychological testing" and require the psychologist to "assume the same degree of responsibility for the validity and reliability of interpretive statement and soundness of inferences, judgments, and recommendations based on computer-generated test results as would be assured if the psychologist had personally examined the client" (Kansas Code, 1985).

The basic problem is that many expert systems are not really very expert. Although a number of these products have been carefully designed and developed, a frightening number have been developed along the lines of what might be termed the "creationist" perspective. That is, on Monday, the system developer (SD) begins the process by selecting and ordering a new microcomputer system. On Tuesday, the system is installed and made operational. On Wednesday, the SD learns to program in BASIC. On Thursday, the SD develops an interpretation program for the MMPI or some other well-known instrument. On Friday, the SD places an ad for the new system in the APA *Monitor*. On Saturday, the SD fills the first order and begins to develop documentation for the system. But then on the seventh day the SD rests (and the documentation is never quite completed).

Unfortunately, this scenario seems to be true for an uncomfortably large number of services and products currently available. Legislation and standards will help improve the quality of offerings. But improved consumer education must occur at the same time to create a more sophisticated and demanding audience for these kinds of products.

Concerns about the potential that exists for misusing such tools have been heard from many different quarters (for example, Eyde and Kowal, 1985; Matarazzo, 1983; Mitchell, 1984). These concerns relate most often to (1) the technical quality of the products that have been produced and the lack of documentation for many of them; (2) the depersonalization of the assessment process; and (3) the loss of control over psychological assessment itself.

VALIDITY AND UTILITY

The first question usually raised is whether the reports produced by computer interpretive systems are valid. However, that is probably too narrow a statement of the problem. We have known for nearly a half century that validity is only one of several related factors that affect the accuracy of decision outcomes (Taylor and Russell, 1939). Moreover, research by O'Dell (1972), Adam and Shore (1976), and Nichols and Knopf (1977), among others, has shown that if validity is taken too narrowly in the usual sense of accuracy, then computer reports are judged most valid when they contain general, nonspecific statements that are true for most people.

For these reasons we need to think in terms of the *utility* of these systems, not just their validity. A quick review of available products and services reveals that there are substantial differences in the organization of different reports, in the amount of information conveyed, and in the manner in which it is conveyed.

The first concern that comes to mind in determining the utility of an interpretive product is whether it addresses some relevant referral issue. Does it address specific user concerns or does it simply provide information about what the system developer knew about the test instrument? If it follows the latter course, the user is left to face the "so what" problem alone instead of being guided reasonably toward answers to questions for which the test was administered in the first place.

Does the system possess discriminative validity? Does the information it presents consist largely of high base-rate statements that are true of most people, or does it correctly reflect real differences among people? In some instances validity for a particular system has been offered by demonstrating that users agree with the content of a report. However, as O'Dell (1972) has argued, that is much less than a sufficient or necessary condition for validity. What must be demonstrated is that the information presented tends to be true for some, but not all, people.

Most of the research conducted so far has asked whether independent experts agree that specific interpretive statements or paragraphs are true for the client. What is needed is an experimental design, for example, one in which classifications or decisions made on the basis of the test report are compared to decisions made without such information. It may be that certain systems are so populated with high base-rate statements that they actually interfere with the correct classification or placement of clients. On the other hand, it may be that the narrative provided by certain systems provides insights into the client that might not otherwise be apparent in the numerical score profile alone. The obvious corollary is that systems may have utility for one group of test users but not for another. While this further complicates the "validation" process, it serves to demonstrate that the validation of interpretive systems is not a simple process.

Finally, what about the "usability" of the product? Some system designers seem to be convinced that more is better. As a result, certain reports intended to help in the career planning process have become so long that it is unlikely the person could even read the material, let along digest it, in the space of an entire lifetime. In other cases, the reading level appears to be inappropriate for the target audience. For example, some reports designed for lay audiences are written at levels that require reading abilities at the sixteenth or seventeenth grade level.

Obviously time and cost also play some role in the utility of interpretive products. There are many factors other than the accuracy of specific sentences in the computer report that influence the impact a computerized test system may have on the accuracy of decisions made about people.

DEPERSONALIZATION

The concern about depersonalization of the assessment process is especially important when human services are in question. Many people feel that the computer may increase the distance between the therapist and the client and lead to a more mechanized, less effective delivery system.

This would appear to be more the therapist's concern than the client's. Research by Skinner and Allen (1983) and Harrell and Lombardo (1984), for example, has suggested that clients actually prefer to face the computer than a live interviewer or a test booklet.

There is even stronger evidence that the depersonalization concern is less important than some have suggested. Research by Wagman (1980, 1982) suggests that even computerized counseling results in about the same gains as are found for more traditional approaches that involve a live therapist. The system he designed teaches the client a general approach to problem solving. The computer interacts with the client much as a human counselor might to answer questions, suggest strategies, and so forth. The findings from Wagman's studies further suggested that clients preferred the computer to a live therapist.

Many other human service systems have had to permit some degree of depersonalization in order to take advantage of more effective diagnostic and treatment techniques. Before radiology, a bone fracture could only be crudely diagnosed by observation and manipulation. Patients have had to trade some of the patient-physician relationship they formerly enjoyed to take advantage of these new techniques, but the overall effect has been to improve the effectiveness of medical practice and the quality of life itself.

The conclusion appears to be that the introduction of any technology, computer included, into psychological assessment is not in itself depersonalizing. In many cases the use of the computer may actually free the practitioner from routine tasks, leaving more time available for interacting with clients.

LOSING CONTROL OF THE TESTING PROCESS

The issue of loss of control over psychological testing itself is perhaps the most significant question that has been raised, and the least satisfactorily explored. Although a number of standards, regulations, and guidelines have been prepared for computerized testing, it isn't always exactly clear what a computerized test is (or, for that matter, exactly what a psychological test is). New products that have begun to appear on the market, such as *Mind Prober* (Johnson, Johnson, and Gallagher, 1984) or *Sell! Sell! Sell!* (Thoughtware, 1985), are likely only to further blur the distinction between psychological and nonpsychological software.

Ultimately the designation of products as psychological in nature rests on the perceived need for professional skills to use them properly. The computer may, of course, provide some of those needed skills, especially in regard to administration and scoring. Under such circumstances, an instrument that is correctly designated as "psychological" in paper-and-pencil form may be appropriate for broader use in computerized form.

This transformation is not without precedent in other fields. One obvious parallel is that an increasing number of medical tests that were formerly conducted only by certified laboratories have now reappeared in diagnostic "kit" form for home use.

Conclusion

Computerized testing is not without its problems and pitfalls, though it certainly has a great deal of promise as well. The computer has contributed greatly to the development of sophisticated instruments for transforming people into numeric profiles. Increasingly, it appears that the computer will help transform these profiles of numbers back into answers to the questions for which the tests were given in the first place.

REFERENCES

Adam, K. M., and Shore, D. L. (1976). The accuracy of an automated MMPI interpretation system in a psychiatric setting. *Journal of Clinical Psychology*, 32, 80–82.

Eyde, L. D., and Kowal, D. M. (1985). *Psychological decision support software for the public: Pros, cons, and guidelines*. Paper presented at the 1985 Convention of the American Psychological Association, Los Angeles.

Gorsuch, R. L. (in press). Psychometric evaluation of scales when their scoring keys are unavailable. *Professional Psychology*.

Harrell, T. H., and Lombardo, T. A. (1984). Validation of an automated 16PF administration procedure. *Journal of Personality Assessment*, 48, 638–642.

Henry, T. J., Henry, V. M., and Krug, S. E. (1984). *GROW: The individualized marriage enrichment program*. Champaign, IL: MetriTech.

Johnson, J. H., and Johnson, K. N. (1981). Psychological considerations related to the development of computerized testing stations. *Behavior Research Methods and Instrumentation*, 13, 421–424.

Johnson, J. H., Johnson, K. N., and Gallagher, R. (1984). *Reading others. Mind Prober* [manual]. Palo Alto, CA: Human Edge Software Corporation.

Kansas Code, §§102-1-16 (1985).

Krug, S. E. (1984a). *The Adult Personality Inventory*. Champaign, IL: Institute for Personality and Ability Testing.

Krug, S. E. (1984b). *Psychware: A reference guide to computer-based products for behavioral assessment in psychology, education, and business*. Kansas City, MO: Test Corporation of America.

Krug, S. E. (1985). *TEST PLUS: A microcomputer based system for the Adult Personality Inventory*. Champaign, IL: MetriTech.

Matarazzo, J. D. (1983). Computerized psychological testing. *Science*, 221, 323.

Mitchell, J. V. (1984). Computer-based test interpretation and the public interest. *Proceedings of the 92nd Annual Convention of the American Psychological Association*.

Nichols, M. P., and Knopf, I. J. (1977). Refining computerized test interpretations: An in-depth approach. *Journal of Personality Assessment*, 41, 157–159.

O'Dell, J. W. (1972). P. T. Barnum explores the computer. *Journal of Consulting and Clinical Psychology*, 38, 270–273.

Skinner, H. A., and Allen, B. A. (1983). Does the computer make a difference? Computerized versus face-to-face versus self-report assessment of alcohol, drug, and tobacco use. *Journal of Consulting and Clinical Psychology*, 51, 267–275.

Taylor, H. C., and Russell, J. T. (1939). The relationship of validity coefficients to the practical effectiveness of tests in selection. *Journal of Applied Psychology*, 23, 565–578.

Thoughtware, Inc. (1985). *Sell! Sell! Sell!* [manual]. Coconut Grove, FL: Author.

Wagman, M. (1980). PLATO DCS: An interactive computer system for personal counseling. *Journal of Counseling Psychology*, 27, 16–30.

Wagman, M. (1982). Solving dilemmas by computer or counselor. *Psychological Reports*, 50, 127–135.

Wiggins, J. S. (1973). *Personality and prediction: Principles of personality assessment*. Reading, MA: Addison-Wesley.

Wiggins, J. S. (1979). A psychological taxonomy of trait-descriptive terms: The interpersonal domain. *Journal of Personality and Social Psychology*, 37, 395–412.

3

Computerized Psychological Assessment: What's Available

Kevin L. Moreland

Introduction

As Fowler (1985) has pointed out, computerized psychological assessment is *not* a recent phenomenon. Elmer Hankes began to use an analog computer to score the Minnesota Multiphasic Personality Inventory (MMPI) and Strong Vocational Interest Blank (SVIB) during the late 1940s. A system for the automated interpretation of the MMPI went into operation at the Mayo Clinic in the early 1960s. The Roche Psychiatric Service Institute first made MMPI interpretations available commercially in 1965. On the other hand, for many years computerized clinical assessment was practically synonymous with large, centrally located scoring and interpretation services for the MMPI. Progress was being made in secluded settings, however, notably at the Psychiatric Assessment Unit (PAU) at the Veteran's Administration Medical Center in Salt Lake City (Johnson and Williams, 1980). In 1977 a group of PAU expatriates started Psych Systems, the first commercial enterprise dedicated solely to computerized psychological assessment. With Psych Systems came some radical departures from the way computerized clinical assessment had been done for over fifteen years.

Before Psych Systems, those wanting to use computerized psychological assessment had a standard paper-and-pencil test completed in the usual manner and mailed the answer sheet to a scoring service, receiving the computerized report by return mail. Psych Systems put computer terminals for on-line test administration into practitioners' offices. Before Psych Systems, clinicians generally sent away for MMPI reports. Psych Systems' computer software at one time included twenty assessment instruments in addition to the MMPI. Other companies were quick to follow their lead, eventually outstripping them in some areas. I believe it is these kinds of innovations that make computerized psychological assessment seem new, and that make a chapter like this one worth writing.

This chapter provides an overview of the types of computerized assessment products and services that are currently available. The first part of the chapter deals with input—that is, the various ways in which psychological assessment data can be entered into a computer. The pros and cons of each of the available methods are highlighted. This is followed by a brief digression into the technical issues surrounding one of the hot topics in computerized assessment today: test administration by computer. The next section of the chapter discusses the output side of computerized assessment—in other words, the types of reports currently available. The validity of computer-based test interpretation (CBTI) systems—perhaps the most talked-about topic in computerized assessment today—receives detailed attention. The chapter winds up with some advice for the would-be consumer of computerized clinical assessment.

Input

There are several means of entering test data into a computer. All have important implications for the cost of computer processing and the time it takes to receive results.

CENTRAL PROCESSING

Central test processing requires that you administer paper-and-pencil tests in the usual fashion. The answer sheets are then mailed to a remote, central location for processing. Test results are returned to the examiner in the same fashion.

Automatic equipment has been used to process tests for many years. The SVIB was first scored by a Hollerith card sorter in the late 1920s. This primitive method required that 420 Hollerith cards corresponding to the responses for a single test be selected from among 1,260 possible cards. Those cards were then run through the sorter three times to score the twenty-two scales then composing the SVIB. As noted earlier, Elmer Hankes, a Minneapolis electrical engineer, first used a computer to score the SVIB in 1946. Hankes's analog computer employed keypunched cards like the Hollerith card sorter, but his equipment required far fewer cards per test. Optical mark reading equipment was introduced in the mid-1950s at E. F. Lindquist's Measurement Research Center (MRC) in Iowa City. These "scanners" permitted the processing of test answer sheets themselves, thus avoiding the cumbersome, error-prone process of keypunching test responses onto cards. The central test processing equipment in use in 1986 is a refinement of the MRC system developed over a quarter century ago.

Central test processing flourished initially because the equipment required was very large and costly. Many universities and other large institutions acquired such equipment in the 1960s, but it remained beyond the means of individual practitioners until the mid-1980s. With the increasing availability of inexpensive microcomputers and optical mark reading equipment, computerized test processing is being decentralized, though the demise of central processing is not yet in sight. Central processing will continue to be attractive when test results are not needed quickly or when a large number of tests must be processed. Academic achievement tests, entrance and competency examinations, licensing and certification examinations, and vocational interest inventories will continue to be processed centrally for the foreseeable future. At present, many thousands of clinical tests are processed centrally each year too. For example, most of the MMPIs processed centrally by National Computer Systems (NCS) come from private practitioners. When clients are being seen only once a week, central processing provides test results quickly enough. NCS also processes large numbers of MMPIs from practitioners who are screening applicants for high-risk jobs. Again, time is not usually at a premium; however, the number of protocols to be processed at one time is large.

Central processing is also economical in the short run since the practitioner need not purchase any computer equipment. With the cost of powerful microcomputers near $1,000 and falling, and the price of data communications terminals considerably less than that, central processing, with its associated mailing costs, will not maintain this advantage for long. Central processing also forces practitioners to stay with tests that have a fixed item sequence. While there are as yet no psychometric tests in general use that are administered using a variable item sequence, there are a number of useful interviews wherein responses determine which questions will be asked and in what order.

Virtually all major test publishers in the United States maintain a central processing service for one or more of their tests. NCS maintains the largest such service, with thirty-one different reports available for twenty-three different tests.*

TELEPROCESSING

Like central processing, teleprocessing makes use of a large, remote computer. Unlike central processing, raw test data are entered locally (for example, in the

* When considering figures like these, the reader needs to keep in mind that new companies and products appear every month—if not more often—and that this chapter was completed in January 1986. Consult appendix A of this volume for a useful listing of many of the computerized assessment products available as of late 1985.

practitioner's office) and test results are printed locally. In between, raw test data are transmitted to the computer over the telephone, are processed, and test results are returned via telephone. Teleprocessing is a relatively new means of processing test data, having been commercially available for only about five years. Given the advantages of teleprocessing, however, its popularity should increase rapidly.

Teleprocessing is an attractive alternative to central processing because test results are available within minutes. It is an attractive alternative to local processing (see the next section) because start-up costs can be lower. The only equipment needed is a data communications terminal. Texas Instruments' Silent 700™ series of 300-baud* data communications terminals with a built-in printer and modem† can be purchased for less than $700. Terminals tend to be inexpensive because they are "dumb"—all they will do is send and receive information. By contrast, microcomputers with enough intelligence to allow local test processing cost at least twice as much as the cheapest terminal. Teleprocessing has the added advantage of allowing the use of virtually any microcomputer (in lieu of a data communications terminal). Software for use in local test processing is typically available for only the most popular brands of microcomputers, such as IBM. Furthermore, there are currently some computerized assessment services available via teleprocessing that are not available locally (see chapter 11, for example). Services other than test processing can also be obtained via teleprocessing. For example, a number of teleprocessing services are available for use in conducting literature searches. The American Psychological Association's PsychInfo is one example of such a service. The Buros Institute for Mental Measurement maintains its data base of test reviews on a computer that can be accessed by teleprocessing. (Consult Lieff [1984] and Pressman [1984] for examples of other services that can be obtained via teleprocessing.)

The main disadvantage of teleprocessing is that you have to pay for the telephone call to the central computer. Fortunately, these charges tend to be modest. My experience is that they currently range from about $0.50 to about $2.50 per test processed. These charges vary according to the test, type of results desired, and the teleprocessing service being used. There is always a charge, though it may be "bundled" with the charge for the test processing.

At present two American test publishers maintain teleprocessing services: NCS and the Institute for Personality and Ability Testing (IPAT). NCS's ARION II™ service is the larger of the two, offering twenty-nine different reports for twenty-three different tests. ARION II can be accessed by virtually any 300- or 1,200-baud data communications terminal, or by most microcomputers having modems and communications software. Raw test data may be entered into ARION II for teleprocessing in two ways: by entering item re-

* "Baud" refers to the speed at which data are transmitted. For example, 300 baud is thirty characters per second. The faster data are transmitted, the lower the telephone charges for teleprocessing.

† A modem is an electronic device that translates (or *mod*ulates) signals from a computer into signals that can be transmitted over ordinary telephone lines. A modem will also *dem*odulate signals received over the telephone so that a computer can read them.

sponses from an answer sheet via a keyboard or by processing answer sheets through local optical mark reading equipment. Raw scores, standard scores, and derived scores (for example, produced by regression equations) are then calculated by NCS's central computer. Those scores and, in many cases, a computerized test interpretation are then returned to the practitioner's office via telephone. The test results can then be printed immediately or, if you are using a microcomputer, stored for later use.

The Teletest™ service can be accessed with either a 1,200-baud telecommunications terminal or a microcomputer. Data can be entered into the Teletest system in two ways. All the available tests and reports can be accessed by entering raw scale scores into the system via a keyboard. Standard scores and derived scores are then calculated by IPAT's central computer and returned to the user's terminal or microcomputer. IPAT has also developed the Teledisk™ to allow clients to take the Sixteen Personality Factor Questionnaire (16 PF) and the Adult Personality Inventory on-line on an IBM Personal Computer. That is, the computer presents test items to the client on the screen and the client responds by pressing the appropriate key on the computer keyboard. The item endorsements are then processed and the results reported via teleprocessing. As of this writing, IPAT is considering expanding the Teledisk to accommodate more tests and different brands of microcomputers.

LOCAL PROCESSING

With local test processing, nothing has to be sent through the mail or over the telephone in order to accomplish all the steps necessary to receive computer-generated test results. For the individual practitioner this means using a microcomputer. Local processing may involve an optical mark reader, but it need not. A microcomputer used for local test processing can also be configured to teleprocess but need not be.

Two big advantages of local processing are practitioner control and flexibility. The local system will never be unavailable due to routine maintenance at an inconvenient time. If the optical mark reader is on the blink the responses can always be key-entered. If for any reason the local system cannot be used to process tests in a timely fashion (perhaps because it lacks the appropriate software), it may be possible to teleprocess those tests. If that is not possible, some practitioners may fall back on central test processing. Hand scoring is an option for many tests but, as is noted in the section on output, hand scoring often means giving up much of the information that is provided by the computer. On the other hand, local software is available to assist in the scoring and interpretation of tests that must be administered and, to some extent, scored by hand. Such software is available in abundance for a number of widely used intelligence scales, such as the Wechsler series, Stanford-Binet, and Kaufman Assessment Battery for Children (K-ABC).

Another advantage of local test processing is that it forces you to own a computer. If the computer is configured for teleprocessing, you can enjoy the nontesting services, such as those described earlier, available over the telephone. Optical mark readers also have many nontesting applications, such as processing of client intake forms. You can also use local software for everything from billing to word processing.

The ability to administer tests on-line is another advantage usually touted for local test processing although, as we saw, on-line administration is also compatible with teleprocessing. There is some professional controversy about the administration of tests by computer that I will deal with in more detail later. There are also some practical advantages and disadvantages to be considered. As noted, a number of useful structured interviews must be administered by a human or a computer—that is, they are not amenable to the paper-and-pencil format (see chapters 7, 8, and 9). The reason a computer is necessary is that these interviews use branching logic. For example, if a client indicates that he or she is married, the computer might then ask whether this is the client's first marriage. If the client, on the other hand, indicates that he or she has never been married, no further questions about marriage are asked. This is obviously quite different from paper-and-pencil tests that have a fixed item pool presented in a fixed sequence. Branching logic allows the use of a very large item pool without exhausting clients with too many inquiries or irritating them with irrelevant questions. Tests that branch on the basis of the psychometric characteristics of the items (rather than rational considerations as in the case of interviews) have been under development by ability testers for many years (see chapter 16). Such "computer-adaptive" tests are not yet available for general use, but clinically oriented researchers are working on the development of such instruments (see Butcher, Keller, and Bacon, 1985). This is surely the wave of the not-too-distant future.

There is one big disadvantage to on-line test administration that typically occurs to people once the high-tech glamour of using the computer to give a test has worn off: test administration monopolizes a microcomputer. As long as a client is taking a test on-line your microcomputer cannot be used to write reports, update patient records, send out bills, balance your books, or anything else. And some popular tests take a long time to administer on-line. Some individuals can take the MMPI on-line in forty-five minutes; however, others may take as long as two hours. It is doubtful that this is a cost-effective use of the computer equipment. By contrast, an experienced clerk can easily key in all 566 MMPI responses from an answer sheet in less than five minutes. An optical mark reader can process an answer sheet in about five seconds.

Currently there exists an embarrassment of riches when it comes to assessment software for local use. Paradoxically, this may be a disadvantage to the potential consumer of computerized assessment. As I alluded to in the introduction, the advent of cheap microcomputers and easy-to-learn computer programming languages has changed things greatly from that time not too long ago when tens of thousands of dollars' worth of equipment and highly specialized knowledge were needed to open a computerized assessment business. Gone are the days when the tremendous investment necessary to develop and market computerized assessment products virtually guaranteed that they had been carefully developed by experts. Much of the software now available for local computerized assessment has been developed by individuals who have no special qualifications. Many of the assessment software companies that have sprung up in the last half-dozen years appear to be located in someone's basement. Furthermore, an alarming number of computer software companies spring up overnight only to disappear just as quickly (Larson, 1984).

This is not to say that none of the new companies can deliver and support a high-quality product. Every company was young once. Psychological Assessment Resources is an example of a company that a few years ago could have been fairly described as a basement operation; today it is rapidly maturing into one of the major competitors in the field of computerized assessment. Other new companies appear to produce high-quality assessment tools that are not psychometric in nature—for example, structured interviews and problem checklists. However, my feeling is that you are on safer ground dealing with established test publishers if their product meets your needs. The established publishers generally have more personnel and expertise to devote to critical issues like quality assurance of software before it is sold and support of that software in the field after it is sold. They also tend to command the best computerized report authors. And, most important, they are unlikely to disappear overnight.

TECHNICAL "INPUT" ISSUES: ON-LINE ADMINISTRATION OF TESTS AND INTERVIEWS

Looked at in the abstract, computer administration of tests and interviews appears to be a nonissue. Procedures for computer administration of tests are developed in the same way that administration procedures for conventional tests are developed, right? In principle. As a matter of fact, most assessment tools that are currently available for on-line administration were developed for conventional administration. Therefore, as a practical matter, practitioners must be concerned that factors indigenous to on-line administration but irrelevant to the purposes of the test may alter test performance. These computer-linked factors may change the nature of a task so dramatically that you cannot say the computer-administered and conventional version of a test are measuring the same construct. For example, scores on a test of divergent thinking (for example, listing uses for common objects within a time limit) will depend heavily on typing ability if administered via a computer keyboard but be completely independent of typing skill if administered in the conventional fashion. In such cases normative, reliability, and validity data cannot be generalized from the conventional to the computer-administered version.

It is also apparent that there are a number of plausible reasons for differences between computerized and conventional item presentation. First, the computer presents items a few at a time, at most. On the other hand, since on conventional tests test respondents often have access to all the questions, some skip around looking for questions they can answer. This may be a boon to the test respondent, as when a later question provides a clue to the answer for a question that was skipped. Skipping around in a personality inventory may create a more consistent response pattern than would otherwise be the case. For example, individuals who describe themselves as "hostile" on an adjective checklist may be more likely to endorse "angry" if the first answer can be reviewed. The computer usually does not permit such item interconnections.

Another difference between administration methods is that the computer usually requires a response—though not necessarily an answer—to each item. The test respondent who wishes to skip an item usually pushes a button to do so. As just noted, the computer does not present an entire test at once, so the respondent has no way of knowing how many items are on the test. On many conventional tests the respondent can see all the items, and the prospect of taking a long test may lead to hurried answers or even omissions. The computer may force more careful attention to each item, which may affect the meaning of individual responses, thus affecting the interpretation of test results.

In both of these instances it is reasonable to suppose that computerized administration may be psychometrically superior to conventional administration. However, it may also cause the results to differ enough from those obtained from conventional administration to make data developed in that mode inapplicable when the test is administered via computer.

There is evidence that certain types of items may function differently depending on the mode of administration regardless of how carefully they were adapted to the computer. Greaud and Green (1984) found large differences in scores on speeded tests between computerized and paper-and-pencil administrations. Their tests involved very simple arithmetic problems, so it is not surprising that the time needed to record a response—a variable that differed greatly as a function of administration mode—significantly affected scores. Hoffman and Lundberg (1976) found the two modes equivalent on multiple-choice and true-false items; however, the computer presentation of items requiring matching responses resulted in significantly lower scores, different numbers of changed answers, and different patterns of changed answers.

There is also increasing evidence that rather subtle differences between on-line and conventional test administrations can produce large differences in test scores produced by the two modes. Studies of on-line administration of the MMPI indicate that providing an explicit "Cannot Say" option produces a greater number of item omissions than is found when that option is less obvious (Biskin and Kolotkin, 1977). Allred and Harris (1984) indicated that a similar phenomenon is encountered when the Adjective Checklist is administered by computer and respondents must, therefore, actively reject an adjective rather than passively fail to endorse it.

The content of items may also have an effect. Early on, Smith (1963) hypothesized that "confession-type" questions might be answered more honestly on the impersonal computer. This is not a very appealing hypothesis where comparisons with paper-and-pencil questionnaires are concerned. There is no a priori reason to believe that questionnaires are any more "invasive" than computers. However, two studies have found some evidence that this is the case (Evan and Miller, 1969; Koson, Kitchen, Kochen, and Stodolsky, 1970). Skinner and Allen (1983), on the other hand, found no differences between subjects' willingness to describe their alcohol and illegal drug use on a paper-and-pencil questionnaire and on a computer. To further muddy the waters, a recent study of on-line administration of the MMPI found patients producing more pathological profiles when the test was administered in the usual fashion than when it was administered via computer (Bresolin, 1984). The data from automated interviews are not consistent in this regard, though the hypothesis that people might respond more honestly to an impersonal computer than to a human interviewer *is* intuitively appealing. Four studies have found individuals admitting more socially undesirable behaviors to a computer than to an interviewer (Carr, Ghosh, and Ancil, 1983; Duffy and Waterton, 1984; Greist and Klein, 1980; Lucas, Mullins, Luna, and McInroy, 1977), while one has not (Skinner and Allen, 1983). Unfortunately, it is not clear whether the former results are due to an increased willingness to admit things to a computer, to the fact that computers can be counted on to ask everyone the same questions while interviewers cannot, or to both.

Despite these inconsistencies, the bulk of the evidence on computer adaptations of paper-and-pencil questionnaires points to the conclusion that nonequivalence is typically small enough to be of no practical consequence, if it is present at all (see also Blankenship, 1976; Katz and Dalby, 1981a, 1981b; Rezmovic, 1977).* Rezmovic (1977) found that computer administration caused extreme scorers to become even more extreme, suggesting that nonequivalence in questionnaires may occur mainly at points in the distribution of scores where measurement is already imprecise. The only consistent finding in the literature is that provision of an explicit "Cannot Say" option on the computer changes MMPI and California Psychological Inventory scores (Biskin and Kolotkin, 1977; Lushene, O'Neil, and Dunn, 1974; Scissons, 1976; White, Clements, and Fowler, 1985). This finding appears to be due to the change in response format between computer-administered and conventional versions of the tests. When care is taken to keep the two administration formats as similar as possible, this problem disappears (Biskin and Kolotkin, 1977; Bresolin, 1984; Rozensky, Honor, Tovian, and Herz, 1982; White, Clements, and Fowler, 1985).

On the other hand, it seems fair to conclude that people tend to be more willing to deal frankly with sensitive material when interacting with an impersonal computer than when talking with another person. This may be a problem even if, as seems likely, the data gathered during the computer interview are more accurate than those gathered face to face (Greist et al., 1973; compare the

* See Hofer and Green (1985) for a different interpretation of these data.

conclusions of Lucas, Mullins, Luna, and McInroy, 1977, with those of Pernanen, 1974). For example, it seems likely that the developers of the third edition of the *Diagnostic and Statistical Manual of Mental Disorders* (DSM III; American Psychiatric Association, 1980) were using implicit norms based on years of experience interviewing patients when they decided that one must possess X number of symptoms of a certain type in order be diagnosed as suffering from Y disorder. Those "cutting scores" may result in overdiagnosis if applied to data from the structured psychiatric interview schedules that are now being computerized (see Erdman, Klein, and Greist, 1985; see also chapter 9).

These conclusions can only be tentative because of the paucity of studies and the fact that only a few of these investigations took individual differences into account. There is some evidence—both direct and indirect—that individual differences may be important. As noted, Rezmovic (1977) found mode effects mainly for extreme scorers. Koson, Kitchen, Kochen, and Stodolsky (1970) found that only their female subjects tended to be more honest on the computer. In addition to this direct evidence, there is a large and rapidly growing body of literature on attitudes toward computer-administered tests and interviews and on the affective reactions engendered by computer test administration. Individuals are generally favorable to being questioned by computer; indeed, many prefer interacting with a computer to conventional assessment (see Bresolin, 1984; Greist, 1975; Lucas, 1977). Individuals have rated interacting with the computer at least as relaxing as other methods of assessment (Bresolin, 1984; Skinner and Allen, 1983), even if the computer initially was somewhat more anxiety provoking than a traditional questionnaire (Lushene, O'Neil, and Dunn, 1974). However, a significant minority of subjects in these same studies report a persistent negative reaction to the computer. The elderly compose one demographic group that is, in general, uncomfortable being questioned by a computer (Carr et al., 1982; Volans and Levy, 1982).* It is reasonable to speculate that such negative reactions may adversely affect the quality of computer-administered assessments. Perhaps people who are frustrated by having a cold, unresponsive computer ask questions or who are daunted by the technology may respond carelessly or be too nervous to devote proper attention to the assessment task.

These same kinds of individual difference considerations no doubt apply to automated administration of ability measures. Indeed, Johnson and Mihal (1973) found that blacks scored higher on a computer-administered ability test than on one administered in the conventional way. When individual differences are ignored, the available evidence for power ability tests that do not require a change in response format for computerized administration consistently indicates that nonequivalence, if present at all, is likely to be small (Moreno, Wetzel, McBride, and Weiss, 1984; Sacher and Fletcher, 1978). As a matter of fact, several studies have demonstrated that computer-adaptive administration of

* It is only fair to point out that we do not know how the elderly feel about traditional assessment; they may not like that much either.

conventional tests typically results in a 50 percent reduction in the number of items administered *and* a decrease in measurement error (see chapter 16 for details of these studies).

In summary, most data indicate that if a computerized administration procedure is comparable to the conventional one, comparable results will be obtained. The data are a little more shaky with regard to personality inventories and interviews than ability tests. This is not surprising given the widely held belief that responses to the former have more complex determinants than responses to the latter regardless of mode of administration. Ability testers have never concerned themselves with issues like social desirability! The assessor needs to be familiar with the different types of test equivalence and their respective implications for the use of interpretive data. Hofer and Green (1985) provide a brief, practical synopsis of this complex topic. If an individual expresses reluctance to interact with the computer, the test or interview should probably be administered in the conventional fashion. In any case, extra care should be taken to ensure that individuals understand the task at hand and are able to respond appropriately. Johnson and White (1980) found that elderly people who received one hour of training in the use of a terminal prior to testing scored significantly higher on the Wonderlic Personnel Test than did those who received no training. Practitioners may find it beneficial to develop several samples of different item types for training in the use of the computer. Equipment and other conditions of testing are important determinants of the quality of any assessment, but computer administration places an extra burden on the assessor to see that testing conditions are optimal. Properly functioning equipment, including a clean, glare-free display of adequate resolution, and clear response devices, perhaps with covers over unused keys, is important.

Output

As with input, there are several different output options available to the consumer of computerized assessment. Choice of the best option depends mainly on the amount of information necessary to discharge the assessment task at hand. Time may also be a consideration. The more detailed the computerized report, the less work a practitioner must put forth to work up a case. In reading what follows, keep in mind the fact that the taxonomy of report types is merely a heuristic device. In practice reports are frequently a combination of the pure types discussed in the following section. In particular, interpretive reports usually report scores.

SCORING REPORTS

Scoring reports present just what their name implies: test scores. The scores may be simply listed or they may be drawn on a profile, but scores are all that you get. Some tests—notably vocational interest inventories with well over one-hundred scales, such as the Kuder Occupational Interest Survey and the Strong-Campbell Interest Inventory—are much too long to score by hand. Thus computer-generated scoring reports are a necessity rather than an option for those tests. Even in cases where the test may be scored by hand, scoring reports will be useful when a practitioner desires to use a large number of scores. You can, for example, get by with hand scoring the fourteen MMPI scales that have been part of the basic profile since the test was first published. However, an increasing number of practitioners feel that they get more out of the test if they have scores on some of the more than six-hundred special scales now available for the test. It takes roughly a minute to hand-score and plot one MMPI scale. Thus you need not use many special scales before computer scoring becomes cost effective. This is to say nothing about the increase in scoring accuracy you can expect from computer scoring (see Greene, 1980, p. 25; Klett, Schaefer, and Plemel, 1985).

EXTENDED SCORING REPORTS

Zachary (1984) defined extended scoring reports as "usually involving the addition [to a scoring report] of deatiled statistical output but little or no case-specific narrative" (p. 9). A portion of an extended scoring report that Zachary helped to develop is presented in chapter 17. You do not often see test profiles like the one in that chapter that include statistical confidence intervals plotted around scores and statistical significance tests. These kinds of data make it possible for practitioners to identify especially meaningful scores at a glance. They should also increase the practitioner's confidence that those scores are, in fact, important. Everyone ought to be willing to admit that statistical significance tests are bound to beat old-fashioned clinical "eyeballing" of profiles! And what busy practitioner is going to calculate confidence intervals by hand—especially for tests with dozens of scales? On the other hand, as Zachary was careful to point out, it is still up to the practitioner to determine the clinical significance of the statistical significance.

The possibilities for reports of this kinds are legion. For example, different confidence intervals might be computed for use in interscale and test-retest comparisons (see Dudek, 1979). Jackson (1984) provides statistical indices of similarity between Jackson Vocational Interest Survey profiles and the mean profiles of a number for occupational clusters and college majors. George Huba and his colleagues at Western Psychological Services (WPS) are applying similar techniques to several personality inventories. This kind of report is widely available for popular ability measures, such as the Wechslers, Stanford-Binet, and K-ABC. It is hoped that reports of this type will become much more common in the near future.

DESCRIPTIVE REPORTS

Unlike the reports already described, descriptive reports provide interpretations of test scores. They may be distinguished from other types of interpretive reports by two factors: each scale on the instrument is interpreted without reference to the other, scale by scale, and comments on any one scale are usually quite cryptic. These interpretations often involve no more than an adverb modifying the adjectival form of the scale name. Such an interpretation of a high score on an anxiety scale might, for example, read: "Mr. Jones reports that he is very anxious." Thus the interpretive comments stick close to empirical data and their origins are obvious. At first blush, this kind of report may seem so simpleminded as to be unhelpful. Not so. This type of report can be especially helpful when a test has a large number of scales or when a large number of tests need to be interpreted in a short period of time. Like extended scoring reports, descriptive reports allow the practitioner to quickly and easily identify the most deviant scales. This kind of report is most helpful if an instrument contains scales that are reported in terms of different types of standard scores (see Ripley and Ripley, 1979) or different normative samples (see chapter 15). The Narrative Scoring Report for the 16 PF is probably the most widely used report of this type.

The output of most nonpsychometric computerized assessment tools can be characterized as descriptive too. The output from structured interviews is frequently a simple playback of what the client reported. Take Mr. Jones. The interpretive statement just reported as the result of a high score on a psychometric anxiety scale could as easily have been generated by a structured interview program if, in response to the question "What brings you here today?" Mr. Jones had typed in "I am very anxious."

SCREENING REPORTS

Like descriptive reports, screening reports are cryptic. They are distinguished from descriptive reports in that relationships among scales are usually considered in the interpretation and the interpretive comments are not usually couched in terms of a single scale name. The Minnesota Personnel Screening Report presented in chapter 10 is a screening report in this sense. Obviously the main body of that report is very cryptic—five six-point rating scales. None of the rating scales corresponds directly to an MMPI scale, however. In fact, the rating on each of the five scales is determined by the configuration of a number of MMPI scales. The rules governing the "Content Themes" presented in that report are also complex. The comment that the client "may keep problems to himself too much" resulted from the consideration of the following set of rules:

L and *K* are greater than *F* and
F is less than 55*T* and
D, *Pa*, *Pt*, and *Sc* are less than 65*T* and

Hy is greater than 69*T* or
*Hy*2 is greater than 63*T* or
Hy is greater than 64*T*, and *Hy*1 or *Hy*5 is greater than 59*T* or
R is greater than 59*T* or
*D*5 is greater than 59*T*

Screening reports will be most helpful in situations where the same decision can be reached by multiple paths. Take the example of screening commercial pilots for emotional fitness. A screening report like the Minnesota Report may deem a candidate's emotional fitness "suspect" if he or she: (1) seems to be a thrill-seeking individual; (2) is so obsessive that he or she is unlikely to respond promptly to in-flight emergencies; or (3) may have a drinking problem. Because of this multifaceted approach to the assessment problem, such reports are also likely to be most helpful when they are truly used for screening rather than for making final decisions. They are too deliberately cryptic to be used for the latter purpose. Further investigation, triggered by a screening report, may lead one to discover that a suspect candidate is a recovering alcoholic who has been dry for ten years.

Like descriptive reports, screening reports need not be based on test results. A structured interview that yields psychiatric diagnoses may be thought of as a screening procedure.

The limited output of screening reports means that their output, while more inferential than that of a descriptive report, stays close to the empirical data about the instrument. The expertise of the system developer comes in mainly in the formation of useful higher-order categories that are impinged upon by the test scales (for example, overall adjustment). The limited output also means that, despite the complex decision rules, the potential consumer can get a feel for the adequacy of a screening report by examining the results for a small number of cases. Formal research is also feasible with these kinds of reports even though publishers seldom make the decision rules available to consumers for fear of piracy.

CONSULTATIVE REPORTS

Dahlstrom, Welsh, and Dahlstrom (1972) contrasted consultative MMPI reports with screening reports in the following fashion: "The intent [of consultative reports] is to provide a more detailed analysis of the test data in professional language appropriate to communication between colleagues" (p. 313). In other words, consultative reports are designed to mimic as closely as possible the reports generated every day by human test interpreters. Well-developed reports of this type are characterized by the smoothly flowing prose and complete exploitation of the data that would be expected from an expert human consultant. Indeed, the chief advantage of these reports is that they can provide busy practitioners with a consultation from someone who has spent years studying and using the instrument in question—an expert to whom the average practitioner would not ordinarily have access. The chapters in part two of this volume abound with examples of consultative reports produced by just such experts.

Choosing a system that produces consultative computerized reports is a risky business. In order to cover all cases most of these systems must fairly frequently fall back on clinical lore and the idiosyncratic practical experience of the system developer. Choosing such a system is especially difficult if you want local computer software. As noted previously, unlike central processing and teleprocessing, anyone who has a couple of thousand dollars and can read a book can get into the local software business. A number of commercial programs written at the consultative level appear to have been developed by someone with a programming guide in one hand and an MMPI "cookbook" in the other. I have come across at least one MMPI software package that was in fact written by a computer programmer who had no knowledge of the MMPI beyond what he copied out of two popular "cookbooks." Thus you need to carefully check the *bona fides* of the system you are proposing to use.

It is unlikely that you will be able to review the interpretive rules used in a consultative system, again because authors and publishers are afraid of having their work stolen. Other than trying a few reports, the best way to evaluate the potential adequacy of these systems is to review the credentials of the system authors. If the authors have no track record as researchers with the instrument in question, you're probably better off looking elsewhere. Reviews of these types of systems are also frequently available in sources like the *Mental Measurements Yearbook*. The size and complexity of consultative systems present formidable obstacles to the would-be researcher (see Moreland, 1985). The Minnesota Clinical Report system described in chapter 10 has hundreds of rules used to trigger thousands of sentences in untold numbers of combinations. Nevertheless, there has been some research—modest in both quantity and quality—on consultative systems. It is that research to which we now turn.

TECHNICAL "OUTPUT" ISSUES: COMPUTER-BASED TEST INTERPRETATION

With very few exceptions current CBTI systems use the method of automated *clinical* prediction, as described by Wiggins (1973): ". . . On the basis of published research, clinical hypotheses, and clinical experience, a skilled [sic] clinician assembles a set of interpretations that are uniquely associated with the input data" (p. 199). It is very important to distinguish between these types of CBTI systems and those that are *actuarial*. A CBTI system is actuarial *if and only if* the interpretive output of the system is completely determined by statistical regularities that have been empirically demonstrated to exist between that output and the input data (Sines, 1966). This distinction is important because many of the interpretations generated by automated clinical systems need to be validated much as a test needs to be validated. The issue with actuarial interpretations is not validity per se but generalizability beyond the population on which they were developed.

David Lachar and his colleagues have expended a great deal of creative effort developing an actuarial CBTI system for the Personality Inventory for Children (see chapter 14). However, most of the empirical correlates used in this system were developed in one clinical setting. Will they be equally applicable in other settings? The jury is out. The same is not true of the various attempts that have been made to interpret neuropsychological data by computer. Several studies have called into question the generalizability of the interpretive approach developed by Russell, Neuringer, and Goldstein (1970). Comparative studies have found that several computerized interpretive systems for the Halstead-Reitan Battery are less accurate than expert human interpreters. (Consult chapter 18 for more details on this work.) It is also worth noting that there are numerous instances in which the clinical judgment of neurologists (Kleinmuntz, 1968) and other physicans (Blois, 1980) has bested the computer.

A very different state of affairs exists with regard to computerized *clinical* interpretation of *personality* tests. Both the means of assessing system validity and the results of validity studies differ from those in neuropsychology and medicine. This may reflect the primitive state of personality assessment relative to neuropsychology and medicine; criterion information is much more definitive in the latter two areas. It may also reflect the comparatively primitive state of computer programs for neuropsychological assessment (see chapter 18) and in some areas of medical diagnosis. Time will tell.

To date studies of the accuracy of computer-based clinical interpretations of personality tests have been limited almost exclusively to the MMPI (but see Green, 1982; Harris et al., 1981; Moreland and Onstad, 1986), and that instrument will be the focus of attention here too. These studies have involved several experimental approaches. A few studies have compared computer-based test interpretation systems with human interpretations using rigorous experimental designs (for example, see Bringmann, Balance, and Giesbrecht, 1972; Glueck and Reznikoff, 1965; Johnson, Giannetti, and Williams, 1978). The "criterion" reports, since they are prepared by human interpreters, may provide a poor standard against which to judge the validity of computer-based interpretations of the MMPI. The validity of a clinician's interpretation of the MMPI is often low enough that a computer-based test interpretation can be at serious variance with it and still be accurate (see Graham, 1967). Labeck, Johnson, and Harris (1983) asked three experts to rate the quality and accuracy of interpretive rules and interpretive statements for the MMPI CBTI system developed by the first author. Though suffering from the same problem as those studies using clinicians' reports as criteria, this study does highlight a useful means of evaluating and improving CBTI systems. This is especially true in light of the fact that most CBTI systems are developed by one individual.

Most of the published studies of CBTI validity have involved asking recipients to rate the accuracy of the computer interpretations on the basis of their knowledge of the test respondents (Green, 1982; Moreland, 1985; Vincent and

Castillo, 1984). Though disparaged by some writers (Lanyon, 1984; Matarazzo, 1983), these studies are considered promising by other experts—especially if

TABLE 3.1
Global Accuracy Ratings of CBTI Systems for the MMPI

Study	*Settings*	*CBTI System*	*No. of CBTIs*	*Percentage "Accurate"*
Webb, Miller, and Fowler, 1969	Settings served by psychiatrists, psychologists subscribing to Roche	Roche	697	87
Webb, Miller, and Fowler, 1970	State hospital, mental health center, settings served by psychiatrists, psychologists subscribing to Roche	Roche	86	80
Webb, 1970	Veterans Administration Medical Centers	Roche	160	77
Fowler and Blaser, 1972	Psychiatric	Roche		
—Australia			NR[a]	81
—Italy			NR	70
Fowler, N.D.	State reformatory	Roche	31	61
Lushene and Gilberstadt, 1972	Veterans Administration Medical Centers	VA		
—first study			599	89
—second study			355	91
Lachar, 1974	Psychiatric and general medical	WPS	1,410	77
Adams and Shore, 1976	Psychiatric hospital	WPS	100	85
Lachar, Klinge, and Grisell, 1976	Psychiatric hospital	WPS		
—adolescent norms			100	58
—adult norms			100	32
Green, 1982[b]	Variety of psychiatric settings	Roche	100	81
		Mayo Clinic	50	64
Moreland and Onstad, 1985	Private practice, mental health center	Minnesota Clinical Report	66	70
		Bogus Minnesota Clinical Report	66	39

[a] NR = not reported.　[b] Summary of Green's table 2.

slightly modified (see Webb, Miller, and Fowler, 1970)—and therefore merit further consideration. These studies are summarized in table 3.1.

The "customer satisfaction" studies (Lanyon, 1984) have been overwhelmingly supportive of CBTI systems, as indicated by the median accuracy rating of 78.5 percent that can be gleaned from table 3.1. Reviewers appear to agree that the major shortcoming of these studies is a failure to control for the well-known P. T. Barnum Effect. That is, reviewers have been concerned that raters would characterize CBTI systems as accurate not because the reports were pointed descriptions of the individuals at issue but rather because they contained glittering generalities (cf. O'Dell, 1972). However, some of these studies have been useful in guiding authors' efforts to improve their CBTI systems for the MMPI (see Moreland, 1985). Furthermore, the last study listed in table 3.1 (Moreland and Onstad, 1985) addressed the issue of base-rate accuracy. The authors found genuine computer-based test interpretations far superior to closely matched, but phony, ones (see chapter 10 for further discussion of this study). Wimbish (1984) has conducted a similar study. Both of the latter two studies have demonstrated that clinicians rate computer-based MMPI interpretations sold by several commercial firms as being considerably more accurate than phony reports.

A few researchers have asked consumers of computer-based MMPI interpretations to complete symptom checklists or Q-sorts based on the computer-generated reports, subsequently comparing those ratings with analogous ones made by clinicians familiar with each patient (see Moreland, 1985). Those studies are summarized in table 3.2.

The "external criterion" studies have typically dealt with the base-rate accuracy problem by comparing the accuracy of report-based ratings with "stereotypical patient" ratings or by presenting multireport-multirating intercorrelation matrices. These studies have been plagued by small samples of test respondents, interpretive statements, and criterion variables, which call into question the generalizability of the results. Further, the results of these studies, considered one at a time, have been decidedly mixed. Two studies have indicated that computer-based test interpretations enjoy modest validity, similar in magnitude to that found for interpretations generated in the traditional fashion (Chase, 1974; Crumpton, 1974; compare Graham, 1967). Two other studies have found computer-based MMPI interpretations to manifest chance accuracy (Anderson, 1969; Hedlund, Morgan, and Master, 1972). And one study found computer-based test interpretations to be valid for one set of criterion variables but no more valid than "stereotypical patient" ratings for another set (Moreland, 1983). Moreland (1983) and Chase (1974) found that ratings made directly from MMPI *profiles* were more valid than those based on computerized *reports*, but Anderson (1969) did not. Chase's (1974) computer-based interpretations were at least as accurate as clinician-generated reports.

Sifting through this mass of evidence, things look pretty good for computer-based MMPI interpretations. Consumers give them high marks, and the results of properly controlled studies indicate that this high acceptance rate is not the

TABLE 3.2
Correlations Between Ratings Made By Clinical Judges and the Same Ratings Made from Computer-Based Test Interpretations of the MMPI and the MMPI Profile

Study	*Setting*	*No. of Cases*	*Rating Source*	*Mean r*
Anderson, 1969	Private psychiatric hospital	28	Roche	0.20
			MMPI profile	
Crumpton, 1974	Private practice	9	Roche	0.30
			Caldwell	0.42
			ICA[a]	0.34
Chase, 1974	General hospital psychiatric inpatient unit	3	Roche	0.30
			Caldwell	0.31
			Behaviordyne	0.42
			Marks and Seeman, 1963	0.39
			clinician reports	0.32
			MMPI profile	0.45
Moreland, 1983	State hospital inpatient			
—Brief Psychiatric Rating Scale		49	Roche	0.25
			WPS	0.25
			MMPI profile	0.27
			patient stereotype	0.22
—Nurse's Observation Scale for Inpatient Evaluation		52	Roche	0.46
			WPS	0.46
			MMPI profile	0.60
			patient stereotype	0.36

[a] ICA = Institute for Clinical Analysis.

result of generalized reports that are equally applicable to most clients (Moreland and Onstad, 1985; Wimbish, 1984). The validity coefficients developed in the external criterion studies are of the magnitude typically found in studies of clinical assessment (see Graham, 1967). The one study that compared clinician- and computer-generated reports the latter to be at least as good as the former (Chase, 1974); and one study found no difference between ratings generated from computer-based *reports* and MMPI *profiles* (Anderson, 1969). There are both theoretical reasons (see Fowler, 1969) and some research evidence (Moreland and Onstad, in press) to suggest that these findings should generalize to CBTI systems for other clinical instruments *if those systems are developed to mimic expert interpretations of thoroughly researched instruments*. For example, I would be willing to wager that the systems described in chapters 11 and 12 would fare well under empirical scrutiny.

Advice to the Would-be Consumer

All the foregoing can be distilled into a few questions that prospective consumers of computerized assessment should ask themselves in deciding what to buy. Ask output kinds of questions first. "What kind of assessment tools do I need?" Once you narrow the range of possibilities to categories like "personality tests for the assessment of psychopathology," ask: "What kind of reports do I need?" Don't begin to consider input options until these questions about the kinds of information you need are settled. Information needs should dictate choice of computer services rather than the other way around. Once output needs are decided upon, you can then decide what sort of computer service to use. Assuming you do not desire technology-dependent information (for example, a social history that requires on-line administration because it uses branching logic), a variety of options will still be available at this point. You can now ask: "What kind of turnaround time do I need? Can I afford to wait a week for central processing or do I need immediate results?" If you need immediate processing you'll need to consider the volume of assessment you do. "Do I process enough tests to make me want to avoid the clerical time and telephone charges involved in teleprocessing? Is my assessment practice small enough to make on-line administration an attractive option or will I need an optical mark reader to handle everything?" Finally, ask yourself some important practical questions about the company you're thinking of dealing with. Do their products evidence good craftsmanship? What kind of technical support do they offer to their customers? Is the company financially sound or is it likely to be gone tomorrow?

I believe that these questions will lead you to choose the right computerized assessment products and services. I hope that considering the issues in this order will also help you to make the right choices quickly and efficiently. Obviously if you need an interpretive report and none exists it is fruitless to worry about how to get your data into the computer!

ACKNOWLEDGMENTS

This article represents the private views of the author and not necessarily those of NCS Professional Assessment Services.

I would like to thank David R. Roble for his help in preparing the section on teleprocessing.

REFERENCES

Adams, K. M., and Shore, D. L. (1976). The accuracy of an automated MMPI interpretation system in a psychiatric setting. *Journal of Clinical Psychology*, 32, 80–82.

Allred, L. J., and Harris, W. G. (1984). *The non-equivalence of computerized and conventional administrations of the Adjective Checklist.* Unpublished manuscript, Johns Hopkins University, Department of Psychology, Baltimore.

American Psychiatric Association (1980). *Diagnostic and statistical manual of mental disorders* (3rd ed.). Washington, DC: Author.

Anderson, B. N. (1969). *The utility of the Minnesota Multiphasic Personality Inventory in a private psychiatric hospital setting.* Unpublished master's thesis, Ohio State University, Columbus.

Biskin, B. H., and Kolotkin, R. C. (1977). Effects of computerized administration on scores on the Minnesota Multiphasic Personality Inventory. *Applied Psychological Measurement*, 1, 543–549.

Blankenship, L. L. (1976). Computer-conducted assessment of life-change psychological stress. *Dissertation Abstracts International*, 37, 2495B. (University Microfilms No. 76–24, 045)

Blois, M. S. (1980). Clinical judgment and computers. *New England Journal of Medicine*, 303, 192–197.

Bresolin, M. J., Jr. (1984). *A comparative study of computer administration of the Minnesota Multiphasic Personality Inventory in an inpatient psychiatric setting.* Unpublished doctoral dissertation, Loyola University, Chicago.

Bringmann, W. G., Balance, W. D. G., and Giesbrecht, C. A. (1972). The computer vs. the technologist: Comparison of psychological reports on normal and elevated MMPI profiles. *Psychological Reports*, 31, 211–217.

Butcher, J. N., Keller, L. S., and Bacon, S. F. (1985). Current developments and future directions in computerized personality assessment. *Journal of Consulting and Clinical Psychology*, 53, 803–815.

Carr, A. C., Ghosh, A., and Ancil, R. J. (1983). Can a computer take a psychiatric history? *Psychological Medicine*, 13, 151–158.

Carr, A. C., Wilson, S. L., Ghosh, A., Ancil, R. J., and Woods, R. T. (1982). Automated testing of geriatric patients using a microcomputer-based system. *International Journal of Man-Machine Studies*, 28, 297–300.

Chase, L. L. S. (1974). An evaluation of MMPI interpretation systems. *Dissertation Abstracts International*, 35, 3009B. (University Microfilms No. 74-26, 172)

Crumpton, C. A. (1974). An evaluation and comparison of three automated MMPI interpretive reports. *Dissertation Abstracts International*, 35, 6090B. (University Microfilms No. 75-11, 982)

Dahlstrom, W. G., Welsh, G. S., and Dahlstrom, L. E. (1972). *An MMPI handbook. Vol. 1: Clinical interpretation (rev. ed.).* Minneapolis: University of Minnesota Press.

Dudek, F. J. (1979). The continuing misinterpretation of the standard error of measurement. *Psychological Bulletin*, 86, 335–337.

Duffy, J. C., and Waterton, J. J. (1984). Under-reporting of alcohol consumption in sample surveys: The effect of computer interviewing in fieldwork. *British Journal of Addictions*, 79, 303–308.

Erdman, H. P., Klein, M. H., and Greist, J. H. (1985). Direct patient computer interviewing. *Journal of Consulting and Clinical Psychology*, 53, 760–773.

Evan, W. M., and Miller, J. R. (1969). Differential effects on response bias of computer vs. conventional administration of a social science questionnaire. *Behavior Science*, 14, 216–227.

Fowler, R. D. (N.D.). *The use of computer-produced MMPI reports with a prison population.* Unpublished manuscript.

Fowler, R. D. (1969). Automated interpretation of personality test data. In J. N. Butcher (Ed.), *MMPI: Research developments and clinical applications* (pp. 105–125). New York: McGraw-Hill.

Fowler, R. D. (1985). Landmarks in computer assisted psychological assessment. *Journal of Consulting and Clinical Psychology*, 53, 748–759.

Fowler, R. D., and Blaser, P. (1972). *Around the world in 566 items.* Paper presented at the Seventh Annual Symposium on Recent Developments in the Use of the MMPI, Mexico City. Cited in J. N. Butcher and P. Pancheri (1976), *A handbook of cross-national MMPI research* (pp. 194–196). Minneapolis: University of Minnesota Press.

Glueck, B. C., Jr., and Reznikoff, M. (1965). Comparison of computer-derived personality profile and projective psychological test findings. *American Journal of Psychiatry, 121*, 1156–1161.

Graham, J. R. (1967). A Q-sort study of the accuracy of clinical descriptions based on the MMPI. *Journal of Psychiatric Research, 5*, 297–305.

Greaud, V. A., and Green, B. F. (1984). *Equivalence of conventional and computer presentation of speed tests*. Manuscript submitted for publication.

Green, C. J. (1982). The diagnostic accuracy and utility of MMPI and MCMI computer interpretive reports. *Journal of Personality Assessment, 46*, 359–365.

Greene, R. L. (1980). *The MMPI: An interpretive manual*. New York: Grune & Stratton.

Greist, J. H. (1975). The computer interview as a medium for collecting questionnaire data on drug use: Predicting adolescent drug abuse. In D. J. Lettieri (Ed.), *Predicting adolescent drug use: A review of issues, methods and correlates* (pp. 147–164). Washington, DC: U.S. Government Printing Office.

Greist, J. H., Gustafson, D. H., Stauss, F. F., Rowse, G. L., Laughren, T. P., and Chiles, J. A. (1973). A computer interview for suicide risk prediction. *American Journal of Psychiatry, 130*, 1327–1332.

Greist, J. H., and Klein, M. H. (1980). Computer programs for patients, clinicians, and researchers in psychiatry. In J. B. Sidowski, J. H. Johnson, and T. A. Williams (Eds.), *Technology in mental health care delivery systems* (pp. 161–182). Norwood, NJ: Ablex.

Harris, W. G., Niedner, D., Feldman, C., Fink, A., and Johnson, J. H. (1981). An on-line interpretive Rorschach approach: Using Exner's Comprehensive System. *Behavior Research Methods and Instrumentation, 13*, 588–591.

Hedlund, J. L., Morgan, D. W., and Master, F. D. (1972). The Mayo Clinic Automated MMPI Program: Crossvalidation with psychiatric patients in an army hospital. *Journal of Clinical Psychology, 28*, 505–510.

Hofer, P. J., and Green, B. F. (1985). The challenge of competence and creativity in computerized psychological testing. *Journal of Consulting and Clinical Psychology, 53*, 826–838.

Hoffman, K. I., and Lundberg, G. D. (1976). A comparison of computer monitored group tests with paper-and-pencil tests. *Educational and Psychological Measurement, 36*, 791–809.

Jackson, D. N. (1984). *Jackson Vocational Interest Survey manual* (2nd ed.). Port Huron, MI: Research Psychologists Press.

Johnson, D. F., and Mihal, W. L. (1973). The performance of blacks and whites in computerized versus manual testing environments. *American Psychologist, 28*, 694–699.

Johnson, D. F., and White, C. B. (1980). Effects of training on computerized test performance in the elderly. *Journal of Applied Psychology, 65*, 357–358.

Johnson, J. H., and Williams, T. A. (1980). Using on-line computer technology in a mental health admitting system. In J. B. Sidowski, J. H. Johnson, and T. A. Williams (Eds.), *Technology in mental health care delivery systems* (pp. 237–249). Norwood, NJ: Ablex.

Johnson, J. H., Giannetti, R. A., and Williams, T. A. (1978). A self-contained microcomputer system for psychological testing. *Behavior Research Methods and Instrumentation, 10*, 579–581.

Katz, L., and Dalby, J. T. (1981a). Computer and manual administration of the Eysenck Personality Inventory. *Journal of Clinical Psychology, 37*, 586–588.

Katz, L., and Dalby, J. T. (1981b). Computer-assisted and traditional assessment of elementary-school-aged children. *Contemporary Educational Psychology, 6*, 314–322.

Kleinmuntz, B. (Ed.) (1968). *Formal representation of human judgment*. New York: Wiley.

Klett, B., Schaefer, A., and Plemel, D. (1985, May). Just how accurate are computer-scored tests? *The VA Chief Psychologist, 8*, 7.

Koson, D., Kitchen, C., Kochen, M., and Stodolsky, D. (1970). Psychological testing by computer: Effect on response bias. *Educational and Psychological Measurement, 30*, 803–810.

Labeck, L. J., Johnson, J. H., and Harris, W. G. (1983). Validity of an automated on-line MMPI interpretive system. *Journal of Clinical Psychology, 39*, 412–416.

Lachar, D. (1974). Accuracy and generalization of an automated MMPI interpretation system. *Journal of Consulting and Clinical Psychology, 42*, 267–273.

Lachar, D. (1984). *Multidimensional description of child personality: A manual for the Personality Inventory for Children* (rev. ed.). Los Angeles: Western Psychological Services.

Lachar, D., Klinge, V., and Grisell, J. L. (1976). Relative accuracy of automated MMPI narratives generated from adult norm and adolescent norm profiles. *Journal of Consulting and Clinical Psychology, 44*, 20–24.

Lanyon, R. I. (1984). Personality assessment. *Annual Review of Psychology, 35*, 667–701.

Larson, E. (1984, January 6). Many firms seek entry into software. *The Wall Street Journal*, p. 23.

Lieff, J. D. (1984). *Computers and other technological aids for psychiatric private practice*. Washington, DC: American Psychiatric Press.

Lucas, R. W. (1977). A study of patients' attitudes to computer interrogation. *International Journal of Man-Machine Studies*, 9, 69–86.

Lucas, R. W., Mullins, P. J., Luna, C. B., and McInroy, D. C. (1977). Psychiatrists and a computer as interrogators of patients with alcohol-related illnesses: A comparison. *British Journal of Psychiatry*, *131*, 160–167.

Lushene, R. E., and Gilberstadt, H. (1972, March). *Validation of VA MMPI computer-generated reports*. Paper presented at the Veterans Administration Cooperative Studies Conference, St. Louis.

Lushene, R. E., O'Neil, H. H., and Dunn, T. (1974). Equivalent validity of a completely computerized MMPI. *Journal of Personality Assessment*, 38, 353–361.

Marks, P. A., and Seeman, W. (1963). *The actuarial description of abnormal personality*. Baltimore: Williams & Wilkins.

Matarazzo, J. M. (1983, July 22). Computerized psychological testing. *Science*, *221*, p. 323.

Moreland, K. L. (1983, April). *A comparison of the validity of two MMPI interpretation systems: A preliminary report*. Paper presented at the 18th Annual MMPI Symposium, Minneapolis.

Moreland, K. L. (1985). Validation of computer-based test interpretations: Problems and prospects. *Journal of Consulting and Clinical Psychology*, 53, 816–825.

Moreland, K. L., and Onstad, J. A. (1985, March). *Validity of the Minnesota Clinical Report, I: Mental health outpatients*. Paper presented at the 20th Annual MMPI Symposium, Honolulu.

Moreland, K. L., and Onstad, J. A. (in press). Validity of Millon's computerized interpretation system for the MCMI: A controlled study. *Journal of Consulting and Clinical Psychology*.

Moreno, K. E., Wetzel, C. D., McBride, J. R., and Weiss, D. J. (1984). Relationship between corresponding Armed Services Vocational Aptitude Battery (ASVAB) and Computerized Adaptive Testing (CAT) subtests. *Applied Psychological Measurement*, 8, 155–163.

O'Dell, J. W. (1972). P. T. Barnum explores the computer. *Journal of Consulting and Clinical Psychology*, 38, 270–273.

Pernanen, K. (1974). Validity of survey data in alcohol use. In R. J. Gibbins, Y. Israel, H. Kalant, R. E. Popham, W. Schmidt, and R. G. Smart (Eds.), *Research advances in alcohol and drug problems, vol. 1* (pp. 355–374). New York: Wiley.

Pressman, R. M. (1984). *Microcomputers and the private practitioner*. Homewood, IL: Dow Jones-Irwin.

Rezmovic, V. (1977). The effects of computerized experimentation on response variance. *Behavior Research Methods and Instrumentation*, 9, 144–147.

Ripley, R. E., and Ripley, M. J. (1979). *Career families: Interpretation manual for the World of Work Inventory* (rev. ed.). Scottsdale, AZ: World of Work.

Rozensky, R. H., Honor, L. F., Tovian, S. H., and Herz, G. I. (1982). *Paper-and-pencil versus computer administered MMPI: A comparison of patient attitudes*. Unpublished manuscript, Evanston Hospital, Evanston, IL.

Russell, E. W., Neuringer, C., and Goldstein, G. (1970). *Assessment of brain damage: A neuropsychological key approach*. New York: Wiley.

Sacher, J., and Fletcher, J. D. (1978). Administering paper-and-pencil tests by computer, or the medium is not always the message. In D. J. Weiss (Ed.), *Proceedings of the 1977 Computerized Adaptive Testing Conference* (pp. 403–419). Minneapolis: University of Minnesota, Department of Psychology, Psychometric Methods Program, Computerized Adaptive Testing Laboratory.

Scissons, E. H. (1976). Computer administration of the California Psychological Inventory. *Measurement and Evaluation in Guidance*, 9, 22–25.

Sines, J. O. (1966). Actuarial methods in personality assessment. In B. Maher (Ed.), *Progress in experimental personality research, vol. 3* (pp. 133–193). New York: Academic Press.

Skinner, H. A., and Allen, B. A. (1983). Does the computer make a difference? Computerized versus face-to-face versus self-report assessment of alcohol, drug, and tobacco use. *Journal of Consulting and Clinical Psychology*, 2, 267–275.

Smith, R. E. (1963). Examination by computer. *Behavioral Science*, 8, 76–79.

Vincent, K. R., and Castillo, I. M. (1984). A comparison of two MMPI narratives. *Computers in Psychiatry/Psychology*, 6(4), 30–32.

Volans, P. J., and Levy, R. (1982). A re-evaluation of an automated tailored test of concept learning with elderly psychiatric patients. *British Journal of Clinical Psychology*, *21*, 93–101.

Webb, J. T. (1970). Validity and utility of computer-produced MMPI reports with Veterans Administration psychiatric populations. *Proceedings of the 78th Annual Convention of the American Psychological Association*, 5, 541–542.

Webb, J. T., Miller, M. L., and Fowler, R. D. (1969). Validation of a computerized MMPI interpretation system [Summary]. *Proceedings of the 77th Annual Convention of the American Psychological Association*, 4, 523–521.

Webb, J. T., Miller, M. L., and Fowler, R. D. (1970). Extending professional time: A computerized MMPI interpretation service. *Journal of Clinical Psychology*, 26, 210–214.

White, D. M., Clements, C. B., and Fowler, R. D. (1985, March). *A comparison of computer administration with standard administration of the MMPI*. Paper presented at the annual meeting of the Southeastern Psychological Association, Atlanta, GA.

Wiggins, J. S. (1973). *Personality and prediction: Principles of personality assessment*. Reading, MA: Addison-Wesley.

Wimbish, L. G. (1984). *The importance of appropriate norms for the computerized interpretation of adolescent MMPI profiles*. Unpublished doctoral dissertation, Ohio State University, Columbus.

Zachary, R. (1984, August). Computer-based test interpretations: Comments and discussion. In J. D. Matarazzo (Chair), *Computer-based test interpretation: Prospects and problems*. Symposium conducted at the annual convention of the American Psychological Association, Toronto.

4

Developing a Computer-Based Test Interpretation System

Raymond D. Fowler

The availability to most psychologists of relatively powerful microcomputers has inspired a broad range of personal and professional uses. Automated stimulus presentation, data recording, and statistical analysis have revolutionized the psychological laboratory. Clinical applications have also proliferated. Computer-based psychological test reports, once available only by mail, can now be produced on the personal computer by means of commercially available diskettes. A growing number of psychologists would like to develop computer programs to produce computer-based test reports for their own use or to sell to others. The purposes of this chapter are to outline some of the issues, problems, and scientific potential inherent in developing a computer-based test interpretation (CBTI) system and to suggest some guidelines and strategies to facilitate the development process.

Types of Psychological Software

Krug (1984) has coined a useful term, psychware, to designate the array of computer-based products used by psychologists. The products currently on the market for use by clinical psychologists may be loosely divided into assessment systems and behavior change systems. Assessment systems are designed to diagnose or evaluate by means of tests, histories, self-descriptions, or standardized observations. The purpose of these systems is to describe or evaluate behavior, not to change it.

Behavior change systems are designed to help individuals eliminate unwanted behaviors or initiate new ones. They may include an assessment component, but their main purpose is to change behavior. This chapter focuses entirely on assessment programs; behavior change programs involve another set of professional and ethical issues and a different set of strategies.

Types of Assessment Instruments

Assessment instruments that make up CBTI systems include standardized tests and a range of other instruments including histories, rating scales, and checklists. *Standardized tests* include published and unpublished psychometric instruments that permit the responses of the test subject to be compared with the responses of other individuals in a systematic manner and in which the same stimuli are administered under the same conditions and scored in the same way from administration to administration. Usually such standardized tests have norms—that is, the response characteristics of certain known groups have been determined, and the test subject's responses may be compared with the responses of the normative group. The Joint Testing Standards endorsed by the American Psychological Association, the National Educational Research Association, and the National Council on Measurement in Education (APA, 1985) provide detailed guidelines for the development and standardization of tests.

Examples of psychometric tests include the Minnesota Multiphasic Personality Inventory (MMPI), the Wechsler Adult Intelligence Scale-Revised (WAIS-R), and the Strong-Campbell Interest Inventory (SCII). Except for a few "public domain" instruments, most psychometric instruments are protected by copyright and may be used legally only with the permission of the copyright holder and, usually, the payment of a fee.

Most of the assessment instruments for which computer interpretation systems have been developed are standardized psychometric tests. Most of the early CBTI systems were developed for personality tests, particularly the MMPI (Fowler, 1985), which was the first assessment instrument for which a computer-based interpretation system was developed (Rome et al., 1965). MMPI reports probably still account for the majority of computer-based reports produced. Early systems were also designed for the Sixteen Personality Factor Questionnaire (Eber, 1964) and the Rorschach (Piotrowski, 1964). The Strong Vocational Interest Blank was the first vocational interest test for which a computer interpretation system was reported (Hansen, 1983; Johansson, 1974). Much of the early work on cognitive and neuropsychological instruments was done in England (Gedye and Miller, 1969), although the focus there was more on computer administration and scoring than on interpretation. By 1985 computer interpretation systems had been developed for most of the standardized tests frequently used by psychologists for clinical and vocational evaluation, and multiple systems existed for the most popular tests (see appendix A).

While computer systems for standardized tests were being developed, other investigators were developing methods for computer administration of various types of histories, symptom checklists, and direct patient interviews and reports on their results. This work is summarized in a recent article by Erdman, Klein, and Greist (1985). The reports on history and interview instruments, which were relatively straightforward presentations of what the subjects had reported about themselves, were generally less sophisticated than the reports on standardized tests. The administration, however, was quite advanced. Complex branching was used, so that whole categories of questions could be omitted or included depending on the subject's response to previous questions. Also, the nonstandardized instruments were interactive from the beginning, while the early systems for standardized tests tended to use paper-and-pencil administration.

These parallel developments in standardized and nonstandardized assessment instruments were brought together in the early 1970s when Johnson and Williams (1975, 1980) developed computer programs to administer, score, and interpret a whole battery of assessment instruments, including the MMPI, the Beck Depression Inventory, the Shipley-Institute of Living Intelligence Test, a social history, a problem checklist, and a structured mental status examination. Psych Systems, the first company to market hardware and software systems to administer, score, and interpret a battery of psychological tests, was an outgrowth of the work of Johnson and Williams. It was followed by other companies and a large number of individual entrepreneurs marketing a sizable array of psychware products. These are summarized in appendix A and described in considerable detail in *Psychware* (Krug, 1984).

Functions of an Automated System

The common feature of CBTI systems is that the input to the computer consists of responses to some assessment instrument and the output presents the results of some type of analysis of those responses. There is considerable variation across systems with respect to how the instrument is administered, how the responses are processed, and how the results are printed.

ADMINISTRATION

The administration of the instrument may be clinical or interactive. In clinical administration, the instrument is administered in the traditional manner, for example, individually administered by a clinician (as is done with the Rorschach) or self-administered on a paper-and-pencil answer sheet (as is done with the MMPI). In interactive administration, the items are presented on a computer screen, and the client responds on the computer keyboard or other peripheral input device.

PROCESSING MODE

Several different configurations are available for processing the data obtained from the subject. If the administration was not interactive, the responses must be put into the computer somehow. This is typically done by means of an optical scanner or by entering the responses on the keyboard of a terminal or the computer. In either case, the computer used to do the processing may be on-site or remote. In the latter case, the data is usually transmitted via telephone lines. A completely automated system is one in which a computer administers and scores the test and generates a report.

TYPE OF REPORT

The *scoring report* simply presents the scores obtained by the subject and, where appropriate, converts them into standard scores by reference to a table of norms. The profile report supplies the same information but presents the scores in a graphic format to simplify comprehension of the results.

The *descriptive report* provides information about what the scales measure and how scale elevations are usually interpreted. The clinician may view the descriptive report as an aid to test score interpretation. For the developer, it may be a step toward producing an interpretive report.

The *interpretive report* represents a more complex analysis of test performance. In describing the test subject, the analysis may take into account patterns of scores and the interaction of several test variables. Most reports available by mail teleprocessing or on commercially available diskettes are interpretive.

The *summary report* brings together information from various sources, such as different tests, histories, demographic data, and behavioral observations. The report consists of summaries of the information found drawn from each instrument. The summaries are brought together in a single report, but the results from one source are not modified by or integrated with the results from other sources. The evaluation report produced by FASTTEST, the software system developed by Psych Systems, fits this description of a summary report.

The *integrated report* is a still more sophisticated effort. The results from various sources are drawn together, compared, and integrated, much as a clinician does when writing a report on a battery of tests. To date no true integrated report system has been developed for the computer.

The principal focus in this chapter is on the development of CBTI systems for *on-line administration*, *scoring*, and *interpretive report* generation for *standardized tests*.

Strategies for Developing a CBTI System

The CBTI system developer must give serious attention to the choice of an instrument, obtaining permission to use it, developing interpretive skills, and structuring the interpretive report.

CHOOSING AN INSTRUMENT

The choice of an instrument for which to develop an interpretation system is the most critical of all. Perhaps the ideal strategy is to develop a new instrument and an interpretation system concurrently, so the data gathering for test development can also enrich the evolving interpretation system. An example of this strategy is the Personality Inventory for Children (Wirt, Lachar, Klinedinst, and Seat, 1984).

However advantageous it may be, this strategy is not practical for many developers who have neither the experience nor the resources to develop a new instrument "from scratch." In this case, the developer will have to choose an existing instrument. Since it is impossible to develop a good interpretation system for a bad test, the developer should carefully examine the manual, the instrument itself, and the published literature to ensure that the instrument is psychometrically sound and adequately normed. If the instrument is sound but lacks supporting literature, the developer may wish to undertake a program of research to provide the necessary research support. This might be done in cooperation with the test author. Many authors would welcome a research colleague and might be willing to provide data or other assistance.

OBTAINING PERMISSION

To make rabbit stew you first need a rabbit, and a rabbit may be easier to obtain than permission to use the instrument for which one wishes to develop a CBTI system. Many psychologists who are accustomed to thinking of psychological tests as "tools of the trade" that may be freely used by qualified professionals are surprised to find that copyright laws give publishers and authors considerable authority over the use of their tests. Copyright is, simplistically, the right to copy. Test authors typically assign their copyright privileges to a publisher who then copies (prints) the test, test materials, and manuals and sells them for use by specific individuals under specified conditions. The most important of these conditions is the agreement by the purchaser not to copy the test material. While it is clear to most people that they may not legally print the tests and sell them to others, it is not uncommon for people to make photocopies for their own use without realizing that this also violates the law. Similarly, some people copy the test material onto a computer disk without realizing that that is as much a violation of the copyright laws as any other form of copying.

In short, there is no legal and ethical way in which test materials that are under copyright protection may be copied or otherwise made a part of a computer system without permission from the copyright holder or his or her representative, usually the test publisher. Ordinarily, permission to copy would be granted in the form of a license or sublicense; persons interested in obtaining a license to use a test must contact the publisher. Unfortunately for the system developer, such requests are likely to be refused. The increasingly competitive environment among the major test publishers and between publishers and the smaller distributors and independent entrepreneurs has put a great deal of pressure on publishers to maintain exclusive rights for the tests they publish. Test licenses that once were obtained easily are now quite difficult for the independent developer to obtain. This is not true for all tests, but the developer should be prepared for a less than enthusiastic response from publishers and, perhaps, a refusal.

On the positive side, the tests for which it is most difficult to obtain a license are the ones for which CBTI systems, sometimes many systems, have been developed. Licenses may be easier to obtain on newer instruments for which no CBTI system has yet been developed.

DEVELOPING INTERPRETIVE SKILLS

After ascertaining that the instrument is psychometrically sound, the developer should be certain that he or she has adequate clinical experience with the instrument and its interpretation. There are large gaps in interpretive literature for even the most extensively researched clinical instrument, the MMPI, and developers of MMPI interpretation systems have had to draw heavily on their clinical experience to fill the gaps. Since most instruments have accumulated only a small fraction of the interpretive literature that is available for the MMPI, clinical experience with the instrument becomes especially important. Using the instrument for two or three years with subjects who cover the range for which it was developed would, for most instruments, provide a solid experiential base. In order for the experience to be useful, however, it is essential that systematic feedback be available on the accuracy of one's interpretations with various populations. For example, when making diagnoses from test results, it is important to compare them with expert diagnoses made on the basis of interviews and external data. Otherwise one runs the risk of becoming very experienced at making incorrect diagnoses, a skill not likely to contribute to a good interpretation system.

Access to a large number of well-written reports by experienced clinicians, as might be available in a large clinic or hospital setting, is an excellent way to expand clinical experience vicariously. Workshops and supervision from more experienced clinicians can also be a very useful way of building interpretive expertise.

In addition to acquiring the clinical skills necessary to develop a good interpretation system, the developer would also be well advised to enhance his or her credibility by such means as publications, presentations at professional meetings, lectures, and workshops. It is also useful for the developer to obtain those credentials that would demonstrate professional competence. A license to practice and membership in the appropriate professional organizations are basic. Becoming a diplomate of the American Board of Professional Psychology, being listed in the National Registry of Health Service Providers, or being elected to Fellow status in the American Psychological Association, the Society for Personality Assessment, or other relevant groups would be appropriate credentials.

In his advice to prospective purchasers of computer-based interpretive services, Moreland (in press) suggests the following:

> First, find out who authored the CBTI system and investigate their qualifications. Does the developer have a record of scholarship with the test instrument in question? In the general area of CBTI? Does the system author have any credentials that indicate special expertise as a practitioner? If the answer to most of these questions is no, one would be well advised to look elsewhere.

DEVELOPING THE NARRATIVE REPORT

Having selected an instrument and obtained a license and having established a high level of interpretive skill and the appropriate professional credentials, the developer is now ready to develop a CBTI report. There are perhaps as many ways to go about this as there are people who do it, and the approach taken is largely a matter of personal style. Some of the following suggestions may be helpful.

1. Assemble all of the interpretive material that will be used and organize it for convenient access. The time spent making an index and an alphabetical file will be amply repaid.
2. Check the scoring routine against a set of answer sheets that have been independently hand-scored several times to eliminate errors. Keep the answer sheets to check your scoring routine periodically.
3. Check the standard scores against the scores that appear in the manual and/or the profile sheet for equivalent scores. If the standard scores differ, don't automatically assume there is an error. Sometimes the standard scores in the manual may be rounded off or estimated and thus not as exact as yours. If you want the scores to be identical to the scores that would be obtained by someone hand-scoring and profiling, you may have to "build in errors" in order to obtain equivalence.
4. Try several formats for the profile or other graphic display of standard scores. A too-busy or cluttered profile sheet is a liability to an otherwise good system.
5. Outline areas you wish to cover in your narrative report and indicate the test sources you will use for each content area. For example, if you have a section

on emotional stability, indicate in your outline the relevant scores, patterns, or other test signs that you will use to make that determination.

6. Make up a prototype of how you want the final product to look. If there are several types of reports, you may need several prototypes.
7. Keep the sentences short, simple in construction, and to the point. Avoid professional jargon. Wherever possible use synonyms or alternate phrases to express the same idea in order to avoid repetitiveness. A book of synonyms or a thesaurus may be useful.
8. Unless the entire report is built around a particular theoretical framework, avoid references to concepts applicable to a specific theory. For example, don't refer to oedipal conflicts unless your report is psychoanalytically based.
9. Use a spelling checker program to check your spelling throughout. Have the entire text read by a proofreader (not yourself). Mispellings, typographical errors, and awkward wording can detract greatly from a report.
10. When you have a working model of the system, run sample reports to be sure all appropriate sections are being printed. Then, following your decision rules, use the same sets of scores to manually produce parallel reports to be sure they are identical to those produced by the computer.
11. Test the limits of the system by introducing deviant scores such as all true or all false scores, extremely high or low scores.
12. Document the entire system so that it could be reproduced from the documentation alone. This will be time-consuming and tiresome, but it will greatly facilitate upgrading and revising the system, modifying it for other populations, or programming it in other languages. This will also greatly facilitate the sale of the program or its commercial use. Be sure to record the sources used in making your interpretations.
13. Use the documentation to develop a "user friendly" manual. Test the manual by asking a computer-naive person to read it and evaluate it for comprehensibility and readability.
14. Copyright your system and copy-protect your disk. The former will be useful if you wish to sell the system, but only copy-protecting (preparing the disk so that it cannot be duplicated) will ensure that your program is not pirated and used for purposes you had not intended. You may need expert legal assistance in getting your material copy-protected, but it is worth the expense.
15. Arrange to have the system tested in the kind of facilities in which it would eventually be used clinically. During the testing phase, you may need to be available as a backup to respond to questions and to correct errors. Feedback from clinicians who read the reports can be facilitated by preparing a standard rating form. The form may examine the degree of satisfaction with the report, the accuracy of specific statements, or both. A comparison of computer reports with regular clinician-written reports or with random computer-generated reports can provide information that is useful and may well be publishable if carefully planned (see Moreland, in press).
16. After the test period, it is useful to observe the system in routine clinical use for a time. Do the staff find the reports useful? Do they continue to use the system after the test period is over? Are they willing to pay for the service when the free trial period is over? If not, the system may have limited commercial value.
17. Finally, it is good to have the system reviewed by a qualified expert. This may be done by requesting that the system be reviewed by one of the journals that

review psychological software, such as *Computers in Human Behavior* (Pergamon Press). The *Ninth Mental Measurements Yearbook* (Mitchell, 1985) also provides reviews for some software, but the publication lag can be quite long. The best solution may be to make arrangements with a qualified reviewer on a consultation basis.

VALIDATING THE SYSTEM

Computer programs are, by their nature, reliable. Barring major equipment malfunctions, the same input will invariably produce the identical output. Validity is another problem altogether. There is broad agreement that the task of validating a computer system is a difficult one. Green (1983) noted that "establishing their validity will not be easy because appropriate methods are not well developed" (p. 1178). Moreland (in press) has summarized the validation work done to date, and provides some useful advice for future validation studies. His article is essential reading for the system developer.

Fowler (1985) observed:

> One important issue that should not be overlooked is the relation of test validity to report validity. CBTI reports on poorly validated tests are unlikely to demonstrate validity regardless of the care with which the interpretive reports are developed. Unless there are well-demonstrated relations of test variables to behavior, the chances of developing valid reports are slight. On the other hand, the system developer who is dealing with a test on which a great deal of empirical research exists has a much easier time. (Pp. 755–756)

MARKETING A NEW PROGRAM

Most people who develop CBTI systems wish to see their systems used by others. Before making a system commercially available, it is important that all of the steps just discussed have been completed. Trying to market an incomplete or poorly documented system that has not been properly tested may result in the rejection of a promising system. Worse, it is professionally irresponsible.

There are several avenues for marketing CBTI systems. The developer might contact the publishers and test distributors who market and distribute existing CBTI systems to determine whether they are interested in a system for this particular instrument. If there is a positive response, a detailed proposal with sample printouts, sources, references, reviews, and the credentials of the developer should facilitate the publisher's decision. The publisher may propose licensing the system with payment in the form of royalties. Unless one is experienced in contracts, some legal advice may be useful at this point.

Having a system distributed by a publisher has some obvious advantages. National advertising, catalogs, sales representatives, telemarketing, an established reputation, and a customer base provide a level of distribution impossible for the independent developer to match.

Since publishers are most interested in systems developed by recognized experts, they look for tests with an established reputation and high potential volume. Most developers will have to look elsewhere for a distribution source. Some developers have formed distribution companies by themselves or with other developers. Others have sold their systems or licensed them to small distributors, and still others have simply advertised their products in professional publications such as the *APA Monitor*. A few developers have made their systems available as public domain software. This form of distribution should be approached with great caution since it could permit the instrument to be used by unqualified persons, thus compromising the instrument's professional character and exposing the developer to charges of unethical behavior.

APA GUIDELINES FOR CBTI SYSTEMS

The APA first adopted interim standards on automated test scoring and interpretation practices in 1966. The focus at that time was on the mail-in services that used mainframe computers, and the standards served well for that purpose for many years. With the advent of microcomputers and the proliferation of CBTI systems, an APA committee was established to develop the guidelines for computer-based tests and interpretations (CBTI Guidelines; APA, 1986) that are cited in appendix B of this volume. The CBTI Guidelines draw from the Ethical Principles of Psychologists (Ethical Principles; APA, 1981) and the Standards for Providers of Psychological Services (Provider Standards; APA, 1977). Although these documents are binding only on APA members, they present sound principles for anyone involved in computer-based test interpretation.

The *Standards for Educational and Psychlogical Testing* (Testing Standards; APA, 1985) is an interorganizational statement on the development, standardization, and professional use of tests. The CBTI Guidelines interpret the Testing Standards as they relate to computer-based test interpretation and draw attention to the Ethical Principles and the Provider Standards that are particularly relevant to such interpretation.

The Testing Standards identify a test developer as any individual or agency who develops, publishes, and markets a test. The CBTI Guidelines further distinguish among the test author who developed this assessment instrument, the software author who developed the CBTI system, and the test publisher who markets the computer software. The guidelines address the responsibilities of each, although in many cases the responsibilities are shared.

The test author is responsible for developing a test that meets the criteria of the Testing Standards. The test author is not necessarily involved in the development of software, although in some cases the same individual may develop both the test and the software.

The CBTI Guidelines are specific and detailed with respect to the responsibilities of the software author. The software author is, first of all, responsible for developing a system consistent with the Testing Standards, the Provider Standards, and the Ethical Principles and the CBTI Guidelines. Some of the specific responsibilities of the software author include:

1. Taking into account human factors and the performance of computer equipment in the administration of tests by computer.
2. Developing procedures to ensure the confidentiality and privacy of the test taker.
3. Ensuring the validity and reliability of the CBTI system and the accuracy of scoring.
4. Demonstrating the comparability of scores from the CBTI system with scores obtained by conventional administration.
5. Providing sufficient information to supply users with a manual reporting the rationale and evidence in support of the CBTI system.
6. Developing the CBTI system around a classification system that is consistent and precise. (The test publisher should provide information about the classification system and its consistency.)
7. Providing the user with a manual that indicates the degree to which statements are based on quantitative research versus expert clinical opinion. Complete disclosure of the interpretive statements and the decision rules should be made available to qualified reviewers under appropriately confidential circumstances. The original test scores and information about how the test scores are derived from those scores and the consistency of interpretations should be available.
8. Ensuring that reports are comprehensible to the user and written in language appropriate to the users' training and experience. Authors and publishers share some of the responsibilities for ensuring that the system is appropriately developed, documented, and administered, but the ultimate responsibility of the software author cannot be delegated. If the system is not administered under the direct supervision of the software author, regular feedback is required to ensure that the guidelines are being followed.

Ethical, Legal and Professional Issues

Since the CBTI Guidelines are in their infancy, the degree to which they will resolve existing problems remains to be seen. In an area of technology as new and rapidly changing as computer software, troublesome problems may be anticipated. Some legal, ethical, and professional problems have already begun to emerge.

LEGAL ISSUES

While the software author cannot be expected to be an authority on the laws associated with the software business, he or she must be aware of some of the legal issues that may arise. The copyright issue has already been addressed: the software author who uses copyright-protected test material without permission can expect problems with the copyright owner. There has not been, to date, very much legal action concerning unauthorized use of test material by software developers. It seems inevitable that this will change as the use of test material without permission increases, thus increasing the pressure on publishers to defend the copyright status of the tests they distribute.

Because some of the legal issues are new and not yet clarified, it is prudent for any test developer to obtain competent legal advice before distributing software. For example, appropriate disclaimers on narrative reports may reduce the liability of the author/distributor for content that may be in error or subject to unanticipated misuse. Also, having adequate copyright protection on one's own material may reduce the risk of unauthorized use.

Legal advice is also important when licensing others to distribute one's work. Contracts usually contain conditions and provisions that are difficult for the nonlawyer to comprehend. A careful reading by an attorney can reduce the chance of costly misunderstandings. Also, contracts usually specify the legal liability for each party in case of suit by a user. It is important for the developer to know what liability has been incurred and to be sure of adequate insurance in case of legal action.

ETHICAL ISSUES

Most licensed psychologists, whether APA members or not, are obligated to adhere to the APA Ethical Principles or a similar set of principles that have been adopted as part of the state licensing laws. Many publishers voluntarily follow the APA Ethical Principles with respect to test usage and require that their customers agree to do so before test materials are sold to them. Thus it is essential that the test developer be familiar with, and adhere to, the Ethical Principles.

The CBTI Guidelines include excerpts from the Ethical Principles that particularly apply to software authors. The most important of these are summarized here, but the developer should be familiar with the whole document. The developer is expected to:

1. Utilize established scientific principles and the relevant APA standards.
2. Make every effort to prevent misuse of assessment results.
3. Be able to produce appropriate evidence for the validity of programs.
4. Prevent use of assessment results by unqualified people.
5. Make certain that any public statements about their system, such as announcements or advertisements, accurately reflect their own qualifications, correctly describe their products, and are presented in a professional manner.
6. Provide individual diagnostic services only in the context of a professional psychological relationship. (The public offering of an automated interpretation service is considered a professional-to-professional consultation.)

PROFESSIONAL ISSUES

One of the most persistent problems associated with CBTI systems is the question of who is qualified to use CBTI reports and systems to produce reports.

It is difficult to deal with this issue without also dealing with the question of who is qualified to use psychological tests. This issue is particularly cogent with respect to the use of psychological tests by psychiatrists.

Some psychologists believe that only psychologists have appropriate training and experience to use psychological tests and that other professionals should be consumers of psychological reports provided by psychologists. The CBTI Guidelines state that the user should be a qualified professional with knowledge, background, and experience in the field of testing and psychopathology. Psychiatrists have extensive background in psychopathology. Few have much training in the field of testing, yet longstanding practice gives psychiatrists equal standing with psychologists in the purchase of tests, and the laws in most states do not prohibit psychiatrists from engaging in testing as long as they do not call themselves psychologists.

This longstanding practice derives from the history of psychological tests. Physicians were closely involved in the development of many of our most important tests, such as the Stanford-Binet, Rorschach, Thematic Apperception Test, and the MMPI. In practice, most publishers made clinical tests available to psychiatrists as well as psychologists, and this caused no particular response from psychologists until the advent of CBTI systems. Most psychologists do not object when psychiatrists receive CBTI reports but do object when psychiatrists purchase CBTI software and provide testing services to other professionals or for their own use. Since the use of psychological tests by psychiatrists is not prohibited by the statutes governing the practice of psychology or psychiatry, the issue becomes one of appropriate and ethical professional practice. Psychiatrists should not use assessments for which their training does not qualify them unless they have a qualified consultant available to them. This area of potential professional friction can best be resolved by a collaboration in which psychologists make themselves available to provide such consultation when it is requested and psychiatrists request the consultation when it is needed.

The use of psychological tests by other professionals or even nonprofessionals who lack training in both psychopathology and testing is an even more vexing issue, one that the software author and the test publisher must address seriously and carefully. The software author must be careful not to include in the report information that requires psychometric training to be comprehended. Test publishers must be prepared to defend a decision to provide—or deny—CBTI materials to nonpsychologists.

Conclusions

Developing a good computer-based test interpretation system can be facilitated by following the guidelines developed by the American Psychological Association and other professional organizations. The system developer should carefully think out the issues of instrument choice, validation, and marketing, and should be aware of the legal, ethical, and professional issues that relate to computer-based test interpretation. With proper preparation and concern for the appropriate guidelines, developing a computer-based test interpretation system can be a useful, rewarding, and professionally stimulating activity.

REFERENCES

American Psychological Association. (1966). Interim standards for automated test scoring and interpretation practices. *American Psychologist*, 22, 1141.

American Psychological Association. (1977). *Standards for providers of psychological services*. Washington, DC: Author.

American Psychological Association. (1981). *Ethical principles of psychologists*. Washington, DC: Author.

American Psychological Association. (1986). *Guidelines for computer-based tests and interpretations*. Washington, DC: Author.

American Psychological Association, American Educational Research Association, and National Council on Measurement in Education. (1985). *Standards for educational and psychological testing*. Washington, DC: American Psychological Association.

Eber, H. W. (1964, September). *Automated personality description with 16-PF data*. Paper presented at the meeting of the American Psychological Association, Los Angeles.

Erdman, H. P., Klein, M. H., and Griest, J. H. (1985). Direct patient computer interviewing. *Journal of Consulting and Clinical Psychology*, 53, 760–773.

Fowler, R. D. (1985). Landmarks in computer-assisted psychological testing. *Journal of Consulting and Clinical Psychology*, 53, 748–759.

Gedye, J. L., and Miller, E. (1969). The automation of psychological assessment. *International Journal of Man-machine studies*, 1, 237–262.

Green, B. F. (1983, December 16). Computer testing [Letter to the editor]. *Science*, p. 1178.

Hansen, J. I. (1983). The measurement of vocational interests: Issues and future directions. In S. D. Brown and R. W. Lent (Eds.), *Handbook of Counseling Psychology* (pp. 99–136). New York: Wiley.

Johansson, C. B. (1974). *Manual for the augmented interpretive report for the Strong Vocational Interest Blanks*. Minneapolis, MN: National Computer Systems.

Johnson, J. H., and Williams, T. A. (1975). The use of on-line computer technology in a mental health admitting system. *American Psychologist*, 30, 388–390.

Johnson, J. H., and Williams, T. A. (1980). Using on-line computer technology in a mental health admitting system. In J. B. Sidowski, J. H. Johnson, and T. A. Williams (Eds.), *Technology in mental health care delivery systems* (pp. 237–249). Norwood, NJ: Ablex.

Krug, S. E. (1984). *Psychware*. Kansas City, MO: Test Corporation of America.

Mitchell, J. V. (1985). *Ninth mental measurements yearbook*. Lincoln, NB: Buros Institute of Mental Measurements, University of Nebraska.

Moreland, K. L. (in press). Computer-based test interpretation: Advice to the consumer. *International Journal of Applied Psychology*.

Piotrowski, Z. A. (1964). A digital computer administration of inkblot test data. *Psychiatric Quarterly*, 38, 1–26.

Rome, H. P., Mataya, P., Pearson, J. S., Swenson, W., and Brannick, T. L. (1965). Automatic personality assessment. In R. W. Stacy and B. Waxman (Eds.), *Computers in biomedical research: vol. 1* (pp. 505–524). New York: Academic Press.

Wirt, R. D., Lachar, D., Klinedinst, J. K., and Seat, P. D. (1984). *Multidimensional description of child personality: A manual for the Personality Inventory for Children*. Los Angeles: Western Psychological Services.

5

Developing Expert Computer Systems to Interpret Psychological Tests

C. David Vale and Laura S. Keller

Professional psychologists have grown comfortable with the computer as a clerical aid, assisting with tasks such as test scoring and record keeping. In recent years, however, the use of computers in psychological testing has progressed from such simple tasks to the automation of interpretive judgments, a domain traditionally reserved for the expert clinician (Butcher, Keller, and Bacon, 1985; Fowler, 1985; Johnson, Giannetti, and Williams, 1976). While all applications have capitalized on the admittedly superior speed, memory capacity, and reliability of the computer, only these recent applications have attempted to tap the computer's intelligence as well.

The most significant contributions of artificial intelligence (AI) programming to the clinical practice of psychology have been expert diagnostic and interpretive systems. These systems, referred to as expert systems (Hayes-Roth, Waterman, and Lenat, 1983; Waterman, 1986), are computer programs that capture the expertise of a human practitioner and perform tasks requiring this expertise. An expert system is, in a very real sense, an apprentice that learns the art of interpretation through communication with experts. In this chapter we discuss apprenticeship techniques by which the computer can be trained in the art of test interpretation.

Why Bother: What Are the Special Skills of a Computer?

A computerized test interpreter can perform better than a human interpreter in at least six ways. The first of these is the standardization and reliability of results. If two human interpreters write reports based on the same set of test scores, it is very unlikely that their interpretations will be identical. This inconsistency can be problematic if it means that different decisions will be made from the same scores depending on who interprets them. In theory, standardization can be achieved if all tests are interpreted by a single expert, but this is impractical in most settings. Reliability is even more difficult to achieve. A single expert's interpretive strategy may vary from one report to another, and his or her interpretation of the same score profile may change from day to day for reasons that are unrelated to valid interpretation. By contrast, a computerized system achieves perfect standardization: it applies its programmed decision rules with total reliability, thereby guaranteeing that all interpretations resulting from the same scores will be identical.

A second advantage that computerized interpretation can offer is accuracy. Even if a single interpreter could produce perfectly reliable reports, it is almost inevitable that personal biases or interpretive errors would compromise the report's accuracy at least to some extent. Additional errors may creep in as a result of burnout; few if any human interpreters can mass-produce interpretations without fatigue and boredom affecting accuracy. Report accuracy could be increased by having experts work on a consensual interpretation to balance out individual errors and biases, but the use of multiple human experts to interpret every individual score profile is impractical. A computerized system, on the other hand, can easily incorporate the expertise of a large number of test experts, and such a consensually developed automated system of interpretations is likely to result in a more accurate final report.

The third advantage a computer can offer is economy. Computers are markedly more efficient than humans at performing certain tasks. This efficiency can result in savings of time, personnel, and, of course, money. Test interpretation is a complex process that requires considerable professional education in testing and many hours of training specific to the test battery in use. The substantial investment in terms of educational costs and the training time required of both trainer and trainee is greatly reduced if a few resident experts can teach their interpretive system to a computer. Training is faster and need be done only once instead of being repeated for every new human interpreter, with the added advantage that the computer version can do the same work that previously required many individual test experts. For example, a clinician may take an hour to produce a narrative interpretation for a test battery. At a conservative estimate of $50 per hour for the expert's time, the report would cost $50. By contrast, once an automated interpretive system has been programmed, the cost of computer time to produce a similar report is approximately 25 cents. If the computerized report is as useful as the clinician's report, the efficiency gain is about 20,000 percent.

A fourth potential advantage of a computerized interpretation system is the currency of the interpretations produced. As was just mentioned, only the original interpretive system needs to be trained. Copies of the system can be produced at virtually no cost, in contrast to the financial investment needed to train several human experts. Thus, when new knowledge becomes available, only one system needs to be updated; all of the rest can be replaced with copies. Automation vastly increases the speed with which new knowledge can be incorporated into a standard interpretive strategy.

Fifth, it is easier to validate a computerized interpretation system than to validate the interpretive schemes of individual psychologists. This is due to the reliability with which computer reports can be generated and because only one version (that is, not all of the copies) needs to be validated. Furthermore, the judgmental rules on which the narrative is based are much more explicit in an automated system and therefore can be tested more easily.

A final advantage of computerization is permanence. Human interpreters may quit their jobs, be transferred, retire, or die, taking all of their interpretive expertise with them. A computerized interpretive system is permanent until it is purposely replaced by an improved version.

Expert Systems: The Computer Science Perspective

The design and development of expert systems is an important area of computer science. An expert system is a knowledge-based reasoning program that emulates the work of a human expert to solve complex problems in a narrow domain. Waterman (1986) lists four characteristics of an expert system: expertise, symbolic reasoning, depth, and self-knowledge. Expertise refers to the skill level with which the expert system solves a problem. High expertise implies that the system will exhibit performance commensurate with that of human experts in its problem domain, will use shortcuts and strategies to apply its knowledge effectively, and will degrade gracefully when pushed to the limits of its ability. Symbolic reasoning is the ability to represent and reformulate knowledge symbolically. The knowledge in an expert system is represented in a form analogous to natural language rather than in a set of equations, and the system solves problems by applying language rules rather than by evaluating an equation. Depth means that the problems encountered by the expert system are difficult and that the rules it applies to solve them are complex. The class of problems is complex enough that people who solve them are considered experts. Finally, self-knowledge refers to the program's ability to examine and explain its own knowledge. A system with self-knowledge not only performs an expert task but also explains how it performed it and why it made each decision.

Test-interpretation systems are expert systems of a sort. Their technology developed independently of expert systems technology in the computer science sense, however, and such systems have several different characteristics. They do exhibit expertise and depth; their interpretations can be indistinguishable from those produced by experts, for example (and people who are skilled in test interpretation are generally considered experts). However, their capacity for symbolic reasoning is typically minimal compared to other expert systems, and they rarely have much self-knowledge. They lack the ability to manipulate symbols because they are typically developed by standard programmers using standard data-processing languages rather than recognized AI languages. They usually lack self-knowledge because most developers of interpretation systems have preferred to keep their rules proprietary and would not want their systems to explain their interpretations.

They also differ from typical expert systems in that they are less interactive. A typical expert system queries the user for information in an adaptive manner, probing for information when it is needed and providing conclusions when they are requested. Currently available test-interpretation systems, on the other hand, typically start with a set of test scores and end with a narrative interpretation, often with no interaction with the user.

"Knowledge engineers" trained in computer science might choose to regard a test-interpretation system as a poor cousin to a "true" expert system because it is not interactive and is not written in the style of an artificially intelligent program. However, a test-interpretation system does contain the essence of an expert system: performance comparable to a human expert in a complex problem domain.

A discussion of expert systems from the computer science perspective can leave the impression that programming is the most time-consuming and difficult part of expert system development. The degree to which this is true depends on the specific application and its similarity to previous successful applications. In fact, both in computer science and in psychology there exist expert system development tools that can dramatically reduce the need for programming (see Assessment Systems Corporation, 1984; Waterman, 1986). If these tools are used, the time-consuming parts of the development effort are the acquisition of expert knowledge and the evaluation and validation of the resulting system.

The development of expert systems is generally considered to be a time-consuming and expensive process. Waterman (1986) estimates that a moderately difficult expert system may take six person-years to develop, and a very difficult system may take thirty person-years. (He did not consider any systems that were less than moderately difficult, possibly because he would not regard anything easier as an expert system.) Our experience is that the development of a test-interpretation system requires one to two person-years of effort, counting the expert's time and the evaluation and validation process. This difference may result because interpretation systems are indeed simpler than typical expert systems. However, we prefer to think it is because in the typical development scenario the knowledge engineer does not have any training in the specific content area to be "taught" to the computer and may spend more than a year overcoming this. In contrast, we (acting as knowledge engineers) begin with substantial familiarity with the interpretation of psychological tests and therefore do not have to devote any time to acquiring this expertise.

Buchanan and associates (1983) suggested five stages of the knowledge-acquisition process: identification, conceptualization, formalization, implementation, and testing. Identification refers to defining the scope of the problem the system will address, identifying sources of expertise, evaluating the resources for system development, and stating the specific goals of the effort. In the conceptualization stage, concepts identified in the identification stage are made explicit. In the formalization stage, concepts and rules are stated formally in a manner such that they can be easily incorporated into the language of an expert system development tool (that is, an authoring language). In the implementation stage, the formalized knowledge is entered as data into the expert system development tool. Finally, the system is evaluated in the testing stage.

Waterman (1986) further suggests that the overall development process goes through five phases, which produce a demonstration prototype, a research prototype, a field prototype, a production prototype, and, finally, a commercial system. The demonstration prototype is a small version of the system designed to convince funding sources that the idea is feasible and to try out preliminary design ideas. It is usually based on a system development tool. The commercial system is the complete and tested system, ready for production use and usually written, for speed, in a standard programming language. The other stages represent an orderly progression between these two stages.

The stages and phases cited by Buchanan and coworkers (1983) and Waterman (1986) are descriptive rather than heuristic, however. Essentially these models suggest that expert system development progresses from abstract to concrete and from crude to refined. Although these models may describe the typical process, the specific stages and phases that may be "highly interdependent and overlapping" (Waterman, 1986) provide little insight into specific techniques for system development.

The technology of expert systems, from the computer science perspective, appears to focus on complex methods of knowledge representation and manipulation; knowledge acquisition is accomplished by the time-consuming process of learning how the expert thinks. Yet it is the knowledge-acquisition process that is most important in capturing expertise for a computer system. In order to develop an expert system, this information must be communicated effectively to the computer.

Narrative Interpretations: A Different Breed of Expert Systems

Techniques for developing psychological test-interpretation systems evolved independently of the expert systems techniques and were not influenced by the multistage models discussed earlier. Interpretation systems appear to have developed in parallel with expert systems starting in the mid-1960s. The development of a computer program to generate test interpretations has been approached in several ways, most of which are variations of techniques used by practitioners to develop manual interpretation systems. In fact, the majority of currently available automated interpretive programs were designed to copy an already established manual interpretive system. While this is a logical starting point, automation of the interpretive process also offers the potential of improving the accuracy and validity of established interpretive practice.

DEVELOPMENTAL STRATEGIES

Most contemporary automated systems for interpreting psychological tests attempt to mimic established clinical practice at various levels of complexity. Roid and Gorsuch (1984) have categorized automated interpretive reports into three types: descriptive, clinician-modeled, and clinical-actuarial. We believe these types are not mutually exclusive, and we have subsumed their taxonomy under our own categorization into nonintegrative, omnibus integrative, and focused integrative types.

NONINTEGRATIVE INTERPRETIVE STRATEGY

A nonintegrative interpretive program (termed descriptive by Roid and Gorsuch) consists of a series of sentences or phrases that each interpret a different single test or scale score. Such interpretations may be based on detailed data addressing the correlates of very specific score elevations, they may be more loosely modeled on clinical lore concerning the meaning of various levels, or they may involve a combination of researched anchor points and extrapolations to other elevations through clinical judgment of appropriate interpretations. Thus even a simple single-scale interpretive program is likely to involve a combination of actuarial data and modeling of clinical judgment.

Nonintegrative programs differ in how much effort is put into tailoring the report to the individual through such devices as gender-specific statements (that is, using "he" or "she" rather than "the client"). The single-scale interpretive phrases may or may not be combined to form a narrative report; usually they are simply listed in succession. The earliest example of a descriptive system that is almost completely nonintegrative was the Minnesota Multiphasic Personality Inventory (MMPI) report developed at the Mayo Clinic (Rome et al.,

1962). The computer generated a profile of scale scores and several interpretive phrases, most of which were based on single-scale elevations. Another example is the automated intelligence assessment described by Gilberstadt, Lushene, and Buegel (1976), which produced a report consisting primarily of a series of statements based on single test scores.

The nonintegrative approach is the least complicated method of computerizing test interpretations, but it is often overly simplistic. Configural (score pattern) interpretations are not included, and narrative reports based solely on single-scale elevations are prone to internal contradictions or repetition, may be disjointed, and will completely miss interaction effects in interpretation. When faced with a profile of test scores, the expert clinician usually integrates information from one scale or test with the pattern of scores obtained on other scales and tests before he or she "outputs" an interpretive report. Creating a computer program that incorporates the integrative capacity of the human expert requires a more complex developmental strategy than the nonintegrative approach.

OMNIBUS INTEGRATIVE INTERPRETIVE STRATEGY

An omnibus integrative strategy is designed to interpret an entire profile of scale scores or a battery of test scores in an integrative fashion. It is not simply an extension of the nonintegrative strategy, however; the simple extension of that strategy would be to cross all scales into a multidimensional configural approach. Such an approach quickly produces more statements than can reasonably be represented on a computer.

Roid and Gorsuch (1984) suggested that an integrative program can be created either by modeling the decision process of an expert clinician or by incorporating actuarial data from research delineating the empirical correlates of various score patterns. Clinician-modeled programs assume that the clinical practitioner can be viewed as an information processor who collects, analyzes, and integrates input data and then outputs an interpretation. If the interpretive expert's strategy can be made explicit, it should be possible to program the computer to model the human practitioner's decision process (Kleinmuntz, 1969, 1975).

Some of the earliest attempts to model the practitioner's thought processes were applied to medical diagnosis. The physician was instructed to "think aloud," and the logical sequence of decisions he or she used in arriving at a final decision was programmed into the computer. Several computerized psychiatric diagnostic interview systems have employed this "logical decision tree" method, assuming that the clinician successively rules out potential classifications and converges on a final category (see Erdman, Klein, and Greist, 1985; Fleiss, Spitzer, Cohen, and Endicott, 1972). Kleinmuntz (1975) used this method to construct a logical decision-tree model of an MMPI expert's strategy for sorting test profiles into adjusted, maladjusted, or unclassified categories. The computer's sequential decision rules were based on hours and hours of tapes of the clinician's verbalizations as he sorted the profiles.

Some researchers question whether the logical decision tree is an appropriate or complete model of the clinician's interpretive strategy. Glueck and Stroebel (1969) suggested that an interpretive program must somehow model the clinician's "hunches": his or her ability to recognize patterns and see them as meaningful gestalts rather than exclusively engaging in a logical stepwise decision process. Karson and O'Dell (1975) developed an interpretive system for the Sixteen Personality Factor Inventory (16 PF) through content and logic analysis of the senior author's actual interpretive reports rather than by having him try to map out his interpretive scheme directly. Goldberg (1970) presented a method of modeling the practitioner using statistical analyses of the expert decision process rather than trusting that the clinician can clearly delineate his or her own interpretive strategy. He developed mathematical models of the prediction process of clinical psychologists attempting to classify MMPI profiles as either neurotic or psychotic, and found that after the human experts' classification rules were specified and programmed, the computerized model outperformed the original clinicians. The automated formula presumably removed human unreliability from the interpretive process.

Similarly, Kleinmuntz (Brooks and Kleinmuntz, 1974; Kleinmuntz, 1975) has pointed out that automating the clinician's judgmental rules allows analysis and improvement of those rules through statistical methods. In the case of the MMPI sorting program just described, he improved the valid positive hit rate of the computerized rules from 63 percent to 91 percent (compared to 80 percent for the clinician) by including optimal weighting. The revised rules outperformed the average clinician on cross-validation as well: "in principle, the computer . . . must excel in this class of clinical activity because it is a more reliable applier of its rules and, paradoxically, it is more flexible than the clinician. Its flexibility is achieved because its decision criteria (i.e., new normative data, critical cutoff points) can be more easily adjusted than those of the clinician" (Kleinmuntz, 1975, p. 382).

The computer is able to improve on clinical judgment not only by applying the practitioner's rules more reliably but also by improving on those rules when appropriate. The validity of a computerized system developed solely by the clinician-modeled strategy rests on the sometimes unjustified assumption that the strategy being modeled is actually valid in predicting relevant criteria. The category of automated systems that Roid and Gorsuch (1984) have labeled clinical-actuarial is designed to avoid this problem by basing all interpretive statements exclusively on empirical research findings for various test scores. Actuarial prediction is "arrived at by some straight-forward application of an equation or table to the data . . . the defining property is that no judging or inferring or weighing is done by a skilled clinician" (Meehl, 1954, pp. 15–16). For example, a system developed to interpret the MMPI might employ only descriptors that have been empirically determined to characterize persons with certain highpoint scale combinations, or "code types."

At this time no purely actuarial computerized narrative interpretive systems exist. The necessary developmental research is prohibitive; the amount of empirical data required by such a system increases geometrically with the number of variables and score levels to be interpreted by the program. Existing actuarial systems such as the MMPI "cookbooks" (see Gilberstadt and Duker, 1965; Marks, Seeman, and Haller, 1974) either leave a large percentage of examinees unclassified or use such broad categories that fine interpretive discriminations are impossible. As a result, the interpretive systems written for even the most popular and well-researched psychological tests are actually a mixture of rules based on actuarially validated relationships and other rules culled from established clinical lore or from the expert author's personal experience with the test.

The vast majority of the currently available automated narrative interpretive reports were developed with this mixed actuarial and clinician-modeled strategy. For example, the MMPI interpretive system developed at Assessment Systems Corporation was modeled on the judgmental strategy of one interpretive expert, James Butcher, but was also actuarial in that he attempted to incorporate into his interpretation all of the accepted actuarial data along with his personal clinical experience (National Computer Systems, 1982). The program is built hierarchically around code-type interpretations: if an examinee's profile fits an established score pattern for which actuarially validated descriptors are available, a standard narrative is invoked fitting that configuration (with a few modifications based on other moderating scale elevations). The MMPI interpretive report used by Psych Systems uses five different schemes, first checking for the profile's fit to a well-known actuarially validated code type and then proceeding to other interpretive strategies, such as linear combinations of single-scale interpretations, if the best-researched code types do not apply (Labeck, Johnson, and Harris, 1983; Miller et al., 1977). The computer-generated interpretations of the Rorschach available through National Computer Systems employ John Exner's actuarial data on his scoring system as well as his clinical interpretive style and judgment (Exner, 1983).

A further refinement of the mixed actuarial and clinician-modeled strategy involves modeling the interpretation on more than one expert. Wiggins (1980) has pointed out that pooling the judgments of several clinicians into a composite model can improve a computer algorithm's predictive power by reducing the effects of idiosyncratic biases and individual unreliability. Such considerations were incorporated into the automated interpretation developed by Assessment Systems Corporation for a retail merchandising company's executive screening battery (Vale and Keller, 1984; Vale, Keller, and Bentz, in press). A committee of testing experts was responsible both for designing the overall report structure and for approving all interpretations included in the final statement library. The developmental procedure is described in more detail later in this chapter.

FOCUSED INTEGRATIVE INTERPRETIVE STRATEGY

Although the omnibus integrative strategy is appropriate for general reports designed to summarize a broad range of test information applicable to many different settings and uses, it is often not the ideal interpretive strategy for a specific testing site or application. Such reports may resemble the wide-band interpretations found in testing manuals rather than address the specific concerns and needs of a particular practitioner's client population. Giannetti and Klingler (1980) predicted that "better returns can be anticipated from the computer applications which provide timely information for facilitating ongoing tasks and optimizing decisions rather than those that simply duplicate existing manual procedures" (p. 269). The focused interpretive strategy is designed to produce reports that address the specific concerns of the test user.

One of the most ambitious attempts to develop a focused integrative system was undertaken at the Salt Lake City Veterans Administration Hospital (Johnson, Giannetti, and Williams, 1979). Rather than continuing to automate a wide variety of potentially redundant and sometimes clinically irrelevant standard assessment devices, Johnson, Giannetti, and Williams developed a new test, the Psychological Systems Questionnaire, specifically for the computer. Before constructing specific system components, they identified content areas and decision-relevant information to be addressed by the program's output and deleted overlapping or unnecessary information. The final report was designed to focus on information relevant to the specific problems and decisions practitioners address.

Several other systems have taken established tests or test batteries and tailored their interpretive reports to address the concerns and needs of specific client populations or particular practitioners' settings. For example, the University of Minnesota publishes an automated MMPI interpretive report focusing on information relevant to personnel decisions rather than information relevant for other purposes, such as discriminating types of severe psychopathology (National Computer Systems, 1984). In developing a concise but useful narrative interpretation, it makes sense to begin by specifying the information that such a report should supply to be most effective as a decision aid in a particular setting.

A focused integrative interpretive report is designed to provide specific information relevant to the concerns of a particular population or practitioner's organization. The first step in developing such a report is to design a list of content areas to be addressed by the final narrative. We have found it useful to think of the interpretive program as an "answer-to-question mapping system" rather than as an automated version of one expert's report-writing style. The basic framework for the report can be provided by designing a list of questions to be answered by a good narrative interpretation.

After content areas and questions within these areas have been specified, the next step is to develop a strategy for answering the questions from the available test data. This involves deciding which scores are relevant for which questions and whether sufficient information can be gained from single-scale scores or whether additive or configural combinations are necessary.

The library of interpretive statements must be written and structured to produce an organized, coherent narrative report. This will involve determining the overall report format and the order of content areas, dealing with possible redundancies and/or contradictions, and tailoring the report to the individual's name, gender, age, or any other relevant variables.

Finally, a program will be required to transform the statement library into narrative reports based on a profile of scores. If the program is expressly intended for the development of interpretations, the statement library and its rules may be written separately and may read like plain English. If such a program is not available, the statement library itself must be programmed. Generally, the first approach is preferable.

The next section provides an example of the process used by Assessment Systems in developing a computerized focused integrative interpretation of a large battery of psychological tests.

APPLICATION OF THE FOCUSED INTEGRATIVE STRATEGY TO A PERSONNEL SCREENING BATTERY

The focused integrative interpretive report to be described was designed to assist personnel managers in making decisions about executive job placement and movement within a large retail merchandising corporation. Traditionally the company's small staff of testing experts interpreted the battery of intellectual, personality, values, and interest tests. The project was designed to crystallize the expertise of these individuals into a computerized report addressing the specific concerns of personnel decision makers.

DEVELOPING THE QUESTION LIST

The first step in developing this automated interpretation was the specification of the information to be covered in the final report. In order to establish broad content areas to be addressed, the reports produced by the company's testing experts were examined. The six major areas identified were overall mental ability, quantitative skills and interests, verbal ability and communication skills, business motivation, personal characteristics and leadership potential, and emotional adjustment. These areas were chosen to be the major sections of the report.

Next the company's interpretive experts met to delineate specific questions to be answered within each section, taking care to include only those questions they felt could be answered by the tests included in the screening battery. This process resulted in approximately sixty questions designed to cover adequately the important information to be provided in the six major content areas. For example, the question list written for the business motivation section included these questions:

1. How does the individual's level of economic motivation compare to the typical businessperson?
2. How does the individual's level of political motivation compare to the typical businessperson?
3. Is the individual interested in scientific and technical areas of activity?
4. Is the individual interested in mechanical problems and in working with his/her hands?
5. Overall, does the individual have a competitive-aggressive interest and motivational pattern?

6. If the individual's aesthetic interests are higher than business interests, is it because he/she has a general cultural orientation?

DEVELOPING A QUESTION-ANSWERING STRATEGY

The general content headings and question lists developed in collaboration with the company's interpretive experts provided a complete description of the overall structure and content of the narrative statement library. The next task was to decide which test scores and scales were to be used to answer each of the questions. The judgment of the company's senior expert provided the initial direction for this phase, as he suggested a scale or set of scales as the source of information for each specific question. Further information was provided by a training manual that the company had developed for interpretation of the screening battery. This manual included a definition of each scale or test and a description of its relevance to executive behavior.

The writing of the statement library began by selecting a question from the list and writing a set of possible answers based on different levels of the relevant scale(s). The training manual provided a small set of interpretive statements considered appropriate for scale scores falling at the tenth, twenty-fifth, seventy-fifth, and ninety-fifth percentiles. It also included some brief descriptions of important scales that might modify the interpretation of other scales and listed a few scale configurations relevant to executive behavior. The sample interpretations did not always directly address the issues raised in the question list, and the library writers modified and extrapolated from this basic material when necessary. They also expanded the interpretive material to provide a richer variety of statements and finer discriminations within each scale. Using the training manual's interpretations as anchor points, they expanded the range of interpretive statements to approximately ten levels per scale.

The preliminary version of the statement library consisted primarily of sets of statements corresponding to all possible score levels of single scales. For example, the first set of statements in the library was composed of ten different answers to the question "How does this person's overall mental ability compare to that of other company executives?" The ten answers each corresponded to a different score on the mental ability test relevant to this question. Obviously, only one of these statements would be invoked for any particular examinee.

For other questions, a more complicated structure was necessary. According to the interpretive experts and the training manual, several interpretations depended on combinations of two or more scales rather than on the elevation of one scale alone. In the simplest case, a set of statements was written for a particular scale but a few words of some of the statements were deleted, modified, or added depending on the level of another scale. Another strategy was to write two or more entire sets of statements for a single scale according to the level of another scale. The third strategy, a configural approach, was to write statements to be used only for the simultaneous occurrence of several scale-score elevations in specified ranges. This strategy was particularly useful for providing summary paragraphs or for emphasizing a particularly meaningful combination of characteristics.

REFINING THE STATEMENT LIBRARY

When preliminary answers had been written to all of the questions on the preliminary list, a meeting of the experts was called to refine both the question list and the library. The experts were asked to look for inadequacies, redundancies, and offensiveness in the question list and in the answers. As a result of this review, a few repetitious questions were removed. After looking at the answers, the experts concluded that a few of the questions could not be answered solely on the basis of test information; these questions and their associated answers were also removed. Finally, a few of the questions were worded in such a way that the experts thought the answers might be considered offensive by some individuals; these questions and their associated answers were revised.

When the question list had been finalized, the experts were asked to concentrate on the statements written to answer the questions. The interpretive statements were divided into three types: those based on a single score, those based on two scores, and those based on a configuration of scores. The experts were given different instructions for each answer type.

For the single-scale answers they were asked to:

1. Read the whole set of answers to get a feel for the content and range.
2. Read each individual answer and make sure it was appropriate regardless of levels of other scores on the test.
3. Eliminate any unnecessary information in the answer.
4. Read the set sequentially and make sure each successive answer indicated a higher score, reordering if necessary.
5. Compare each successive pair of answers to see if there was room interpretively between them for another answer, adding one if so.
6. Compare successive triples, eliminating the middle if the outer two adequately covered the range of interpretability.
7. Edit out any unnecessary harshness or evaluative connotation and make sure none of the answers were too strong.

For the two-scale questions, the answers were arranged in a matrix with levels of the first scale on one side and levels of the second scale along the top. The experts were asked to read the answers in a column of the matrix to get a feel for the level of the secondary scale and then to hold that scale constant in their minds while doing single-scale editing on the column. As with the single-scale answers, they were asked to ensure that all levels of both scales were covered and to write more answers if they were not.

For the configural answers, the experts were asked to evaluate whether the answer added anything unique to the interpretation that could not be obtained from single- or two-scale answers. If it did, they were asked to evaluate the scales contained in the configuration and to revise the configuration if necessary. No score levels were discussed at this point, however.

When this review session was completed, all of the questions and answers had been approved by the experts, and the narrative portion of the statement library was considered final. All that remained was to add the score levels that would complete the decision rules.

COMPLETING THE DECISION RULES

The decision rules that determined which statements from the library would be included in the final narrative had been constructed during the previous efforts, except for the specific score levels. To set these levels, the entire statement library was assembled into a rating packet. Each page contained one question and its associated answers. The header on the page listed the question and gave explicit instructions about how to rate the answers that followed. In general, the statements were ordered on the page from those indicated by low scores to those indicated by high scores. Beside each question were two rating blanks for indicating the lowest and highest scores that would be appropriate for each answer. Raters were instructed to make their ratings contiguous so that the high rating of one answer was equal to the low rating of the next. Although this resulted in redundant ratings, experts preferred this over a single cut-score rating because they found it easier to understand.

Two-scale questions were contained on several pages; each page corresponded to a level of the secondary score. Configural questions generally had only one answer, which was either applicable or not. Raters were instructed to indicate score levels of the configuration for which the answer applied.

All experts evaluated all answers in the rating packet. The mean and standard error of each rating was computed across all raters. If the standard error was low enough, the mean rating was taken as the cutoff score for the decision rule. Mean ratings with larger standard errors were further scrutinized.

This further scrutiny involved looking at the individual ratings to see if any one expert's rating was discrepant; if so, he or she was asked to reconsider the rating. This resolved a few of the discrepancies. When the discrepancies appeared to reflect a general disagreement rather than an outlier, however, the entire set of statements surrounding the problematic one was examined to see if the problem could be ameliorated by adding another interpretive level or by rewording the existing statements. If this appeared to help, the entire new set of statements for the question was redistributed to the experts for rerating. If a large standard error still resulted, the senior expert was consulted. If he felt that the mean rating was accurate, despite its large standard error, it was adopted. If not, he provided another rating and the average of his and the mean rating was taken as the official value.

FINAL REFINEMENT OF THE REPORT

When the statement library was complete, several test cases were interpreted as a tool for refining the reports. The reports were first reviewed internally by library writers to ensure their overall readability and smoothness of style. Small stylistic changes, unrelated to content, were made.

The reports were then submitted to the senior interpretive expert for his evaluation. On the basis of his comments, a few minor wording changes were made. Because he felt that some of the configural statements were invoked too rarely, the rules associated with them were made slightly more lenient to place additional emphasis on the qualifications of outstanding executive candidates.

With these final adjustments, the development of the report was considered complete.

VALIDATION OF THE REPORT

Before a successful validation can be done, some consideration must be given to the objectives of the entity being validated and how to best evaluate the achievement of those objectives. The basic goal of an expert system is to perform its assigned tasks in an expert manner. In the case of a narrative interpretation system, the goal is to interpret a set of test scores in a manner at least as thorough, coherent, readable, and accurate as could be done by a human expert.

The quality of the narrative interpretation system was evaluated by comparing reports it produced with reports produced by human experts on those four criteria. First, the senior expert chose eighteen profiles from the company archives that represented the range of ability and personal characteristics typical of the executive candidate population. Each of six experts was then asked to write a narrative interpretation of three of those profiles. One profile was lost because of logistic difficulties; seventeen were thus interpreted in a useful form. The computerized system interpreted the same seventeen profiles. Each expert was then given twenty-eight or thirty reports (all pairs that he or she had not interpreted previously) and asked to rate them on their thoroughness, readability, and coherence. To evaluate the accuracy of the reports, the experts were asked to reproduce the profile of scores that they thought would most likely have generated each of the interpretations.

The computer-generated interpretations were rated significantly more thorough than the manually generated ones. There was no significant difference in the readability ratings across the two modes. The manual interpretations were rated as significantly more coherent. The accuracy of the profile reproduction was significantly greater for the computer-generated interpretations.

Discovering that the computer-generated reports were more accurate and more thorough was rewarding but not surprising. What was surprising, however, was that the manually generated reports were considered more coherent. Two possible explanations for this are that the computerized version failed to integrate interpretive concepts as well or that human experts tend to force a coherent interpretation even when the data do not support it. No analyses were done to determine which explanation is correct. Further details of the development and validation process for this system can be found in Vale and Keller (1984) and Vale, Keller, and Bentz (in press).

Further Thoughts on Validation

That narrative interpretations of psychological tests should be validated is self-evident. How this should be accomplished is a controversial subject, however.

Moreland (1985) summarized the work that has been published on validating computerized interpretations of the MMPI. He grouped the studies into four types: anecdotal, comparisons with human-produced reports, customer satisfaction, and external criterion. He considered anecdotal studies unscientific and therefore did not discuss them. He felt that comparisons with human-produced reports were poorly designed because they do not take into consideration the fact that a computerized report can be substantially different from a human interpreter's report and still be valid. (It should be noted, however, that he was referring to the design in which the human-generated report is considered the ideal rather than a design that uses the level of human performance as a base of comparison.) Customer-satisfaction studies ask consumers (that is, clinicians) to rate the accuracy of reports based on their knowledge of the clients described by the report; Moreland suggested that the lack of control for base-rate statements (those that would accurately describe most people) is a serious problem with this design. Finally, external criterion studies compare ratings of the report and of the patient on a common symptom-evaluation scale. According to Moreland, inadequate coverage of the domain of the report is the most significant problem with this design.

The views on validation implicit in Moreland's review and in the research he cites are perhaps somewhat more ambitious than is necessary or desirable. This implicit view is that a computerized interpretation is a prediction system, which, like a set of prediction equations, can be evaluated on the accuracy of the predictions it makes. However, a clinical approach to assessment is most useful when statistical prediction equations are not available. We view a narrative interpretation as an expert system that attempts to emulate the experts it is modeled after, and it should be evaluated by the success with which it achieves this goal. The former view is, in the ideal world, probably closer to the ultimate goal of interpretation. It is more useful as an approach to improving the predictions of an interpretation system, however, after its basic validity has been established.

Therefore, the most appropriate model for initial validation is one that compares the accuracy of computer-generated reports with that of human-generated ones. To suggest that a report's statements should prove true empirically is not wrong; however, it is unreasonable to expect that an expert system will be more accurate than the expertise it was given. Thus the initial goal of validation should be to establish that the performance of an expert system mimics that of an expert. A system should be considered minimally accurate if it can do that. Further comparisons with empirical observations extend beyond the scope of validation into the realm of further improvement.

We suggest that a proper model for validation of a narrative report must have an objective, a basis, and a criterion. The objective, which may be multifaceted, suggests what dimensions of quality must be evaluated. The basis provides a method for evaluation. The criterion provides a level at which the evaluation will be judged satisfactory.

The basis, as we have already suggested, is that an expert system should perform like the experts on whom it is modeled. Although, as Moreland pointed out, reports can be substantially different and still be accurate, all such reports should reflect the same score profile. Therefore, while the profile-to-report path may be a one-to-many mapping, the reverse path should be many to one.

Similarly, we have already suggested the criterion: An expert system should perform as well as the experts it is intended to replace. In one facet of evaluation, this suggests that the computer-generated reports should describe the profile as accurately as do the human-generated ones.

As facets of the objective we suggest accuracy, utility, and safety. A report is accurate to the extent that the statements it makes are the same as those that would have been made by the experts. In a properly developed interpretation, then, the validity can be built in. That is, if a group of experts agree that they would make a statement in response to a particular pattern of test scores, that statement and its decision rule are accurate. If such agreements are obtained for every statement in the report, and if none of the statements contradict the others in any real profile, the entire report is accurate. Validation through the consensus of experts is not unlike test validation through the content-validation paradigm.

A narrative report is more than the sum of its parts, however, because the individual statements interact: this interaction is the essence of the integrative report. Thus the report must be evaluated as a whole. Its overall accuracy can be evaluated by asking experts to reproduce the score profile from the narrative report and computing how deviant this profile is from the true one. Although such an accuracy statistic provides only relative information, it offers a useful comparison when the accuracy of computer-generated reports is compared to the accuracy of reports written by clinicians.

However, this type of accuracy evaluation has a weakness from a logical perspective: it is not meaningful separate from an evaluation of utility. By utility, we mean the usefulness of the report to its consumers. The statement "Mr. Jones's verbal score was 95" would produce nearly perfect profile reproducibility with virtually no utility over the raw test score. The problem is not unlike the problem with internal consistency reliability. The best way to maximize reliability is by asking the same question repeatedly. This problem has not hampered the utility of internal consistency reliability. Thus, although the technique of accuracy evaluation is susceptible to abuse, it is still a good indicator of the accuracy of the interpretation.

In the project described earlier (Vale and Keller, 1984), utility was not evaluated directly but was assumed to be built in. All of the questions that the personnel experts felt could and should be answered were answered as far as possible. As an independent check, it would be feasible to ask an independent group of experts (assuming more experts exist) to evaluate the utility of the question list and of the answers. For any effort that is thorough enough to develop a question list and answer the questions to the greatest degree of resolution reasonable, this analysis is likely to be superfluous.

By safety we mean that the report must not say anything that will cause its recipient to take any adverse action. Safety has, to a large extent, been neglected in validation studies to date. When narrative reports are directed at professionals, safety is less of an issue; a trained professional should recognize the limits of an interpretation of a test. It is unreasonable to think that narrative reports will be limited to use by professionals, however, and some reports may be beneficial in the hands of the ultimate consumer. To develop professional guidelines (APA, 1985) that inflexibly adhere to APA Ethical Principal 8e (APA, 1981), which states in part that a narrative interpretation is a professional-to-professional consultation, is to force the development of interpretations intended for the client out of the province of professional jurisdiction. A better approach is a direct one in which professional guidance is provided to developers of interpretations regarding what constitutes safety. We suggest that one approach is to evaluate each statement in the statement library on its safety, in much the same way that utility or cutting scores might be evaluated. Joint consideration of safety and utility would provide a practical limit to the naïveté of the audience to which the report could be given; if the statements have to be weakened for safety to the point that they have no utility, it indicates that the audience is too naïve to receive the report.

Taken together, what do the objective, basis, and criterion suggest for a validation paradigm? The procedures used by Vale and Keller (1984) provide a starting point for this design. Although their approach had a few shortcomings as a general model for validation, it provides a concrete example on which to build. If validity is the goal, the development process should build the validity in. Utility can be ensured by developing a list of useful questions that the report must answer. Vale and Keller worked with personnel testing experts to build a comprehensive question list; the notable shortcoming of the approach with regard to utility was that the end users (the employment managers) had no input. Similarly, accuracy was incorporated into the development by obtaining group consensus on the decision rules and group averages on the cutting scores. Safety, however, was not explicitly considered.

Safety could be built in in much the same way as accuracy. The experts could be asked to evaluate the safety of each proposed statement, considering the extent to which extra-test information might influence the accuracy of the statements and whether each of the statements is mild enough to be received directly by the consumer.

Although system development as described would build in much of the required validity, an independent evaluation would still be necessary. Accuracy can be evaluated by having experts attempt to reproduce the original scale scores. Safety can be evaluated by having experts rate the safety of what they consider to be the most sensitive statement in each report. Similarly, utility can be evaluated by having experts or consumers rate the utility of the report overall; better yet, the consumers could rate the adequacy of the report in answering each of the questions it was designed to answer.

The criterion for comparison in this design should be the reports written by human experts. Although it is unreasonable to expect the initial computerized reports to be better than the consensual reports, as has been demonstrated several times, the computerized report can be better than the typical report written by an individual expert.

A study so conducted avoids many of the problems in validation identified by Moreland (1985). Evaluation of the accuracy of profile reproduction ensures that the reports will be better than a base-rate report. Utility evaluation, especially if it is directed at the entire question list, ensures adequate coverage of the domain of the interpretation. Furthermore, the concept of safety evaluation opens the possibility of having reports directed to the client. Thus, although this validation design is less ambitious than others, it provides a good foundation for establishing minimum criteria for validity.

REFERENCES

American Psychological Association. (1981). Ethical principles of psychologists. *American Psychologist*, *36*, 633–638.

American Psychological Association. (1985, October). *Guidelines for computer-based tests and interpretations* (draft). Washington, DC: Author.

Assessment Systems Corporation. (1984). *User's manual for the MicroCAT Testing System*. St. Paul, MN: Author.

Brooks, R., and Kleinmuntz, B. (1974). Design of an intelligent computer psychodiagnostician. *Behavioral Science*, *19*, 16–20.

Buchanan, B. G., Barstow, D., Bechtel, R., Bennett, J., Clancey, W., Kulikowski, C., Mitchell, T., and Waterman, D. A. (1983). Constructing an expert system. In F. Hayes-Roth, D. A. Waterman, and D. B. Lenat (Eds.), *Building expert systems* (pp. 127–167). Reading, MA: Addison-Wesley.

Butcher, J. N., Keller, L. S., and Bacon, S. F. (1985). Current developments and future directions in computerized personality assessment. *Journal of Consulting and Clinical Psychology*, *53*, 803–815.

Erdman, H. P., Klein, M. H., and Greist, J. H. (1985). Direct patient computer interviewing. *Journal of Consulting and Clinical Psychology*, *53*, 760–773.

Exner, J. (1983). *The Exner report for the Rorschach comprehensive system*. Minneapolis, MN: National Computer Systems.

Fleiss, J. L., Spitzer, R. L., Cohen, J., and Endicott, J. (1972). Three computer diagnosis methods compared. *Archives of General Psychiatry*, *27*, 643–649.

Fowler, R. D. (1985). Landmarks in computer-assisted psychological assessment. *Journal of Consulting and Clinical Psychology*, *53*, 748–759.

Giannetti, R. A., and Klingler, D. E. (1980). A conceptual analysis of computerized mental health care systems. In J. B. Sidowski, J. H. Johnson, and T. A. Williams (Eds.), *Technology in mental health care delivery systems* (pp. 267–288). Norwood, NJ: Ablex.

Gilberstadt, H., and Duker, J. (1965). *A handbook for clinical and actuarial MMPI interpretation*. Philadelphia: Saunders.

Gilberstadt, H., Lushene, R., and Buegel, B. (1976). Automated assessment of intelligence: The TAPAC test battery and computerized report writing. *Perceptual and Motor Skills*, *43*, 627–635.

Glueck, B. C., and Stroebel, C. F. (1969). The computer and the clinical decision process: II. *American Journal of Psychiatry*, *125*(supp. 7), 2–7.

Goldberg, L. R. (1970). Man vs. model of man: A rationale, plus some evidence, for a method of improving on clinical inferences. *Psychological Bulletin*, *73*, 422–432.

Hayes-Roth, F., Waterman, D. A., and Lenat, D. B. (Eds.). (1983). *Building expert systems*. Reading, MA: Addison-Wesley.

Hedlund, J. L., Evenson, R. C., Sletten, I. W., and Cho, D. W. (1980). The computer and clinical prediction. In J. B. Sidowski, J. H. Johnson, and T. A. Williams (Eds.), *Technology in mental health care delivery systems* (pp. 201–235). Norwood, NJ: Ablex.

Johnson, J. H., Giannetti, R. A., and Williams, T. A. (1976). Computers in mental health care delivery: A review of the evolution toward interventionally relevant on-line processing. *Behavior Research Methods and Instrumentation*, 8, 83–91.

Johnson, J. H., Giannetti, R. A., and Williams, T. A. (1979). Psychological Systems Questionnaire: An objective personality test designed for on-line computer presentation, scoring, and interpretation. *Behavior Research Methods and Instrumentation*, 11, 257–260.

Karson, S., and O'Dell, J. W. (1975). A new automated interpretation system for the 16PF. *Journal of Personality Assessment*, 39, 256–260.

Kleinmuntz, B. (Ed.). (1969). *Clinical information processing by computer: An essay and selected readings*. New York: Holt, Rinehart, & Winston.

Kleinmuntz, B. (1975). The computer as clinician. *American Psychologist*, 30, 379–387.

Labeck, L. J., Johnson, J. H., and Harris, W. G. (1983). Validity of a computerized on-line MMPI interpretive system. *Journal of Clinical Psychology*, 39, 412–416.

Marks, P. A., Seeman, W., and Haller, D. L. (1974). *The actuarial use of the MMPI with adolescents and adults*. New York: Oxford University Press.

Mathisen, K. S. (1985, June). *Issues in research on clinical computer applications for mental health*. Paper presented at the conference on Research on Mental Health Computer Applications sponsored by the Division of Biometry and Epidemiology of the National Institutes of Mental Health, Madison, WI.

Meehl, P. M. (1954). *Clinical versus statistical prediction: A theoretical analysis and a review of the evidence*. Minneapolis, MN: University of Minnesota Press.

Miller, D. A., Johnson, J. H., Klingler, D. E., Williams, T. A., and Giannetti, R. A. (1977). Design of an on-line computerized system for MMPI interpretation. *Behavior Research Methods and Instrumentation*, 9, 117–122.

Moreland, K. L. (1985). Validation of computer-based test interpretations: Problems and prospects. *Journal of Consulting and Clinical Psychology*, 53, 816–825.

National Computer Systems. (1982). *User's guide for the Minnesota report*. Minneapolis, MN: University of Minnesota Press.

National Computer Systems. (1984). *User's guide: The Minnesota report personnel selection system*. Minneapolis, MN: University of Minnesota Press.

Roid, G. H., and Gorsuch, R. L. (1984). Development and clinical use of test-interpretive programs on microcomputers. In M. D. Schwartz (Ed.), *Using computers in clinical practice* (pp. 141–149). New York: Haworth.

Rome, H. P., Swenson, W. M., Mataya, P., McCarthy, C. E., Pearson, J. S., Keating, F. R., and Hathaway, S. R. (1962). Symposium on automation technics in personality assessment. *Proceedings of the Staff Meetings of the Mayo Clinic*, 37, 61–82.

Vale, C. D., and Keller, L. S. (1984). *Development and validation of a computerized narrative interpretation system for the Sears Executive Screening Battery*. St. Paul, MN: Assessment Systems Corporation.

Vale, C. D., Keller, L. S., and Bentz, V. J. (in press). Development and validation of a computerized interpretation system for personnel tests. *Personnel Psychology*.

Waterman, D. A. (1986). *A guide to expert systems*. Reading, MA: Addison-Wesley.

Wiggins, J. S. (1980). *Personality and prediction: Principles of personality assessment*. Reading, MA: Addison-Wesley.

PART II

A SURVEY OF COMPUTER-BASED CLINICAL DATA GATHERING METHODS

6

An Automated Problem-Rating Interview: The DPRI

D. Robert Fowler, Allan Finkelstein, Walter Penk, William Bell, and Bonnie Itzig

Introduction

Most clinicians agree that a lot of information is necessary to adequately evaluate and treat patients with psychiatric problems. There is frequently wide disagreement among mental health professionals, however, about which information is important and about how clinical information can best be used to plan and deliver treatment. Clinicians' methods of collecting and managing clinical information are influenced by training, experience, theoretical approach, time, resources, treatment setting, and a myriad of other factors that play a role in how they practice their craft. There is little wonder that a remarkably poor interclinician reliability obtains when clinicians are compared in the way they evaluate and treat patients, since even the type of information considered important varies so much from one clinician to another. Over the years, a number of solutions to this problem of interclinician reliability have been proposed.

In the past twenty years the mental health professions have seen two major entries into an area that might be called clinical information management. One, the problem-oriented system (Ryback, Longabaugh, and Fowler, 1981; Weed, 1969), attempts to structure clinical information by defining an idiosyncratic list of problems for each patient. The other, the diagnostic criteria system, introduced by the publication of the third edition of the *Diagnostic and Sta-*

tistical Manual of Mental Disorders (DSM-III; American Psychiatric Association, 1980), attempts to structure clinical information by using a predefined set of explicit criteria to judge whether a patient fits into one or more of a finite set of diagnostic categories. The objectives of these two methods of organizing clinical information are the same—to assist clinicians in determining which information is important for evaluation and treatment of a particular patient, and to provide a framework on which the information can be organized and synthesized. Each of these two approaches has had its proponents and critics.

Enthusiasm for the use of the problem-oriented record system reached its peak in the mid-1970s. Inconsistencies in data collection, disagreement among clinicians regarding the importance attached to certain clinical information, and poor reliability in problem definition have disillusioned many of the system's early proponents. These difficulties in reliable data collection and synthesis, along with the large amount of time required to document systematically the wide range of problems presented by psychiatric patients, have, for practical purposes, relegated to history widespread use of the problem-oriented record in mental health care. The appearance of DSM-III in 1980, which demonstrated increased reliability among clinicians over previous diagnostic classification systems, furthered the decreasing popularity of the problem-oriented record.

At least two features of the problem-oriented system, however, provide important advantages over diagnoses alone for the organization of clinical information. First, the problem-oriented system allows for identification and definition of a wide range of clinical problems. Diagnoses focus on a more restricted range of problems. Indeed, a major reason for the increased reliability of DSM-III over its predecessors is the fact that, by its inclusion and exclusion criteria, only a restricted range of symptoms (problems) is allowed within diagnostic categories. A problem-focused approach, allowing for definition of a more comprehensive range of problems, provides a broader view of the difficulties confronting patients with psychiatric disorders. Studies by the Longabaugh group (Longabaugh, Fowler, Stout, and Kriebel, 1983; Longabaugh et al., 1986) have demonstrated that such an approach facilitates improved treatment planning and effectiveness over a diagnostic approach alone.

Second, by focusing on specific problems instead of diagnostic groupings, the problem-oriented system permits tracking of treatment response (improved, worse, or unchanged) in a far more detailed and comprehensive manner than that permitted by diagnostic categories alone. Evaluation of treatment by using more global measures, or by focusing on a limited area, may give a misleading picture of treatment response or fail to provide necessary information for revising treatment.

The Dallas Problem Rating Interview (DPRI) was developed to utilize these potential advantages of the problem-oriented system by providing clinicians an efficient means of identifying the problems presented by psychiatric patients and to assist in synthesizing that information in a format that facilitates evaluation of responses to treatment. Since our goal was to devise an instrument that would be comprehensive without unduly burdening clinicians, we reviewed previous experiences with automated problem-focused interviews. Attempts to utilize computers for identifying psychiatric problems date back to 1973, when Greist, Klein, and Van Cura reported a computer interview to identify psychiatric target symptoms. Other developers of problem-focused computer psychiatric interviews since that time include Angle, Ellinwood, and Carrol (1978), Hay, Hay, Angle, and Ellinwood (1977), Johnson and Williams (1980), and McCullough (1984). These interviews have focused primarily on the identification of general or specific problem areas by having patients list symptoms (in free text) or endorse the presence or absence of specific items presented in the form of questions on a computer screen.

Patient acceptance of this form of data collection has been uniformly high. Studies comparing the items identified by computer interview with those identified by human interviewers (for example, see Angle, Ellinwood, and Carrol, 1978) indicate that the computer interview consistently identifies significantly more problems than are identified by human interviewers. Our survey of the literature, however, also indicates that insufficient attention to the validity of automated instruments has diminished the overall value of these techniques in clinical practice (Clavell and Butcher, 1976; Hedlund, Vieweg, and Cho, 1985). The application of computer technology in administering and interpreting a psychological test or interview does not exempt its developer from sufficiently demonstrating the instrument's psychometric properties.

We wanted to develop a psychometrically sound instrument that would identify and rate the intensity, frequency, and severity of a comprehensive range of psychiatric problems and that would be able to track problem-specific changes that might occur as a result of treatment. The instrument should make efficient use of personnel in its administration and provide reliable observations regarding patient response to treatment. The following sections detail development of the DPRI and describe its psychometric properties.

Selection of Interview Items

The DPRI is administered to patients via computer terminal. The items identified by the interview were derived from a Problem Indicator Classification scheme developed by the senior author (DRF) from a number of sources, including DSM-III, the Diagnostic Interview Schedule (Robins et al., 1979), and the Butler Hospital Problem Code (Longabaugh et al., 1981). "Problem indicators" represent items of information about a patient from which a clinician might infer that the patient has a problem (Ryback, Longabaugh, and Fowler, 1981, p. 25). In general, these items represent observable behaviors (such as restlessness) or patient-reported experiences (such as auditory hallucinations or depressed mood) that are defined at a relatively low level of inference, but they may also denote social or family role-related behaviors (such as misses work frequently or is dysfunctional in parent role). To be included as a problem indicator in the classification scheme, an item was selected only if it met the criterion of "clinical relevance" just mentioned and appeared to be "sensitive to change"—that is, could be expected to change in response to successful treatment of a psychiatric problem.

Approximately 245 nonoverlapping items meeting these criteria were selected from the sources just mentioned and organized into fourteen major problem areas (see figure 6.1). For conceptual clarity and completeness, these items

```
 1.  MOOD/AFFECT PROBLEMS
 2.  SPEECH AND THOUGHT PROBLEMS
 3.  IMAGERY/PERCEPTION PROBLEMS
 4.  SOCIAL BEHAVIOR PROBLEMS
 5.  OVERT BEHAVIOR PROBLEMS
 6.  FOOD AND SUBSTANCE USE PROBLEMS
 7.  SEXUAL BEHAVIOR PROBLEMS
 8.  SLEEP PROBLEMS
 9.  INTELLECTUAL PERFORMANCE/SENSORIUM/MEMORY PROBLEMS
10.  PHYSICAL SYMPTOMS/SIGNS/OTHER
11.  FAMILY ROLE PROBLEMS
12.  SOCIAL ROLE PROBLEMS
13.  LIFE TASK PROBLEMS
14.  SUBSISTENCE PROBLEMS
```

Figure 6.1. Major problem areas covered in the problem indicator classification code.

were further organized hierarchically into a four-level classification system and coded for ease of cross-referencing. Figure 6.2 provides an example of one problem area of the code, illustrating the four levels of classification: problem area, problem category, problem indicator, and problem indicator descriptor.

```
14  OVERT BEHAVIOR PROBLEMS

    1410   EXCESSIVE BEHAVIOR
           141010  INCREASED MOTOR ACTIVITY (RESTLESSNESS/
                     AGITATION)
           141011  DYSKINESIAS
                 14101110  TONGUE
                 14101111  MOUTH
                 14101112  FACE
                 14101113  EYELID
                 14101114  TRUNK
           141012  AKATHISIA
           141013  TREMOR
           141014  CHOREA (CHOREIFORM MOVEMENTS)
           141015  ATHETOSIS
           141016  TICS
           141017  FACIAL GRIMACES
           141018  MUSCLE RIGIDITY OR DYSTONIA

    1411   INSUFFICIENT BEHAVIOR

           141110  DECREASED MOTOR ACTIVITY
                     (MOTOR RETARDATION/AKINESIA)
           141111  CATAPLEXY

    1412   INAPPROPRIATE (INCONGRUOUS) BEHAVIOR

           141210  INAPPROPRIATE (BIZARRE) BEHAVIOR
           141211  COMPULSIVE BEHAVIOR
           141212  INAPPROPRIATE CRYING
```

Figure 6.2. Overt behavior problem area of the problem indicator classification code.

Problem areas (two-digit numbers) are the major classification level. Problem categories (four-digit numbers) define the type of problem indicator (for example, behavioral excesses, deficiencies, or incongruities). Problem indicators (six-digit numbers) represent the key level of the code, the items on which the interview and ratings are based. Problem indicator descriptors (eight-digit numbers) add descriptive information about problem indicators that may be important for evaluation or treatment (such as type of dyskinesia, delusion, or phobia).

Interview Questions and Branching Logic

The next step in creating the DPRI was to write the items in interview format. Questions were written to elicit whether a patient had recently experienced the problem described by each problem indicator in the classification scheme. To permit more efficient administration of the interview, "branching" questions were inserted prior to major sections of the interview. These branching questions (such as "Do you have a problem with your feelings, for example, with feeling depressed, sad, nervous, or anxious?") allow the patient to skip irrelevant sections of the interview. (For other views on the subject of branching, see Angle, Ellinwood, and Carrol, 1978, and Erdman, Klein, and Griest, 1985.)

Since the order of the interview questions followed the order of the classification scheme, it was rather easy to devise branching questions to fit problem categories. The accuracy of these branching questions was studied empirically by orally reading the interview to a pilot sample of thirty subjects (patients). The branching questions were asked without branching occurring. If a patient answered "no" to a branching question but "yes" to a subset question, either the branching question was discarded or the subset question was removed from the branching. To illustrate—the question "Are you bothered by having spells in which you lose your memory (for example, blackouts)?" was initially included as a subset of the branching question "Do you have problems with your memory?" A few patients answered "no" to the branching question but "yes" to the subset question. Consequently, this subset question was removed from the branching logic. Both the branching logic and the wording of the questions were revised after the pilot phase to increase the accuracy and clarity of the interview; then a computer program was written to present the questions on a computer video terminal.

Patients taking the computer interview indicate whether a particular item has been a problem for them by pressing the "Y" (yes) or "N" (no) key on the keyboard. If the patient endorses a problem indicator that has further descriptors (see, for example, figure 6.2), he or she is also asked to endorse whether or not that item (descriptor) applies. Intensity and frequency ratings, however, are obtained only for problem indicators. For each item at the problem indicator level that the patient endorses as being a problem, he or she is asked to rate

```
                 THREE DAY RATING PERIOD

      INTENSITY                         FREQUENCY

1.  VERY MINIMAL               1.  NONE IN THE PAST 3 DAYS
2.  MILD                       2.  JUST A LITTLE OF THE TIME
3.  MODERATE                   3.  SOME OF THE TIME
4.  SEVERE                     4.  MOST OF THE TIME
5.  EXTREMELY SEVERE           5.  ALL OF THE TIME
```

Figure 6.3. Intensity and frequency rating scales.

the greatest intensity of the problem (see figure 6.3) and its frequency over the past three days. Patients indicate their rating, presented in the form of a five-point scale, by pressing the relevant numeric key on the keyboard. A few questions, such as those related to episodic symptoms or behaviors (for example, episodes of depressed mood) or role-related items (for example, vocational functioning) also ask for intensity and frequency ratings over the past year.

Each question was written to require that patients endorse not only that they are experiencing the item (symptom, behavior, and so forth), but also that it represents a problem (dysfunction) for them. This concept of a "threshold" level for identification of a problem is addressed in the introduction to the DPRI (figure 6.4) by implying that patients can experience a symptom or behavior

```
   D A L L A S   P R O B L E M   R A T I N G   I N T E R V I E W

   I AM GOING TO ASK YOU A NUMBER OF QUESTIONS ABOUT PROBLEMS
   THAT DIFFERENT PEOPLE HAVE.  I USE THE WORD, "PROBLEM", TO
   MEAN ANYTHING THAT CAUSES YOU TO FEEL PARTICULARLY BAD OR
   THAT INTERFERES WITH YOUR ABILITY TO DO THINGS OR TO GET
   ALONG WITH PEOPLE.  OBVIOUSLY, NO ONE WILL HAVE ALL OF THE
   PROBLEMS THAT I WILL ASK YOU ABOUT, BUT SINCE I DON'T KNOW
   WHICH ONES YOU MIGHT HAVE, I WILL ASK YOU ALL OF THE
   QUESTIONS.  PLEASE DO YOUR BEST TO ANSWER THE QUESTIONS
   AS WELL AS YOU CAN.

   FIRST, I AM GOING TO ASK YOU ABOUT PROBLEMS WITH THE WAY
   THAT YOU FEEL OR SHOW YOUR FEELINGS (PROBLEMS WITH YOUR
   MOOD OR EMOTIONS).  PLEASE ANSWER "Y" (YES) TO THE FOLLOWING
   QUESTIONS IF YOU HAVE HAD THESE PROBLEMS RECENTLY (IN THE
   PAST FEW MONTHS).

PRESS THE SPACE BAR TO CONTINUE.
```

Figure 6.4. Introduction to the DPRI.

(such as depressed mood) yet not consider it problematic. By requesting that patients make this distinction in identifying problem indicators, we are attempting to distinguish between inconsequential and clinically relevant information.

Since the interview is branching, depending on the number of items endorsed as being problematic, the patient may answer as few as 119 questions or as many as 396. Time required for taking the interview has ranged from about twenty minutes to about two hours, varying by the number of items endorsed and the patient's ability to focus attention. Most patients complete the interview in less than forty-five minutes.

A follow-up version of the DPRI (the DPRI-F) was developed to record problem-specific changes. The DPRI-F is constructed to ask whether each

```
THIS INTERVIEW IS A FOLLOW-UP TO THE LAST ONE I GAVE YOU TO SEE
   HOW YOU ARE DOING NOW IN THE PROBLEM AREAS THAT YOU REPORTED
   LAST TIME.


   FIRST I WILL ASK YOU WHICH OF THE PROBLEMS YOU REPORTED LAST
   TIME ARE STILL PROBLEMS FOR YOU NOW.
   THEN I WILL ASK YOU TO RATE THE INTENSITY AND FREQUENCY OF
   THE PROBLEMS THAT STILL BOTHER YOU.

   PRESS THE SPACE BAR TO CONTINUE.

                        FEELING DEPRESSED

        PREVIOUSLY YOU SAID THAT THE ABOVE WAS A PROBLEM FOR
        YOU.  IS THIS A PROBLEM FOR YOU NOW?


    ANSWER (YES/NO)= Y
```

Figure 6.5. Introduction to the DPRI-F.

previously identified problem is currently a problem (see figure 6.5). If the past problem is still a current one, the patient then rates, on a five-point scale, the intensity and frequency of that problem over the three previous days, as was done in the DPRI. In order to identify problems that have arisen since the previous interview (for example, medication side effects), the patient is then asked whether any previously unendorsed problems have subsequently become a problem (see figure 6.6). For new items endorsed on the DPRI-F, the patient

```
NOW I WILL ASK YOU TO REPORT ANY NEW PROBLEMS THAT WERE NOT THERE
AT THE TIME OF THE LAST INTERVIEW.  IF THERE ARE ANY NEW ONES, I
WILL ASK YOU TO RATE THEIR INTENSITY AND FREQUENCY OVER THE PAST
3 DAYS.

LOOK OVER THE LIST OF POSSIBLE NEW PROBLEMS CAREFULLY.  IF YOU
SEE ANY IN THE LIST THAT HAVE BOTHERED YOU SINCE THE LAST TIME,
ANSWER "YES (Y)" TO THE LIST.

THEN I WILL ASK YOU ABOUT EACH PROBLEM IN THE LIST.  ANSWER "NO
(N)" TO EACH ONE THAT DOESN'T BOTHER YOU AND "YES (Y)" TO EACH
ONE THAT DOES.

PRESS THE SPACE BAR TO CONTINUE.


SINCE THE LAST TIME YOU ANSWERED THESE QUESTIONS, HAVE YOU
NOTICED ANY NEW PROBLEMS THAT YOU DID NOT HAVE BEFORE WITH

   YOUR FEELINGS OR MOODS such as:

     C. FEELING ANGRY OR IRRITABLE
     D. FEELING TOO GOOD
     F. NOT SHOWING ANY FEELINGS
     G. NOT ENJOYING OR FINDING PLEASURE IN ANYTHING
     H. NOT SHOWING AFFECTIONATE OR LOVING FEELINGS
     I. NOT SHOWING YOUR ANGRY FEELINGS
     J. NOT SHOWING YOUR ANXIOUS OR NERVOUS FEELINGS
     K. NOT SHOWING YOUR SAD FEELINGS

                                        ANSWER (YES/NO)= N


   NB: (Indicators A and B [Depressed Mood and Anxious mood]
        do not appear on this list, since they were previously
        endorsed)
```

Figure 6.6. Introduction to new problems on the DPRI-F.

again rates the intensity and frequency (five-point rating scale) over the previous three days.

Factor Development

The studies to be described were conducted on the inpatient units of the Psychiatry Service, Veterans Administration Medical Center (VAMC), Dallas. These inpatient programs have 170 beds, divided into three acute general psychiatry units, a psychiatric rehabilitation unit, an alcohol dependency treatment unit, and a drug dependency treatment unit. Approximately two thousand patients are admitted and discharged each year.

Since 1981 the Dallas VAMC Psychiatry and Psychology services have served as an Automated Medical Information System demonstration and development site. Components of this system include thirty-five computer terminals on patient wards, in testing areas, in clinics, and in offices. Psychological tests and interviews are routinely administered to patients on the terminals. Hardware includes a PDP-11/44 minicomputer with an 80-megabyte disk drive. Patients participating in the concurrent validity studies, therefore, were accustomed to data collection via computer terminal. Diagnostically, most of the patients on this service comprise the major DSM-III categories—Schizophrenic Disorders (12 percent), Affective Disorders (15 percent), Anxiety Disorders (8 percent), and Substance Abuse (Alcohol and Drug) Disorders (46 percent).

FACTOR STABILITY

In order to test the DPRI's representativeness and the stability of its factor structure, we administered the interview to 482 patients shortly after admission to either the alcohol unit or one of the general psychiatry units. This sample of patients was randomly divided into equal subsets, the second subset serving as a cross-validation sample. Since correlation matrices can be severely distorted by either single "outliers" or "idiosyncratic collections of subjects" (Comrey, 1978), each subset was submitted to a cluster analysis in order to identify such outliers, thereby providing a homogeneous group thought to be representative of psychiatric inpatients. The cluster analysis performed, using the IMSL software (International Mathematical and Statistical Libraries, Inc., 1984), was a complete linkage (maximum distance or farthest neighbor), agglomerative hierarchical method on patients by intensity scores on the DPRI. The similarity measure used was the Euclidean distance of DPRI patient responses from each other. The cutoff point selected in each split half was 0.45.

This procedure resulted in retaining 192 patients (80 percent) in the first subset of 242 patients ("developmental" sample) and 191 (80 percent) in the second subset of 240 patients ("validation" sample). Inspection of the eliminated subjects indicated that they were distinguishable by their interview response tactics—either tending to answer "yes" to all of the items or "no" to all of them. Analysis of data regarding these patients as "underreporters" and "overreporters" will be presented elsewhere.

Results of an earlier, preliminary factor analysis had indicated that "psychopathological" items could be analyzed separately from social role dysfunctions. This previous analysis had shown that the Family Role, Social Role, Life Task, and Subsistence problem indicators loaded separately from the psychopathological items (such as problems in mood, thought, overt behavior, sleep, substance use, physical, and so forth). Furthermore, in future studies we intend to examine the effects of psychopathological problems on Family and Social Role dysfunctions. We believe that separating the factor analysis of these two "domains" of items at this stage of DPRI development will facilitate these future studies. For these reasons, we restricted subsequent factor analyses to items in the first ten problem areas (problem areas 1 through 10, figure 6.1). Moreover, we chose to diminish the influence of infrequent items by choosing only those indicators endorsed by at least 20 percent of the patients, except for certain items (for example, visual hallucinations, violent behavior, and so forth) that were thought to have high clinical significance. The intensity ratings for 111 items were submitted to factor analysis (with Varimax rotation) on each of the two subsets of patients, using the SAS statistical package (Statistical Analysis System, 1982).

Factor analysis of the developmental sample yielded eighteen factors consisting of two or more items with a factor coefficient equal to or greater than 0.4. Factor analysis of the validation sample yielded twenty-one factors meeting the same criteria. Although the factors yielded by the two subsets of patients were not identical, there was sufficient overlap to indicate these randomly grouped patients had a comparable factor structure. Considering the size limitation of the two samples, minor differences in item composition and number of factors were expected. (Comrey, 1978, has noted that descriptive factors derived from a subject population may not be expected to stabilize until sample sizes of two thousand or more are reached.)

For a more precise comparison, the item factor coefficients were correlated for each of the eighteen factors on both the developmental and the validation samples. All of the correlation coefficients were significant, ranging from a low of 0.26 to a high of 0.85. Three factors correlated above 0.80, three from 0.70 to 0.79, seven from 0.60 to 0.69, and one obtained an r of 0.59. Only five of the eighteen factors correlated in the range of 0.26 to 0.58.

FACTOR STRUCTURE

Since the factors appeared to be sufficiently stable, we performed a final factor analysis on the larger group (both subsets combined) of homogeneous patients (N = 383), entering the same items selected in the previous factor analysis. Our patients were mostly male (99 percent), with ages ranging from twenty-two to seventy-eight. Twelve percent of the patients were in the age group twenty to twenty-nine, 42 percent were thirty to thirty-nine, 16 percent were forty to forty-nine, 19 percent were fifty to fifty-nine, and less than 2 percent were over sixty years old. The majority of patients received a primary discharge diagnosis of Alcohol Dependency (55 percent). Other diagnostic categories represented were: Drug Abuse (11 percent), Schizophrenic Disorders (8 percent), Major Affective Disorders (10 percent), Anxiety Disorders (6 percent), and Personality Disorders (6 percent).

This analysis yielded a factorial structure of twenty-one factors among the 111 items (using factor loadings of 0.40 or greater and factors with two or more items). Table 6.1 shows items by factors and factor coefficients for each item.

TABLE 6.1

Factor Structure of DPRI: Factor, Question Number,[a] Item and Factor Coefficient[b]

1. *Depression*: (43) Hopelessness .77; (44) Helplessness .72; (42) Low Self Esteem .70; (46) Ideas of Guilt .65; (49) Thoughts of Harming Self .55; (2) Depressed Mood .50; (5) Anxious Mood .46
2. *Affective Constriction*: (18) Deficient Recognition of Anger .76; (17) Deficient Recognition of Intimate Feelings .69; (15) Blunted or Flat Affect .60; (14) Inappropriate Affect .60; (16) Anhedonia .57
3. *Sleep Disturbances*: (167) Frequent Awakening .78; (168) Early Awakening .77; (169) Difficulty Falling Asleep .77; (165) Distress About Sleep .76
4. *Disturbed Thinking*: (23) Slowed Thoughts .77; (22) Derailment .69; (24) Racing Thoughts .63; (186) Poor Memory .62
5. *Alcohol Use Problem*: (121) Problems with Stopping Alcohol Use .82; (120) Concern About Alcohol Use .80; (258) Intoxication .77; (250) Tolerance to Alcohol .70; (189) Episodes of Memory Loss .43
6. *Anorexia*: (257) Underweight .77; (254) Weight Loss .75; (142) Undereating .70; (248) Decreased Appetite .66
7. *Motor Restlessness*: (101) Dyskinesias .82; (108) Tremor .80; (107) Akathisia .75
8. *Aggressiveness*: (87) Excessive Aggressiveness .78; (86) Insufficient Tolerance of the Needs of Others .76; (89) Negativism .71
9. *Social Avoidance*: (83) Social Withdrawal .76; (84) Social Isolation .76; (85) Insufficient Assertiveness .45
10. *Respiratory Complaints*: (209) Dyspnea .81; (208) Shortness of Breath .79; (203) Cough .72
11. *Overeating*: (141) Overeating .80; (256) Obesity .73
12. *Hyperarousal*: (174) Night Terrors .73; (193) Hypervigilance .64; (176) Nightmares .62
13. *Self-Destructiveness*: (91) Self-Injurious Behavior .72; (94) Threats of Harming Self .49; (49) Thoughts of Harming Self .54
14. *Lassitude*: (247) Fatigue .60; (53) Low Energy Level .60; (98) Decreased Motor Activity .48
15. *Threatening to Others*: (50) Thoughts of Harming Others .65; (95) Threats of Harming Others .64
16. *Cardiovascular Complaints*: (211) Tachycardia .74; (212) Palpitations .67; (210) Dizziness .47
17. *Pain Complaints*: (207) Acute Pain .76; (206) Chronic Pain .70; (204) Headache .42
18. *Hypomania*: (9) Elevated Mood .78; (45) Inflated Self Esteem .44
19. *Drug Use Problems*: (137) Concern About Drug Use .88; (126) Use of Street Drugs .83
20. *Cigarette Smoking*: (125) Problems with Stopping Cigarette Smoking .86; (124) Problems with Smoking Cigarettes .84
21. *Imagery Problems*: (70) Illusions .68; (72) Auditory Hallucinations .66

[a] Numbers in parentheses refer to interview question number.
[b] Numbers not in parentheses represent factor coefficients.

Numbers in parentheses refer to the DPRI question number. Table 6.2 provides the means and standard deviations for each of the twenty-one factors. Since no single item on the interview was endorsed by over 60 percent of the patients, and most of the items by less than 50 percent, the modal response for each item was zero. As a result, with the exception of the first factor, standard deviations were greater than the mean intensity score for each factor.

FACTOR RELIABILITY

To examine test-retest reliability of items and factors, the DPRI was administered to fifty patients on consecutive days (within twenty-four hours). Correlation coefficients (Pearson *r*) were calculated for each of the twenty-one factors and each of the seventy-one items making up the factors, based on the intensity ratings (five-point scale) for each item endorsed by each patient. As shown in Table 6.2 (column 3), factors were quite stable (*r*'s ranged from 0.39 to 0.93, all correlations significant beyond *p* levels of 0.01).

Inspection of the factor structure derived from the interview items (table 6.1) shows that the factors appear to reflect a broad range of problem areas representative of those identified in hospitalized psychiatric and alcohol-abusing patients.

TABLE 6.2

Mean, Standard Deviation, and Test-Retest Reliability of Factors

Factor	*Mean*	*Standard Deviation*	*Coefficient (r)*
1. Depression	1.352	1.150	0.92
2. Affective Constriction	0.812	1.009	0.80
3. Sleep Disturbances	1.257	1.402	0.84
4. Disturbed Thinking	0.643	0.866	0.88
5. Alcohol Use Problems	1.010	1.025	0.91
6. Anorexia	0.516	0.907	0.82
7. Motor Restlessness	0.598	1.049	0.62
8. Aggressiveness	0.283	0.644	0.52
9. Social Avoidance	0.611	1.011	0.58
10. Respiratory Complaints	0.396	0.848	0.85
11. Overeating	0.384	0.711	0.86
12. Hyperarousal	0.357	0.791	0.91
13. Self-Destructiveness	0.369	0.741	0.86
14. Lassitude	0.297	0.703	0.81
15. Threatening to Others	0.262	0.607	0.87
16. Cardiovascular Complaints	0.501	0.885	0.66
17. Pain Complaints	0.394	0.815	0.87
18. Hypomania	1.46	1.559	0.39
19. Drug Use Problems	0.238	0.637	0.93
20. Cigarette Smoking	0.286	0.394	0.93
21. Imagery/Perception Problems	0.286	0.440	0.76

TABLE 6.3

Pearson Correlations Between the DPRI Factors and the MMPI Scales

DPRI Factors	L	F	K	HS	D	HY	PD	MF	PA	PT	SC	MA	SI
Depression	31[c]	41[c]	−40[c]	15[b]	49[c]	19[b]	31[c]	12[a]	40[c]	54[c]	43[c]	09	47[c]
Affective Constriction	−15[b]	33[c]	−25[c]	12[a]	25[c]	11[a]	14[a]	02	28[c]	34[c]	34[c]	11[a]	31[c]
Sleep Disturbances	−10	24[c]	−18[b]	26[c]	42[c]	27[c]	18[b]	03	21[c]	41[c]	27[c]	08	24[c]
Disturbed Thinking	−16[b]	40[c]	−28[c]	24[c]	37[c]	22[c]	11[a]	06	31[c]	45[c]	46[c]	14[a]	30[c]
Alcohol Use Problems	−15[b]	07	−14[a]	04	10	04	03	−14[a]	04	04	03	06	11[a]
Anorexia	−11[a]	12[a]	−10	28[c]	31[c]	23[c]	12[b]	02	11[a]	22[c]	17[b]	02	10
Motor Restlessness	−13[a]	15[b]	−11[a]	20[b]	18[b]	21[b]	02	−09	19[b]	22[c]	22[c]	11[a]	07
Aggressiveness	−14[a]	28[c]	−25[c]	03	11[a]	−02	10	06	20[b]	14[a]	21[c]	13[a]	21[c]
Social Avoidance	−20[b]	36[c]	−29[c]	08	27[c]	05	22[c]	07	26[c]	29[c]	34[c]	11[a]	41[c]
Respiratory Complaints	−10	−01	−07	34[c]	17[b]	27[c]	01	02	05	07	04	−03	04
Overeating	−17[b]	13[a]	−16[b]	07	08	−01	−01	07	05	11[a]	08	06	07
Hyperarousal	−09	33[c]	−13[a]	24[c]	31[c]	26[c]	21[c]	07	32[c]	42[c]	41[c]	20[b]	21[c]
Self-Destructiveness	−10	33[c]	−19[b]	15[b]	32[c]	19[b]	23[c]	03	30[c]	37[c]	36[c]	06	26[c]
Lassitude	−15[b]	22[c]	−11	47[c]	48[c]	47[c]	16[b]	13[a]	28[c]	44[c]	34[c]	−02	30[c]
Threatening to Others	−09	28[c]	−16[b]	−00	01	−02	08	05	28[c]	18[b]	29[c]	29[c]	08
Cardiovascular Complaints	−03	00	−06	37[c]	18[b]	28[c]	−00	−07	02	13[a]	09	−03	00
Pain Complaints	−02	10	−05	33[c]	24[c]	25[c]	12[a]	08	18[b]	12[a]	21[c]	22[c]	09
Hypomania	−12[a]	20[b]	−20[b]	08	01	01	−04	06	12[a]	12[a]	21[c]	22[c]	−02
Drug Use Problems	−05	12[a]	−05	−03	−14[a]	−03	17[b]	07	17[b]	06	12[a]	27[c]	−08
Cigarette Smoking	−07	11[a]	−15[b]	14[a]	14[b]	15[b]	15[b]	02	09	08	08[a]	−02	08
Imagery/Perception Problems	−05	27[c]	−13[a]	09	12[a]	08	01	−09	17[b]	18[b]	23[c]	11[a]	12[a]

NOTE: Decimals have been omitted. [a] $p \leq 0.05$ [b] $p \leq 0.01$ [c] $p \leq 0.001$

Concurrent Validity of the DPRI

We are testing the DPRI's validity by several means and have completed a series of concurrent validity studies. Concurrent validity was first tested with the most widely used adjustment measure, the Minnesota Multiphasic Personality Inventory (MMPI; Hathaway and McKinley, 1951). Canonical correlational analyses were performed to address whether the DPRI factors (table 6.1) overlap with MMPI validity and clinical scales and the substantive content of such overlap. The results of our analyses (table 6.3) show that DPRI factors and MMPI scales obtain a high degree of association. Of 273 bivariate pairs, 179 attain significance at the 0.05 level of significance or greater. (Of these, 133 correlate at 0.01 or more.)

From these correlations, five (nearly six) canonical factors were found to be significant in a sample of 283 recently admitted male psychiatric and substance abuse inpatients. The DPRI accounted for 67 percent of the MMPI variance and the MMPI accounted for 43 percent of the DPRI variance. Areas of redundancy between the DPRI and the MMPI were as follows (canonical correlations squared [r_c^2] given in parentheses): depression (0.58), somatic symptoms (0.42), irritability and interpersonal anger (0.33), addictive behaviors associated with antisocial attitudes and behaviors (0.19), addictive behaviors associated with neuroticlike symptoms (0.16), and social avoidance (0.16). More detailed information on canonical structure coefficients and interpretations of areas of overlap are given in Fowler and associates (1986). These results were interpreted as establishing concurrent validity for the DPRI with another self-report clinical assessment scale, the MMPI.

Concurrent validity was also studied with measures based on clinician ratings, by using the Brief Psychiatric Rating Scale (BPRS; Overall and Gorham, 1962). Results showed a significant degree of overlap. Table 6.4 presents canonical correlation results using the four BPRS syndrome scores (Thinking Disturbance, Anxious Depression, Paranoid Disturbances, and Withdrawal Retardation) derived from the BPRS scales.

Twenty-six of eighty-four possible bivariate correlations are significant at the 0.05 level or greater (using one-tailed tests, based on specific predictions for BPRS syndrome scale-DPRI overlap). Two significant canonical variates emerged—one overlap between the BPRS Anxious Depression syndrome and the DPRI factor of Depression, and the other between the BPRS Thinking Disturbance syndrome and the DPRI factors of Tremor/Restlessness, Imagery/Perception, and Self-destructiveness. This second significant variate provides concurrent validation of the DPRI's capacity to assess dimensions associated with psychotic symptoms. The BPRS explained 40.6 percent of the variance in the DPRI, and the DPRI explained 15.3 percent of the variance in the BPRS.

TABLE 6.4
DPRI–BPRS Syndrome Score Correlational Matrix

	BPRS Syndrome Scores			
DPRI Factors	*Thinking Disturbances*	*Anxious Depression*	*Paranoid Disturbances*	*Withdrawal Retardation*
1. Depression	00	45[b]	10	08
2. Affective Constriction	01	22[b]	07	06
3. Sleep Disturbances	00	19[a]	00	02
4. Disturbed Thinking	13[a]	13[a]	19[a]	13[a]
5. Alcohol Use Problems	−09	13[a]	−10	−05
6. Anorexia	07	15[a]	−10	−08
7. Motor Restlessness	11	21[b]	−10	08
8. Aggressiveness	08	10	13[a]	14[a]
9. Social Avoidance	−05	32[b]	12	14[a]
10. Respiratory Complaints	−11	05	08	−01
11. Overeating	−03	07	−07	−01
12. Hyperarousal	10	27[b]	05	−05
13. Self-Destructiveness	13[a]	23[b]	02	05
14. Lassitude	00	20[a]	04	14[a]
15. Threatening to Others	20[a]	04	25[a]	08
16. Cardiovascular Complaints	08	03	−06	−04
17. Pain Complaints	05	25[b]	02	−05
18. Hypomania	10	−05	−02	−13[a]
19. Drug Use Problems	07	16[a]	14[a]	05
20. Cigarette Smoking	−12	06	02	−02
21. Imagery/Perception Problems	22[b]	−06	06	10

NOTE: Decimals have been omitted. [a] $p < 0.05$ [b] $p < 0.01$

The degree of BPRS-DPRI association was lower than that of the MMPI-DPRI. Nevertheless, the BPRS-DPRI strength of association was quite similar to MMPI-BPRS associations. Two significant canonical variates were found between the MMPI and BPRS—one overlap between the BPRS Anxious Depression syndrome with the MMPI Psychasthenia, Depression, and *F* scales, and the other between the BPRS Paranoid Disturbance Syndrome and the MMPI Schizophrenia and *F* scales. Thus the canonical structure between these two well-established instruments was quite similar to the canonical structure of the DPRI and the BPRS.

The DPRI as a Change Measure

A major objective in developing the DPRI was to make use of the problem-oriented system's potential for tracking treatment response (or lack thereof) by specific problem. Studies of the validity of the instrument as a change measure are in progress. The concept of problem severity, which has already been defined (Fowler et al., 1986), is essential to a discussion of problem change. This earlier, preliminary study, using intensity and frequency scores from patients administered the DPRI and DPRI-F at two points during the course of treatment, produced patterns of differences that indicated the feasibility of deriving severity ratings from a combination of intensity and frequency ratings.

A more recent study (Fowler et al., May 1986), involving results from DPRI and DPRI-F administration at two points during the treatment course of psychiatric and substance abuse inpatients, examines concurrent validity of the DPRI change measures by using DPRI intensity ratings only. In this study, the DPRI and DPRI-F were administered concurrently with the MMPI and the BPRS shortly after admission and once again between fourteen and forty-five days after the initial administration. Initial and follow-up DPRI and MMPI scales were given to 249 patients. Initial and follow-up DPRI and BPRS scales were given to 80 patients.

In order to diminish reliability problems encountered in the analysis of difference scores, we followed the recommendations of Cohen and Cohen (1983) and Ellsworth (1975) by using *residual scores* for analyzing concurrent validity of the DPRI as a measurement of change. We determined a "severity" score for each of the twenty-one factors for each patient on both the initial interview and the follow-up interview, here using intensity ratings only. Using these ratings, we then calculated residual scores for each factor on each patient. Residual scores were likewise calculated for the concurrently administered MMPI and BPRS scales. Canonical correlation analysis was employed to compare the residual scores of the DPRI and MMPI and the DPRI and BPRS.

Analysis of the correlation between the DPRI and MMPI residuals yielded three significant canonical variates (all with p values less than 0.005). The three variates produced the following overlaps: (1) the DPRI Depression, Affective Constriction, Lassitude, and Pain Complaint factors with the MMPI *F*, *D*, and *Hy* scales; (2) the DPRI Overeating, Hyperarousal, and Threatening to Others factors with the MMPI *F*, *Pd*, and *Si* scales; and (3) the DPRI Pain and Hypomania factors with the MMPI *Hs*, *Pd*, and *MF* scales. These results indicate that the DPRI and MMPI overlap significantly as instruments to measure change, using only intensity scores from the DPRI.

The canonical correlation of the DPRI-BPRS residuals produced only one canonical variate near the 0.05 level of significance. This variate ($p \leq 0.06$) showed overlap between the DPRI Social Avoidance, Threatening to Others, Pain Complaints, and Imagery/Perception Problems factors with the BPRS Thinking Disturbance and Paranoid Disturbances syndromes. Although this correlation did not meet our criterion level of significance, the variate overlap shows clinical relevance. We hope that the analyses of residuals based on DPRI severity ratings (incorporating frequency ratings) will produce better correlations with the BPRS.

Other Studies

Results from concurrent validity studies and other studies in progress provide empirical evidence of the validity of the DPRI as an instrument for measuring problem dimensions. It must be noted, however, that concurrent validity is but one method of establishing the usefulness of any clinical instrument. Other forms of validity—such as predictive validity, construct validity of the various factors, discriminant validity, and so forth—must be tested.

Although the degree of association between the DPRI and the MMPI and between the DPRI and the BPRS was significant, concurrent validity studies also implied that the DPRI measures problem dimensions other than those attaining significance, as shown in the canonical correlational analyses. This latter point can readily be inferred from the moderate degree of variance in the DPRI accounted for by the MMPI and the BPRS, as well as from the fact that the MMPI and BPRS accounted for somewhat different DPRI dimensions.

These observations suggest additional concurrent validity studies, which are now underway. Other studies, using different combinations of frequency and intensity to determine the best measure of problem severity for demonstrating change, are also required. New factors, developed from larger and more homogeneous patient samples (for example, all general psychiatry inpatients, all alcohol treatment program patients, or all drug treatment program patients), are also being analyzed. Further norms, using outpatient and nonpatient populations, will need to be developed.

Reporting Format

We developed the DPRI so that clinicians could efficiently gather the patient information necessary to take advantage of the strengths of the problem-oriented system. These strengths include providing a structure that encourages identification of a comprehensive range of problems and a method for linking data about problems with treatments for those problems. Furthermore, the DPRI, with its follow-up format, the DPRI-F, was also designed to provide a method for problem-specific assessment of treatment impact. Empirical development of factors is one way to assist clinicians in information synthesis.

The most efficient and valid instrument loses its value to clinicians, however, if the feedback mechanism (the report) is confusing or overwhelming to the staff for whom it is intended. We are experimenting with several report formats in order to determine those that are likely to be most useful (and used). Figure 6.7 illustrates part of a report that emphasizes the "microscopic" view of how the patient has responded to the interview.

```
000-00-0000  CASE,SAMPLE                M AGE 38 01/06/86    09/07/83

                *** PROBLEM INDICATOR FOLLOW-UP INTERVIEW ***

DEPRESSED MOOD
     09/07/83                RESOLVED                   RESOLVED
     08/29/83                INTENSITY= 3 ######        FREQUENCY= 2 ####
     08/04/83                INTENSITY= 3 ######        FREQUENCY= 3 ######
     07/21/83 INITIAL        INTENSITY= 5 ##########    FREQUENCY= 4 ########

ANXIOUS MOOD
     09/07/83                INTENSITY= 2 ####          FREQUENCY= 1 ##
     08/29/83                INTENSITY= 2 ####          FREQUENCY= 3######
     08/04/83                INTENSITY= 3 ######        FREQUENCY= 3 ######
     07/21/83 INITIAL        INTENSITY= 5 ##########    FREQUENCY= 3 ######

IRRITABLE MOOD
     09/07/83                RESOLVED                   RESOLVED
     08/29/83                INTENSITY= 3 ######        FREQUENCY= 2 ####
     08/04/83                INTENSITY= 3 ######        FREQUENCY= 2 ####
     07/21/83 INITIAL        INTENSITY= 3 ######        FREQUENCY= 3 ######
```

Figure 6.7. DPRI-F report showing problem indicators.

In this format, the patient's rating of each problem indicator, both intensity and frequency (ultimately severity), is reported. Such a detailed report would be overwhelming and impossible for most clinicians to synthesize, but it might be important for some purposes (such as for certain drug studies or for specific behavioral treatments).

In most instances a more synthesized view of the patient's responses would be appropriate. Figure 6.8 illustrates part of one such report, in which factor severity scores (in this case, intensity scores alone) are presented. In addition, so that the clinician can see the items (problem indicators) that constitute each factor, the initial and final scores for each indicator are also given.

For some clinicians, even this level of detail is unnecessary. We are also testing more general reports (for example, giving only those factors that are improving, staying the same, or getting worse). We want to take advantage of

```
000-00-0000  CASE,SAMPLE                M AGE 38 01/06/86    09/07/83

                *** DPRI-F FACTOR REPORT ***

DEPRESSION                               3       5       7       9       110
                                T    :---0---:---0---:---0---:---0---:---:---+
 JUL 21,1983 Initial        76.23    ***********************
 AUG 4,1983    +14          72.73    **********************
 AUG 29,1983   +25          66.12    *******************
 SEP 7,1983    +9 (+48)     43.98    *********

Problem Indicators:                                  Initial/Final Ratings:
 HOPELESSNESS                                        Initial= 4  Final= 0
 HELPLESSNESS                                        Initial= 3  Final= 0
 LOW SELF-ESTEEM                                     Initial= 5  Final= 0
 IDEAS OF GUILT OR SELF-BLAME                        Initial= 5  Final= 3
 THOUGHTS OF HARMING SELF                            Initial= 4  Final= 0
 DEPRESSED MOOD                                      Initial= 5  Final= 0
 ANXIOUS MOOD                                        Initial= 5  Final= 2
```

Figure 6.8. DPRI-F report showing factors and problem indicators.

one of the major strengths of the computer—the ability to sort and display information from a variety of perspectives. During this early phase of test development, we are primarily interested in usefulness and acceptability to clinicians. Later we will be testing the value to clinicians by examining the effects of various report formats on clinician behavior and treatment (see McCullough, 1984).

Discussion

The DPRI was formulated to facilitate a problem-focused approach to evaluation and treatment, not merely to aid in the use of the problem-oriented record. We believe that, compared to the predominant approach that emphasizes diagnostic classification alone, the problem-oriented approach greatly improves clinicians' abilities to formulate and plan treatment. Where criteria-based diagnostic classification ensures homogeneous groups of very similar psychopathological manifestations, a problem-oriented approach permits tracking of symptoms and behaviors that do not necessarily constitute a single syndrome. By following patients at this level, a great deal of information usually lost through the data reductions of diagnosis and similar methods heuristically used by clinicians is retained. The diagnostic method of reduction has been valuable because it has allowed clinicians to process large amounts of data and to make generalizations from them.

The use of automated procedures can diminish this need for early data reduction to manage information, and encourages descriptions rather than classification of patients. Remaining closer to the data also permits its reduction through statistical analysis rather than through heuristic (that is, clinical) means. Factorial and cluster analysis also lead to data reduction, but without a priori assumptions about symptom clusters. In the scope of patient description, assessment, and treatment planning, remaining closer to the data has been shown to lead to significantly more successful clinician behaviors (McCullough, 1984). When it is presented in an acceptable way, clinicians respond appropriately to the increased information—and the computer is well suited to present data clearly.

The DPRI, and especially its follow-up form, the DPRI-F, are computer-based interviews. They were constructed to maximize the interactive properties available with computerized administration. The branching nature of the test individualizes each administration, based on previous answers and demographic information. Although the questions and branching logic are available in written form, the test can be given only by computer. The philosophy underlying the construction of the DPRI was that it should be a part of a larger clinical data base and, therefore, should be easily accessible and follow good data base management rules. In order to be useful to the entire psychometric field, computerized tests must be available, of reasonable cost, and open to scientific inspection. We believe that we have met these goals with the DPRI.

The DPRI was written in the MUMPS computer language. While MUMPS is not as familiar to most people as BASIC or PASCAL, it is a good choice for test construction and data manipulation. MUMPS is an American National Standards Institute (ANSI) standard language and will run on all computers running this standard. Nonproprietary MUMPS language systems are available for most microcomputers, including the IBM PC with PC-DOS and the Apple II computers with CPM. Proprietary MUMPS implementations are available on a range of micro, mini, and mainframe computers. All these ANSI implementations will run the DPRI software.

The DPRI was written to take advantage of two other nonproprietary software packages—the VA File Manager and the VA Psychodiagnostic testing package, which are available at nominal cost and are standard MUMPS implementations. While not necessary to run the DPRI, these packages are very useful. The File Manager is an extensive data base management system upon which full hospital information systems, including Laboratory, Pharmacy, Admissions, and Outpatient Scheduling packages, have been developed. The VA also has an extensive Mental Health software package that is compatible with its File Manager. The File Manager allows searching, sorting, and reporting of the DPRI data in ways that do not require programming skills.

The VA Psychodiagnostic Testing package is an on-line administration, scoring, and authoring system for tests and interviews. It has been in use for the past decade by clinicians across the country. Other interviews and tests can be constructed by using these two complementary software packages.

Care was taken to make the DPRI software portable to other computers. The package was developed on an 11/44 minicomputer, using ISM-11 MUMPS. It has now been transported to a full DEC system and to an IBM PC–compatible microcomputer, using MS-DOS, version 2.11. The minimum system requirement for microcomputers is based on mass storage. The required routines use approximately 50 kilobytes of disk space, and the data files require another 220 kilobytes. Storage of patient responses requires 3 kilobytes per average administration. An IBM PC or compatible with two floppy disk drives can, therefore, run the interview quite nicely and store data on over forty-five interview administrations. A hard disk of at least 5 megabytes is required to run the two optional packages (File Manager and Psychodiagnostic Testing) or to store interview results on a larger number of patients.

The field of automated psychological tests and interviews has produced many poorly validated instruments. A number of others are well conceived and validated but, since they are proprietary, they are difficult to obtain and impossible to verify because decision rules remain hidden. The DPRI is unique in that it was constructed to maximize computer usage, is nonproprietary, and is portable to so many different hardware configurations. The logic of the DPRI is open for inspection and verification. Validation studies as reported here continue, and data is solicited from others as the software becomes available to other facilities.

ACKNOWLEDGMENTS

This investigation was supported in part by Biomedical Research Support Grant 2 S07 RR-5426-21 (Dr. Fowler) and a Veterans Administration Merit Review (Dr. Penk). Dovalee Dorsett, Ph.D., Statistics Department, Southern Methodist University, provided statistical consultation for this project. Harriet Warren and the Veterans Administration Data Processing Center, Austin, Texas, provided computer processing and statistical analyses.

REFERENCES

American Psychiatric Association. (1980). *Diagnostic and statistical manual of mental disorders* (3rd ed.). Washington, DC: Author.

Angle, J. V., Ellinwood, E. H., and Carrol, J. (1978). Computer interview problem assessment of psychiatric patients. In F. C. Carrol (Ed.), *Proceedings of the Second Annual Symposium on Computer Applications in Medical Care* (pp. 137–148). New York: Institute of Electrical & Electronics Engineers.

Clavell, R. R., and Butcher, J. N. (1976). An adaptive typological approach to psychiatric screening. *Journal of Consulting and Clinical Psychiatry*, 45, 851–859.

Cohen, J., and Cohen, P. (1983). Applied multiple regression/correlation. *Analysis for the behavioral sciences* (2nd ed.). Hillsdale, NJ: Lawrence Erlbaum.

Comrey, A. L. (1978). Common methodological problems in factor analytic studies. *Journal of Consulting and Clinical Psychiatry*, 46, 648–659.

Ellsworth, R. B. (1975). Consumer feedback in measuring the effectiveness of mental health programs. In M. Guttentag and G. L. Struening (Eds.), *Handbook of Evaluation Research, vol.* 2 (pp. 239–274). Beverly Hills, CA: Sage.

Erdman, H. P., Klein, M. H., and Griest, J. H. (1985). Direct patient interviewing. *Journal of Consulting and Clinical Psychology*, 53, 760–773.

Fowler, D. R., Bell, W., Finkelstein, A. S., and Penk, W. (1986, May). *Measuring treatment response by computer interview*. Paper presented at the annual meeting of the American Psychiatric Association, Washington, DC.

Fowler, D. R., Finkelstein, A. S., Penk, W., Itzig, B., and Bell, W. (1986). Problem tracking by computer: The Dallas problem rating interview. In J. E. Mezzich (Ed.), *Clinical care and information systems in psychiatry*. Washington, DC: American Psychiatric Press.

Fowler, D. R., Finkelstein, A. S., Penk, W., Itzig, B., Bell, W., and Dorsett, D. (1985). *Correlates and canonical variates for domains of problems and personality*. Unpublished manuscript.

Griest, J. H., Klein, M. H., and Van Cura, L. J. (1973). A computer interview for psychiatric patient target symptons. *Archives of General Psychiatry*, 29, 247–253.

Hathaway, S. R., and McKinley, J. C. (1951). *The Minnesota Multiphasic Personality Inventory*. New York: Psychological Corporation.

Hay, W. M., Hay, L. R., Angle, H. V., and Ellinwood, E. H. (1977). Computerized behavioral assessment and the problem oriented record. *International Journal of Mental Health*, 6, 49–63.

Hedlund, J. L., Vieweg, B. W., and Cho, D. W. (1985). Mental health computing in the 1980's. II. Clinical applications. *Computers in the Human Services*, *1*(2), 1–31.

International Mathematical and Statistical Libraries. (1984). *IMSL Users Guide*. (Available from author, NBC Building, 7500 Bellaire Boulevard, Houston, TX.)

Jackson, D. N. (1971). The dynamics of structured personality tests. *Psychiatry Reviews*, 78, 229–248.

Johnson, J. G., and Williams, T. A. (1980). Using on-line computer technology to improve service response and decision-making effectiveness in a mental health admitting system. In J. B. Sidowski, J. H. Johnson, and T. A. Williams (Eds.), *Technology in mental health care delivery systems*, (pp. 237–249). Norwood, NJ: Ablex.

Longabaugh, R., Fowler, D. R., Stout, R., and Kriebel, G. (1983). Validation for a problem-focused nomenclature. *Archives of General Psychiatry, 40,* 453–461.

Longabaugh, R., Fowler, D. R., Kriebel, H., Westlake, R., and Stout, R. (1981, February). The Butler hospital code for psychiatric problems (MS No. 2207). *JSAS Catalogue of Selected Documents in Psychology.*

Longabaugh, R., Stout, R., Kriebel, G. W., McCullough, L., and Bishop, D. (in press). DSM-III and clinically-identified problems as a guide to treatment. *Archives of General Psychiatry.*

McCullough, L. (1984, November). Systematic evaluation of the impact of computer-acquired data on psychiatric care. *Proceedings of the Fifth Annual Symposium of Computer Applications in Medical Care,* 426–430.

Overall, J. E., and Gorham, D. R. (1962). The Brief Psychiatric Rating Scale. *Psychological Reports, 10,* 799–812.

Robins, L. N., Helzer, J. E., Croughan, J. L., *et al.* (1979). *The NIMH Diagnostic Interview Schedule.* Bethesda, MD: National Institute of Mental Health.

Ryback, R. S., Longabaugh, R., and Fowler, D. R. (1981). *The problem oriented record in psychiatry and mental health care* (rev. ed.). New York: Grune & Stratton.

Statistical Analysis System. (1982). *SAS users guide: Statistics.* Cary, NC: SAS Institute.

Weed, L. L. (1969). *Medical records, medical education and patient care.* Cleveland, OH: Case Western Reserve University Press.

7

Lifestyle Assessment Using Microcomputers

Barbara Allen and Harvey A. Skinner

Lifestyle issues have captured a great deal of public attention. A perusal of any popular magazine or television news program will reveal the latest strategies for losing weight, keeping fit, eating better, avoiding stress, quitting smoking, drinking less, and enjoying life more. Lifestyles are also a topic of growing concern among policy makers and health care providers. Research linking specific lifestyle activities to increased risk of disease and mortality has stimulated various calls for health-promotion and disease-prevention programs. The goal of health promotion is education, while disease prevention focuses on the modification of risk factors and early intervention when prognosis is more favorable.

This chapter describes an application of microcomputer technology to lifestyle screening and assessment. Over the past six years, we have systematically developed a computer program that conducts a comprehensive assessment of lifestyle activities. The program was designed so that it could be used as a part of health-promotion and disease-prevention programs in busy clinical settings. The chapter is divided into four major sections. First, the importance of assessing lifestyle behaviors is addressed as a "new perspective" on health care. Then results are briefly reviewed from several evaluations of the computerized lifestyle assessment. The third portion of the chapter is devoted to a detailed description of a computer program that was designed to provide an easy-to-use yet comprehensive lifestyle assessment. Finally, future developments are outlined where the computerized lifestyle assessment is being linked with brief intervention strategies.

Why Assess Lifestyles?

Interest in disease prevention is not a recent phenomenon. As early as two centuries ago, Johan Frank said, "Since it is infinitely easier to prevent physical illnesses than to remedy them once they have arrived, preventive medicine is the most important part of medicine" (Yankauer, 1983, p. 1032). Indeed, prevention and health promotion have proven to be invaluable strategies for disease control. During the early 1900s infectious and communicable diseases were the leading cause of death and disability in North America. With immunization, improved sanitation, better nutrition, and public health programs, the mortality rate from these diseases plummeted to only about 1 percent of deaths in persons under seventy-five years of age (U.S. Surgeon General, 1979).

The mortality pattern has changed during the past eighty years. Today the leading causes of death and illness are chronic noncommunicable disorders (heart disease, cancer, cerebrovascular disease) and accidents (Jonas, 1982; Lalonde, 1974). Before the major underlying causes of these diseases were established, little attention was given to preventive initiatives. Consequently, health care professionals' time and government expenditures have been largely devoted to treatment (Taylor, Ureda, and Denham, 1982).

In 1974 Marc Lalonde, the National Minister of Health and Welfare Canada, published a now-classic paper on the health of Canadians. He distinguished among lifestyle, human biology, and the environment as major causes of sickness and death. When American experts analysed the ten leading causes of death in the United States, they found that "perhaps as much as half of U.S. mortality in 1976 was due to unhealthy behavior or lifestyle; 20 percent to environmental factors; 20 percent to human biological factors; and only 10 percent to inadequacies in health care" (U.S. Surgeon General, 1979, p. 9). Although multiple risk factors underlie chronic diseases, the fact that behavioral components underlie so much of the mortality rate leads to the supposition that many of the physical and mental disorders being treated today are preventable (Taylor, Ureda, and Denham, 1982).

Preventive strategies aimed at lifestyle modification may have more impact on reducing illness and mortality than current treatment approaches (Schweiker, 1982). The U.S. Surgeon General (1979) called cigarette smoking "the single most important preventable cause of death." A clear link has been established between cigarette smoking and cancer, chronic bronchitis, and emphysema (U.S. Surgeon General, 1982, 1983, 1984). Cigarette smoking also elevates the risk of heart disease, especially among men. With respect to alcohol consumption, excessive use can lead to a wide range of physical morbidity, such as liver disease (Ashley et al., 1981), and a reduction in alcohol consumption among heavy drinkers will reduce their alcohol-related mortality rate (Stewart, 1980). The influence of alcohol is noted in approximately 50 percent of road traffic accidents (Fitzgerald et al., 1984). Failure to use seat belts increases the risk of serious injuries and death from traffic accidents (Sherk, Thomas, Wilson, and Evans, 1985). Although there is still a great need for epidemiological and clinical studies (Relman, 1982), it is clear from the research to date that some lifestyle choices can have severe yet preventable health consequences.

A prospective study of 6,928 adult residents of Alameda County, California, showed that a few simple health habits can reduce the risk of disease and mortality (Belloc, 1973; Belloc and Breslow, 1972; Berkman and Breslow, 1983). A nine-year follow-up found that getting seven to eight hours of sleep each night, maintaining desirable weight (in relation to height), not smoking cigarettes, moderate or no use of alcohol, and getting regular exercise were positively and strongly associated with good health (Berkman and Breslow, 1983). Furthermore, the effect was cumulative: the greater the number of personal health habits practiced, the greater the probability of leading a longer life (Breslow and Enstrom, 1980). With respect to social relationships, Berkman and Syme (1979) reported a link between social networks and mortality. Marital status, contacts with close friends and relatives, church membership, and membership in four types of groups were used to form the social network index. In the nine-year follow-up period, lower mortality rates were observed among persons with more extensive social contacts. The relationship between mortality and social networks was not dependent on initial health status, year of death, health practices, or socioeconomic status.

Many of the lifestyle factors implicated in disease and mortality involve simple daily habits over which individuals have personal control. Yet health care expenditures are largely devoted to treatment of disease rather than to preventive strategies (U.S. Surgeon General, 1979). A "new perspective" is called for that gives more emphasis to health-promotion and disease-prevention programs. Roemer (1984) argues that an ideal opportunity for health promotion arises when patients seek help in hospitals and general practices. The family physician is in an excellent position to identify patients who exhibit health-risk behaviors and to take action with education and early intervention programs (Russell, Wilson, Taylor, and Baker, 1979; Skinner and Holt, 1983).

A survey of 433 physicians considered the extent to which they view their role as health promoters. Nearly three-quarters felt it was definitely the responsibility of physicians to educate patients about lifestyle risk behaviors such as smoking, alcohol, drugs, stress, exercise, and diet (Wechsler et al., 1983). But only a fourth (27 percent) reported that they routinely gathered information about all these behaviors. Questions about diet, exercise, and stress were asked least often. This study suggests that routine screening of a broad range of health-risk behaviors is not a standard procedure in clinical practice. Other studies have shown that some physicians wrongly associate negative patient characteristics with alcohol and drug abuse problems (Skinner, Allen, McIntosh, and Palmer, 1985b). Physicians' stereotypes about their patients may hinder early detection of substance abuse and perhaps other health-risk habits.

Wallace and Haines (1984) investigated patients' perspective on lifestyle activities. Although most felt physicians should be interested in weight control, cigarette smoking, alcohol use, and physical exercise, less than half reported that their physician had seemed concerned with these issues. If physicians engage in only "selective" screening of lifestyle issues, then certain cases may be missed.

Evaluation of the Computer Program

Routine lifestyle screening using low-cost microcomputers has great potential for assisting the busy clinician with early identification of health-risk behaviors. Over the past six years we have developed a lifestyle assessment in which subjects respond to questions administered by a microcomputer. The assessment examines a broad range of factors including nutrition, caffeine use, exercise, weight, sleep, cigarette smoking, and alcohol and nonmedical drug use. Major evaluations of the software have concentrated on the accuracy and acceptability of the computerized assessment.

Computers are a particularly attractive method of assessing lifestyles because patients may be more honest in divulging potentially sensitive information (for example, alcohol use) to a medium that affords privacy (Lucas, Mullin, Luna, and McInroy, 1977). Because of respondents' tendency to underreport alcohol use (Pernanen, 1974), we hypothesized that greater and presumably more accurate substance use (alcohol, drugs, and tobacco) would be reported to the computer than to a human interviewer or on a paper-and-pencil questionnaire (Skinner and Allen, 1983). Patients who voluntarily sought help for an alcohol or drug problem at the Addiction Research Foundation in Toronto were randomly assigned to one of the three assessment formats. Analyses showed no important differences in reported alcohol, drug, or tobacco consumption patterns, or in the level of related problems.

Because the 150 patients in this study were voluntarily seeking help for substance use problems, they might be less likely to distort or minimize consumption patterns. Consequently, the study was replicated using general medical patients at the Family Practice Service of Toronto General Hospital (Skinner, Allen, McIntosh, and Palmer, 1985a,b). Again, patients were randomly assigned to a computer assessment ($N = 60$), face-to-face interview ($N = 60$), or a self-completed questionnaire ($N = 60$). Results from this study confirmed the earlier work. No significant differences in alcohol, drug, or tobacco consumption levels or related problems were reported across the three assessment formats.

Another issue relating to the accuracy of computerized assessment concerns the reliability of screening instruments used in the interview. Coefficient alpha (Cronbach, 1970), a measure of the degree of consistency in responding to items, was examined by Selzer (1971) for the twenty-four-item Michigan Alcoholism Screening Test (MAST). A reliability estimate of 0.90 was obtained on the MAST when it was administered via the computer, the face-to-face interview, and the self-completed questionnaire (Skinner and Allen, 1983). This suggests that the type of assessment format does not influence patients' consistency in answering items.

In addition to assessment accuracy, we were concerned with the acceptability of the computerized assessment to both patients and staff. Certainly if patients have major concerns about answering questions on a computer, or if staff are resistant or uncomfortable in using the software, then computerized lifestyle assessments would not be feasible. Our evaluation showed that patients have both positive and negative attitudes toward computerized assessment (Skinner, Allen, McIntosh, and Palmer, 1985a). Prior to being asked any questions about lifestyle, patients rank-ordered their preference of three assessment formats (computer, interview, and questionnaire) on a paper-and-pencil questionnaire. While most patients selected face-to-face interviews as their first choice, only a few selected the computer. However, when preferences were reranked after the lifestyle assessment, there was a significant increase (13 percent to 43 percent) in preference for the computer among those completing the computerized interview (see figure 7.1). The greatest increase in preference for the computer was among those with no previous computer experience. This suggests that direct, "hands-on" experience increases the acceptance of computerized interviews.

For some patients, negative attitudes were so strong that they refused the computer interview. Roughly 5 percent of patients assigned to the computer assessment fell into this category. Research has shown that computers are not well accepted by nervous or highly stressed patients (Cruickshank, 1982). These patients might better be assessed using some other method. Table 7.1 lists some

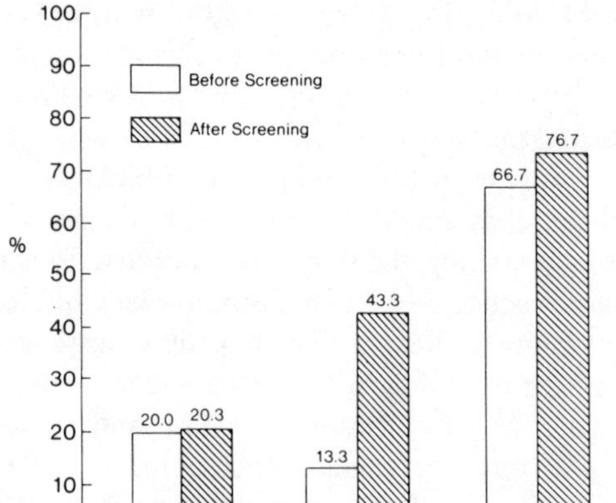

Figure 7.1. Change in patients' preference (first choice) for mode of assessment following administration of the lifestyle assessment.
NOTE: Reprinted, by permission of the publisher, from H. A. Skinner, B. A. Allen, M. C. McIntosh, and W. H. Palmer, "Lifestyle Assessment: Applying Microcomputers in Family Practice," *British Medical Journal* 290 (1985): 212.

TABLE 7.1
Reasons Given by Patients for Liking or Disliking Computerized Assessment

Like	*Dislike*
"Think it would be interesting"	"Frightening. Information can be called upon by anyone for malicious use"
"Have never tried it"	"It's a machine and I would feel stupid talking to machine"
"Fast, private"	"I loathe technology"
"Tendency to be more honest"	"Computers take away employment"

NOTE: Reprinted, by permission of the publisher, from H. A. Skinner, B. A. Allen, M. C. McIntosh, and W. H. Palmer, "Lifestyle Assessment: Applying Microcomputers in Family Practice," *British Medical Journal* 290 (1985):213.

of the reasons patients offered for liking and disliking computerized assessment. Attitudes toward the computer assessment were not associated with patient age, sex, marital status, education, or occupation (Skinner, Allen, McIntosh, and Palmer, 1985a).

Patients also evaluated the computer interview on a five-point semantic differential scale. The computer was rated as mechanical and impersonal, but it was also reported to be more interesting than the personal interview and the paper-and-pencil questionnaire. Although the computer was rated as friendly, the rating showed it to be the least friendly of the assessment formats. In general, however, patients rated the computer interview favorably.

No formal investigation of staff acceptance of the computerized assessment was conducted. Before any testing began, the initial reactions of physicians, nurses, and receptionists ranged from enthusiastic acceptance to indifference, to overt dislike and mistrust. However, many of the staff who initially held negative opinions voiced interest and more favorable attitudes once they personally completed the computer interview. After patients were being assessed and computer-generated reports of their lifestyle habits were made available to physicians, several doctors spontaneously approached the research team expressing interest in the software and willingness to discuss advantages of computerized lifestyle screening.

What are the advantages? On-line computer software relieves the physician and allied health professionals from routine information-gathering activities. Individualized summary reports printed immediately after the assessment is completed can be available for the physician's perusal and can assist in identifying patients with health-risk behaviors. Once these patients are identified, physicians can concentrate on more in-depth assessment and intervention strategies. Because the computer is a tireless but rapid interviewer, many patients can be assessed in the physician's waiting room. The computer's capacity to generate both graphic and textual feedback on the monitor makes it a viable tool for patient education. Immediately after completing questions about specific health habits, patients can compare their own judgment of health-risk behaviors with the computer's assessment. Other advantages of computerized assessments, such as tailored testing, are discussed by Skinner and Pakula (1986) and in a special series edited by James Butcher in the December 1985 issue of the *Journal of Consulting and Clinical Psychology*.

Description of the Computer Program

The Computerized Lifestyle Assessment conducts an on-line interview of a broad range of lifestyle activities, scores content areas, provides graphic feedback at various points during the interview, and generates printed reports. Although originally designed as a research tool, the computer program has practical value for both the health care professional and the patient. The computerized interview provides the busy clinician with a brief yet systematic method to assess health-risk behaviors. Information from the printed report can be used as a starting point for a more detailed assessment of specific risk behaviors and for facilitating physician-patient dialogue on lifestyle issues and related health problems. With regard to the patient, the lifestyle program was designed to stimulate self-examination of lifestyle choices that influence physical and mental well-being. The graphic feedback on selected lifestyle behaviors and the concluding review of lifestyle strengths and weaknesses function as an educational component. For the researcher, the computerized lifestyle program provides an efficient means of acquiring information on the prevalence of health-risk behaviors among clinical populations.

The current version of the Computerized Lifestyle Assessment is based on earlier work by the authors on computer-assisted testing. The original twenty-three-item questionnaire provided a brief assessment of consumption patterns and related problems within the domains of alcohol, drug, and tobacco use (Skinner and Allen, 1980). The current version is greatly expanded and takes approximately twenty minutes to complete. The seventeen content domains described in table 7.2 include: substance use (alcohol, cigarettes, caffeine, nonmedical drugs), social issues (social relationships, family functioning, physical abuse, sexual activities), psychological well-being (stress, depression, life satisfaction), health-promoting practices (nutrition, weight control, physical activity, sleep) and preventive activities (seat-belt use, dental checkups). Questions in the item pool were adapted from earlier questionnaires by the authors (Skinner and Allen, 1983; Skinner, Allen, McIntosh, and Palmer 1985a), the Health of Canadians Survey (Canada Health Survey, 1981), and the Alameda County Study (Berkman and Breslow, 1983). Items in the alcohol section include the CAGE (Mayfield, McLeod, and Hall, 1974), which is a brief screening instrument for the detection of alcohol problems, ten items from the Alcohol

TABLE 7.2
Computerized Lifestyle Assessment Content Areas

1. Nutrition
   - Balanced diet
   - Frequency of eating breakfast
   - Limit use of salt, sugar, and animal fats
   - Self-rating of nutrition
2. Caffeine Use
   - Amount of caffeine from coffee, tea, and cola
   - Caffeine-related health problems
3. Physical Activity
   - Frequency of activity
   - Physical limitations
   - Exercise-related health problems
4. Weight/Height
   - Current and desired weight
   - Weight-related health problems
5. Eating Disorders
   - Anorexia and bulimia
6. Sleep Habits
   - Quantity per twenty-four-hour period
   - Sleep-related health problems
7. Seat-belt Use
   - Motor vehicles
8. Dental Checkups
   - Regular care
9. Social Relationships
   - Marital status
   - Number of close friends/relatives and frequency of contact
   - Group involvement (church, social, community, etc.)
10. Family Functioning
    - Persons living with
    - Caring, problem resolution, family satisfaction
11. Physical Abuse
    - Frequency of abuse
    - Sought medical treatment
    - Reported to doctor
12. Cigarette Smoking
    - Type (never, occasional, daily, etc.)
    - Quantity
    - Dependence
    - Smoking-related health problems
13. Alcohol Use
    - Frequency in past twelve months
    - Consumption in a typical month
    - Consequences from drinking
    - Dependence symptoms
14. Nonmedical Drug Use
    - Frequency of use of seven drug types
    - Consequences of nonmedical drug use
15. Anxiety, Depression, Work-related Stress
    - Critical items
16. Sexual Activities
    - Health concerns
17. Life Satisfaction
    - Personal accomplishments
    - Job satisfaction
    - Pleasure from daily activities

Dependence Scale (Skinner and Horn, 1984) that correlate (0.94) with the original twenty-five-item scale, and fifteen items covering adverse consequences from drinking (Polich and Orvis, 1979). Finally, the Drug Abuse Screening Test (Skinner, 1982) provides a quantitative index of problems related to drug abuse.

The computer program engages in two levels of lifestyle assessment. First, *brief screening* questions are posed to determine current health practices and self-identified concerns. Critical items are used to decide if a particular lifestyle practice presents a potential problem. For example, the alcohol section uses three criteria to identify "potential" problem drinkers: (1) consumption levels (40 g ethanol per day for women; 60 g ethanol per day for men), (2) CAGE score of 2 or more, and (3) self-identified concern over drinking. Patients flagged for problems continue with the second level (*basic assessment*), which is aimed at establishing the extent and severity of problems. For example, patients with alcohol problems are administered the Alcohol Dependence Scale to obtain a quantitative rating of the severity of alcohol dependence. By employing a two-stage assessment process, detailed information need be obtained only for patients with identified or suspected health-risk behaviors.

A WALK THROUGH THE PROGRAM

The Computerized Lifestyle Assessment program was developed on an IBM PC microcomputer using the version of BASIC supplied with IBM PC DOS 1.1. A parallel version of the software has been developed in Borland International's Turbo PASCAL. Hardware requirements to run the software are an IBM PC (or compatible) with two 360K floppy disk drives, 256K of random access memory (RAM), a color graphics card, and a color monitor. Although the software may be used with a monochrome monitor, the impact of the graphics is not as striking and the interview loses much of its attractive visual appeal. To obtain printed reports at the completion of the interview, a printer and printer cable linked to the microcomputer are also required.

Procedures for running the Computerized Lifestyle Assessment program are simple and easy to learn. The interview can be set up and administered by individuals with no previous programming or computer experience. Thus nurses, receptionists, or ward assistants could easily manage routine administration of the software.

The following sections briefly describe the eight major components of the program. Because it is self-driven, most of the program segments automatically progress to the next. Only in the first two segments (Startup and Patient Introduction to the Computer) and the final segment (Report Writing) is intervention by the test administrator required. However, the intervention is minimal and is always prompted by the computer.

Startup. To begin, the program disk must be placed in the A disk drive before the computer is powered on. At the DOS prompts, the test administrator enters the date and time. These data are only required at the beginning of each day and can be entered before patients arrive. The date is later incorporated into each patient's data record. The time is used for calculating the number of seconds each patient requires to answer assessment items. These data are also recorded in the patient record. Once the date and time are correctly entered, a strike of the ENTER/RETURN key will result in the automatic execution of the Lifestyle Assessment program.

Introduction to the Computer. While the patient watches, the test administrator begins the on-line interview by entering data in response to three prompts. First, the patient's name is typed on the keyboard: given name first and surname last. As each letter is typed, it appears on the monitor. Although the patient's first name is later used in the interview to make it user friendly, only the initials are retained for the data file. Next, the computer prompts for the study phase number. This was important for our research, but requests for this information can be suppressed or easily adapted to suit requirements for other installations (for example, location code). Finally, the test administrator is prompted for the patient's six-digit identification number. If too many or too few digits are entered, the computer erases the number and requests that it be entered again. Once this information has been entered and verified as correct, the test administrator strikes the ENTER/RETURN key to proceed to the next segment of the program.

Instructions. After entering the basic data, the test administrator places a special wood cover over the keyboard that allows access to only those keys required for answering the interview questions (the numbers from 0 to 9 and the ENTER/RETURN key). At this point the patient can begin to interact with the computer.

The instruction segment of the program begins with a welcoming frame or "page" that starts with "Hi" followed by the patient's first name. Although test administrators can give basic verbal instructions to patients, they are not necessary as patients can read instructions printed on the monitor's screen. Patients progress through each frame of the instructions at their own pace by pressing the ENTER/RETURN key when they are ready for more information. The program was engineered to make answering questions on the computer very easy. Some questions are multiple choice and others are open-ended (for example, How many hours of sleep do you get each night or each twenty-four-hour period?). For all questions, regardless of type, patients answer by entering a number, then striking the ENTER/RETURN key. Patients are instructed to check their answer, which shows up on the monitor next to the answer prompt. As an additional check for multiple-choice items, a happy face shows next to the endorsed category. If patients wish to change their answer, they simply type a new numerical response and strike the ENTER/RETURN key. This replaces the old response with the corrected answer and moves the location of the happy face (for multiple-choice items). When the patient is satisfied that he or she has correctly entered the answer, an additional strike of the ENTER/RETURN key advances the interview to the next question.

Trial Run on Sample Questions. A few sample questions allow patients to test their understanding of the instructions and to become more familiar with the computer. At the same time, the sample questions provide the tester with an opportunity to collect basic demographic data (age and sex and, if female, number of pregnancies), to observe whether or not the instructions were adequately understood and carried out, and to point out any errors in usage and offer further instructions as required. In our experience, the vast majority of patients grasped the instructions by the time they completed the sample questions and did not encounter difficulties with the mechanics of computer use during administration of the lifestyle items.

When the sample questions are completed, patients are given one final instruction. If for any reason they do not want to answer a question, it can be skipped over simply by entering "999." This code instructs the software to present the next question. We offered the option of skipping questions in two studies (Skinner and Allen, 1983; Skinner, Allen, McIntosh, and Palmer, 1985a) involving a total of 330 patients. Only four patients used the option.

Lifestyle Assessment. The lifestyle component contains 130 items grouped into twelve sections. Each section is introduced with a "title" page (for example, "The next section is about your physical activity"). Within sections, items appear individually on the computer monitor. The interview will not progress until each question is answered with a response acceptable to the computer (a valid answer or "999"). At the completion of selected content areas, a graphic rating of reported health practices is displayed.

Because of the potential for patient boredom and fatigue, this phase of the program must be executed efficiently, while ensuring maximum accuracy of the data collected. In order to meet these needs, the assessment was engineered with several special features. One of the more expedient features of the software is the branching logic that determines the order of item presentation. In some instances the branching is simple. A response to a single item will result in skipping a subsequent question. For example, patients who answer "male" to the sex item are not presented with the subsequent question about pregnancy. Responses to single items can also result in skipping a series of questions or branching to response specific lines of inquiry. For example, patients reporting that they have never smoked cigarettes are not presented with any of the detailed questions about cigarette smoking. On the other hand, patients who indicate that they are current daily smokers answer a different set of questions from those who indicate that they are only occasional smokers. The software also uses complex branching strategies. For example, item selection can be based on a mathematical equation, a score derived from a series of questions, or a combination of the two. Branching logic allows the interview to be tailored to each patient's responses. Because it is quickly executed, patients are unaware that they are answering individually selected items. This branching logic underlies the progression from brief screening to basic assessment of specific behaviors. Because detailed questions are presented only when a problem area is flagged, the time required to complete the interview is minimized.

Three features are used to maximize accuracy of the data. The first method is a simple range check of responses. As each answer is entered at the keyboard, it is checked to ensure that it falls within a valid range of responses for that item. When the response is out of range the computer "beeps" to indicate an error. Then it erases the invalid answer from the screen and prompts for a new response, giving the valid range as a guide. The second method of data checking is used with only a few selected items (for example, For how many years have you smoked cigarettes?). For these items a comparison is made with the patient's age to ensure that the response is logically valid. The final strategy used to enhance data accuracy relies upon patients checking their own answers. The program was designed such that patients must double strike the ENTER/RETURN key before progressing to subsequent questions. Thus patients can check each answer after the first strike and correct errors as necessary.

One of the more interesting facets of the assessment is the color graphics

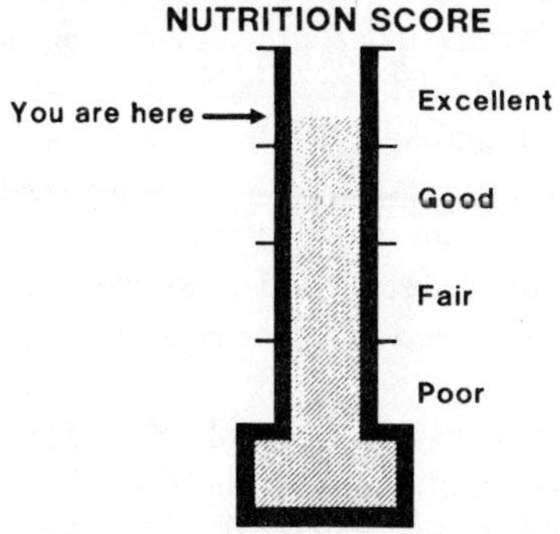

Figure 7.2. Illustration of the "thermometer" graphic used for giving feedback to patients.

displayed at the completion of selected content areas. For three sections, feedback is in the form of a magenta thermometer on a blue background. A yellow bar rises to the level scored and a white arrow points to the top of the bar with the words "YOU ARE HERE." Degrees of the thermometer are described to its right (see figure 7.2). Four other sections of the interview are concluded with feedback in the form of a black-edged stoplight on a blue background. Each section of the stoplight is a different color (red, yellow, green) and represents the risk levels that label the graphic (see figure 7.3). The stoplight blinks the color representing the patient's health-practice score and, as in the thermometer graphic, an arrow points to the flashing color with the words "YOU ARE HERE." The graphic feedback is both informative and visually pleasing. Furthermore, it has potential for making a strong impact because it is presented immediately following the assessment of specific lifestyle behaviors.

Color is used liberally throughout the questionnaire. The background color for all pages is blue. Instructions and title pages are printed in white characters while questions and response prompts are printed in yellow. Responses and happy faces appear in white and a reminder to change wrong answers or restrike the ENTER/RETURN key is in cyan. Color is useful for differentiating separate

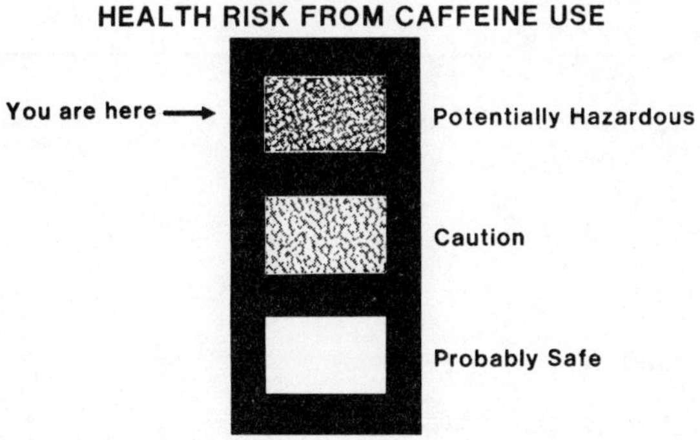

Figure 7.3. Illustration of the "stoplight" graphic used for giving feedback to patients.

stages in the assessment (instructions or title pages versus questions). Moreover, because color is used to identify different segments of each item (question, response prompt, response, reminder), the readability of the screen is increased.

A final feature of the program is its flexibility and adaptability to the needs of the patient. First, the pace of the interview depends entirely on the patient. It will progress as quickly or slowly as the patient is able to answer questions. Second, the patient can avoid answering any question by entering "999." With this feature, patients are not forced to lie or answer questions they prefer to leave blank.

Data Storage. Once the interview is completed, a data record is written to the end of a random access file on a disk in the B drive. (Random access files make efficient use of disk space and allow quick access to records.) Data written to the disk for each patient includes patient number, study phase, year, month and day of assessment, patient's initials, age, sex, pregnancy, time in seconds required to complete the assessment items, and raw responses to items. Responses to the questions patients chose not to answer are written as "999," while "777" is used to designate items not presented to the patient because of the branching logic.

Lifestyle Review. At the completion of the item pool, lifestyle habits are reviewed on the monitor (see figure 7.4). First, habits that patients scored well on are listed under the heading "YOUR LIFESTYLE STRENGTHS ARE." When the patient is ready to continue, a strike of the ENTER/RETURN key lists "LIFESTYLE AREAS YOU SHOULD LOOK AT FURTHER AND POSSIBLY CHANGE." Items under this heading are those on which the

LET'S REVIEW YOUR LIFESTYLE. YOUR STRENGTHS ARE:

- Excellent Nutrition
- Regular Medical and Dental Check-ups
- Good Social Relationships
- Good Family Functioning
- Moderate Drinker
- Avoiding Non-Medical Drug Use

HIT ENTER KEY TO CONTINUE

LIFESTYLE AREAS YOU SHOULD LOOK AT FURTHER AND POSSIBLY CHANGE:

- Caffeine Use
- Exercise
- Weight
- Sleep
- Seat Belt Use
- Cigarette Smoking
- Work-Related Stress

HIT ENTER KEY TO CONTINUE

Figure 7.4. Example of the lifestyle review on the computer screen.

patient scored poorly. Lifestyle activities on which the patient scored in the middle of the range (that is, neither excellent, nor poor) are not reported in the final review.

Hard Copy Report. The Computerized Lifestyle Assessment gives the user the option of rerunning the assessment for another patient or printing a hard copy report. The printed report provides a summary of the patient's lifestyle strengths and weakness. Lifestyle activities in which the patient identified a concern are highlighted. Finally, patient responses are listed under relevant content area labels (for example, nutrition, caffeine, exercise, and so forth). In our research, we print hard copy reports on two-part paper. This allows the patient to retain a copy. The other copy is filed in the medical record. The average length of printed reports is two to three pages, depending on each patient's lifestyle habits.

Future Developments

The Lifestyle Assessment software is part of an ongoing program of research into the application of microcomputer technology to health care. A large-scale project that links the computerized lifestyle assessment with an evaluation of brief intervention methods for alcohol problems is currently underway at the Family Practice Service of Toronto General Hospital (Skinner, Sanchez-Craig, McIntosh, and Palmer, 1985). The project consists of two phases. In phase 1, approximately one thousand patients are completing the computerized lifestyle assessment. Patients are randomly assigned to receive *assessment only* or *assessment plus feedback*, which includes computer graphics and a printed report. From the lifestyle assessment, one hundred patients with drinking problems (fifty per condition) will be identified. These patients are being followed up six months later in order to evaluate the impact of assessment feedback in reducing alcohol consumption and other lifestyle-related problems.

In phase 2, approximately 1,500 patients are undergoing the computerized lifestyle assessment without any feedback. From this assessment, 150 patients who have drinking problems are randomly assigned to one of three interventions: *physician advice*: brief, five-minute advice from the physician about hazardous and safe levels of alcohol use, plus instruction to cut down or abstain; *computerized intervention:* two thirty-minute sessions with a microcomputer that include identification of risk situations for excessive drinking and advice on strategies for moderating alcohol intake; or *physician intervention:* two thirty-minute sessions with the physician that include the identification of risk situations and existing competencies, the setting of goals regarding alcohol use, and a discussion of strategies for goal attainment. All patients are followed up at six and twelve months following the intervention. Thus a major thrust of this research is to extend the use of microcomputers from initial screening and assessment to their use for brief intervention with identified problem areas.

In conclusion, the overriding objective of our research is to develop computer software packages for assisting health care professionals with the identification and management of health-risk behaviors related to lifestyles. The computerized lifestyle assessment covers seventeen different areas and incorporates several innovative features, such as the use of color graphics for feedback. Evaluation studies conducted over the past six years have supported both the accuracy and the acceptability of using microcomputers for assessment in busy clinical settings. Routine use of the computerized lifestyle assessment could make significant inroads on reinforcing healthy lifestyles and on motivating patients to change health-risk behaviors.

REFERENCES

Ashley, M. J., Olin, J. S., LeRiche, W. H., Kornaczewski, A., Schmidt, W., Corey, P. N., and Rankin, J. G. (1981). The physical disease characteristics of inpatient alcoholics. *Journal of Studies on Alcohol*, 42, 1–14.

Belloc, N. B. (1973). Relationship of health practices and mortality. *Preventive Medicine*, 2, 67–81.

Belloc, N. B., and Breslow, L. F. (1972). Relationship of physical health status and health practices. *Preventive Medicine, 1(3)*, 409–421.

Berkman, L. F., and Breslow, L. (1983). *Health and ways of living. The Almeda County study*. New York: Oxford University Press.

Berkman, L. F., and Syme, L. (1979). Social networks, host resistance, and mortality: A nine-year follow-up study of Alameda County residents. *American Journal of Epidemiology*, *109(2)*, 186–204.

Breslow, L., and Enstrom, J. E. (1980). Persistence of health habits and their relationships to mortality. *Preventive Medicine*, 9, 469–483.

Butcher, J. N. (Ed.) (1985). Special series: Perspectives on computerized psychological assessment. *Journal of Consulting and Clinical Psychology*, 53, 745–950.

Canada Health Survey. (1981). *The health of Canadians*. Ottawa: Minister of Supply and Services Canada and Minister of National Health and Welfare, Catalogue No. 82-538E.

Cronbach, L. J. (1970). *Essentials of psychological testing*. New York: Harper & Row.

Cruickshank, P. J. (1982). Patient stress and the computer in the consulting room. *Social Science and Medicine*, *16*, 1371–1376.

Fitzgerald, D., Litt, J., Ciliska, D., Delmore, B., and Butson, T. (1984). Health consequences of selected lifestyle factors: A review of the evidence. *Canadian Family Physician*, 30, 2548–2554.

Jonas, S. (1982). A perspective for educating physicians for prevention. *Public Health Reports*, *97(3)*, 199–204.

Lalonde, M. (1974). *A new perspective on the health of Canadians: A working document*. Ottawa: Government of Canada.

Lucas, R. W., Mullin, P. J., Luna, C. B. X., and McInroy, D. C. (1977). Psychiatrists and a computer as interrogators of patients with alcohol-related illnesses: A comparison. *British Journal of Psychiatry*, *131*, 160–167.

Mayfield, D., McLeod, G., and Hall, P. (1974). The CAGE questionnaire: Validation of a new alcoholism screening test. *American Journal of Psychiatry*, *131*, 1121–1123.

Pernanen, K. (1974). Validity of survey data on alcohol use. In R. J. Gibbins et al. (Eds.), *Research advances in alcohol and drug problems, vol. 1* (pp. 355–374). New York: Wiley.

Polich, J. M., and Orvis, B. R. (1979). *Alcohol problems: Patterns and prevelance in the U.S. Air Force*. (No. R-2308-AF). Santa Monica, CA: The Rand Corporation.

Relman, A. S. (1982). Encouraging the practice of preventive medicine and health promotion. *Public Health Reports*, *97(3)*, 216–219.
Roemer, M. I. (1984). The value of medical care for health promotion. *American Journal of Public Health*, *74(3)*, 243–248.
Russell, M. A. H., Wilson, C., Taylor, C., and Baker, C. D. (1979). Effect of general practitioner's advice against smoking. *British Medical Journal*, 2, 231–234.
Schweiker, S. (1982). Disease prevention and health promotion. *Journal of Medical Education*, 57, 15–19.
Selzer, M. L. (1971). Michigan Alcoholism Screening Test. The quest for a new diagnostic instrument. *American Journal of Psychiatry*, *127*, 1653–1658.
Sherk, C., Thomas, H., Wilson, D. M. C., and Evans, C. E. (1985). Health consequences of selected lifestyle factors: A review of the evidence, Part 2. *Canadian Family Physician*, *31*, 129–139.
Skinner, H. A. (1982). The Drug Abuse Screening Test. *Addictive Behaviors*, 7, 363–371.
Skinner, H. A., and Allen, B. A. (1980). *An evaluation of computer-assisted testing with alcohol and drug use items. Program description*. Unpublished manuscript. Addiction Research Foundation, Toronto.
Skinner, H. A., and Allen, B. A. (1983). Does the computer make a difference? Computerized versus face-to-face versus self-report assessment of alcohol, drug and tobacco use. *Journal of Consulting and Clinical Psychology*, *51*, 267–275.
Skinner, H. A., Allen, B. A., McIntosh, M. C., and Palmer, W. H. (1985a). Lifestyle assessment: Applying microcomputers in family practice. *British Medical Journal*, *290*, 212–214.
Skinner, H. A., Allen, B. A., McIntosh, M. C., and Palmer, W. H. (1985b). Lifestyle assessment: Just asking makes a difference. *British Medical Journal*, *290*, 214–216.
Skinner, H. A., and Holt, S. (1983). Early intervention for alcohol problems. *Journal of the Royal College of General Practitioners*, *33*, 787–791.
Skinner, H. A., and Horn, J. L. (1984). *Alcohol Dependence Scale Users Guide*. Unpublished manuscript. Addiction Research Foundation, Toronto.
Skinner, H. A., Sanchez-Craig, M., McIntosh, M., and Palmer, W. (1985). *Computerized lifestyle assessment in family practice: Early intervention for alcohol problems*. Research grant proposal. Health and Welfare, Canada.
Skinner, H. A., and Pakula, A. (in press). Challenge of computers in psychological assessment. *Professional Psychology: Research and Practice*, *17(1)*.
Stewart, W. L. (1980). A major role for family medicine in the 1980's. *Journal of Family Practice*, *11(2)*, 325–327.
Taylor, R. B., Ureda, J. R., and Denham, J. W. (1982). *Health promotion: Principles and clinical applications*. Norwalk, CT: Appleton-Century-Crofts.
U.S. Surgeon General. (1979). *Healthy people. The Surgeon General's report on health promotion and disease prevention* (DHEW [PHS] Publication No. 79-55071). Washington, DC: U.S. Department of Health, Education and Welfare.
U.S. Surgeon General. (1982). *The health consequences of smoking: Cancer* (DHHS [PHS] 82-50179). Rockville, MD: U.S. Department of Health and Human Services.
U.S. Surgeon General. (1983). *The health consequences of smoking: Cardiovascular disease* (DHHS [PHS] 84-50204). Rockville, MD: U.S. Department of Health and Human Services.
U.S. Surgeon General. (1984). *The health consequences of smoking: Chronic obstructive lung disease* (DHHS [PHS] 84-50205). Rockville, MD: U.S. Department of Health and Human Services.
Wallace, P. G., and Haines, A. P. (1984). General practitioner and health promotion: What patients think. *British Medical Journal*, *289*, 534–536.
Wechsler, H., Levine, S., Idelson, R. K., Rohman, M., and Taylor, J. O. (1983). The physician's role in health promotion—a survey of primary-care practitioners. *New England Journal of Medicine*, *308(2)*, 97–100.
Yankauer, A. (1983). Public and private prevention. *American Journal of Public Health*, *73(9)*, 1032–1034.

8

The GOLPH Psychosocial History: Response-Contingent Data Acquisition and Reporting

Ronald A. Giannetti

Introduction

The psychosocial history is indispensable in the proper evaluation of a patient, whereas psychometric tests and laboratory studies are, for the most part, elective procedures. Standard textbooks emphasize the central role of history taking in clinical practice. According to Korchin (1976), "Knowing the history of a person is important to the understanding of his current personality structure and functioning. Similarly important is knowledge of his current life situations, the stresses and realities within which he lives" (p. 172). Kolb and Brodie (1982) state that "the purpose of the psychiatric examination is . . . to secure a biographical-historical perspective of the personality, a clear psychological picture of the living person as a specific human being with individual problems" (p. 184). And Kaplan and Sadock (1981) believe that "the psychiatric history strives to convey the more elusive picture of the patient's individual personality characteristics, including both his strengths and his weaknesses. It provides insight into the nature of his relationships with those closest to him, and includes all of the important people in his past and present life" (p. 185).

The role of the psychosocial history in clinical assessment can be contrasted with that of psychological tests. Tests provide standardized estimates on a set of personality, intellectual, or symptomatic variables. They inform us about the person's internal characteristics, resources, and patterns of behavior in a normative framework. The psychosocial history, on the other hand, provides information on the long series of external stimuli, events, and individuals with which the person has interacted, including the consequences of those interactions. It describes how internal characteristics, resources, and patterns of behavior measured by psychological tests have been externally applied and shaped.

Of course, the history has a purpose beyond simple description. It has an inferential, or predictive, value as well. Clinical hypotheses, diagnoses, and formulations are derived from this material. Two studies on the incremental predictive value of psychological tests have also provided evidence on the history's predictive value. Using a Latin-square design, Kostlan (1954) studied the accuracy of twenty clinical psychologists in predicting various criteria on five patients from different combinations of tests frequently found in test batteries: social case history, Minnesota Multiphasic Personality Inventory (MMPI), Rorschach, and sentence completion. The predictive value of any combination of tests was measured as the increment in validity over predictions made from a biographical face sheet containing only age, marital status, occupation, education, and referral source. Only two combinations produced predictive accuracy greater than simple biographical data alone: social history, MMPI, and either the sentence completion or Rorschach. If either the MMPI or social history was not part of a battery, predictive accuracy did not exceed that obtainable from face sheet data alone.

In a similar study Sines (1959) had five clinicians use different combinations of a biographical data sheet, interview, MMPI, and Rorschach to predict therapists' Q-sort descriptions of thirty patients. He found only two combinations yielding average predictive validities significantly greater than that obtainable from the biographical data sheet alone (0.396): biographical data plus interview (0.566) and biographical data plus interview plus MMPI (0.595). Thus these studies suggest that biographical data have considerable predictive value independent of psychological tests. Garb's (1984) recent review of incremental validity studies supports this conclusion. Numerous other studies have demonstrated the value of psychosocial history data in classification and prognosis (Strauss, Carpenter, and Nasrallah, 1978).

Although computers have been used for decades to facilitate the scoring and interpretation of psychological tests, the psychosocial history has been virtually ignored. There is a simple reason for this phenomenon. The tests that have been computerized are primarily those that can be administered via self-report, consist of items that can be answered independently of one another, and have invariable scoring procedures. These features make computerization relatively straightforward. The characteristics of the psychosocial history are another matter entirely. With the exception of the Minnesota-Briggs (Briggs, Rouzer, Hamberg, and Holman, 1972), a self-report history consisting of independently answered items, no standardized self-report history exists. Furthermore, an examination of the literature on the psychosocial history reveals no theory or model providing a rationale for specifying its content. Even if the content were specified, however, a comprehensive history could not be reduced to a set of independently answered true-false or multiple-choice self-report items that constitute the typical psychological test. Questions asked to collect history data are necessarily interdependent or response-contingent. One does not ask about a patient's marital relationship without first inquiring if the patient is married. In the past this interdependence required that historical data be collected by an interviewer who could select questions based on the patient's prior responses.

Because of this response-contingent structure, routine collection of comprehensive history data via self-report was impractical until on-line, interactive computer technology became inexpensive and generally available. With on-line technology the branching capabilities of the computer could be used to administer items contingent upon responses to previous items in order to collect highly detailed historical data (Giannetti, Klingler, Johnson, and Williams, 1976).

The technological feasibility of a computerized procedure is insufficient to justify its development (Giannetti and Klingler, 1980). There is evidence, however, that an automated self-report psychosocial history would have advantages for both clinical practice and research. First, previous research has clearly established that most patients, both medical and mental health, accept and enjoy responding to on-line computerized questionnaires and frequently prefer them over clinical interviews or paper-and-pencil questionnaires.* A majority of inpatients, including many of the more chronic and severely disturbed ones, can answer computer-presented questions without assistance (Carr, Ghosh, and Ancill, 1983; Stillman, Roth, Colby, and Rosenbaum, 1969). Second, development of a computerized questionnaire requires the imposition of a specific structure on the information to be gathered. Structured techniques have been shown to produce more thorough coverage than unstructured interviews (Briggs et al., 1972; Carr, Ghosh, and Ancill, 1983; Climent et al., 1975). Furthermore, there are indications that respondents may be more likely to report socially undesirable behavior to a computer. Two studies using alcohol questionnaires have shown that respondents report greater alcohol consumption to computers than to interviewers (Duffy and Waterton, 1984; Lucas, Mullin, Luna, and McInroy, 1977), although a third study found no difference (Skinner and Allen, 1983). Third, self-report and interviewer-collected history data show high agreement. Grady and Ephross (1977) found a 94.6 percent correspondence between a self-report and interviewer history collected on the same sample of patients. Fourth, a history would be less expensive to collect by computer than by traditional means (Elwood and Griffin, 1972; Johnson and Williams, 1980; Space, 1981). In summary, a computerized self-report psychosocial history is likely to prove acceptable to patients and be more reliable and thorough, as accurate, and less expensive than a history obtained by the traditional interview method.

* See Angle et al., 1977; Card et al., 1974; Erdman, Klein, and Greist, 1983; Greist et al., 1973; Lucas, 1977; Lukin, Dowd, Plake, and Kraft, 1985; and Slack and Van Cura, 1968.

A Sample History

The considerations and procedures for developing an on line psychosocial history will be discussed later. That discussion will be facilitated if the reader has already seen a sample of output. The following is a mock-up of the output of the Giannetti On-Line Psychosocial History (GOLPH), version 2.0 (Giannetti, 1985). This is a revision of an experimental version developed in 1983 with COMPU-PSYCH, Inc. Programming of this revised version by National Computer Systems was not complete at the time this volume went to press. Therefore, the mock-up that follows is a prototype and does not present data from an actual patient. Rather, responses have been selected so that all major sections of the history are shown and a sample of the content in each of these sections is presented in the output. As a consequence, this report is longer than most reports that actual patients would produce.

The report consists of two sections. The first section is the narrative report, which can be used for the same purposes as a narrative report produced by a clinician. The second section is the Follow-up Summary, which rearranges the data into a format more useful for follow-up of positive findings in subsequent interviews and for consideration of the differential diagnostic implications of these data. This section can be discarded after it has served its purpose.

SAMPLE HISTORY

GOLPH
Psychosocial History
(Version 2.0)

Identifying Data

Joseph Sample is a 42-year-old white Presbyterian male. He is employed full-time, working 40 hours per week as a stockhandler and warehouseman, taking home $1650 per month. Income other than from personal employment includes $900 per month from his spouse's employment and investments. He is a part-time vocational school student studying electronics. The client is married and has had 2 natural children, 1 adopted child, and 2 stepchildren. He resides in a multiple-family dwelling, which he occupies in exchange for services, and has lived there for 10 months. He lives with his spouse, spouse's mother, 1 natural child from his current spouse, 2 unrelated children (spouse's, adopted), and 1 nonrelative. He has had no previous psychiatric hospitalizations and no previous outpatient mental health services. Currently, he is under a physician's care for a health problem and using prescription medication.

Family of Origin

During childhood and adolescence, the client was raised by his natural mother, 1 stepfather, and a maternal grandmother. The natural father never lived with the client because he died in an accident before the client was born. The natural mother is still living. He has 1 older brother, 2 younger stepbrothers, and 1 younger half sister. One sibling died before the client was 18. The natural mother suffered from depression.

He considers himself to have been raised primarily by his natural mother and his stepfather. When the client was born, his mother was 20 years old. He describes his mother as shy, cautious, and quiet, yet also warm and gentle. She was mostly unhappy and insecure. The client perceives his mother as having loved him. The mother was physically affectionate and was giving of time and attention. The client could talk to her about few problems. She was overly fault finding. His mother was interested in the client's activities and occasionally praised him for his accomplishments. She was not very strict and gave the client more freedom of action than desirable. When they disagreed, the client could usually get her to give in. If the client misbehaved, punishment was infrequent. To punish the client psychologically, the mother would yell at him and make him feel that she had been hurt. She never used corporal punishment.

When the client was born, his stepfather was 24 years old. He describes his stepfather as being outgoing and energetic, yet also impatient and hard. He was responsbile and hardworking, yet a poor money manager and insecure. The client perceives his stepfather as having disliked him. He was never physically affectionate and made him feel neglected. The client could talk to him about few problems. He criticized the client over almost everything. He was interested in the client's activities, but resented his accomplishments as if they were in competition. He was an extremely strict disciplinarian who gave the client little freedom of action. When they disagreed, the client didn't dare to voice it. If the client misbehaved, punishment was inevitable. To punish the client psychologically, the stepfather would embarrass him and take away privileges. Typical corporal punishments were spanking and shoving. The client reports that the stepfather punched him.

The client's family strongly valued being religious, being ambitious, and obeying authority. He thinks that working hard and trying your best, asserting your beliefs, and being "manly" and tough were overemphasized to the point of annoyance.

Developmental History

The client was a planned child. While pregnant with him, the mother was injured and underwent surgery. At birth he was delivered by C-section and was premature and underweight. He was put in an incubator and had no birth defects. He is not aware of problems learning to sit up, crawl, stand, walk, talk, toilet, feed himself, or dress himself. Before age 13 he considers himself to have been somewhat unhappy. He reports problems with frequent nightmares. He admits to frequent stomachaches and repeated eating of nonfood substances, including plaster and paint. He denies difficulty with coordination, excitability, and overactivity. He admits to no antisocial or daredevil behavior. He was rarely ill. As a child and teenager he reports suicidal preoccupations and denies sexual molestation, running away from home, deliberate self-injury, and attempted suicide. He reports 2 episodes of suicidal preoccupation beginning at age 12.

As a teenager, he was very healthy, had no unusual eating habits, and considered himself too thin and unattractive. He describes himself as active, timid, unhappy, and unsure of himself. His caretakers were strict about rules and acted as if the client's judgment could be trusted only a little. He began to physically mature at about age 13, at roughly the same time as most of the boys he knew. He first learned about sex from a friend and received a somewhat incorrect explanation. He felt he could discuss nothing about sex with his parents. He began dating at age 16. On the average he dated less than once per month. His parents did not comment upon the people he dated. His dating pattern had been to play the field. He first had heterosexual intercourse at age 18 and reports feeling happy and nervous afterward. He reports having had 3 sex partners. Currently, he usually enjoys sex. He denies having homosexual experience before age 18 or afterward. Before age 18 he claims to have had 1 very close friend with whom he could discuss nearly anything. He has no such friend now.

Educational History

The client graduated from elementary school in 1957 and from high school by examination (GED) in 1963. He quit high school in the 12th grade. He never attended college. Some elementary education was completed in a foreign country. The client has also attended a school operated by his employer.

He completed his elementary education in 2 schools (public, military). He reports that his performance was uneven. He was held back 1 semester. He admits to repeated truancy, but took no special classes for behavior problems. Socially, he describes himself as shy, not liked nor disliked by most schoolmates, and having one or two close friends. In general he had mixed feelings about elementary school. The client attended 1 high school (public). His academic performance was in the B range. Extracurricular activity consisted of clubs and ROTC. He had difficulty in school due to serious injury and problems at home. He describes himself as shy, not popular nor unpopular with other students, and as having a miserable experience in high school.

Marital History

The client's current marriage began when he was 26 years old and his spouse was 25 years old. He was previously married 1 time. The previous marriage began when he was 21 years old and his former spouse was 18. The marriage ended in divorce when he was 23. They had one child and the spouse received custody. The client did receive visitation privileges and visited regularly.

The client's partner is a 42-year-old white Eastern Orthodox female. She has a high school education. She works full-time for 40 hours per week. He describes his partner as outgoing, talkative, and generous, yet impatient. She is hardworking, strong, and secure.

In their relationship they both have problems with the amount of time spent together. The client admits to problems with drinking and with talking about feelings. He states that his partner has problems with having trust. The primary caretakers of the children in the home are the client, his partner, and the babysitter. Child rearing has been problematic because frequent illnesses occurred.

Occupational History

The client works for an employer and is paid in the form of hourly wages. He is a union member. He has had this job for 10 years, is somewhat dissatisfied with it, and is thinking about changing jobs. The positive aspects of the job are the benefits, security, and relationships with coworkers. The negative aspects are the bad hours and lack of future prospects in it. He has been promoted on this job. Complaints have been made about him regarding tardiness, but he reports no action taken against him. He attributes this to personal problems.

He has had 3 previous jobs in 2 different occupations. He quit previous jobs because of opportunity for a better job and dissatisfaction with an entire line of work. He has been laid off 2 times and fired once.

Income supports 5 people, has increased somewhat over the past year, and is more than sufficient to pay for basic necessities. Primary responsibility for money management resides with the partner.

Military History

The client enlisted and served on active duty and in the reserves in the Army. He entered the service at age 18 because he wanted training, wanted discharge benefits, and wanted to get away from home. Upon entering the service he had less than a high school education. While in the service he completed high school. He attained the rank of E-5 and completed 3 years of active duty. He received a general discharge under honorable conditions. He has a 10% service-connected disability. While in the service he was involved in wartime face-to-face combat, medical care/evacuation, patrol assignments, and ambushes. He witnessed American, enemy, and civilian casualties and was personally wounded. He was not treated for psychological problems. Events experienced in the service are currently distressing him. Disciplinary proceedings were initiated against him 2 times for unauthorized absence (AWOL) and disrespect. He received a nonjudicial punishment resulting in a fine.

Legal History

The client denies being sued, bankruptcies, court-ordered psychological evaluations, and civil commitments. He has initiated a lawsuit 1 time, been arrested and charged 2 times, and been convicted 2 times. He has sued for child custody and lost. He has been arrested and charged as an adult for driving while intoxicated. He was convicted and was forbidden to drive and put on probation.

Symptom Screen

Last physical exam was within the last week and the physician did say that problems were detected. Within the last year he has visited a dentist, and he is having no dental or gum problems. He has had 2 surgeries. Current health is rated as fair. He reports blood relatives with diabetes, hypertension, cancer, and gout. He reports being allergic to foodstuffs. The client complains of being overweight, continuously being moist or sweaty, and intolerant of heat. Recently, he has experienced hearing loss. He has a history of head injury with loss of consciousness. He has been experiencing swollen ankles. He recently had increased frequency of urination. He complains of recent back pain, muscle weakness, and muscle cramps.

He began drinking alcohol at age 17 and now drinks daily. He drinks beer and hard liquor. He reports a need to drink daily, difficulty controlling intake, having drunk throughout the day for more than one day, and having drunk a fifth or equivalent in one day on more than one occasion. There has been some increase in tolerance over time. Upon discontinuation of drinking he has expereinced tremulousness, nausea, malaise, sweating, and nightmares. He has used minor tranquilizers, cocaine, and cannabis. He began taking drugs at age 18, but does not use any now. He denies signs of pathological drug use and psychosocial impairment. He reports one episode of persistent depressed mood, diminished energy level, anorexia, and sleep disturbance accompanied by a significant weight change, difficulty concentrating, guilt feelings, loss of libido, and social withdrawal. He reports no history of suicide attempts. He denies periods of elated mood and hyperactivity. He admits to sustained experience of thought insertion, but not feelings of being controlled, thought broadcasting, thought withdrawal, auditory distortions/hallucinations, grandiose beliefs, and persecutory beliefs. He denies specific phobias, denies repetitive thoughts, and denies repetitive acts. He reports experiencing a highly stressful situation with prolonged consequences including recurrent dreams and avoidance of certain situations.

Follow-up Summary
Indeterminate Responses

None found.

Adult Problems

Substance Use (291.xx; 292.xx; 303.xx; 304.xx; 305.xx)
- Alcohol
  - Pathological Use
    - need to drink daily
    - difficulty cutting down
    - drank all day, more than one day
    - drank fifth or equivalent per day more than once
  - Psychosocial Impairment
    - missed work
    - trouble on job
    - trouble with law
  - Tolerance/Withdrawal
    - needs more for same effect
    - tremulousness
    - nausea
    - malaise
    - sweating
    - nightmares
- Drugs
  - Types
    - minor tranquilizers
    - cocaine
    - cannabis

Psychotic Symptomatology (293.xx; 295.xx; 297.xx; 298.xx)
- thought insertion

Affective Symptomatology (293.xx; 296.xx; 300.xx; 301.xx)

Depression
- depressed mood
- diminished energy
- anorexia
- sleep disturbance
- weight change
- guilt
- loss of libido
- social withdrawal

Anxiety Disorders (300.xx; 308.30; 309.81)

Traumatic Stress
- frightening situation followed by:
  - repetitive dreams
  - avoidance of situations

Possible anxiety-related somatic symptoms if physical etiology ruled out
- frequent urination
- muscle cramps

Somatoform Disorders (300.xx) (If R/O physical etiology, somatization disorder requires 14 symptoms for women and 12 for men)

Conversion/pseudoneurological
- hearing loss

Gastrointestinal
- food allergy

Pain
- neck pain
- back pain

Psychosexual Disorders (302.xx; 306.51)

Denied

Antisocial Personality (301.70)
- truancy (grammar school)
- arrested-DUI

Other Potential Adult Stressors

Domestic
- divorce
- frequent arguments with spouse/partner
- child(ren) frequently ill

Occupational/Financial/Legal
- job dissatisfaction
- fired from job

Interpersonal
- no close friends

Other
- wounded in service
- currently bothered by military experience

Potential Developmental Problems

Activity Level/Lability (314.00)
Denied

Conduct/Aggressive/Non-aggressive) (312.xx)
Grammar school
repeated truancy

Anxious/Avoidant (309.xx; 313.xx)
frequent stomachaches
frequent nightmares
timid

Eating/Weight (307.xx)
ate nonfood substances (age < 13)
plaster
paint
considered self skinny (teen)

Movement Disorders/Physical Manifestations (307.xx)
frequent nightmares

Other Disorders/Delays
suicidal preoccupation

Other Potential Developmental Stressors
natural mother depressed
natural father died
not raised by natural father
death of sibling
mother injured during pregnancy
mother had surgery during pregnancy
born premature
born underweight
put in incubator
held back in grammer school
disliked grammar school
high school viewed negatively
serious injury as teenager

Development

Content specification was the first consideration in the development of the GOLPH. As noted, no theory or model exists that would dictate this content; therefore, it had to be determined by consensus. History outlines were obtained from standard textbooks and from clinical facilities. Underscoring the perceived importance of providing examiners with structured interviewing guides rather than leaving the content of histories to chance and memory, virtually every hospital, clinic, and mental health center contacted had developed its own outline. Outlines were also obtained from several specialty settings such as pediatric, neuropsychological, and forensic services. In all, forty-two such outlines were collected.

A content analysis of these history outlines was performed by writing each item from each history on a three- by five-inch card. Initial category titles were developed and the cards were sorted accordingly. After examining the cards that were unclassifiable, category titles were revised and the cards resorted. A few repetitions of this process resulted in a set of ten categories that were reasonably mutually exclusive and exhaustive. The titles assigned to these final categories are shown in figure 8.1.

1. Identifying demographic data/current living arrangements
2. Family of origin
3. Client development
4. Educational history
5. Marital history/current family functioning
6. Occupational history/current financial circumstances
7. Military history
8. Legal/criminal history
9. Physical illnesses/current somatic symptoms
10. Psychological symptoms/treatments

Figure 8.1. Major psychosocial history categories.

Originally there was an eleventh category composed of items whose content could be termed lifestyle. It included items about health habits, such as diet and exercise, and typical leisure or recreational activities. This category was eliminated for three reasons. First, health-risk appraisal instruments already existed. Second, while patients rarely present primarily with recreational problems, recreational activities are so varied that a large number of items would be required to generate specific statements; therefore, the return from these items would be small. Third, the amount of material in the other categories indicated that the program would already be very large.

The items in each category were reviewed to eliminate duplicates. Items that would require an observer's judgment (that is, could not reasonably be obtained by self-report) were also eliminated. A content outline of that area was then developed. A sample outline of the Developmental History content is shown in figure 8.2.

At this point a good deal of additional research was required in order to produce logically interrelated self-report items that could generate a narrative

Complications of pregnancy and birth	Eating/feeding problems
Presence of birth defects	Aggressive behavior
Developmental delays	Antisocial behavior
Manifestations of anxiety	Substance use/abuse
Manifestations of depression	General physical health
Activity levels/movement disorders	Sexual development/preference/abuse
Emotional lability	Peer relationships

Figure 8.2. Developmental history content areas.

high in specificity. Major shortcomings of computer-produced narratives are indeterminacy and ambiguity. To read that a patient lives in an "other" type of residence and has lived there "from 3 to 5 years" is irritating. The report is marred by the use of "computerese" rather than standard English. The only solution to this problem was to generate items whose response alternatives are mutually exclusive and exhaustive whenever possible. For example, producing a definite statement about the type of discharge received from the military requires an item that contains all possible discharge types as alternatives. For an item in which an exhaustive list is impossible (for example, type of residence), then the statistically most frequent alternatives must be identified. This minimizes the probability of "other" being endorsed in response to the item.

In order to construct items containing response alternatives that were as exhaustive as possible, a variety of sources, such as the census bureau, almanacs, military regulations, arrest statistics, and epidemiological data, were consulted. After the items were constructed experts in each content area reviewed them for potential omissions. For example, the military history was reviewed by a military psychologist and a Veterans Administration psychologist. The educational history was reviewed by elementary and secondary school teachers and a school psychologist. This process resulted in the use of "other" only sixty times in over 2,400 response alternatives, or approximately 2.5 percent. In addition, using the most probable response alternatives in an item further minimized the likelihood of "other" being endorsed.

As an example, the logic for determining type of residence is shown in figure 8.3, which was constructed using U.S. census data. There are five items with a total of twenty-five response options. These will produce a highly specific statement about where the patient currently lives. Because of the structure, the patient will be presented with two items at most. Also, the item alternatives cover the preponderance of possible types of residences, making it very unlikely that "other" will be endorsed.

Construction of the actual questionnaire and narrative came next. The process is difficult to describe, but essentially it involves two related procedures. First, a decision structure was developed that determined the logical branching relationships among sets of items with similar content. This was constructed to minimize the number of responses required to cover that content. Second, instructions were developed for construction of a narrative statement or statements based on these items. These instructions must produce an understandable

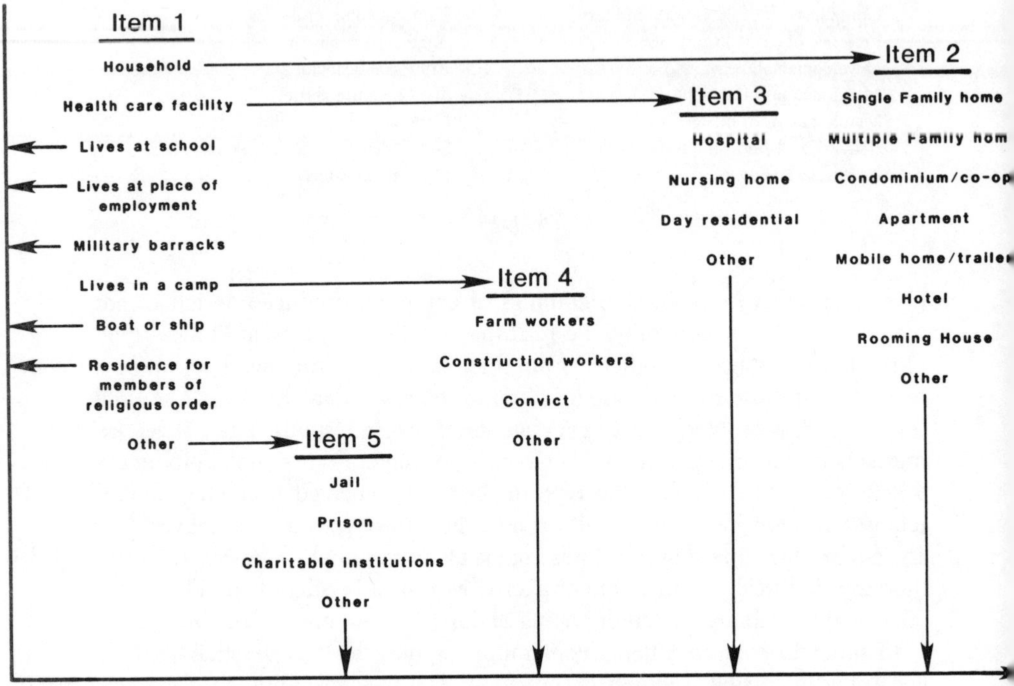

Figure 8.3. Logic for determining current residence.

statement for all allowable combinations of item responses. Care was taken to produce a narrative that reported item responses in as few words as possible. Although described separately, item hierarchy construction and narrative construction were iterative processes that continued until a reasonably efficient set of items resulted in a sensible and compact narrative statement.

An example may clarify this. Figure 8.4 shows a set of items from the Family of Origin section. This set of items is entered if, and only if, the respondent indicates that he or she was not raised by the biological father. It is part of a larger set of items that determines all of the individuals who served as caretakers for the respondent from birth to age eighteen. The instructions in brackets are the branching instructions for each item. For example, the instructions for item 18 are interpreted as follows: "If response alternative 1 or 2 was endorsed in item 17, then administer item 18; otherwise, go to item 22." Only the question and the response alternatives actually appear on the computer screen. The branching instructions do not.

Figure 8.5 shows the instructions for producing a narrative statement from the items in figure 8.4. The sentence fragment on each line is printed if the corresponding response alternative has been endorsed. For example, if alternative 1 in item 17 was endorsed (17.1), then "never lived with the client" is printed. Note the expression "him/her" in 17.3. In printing this fragment the program selects the correct pronoun according to the sex of the respondent. Finally,

17. [If not 1.2 continue, else 22]
You indicated that your natural father did not raise you.
Was that because:
1. He never lived with you
2. He lived with you, but only when you were very young
3. He lived with you, but he did not take care of you much

18 [If 17.1 or 17.2 continue, else 22]
Why didn't your natural father live with you?
1. He died
2. He never married your mother
3. He divorced your mother or left her
4. He put you up for adoption
5. He gave you away
6. Other

19. [If 18.1 continue, else 22]
What did your father die from?
1. Illness
2. Accident
3. Suicide
4. Killed in war
5. Killed by another person
6. I don't know
7. Other

20. Did he die
1. Before you were born
2. Before you were one year old
3. After that
4. I don't know

21. [If 20.3 continue, else 22]
[Do not accept response of 0]
How old were you when he died? Enter number, then press enter.

Figure 8.4. Sample items from family of origin.

17. The natural father
17.3 lived with the client, but was not considered a caretaker by him/her.
17.2 lived with the client only briefly
17.1 never lived with the client
18. because he
18.2 never married the mother.
18.3 left the mother.
18.4 put the client up for adoption.
18.5 gave the client away.
18.6 (? reason).
18.1 died
19.1 from illness
19.2 in an accident
19.3 by suicide
19.4 in war
19.5 from another person's actions
19.6 from an unknown cause
19.7 from (? cause)
20.1 before the client was born.
20.2 before the client was a year old.
20.3 when the client was <u>21</u> year/years old.
20.4 .

Figure 8.5. Narrative construction logic for items in figure 8.4.

note the underlined number, 21, in fragment 20.3. If this fragment is printed, the program inserts into it the number input in response to item 21 and selects the correct singular or plural from "year/years."

The interested reader can obtain an impression of how the history operates by creating alternative sets of responses to the items in figure 8.4 and then translating these into narrative using the instructions in figure 8.5. Note that a complete sentence is generated no matter which combination of permitted responses is made.

Version 2.0

The initial experimental version of the GOLPH was programmed by COMPU-PSYCH, Inc., for use on their Psychometer 3000 computer. After approximately one thousand administrations of the history, a questionnaire was sent to thirty users requesting their recommendations for revisions.* Fifteen users returned the questionnaire and three others provided their opinions by phone. Their recommendations were incorporated into the latest version (2.0).

Users agreed that three areas required revision. They strongly favored having the entire history collected by self-report. The initial version required the user, rather than the patient, to provide part of the input into the first section of the history, Identifying Data. This collected highly specific information requiring some typing (for example, address, phone number, name of an emergency contact, and so forth). Since most of the information requiring typing was collected by the users or their staff prior to the initial patient interview, it could be removed from the history without consequence. Accordingly, the Identifying Data section of Version 2.0 has been streamlined, and all information is collected via self-report.

Users concurred that the descriptors of the respondent's parents or caretakers were overly detailed and sometimes contradictory. This section was shortened considerably and programmed to prevent contradictions. Finally, users agreed that the alcohol and drug histories needed expansion. More questions were added detailing pathological use, psychosocial impairment, and evidence of tolerance and withdrawal. The Follow-up Summary section was added to the new version on the author's initiative.

Clinical Use

The GOLPH is designed to be administered after the initial interview. In the typical initial interview the patient is primarily interested in discussing the reasons

* I am indebted to Ms. Carol Watson, Clinical Marketing Manager for National Computer Systems, for conducting this survey.

for seeking treatment. It is undesirable to attempt to obtain detailed historical information during this session. Knowing that a reasonably comprehensive set of historical data will be forthcoming, the clinician is free to focus on the chief complaint and current episode and upon establishment of a therapeutic and contractual relationship.

During this initial interview the clinician is likely to collect sufficient behavioral observations and mental status information to judge the patient's capacity to produce valid self-report data. Obviously, patients who have attention or memory deficits, are acutely psychotic, or are otherwise judged to be poor historians are not suitable candidates. Testing might also be delayed for patients who are experiencing extreme anxiety or exhibiting psychomotor retardation. Finally, the clinician might delay evaluation based on judgments about the adequacy of the patient's trust in him or her.

The GOLPH is intended for use with individuals who are at least sixteen years old, have a sixth-grade reading level, and are seeking mental health services. It was not designed for use in other evaluative contexts. Administration to patients between the ages of thirteen and sixteen may be attempted, but the results should be viewed with caution. The internal logic of the program precludes its use with patients under thirteen years of age.

The GOLPH can be administered by the clinician or a suitably trained support staff member. The clinician should give the patient a credible rationale for completing this task conscientiously. This should appeal to the patient's self-interest, as the validity of the data depends primarily on the patient's trust and involvement. After orientation to the computer equipment, administration can proceed.

The program begins by offering the clinician the option to delete administration of any sections of the history except for the Identifying Data section. Any sections deemed irrelevant to the type of evaluation being conducted may be deleted. Deletion of sections is inadvisable, however, until clinicians gain some experience and familiarity with the GOLPH. A possible exception to this is the Physical Symptom section, which contains items on family history of physical illnesses, patient's past physical illnesses, and current physical and psychophysiological symptoms. It may be redundant, for example, in an inpatient facility in which a separate medical history and physical exam are routine components of the evaluation.

The amount of time required to complete the history will vary with the patient's test-taking skills and clinical condition and the complexity of his or her history. The program presents the fewest questions to younger, less educated individuals who have never worked, been married, or had children and have not been involved with the military, legal, or mental health systems. If any of these conditions do not obtain, more questions will be asked. In general, most patients should be able to complete the history in fifty to ninety minutes, approximately the time needed to complete an MMPI. If the history cannot be completed in the time available, administration can be discontinued and completed later without loss of data.

After the history is complete the narrative output provides an overview of the patient's history. After reviewing this, the clinician can use the Follow-up Summary (see the earlier sample history) as a checklist for subsequent interviews. The first section of the summary, Indeterminate Responses, shows those items for which the program could not elicit a specific response (that is, the patient responded "other"). The next two sections, Adult Problems and Potential Developmental Problems, summarize positive findings. Each of these sections is divided into two subsections. The first groups findings according to their potential relevance for various DSM-III categories. The second, Potential Stressors, contains positive findings that may be significant for the patient but that are not of direct relevance to a diagnostic category. The clinician can pursue these findings and note their significance directly on the sheet.

For practitioners with word processing software, the narrative section can be transferred to it as a file and modified to accommodate findings from follow-up interviews. If indeterminate responses appear in the narrative, each of these is identified by a "?" (for example, see narrative fragment 19.7 in figure 8.5). These can be located quickly by setting the word processing program's "search" or "find" function to "?" and can be corrected or deleted. Clinician observations and narrative output from psychological tests can be added to create a more comprehensive report.

Interpretive Cautions

Despite the demonstrable descriptive and predictive qualities of psychosocial history data, there are certain limitations on their interpretation. These limitations accrue from absence of empirical scaling, potential ambiguities in the meaning of an item, the historical accuracy of a response, and the etiological significance of the data. They argue for the use of these data in clinical hypothesis formation rather than confirmation. Clinical hypotheses derived from these data require corroboration from other sources.

In interpreting the output from the GOLPH the clinician should keep in mind that this is not a psychological test in the usual sense. Whereas psychological test results describe a sample of behavior with an empirically derived numerical scale or category system, the GOLPH output is a direct translation of item responses into narrative statements. It is a face-valid display of raw data similar to a listing of responses to a personality inventory. It is *not* an interpretation of these responses.

Potential ambiguity in the meaning of an item limits interpretation. The meaning the patient attributes to a response alternative is not necessarily the same meaning the clinician would attribute to it. For more factual items, such as religion and marital status, this is not a problem. For items describing a symptom or behavior, however, this can be. For example, the patient may endorse the item about experiencing surroundings as if they were not real. This may refer to a bona fide derealization experience with serious implications or to another type of experience with completely benign implications. Even when the patient and clinician are referring to the same phenomenon, misinterpretation is still possible. For instance, psychotic patients may endorse items about experiencing visual and auditory hallucinations, but so might nonpsychotic individuals with extremely high hypnotic ability (Wilson and Barber, 1981).

Patient recall of remote events, particularly those occurring in childhood, may not be historically accurate or in agreement with the recall of other family members. Robins and associates (1985) interviewed adults in their forties who had been child guidance clinic patients thirty years earlier. Agreement between interview and clinic record items varied from 20 percent to 91 percent. They also compared agreement between individuals and their close-aged siblings on early home environment items in both patient and nonpatient samples. Sibling agreement measured by weighted kappa was significant for about half of the items. Patient status did not affect agreement. Thus, while patients might be reporting their actual recollection of remote events, these may not be congruent with other sources.

Finally, the clinician must exercise caution in making inferences about causal, etiological connections between a patient's life experiences and current psychopathology. Schofield and Balian (1959) compared schizophrenic patients and a matched sample of nonpsychiatric patients on over one hundred historical items. A number of statistically significant differences emerged. Yet the distributions of the two groups overlapped markedly rather than showing a preponderance of "traumatic" events in the schizophrenic group. These results generally contraindicate attributing major pathogenic significance to any single historical event.

These interpretive limitations have implications for the qualifications of the GOLPH's user. In clinical practice a variety of individuals (professionals, paraprofessionals, and technicians) might collect historical data from a patient. Nevertheless, these data are part of a more comprehensive evaluation leading to diagnostic and treatment decisions. In view of the ultimate purpose and consequences of such an evaluation and the need for proper contextual interpretation and corroboration of psychosocial history data, the GOLPH should be used by clinicians who are qualified to practice independently. All other users should be under the supervision of a competent, independent practitioner.

Future Directions

The clinical adequacy and acceptability of the GOLPH now require investigation. While the objections to the earlier version have been corrected, that is no substitute for systematic data comparing this history to those acquired by traditional methods on such variables as patient acceptability, completeness, reliability, and cost efficiency. There is also a need, however, to begin moving beyond these process studies to determine if this and other computer-based patient evaluation methods have positive effects on clinical decision making and therapeutic outcomes.

If the GOLPH proves to be generally acceptable and effective, development of additional applications is possible. Scales can be developed from the items to normatively measure a variety of potential constructs, such as level of functioning in various social roles. Subsets of questions about current level of role functioning, say in marriage or work, or symptomatic status could be readministered periodically to monitor treatment progress and outcome.

The item set could be modified for use in other populations. The current version can be conceptualized as consisting of two sets of items. One set consists of general items that would be collected in virtually any situation requiring a history. The second set consists of items relevant for evaluating patients in a general psychiatric population. This second set could be modified to apply to specialized clinical contexts, such as behavioral medicine or neuropsychology, or to nonclinical evaluative contexts, such as in organizational or industrial settings.

The GOLPH can be used in the management of a mental health facility. Given the data collected on a sample of patients, it would be simple to determine the number and percentage of patients who are unemployed, homeless, disabled, veterans, in trouble with the law, in abusive relationships, have suicidal ideation, complain of sexual problems, and so forth. Such information can be invaluable in planning the types and mix of services that a facility should offer and in reviewing resource utilization. These are also the very same types of information required by external funding and accrediting agencies and internal quality-assurance groups. Often these data can be obtained only through labor-intensive special studies, such as chart reviews and staff surveys, requiring substantial time and expense. Analyses are complicated and results are obscured if these data have been charted unreliably or in inconsistent formats. Routine use of the GOLPH would ensure reliable collection of these data in a standard and easily analyzable format with no additional investment of staff time.

Finally, the potential research applications of the history are quite broad. Two general areas will be mentioned here. Historical data collected retrospectively can be used to develop hypotheses about experiences and environments that foster psychological disorders before proceeding to very costly prospective studies (Robins et al., 1985). The GOLPH can also facilitate research into the predictive value of historical data in diagnosis, treatment decision making, and prognosis. As noted previously, many studies have related these data to important clinical outcomes. However, both retrospective and predictive studies rarely use a common data-collection instrument. Rather, they typically use idiosyncratic data sets, which precludes comparison of results across studies. When standard structured methods have been used, they have required data collection by interviewers. By taking advantage of contemporary computer capabilities and using a standard self-report item set, these studies can produce results that are comparable, eliminate the variance introduced by different interviewers with differing techniques and styles, and do so at a much lower cost.

REFERENCES

Angle, H. V., Ellinwood, E. H., Hay, W. M., Johnsen, T., and Hay, L. R. (1977). Computer-aided interviewing in comprehensive behavioral assessment. *Behavior Therapy*, *8*, 747–754.

Briggs, P. F., Rouzer, D. L., Hamberg, R. L., and Holman, T. R. (1972). Seven scales for the Minnesota-Briggs History Record with reference group data. *Journal of Clinical Pyschology*, *28*, 431–448.

Card, W. I., Nicholson, M., Crean, G. P., Watkinson, G. E., Evans, C. R., and Russell, D. (1974). A comparison of doctors and computer interrogation of patients. *International Journal of Biomedical Computing*, *5*, 175–181.

Carr, A. C., Ghosh, A., and Ancill, R. J. (1983). Can a computer take a psychiatric history? *Psychological Medicine*, *13*, 151–158.

Climent, C. E., Plutchik, R., Estrada, H., Gaviria, L. F., and Arevalo, W. (1975). A comparison of traditional and symptom-checklist-based histories. *American Journal of Psychiatry*, *132*, 450–453.

Duckworth, G. S., and Kedward, H. B. (1978). Man or machine in psychiatric diagnosis. *American Journal of Psychiatry*, *135*, 64–68.

Duffy, J. C., and Waterton, J. J. (1984). Under-reporting of alcohol consumption in sample surveys: The effect of computer interviewing in fieldwork. *British Journal of Addictions*, *79*, 303–308.

Elwood, D. L., and Griffin, R. H. (1972). Individual intelligence testing without the examiner: Reliability of an automated method. *Journal of Consulting and Clinical Psychology*, *38*, 9–14.

Erdman, H., Klein, M. H., and Greist, J. H. (1983). The reliability of a computer interview for drug use/abuse information. *Behavior Research Methods and Instrumentation*, *15*, 66–68.

Garb, H. N. (1984). The incremental validity of information used in personality assessment. *Clinical Psychology Review*, *4*, 641–655.

Giannetti, R. A. (1985). *Giannetti on-line psychosocial history: GOLPH (Version 2.0)*. Unpublished manuscript.

Giannetti, R. A., and Klingler, D. E. (1980). A conceptual analysis of computerized mental health care systems. In J. B. Sidowski, J. H. Johnson, and T. A. Williams (Eds.), *Technology in Mental Health Care Delivery Systems* (pp. 267–288). Norwood, NJ: Ablex.

Giannetti, R. A., Klingler, D. E., Johnson, J. H., and Williams, T. A. (1976). The potential for dynamic assessment systems using on-line computer technology. *Behavior Research Methods and Instrumentation*, *8*, 101–103.

Grady, M., and Ephross, P. H. (1977). A comparison of two methods for collecting social histories of psychiatric hospital patients. *Military Medicine*, *142*, 524–526.

Greist, J. H., Gustavson, D. H., Stauss, F. F., Rowse, G. L., Laughren, T. P., and Chiles, J. A. (1973). A computer interview for suicide-risk prediction. *American Journal of Psychiatry*, *130*, 1327–1332.

Johnson, J. H., and Williams, T. A. (1980). Using on-line computer technology to improve service response and decision-making effectiveness in a mental health admitting system. In J. B. Sidowski, J. H. Johnson, and T. A. Williams (Eds.), *Technology in Mental Health Care Delivery Systems* (pp. 237–249). Norwood, NJ: Ablex.

Kaplan, H. I., and Sadock, B. J. (1981). *Modern synopsis of comprehensive textbook of psychiatry* (3rd ed.). Baltimore: Williams & Wilkins.

Kolb, L. C., and Brodie, H. K. H. (1982). *Modern clinical psychiatry* (10th ed.). Philadelphia: W. B. Saunders.

Korchin, S. J. (1976). *Modern clinical psychology*. New York: Basic Books.

Kostlan, A. (1954). A method for the empirical study of psychodiagnosis. *Journal of Consulting Psychology*, *18*, 83–88.

Lucas, R. W. (1977). A study of patients' attitudes to computer interrogation. *International Journal of Man-Machine Studies*, 9, 69–86.

Lucas, R. W., Mullin, P. J., Luna, C. B. X., and McInroy, D. C. (1977). Psychiatrists and a computer as interrogators of patients with alcohol-related illnesses: a comparison. *British Journal of Psychiatry*, *131*, 160–167.

Lukin, M. E., Dowd, E. T., Plake, B. S., and Kraft, R. G. (1985). Comparing computerized versus traditional psychological assessment. *Computers in Human Behavior*, *1*, 49–58.

Robins, L. N., Schoenberg, S. P., Holmes, S. J., Ratcliff, K. S., Benham, A., and Works, J. (1985). Early home environment and retrospective recall: A test for concordance between siblings with and without psychiatric disorders. *American Journal of Orthopsychiatry*, 55, 27–41.

Schofield, W., and Balian, L. (1959). A comparative study of the personal histories of schizophrenic and nonpsychiatric patients. *Journal of Abnormal and Social Psychology*, 59, 216–225.

Sines, L. K. (1959). The relative contribution of four kinds of data to accuracy in personality assessment. *Journal of Consulting Psychology*, 23, 483–492.

Skinner, H. A., and Allen, B. A. (1983). Does the computer make a difference? Computerized versus face-to-face versus self-report assessment of alcohol, drug, and tobacco use. *Journal of Consulting and Clinical Psychology*, 51, 267–275.

Slack, W. V., and Van Cura, L. J. (1968). Patient reaction to computer-based medical interviewing. *Computers and Biomedical Research*, *1*, 527–531.

Space, L. G. (1981). The computer as psychometrician. *Behavior Research Methods and Instrumentation*, 13, 595–606.

Stillman, R., Roth, W. T., Colby, K. M., and Rosenbaum, C. P. (1969). An on-line computerized system for initial psychiatric inventory. *American Journal of Psychiatry*, *125* (Suppl.), 8–11.

Strauss, J. S., Carpenter, W. T., and Nasrallah, A. T. (1978). How reliable is the psychiatric history? *Comprehensive Psychiatry*, *19*, 213–219.

Wilson, S. C., and Barber, T. X. (1981). Vivid fantasy and hallucinatory abilities in the life histories of excellent hypnotic subjects ("somnambules"): Preliminary report with female subjects. In E. Klinger (Ed.), *Imagery: Vol. 2, Concepts, results, and applications* (pp. 133–149). New York: Plenum Press.

9

Computer-Assisted Diagnosis for Children and Adolescents

Steven J. Stein

The interview is perhaps the most widely used clinical assessment technique in the mental health field. All levels of mental health professionals continue to use unstructured clinical interviews even though there have been many criticisms of their reliability and validity (Matarazzo, 1983). It seems likely that the diagnostic interview will reign supreme in spite of any data supporting or refuting its "psychometric test" properties. It is clear that clinicians, no matter what their theoretical perspective, have found interviews to be a flexible and useful way in which to collect necessary information.

Recently there has been some movement in psychiatry and psychology toward the development of "structured" and "semistructured" interviews. The introduction of this concept initiated a great deal of criticism and resistance from clinicians who were concerned about such issues as the rigidity and restrictiveness of the approach as well as the reduced emphasis given to nonverbal cues and clinical judgment. In research, however, where there has long been a desire to deal more objectively with the criteria required to meet various diagnostic categories being investigated, the use of structured interviews is flourishing. Thus when considering whether to use treatments reported in the literature, clinicians will have an increasing ability to base their decisions on the rather clear selection criteria delineated in the research.

With the advent and increased availability of microcomputers, dramatic changes have begun to take place in the assessment and diagnosis of emotional problems in adults and children. These changes have largely been due to the easier access to computers by clinicians and their availability for conducting actual patient inquiries. One of the first descriptions of the possible use of computers for psychiatric interviewing was given by Kleinmuntz and McLean (1968). They conceptualized a structured interview that consisted of a directed search through all possible questions presented to the patient. They believed that the computer, which would allow for branching, storage, and retrieval of information, was well suited for this type of interview. Other advantages they saw in the computer interview included the objectivity found in this type of standardized testing situation. Not only would the computer interview be comprehensive, but it was also seen as fast and efficient. A final benefit was cost. The authors felt it would probably be much less expensive for a computer to conduct an intensive interview than a highly skilled clinician.

This chapter focuses on the use of microcomputers for conducting diagnostic interviews of emotionally disturbed children/adolescents and their parents. While computers have begun to have an impact on clinical assessment through their use in the administration, scoring, and interpretation of standard psychological tests, little work has been carried out on their use for sophisticated diagnostic interviewing.

Review of Diagnostic Interviews for Children

With the advent of the third edition of the *Diagnostic and Statistical Manual of Mental Disorders* (DSM-III), a number of established psychiatric/psychological interviews have been updated and some new ones have emerged. Unlike what has occurred in adult psychiatry, there has been little consensus among clinicians and researchers in child and adolescent psychiatry over the use of a standard interview for the field. Table 9.1 provides a listing of the various

TABLE 9.1
Diagnostic Interviews for Children and Adolescents

Interview	*Authors*	*Year*
Rutter-Graham Child Questionnaire	Rutter and Graham	1968
Diagnostic Interview for Children and Adolescents	Herjanic, Herjanic, Brown, and Wheatt	1975
Psychological Screening Inventory	Langer, Gersten, McCarthy, Eisenberg, Green, Hersen, and Jameson	1976
Mental Health Assessment Form	Kestenbaum and Bird	1978
Schedule for Affective Disorders and Schizophrenia for School-Aged Children	Chambers, Puig-Antich, and Tabrizi	1978
Child Assessment Schedule	Hodges, Kline, Fitch, McKnew, and Cytryn	1981
Interview Schedule for Children	Kovacs	1982
Diagnostic Interview Schedule for Children	Costello, Edelbrook, Kalas, Kessler, and Klaric	1982

interviews that have been reported in the child psychiatry/psychology literature and their authors.

The development of these interviews has been stimulated by the need for reliable and valid ways in which to classify children and adolescents. Published data are available on the reliability of the Child Assessment Schedule (Hodges, Kline, Stern, Cytryn, and McKnew, 1982), the Diagnostic Interview for Children and Adolescents (DICA; Herjanic, Herjanic, Brown, and Wheatt, 1975; Herjanic and Campbell, 1977; Herjanic and Reich, 1982; Reich, Herjanic, Welner, and Gandhy, 1982), the Psychological Screening Inventory (Langer et al., 1976), the Schedule for Affective Disorders and Schizophrenia for School-Aged Children (Orvaschel, Puig-Antich, Chambers, Tabrizi, and Johnson, 1982), and the Rutter-Graham Child Questionnaire (Rutter & Graham, 1968). For a more detailed discussion of these interviews, see Edelbrock and Costello (1984).

Background of the Diagnostic Interview for Children and Adolescents

The DICA was selected as a good interview for computerized administration as it is highly structured and was designed primarily to accept "yes" or "no" answers. The interview covers: (1) factual information, including age, reason for coming, source of referral; (2) description of behavior and relationships at home, with peers, and at school; school progress; and social behavior in the community; and (3) a wide range of psychiatric symptoms, such as phobias, obsessions, compulsions, depression, suicidal thoughts, somatic complaints, and enuresis and encopresis.

In addition, the parent's interview includes questions about pregnancy, birth, development of the child, and family history, as well as all of the questions asked of the child (appropriately reworded for adults).

One of the factors important in the decision to computerize the DICA was the amount of data available regarding the interview. Previous studies by Herjanic and Campbell (1977) have, among other things, examined the ability of an early version of the DICA to differentiate between psychiatric and pediatric samples of children. In addition, in a study by Herjanic, Herjanic, Brown, and Wheatt (1975) comparing child versus parent interviews, it was found that there was an average of 80 percent agreement between child and parent reports to separate interviewers. Agreement was highest on factual information and lowest on questions related to mental status. Girls were found to be more reliable reporters than boys.

Other factors important in the selection of the DICA included, as mentioned, its yes/no answer format, its structure by diagnostic category (so that a logical sequence prevails throughout the questioning), its natural flow as an interview, its readability for adolescents and parents, its DSM-III–based scoring, and its wide age range.

Review of Computer-Administered Interviews

PATIENT ACCEPTABILITY

One of the reasons why many clinicians still avoid using computers to perform direct patient interviews is their concern about patient reactions. To many clinicians, computerized interviewing is a cold, unempathic, and mechanistic way of dealing with people. They tend to prefer more traditional approaches of gathering information, such as the Wechsler Intelligence Scale for Children (Revised) or the Rorschach. Many clinicians also prefer interviewing their clients before video cameras or viewing groups of people through one-way mirrors. Evaluation through client satisfaction or attitude scales of the effects on patients of these commonly used assessment techniques might prove interesting.

Fortunately, there are data on patient acceptability of computerized information collecting. A number of these studies are summarized in table 9.2. Space (1981) presents many of the arguments for and against the use of computers in assessing patients.

RELIABILITY AND VALIDITY

Some studies have looked at the reliability of computerized interviews (or checklists) by comparing the results of the computer version with those of the face-to-face (or questionnaire) version. For example, Carr, Ancill, Ghosh, and Margo (1981) found correlations of 0.81 between experienced clinicians using a rating scale as part of their clinical examination and a computerized self-administered version of the Hamilton Depression Questionnaire. Erdman, Klein, and Greist (1983) did a similar study with a drug use questionnaire. They found both methods similar in diagnostic accuracy. The difficulty in this kind of study is the determination of which administration type is more correct, to be used as the "gold standard."

A number of studies have looked at the completeness of computerized interviews when compared with those of clinicians. For example, when comparing medical symptom checklists (Meikle and Gerritse, 1970; Grossman, Barnett, McGuire, and Swedlow, 1971; and Maultsby and Slack, 1971), it was found that the automated interviews produced additional information that was clinically useful. Studies have found that patients admit more complete (and sensitive) information to computers than to clinical interviewers (Carr, Ghosh, and Ancill, 1983; Greist et al., 1973, and Slack and Van Cura, 1968). More recent studies in the addiction field have found no difference between information given to an interviewer (using a structured interview) and to a computer (Skinner and Allen, 1983).

TABLE 9.2
Patient Views of Computer Interviews

Authors	N	*Patients*	*Findings (patient response)*
Slack, Hicks, Reed, and Van Cura (1966)	40	Medical	36% prefer machine, 24% prefer physician, 40% no opinion
Mayne, Weksel, and Sholtz (1968)	159	Medical	Patients report favorable response
Haessler (1969)	200	Medical	66% no preference for machine or physician, 29% prefer machine, 10% prefer physician, 5% prefer nurse; 79.5% report computer interesting
Grossman, Barnett, McGuire, and Swedlow (1971)	250	General medical	91% enjoyed
Yarnall, Samuelson, and Wakefield (1972)	98	General medical	98% comfortable; 24% less comfortable than with physician; discoveries about psychiatric and sex problems
Maultsby and Slack (1971)	69	Medical/Psychiatric	80% not difficult, enjoyable, interesting; 50% prefer machine, 30% prefer physician
Coddington and King (1972)	80	Mothers of normal and psychiatric children	67% as honest as with physician, 15% more honest; 50% found interaction easier, 37.5% harder
Stead, Heyman, Thomson, and Hammond (1972)	50	Headache	98% interesting and enjoyable
Card et al. (1974)	75	Dyspepsia	99% interesting, 94% acceptable
Lucas (1977)	67	Dyspepsia	82% acceptable; preferred most by male manual workers, under 30; 50% preferred computer to physician
Dove et al. (1977)	60	General medical	Therapeutic effect; removed apprehension prior to seeing physician
Moore, Summer, and Bloor (1984)	59	Antenatal	59% positive, 22% interesting, 3% constructive, 7% reservations, 5% negative, 4% don't know

Griest and associates (1973) reported on a computerized interview that was used for the prediction of suicide potential in patients. The patients were interviewed by a computer monitor and responded to the multiple-choice and open-ended questions on a keyboard. The study compared computer and clinician predictions of suicide attempts for twenty-two patients expressing suicidal ideas and forty-three nonsuicidal psychiatric patients. The computer was 70 percent accurate in predicting suicide attempters while the clinicians' hit rate was 40 percent. When it came to predicting nonattempters, however, the clinicians did slightly better than the computer, with predictions of 94 percent compared to the computer's 90 percent. The goal of the study was to demonstrate the potential effectiveness of computers in the planning of treatment interventions.

Another study directly addressed the issue of the nature or content of clinicians' interviews as compared to the computer. Slack and Slack (1977) compared structured interviews given by computer with those given by a physician. Their data showed that what the physician was told was affected by the time of day and by interviewing sequences, whereas this was not the case for the computer.

In what may become a classic study, Carr, Ghosh, and Ancill (1983) compared answers given by psychiatric patients to a computerized psychiatric history with information that had been recorded in the clinical file by each patient's psychiatric team. They found 90 percent agreement between the responses on the computer and the clinical file. Approximately 9 percent of the difference was due to "discoveries" that were made by the computer and reconfirmed in a follow-up session. These "discoveries" were generally found to be in the areas of sexual difficulties, criminal or unethical behavior, drinking and drug problems, and previous suicidal attempts.

Issues Important in Adapting Interviews to Computer Format

At this time no published studies have made use of the recent advances in diagnostic interviews (since the advent of DSM-III) and computerized administration of the interview. With the development of more specific diagnostic criteria and the establishment of the reliability of some of these interviews, it is only a natural next step to compare the reliability and validity of computerized administration of these interviews.

A number of issues must be considered when adapting a diagnostic interview to a computer-administered format. First, all of the questions must be clear and make grammatical sense when coming from the computer. Very often, the computer interviewer is treated like a person, and adolescents may react to the machine in the same way they treat an unintelligent person who asks silly, repetitive, or out-of-sequence questions. They may call it names, laugh at it, or simply ask if it is "stupid or what?"

Mental health professionals often assume that their patients are morons who will always have difficulty in relating to a computer keyboard. My experience has been that when a well-constructed tutorial is presented at the beginning of the program, patients have little trouble getting through the interview. Many adolescents are familiar with computers or, at the very least, with typewriters, and have adapted well to the IBM PC keyboard that I use.

A program should always have the ability to back up and correct answers.

People tend to get very frustrated if they cannot check and/or change previous responses. In a branching program, the ability to branch backward as well as forward is extremely important. A good program usually appears deceptively simple. The screens are clean and uncluttered and they move quickly from one to the other. The program should be virtually crashproof—that is, it should continue to function even after someone tampers with the keyboard, pushing various keys at random. Also many features should be accessible to the clinician. For example, it should be possible to stop the interview at any place and have it return to the same question at another time. If it is a long interview, it should be able to be configured so as to administer only the most relevant sections (for example, if time is at a premium).

Initial Experiences in Computer Assessment with Adolescents

The first experience my assistant and I at Thistletown Regional Centre had in using computerized assessment with an adolescent in residential treatment was a lesson in humility. The program was one of the first commercially available Minnesota Multiphasic Personality Inventory (MMPI) administration programs, and it ran on an Apple computer. Our experience at that time was limited to mainframe computers; we had little knowledge of microcomputers, which were still relatively new.

We were very much concerned about the effects of asking an emotionally disturbed adolescent to submit to a test by computer and took great lengths in preparing him for the experience. After being given an explanation of the process and ample time in which to change his mind, he impatiently asked if he could see the diskette. He then grasped the diskette, opened the disk drive door, put it in, turned on the computer, and watched the screen as the diskette whirled in the drive. Suddenly a message came on the screen and he exclaimed, "Oh, good, a self-booting diskette." At the time I was not aware of what a "self-booting diskette" was or what that implied. In any event, he proceeded to work through the program, completing the MMPI in one sitting and making several suggestions for improving the program (which were forwarded to the publisher of the program and implemented).

How to Integrate a Computerized Diagnostic Interview into a Clinical Practice

There are several ways in which a computerized diagnostic interview can be incorporated into a clinical practice. One possibility is to have the parent and/

or child complete the interview just prior to the first clinical session. A well-trained secretary or assistant can make the family feel comfortable on arrival and introduce them to the computer. The clinician can review the printout and identify areas of importance just prior to meeting the family.

Some clinicians, however, feel more comfortable keeping their first session as their traditional initial interview. At the end of the session they can introduce the computer interview as something to be completed at the beginning of their next session. A time could then be scheduled just prior to the second appointment for the parent and/or child to take the interview. A printout would then be available for the second session, during which time any important issues that were missed during the first interview could be focused on.

The information collected by the computerized interview can then be used in negotiating a treatment plan with the family. In my own work I have sometimes found that parents and clinicians have had different agendas after the implementation of a treatment plan. It usually does not take long for the treatment process to break down if the parents have different expectations regarding the nature of their child's (or family's) problems. The computer interview helps parents and adolescents feel that they have been heard and gives them a sense of having been examined fairly thoroughly. If the clinician uses the information provided by the interview constructively when negotiating treatment plans, it may ensure that sufficient attention be paid to the family's needs.

Interviews alone, whether given by computers or clinicians, do not represent a complete diagnostic workup. Rather it is expected that the interview will identify those diagnostic categories for which an individual may meet specific inclusion or exclusion criteria. Thus several DSM-III categories may be listed as potential areas to explore further. However, the primary diagnostic category will need to be determined on the basis of more than just a psychiatric interview. For example, specific weight-loss criteria will be important in the establishment of a diagnosis of anorexia nervosa, neuropsychological assessment may be requested to confirm certain diagnoses such as organic mental disorder, and so forth. One of the advantages of using a computerized diagnostic interview is that it is a relatively short, broad-banded screening method that encompasses a majority of possible patient complaints.

The Diagnostic Interview for Children and Adolescents: Computer Version

The DICA: Computer Version (Herjanic, 1985) was developed in order to provide an easier and more efficient way of collecting information important in establishing a child or adolescent's diagnosis. The interview consists of a total of 940 questions and probes. In practice, with a clinical population, approximately half of the questions may actually be administered. For example, if the youth does not drink alcohol, a series of questions relating to alcohol use and abuse would not be triggered. In my experience the interview takes approximately one and a half hours for adolescents and two hours for parents to complete. Generally adolescents are much more familiar with the use of computers and are able to proceed more quickly than their parents. In addition, parents prefer to discuss many of the questions with each other prior to committing themselves to an answer.

The computerized interview has been adapted slightly from the original in-person version in order to make it more presentable in computer format. The reading level of the computer interview has been assessed and ranges from grade 6 in its most difficult section (psychoses) to grade 4 in most others. The program has been divided into sections, as indicated in figure 9.1; the clinician

Please Select Diagnostic Interviews to Administer:

Y . .	Demographics	Y . .	Enuresis, Encopresis
Y . .	Attention Deficit Disorders	Y . .	Gender, Sexual Expression
Y . .	Oppositional Disorders	Y . .	Psychosis
Y . .	Conduct Disorders	Y . .	Psychosocial Stressors
Y . .	Substance Abuse	Y . .	Developmental History
Y . .	Affective Disorders	Y . .	Pervasive Developmental
Y . .	Anxiety Disorders	Y . .	Elective Mutism
Y . .	Eating Disorders	Y . .	Pica
Y . .	Somatization	Y . .	Stereotyped Movement Disorders

→ For Previous Screen

Figure 9.1. Diagnostic selection screen from DICA: Computer version. Copyright Multi-Health Systems, Inc. Toronto, Canada.

has the option of selecting those sections most relevant for the client being assessed. For example, the sections on pica and pervasive developmental disorder may be irrelevant for suspected conduct-disordered adolescents. In my use of the instrument, which has been primarily for research purposes, the entire interview is administered.

The clinician can select several options in the program prior to administration. The first of these is whether or not the computer will "beep" upon receiving an appropriate answer to each question. I have found this useful in that the administrator can hear whether or not the interviewee is completing the interview correctly without having to watch him or her. Some patients guard the privacy they are afforded in completing the interview. They seem to treat the computer as a person they are having a private conversation with and prefer as little intrusion as possible from others.

The second option allows for the presentation of a short tutorial introducing the interviewee to the keyboard. If selected, the program then begins with an interactive introduction that must be completed prior to initiating the interview. This serves the purpose of both familiarizing the client with the keys to be used and determining his or her ability to interact with the machine. Once this section has been completed the questions are then presented, beginning with the first section selected.

The questions are primarily answered with "yes/no" keys, with "1" representing "yes" and "2" "no." A sample item from the section on oppositional disorders can be found in figure 9.2. There are some multiple-choice questions

---

Does he often break the rules at home such as not doing something he has been told to do; going out when he was told to stay in; or not coming back when he was supposed to?

Instructions

Yes 1   No 2

Answer: —

F9 To Back Up   F10 To Skip Ahead

Figure 9.2. Sample item from oppositional disorder section of the parent version of DICA: Computer version. Copyright Multi-Health Systems, Inc. Toronto, Canada.

as well as fill-in answers. Patients seem to have little difficulty in typing answers to questions such as "What would you say bothers you the most?" Some of the answers I have received on this particular question have included such things as "mother," "deaths," and "not making people happy." Patients (or parents) have the option of skipping any question they feel uncomfortable with or backing up to any previous questions they want to review or change. In practice, few questions actually get skipped. The skip and backup functions have been designed to keep the forward and backward branching intact.

At the completion of the interview, the subject is instructed to call the examiner, who can enter a code signaling the end of the interview. If the interview cannot be completed in a single session, it can be stopped and picked up again at a later date, starting with the last item administered. The interview can be stopped any number of times and restarted without losing its place.

The printout produced by the program consists of several sections. The first part summarizes the basic information about the child or adolescent and the interview. For example, it lists the child's sex and age, date of the interview, and sections that were administered.

The second section lists all of the diagnostic categories for which the DICA criteria have been met. Also listed are the various exclusion and inclusion criteria for each of the categories. A sample can be found in figure 9.3. It is

Client: 85107

- -

This child meets the DICA criteria for the following diagnostic categories:

- -

312.21 Conduct Disorder, Socialized, Nonaggressive

Duration of symptoms must be at least six (6) months

- -

Alcohol Use

305.0x Alcohol Abuse

303.9x Alcohol Dependence

305.2x Marijuana Use

- -

309.00 Adjustment Disorder with Depressed Mood

- -

300.xx Phobia

Rule out: Schizophrenia, Obsessive Compulsive Disorder

- -

300.81 Somatization Disorder

Current

- -

307.60 Enuresis

Rule out: Physical Disorder such as Diabetes or seizures

- -

Possible Schizophrenia or other psychotic experience

Auditory Hallucinations
Visual Hallucinations
Body Sensations other than auditory or visual hallucinations
Delusions

Rule out: Organic Mental Disorder, Mental Retardation, Substance Abuse, Mood Disorder. If present, the Mood Disorder must have been brief in duration or developed after the psychotic symptoms.

- -

Has experienced psychosocial stress that caused worry, sadness, or anxiety.

- -

Figure 9.3. Sample listing of diagnostic categories meeting DICA criteria, with exclusion and inclusion criteria for each category. Copyright Multi-Health Systems, Inc. Toronto, Canada.

important to reaffirm at this point that the process we are discussing is computer-assisted diagnosis and not computer diagnosis. Thus, while a number of potential diagnostic categories are selected, it is the clinician's responsibility to determine which ones apply. In most cases more complete information than that provided by an interview is needed to determine a differential diagnosis. For example, in order to confirm a diagnosis of schizophrenia or attention deficit disorder, psychological assessment may be required.

The third section of the interview consists of a listing of all questions asked and their responses. This allows the clinician to see which questions led to the triggering of specific diagnostic categories. Thus, if the criteria have been met for oppositional disorder, the specific responses that led to that decision could be evaluated. In some cases, this serves as a cue for further investigation regarding a problem area.

One of the major advantages of this computerized interview is its ability to tap a wide range of problem areas in a relatively short time. It is highly unlikely that an interviewer would cover the full range of diagnostic possibilities through his or her usual intake procedure. In the course of my own research, the computer interview made one rather dramatic discovery that probably would have been missed using more traditional techniques. In this case a nineteen-year-old patient had been in a day treatment program for three years. He had displayed problems of a psychotic nature as well as low intellectual functioning. Due to his low reading ability, he required assistance to complete the computer interview. The youth controlled the pace of the interview by taking responsibility for pushing the answer keys, while questions were read by the research assistant. In the section on sexual expression, the patient reported that he had been sexually abused. I believe that it is unlikely that we would have uncovered this information had it not been for the computer. The reason is that it was not common practice to ask males about sexual abuse. The allegation was confirmed by the adolescent in further questioning.

Future Work and Research on Diagnostic Interviewing of Children, Adolescents, and Their Parents

The use and implications of diagnostic interviewing by computer are still in the early stages. There are still many issues to be explored. As time goes on, it is inevitable that computers will increasingly affect the lives of all of us. While many basic research questions are currently being explored—such as the reliability, concurrent validity, and normative aspects of the computerized version of DICA interviews—there will be a host of new issues to explore. The effects of different forms of computer presentation, such as animation, color, and graphics, on individual responses may prove interesting. Also, varying amounts of computer feedback may be a way to increase patients' comfort level as well as to help educate them in certain areas. Another interesting phenomena that is worth exploring is computerphobia (or computer resistance), an ailment we see more frequently among mental health practitioners than in the patients being treated.

I anticipate a greater use of on-line assessment techniques that go beyond traditional tests and interviews. The computer is an ideal medium for assessing memory functions and reaction time. With the more sophisticated graphics abilities that are becoming available, computer testing will be used for other intellectual functioning areas, such as spatial relations. The mental status interview will take on new dimensions with more sophisticated on-line capabilities and the instant feedback available. Mental health practitioners located in remote areas will have in-house "laboratory" facilities that will allow them to conduct workups as comprehensive as those done in many large urban hospitals.

A great deal of research and development is possible in the area of computer-assisted diagnosis and assessment. As the power and accessibility of the technology increase and our classification systems become more delineated, it is hoped that the precision of our evaluations will be improved.

REFERENCES

Card, W. I., Nicholson, M., Crean, G. P., Watkinson, G., Evans, C. R., Wilson, J., and Russel, D. (1974). A comparison of doctor and computer interrogation of patients. *International Journal of Bio-Medical Computing*, 5, 175–197.

Carr, A. C., Ancill, R. J., Ghosh, A., and Margo, A. (1981). Direct assessment of depression by microcomputer: A feasibility study. *Acta Psychiatrica Scandinavica*, *64*, 415–422.

Carr, A. C., Ghosh, A., and Ancill, R. J. (1983, February). Can a computer take a psychiatric history? *Psychological Medicine*, 157–158.

Chambers, W., Puig-Antich, J., and Tabrizi, M. A. (October, 1978). *The ongoing development of the KIDDIE-SADS*. Paper presented at the meeting of the American Academy of Child Psychiatry, San Diego.

Coddington, R. D., and King, T. L. (1972). Automated history taking in child psychiatry. *American Journal of Psychiatry*, *129*, 276–282.

Costello, A. J., Edelbrock, C., Kalas, R., Kessler, M. D., and Klaric, S. (1982). *The NIMH diagnostic interview for children (DISC)*. Pittsburg: Author.

Dove, G. A., Wigg, P., Clarke, J. H. C., Constantinidou, M., Royappa, B. A., Evans, C. R., Milne, J., Goss, C., and Gordon, M. (1977). The therapeutic effect of taking a patient's history by computer. *Journal of the Royal College of General Practitioners*, 27, 477–481.

Edelbrock, C., and Costello, A. J. (1984). Structured psychiatric interviews for children and adolescents. In G. Goldstein and M. Hersen (Eds.), *Handbook of Psychological Assessment* (pp. 276–290). Elmsford, NY: Pergamon Press.

Erdman, H. P., Klein, M. H., and Greist, J. H. (1983). The reliability of a computer interview for drug use/abuse information. *Behavior Research Methods and Instrumentation*, *1*, 66–68.

Greist, J. H., Gustafson, D. H., Straus, F. F., Rowse, G. L., Langren, T. P., and Chiles, J. A. (1973). A computer interview for suicide-risk prediction. *American Journal of Psychiatry*, *130*, 1327–1332.

Grossman, J. H., Barnett, G. O., McGuire, T., and Swedlow, D. B. (1971). Evaluation of computer-acquired patient histories. *Journal of the American Medical Association*, *215*, 1286–1291.

Haessler, H. A. (1969). Recent developments in automating the medical history. *Computers and Automation*, *18*, 24–27.

Herjanic, B. (1985). *Diagnostic Interview for Children and Adolescents: Computer Version* [computer program]. Toronto, Ont.: Multi-Health Systems.

Herjanic, B., and Campbell, W. (1977). Differentiating psychiatrically disturbed children on the basis of a structured interview. *Journal of Abnormal Child Psychology*, 5, 127–134.

Herjanic, B., Herjanic, M., Brown, F., and Wheatt, T. (1975). Are children reliable reporters? *Journal of Abnormal Child Psychology*, 3, 41–48.

Herjanic, B., and Reich, W. (1982). Development of a structured psychiatric interview for children: Agreement between child and parent on individual symptoms. *Journal of Abnormal Child Psychology*, 10, 307–324.

Hodges, K., Kline, J., Fitch, P., McKnew, D., and Cytryn, L. (1981). The Child Assessment Schedule: A diagnostic interview for research and clinical use. *Catalog of Selected Documents in Psychology*, 11, 56.

Hodges, K., Kline, J., Stern, L., Cytryn, L., and McKnew, D. (1982). The development of a child assessment interview for research and clinical use. *Journal of Abnormal Child Psychology*, 10, 173–189.

Kestenbaum, C. J., and Bird, H. R. (1978). A reliability study of the mental health assessment form for school-age children. *Journal of the American Academy of Child Psychiatry*, 7, 338–347.

Kleinmuntz, B., and McLean, R. S. (1968). Diagnostic interviewing by digital computer. *Behavioral Science*, 13, 75–80.

Kovacs, M. (1982). *The longitudinal study of child and adolescent psychopathology: I. The semi-structured interview schedule for children (ISC)*. Unpublished manuscript.

Langner, T. S., Gersten, J. C., McCarthy, E. D., Eisenberg, G., Greene, E. L., Hersen, J. H., and Jameson, J. D. (1976). A screening inventory for assessing psychiatric impairment in children six to eighteen. *Journal of Consulting and Clinical Psychology*, 44, 286–296.

Lucas, R. W. (1977). A study of patients' attitudes to computer interrogation. *International Journal of Man-Machine Studies*, 9, 69–86.

Matazarro, J. D. (1983). The reliability of psychiatric and psychological diagnosis. *Clinical Psychology Review*, 3, 103–145.

Maultsby, M. C., and Slack, M. V. (1971). A computer-based psychiatry history system. *Archives of General Psychology*, 25, 570–572.

Mayne, J. G., Weksel, W., and Sholtz, P. H. (1968). Toward automating the medical history. *Mayo Clinic Proceedings*, 43, 1–25.

Meikle, S., and Gerritse, R. (1970). A comparison of psychiatric symptom frequency under narrative and check list conditions. *American Journal of Psychiatry*, 127, 379–382.

Moore, N. C., Summer, K. R., and Bloor, R. N. (1984). Do patients like psychometric testing by computer? *Journal of Clinical Psychology*, 40, 875–877.

Orvaschel, H., Puig-Antich, J., Chambers, W., Tabrizi, M. A., and Johnson, R. (1982). Retrospective assessment of prepubertal major depression with the KIDDIE-SADS-E. *Journal of the American Academy of Child Psychiatry*, 21, 392–397.

Reich, W., Herjanic, B., Welner, Z., and Gandhy, P. R. (1982). Development of a structured psychiatric interview for children: Agreement on diagnosis comparing child and parent interviews. *Journal of Abnormal Child Psychology*, 10, 325–336.

Rutter, M., and Graham, P. (1968). The reliability and validity of the psychiatric assessment of the child: I. Interview with the child. *British Journal of Psychiatry*, 114, 563–579.

Skinner, H. A., and Allen, B. A. (1983). Does the computer make a difference?: Computerized vs. face-to-face vs. self-report assessment of alcohol, drug and tobacco use. *Journal of Consulting and Clinical Psychology*, 51, 267–275.

Slack, W. V., Hicks, G. P., Reed, C. Z., and Van Cura, L. J. (1966). A computer-based medical history system. *New England Journal of Medicine*, 274, 194–198.

Slack, W. V., and Slack, C. W. (1977). Talking to a computer about emotional problems: A comparative study. *Psychotherapy: Theory, Research and Practice*, 14, 156–164.

Slack, W. V., and Van Cura, L. J. (1968). Patient reaction to computer-based medical interviewing. *Computers and Biomedical Research*, 1, 527–531.

Space, L. G. (1981). The computer as psychometrician. *Behavior Research Methods and Instrumentation*, 13, 595–606.

Stead, W. W., Heyman, A., Thomson, H. K., and Hammond, W. E. (1972). Computer-assisted interview of patients with functional headache. *Archives of Internal Medicine*, 129, 950–955.

Yarnall, S. R., Samuelson, P., and Wakefield, J. S. (1972). Clinical evaluation of an automated screening history. *Northwest Medicine*, 17, 186–191.

PART III

COMPUTER INTERPRETATION OF PERSONALITY AND INTEREST TESTS

10

Computerized Clinical and Personality Assessment Using the MMPI

James N. Butcher

It was no accident that the developers of the first computerized personality assessment programs chose the Minnesota Multiphasic Personality Inventory (MMPI) as the instrument to use for computer scoring and automated interpretation (Rome et al., 1962). There are several reasons for their choice. First, the MMPI was—and is—the most widely researched objective personality questionnaire available. The inventory was originally published in 1943, after several years of developmental work by Starke Hathaway and J. C. McKinley, as an aid to psychological screening for professionals in the mental health fields and general medical practice. Work with the MMPI has continued, and over the past four decades a great deal of empirical research has been published in a wide variety of clinical settings. Over ten thousand articles and books document its use. The MMPI has become the most frequently administered psychological test (Lubin, Larson, and Matarazzo, 1984). Its well-researched empirical data base establishes the MMPI as a psychological test that lends itself particularly well to actuarial prediction approaches.

The second reason for the broad use of the MMPI in computer-based assessment came from the strong rationale for actuarial interpretation that Meehl (1954) provided over thirty years ago in a monograph contrasting two approaches to clinical prediction: the clinical approach versus actuarial methods in predicting behavior. Meehl forcefully demonstrated that objective methods of actuarially combining data produced more adequate predictions than did those based on clinical methods.

Empirical Data Base for MMPI Interpretation

A number of sources of empirical information regarding the MMPI can be incorporated into an automated interpretation system.

MMPI SCALE INTERPRETATION

The primary ingredient of the MMPI interpretive data base consists of the extensive work published on the empirical correlates of the clinical scales. From the beginning, early researchers sought to establish the validity of MMPI scales and test indices by determining their objective, external test correlates. Numerous studies demonstrating the adequacy of MMPI scales for describing and predicting clinically relevant behavior have been published (for an overview of the MMPI validation data, see Dahlstrom, Welsh, and Dahlstrom, 1972; Graham, 1977; Greene, 1980; and Lachar, 1974). For example, if a clinician obtains a profile elevation on a particular scale, such as Scale 2 (the Depression scale), it is very easy to locate in the published MMPI literature a number of relevant behavior correlates that could be applied to the case depending on the specific elevation.

ILLUSTRATIVE BEHAVIORAL CORRELATES FOR VARIOUS RANGES OF DEPRESSION SCALE SCORES[*]

Scale Elevations with T-score Between 65 and 69. Persons with scales in this range may be considered unhappy, moody, dissatisfied with life, withdrawn, lacking in self-confidence, quiet, not outgoing, fearful, silent, unfriendly, despondent, self-pitying, forgetful, immature, shy, spineless, deliberate, objective, contemplative, realistic, critical, anxious, depressed, and pessimistic.

Scale Elevations with T-scores Between 70 and 79. Persons with scores in this range exhibit moderate clinical depression and dysphoric mood. They are self-depreciatory, present with some somatic complaints such as weakness, fatigue, or loss of energy, are agitated, tense, highstrung, irritable, prone to worry, introverted, seclusive, aloof, indecisive, and readily make concessions. They feel useless, view themselves as failures, avoid interpersonal involvement, see themselves as needy, express dissatisfaction with life, lack self-confidence, and are withdrawn, unhappy, quiet, not outgoing, fearful, silent, unfriendly, despondent, self-punishing, bitter, unenthusiastic, self-pitying, forgetful, immature, shy, spineless, deliberate, objective, contemplative, realistic, critical, anxious, depressed, and pessimistic.

Scale Elevations with T-scores over 80. Persons with scores this high exhibit serious clinical depression, suicidal ideation, and dysphoric mood. They are self-depreciatory, present with somatic complaints such as weakness, fatigue, or loss of energy, are agitated, tense, highstrung, irritable, prone to worry,

[*] This material has been compiled from Dahlstrom, Walsh, and Dahlstrom, 1972; Graham, 1977; Graham and McCord, in press; and Lewandowski and Graham, 1972.

introverted, seclusive, aloof, and secretive. They feel useless and unable to function, view themselves as failures, maintain psychological distance, avoid interpersonal involvement, make concessions, see themselves as needing help, and lack self-confidence. They are indecisive, unhappy, dissatisfied with life, withdrawn, quiet, not outgoing, fearful, silent, unfriendly, despondent, self-punishing, bitter, unenthusiastic, self-pitying, forgetful, immature, shy, spineless, deliberate, objective, contemplative, realistic, critical, anxious, depressed, and pessimistic.

Empirical correlates such as these have been established for the MMPI clinical scales and many special or experimental scales, such as the MacAndrew Addiction Proneness scale (MacAndrew, 1965). The empirical scale correlates are particularly valuable sources of information for use in a computerized MMPI interpretive system since many profiles to be interpreted will have prominent elevations on a single clinical scale. In these instances the basic MMPI correlates provide a great deal of valid, descriptive, and useful personality and symptomatic information on the client.

CODE-TYPE INTERPRETATION

The early developers of the MMPI found that more than one clinical scale was elevated above a T-score of 70 on the profiles of many patients. In order to fully evaluate the patient's response patterns, it is important to consider the profile configuration or pattern of scale-score elevations. Profile or configural interpretation thus became preferred over simple scale-by-scale analyses. In the late 1950s and early 1960s several investigators began to accumulate empirical data on MMPI profile patterns. The profile configuration was summarized in the form of a profile code, and several "classic" profile types were studied extensively. The empirical literature on the correlates of MMPI code types is, therefore, extremely important to computerized MMPI interpretation. Code types are MMPI variables that summarize the prominent scale elevations and their shape in the MMPI profile. They are obtained by rank ordering the MMPI clinical scales in terms of scale elevation and using symbols to denote level of elevation. Most of the empirical research on MMPI code types included only the eight MMPI scales that were traditionally designated clinical scales: *Hs, D, Hy, Pd, Pa, Pt, Sc,* and *Ma*. However, some research incorporating other scales (*Mf* and *Si*) has been published on special populations, such as college students.

Research on the scales making up the code types has usually involved studying correlates of clinical scale elevations above the T equals 70 range; however, Graham and McCord have reported data extending behavioral descriptions to code types downward into the 65 to 69 T-score range.

A number of code types have been well described empirically. The *two-point code type* indicates when two clinical scales, such as *D* and *Pt*, are elevated in the interpretive range, producing a two-point code of 2-7/7-2. The *three-*

point code type is used when three clinical scales are prominent in the profile; for example, scales *D*, *Pd*, and *Pt* are described as a three-point code of 2-4-7. The *four-point code* type, some of which are relatively common in some clinical settings—for example, the 1-2-3-4 code type (which is a combination of *Hs*, *D*, *Hy*, and *Pd* scales)—has also received some research attention.

A large number of MMPI code types have been tied to useful empirical behavioral correlates. Research in this area has typically involved studying homogeneous groups of patients, that is, people who have common code types, and obtaining behavioral descriptions, Q-sort ratings, history information, and other pertinent clinical information on them. These empirical descriptions are then applied to new cases that meet the criteria for inclusion into the code-type classification. For a more detailed description of the code books on MMPI profile types, see Gilberstadt and Duker, 1965; Halbower, 1955; and Marks, Seeman, and Haller, 1974).

Lack of sufficient research on some of the MMPI code types limits the scope of a comprehensive, practical, computer interpretation system based entirely on the actuarial approach to clinical assessment. There are three major problems with current computer interpretation systems.

The primary limitation is that the empirical correlates for the entire range of MMPI code types have not been explored sufficiently. Relatively few codes have been empirically studied and described at this time. Consequently only a limited amount of actuarial classification information is available. Any computerized MMPI interpretation system that aims at comprehensive appraisal of clinical cases must go beyond strict actuarial interpretation by incorporating "clinical" experience for profile types that have evaded actuarial description. This combined actuarial-clinical approach has been referred to as "the automated clinician" (Fowler, 1969). Most computer-based MMPI interpretive systems have been developed following a combined actuarial system and an "automated clinician."

The MMPI profile contains additional information (for example, on the *Mf*, *Si*, and *MAC* scales) that is not included in the code type. MMPI interpretation systems incorporate more information than is available through the code-type literature.

Finally, in some settings where the MMPI is widely used there are few MMPI correlates for the various code types. For example, MMPI code-type correlates are underrepresented in such settings as adolescent populations and medical programs.

In interpreting MMPI code types, it is important to take into consideration a number of factors.

First, the ordering of the scales within the code type can make an important difference when descriptors are applied to a particular case. For example, in interpreting the 3-4/4-3 code type, it makes a difference whether the 3 or 4 scales appear first in the profile code. The same descriptors cannot be applied for the 3-4 code type and the 4-3 code type without losing important specific information. In this combination of MMPI scales the relative prominence of scale 3 over scale 4 provides information as to whether the individual is exercising self-control or whether acting-out behavior is expected.

Second, the elevation range of the code type and the relative elevation of the scales making up the code type can alter the relevant descriptors. For example, in a 2-7/7-2 code type, a somewhat different set of descriptors would be applied to the patient if the Depression scale were in the 70 to 79 T-score range than if it were in the greater than T equals 80 range. In the latter case a more severe depression pattern would be highlighted.

The MMPI code-type literature is not conveniently organized for efficient clinical use. It is impossible for a clinician to commit to memory all of the relevant descriptors for the various profile types. In interpreting an MMPI profile, clinicians usually must refer to a standard reference source to ensure that they apply full and appropriate clinical descriptors. Computerized interpretations can provide clinicians with a convenient summary of the most likely personality descriptors or symptoms that would apply to the typical case. A computerized narrative report organizes the empirical information into a standard "format" for particular clinical applications. Clinicians using a computerized narrative report need to tailor the output to their own setting to ensure that the descriptors apply for their particular case.

Third, MMPI special scales should be considered. A number of additional MMPI scales have been widely researched and can provide useful descriptive information on a patient's problems. These scales, often referred to as special scales, include such measures as the MacAndrew Addiction Proneness scale (MAC; MacAndrew, 1965) or the Wiggins Content scales (Wiggins, 1966). These scales provide more specific information or correlates than do the MMPI validity or clinical scales.

Fourth, MMPI indices and computer-based decision rules must be considered. A number of scale or profile indices have been developed to provide specific diagnostic decisions, such as classification as "psychotic or neurotic" or whether to classify individuals into a psychopathology group. These indices range from extensively researched techniques such as the Goldberg Index (Goldberg, 1965) and the Megargee's Classification System (Megargee and Bohn, 1977), to clinically derived sets of classification rules, such as the Henrichs Rules (Henrichs, 1964, 1966) for discriminating among psychiatric cases or Welsh's Internalization Ratio (Welsh, 1956). These test indices are relatively easy to program for evaluation by a computer and may provide the report user with highly specific information that could guide diagnostic classification or other decision-making processes. It is important for the test report user to be aware of the power of the index in question and the conditions under which valid decisions can be made from it.

And finally, MMPI pathogonomic item responses or "critical items" should be taken into account. The content of the individual's responses can be an important interpretive element in any clinical evaluation. The individual's attitudes, beliefs, and symptoms, as reflected in his or her MMPI responses, can provide important clues in a diagnostic study. Several approaches to appraising a subject's response to individual items have been developed. The critical item approach has been used for some time in clinical MMPI interpretation. The earliest list of critical items was generated by Grayson (1951) using a rational method, that is, by simply reading through the items and deciding intuitively what items were significant. The Grayson Critical Item list, though widely scored on many early computer scoring systems, was never empirically validated against external criteria.

Broader and more empirically valid sets of critical items have been developed. Koss and Butcher (1973), Koss, Butcher, and Hoffman (1976), and Lachar and Wrobel (1979) employed empirical methods to develop lists of items that were tied to objective criteria, such as presenting complaints or problem behavior. The Koss-Butcher and Lachar-Wrobel item sets provide information about a wider range of problems or behaviors reported by the individual than previous lists.

Early Computerized MMPI Scoring and Interpretation Systems

The early MMPI scoring and interpretation systems published by the Mayo Clinic (Pearson et al., 1965) and by Roche Laboratories (Fowler, 1965, 1967) were, in spite of their limitations, innovative pioneers in the field of personality assessment by electronic computer. They demonstrated the practicality of computers in providing personality appraisals in a useful, objective summary format. In part, these early approaches to computerized personality assessment were readily accepted by users because they saved time. However, many users also came to realize that the computer-based report was generally a valid "outside opinion" regarding the nature and extent of the client's problems.

A number of limitations were apparent in the early computerized MMPI systems. The first computerized personality appraisal program, developed by the Mayo Clinic, simply listed a number of personality characteristics or symptoms (usually about six) for a particular profile. Narrative reports today are both more comprehensive and more readable.

Some of the early scoring and interpretation systems also incorporated many less well validated scales or indices in their programs. For example, the *Lb* scale was widely included in early programs although the measure was not sufficiently validated for clinical use and subsequently has been shown not to have much predictive power or utility. Similarly, other indices, such as the Subtle-Obvious keys, with little empirical research and even less proven clinical utility, were computerized. As in the case of the *Lb* scale, subsequent research has shown the subtle item to have little predictive power in a clinical context (see Gynther and Burkhart, 1983).

Another problem with many early MMPI computer-based systems was the uncritical acceptance and printing out of the MMPI "critical items." It is a relatively easy matter for machines to list items that have been endorsed by the patient. The only way to view the patient's item responses was Grayson's Critical Item listing. As mentioned, this early set of items was developed by rational scale construction methods. The critical item lists in use today—those developed by Koss and Butcher and by Lachar and Wrobel—provide items that were developed by empirically validating them against clinically relevant criteria.

As interest in computer-based MMPI applications increased and a number of new scoring and administration formats became available, other problems were noted. For example, some unauthorized MMPI scoring software was sold that actually included errors in scoring. Individuals who purchase computer software to score or interpret any psychological test should be aware of possible scoring errors and verify the scoring against a known hand-scoring template before placing reliance in the procedure.

COMPONENTS OF A GOOD MMPI REPORT

What are the components of a practical and appropriate—a clinician-friendly and clinically useful—computer-based MMPI report? Although the discussion here focuses largely on narrative reports, I believe that the same components are necessary in programs that simply list relevant descriptive correlates.

Automated clinical reports are predetermined or "canned" statements or descriptions that are applied to individuals who obtain established personality test scores. The statements or paragraphs contained in the narrative report are stored in computer memory and automatically retrieved and matched to scores for individuals who obtain similar scale elevations, profile types, or scale indices.

Ideally, narrative report information is based on empirical test correlates or actuarial data that have been established for the test scales or patterns. An example of this is the behavioral correlates for MMPI scales and code types (see Gilberstadt and Duker, 1965; Halbower, 1955; Lewandowski and Graham, 1972; and Marks, Seeman, and Haller, 1975). The validity of automated reports depends on a number of factors, including how well the test instrument has been validated for the uses involved (in the case of the MMPI there is a substantial validity data base) and how closely the developers of the computerized interpretive program have adhered to acceptable test practices and followed the test's data base in compiling the narrative information.

It is important that computerized interpretive reports be used only in an adjunct or "advisory" way and not as the *final* word on the patient. The computerized report should be used only in conjunction with clinical information obtained from other sources.

Automated MMPI clinical reports are designed *only* for use by professionals who are knowledgeable in the inventory's interpretive background. Most narrative computer reports are written for professional use only and not designed for use by nonprofessionals or patients. MMPI interpretation services are generally sensitive about this need and typically evaluate the qualifications of potential system users. Caution should also be taken in the storing of patient records so as not to allow computerized psychological reports to fall into the hands of untrained people. Misinterpretations and incorrect emphases are likely to result.

One of the most important features of a clinically usable MMPI report is that it should incorporate the most valid descriptive information obtainable from the extensive experimental and clinical literature on the test. In addition, the report program should include as much of the actuarial-based information and empirically derived decision rules as possible. The validity and utility of a computerized personality assessment system will depend to a large extent on the validity of the measure itself. In the computerization of any personality measure, the end product, the narrative report, can only be as valid as the inferences for the test itself. Computerized reports based on an unvalidated psychological test are not likely to be valid themselves. The great strength of the MMPI lies in the extensive test validation information that has accumulated.

Computerized report narratives should employ conservatively framed clinical descriptions and predictions and include untested hypotheses sparingly. Inferences included in the narrative MMPI report should be as close to the data and as devoid of speculation as possible. As discussed, the computerized report is not provided as a substitute for clinical judgment but rather as a source of information for the clinician to employ in developing his or her clinical evaluation. Clinical conjecture and "best hunches" about personality dynamics, treatment projections, and so forth, are certainly important elements in any clinical evaluation. However, this activity should be left, as much as possible, to the clinician who has the personal contact with the patient and the opportunity to verify the veridicality of the hypotheses.

The most useful clinical reports, whether they are generated by a computer or by a clinician, are those that are tailored to fit the individual's demographic characteristics and the setting in which the test was administered. Although MMPI descriptors have a high degree of validity generalization across settings, more specific predictions and more accurate descriptions can be made if the setting and relevant demographic characteristics are taken into account.

Similarly, reports that consider the varying reasons for referral and attempt to focus description, classification, or predictions on test-taking parameters will provide more accurate and valid test reports. For example, the clinician who administers an MMPI to a father suspected of abusing his child knows to expect that the profile is likely to reflect test defensiveness (for example, has an elevated *K* score). Computer-based interpretive systems become more accurate and pointed in their focus if such relevant variables are accounted for. Of course, it is very difficult to incorporate information pertinent to all settings and referral situations. However, the more of these relevant factors that are included, the more pointed the reports can be.

Narrative reports, if they are to be useful, must be internally consistent and free from contradictory statements. The MMPI has a vast number of potential descriptors and correlates that can be applied to a particular case. The potential descriptors contain varying degrees of validity and relevance for a particular profile type. It is conceivable that an MMPI interpreter, particularly one who incorporates information from the numerous special scales, will encounter contradictory descriptors in the test literature. For example, it is possible to have a profile that contains a moderately elevated *D* score, which would call for describing the individual as depressed, but also a low Wiggins *DEP* score, which would result in a statement that the individual is not depressed. The fact that the two scales are measuring "depression" differently can escape an unwary interpreter and will escape a computer that is programmed only to interpret the various scale elevations in sequence. Resolving test contradictions is important to clinical test interpretation and can often provide the clinician with an unusual opportunity to gain insight into his or her client's problem situation. As computers are not insightful, they are not very good at resolving such contradictions. Therefore the computer report might appear inaccurate and stupid. Developers of computer-based personality assessment systems usually spend a great deal of time and effort resolving internal contradictions. This task usually requires having extensive knowledge of test correlates and the psychometric properties of the instrument and also involves reviewing a large number of narrative reports to eliminate conflicting information.

Whether they are generated by a computer or by a clinician, reports that incorporate practical suggestions, are most useful to the working clinician. It is important not to provide general personality descriptions that tend to fit anyone. The most useful automated report provides the clinician with ideas or perspectives he or she has not or cannot obtain from examining the profile.

A computer-based MMPI interpretation system should be "alive," flexible, and open to modification, should the circumstances warrant. An instrument like the MMPI is used in many research studies as a criterion of psychopathology. Every year an extensive amount of relevant research providing clinically useful interpretive information that could alter some aspect of the test's use is published. Flexibility in the way the computer interpretation program is written will ensure that revision can be undertaken readily as changes are required.

The Minnesota Report for Clinical Settings

Several goals were kept in mind during the development of the Minnesota Clinical Interpretive Report (University of Minnesota Press, 1982). It was developed as a means for interpreting MMPI profiles in keeping with American Psychological Association standards for psychological test usage and for computer-based scoring and interpretation services.

Several forms of the report were designed to provide information to psychological and medical practitioners that could be integrated with other relevant clinical information about a case. The Minnesota Report was designed as an "MMPI consultation"—to provide the most well-validated personality information and relevant clinical descriptors for the profile in question. It was not designed to stand alone as a complete diagnostic study but rather to be one source of clinical diagnostic information about the client, used in conjunction with information obtained from other sources.

The report was designed to provide potentially informative descriptions and hypotheses about a client in a clinically meaningful format. The major sections of the report were chosen because of their relevance to a practitioner's activities in most clinical settings. An effort was made to summarize information pertinent to a number of clinical settings in order to make the reports more specific than ones written on the basis of MMPI scores alone.

The computer programs for the Minnesota Report were written in a form that would allow for relatively easy revision and periodic updates as new information on the MMPI becomes available. One such revision, involving an expansion of the treatment considerations sections of the clinical report, was undertaken in 1984–85.

USE OF THE MMPI IN TREATMENT EVALUATION

John W., the patient, was a twenty-eight-year-old payroll clerk who was self-referred for therapy because of his inability to function well at work. He had been employed by his company for four years but was recently promoted to payroll clerk. His troubles came when, during the peak work period at the end of each month, he became quite concerned that he would be unable to perform his job. He felt insecure and inadequate to deal with the scheduling problems and was concerned that he would be fired. His tension, anxiety, and low mood were so severe that he was unable to go to work one morning. He decided to seek help for his problems.

John was extremely tense in the initial interview. In a high, breaking voice, he reported great concern that he was going to be fired. Even after acknowledging that he had done a good job in his previous position and was promoted because of his past work efforts, he still expressed concern that he was going to fail. He related his present fears to concerns over rejection and his never having been able to please his mother and father. John also mentioned difficulty he was having in relationships with women. A somewhat shy and unassertive individual, he was spending a great deal of time alone because of his inability to meet and talk with women. He appeared to be highly motivated for treatment. The MMPI was administered following his initial interview (see figure 10.1).

John's evident distress and his apparent inability to deal with his present stressful situation were considered central problems to be dealt with in treatment. The treatment referral stressed the need to provide "stress inoculation" therapy in order to help prepare him to deal more effectively with his job problems. Moreover, John was referred to a female therapist for treatment with the idea

```
                           TM*
         THE MINNESOTA REPORT                          Page  1
                                            TM
for the Minnesota Multiphasic Personality Inventory  :  Adult System

         By James N. Butcher, Ph.D.

Client No. : 012345678                       Gender : Male
Setting : Medical                            Age :  28
Report Date :  3-JAN-86
PAS Code Number : 00020894 409 0005
```

PROFILE VALIDITY

The client has responded to the items in a frank and open manner, producing a valid MMPI profile. He appears to have a strong need to cooperate with the test administration and to endorse psychological symptoms. He may be "letting down his defenses" in an attempt to get help for his problems, and there may be a tendency on his part to be overly self-critical. These hypotheses should be kept in mind when evaluating the clinical patterns reflected in the profile.

SYMPTOMATIC PATTERN

A pattern of chronic psychological maladjustment characterizes individuals with this MMPI profile. The client is overwhelmed by anxiety, tension, and depression. He feels helpless and alone, inadequate and insecure, and believes that life is hopeless and that nothing is working out right. He attempts to control his worries through intellectualization and unproductive self-analyses, but he has difficulty concentrating and making decisions.

He is functioning at a very low level of efficiency. He tends to overreact to even minor stress, and may show rapid behavioral deterioration. He also tends to blame himself for his problems. His life-style is chaotic and disorganized, and he has a history of poor work and achievement.

He may be preoccupied with occult ideas. Obsessive-compulsive and phobic behavior are likely to make up part of the symptom pattern. He has a wide range of interests, and appears to enjoy aesthetic and cultural activities. Interpersonally, he appears to be sensitive, concerned, and able to easily express his feelings toward others. He appears to have no sex-role conflict.

His response content indicates that he is preoccupied with feeling guilty and unworthy, and feels that he deserves to be punished for wrongs he has committed. He feels regretful and unhappy about life, complains about having no zest for life, and seems plagued by anxiety and worry about the future. He has difficulty managing routine affairs, and the item content he endorsed suggests a poor memory, concentration problems, and an inability to make decisions. He appears to be immobilized and withdrawn and has no energy for life. According to his response content, there is a strong possibility that he has seriously contemplated suicide. A careful evaluation of this possibility is suggested.

INTERPERSONAL RELATIONS

NOTE: This MMPI interpretation can serve as a useful source of hypotheses about clients. This report is based on objectively derived scale indexes and scale interpretations that have been developed in diverse groups of patients. The personality descriptions, inferences and recommendations contained herein need to be verified by other sources of clinical information since individual clients may not fully match the prototype. The information in this report should most appropriately be used by a trained, qualified test interpreter. The information contained in this report should be considered confidential.

Figure 10.1. Computer printout of the Minnesota Report for John W., a mental health outpatient.

Client No. : 012345678 Report Date : 3-JAN-86 Page 2

Problematic personal relationships are also characteristic of his life. He seems to lack basic social skills and is behaviorally withdrawn. He may relate to others ambivalently, never fully trusting or loving anyone. Many individuals with this profile never establish lasting, intimate relationships.

He is a rather introverted person who has some difficulties meeting other people. He is probably shy and may be uneasy and somewhat rigid and overcontrolled in social situations.

The content of this client's MMPI responses suggests the following additional information concerning his interpersonal relations. He views his home situation as unpleasant and lacking in love and understanding. He feels like leaving home to escape a quarrelsome, critical situation, and to be free of family domination.

BEHAVIORAL STABILITY

This is a rather chronic behavioral pattern. Individuals with this profile live a disorganized and pervasively unhappy existence. They may have episodes of more intense and disturbed behavior resulting from an elevated stress level.

DIAGNOSTIC CONSIDERATIONS

Individuals with this profile show a severe psychological disorder and would probably be diagnosed as severely neurotic with an Anxiety Disorder or Dysthymic Disorder in a Schizoid Personality. The possibility of a more severe psychotic disorder, such as Schizophrenic Disorder, should be considered, however.

Individuals with this profile present some suicide risk and further evaluation of this possibility should be undertaken.

The content of his responses to the MMPI items suggests symptoms (convulsions, paralysis, clumsiness, and double vision) that are associated with neurological disorder. Vague pain symptoms, nausea, etc. that are found in neurotic conditions are also present, however. Further neurological evaluation would be needed to make a clear differentiation.

TREATMENT CONSIDERATIONS

Individuals with this MMPI profile often receive psychotropic medications for their depressed mood or intense anxiety. Many patients with this profile seek psychological treatment for their problems. Indeed, individuals with this profile usually require psychological treatment for their problems along with any medication that is given. Since many of their problems tend to be chronic ones, an intensive therapeutic effort might be required in order to bring about any significant change. Patients with this profile typically have many psychological and situational concerns; thus it is often difficult to maintain a focus in treatment.

He probably needs a great deal of emotional support at this time. His low self-esteem and feelings of inadequacy make it difficult for him to get energized toward therapeutic action. His expectancies for positive change in therapy may be low. Instilling a positive, treatment expectant attitude is important for him if treatment is to be successful.

Individuals with this profile tend to be overideational and given to unproductive rumination. They tend not to do well in unstructured, insight-oriented therapy and may actually deteriorate in functioning if they are asked to be introspective. He might respond more to supportive treatment of a directive, goal-oriented type.

Individuals with this profile present some suicide risk and precautions should be considered.

NCS Professional Assessment Services, P.O. Box 1416, Mpls, MN 55440

THE MINNESOTA REPORT Page 3

for the Minnesota Multiphasic Personality Inventory : Adult System

By James N. Butcher, Ph.D.

CLINICAL PROFILE

Client No. : 012345678 Gender : Male
Setting : Medical Age : 28
Report Date : 3-JAN-86

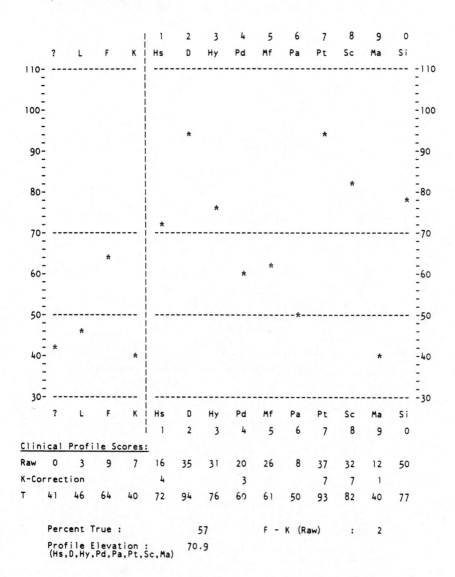

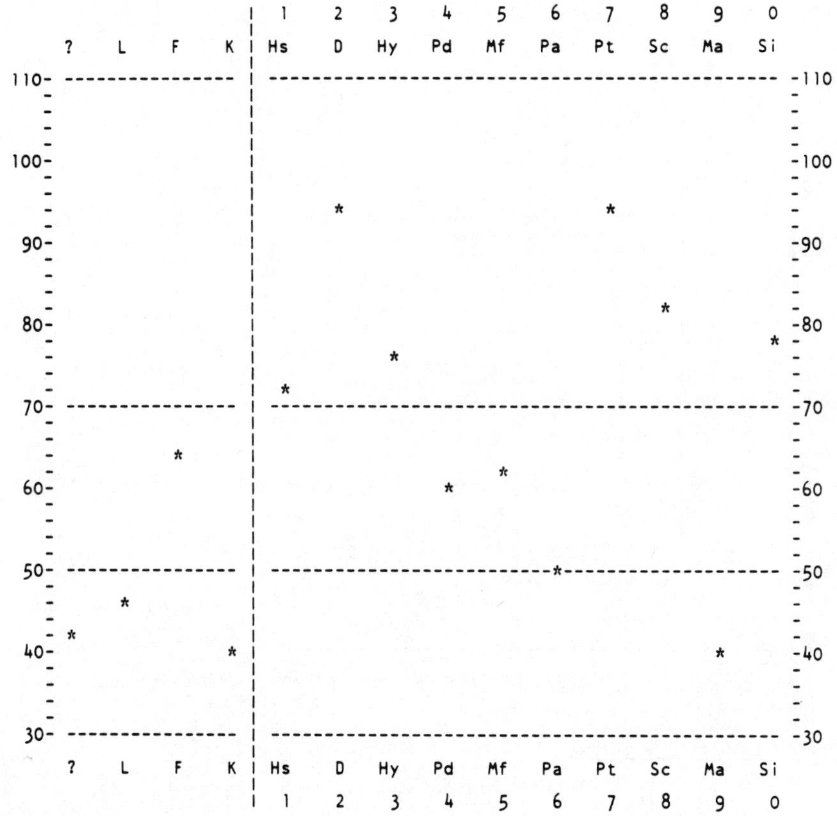

Clinical Profile Scores:

	?	L	F	K	Hs	D	Hy	Pd	Mf	Pa	Pt	Sc	Ma	Si
Raw	0	3	9	7	16	35	31	20	26	8	37	32	12	50
K-Correction					4			3			7	7	1	
T	41	46	64	40	72	94	76	60	61	50	93	82	40	77

Percent True : 57 F - K (Raw) : 2

Profile Elevation : 70.9
(Hs,D,Hy,Pd,Pa,Pt,Sc,Ma)

Welsh Code : 27*8"031'54-6/9: F-L?K:

The Minnesota Multiphasic Personality Inventory

SUPPLEMENTAL PROFILE

Client No. : 012345678 Report Date : 3-JAN-86 Page 4

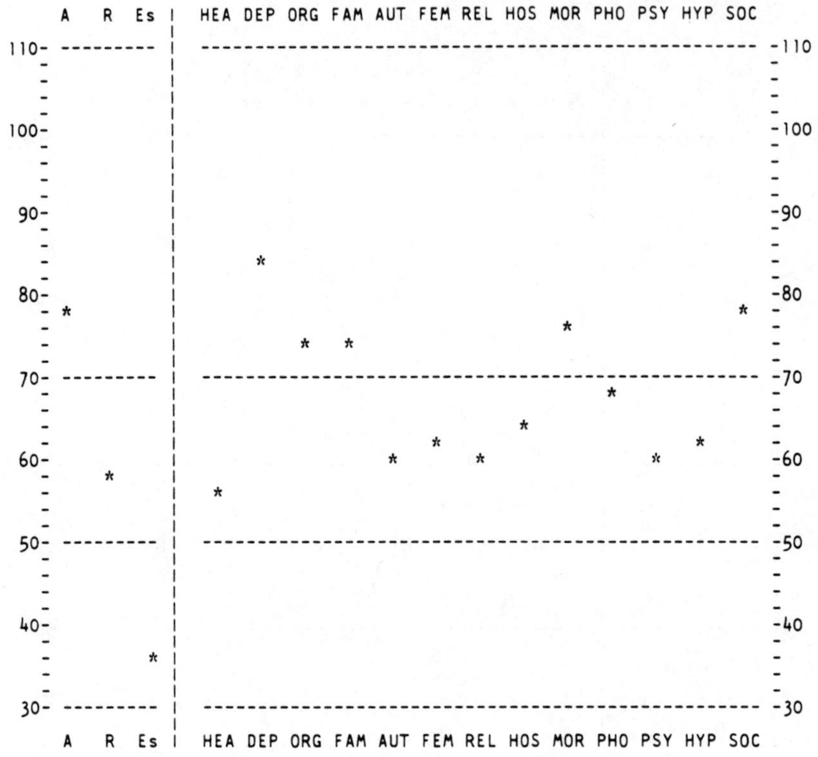

Supplemental Profile Scores:

	A	R	Es	HEA	DEP	ORG	FAM	AUT	FEM	REL	HOS	MOR	PHO	PSY	HYP	SOC
Raw	34	19	35	7	24	15	9	13	13	9	16	21	12	13	17	22
T	77	57	35	55	83	73	73	59	61	59	63	76	67	59	62	78

The Minnesota Multiphasic Personality Inventory

EXTENDED SCORE REPORT

Client No. : 012345678 Report Date : 3-JAN-86 Page 5

Supplementary Scales:	Raw Score	T Score
Dependency (Dy)	48	81
Dominance (Do)	11	39
Responsibility (Re)	19	47
Control (Cn)	31	66
College Maladjustment (Mt)	36	75
Overcontrolled Hostility (O-H)	14	56
Prejudice (Pr)	25	75
Manifest Anxiety (MAS)	41	87
MacAndrew Addiction (MAC)	17	36
Social Status (St)	14	42
Depression Subscales (Harris-Lingoes):		
Subjective Depression (D1)	21	91
Psychomotor Retardation (D2)	12	87
Physical Malfunctioning (D3)	5	63
Mental Dullness (D4)	10	90
Brooding (D5)	8	82
Hysteria Subscales (Harris-Lingoes):		
Denial of Social Anxiety (Hy1)	0	31
Need for Affection (Hy2)	1	34
Lassitude-Malaise (Hy3)	11	87
Somatic Complaints (Hy4)	12	87
Inhibition of Aggression (Hy5)	4	60
Psychopathic Deviate Subscales (Harris-Lingoes):		
Familial Discord (Pd1)	6	74
Authority Problems (Pd2)	1	30
Social Imperturbability (Pd3)	1	23
Social Alienation (Pd4a)	10	66
Self Alienation (Pd4b)	10	74
Masculinity-Femininity Subscales (Serkownek):		
Narcissism-Hypersensitivity (Mf1)	14	100
Stereotypic Feminine Interests (Mf2)	2	41
Denial of Stereo. Masculine Interests (Mf3)	6	73
Heterosexual Discomfort-Passivity (Mf4)	1	33
Introspective-Critical (Mf5)	3	46
Socially Retiring (Mf6)	2	28
Paranoia Subscales (Harris-Lingoes):		
Persecutory Ideas (Pa1)	2	50
Poignancy (Pa2)	4	62
Naivete (Pa3)	1	36
Schizophrenia Subscales (Harris-Lingoes):		
Social Alienation (Sc1a)	7	65
Emotional Alienation (Sc1b)	3	57
Lack of Ego Mastery, Cognitive (Sc2a)	9	97
Lack of Ego Mastery, Conative (Sc2b)	8	83
Lack of Ego Mastery, Def. Inhib. (Sc2c)	4	67
Bizarre Sensory Experiences (Sc3)	3	52
Hypomania Subscales (Harris-Lingoes):		
Amorality (Ma1)	1	45
Psychomotor Acceleration (Ma2)	6	66
Imperturbability (Ma3)	0	30
Ego Inflation (Ma4)	3	52
Social Introversion Subscales (Serkownek):		
Inferiority-Personal Discomfort (Si1)	26	127
Discomfort with Others (Si2)	10	87
Staid-Personal Rigidity (Si3)	8	45
Hypersensitivity (Si4)	8	88
Distrust (Si5)	8	71
Physical-Somatic Concerns (Si6)	5	79

The Minnesota Multiphasic Personality Inventory

CRITICAL ITEM LISTING

Client No. : 012345678 Report Date : 3-JAN-86 Page 6

The following Critical Items have been found to have possible significance in analyzing a client's problem situation. Although these items may serve as a source of hypotheses for further investigation, caution should be taken in interpreting individual items because they may have been inadvertently checked. Critical item numbers refer to The Group Form test booklet. Corresponding item numbers for Form R (only items 367-566 differ) can be found in the MMPI "Manual" or Volume I of "An MMPI Handbook." Corresponding item numbers for the Roche Testbook can be found in "The Clinical Use of the Automated MMPI."

ACUTE ANXIETY STATE (Koss-Butcher Critical Items)

3. I wake up fresh and rested most mornings. (F)
5. I am easily awakened by noise. (T)
13. I work under a great deal of tension. (T)
29. I am bothered by acid stomach several times a week. (T)
43. My sleep is fitful and disturbed. (T)
72. I am troubled by discomfort in the pit of my stomach every few days or oftener. (T)
152. Most nights I go to sleep without thoughts or ideas bothering me. (F)
230. I hardly ever notice my heart pounding and I am seldom short of breath. (F)
238. I have periods of such great restlessness that I cannot sit long in a chair. (T)
242. I believe I am no more nervous than most others. (F)
337. I feel anxiety about something or someone almost all the time. (T)
506. I am a high-strung person. (T)
543. Several times a week I feel that something dreadful is about to happen. (T)
555. I sometimes feel that I am about to go to pieces. (T)

DEPRESSED SUICIDAL IDEATION (Koss-Butcher Critical Items)

41. I have had periods of days, weeks, or months when I couldn't take care of things because I couldn't "get going". (T)
76. Most of the time I feel blue. (T)
84. These days I find it hard not to give up hope of amounting to something. (T)
107. I am happy most of the time. (F)
142. I certainly feel useless at times. (T)
158. I cry easily. (T)
236. I brood a great deal. (T)
252. No one cares much what happens to you. (T)
259. I have difficulty in starting to do things. (T)
301. Life is a strain for me much of the time. (T)
318. My daily life is full of things that keep me interested. (F)
418. At times I think I am no good at all. (T)
526. The future seems hopeless to me. (T)

THREATENED ASSAULT (Koss-Butcher Critical Items)

145. At times I feel like picking a fist fight with someone. (T)
234. I get mad easily and then get over it soon. (T)

SITUATIONAL STRESS DUE TO ALCOHOLISM (Koss-Butcher Critical Items)

137. I believe that my home life is as pleasant as that of most people I know. (F)

MENTAL CONFUSION (Koss-Butcher Critical Items)

100. There is something wrong with my mind. (T)
328. I find it hard to keep my mind on a task or job. (T)
335. I cannot keep my mind on one thing. (T)

Client No. : 012345678 Report Date : 3-JAN-86 Page 7

345. I often feel as if things were not real. (T)
349. I have strange and peculiar thoughts. (T)
356. I have more trouble concentrating than others seem to have. (T)

PERSECUTORY IDEAS (Koss-Butcher Critical Items)

136. I commonly wonder what hidden reason another person may have for doing something nice for me. (T)
265. It is safer to trust nobody. (T)
278. I have often felt that strangers were looking at me critically. (T)
284. I am sure I am being talked about. (T)

CHARACTEROLOGICAL ADJUSTMENT -- ANTISOCIAL ATTITUDE
(Lachar-Wrobel Critical Items)

28. When someone does me a wrong I feel I should pay him back if I can, just for the principle of the thing. (T)
250. I don't blame anyone for trying to grab everything he can get in this world. (T)
280. Most people make friends because friends are likely to be useful to them. (T)

CHARACTEROLOGICAL ADJUSTMENT -- FAMILY CONFLICT
(Lachar-Wrobel Critical Items)

21. At times I have very much wanted to leave home. (T)
137. I believe that my home life is as pleasant as that of most people I know. (F)
245. My parents and family find more fault with me than they should. (T)

SEXUAL CONCERN AND DEVIATION (Lachar-Wrobel Critical Items)

20. My sex life is satisfactory. (F)
133. I have never indulged in any unusual sex practices. (F)
179. I am worried about sex matters. (T)
297. I wish I were not bothered by thoughts about sex. (T)

SOMATIC SYMPTOMS (Lachar-Wrobel Critical Items)

23. I am troubled by attacks of nausea and vomiting. (T)
29. I am bothered by acid stomach several times a week. (T)
47. Once a week or oftener I feel suddenly hot all over, without apparent cause. (T)
55. I am almost never bothered by pains over the heart or in my chest. (F)
62. Parts of my body often have feelings like burning, tingling, crawling, or like "going to sleep." (T)
72. I am troubled by discomfort in the pit of my stomach every few days or oftener. (T)
114. Often I feel as if there were a tight band about my head. (T)
154. I have never had a fit or convulsion. (F)
174. I have never had a fainting spell. (F)
189. I feel weak all over much of the time. (T)
190. I have very few headaches. (F)
243. I have few or no pains. (F)

NCS Professional Assessment Services, P.O. Box 1416, Mpls, MN 55440

that he might work on his social relationships more effectively with a woman. More will be said of this case later when retesting or follow-up evaluation is discussed.

APPLICATIONS OF THE MMPI CLINICAL NARRATIVE REPORT

Clinicians can incorporate computerized MMPI reports into their clinical practice in many ways. As previously noted, the computerized report serves as an aid to diagnostic decisions and treatment planning. It is the clinician's responsibility to ascertain the relevance of the computer-generated information for the patient in question.

The Minnesota Report was developed as a summary view of the empirical scale and code-type correlates and the important content themes patients communicate through their responses. The availability of an MMPI report on a patient in the early stages of clinical contact can provide valuable information to guide the clinician in both the diagnostic and the treatment process.

Diagnostic Overview. Although formal clinical diagnosis is seldom the ultimate goal of a clinical psychological assessment, the report may provide information regarding likely DSM-III classification. The clinician will probably find the descriptive diagnostic information more useful for arriving at a clinical picture. Symptom patterns and problems described enable the clinician to gain an understanding of the patient's mental status and relationship problems. The report is written in a form that provides information tailored, as well as data permit, to the setting or the relevant clinical population.

Treatment Planning. The clinician may find the information provided in the treatment considerations section of the Minnesota Report valuable in determining if the patient is expressing problems that are amenable to psychological treatment and is cooperating sufficiently with the evaluation to cooperate with treatment. The MMPI also provides a great deal of information about the quality of the patient's interpersonal relationships. This is important in determining how readily the patient can become engaged in a therapeutic relationship.

Providing Patient Feedback. The computerized psychological report is a valuable aid in presenting feedback to the patient in early therapy contacts. Patients, as a rule, appreciate receiving personality information from the therapist. Actually, many people expect the expert to provide this service. Patients usually like to gain a new perspective on their problems from the vantage point of an objective test. Even patients who are less insightful and require some confrontation of their problem may find such information informative. In either case, the MMPI report is usually valuable in early therapy sessions in that it highlights problems the patient has endorsed; places these problems in the context of patient responses generally; assists in engaging the patient in treatment (or in some cases indicates a lack of need for psychological therapy); and provides some focus for therapy and may assist in the formulation of treatment goals.

As noted, patients usually respond favorably to feedback on their testing, especially if the clinician is sensitive and tactful.

In conducting feedback sessions, clinicians should:

1. Remind patients that the MMPI was administered to them in the first place in order to better understand their problems.
2. Explain briefly why the MMPI was chosen as a test for their problem. Indicate that the MMPI is the most widely used psychological test with a broad base of research.
3. Briefly describe how the MMPI was constructed by comparing the responses of patients with many types of problems.
4. Orient patients by referring to the clinical profile, showing the range of "average" scores, and highlighting any scale elevations prominent in their profile.

Although referring to the profiles and the narrative statements in the report can be very valuable for focusing patients' attention on the evaluation, it is not a good idea to allow them to review or keep a copy of the report. Patients do not have the expertise to understand the protocol and will likely misinterpret or inappropriately dwell on some insignificant element in the report. Legally, psychologists are not required to give test data to patients (Schwitzgebel and Schwitzgebel, 1980). Patients who are dissatisfied can be informed that test results can be reviewed again at a later date if the need arises.

It is a good idea to avoid technical terms or jargon when providing patient feedback. The Minnesota Report was written with the goal of eliminating as much "psychologese" as possible. Although technical expressions are often required to accurately convey information to clinicians, in most cases information is best relayed to patients in lay language rather than in technical terms.

Follow-up Testing. In some situations it is desirable to retest the patient during the course of treatment or at the end of therapy to assess change (or lack of movement). Most patients are willing to retake the test since it gives them an opportunity to view themselves at a later and hopefully better point. Follow-up testing on the MMPI usually shows marked change, and the report will probably show a reduction of the original pathology. The report may, of course, reflect "residual" problems or character problems that need to be dealt with.

John W., the patient described earlier, was seen in a cognitive-behavior treatment program for about five months.* During the first phase of therapy, for about eight sessions, the focus was on helping him acquire more adaptive skills for managing the problems he was encountering at work and for obtaining more realistic ways of appraising his own abilities. He appeared to enter into treatment in an enthusiastic and effective manner and followed homework assignments consistently. After about eight sessions his problems at work lessened. He was no longer obsessing about the inadequacies he felt and was performing the required tasks with confidence. He was receiving verbal rewards from coworkers and supervisors about his strong performance. He was retested on the MMPI at that point and produced the MMPI report shown in figure 10.2. Although dramatic improvement was shown in his level of tension and

* I wish to thank Susan Ogata, Department of Psychology, University of Minnesota, for providing information on this case.

THE MINNESOTA REPORT[TM*] Page 1

for the Minnesota Multiphasic Personality Inventory[TM]: Adult System

By James N. Butcher, Ph.D.

Client No. : 012345678 Gender : Male
Setting : Medical Age : 28
Report Date : 7-JAN-86
PAS Code Number : 111 0003

PROFILE VALIDITY

This is a valid MMPI profile. The client was quite cooperative in describing his symptoms and problems. His frank and open response to the items can be viewed as a positive indication of the individual's involvement with the evaluation. The MMPI profile is probably a good indication of his present personality functioning and symptoms.

SYMPTOMATIC PATTERN

A pattern of chronic psychological maladjustment characterizes individuals with this MMPI profile. The client is overwhelmed by anxiety, tension, and depression. He feels helpless and alone, inadequate and insecure, and believes that life is hopeless and that nothing is working out right. He attempts to control his worries through intellectualization and unproductive self-analyses, but he has difficulty concentrating and making decisions.

He is functioning at a very low level of efficiency. He tends to overreact to even minor stress, and may show rapid behavioral deterioration. He also tends to blame himself for his problems. His life-style is chaotic and disorganized, and he has a history of poor work and achievement.

He may be preoccupied with occult ideas. Obsessive-compulsive and phobic behavior are likely to make up part of the symptom pattern.

He may experience some conflicts concerning his sex-role identity. He seems somewhat insecure in his masculine role, showing a generally feminine pattern of interests. He may be somewhat uncomfortable in relationships with women.

He has difficulty managing routine affairs, and the item content he endorsed suggests a poor memory, concentration problems, and an inability to make decisions. He appears to be immobilized and withdrawn and has no energy for life. According to his response content, there is a strong possibility that he has seriously contemplated suicide. A careful evaluation of this possibility is suggested. He views his physical health as failing and reports numerous somatic concerns. He feels that life is no longer worthwhile and that he is losing control of his thought processes.

INTERPERSONAL RELATIONS

Problematic personal relationships are also characteristic of his life. He seems to lack basic social skills and is behaviorally withdrawn. He may relate to others ambivalently, never fully trusting or loving anyone. Many

---

NOTE: This MMPI interpretation can serve as a useful source of hypotheses about clients. This report is based on objectively derived scale indexes and scale interpretations that have been developed in diverse groups of patients. The personality descriptions, inferences and recommendations contained herein need to be verified by other sources of clinical information since individual clients may not fully match the prototype. The information in this report should most appropriately be used by a trained, qualified test interpreter. The information contained in this report should be considered confidential.

* "The Minnesota Report," "MMPI," and "Minnesota Multiphasic Personality Inventory" are trademarks owned by the University Press of the University of Minnesota.

Figure 10.2. Computer printout of the Minnesota Report (Narrative Report Section and MMPI Profile) for John W., at retest following eight weeks of stress inoculation treatment.

individuals with this profile never establish lasting, intimate relationships.

He is a rather introverted person who has some difficulties meeting other people. He is probably shy and may be uneasy and somewhat rigid and overcontrolled in social situations.

BEHAVIORAL STABILITY

This is a rather chronic behavioral pattern. Individuals with this profile live a disorganized and pervasively unhappy existence. They may have episodes of more intense and disturbed behavior resulting from an elevated stress level.

DIAGNOSTIC CONSIDERATIONS

Individuals with this profile show a severe psychological disorder and would probably be diagnosed as severely neurotic with an Anxiety Disorder or Dysthymic Disorder in a Schizoid Personality. The possibility of a more severe psychotic disorder, such as Schizophrenic Disorder, should be considered, however.

Individuals with this profile present some suicide risk and further evaluation of this possibility should be undertaken.

TREATMENT CONSIDERATIONS

Individuals with this MMPI profile often receive psychotropic medications for their depressed mood or intense anxiety. Many patients with this profile seek psychological treatment for their problems. Indeed, individuals with this profile usually require psychological treatment for their problems along with any medication that is given. Since many of their problems tend to be chronic ones, an intensive therapeutic effort might be required in order to bring about any significant change. Patients with this profile typically have many psychological and situational concerns; thus it is often difficult to maintain a focus in treatment.

He probably needs a great deal of emotional support at this time. His low self-esteem and feelings of inadequacy make it difficult for him to get energized toward therapeutic action. His expectancies for positive change in therapy may be low. Instilling a positive, treatment expectant attitude is important for him if treatment is to be successful.

Individuals with this profile tend to be overideational and given to unproductive rumination. They tend not to do well in unstructured, insight-oriented therapy and may actually deteriorate in functioning if they are asked to be introspective. He might respond more to supportive treatment of a directive, goal-oriented type.

Individuals with this profile present some suicide risk and precautions should be considered.

THE MINNESOTA REPORT Page 3

for the Minnesota Multiphasic Personality Inventory : Adult System

By James N. Butcher, Ph.D.

CLINICAL PROFILE

Client No. : U12345678
Setting : Medical
Report Date : 7-JAN-86

Gender : Male
Age : 28

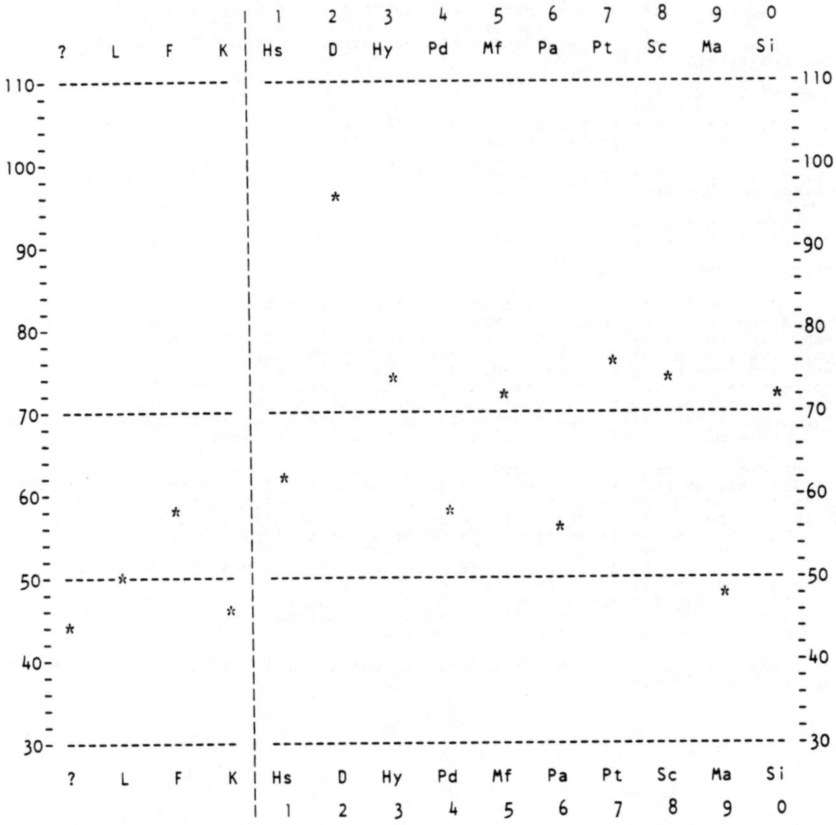

Clinical Profile Scores:

	?	L	F	K	Hs	D	Hy	Pd	Mf	Pa	Pt	Sc	Ma	Si
Raw	16	4	6	10	11	36	29	18	31	10	25	25	14	45
K-Correction					5			4			10	10	2	
T	44	50	58	46	62	96	73	57	71	56	75	74	48	72

Percent True : 50 F - K (Raw) : -4

Profile Elevation : 67.6
(Hs,D,Hy,Pd,Pa,Pt,Sc,Ma)

Welsh Code : 2*78305'1-46/9: FL/K?:

The Minnesota Multiphasic Personality Inventory

SUPPLEMENTAL PROFILE

Client No. : 012345678 Report Date : 7-JAN-86 Page 4

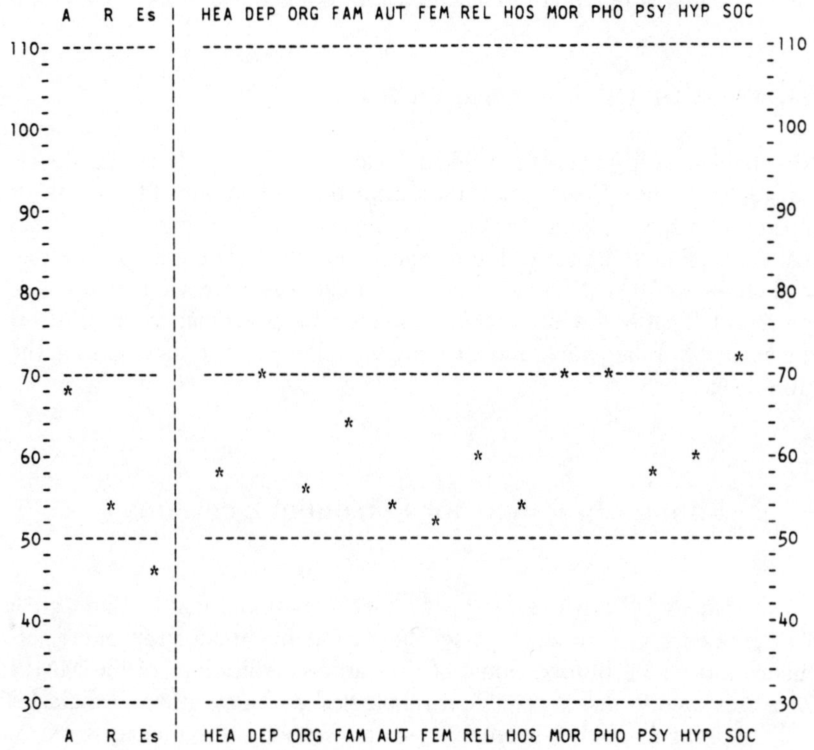

Supplemental Profile Scores:

	A	R	Es	HEA	DEP	ORG	FAM	AUT	FEM	REL	HOS	MOR	PHO	PSY	HYP	SOC
Raw	26	17	41	8	17	8	7	11	10	9	11	18	13	12	16	19
T	67	53	45	58	69	56	64	54	52	59	53	70	70	57	59	72

anxiety (reflected in the lowered score on scale 7), he still showed some problems with social skills and his depressed mood. The therapist provided him feedback on the MMPI, noting both the reduction in anxiety and tension and more confidence in himself probably resulting from his increased capability of dealing with stress at work. The retesting also showed that he still had some psychological discomfort and low mood along with some social isolation. The focus in treatment was shifted at that point to dealing with his loneliness, isolation, and low mood.

VALIDATION OF THE MINNESOTA REPORT

Moreland and Onstad (1985) studied the accuracy of the Minnesota Report by having clinicians rate sections of the narrative report on one of their patients compared to a second bogus report. The bogus report was constructed from modal descriptions relevant to the patient's code type. The authors reported that all sections of the Minnesota Report were rated as more accurate than the bogus report. That is, the interpretations in the patient's actual narrative report fit the behavior of the patient more closely than the narrative statements in the bogus report.

Minnesota Report for Personnel Decisions

The use of the MMPI in screening personnel for positions that require a great deal of public trust or in which personality factors might adversely affect performance has a long history. Some of the earliest applications of the MMPI involved research to detect possible psychological problems among candidates for pilot training or nuclear submarine warfare school in the military services. An extensive literature also exists on using the MMPI for screening in civilian occupations such as police and security guards, nuclear power plant employees, and air traffic controllers, where psychological screening is often required by statute. In these careers judgment factors are often critical; emotional instability could produce catastrophic results.

The use of the MMPI in screening sensitive occupations has been well documented (Beutler et al., 1985; Butcher, 1979, 1985; McCormick, 1984), and there is a growing empirical basis of research support for using the instrument as an aid to personnel decisions.

The Minnesota Personnel Reports (University of Minnesota Press, 1984) were developed as an aid to psychological screening of applicants for positions that require emotional stability. The reports were designed as screening aids or consultations to the clinical or industrial psychologist responsible for the screening and are not recommended as a substitute for clinical judgment in the assessment process.

Two types of screening reports were developed to meet differing MMPI consultation requirements: The Minnesota Personnel Interpretive Report (University of Minnesota Press, 1984) provides scoring of a number of MMPI scales and indices and prints out a comprehensive narrative report on the individual, and the Minnesota Personnel Screening Report (University of Minnesota Press, 1984) scores the MMPI and provides a summary evaluation in the form of ratings on several dimensions pertinent to personnel decisions. Each of these MMPI personnel report forms will be discussed and illustrated to give the reader an idea of the range and format of information they provide.

THE MINNESOTA PERSONNEL INTERPRETIVE REPORT

The Minnesota Personnel Interpretive Report provides the user with the following information:

1. An MMPI profile with both raw and T-scores for the MMPI validity and clinical scales.
2. A profile of the Wiggins Content scales, the A and R scales, and the *Es* scale. In addition, a number of additional scales are scored: the MacAndrew Scale, Dominance, Responsibility, Cynicism, Prejudice scales, and the Taylor Manifest Anxiety scale.
3. A list of potentially significant content themes. This list is summarized from a number of content indicators in the MMPI (such as the Harris-Lingoes subscales, the Wiggins scales, and the Koss-Butcher Critical Items) and reflects item content endorsed by the applicant that might signal problem areas or points of concern.
4. A narrative report that describes the individual's personality. The report begins with an analysis of the individual's test-taking attitudes. The individual's interpersonal relationships and social adjustment are next considered. Personal stability and possible adjustment problems and symptoms are described, and the report concludes with a statement of possible employment problems that might arise with this individual.

   The narrative report is tailored to the specific occupation being screened. Seven occupational contexts are included in the system in order to allow for tailoring of the report to various settings. These occupations are law enforcement, airline pilot, air traffic controller, fire department personnel, seminary applicant, medical or mental health professional, and other.

USE OF THE MINNESOTA PERSONNEL INTERPRETIVE REPORT

Jack W., age thirty-five, an experienced pilot for a small air cargo firm, was applying for a job with a large, international air carrier. He had the requisite flying background and met the educational requirements of a four-year college degree. Jack was single and had been working for his current employer for about six months. Prior to his current job he had worked for three other air freight companies since his graduation from college.

On cognitive ability testing Jack showed some deficits in the area of Visual

Motor Performance. He obtained only a scale score of 6 on the Wechsler Block Design Test and a scale score of 7 on the Coding Subtest. The relatively low scores on these subtests suggests that he would have difficulty learning and performing important aviation-related tasks. His performance appeared to be lowered by carelessness and premature indication that he was finished on some Block Designs that were, in fact, incomplete. In addition to the impulse control problem that showed up on the MMPI report (see figure 10.3), Jack showed some indication of an impulsive lifestyle: he had received four speeding tickets in the past two years.

THE MINNESOTA PERSONNEL SCREENING REPORT

The Minnesota Personnel Screening Report was developed to provide low-cost summary evaluations of applicants on several relevant variables. The report contains all of the elements of the MMPI Personnel Interpretive Report except the narrative report. Decision rules for evaluating aspects of the clinical profile and a number of special MMPI scales were programmed. The decision rules were compiled through a review of the MMPI personnel selection research literature and through clinical experience in using the MMPI with relevant clinical and applicant populations. Five areas of behavior are rated:

Openness to Evaluation. These ratings are based on decision rules to evaluate the individual's test-taking responses and provide an assessment of the credibility of the evaluation.

Social Facility. The decision rules underlying this rating incorporate information as to the applicant's social skills and social adjustment. Information for this dimension is obtained from several interpretive areas of the MMPI including the *Si* scale, the MMPI scale elevations, the Wiggins Content scales, and the Serkownek scales.

Addiction Potential. This rating is based on interpretation of the MacAndrew Alcoholism scale and the various MMPI codes that have been associated with substance abuse.

Stress Tolerance. This complex rating is designed to assess the individual's ability to tolerate stress and frustration. The MMPI factors that comprise this rating include: the individual's characteristic mode of defense, tendency to act impulsively, feelings of confidence and self-esteem, tendency to feel alienated, and other psychopathological factors. Personality characteristics that may predispose the individual to react negatively under stressful situations are taken into account.

Overall Adjustment. Each individual is classified into one category of overall adjustment based on the MMPI profile and other MMPI-based indices. The adjustment ratings are excellent, good, adequate, problems possible, poor, and indeterminate.

THE MINNESOTA PERSONNEL INTERPRETIVE REPORT TM* Page 1

for the Minnesota Multiphasic Personality Inventory TM

By James N. Butcher, Ph.D.

Client No. : 000067890 Gender : Male
Report Date : 7-JAN-86 Age : 23
PAS Code Number : 531 0002
Occupation : Flight Crew

PROFILE VALIDITY

This is a highly defensive MMPI profile that is characteristic of some individuals who are being evaluated at the request of another person or agency. The applicant responded so defensively that the resulting clinical profile is likely to be an underestimate of his problems and personal maladjustment. He has attempted to minimize his faults and to present a very positive self-image.

The applicant has not cooperated in a frank and open manner, and has failed to admit to problems and faults that most people would endorse. Consequently, his self-appraisal should be considered an incomplete view of his personal adjustment.

PERSONAL ADJUSTMENT

The applicant may be somewhat immature and impulsive and may act in a selfish and pleasure-oriented way. He appears to have a low tolerance for frustration and may manipulate others for his own ends. He may not accept responsibility for his own problems but tends to blame others. His behavior may be unreliable and may result in a spotty work or achievement record and other job difficulties. He seems to lack clear goals and may drift from job to job. Individuals with this profile are often viewed as aggressive and may behave in a hostile manner at times, creating difficulties for others.

INTERPERSONAL RELATIONS

He is likeable and effective at creating a good impression. Despite his charm, he may not have a genuine interest in or concern for others, tending to use them instead for his own gains. He may have disrupted family or social relationships since he accepts little responsibility for his interpersonal difficulties and has problems forming warm, close relationships.

Quite outgoing and sociable, he has a strong need to be around others. Although he is gregarious and effective at gaining recognition from others, his personal relationships may appear somewhat superficial. He may be rather spontaneous and expressive and may manipulate others, especially to gain social attention.

The content of this applicant's MMPI responses suggests the following additional information concerning his interpersonal relations. He meets people with ease and fits into most social situations comfortably. He

---

NOTE: This MMPI interpretation can serve as a useful source of hypotheses about clients applying for positions in which stable pysychological adjustment has been determined to be essential for success on the job. The MMPI was not originally developed for use in personnel selection, however, and contains a number of items that some people believe to be irrelevant or inappropriate for that purpose. This report is based upon empirical descriptions derived largely from clinical populations. Caution should be taken in applying these interpretations in a pre-employment screening situation. The MMPI should NOT be used as the SOLE means of determining a candidate's suitability for employment. The information in this report should be used by qualified test interpretation specialists ONLY.

Figure 10.3. Computer printout of the Minnesota Personnel Report for Jack W., an airline pilot applicant.

enjoys being with other people and has little discomfort in groups. His tendencies toward expressive behavior, impulsiveness and exhibitionism make him, at times, the "life of the party." He tends to be interpersonally dominant, asserting a high degree of self-confidence and forcefulness. He willingly expresses strong opinions. He reports that his family relationships are good and that his home life is pleasant. He does not view himself as being overly competitive or aggressive toward others.

BEHAVIORAL STABILITY

He may have frequent social and personal conflicts and may find it difficult to maintain a steady, trouble-free life. The MMPI profile itself is quite stable, however, and not likely to change much over time.

POSSIBLE EMPLOYMENT PROBLEMS

Flight crew applicants with this MMPI profile should be carefully evaluated for the possibility of impulsive behavior or poor judgment. A history of nonconforming or acting-out behavior is possible with this profile.

Because this applicant tends to become bored easily and seeks thrills, he may have problems keeping a steady pace in life and is likely to be considered unreliable at times. He may have difficulties with authority and may resist convention and rules, which might cause interpersonal problems at work.

THE MINNESOTA PERSONNEL INTERPRETIVE REPORT Page 3

for the Minnesota Multiphasic Personality Inventory

By James N. Butcher, Ph.D.

CLINICAL PROFILE

Client No. : 000067890
Report Date : 7-JAN-86
Occupation : Flight Crew

Gender : Male
Age : 23

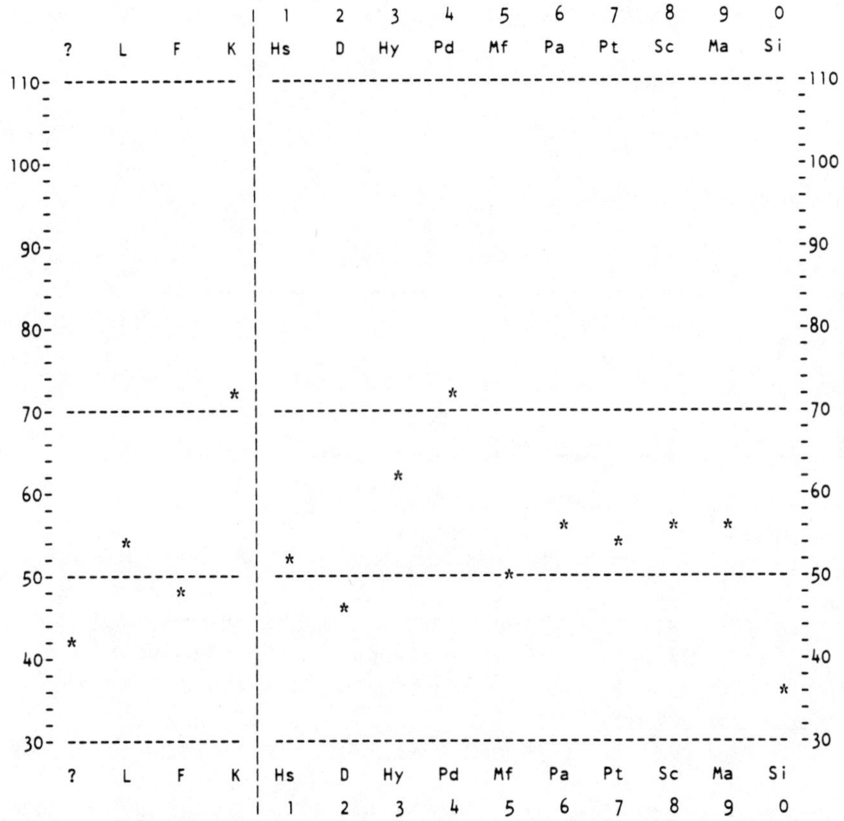

Clinical Profile Scores:

	?	L	F	K	Hs	D	Hy	Pd	Mf	Pa	Pt	Sc	Ma	Si
Raw	0	5	2	24	0	15	23	18	20	10	1	1	14	11
K-Correction					12			10			24	24	5	
T	41	53	48	72	52	46	62	71	49	56	54	55	55	36

Percentage True : 29

F - K (Raw) : -22

Average Profile Elevation : 56.4
(Hs,D,Hy,Pd,Pa,Pt,Sc,Ma)

Disturbance Index (DsI) : 460

Welsh Code : 4'3-68971/52:0# K'L/F?:

The Minnesota Multiphasic Personality Inventory
SUPPLEMENTAL PROFILE

Client No. : 000067890   Report Date : 7-JAN-86   Page 4

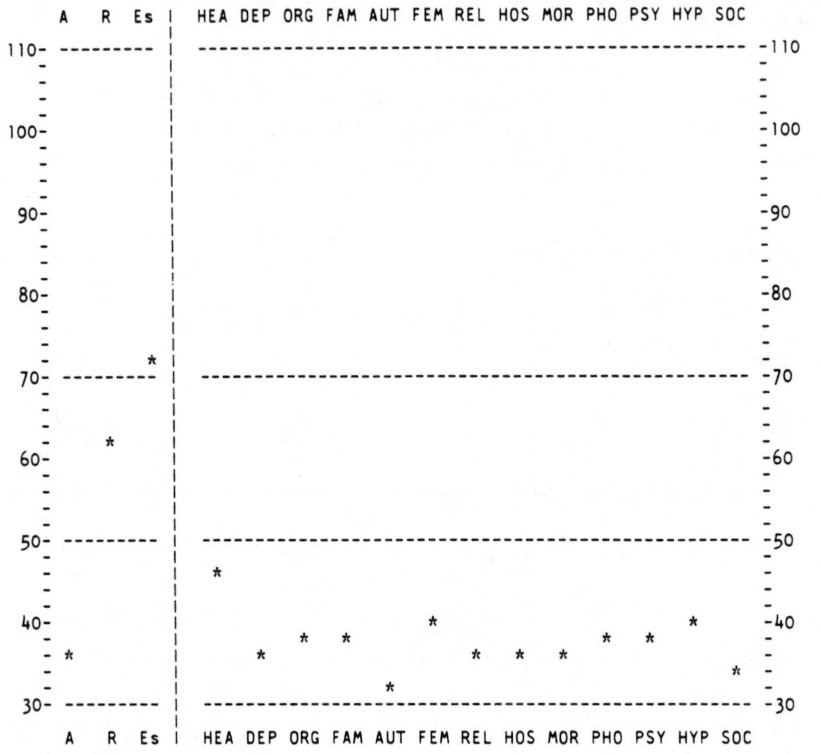

Supplemental Profile Scores:

Raw	0	21	58	3	0	0	1	2	5	2	2	1	1	1	7	1
T	35	61	72	45	36	37	38	31	39	36	35	36	38	38	39	34

The Minnesota Multiphasic Personality Inventory

EXTENDED SCORE REPORT

Client No. : 000067890 Report Date : 7-JAN-86 Page 5

Supplementary Scales:	Raw Score	T Score
Dependency (Dy)	1	30
Dominance (Do)	21	68
Responsibility (Re)	23	57
College Maladjustment (Mt)	1	31
Overcontrolled Hostility (O-H)	17	66
Prejudice (Pr)	2	32
Manifest Anxiety (MAS)	3	34
MacAndrew Addiction (MAC)	18	39
Cynicism (CYN)	0	26
Social Status (St)	24	64
Favorable Impression (Fi)	19	77
Depression Subscales (Harris-Lingoes):		
Subjective Depression (D1)	1	33
Psychomotor Retardation (D2)	6	54
Physical Malfunctioning (D3)	2	42
Mental Dullness (D4)	0	40
Brooding (D5)	0	38
Hysteria Subscales (Harris-Lingoes):		
Denial of Social Anxiety (Hy1)	6	64
Need for Affection (Hy2)	12	79
Lassitude-Malaise (Hy3)	0	41
Somatic Complaints (Hy4)	0	39
Inhibition of Aggression (Hy5)	3	53
Psychopathic Deviate Subscales (Harris-Lingoes):		
Familial Discord (Pd1)	1	45
Authority Problems (Pd2)	9	80
Social Imperturbability (Pd3)	11	64
Social Alienation (Pd4a)	2	38
Self Alienation (Pd4b)	1	39
Masculinity-Femininity Subscales (Serkownek):		
Narcissism-Hypersensitivity (Mf1)	1	28
Stereotypic Feminine Interests (Mf2)	1	34
Denial of Stereo. Masculine Interests (Mf3)	2	43
Heterosexual Discomfort-Passivity (Mf4)	2	46
Introspective-Critical (Mf5)	3	46
Socially Retiring (Mf6)	8	70
Paranoia Subscales (Harris-Lingoes):		
Persecutory Ideas (Pa1)	0	41
Poignancy (Pa2)	1	42
Naivete (Pa3)	8	71
Schizophrenia Subscales (Harris-Lingoes):		
Social Alienation (Sc1a)	0	35
Emotional Alienation (Sc1b)	0	31
Lack of Ego Mastery, Cognitive (Sc2a)	0	41
Lack of Ego Mastery, Conative (Sc2b)	0	39
Lack of Ego Mastery, Def. Inhib. (Sc2c)	0	41
Bizarre Sensory Experiences (Sc3)	0	40
Hypomania Subscales (Harris-Lingoes):		
Amorality (Ma1)	2	52
Psychomotor Acceleration (Ma2)	3	45
Imperturbability (Ma3)	6	65
Ego Inflation (Ma4)	1	40

The Minnesota Multiphasic Personality Inventory

Client No. : 000067890 Report Date : 7-JAN-86 Page 6

Social Introversion Subscales (Serkownek):

Inferiority-Personal Discomfort (Si1)	0	13
Discomfort with Others (Si2)	0	24
Staid-Personal Rigidity (Si3)	7	39
Hypersensitivity (Si4)	1	35
Distrust (Si5)	2	32
Physical-Somatic Concerns (Si6)	1	44

CONTENT THEMES

The following Content Themes may serve as a source of hypotheses for further investigation. These content themes summarize similar item responses that appear with greater frequency with this applicant than with most people.

May keep problems to himself too much.

May harbor hostility toward others.

May have antisocial attitudes.

May have some unconventional beliefs or attitudes.

May show irresponsible attitudes.

May have problems with authority.

May be overly sensitive to criticism.

NCS Professional Assessment Services, P.O. Box 1416, Mpls, MN 55440

The rating section of the Minnesota Personnel Screening Report is illustrated in figure 10.4. The MMPI profile of the client who was described in the Minnesota Personnel Interpretive Report section, Jack W., an airline pilot applicant, was processed through the decision rules. It can be seen that the Overall Adjustment rating shows problems possible and suggests that additional screening is indicated.

VALIDATION OF THE MINNESOTA PERSONNEL SCREENING REPORT

Research demonstrating that the MMPI Screening Report effectively discriminates individuals and appropriately classifies them into correct groups has been conducted. Butcher and Moreland (1985) provided some illustrative classification rates for several different groups, both patient and nonpatient. They used the decision rules to classify a number of known clinical and normal groups in order to determine how the classification rates compared for the groups. They reported the percentages of individuals who were correctly classified as having possible problems according to the Minnesota Personnel Report decision rules in a wide variety of personnel and clinical settings. For example, 76.4 percent of inpatients and 75 percent of outpatients were classified by the decision rules as having psychological adjustment problems, while 24 percent of nuclear power applicants and 29.6 percent of police applicants were so classified. These rates of maladjustment among job applicants were comparable to the rates found among normal populations in the national epidemiological studies of mental disorder (Meyers et al., 1984; Regier et al., 1984).

In another recent empirical study Muller and Bruno (1986) compared the effectiveness of the Minnesota Screening Rules with the Inwald Personality Inventory (IPI) in detecting psychopathology among police applicants. They found that the MMPI and IPI agreed on about 69 percent of the cases in which about 52 percent of the applicants were considered problem-free and 17 percent of cases were problematic. The IPI was found to be more susceptible to faking good. Both the MMPI and IPI were effective at identifying problems within the normal range of profiles. Of the twenty cases the study rejected as unfit for duty as a police officer, both the MMPI and IPI agreed on fifteen cases. However, the MMPI correctly identified all twenty cases. In addition, the MMPI Screening Rules were "remarkably accurate" (85 percent) for detecting addiction potential.

```
                                                 TM*
            THE MINNESOTA PERSONNEL SCREENING REPORT          Page  1
                                                           TM
       for the Minnesota Multiphasic Personality Inventory

                    By James N. Butcher, Ph.D.

 Client No. : 000067890                          Gender : Male
 Report Date :  7-JAN-86                         Age :  23
 PAS Code Number :            531 0002
 Occupation : Flight Crew


                      ******************************
                      *                            *
                      *   OPENNESS TO EVALUATION   *
                      *                            *
                      ******************************

OVERLY     QUITE                      OVERLY
FRANK      OPEN       ADEQUATE        CAUTIOUS      GUARDED      INDETERMINATE
-----------------------------------X---------------------------------


                      ******************************
                      *                            *
                      *      SOCIAL FACILITY       *
                      *                            *
                      ******************************

                                    PROBLEMS
EXCELLENT      GOOD       ADEQUATE   POSSIBLE      POOR      INDETERMINATE
---------------------------------------------------X-------------------


                      ******************************
                      *                            *
                      *    ADDICTION POTENTIAL     *
                      *                            *
                      *      (STANDARD LEVEL)      *
                      ******************************

        NO APPARENT       PROBLEMS
LOW       PROBLEM         POSSIBLE      MODERATE      HIGH      INDETERMINATE
---------------------------X-------------------------------------------------

    This index is associated with Addiction Potential, it does not
confirm existing abuse.

 ------------------------------------------------------------------
 NOTE:  This MMPI report can serve as a useful guide for employment
 decisions in which personality adjustment is considered important for
 success on the job.  The decision rules on which these classifications
 are based were developed through a review of the empirical literature on
 the use of the MMPI with "normal-range" individuals (including job
 applicants) and the author's practical experience using the test in
 employment selection.  The report can assist psychologists and physicians
 involved in personnel selection by providing an "outside opinion" about
 the applicant's adjustment.  The MMPI should NOT be used as the SOLE
 means of determining the applicant's suitability for employment.  The
 information in this report should be used by qualified test interpretation
 specialists ONLY.

              MINNESOTA MULTIPHASIC PERSONALITY INVENTORY
                  Copyright THE UNIVERSITY OF MINNESOTA
          1943, Renewed 1970.  This Report 1983.  All rights reserved.
   Scored and Distributed Exclusively by NCS PROFESSIONAL ASSESSMENT SERVICES
                Under License From The University of Minnesota

*     "The Minnesota Personnel Screening Report," "MMPI,  " and "Minnesota
 Multiphasic Personality Inventory" are trademarks owned by the University
 Press of the University of Minnesota.
```

Figure 10.4. Computer printout of the Minnesota Personnel Screening Rules for airline pilot applicant Jack W.

```
Client No. : 000067890            Report Date :  7-JAN-86          Page  2


                              ******************************
                              *                            *
                              *     STRESS TOLERANCE       *
                              *                            *
                              ******************************

                                              PROBLEMS
HIGH         GOOD         ADEQUATE            POSSIBLE         LOW        INDETERMINATE
------------------------X------------------------------------------------------------


                              ******************************
                              *                            *
                              *    OVERALL ADJUSTMENT      *
                              *                            *
                              ******************************

                                              PROBLEMS
EXCELLENT        GOOD        ADEQUATE         POSSIBLE         POOR       INDETERMINATE
------------------------------------------------------------X-----------------------

     His MMPI responses indicate that his psychological adjustment is
likely to be poor.

     This applicant should be evaluated further to determine if he
has adjustment problems.

   NCS Professional Assessment Services, P.O. Box 1416, Mpls, MN  55440
```

Summary

The MMPI became the early focus of attention among computer system developers because of its broad research base and frequency of use. A wealth of empirical research—over ten thousand books and articles—support its application in a wide variety of clinical settings. Moreover, in 1954 Meehl provided strong theoretical justification for actuarial interpretation when he demonstrated that objective methods of actuarially combining data produced more adequate predictions than those based on clinical methods. Several early MMPI interpretation systems became available in the 1960s and were readily accepted by clinical practitioners. These early interpretation systems, though somewhat rudimentary compared with the more extensive interpretation systems available today, were innovative landmarks in the history of psychological assessment. The MMPI interpretation systems discussed and illustrated in this chapter, the Minnesota Reports, were developed in an effort to provide a more extensive set of clinical descriptors for a wide range of clinical and normal populations.

REFERENCES

Beutler, L., Storm, A., Kirkish, P., Scogin, F., and Gaines, J. A. (1985). Parameters in the prediction of police officer performance. *Professional Psychology*, *16*(2), 324–335.

Butcher, J. N. (1979). The use of the MMPI in personnel selection. In J. N. Butcher (Ed.), *New developments in the use of the MMPI* (pp. 165–202). Minneapolis, MN: University of Minnesota Press.

Butcher, J. N. (1985). Personality assessment in industry: Theoretical issues and illustrations. In H. J. Bernardin and D. A. Bownas (Eds.), *Personality assessment in organizations* (pp. 277–310). New York: Praeger.

Butcher, J. N., and Moreland, K. L. (1985). *Screening for psychopathology: Detection of potential problems in applicants for critical occupations*. Paper presented at the Workshops on Clinical Applications of the MMPI, Minneapolis, MN.

Dahlstrom, W. W., Welsh, G. S., and Dahlstrom, L. E. (1972). *An MMPI handbook: Vol. 1*. Minneapolis, MN: University of Minnesota Press.

Fowler, R. D. (1965). *Purposes and usefulness of the Alabama program for the automatic interpretation of the MMPI*. Paper presented at 73rd annual meeting of the American Psychological Association, Chicago.

Fowler, R. D. (1967). Computer interpretation of personality tests: The automated psychologist. *Comprehensive Psychiatry*, 8, 455–467.

Fowler, R. D. (1969). Automated interpretation of personality test data. In J. N. Butcher (Ed.), *MMPI: Research developments and clinical applications* (pp. 105–126). New York: McGraw-Hill.

Gilberstadt, H., and Duker, J. (1965). *A handbook for clinical and actuarial MMPI interpretation*. Philadelphia: Saunders.

Goldberg, L. R. (1965). Diagnosticians vs. diagnostic signs: The diagnosis of psychosis vs. neurosis from the MMPI. *Psychological Monographs*, 79 (W 602).

Graham, J. R. (1977). *The MMPI: A practical guide*. New York: Oxford University Press.

Graham, J. R., and McCord, G. (in press). Interpretation of moderately elevated MMPI scores for normal subjects. *Journal of Personality Assessment*.

Grayson, H. M. (1951, June). *Psychological admissions testing program and manual*. Los Angeles: Veterans Administration Center, Neuropsychiatric Hospital.

Greene, R. L. (1980). *The MMPI: An interpretive manual*. New York: Grune & Stratton.

Gynther, M. and Burkhart, G. (1983). Are subtle MMPI items expendable? In J. N. Butcher and C. D. Spielberger (Eds.), *Advances in personality assessment: Vol. 2* (pp. 115–132). Hillsdale, NJ: Lawrence Erlbaum.

Halbower, C. C. (1955). *A comparison of actuarial versus clinical prediction to classes discriminated by MMPI*. Unpublished doctoral dissertation, University of Minnesota.

Henrichs, T. (1964). Objective configural rules for discriminating MMPI profiles in a psychiatric population. *Journal of Clinical Psychology*, 20, 157–159.

Henrichs, T. (1966). A note on the extension of MMPI configural rules. *Journal of Clinical Psychology*, 22, 51–52.

Koss, M. P. (1980). Assessing psychological emergencies with the MMPI. *Clinical Notes on the MMPI*. (Roche Psychiatric Service Institute Monograph Series).

Koss, M. P., and Butcher, J. N. (1973). A comparison of psychiatric patient's self report with other sources of clinical information. *Journal of Research in Personality*, 7, 225–236.

Koss, M. P., Butcher, J. N., and Hoffman, N. G. (1976). The MMPI critical items: How well do they work? *Journal of Consulting and Clinical Psychology*, 44, 921–928.

Lachar, D. (1974). *The MMPI: Clinical assessment and automated interpretation*. Los Angeles: Western Psychological Services.

Lachar, D., and Wrobel, T. A. (1979). Validating clinician's hunches: Construction of a new MMPI critical item set. *Journal of Consulting and Clinical Psychology*, 47, 227–284.

Lewandowski, D., and Graham, J. R. (1972). Empirical correlates of frequently occurring two-point MMPI code types: A replicated study. *Journal of Consulting and Clinical Psychology*, 39, 467–472.

Lubin, B., Larsen, R. M., and Matarazzo, J. (1984). Patterns of psychological test usage in the United States 1935–1982. *American Psychologist*, 39, 451–454.

MacAndrew, C. (1965). The differentiation of male alcoholic outpatients from nonalcoholic psychiatric patients by means of the MMPI. *Quarterly Journal of Studies on Alcohol, 26,* 238–246.

McCormick, A. (1984). *Good-cop/bad-cop: The use of the MMPI in the selection of law enforcement officers*. Paper presented at the 19th Annual Symposium in Recent Developments in the Use of the MMPI, St. Petersburg, FL.

Marks, P. A., Seeman, W., and Haller, D. (1975). *The actuarial use of the MMPI with adolescents and adults*. Baltimore: Williams & Wilkins.

Meehl, P. E. (1954). *Clinical versus statistical prediction: A theoretical analysis and review of the evidence*. Minneapolis, MN: University of Minnesota Press.

Megargee, E. I, and Bohn, M. J. (1977). A new classification for criminal offenders, IV: Empirically determined characteristics of the ten types. *Criminal Justice and Behavior*, 4, 149–210.

Meyers, J. K., Weissman, W. M., Tischler, G. L., Holzer, C. E., Leaf, P. J., Orvaaschel, H., Anthony, J. C., Boyd, J. H., Burke, J. D., Kramer, M., and Stoltzman, R. (1984). Six-month prevalence of psychiatric disorders in three communities. *Archives of General Psychiatry*, *41*, 959–967.

Moreland, K. L., and Onstad, J. A. (1985, March). *Validity of the Minnesota Clinical Report. I: Mental health outpatients*. Paper presented at the 20th Annual Symposium on Recent Developments in the Use of the MMPI, Honolulu.

Muller, B. P., and Bruno, L. N. (1986). *The MMPI and Inwald Personality Inventory (IPI) in the psychological screening of police candidates*. Paper presented at the 21st Annual Symposium on Recent Developments in the Use of the MMPI, Clearwater, FL.

Pearson, J. S., Swenson, W. M., Rome, H. P. Mataya, P., and Brannick, T. L. (1965). Development of a computer system for scoring and interpretation of the Minnesota Multiphasic Personality Inventories in a medical clinic. *Annals of the New York Academy of Sciences*, *126*, 682–692.

Regier, D. A., Meyers, J. K., Kramer, M., Robins, L. N., Blazer, D. G., Hough, R. L., Eaton, W. W., and Locke, B. Z. (1984). The NIMH epidemiologic catchment area program. *Archives of General Psychiatry*, *41*, 934–941.

Rome, H. P., Swenson, W. M., Mataya, P., McCarthy, C. E., Pearson, J. S., Keating, F. R., and Hathaway, S. R. (1962). Symposium on automation technics in personality assessment. *Proceedings of the Staff Meetings of the Mayo Clinic*, *37*, 61–82.

Schwitzgebel, R. L., and Schwitzgebel, R. K. (1980). *Law and psychological practice*. New York: Wiley.

University of Minnesota Press. (1982). *User's Guide for the Minnesota Report*. Minneapolis, MN: National Computer Systems.

University of Minnesota Press. (1984). *User's guide for the Minnesota Report: Personnel selection system*. Minneapolis, MN: National Computer Systems.

Welsh, G. S. (1956). Factor dimensions A and R. In B. S. Welsh and W. G. Dahlstrom (Eds.), *Basic readings on the MMPI in psychology and medicine* (pp. 264–281). Minneapolis, MN. University of Minnesota Press, 1956.

Wiggins, J. S. (1969). Content dimensions in the MMPI. In J. N. Butcher (Ed.), *MMPI: Research Developments and Clinical Applications* (pp. 127–180). New York: McGraw-Hill.

11

Computer-Based Interpretation of the 16 PF: The Karson Clinical Report in Contemporary Practice

Samuel Karson and Jerry W. O'Dell

The Karson Clinical Report (KCR) is a popular interpretation system for the Sixteen Personality Factor Questionnaire (16 PF). It was developed in the early 1970s because of the writers' dissatisfaction with computer personality interpretation programs existing at the time. As we shall explain later in this chapter, most other systems of the period centered on the Minnesota Multiphasic Personality Inventory (MMPI), a test that says comparatively little about the normal, positive aspects of personality. The 16 PF covers the normal personality well, but early writings about it were often highly abstract and difficult for clinicians to understand. We hoped to alleviate this situation with the automated program.

Unlike many interpretation systems that use elaborate sets of configural rules to generate comments, the KCR is "clinician-modeled." That is, the program attempts to emulate the thought processes of a single clinician (SK) as he interprets a 16 PF protocol. This is a somewhat novel approach to the problem of automated interpretation, but we have found it useful.

Work on the KCR was greatly enhanced by our program of research on the 16 PF, published in the late 1960s and early 1970s, and also by the writing of our book, A *Guide to the Clinical Use of the 16 PF* (Karson and O'Dell, 1976). In a sense, we both totally immersed ourselves in the test for several years. We believe that this sort of concentration is essential for development of any satisfactory interpretation system.

Finally, we must admit that we developed the KCR, in large measure, simply because it was a challenge. The computer was a comparatively new device at the time, and it was fun to discover just how closely a machine could emulate the workings of one clinician's mind.

Rationale and Development of the 16 PF

Here we briefly discuss the development of the 16 PF test itself. The reader wishing more detail on these issues may consult the writings of Raymond B. Cattell (1946, 1957) or Karson and O'Dell (1976).

Cattell's goal was to construct measures of *normal* personality, and he attacked this problem very ingeniously. According to Cattell (1946), a test for the normal personality should attempt to describe *all* major dimensions in human personality. To achieve this goal, one must first obtain a list of all possible personality characteristics. But where could such a list be found?

The answer is very simple, but so obvious that only a man of Cattell's intellectual stature would have thought of it. A complete list of human personality characteristics may be found in any dictionary. Allport and Odbert (1936) had prepared a list of roughly 4,500 words that seemed to be descriptive of personality. But 4,500 words is far too many for any practical use, certainly for the computing resources available in the early 1940s.

The problem, then, was to somehow reduce these 4,500 words to a smaller, more useful subset. Cattell did this through a complex mathematical procedure called factor analysis. We cannot hope to explain factor analysis in this short chapter. Suffice it to say that it can take a large number of variables, such as the four thousand English adjectives, and reduce them to a smaller number of variables that will account for most of the information in the original set. Through his factor analysis, Cattell found that about sixteen "factors" seemed to underlie English personality descriptions. Thus we have the Sixteen Personality Factor Questionnaire (Cattell, 1946).

These underlying bipolar factors, with their identifying labels, include:

A Warmth vs. Aloofness
B Intelligence
C Ego Strength vs. Emotional Instability
E Dominance vs. Submissiveness
F Impulsivity vs. Deliberateness
G High Group Conformity vs. Low
H Social Boldness vs. Shyness
I Emotional Sensitivity vs. Toughness
L Suspiciousness vs. Trust

M Imagination vs. Practicality
N Sophistication vs. Naïveté
O Guilt Proneness vs. Untroubled Adequacy
Q1 Criticality vs. Respect for Tradition
Q2 Self-Sufficiency vs. Group Dependency
Q3 Ability to Bind Anxiety vs. Lack of Control
Q4 Free-Floating Anxiety vs. Low Tension

We have used the more clinically oriented notation for the factors we adopted (Karson and O'Dell, 1976). To prevent confusion with older writings, Cattell preferred to use new words to describe many of these factors. Thus, for Factor L, which we call Suspiciousness vs. Trust, Cattell prefers the terms "Alaxia vs. Protension." Or, for Factor I, Emotional Sensitivity vs. Toughness, Cattell uses "Harria vs. Premsia." We agree with Cattell's desire for precision but feel that the use of all of these new terms unnecessarily confuses the beginner.

One more technical detail must be mentioned. In a factor analysis, factors may be developed that are completely independent from one another (that is, $r = 0.00$ between them). Alternatively, the factors may be correlated. There is a great deal of debate among factor analysts about which method is preferable, but for his purposes Cattell preferred correlated factors.

If the sixteen factors are allowed to be correlated, we may then proceed to factor analyze the sixteen original factors. This is called a second-order analysis and yields what are called second-order factors (Karson and O'Dell, 1976).

Cattell has identified five major second-order factors, in addition to a number of minor ones. Two of these are particularly important. The first is "Extraversion vs. Introversion," and the second is "Anxiety vs. Dynamic Integration." As we shall see, similar factors generally arise from factor analyses of MMPI scales.

Utility of the 16 PF with Normal Subjects

Practicing clinical psychologists in the 1980s seem largely to have adopted the MMPI as their primary paper-and-pencil personality test. Consequently, it might be asked why we often prefer the 16 PF. There are three main reasons for this.

First, as mentioned, the MMPI was developed largely for use with patients with moderate to severe psychopathology. Yet many patients in modern clinical practice do not show "schizophrenia," "hysteria," or any of the other original MMPI categories. A growing number of patients suffer from milder personality disorders. Others express a feeling of what Jung has called "the senselessness and aimlessness of life." The MMPI is simply not an appropriate test for such people. The 16 PF, developed for the normal personality, seems a better choice (Karson and O'Dell, in press).

Second, the 16 PF has a comparatively sound theoretical basis, carefully detailed in Cattell's many writings. The MMPI, on the other hand, prides itself on a lack of theory, on its derivation through the "empirical" method of test construction. There is nothing inherently wrong with the empirical method. Still, science in our time is built upon theories, and those of us who consider ourselves scientists become rather uneasy at times with the MMPI's complete lack of theory.

Finally, practicing clinicians often seem unaware that there are serious psychometric problems with the MMPI. These problems have been well covered by Cronbach (1958), Norman (1972), and others. Many problems are of sufficient severity that a number of psychologists feel that the test may be simply outdated. We do not share this view nor do we intend to belabor the issue here. However, the 16 PF does not suffer from many of the technical difficulties inherent in the MMPI, and thus we prefer it.

This is not to say that the 16 PF is without its faults. There are questions about its validity, just as with the MMPI. Cattell's writings typically are very difficult for many clinicians to digest. He assumes that one has great mathematical and scientific sophistication (if you don't know matrix algebra fluently, you're in trouble!), he uses hundreds of novel words in his writings, and he employs an elaborate taxonomic system that takes the average clinician a great deal of time to learn.

In short, the 16 PF is a very different instrument from the MMPI, with virtues and deficiencies all its own.

Combined Use of the 16 PF and MMPI in Clinical Practice: A Useful Battery

As mentioned, the MMPI was designed to detect pathology in patients; consequently, it is often difficult to use it to detect normality. Moreover, it does not even purport to measure intelligence, a fact that must be regarded as a serious shortcoming. Statements about a patient's strengths are generally absent from MMPI test reports. The interpretation of scores below a T-score of 50 has always been problematic. Do low scores imply normality, the opposite of the trait measured by the scale, or something quite different?

The 16 PF, which measures the personality traits found in normal people, therefore makes an excellent complement to the Minnesota test. It is especially helpful in situations involving personnel selection, in which prospective employers are interested in the good points about people as well as the bad ones.

In addition, numerous studies have shown that in many samples the MMPI and 16 PF measure very much the same domain. A good example of this is a paper of ours (O'Dell and Karson, 1969), in which the MMPI and 16 PF scales were factor analyzed together.

The first and most important factor was called MMPI Pathology and consisted *entirely* of MMPI scales. This supports the idea that the MMPI is more likely to focus on pathology. The remainder of the factors contained loadings on both 16 PF and MMPI scales. The next two factors, in terms of importance, were "Anxiety," with loadings on MMPI scales such as *K* and *L*, and 16 PF scales including Q4 and O, and "Extraversion," again with salient loadings from both tests.

Thus to some extent both instruments measure the same dimensions. The MMPI has the edge in assessment of gross pathology, while the 16 PF helps to get at the patient's strengths and weaknesses in general. The two tests together make an excellent battery (Karson and O'Dell, 1976).

Validation of the Karson Clinical Report

Validation of automated clinical reports is made difficult by the fact that there is little agreement among clinical psychologists about proper report makeup. Reports on psychological testing in general are rather long, and yet Tallent (1983, p. 76) gives a fascinating example of a very short yet pithy report written by a surgeon, describing the results of an operation. The surgeon's report covers the whole procedure in about four lines! Testing reports generally include references to level of intellectual functioning, personality dynamics, prognosis, and recommended type of treatment. But there is no real agreement about the expected contents or structure of these reports, which occur in a wide variety of settings, and this makes their evaluation most difficult.

Webb, Miller, and Fowler (1969), Webb (1970), Hedlund, Morgan, and Master (1972), Green (1982), and others have attempted to validate MMPI automated report systems. These studies generally follow the same pattern: The MMPI is given to a number of patients who are currently being seen by clinicians. The MMPI protocols are then interpreted by an automated interpretation system. The clinicians working with the patients then rate the accuracy of the reports on a number of dimensions. In studies of this type the reports appear to be very precise, and as a result many people have concluded that the interpretation systems must be valid.

There are several flaws in this conclusion. First of all, the automated interpretation systems generally are based on configural rules such as those provided by Gilberstadt and Duker (1965) or Marks and Seeman (1963). But most modern clinicians are trained to use precisely these rules when interpreting the MMPI. Thus, to the extent that the automated report raters are clinical psychologists, it is not surprising that they find substantial agreement between the automated reports and the patients. It should be kept in mind that, no matter how widespread the use of these configural rules, there is actually comparatively little evidence supporting them.

An even more cogent criticism of this kind of research is provided by Butcher (1978) in the *Eighth Mental Measurements Yearbook*. His comments should be required reading for every practicing clinician who uses automated testing.

His reasoning proceeds as follows: In studies of the sort just mentioned, the clinician is presented with only *one* report describing the personality of the patient in question. Butcher likens this situation to the case of an inexperienced police officer who shows a photograph of only one suspect to witnesses to a crime. Witnesses are much more likely to identify the pictured subject as the criminal than they would be if they were presented with several photographs or a line-up of prisoners. Testimony based on viewing only one photograph is not convincing in a court of law. Similarly, a better method of scrutinizing automated reports would be to present several reports to the clinicians and let them choose the best. This is rarely done in validation research.

Thus it is hardly surprising for the reports to be approved if only one is presented to the rater at a time. The whole situation is reminiscent of the old Sherif (1935) study on the autokinetic effect, in which, in a vague situation, raters converged on the only consistent source of information. It would be far better to present several different interpretations, as, indeed, Green (1982) did.

A third problem in this sort of research arises from the Barnum or "Aunt Fanny" effect. While several of the studies mentioned earlier have purported to show that this effect is not important in automated interpretations, in general, their efforts have not been impressive. It is likely that a clever creator of an automated system can make up Barnum statements of a very sophisticated nature, aimed directly at most clinicians' blind spots, which will pass muster as valid and yet still say almost nothing unique about the testee. A striking example of this sort of report was constructed by Sundberg (quoted by Tallent, 1983, p. 70).

The Dana, Bolton, and West Study on the Karson Clinical Report

A research design circumventing many of the problems just mentioned has been used to assess the validity of the KCR. This innovative study was conducted by Dana, Bolton, and West (1983) at the University of Arkansas. It is an extremely clever one and follows the general procedures Dana has advocated since 1966. In a context of teaching proper Rorschach interpretation, these workers proceeded as follows.

Rorschach records were obtained on four "assessees," each presumably a student or faculty member at the University of Arkansas. The four Rorschach protocols were scored and interpreted by twelve clinical psychology graduate students. At the same time, KCRs were obtained on the twelve "assessors," that is, the students writing the Rorschach reports.

All major concepts were "abstracted," or separated out, from all human and computer reports. This is a simple, clerical process, so that the reliability of sorting out the concepts is in the range of $r = .95$.

The abstracted concepts were then "clustered." That is, one statement in a given report might say that a person was "introversive," while another statement might indicate that the person "does not interact well with others." Both are similar and hence could be clustered together as one concept. This process involves comparatively little judgment, and the reliability of clustering is thus typically $r = .90$.

Two types of concepts were defined from those remaining from the clustering process: "consensus" concepts were those occurring in at least eight reports generated on one protocol, while "unique" concepts were those occurring in only one report.

Dana, Bolton, and West concluded that the KCR performed well in this situation. It provided a large number (46) of unique concepts on the twelve assessors. Generally, 16 PF concepts occurred less than four times. Both of these pieces of information suggest that Barnum processes are minimal in the KCR. These authors noted also that the reports of the KCR agree strongly with impressions of the students by their clinician-instructors, who had observed them in a variety of settings.

In this study, the focus was on the effect of the assessor's own emotional structure (as assessed by the KCR) on his or her Rorschach interpretation. The presumption is that if a student clinician has severe emotional conflicts, these conflicts should "project" themselves into the final Rorschach interpretation (eisegesis, in Dana's terminology), leading to faulty conclusions.

The results of this study are best shown in two tables, showing the performance of a mentally stable clinical student (table 11.1) and a student with emotional problems (table 11.2). At the top of each table are the KCR clusters on the student, followed by the unique Rorschach clusters generated by that student. If the student is projecting his or her own feelings into the test, the correspondence should be obvious—the Rorschach should reflect the interpreter's problems rather than the subject's. Note that both students project their own problems into the reports, but the situation seems much worse in the case of Assessor Y.

A novel feature of these tables is found in the "Assessee Reject/Accept" column under the Rorschach data. Dana, Bolton, and West had the *people who had served as subjects* for the original Rorschach protocols rate the accuracy of the clusters—truly a unique approach. Notice that with the well-adjusted interpreter (X), the assessees found that the concepts fitted them well; in this case, the idea of "strong positive emotional tone" was accepted by eleven assessees and rejected by only one. Not so with the poorly adjusted interpreter: The assessees apparently rejected his or her ideas as often as they accepted them.

TABLE 11.1
Assessor X: Composite of KCR Unique Concepts and Clustered Rorschach Unique Concepts

KCR Unique Concepts (N = 4)

—Good potential for handling emotional conflicts and interpersonal relations.

—Requires much dependency gratification from people, particularly in his job.

—Major problem: strong feelings of assertiveness and need for control.

—Higher than average feelings of tension and frustration.

Rorschach Unique Concepts (N = 47)

# Items in Cluster	*Cluster Label*	*Assessee Reject/Accept*
16	Problems with strong need for attention that includes minimal distancing from others	5/7
12	Strong positive emotional tone	1/11
7	Anxiety/tension	4/3
5	Control Problem	2/3
7	Miscellaneous	5/2

Summary

16 PF suggests balance of good ego strength and good overall functioning with mild concerns re self-control and tension/frustration coupled with strong needs for dependency gratification. Rorschach eisegesis shows balance between strong positive emotional tone (12 concepts) and problems with meeting high needs for affection/attention (16 concepts). Anxiety/tension clearly present (7 concepts) as is a control problem (5 concepts). Note trend for more unique concepts to be accepted by assessees than rejected. This suggests that intensity of own problems does not usually distort perception of assessee.

NOTE: Reprinted, by permission of the publisher, from R. Dana, B. Bolton, and V. West, "Validation of Eisegesis Concepts in Assessment Reports Using the 16 PF: A Training Method with Examples," *Proceedings of the Third International Conference on the 16 PF Test* (Champaign, IL: Institute for Personality and Ability Testing, 1983), 27.

TABLE 11.2
Assessor Y: Composite of KCR Unique Concepts and Clustered Rorschach Unique Concepts

KCR Unique Concepts (N = 6)

—Withdrawal must be considered as is cautious, shy, and unwilling to take risks.

—Too much of his potential wasted on impractical daydreams as he engages in fantasy activity rather than constructive use.

—Below average ego strength in this person indicative of some emotional instability and unresolved neurotic conflicts with limited frustration tolerance and a below average capacity for handling emotional problems in a mature manner.

—Free floating anxiety interfering with functioning efficiency.

—Naive individual.

—Too forthright and direct implying childishness.

Rorschach Unique Concepts (N = 36)

# Items in Cluster	*Cluster Label*	*Assessee Reject/Accept*
14	Affectional needs unmet: resentment struggle/conflict/denial	10/4
10	Anxiety	7/2
7	Underlying anger and control attempts	3/4
6	Miscellaneous	2/4

Summary

16 PF suggests difficulty in everyday functioning and extent of anxiety, fantasy, isolation, and inertia. Rorschach eisegesis suggests basis for these difficulties and some of the struggle, conflict, denial, and resentment expressed in attempting to be accepted/loved/have good relationships with others. Strong anxiety and submerged anger are unaccepted as evidenced by predominant rejection of these concepts by assessees. Assessees are perceived as somewhat out-of-focus as a result of intensity of own problems.

NOTE: Reprinted, by permission of the publisher, from R. Dana, B. Bolton, and V. West, "Validation of Eisegesis Concepts in Assessment Reports Using the 16 PF: A Training Method with Examples," *Proceedings of the Third International Conference on the 16 PF Test* (Champaign, IL: Institute for Personality and Ability Testing, 1983), 28.

Does the Karson Clinical Report Meet the Standards?

Over the years several sets of standards have been proposed for the evaluation of automated clinical reports. We focus here on the two that seem to have the greatest applicability to our situation: the *Standards for Educational and Psychological Testing* (APA, 1985) and the *Guidelines for Computer-Based Tests and Interpretations* (APA, 1986; see appendix B).

In reality, any automated interpretation based on a widely used psychological test must be scrutinized from two completely different viewpoints—one for the test itself and one for the automated interpretation. Clearly, the interpretation can be no better than the test upon which it is based. Fortunately, the construction and validity of the 16 PF have been carefully documented; the interested reader need only consult the *16 PF Handbook* (Cattell, Eber, and Tatsuoka, 1970) for information on these matters. In general, the 16 PF has proved to be a valid and reliable instrument, fully as good as any of its competition in the personality test realm. Questions have been raised about its utility in certain specialized selection situations, but of course that is the case with any modern personality assessment technique. Thus we may conclude that by and large the 16 PF meets most standards applicable to it.

Evaluation of the KCR itself is made difficult because there are so few standards applicable to automated interpretations. We shall, however, comment on those that appear relevant.

First, let us look at the *Standards for Educational and Psychological Testing*. These deal primarily with the construction of tests themselves and say little about computerized interpretations. Standard 3.16 notes that computerized reports should facilitate appropriate interpretations, which presumably means they should be understandable. We feel that the KCR clearly meets this standard, both in the generated report and in its manual. In Section 5 the *Standards* place much emphasis on the quality of manuals accompanying the interpretation. The KCR does have a manual available (Standard 5.1), which fully describes the rationale behind the test and the interpretations generated (Standard 5.11). The KCR uses cutting scores only in comments on the validity scales, and thus the *Standards*'s many cutting-score comments are largely irrelevant to the KCR. Only by a very large stretch of the imagination do any of the other *Standards* apply to automated personality test interpretations, and thus we may assume that the KCR meets the qualifications in the *Standards*.

The *Guidelines for Computer-Based Tests and Interpretations* do have a number of relevant points. Guideline 13 requires that an automated interpretation be used only by qualified professionals. The very first comment in the current edition of the KCR states that "this confidential report is designed for use by appropriately qualified professionals," meeting the guideline. In addition, the KCR limits its target population: it is intended to be used primarily only by psychologists, psychiatrists, physicians, and psychiatric social workers.

Just as with the *Standards*, the *Guidelines* (see guideline 21) are greatly concerned with the availability of adequate manuals, and we have seen that the KCR does indeed have a usable manual. Guideline 24 states that the original scores should be provided to the professional user, and this is done in the KCR. Guideline 25 repeats the requirement of a description of the way in which the interpretive statements are obtained from the original scores; as mentioned, such a description is provided in the KCR manual. Guideline 27 requires that, if an interpretation is based on expert clinical opinion, this fact should be made clear. Of course, the KCR was derived in precisely that fashion, and this is stated explicitly in its manual. Guideline 30 states that reports should be comprehensible both to the test user and the test taker; this is certainly the case for the KCR user. Further, the first page of the KCR clearly states that the report is *not* to be shown to the testee, and thus this standard is met. Finally, Guideline 31 indicates that any automated interpretation system should provide for scholarly review of statement libraries, cutting rules, and so on. The senior author wishes to make this information available to any qualified professional; however, permission from the publisher, namely the Institute for Personality and Ability Testing is necessary for such review.

The KCR appears to run afoul of the *Guidelines* in only one respect. Guideline 26 states that a report should provide warnings about common errors of interpretation. The KCR itself and its manual do not currently provide this information, since only limited feedback is available for providing such data. Moreover, we believe our book (Karson and O'Dell, 1976) serves this purpose.

Thus, in general, the KCR and its manual meet almost all of the applicable standards rather well. In all honesty, it is a bit difficult to say this with a great deal of confidence, for the *Standards* and, more especially, the *Guidelines* are confusing or mutually contradictory in a number of crucial places. This is perhaps to be expected in the case of any "draft" document, but it makes the automated interpretation constructor's job very difficult indeed.

The Development of the Karson Clinical Report

Work on the KCR began in about 1968. The senior author had, for over a decade, made a practice of doing "blind" interpretations from thousands of 16 PFs that he had given in his consulting work with the Federal Aviation Administration. Approximately one hundred of these interpretations were available as work began.

The junior author, looking over these reports, noted a remarkable consistency in the way the reports were written. It appeared that the senior author was working very much as a computer would function, making comments on certain scale-score combinations that were very similar from one report to the next. This may easily be seen by looking at some of the statements themselves.

Thus, for Scale A (warmth), sten score of 1, the following interpretations were found in three separate reports:

> Shows very little warmth; that is, he is markedly reserved. The extremely low A score suggests a history of "burnt child reaction", e.g., of unsatisfactory relationships with others in gratifying his dependency needs.

> He seems to be a person with very little warmth (A = 1) who probably has a history of early conflictual family relations which has resulted in a marked turning away from people.

> Indicates that he has developed a "burnt child reaction" in that he steers away from people to such an extreme that one can only hypothesize that he has a history of unsatisfactory family and peer relationships.

Note the great similarity between these statements, developed on widely differing clients.

The similarities are so fascinating that a few more examples will be given. Thus, for Scale G (group conformity), sten score of 2, we found the following statements, in reports on separate patients: "very low group conformer," "low group conformity," and "low group conformity."

For Scale Q1 (rebelliousness), sten score of 10: "tends to be especially critical and rebellious, with a strong unresolved Oedipal complex," and "especially rebellious and critical with a strong unresolved Oedipal conflict."

For Scale Q3 (ability to bind anxiety), sten score of 1: "shows almost no ability to bind anxiety and undoubtedly feels very lax and unsure of herself," "severe inability to bind anxiety," "low ability to bind anxiety," and "low ability to bind anxiety."

And, finally, for Scale Q4 (free-floating anxiety), sten score of 10: "this woman is suffering from extremely high free-floating anxiety," "high free-floating anxiety," and "much free-floating anxiety."

After looking over these excerpts, the reader may surmise, as the junior author did, that it might well be possible to automate the process.

To systematize things, *all* statements that could be identified as comments on a single scale and a single score were taken from all reports available to us and typed on cards. These were then collected so that all identifiable statements about, say, Scale Q2 (self-sufficiency) were typed on the same page. This crude "content analysis" allowed us to see just how consistent the senior author was in his statements.

Consistency was crucial. If the senior author was not consistent in his comments, things would have been hopeless. Happily, he was quite predictable in the things he said.

As described in a previous paper (Karson and O'Dell, 1975), a number of things became apparent from this work.

First, most of the remarks were simple declarative comments on a *single* scale.

Second, there were comparatively few comments on "combinations" of scores. By this we mean comments such as the following:

> He shows a low group conformity coupled with high superego introjection which suggests that he is caught up in a vicious cycle where he punishes himself for his nonconforming behavior. (Scale G, score of 4, and Scale O, score of 9)

> High G coupled with a high Q1 makes one wonder about the avenues through which his critical tendencies are expressed. (Scale G, score of 8 and Scale Q1, score of 8)

> I get the feeling that she is somewhat confused over her own sex role, which fact is suggested to me by her low I score combined with a high M score. (Scale I, score 4, and Scale M, score 9)

MMPI interpretation has long used configural interpretation of this sort, for example in Fowler's (1969) computer interpretation system. A good example is the combination of high Scale 1, low Scale 2, and high Scale 3, which makes up the "hysteroid valley."

Configural analysis can be a staggering problem for the programmer attempting to make up a simple computer interpretation system. Each 16 PF scale has ten possible sten scores; thus there are 160 possible scale-score combinations on the 16 PF. If we consider all possible combinations of these, we would have to take into account 160 times 160, or 25,600 combinations. It is doubtful that any but the largest computer systems or most devoted programmer could handle all of these "two-point codes." Dealing with all possible "three-point" codes is unthinkable.

Fortunately, the senior author made comparatively few configural statements. These too were listed and fell into patterns, much as did the single-score comments. Generally, these comments mirrored the second-order factors, which were to be commented upon in any event.

Finally, and happily for our simpleminded system, the senior author commented on the scores in a very systematic way. The most deviant scores (sten of 1 or 10) were almost always discussed first, followed by those with a sten of 2 or 9, and so on. And, in general, almost all scores in the profile were discussed, even those that did not deviate markedly from the mean of 5.5 (sten of 5 or 6).

Following the rules implicit in the preceding discussion, a FORTRAN program was written to perform an automated interpretation and was then tested for a number of years.

Changes in the Institute for Personality and Ability Testing Version of the KCR

In about 1978 it appeared that the system had been sufficiently well tested so that it could be made commercially available. The Institute for Personality and Ability Testing (IPAT), publishers of the 16 PF, agreed to do this. In the process, the KCR was enlarged and changed in several ways:

1. The printout of the scores, profiles, and so forth, was greatly improved, to make it more pleasing to the eye.
2. The senior author expended a great deal of effort in revising the statement library. No substantive changes were made, but the statements were generally clarified and sharpened.

3. Proper warnings referring to use only by qualifed professionals, and so forth, were inserted at the beginning of the report.
4. The section of the report on test-taking attitudes was expanded and clarified.
5. Finally, IPAT added a chart of scores for various "need patterns" at the end of the report, to enhance its saleability. These scores originated in unpublished work, done at IPAT, estimating certain of Murray's needs from the 16 PF scores. We consider these scales to be still experimental.

Thus changes in the commercial version of the KCR were largely cosmetic, or designed to meet certain ethical or professional requirements.

Machine Implementation of the KCR: Hints for Programmers

The key person in the implementation of any automated interpretation system is the programmer. It is he or she who will take the clinician's, or the actuarial system's, set of rules and turn them into a readable report.

People who like to do programming are a special, perhaps peculiar group of people. Indeed, DSM-III (American Psychiatric Association, 1980, p. 308) suggests that people "interested in mechanical devices, electronics, and automation" may well have paranoid personality disorders! The junior author, who is writing this section, must plead guilty to an interest in all of these topics and thus finds this point of view rather distressing. Yet there may be more than a grain of truth to it.

In my experience, few psychologists, and even fewer *clinical* psychologists, have any interest in programming. Programming requires a severely logical sort of mind, almost obsessive attention to detail, and complete mastery of the set of rules involved in the programming language. Indeed, this last criterion is precisely the characteristic that should be required in someone interested in an actuarial approach to diagnosis (see Meehl, 1954). One thing is sure: in the development of an automated interpretation system, a clinical psychologist who knows how to program has a tremendous advantage over one who does not.

The absolute desideratum in the construction of any valid interpretation system is a thoroughly comprehensive and consistent set of decision rules. Just as a machinist in a shop cannot work from a flawed set of blueprints (a three-inch hole can't be drilled in a piece of metal two inches wide), the programmer must have the almost perfect set of decision rules. Without them, the computer will simply refuse to do the task. This writer feels strongly that an excellent test of the validity of any set of actuarial rules might well be the ease with which they may be converted to a computer program. When put into computer language, the rules either work or they do not. And if they don't work, they fail in a big way. As Phil Stone (developer of the "General Inquirer") once said, "to err is human, but if you really want to mess things up, use a computer."

What happens when the decision rules are not consistent, not mutually exclusive? Anyone who has programmed automatic test interpretations will tell you in a second: "The final report will be full of contradictions!" In one part of the report, the patient will be called schizophrenic, while somewhere else the statement "no schizophrenic trends are evident" will appear. The large computer in our head, the brain, rebels absolutely at such inconsistencies, and the clinician receiving the report will reject it out of hand. (Not always: See the inconsistencies in the human clinician's report in the Case Example section.) Contradictions are the bane of the computer interpretation programmer's existence.

In the initial stages of the construction of the KCR, we were very fortunate in modeling the behavior of a *very* consistent interpreter. We had no clear-cut set of "actuarial" rules, but we did know rather well that Sam Karson wrote predictable 16 PF reports.

What does one do without such a set of rules? Let us take the case of the multitudinous MMPI computer interpretation systems. In spite of voluminous writings on the topic (Gilberstadt and Duker, 1965; Marks, Seeman and Haller, 1974; Meehl, 1956, and so forth) no single, mutually consistent set of decision rules exists for the interpretation of MMPI profiles, much less a valid set. People writing automated systems for the MMPI, then, must fall back on a number of rather clever ways of avoiding the pitfalls involved in an inconsistent set of decision rules. Let us list a few of these.

One simple solution to the problem is to greatly increase the amount of printed output, the verbiage of the report. The best possible automated report would no doubt be one that stated only 295.3 Schizophrenia, Paranoid Type. But our diagnostic system is not yet that highly developed.

I suspect that the average clinician assumes, generally, that "more is better." A clinician paying twenty dollars for an interpretation that was only one line long might well feel cheated. Consequently, many, if not all, interpretation systems pad their output. An increase in verbiage of this sort might seem difficult to do, but it is not. A clever programmer simply thinks of longer ways of saying rather simple things. It is amazingly easy to convert a two-word phrase into three rather long paragraphs, given the need to do so. To increase the bulk even more, long lists of supposedly "critical items," extra scale scores, and so on and on can be added.

It is greatly to the senior author's credit that, in the early development of the KCR, he strongly resisted my many (very many!) attempts to increase the report length. He wanted them to be short and accurate, as they should be.

There is one disadvantage to increasing the length of the report: doing so greatly increases the possibility of internal contradictions. And contradictions are unacceptable. Fortunately, there is a way around this problem.

If plagued by contradictions in the report, simply reduce statement specificity, using more and more of the Barnum effect (Meehl, 1956; O'Dell, 1972).

Barnum statements are statements that are true of almost everyone—comments such as "latent homosexual tendencies," "great amounts of suppressed anger," "difficulties in relating to the opposite sex." Of course, all human beings probably have all of these problems to some extent, but when written in a psychological report, they sound absolutely wonderful while meaning nothing at all! They take a stand on nothing.

To the programmer's practiced eye, statements of this type are rampant in all-too-many automated reports. They even occur in the KCR, when scale values near the average are interpreted, as they typically are at the end of the report.

While of no clinical or scientific importance, the physical form of the report may be of great marketing importance. Early automated interpretations were produced on large computer line printers or teletype machines and were unattractive. A good example of this was the early Mayo Clinic reports (Pearson and Swenson, 1967). Anyone developing an automated system is well advised to use a high-quality printer and give careful attention to formatting the page. And yet simple appearance adds nothing to the usefulness of the report.

I could go on at great length about the tricks of the trade; certainly there are programmers who know ten times as many of these as I do.

What sort of computer and computer language are needed for the generation of automated reports? In the early days, large, expensive computers had to be used, simply because nothing else existed. Today perhaps 50 percent of all interpretations systems could be implemented on a Commodore 64 (about $500), and almost all the rest could be fitted into a machine such as an IBM PC-XT (about $4,000). The programming language used is not highly important; indeed, most of them are pretty much the same. In the early days we used FORTRAN; today BASIC would do the job nicely, although PASCAL might be easier to maintain.

Case Example

The usefulness of the KCR may be seen in the following illustration. The case is reported in relatively skeletal fashion, with the report of a traditional clinical psychologist and the report generated by the KCR program. It may be interesting to attempt to guess which report is generated by the clinician and which by the computer.

The patient was a forty-one-year-old white female, hospitalized for depression. The clinical psychologist writing the report administered the revised Wechsler Adult Intelligence Scale, MMPI, Bender-Gestalt, House-Tree-Person, Rorschach, and Thematic Apperception Test (note that the 16 PF had been given earlier and was not included in the battery).

The patient's 16 PF was administered several days prior to her hospitalization. The scores were as follows:

	Factor	*Sten Score*
A	Warmth	5
B	Intelligence	5
C	Ego Strength	3
E	Dominance	3
F	Impulsivity	9
G	Group Conformity	9
H	Boldness	5
I	Emotional sensitivity	5
L	Suspiciousness	9
M	Imagination	6
N	Shrewdness	3
O	Guilt Proneness	9
Q1	Rebelliousness	2
Q2	Self-Sufficiency	6
Q3	Ability to Bind Anxiety	8
Q4	Free-Floating Anxiety	9

Faking Good: 5 (raw) Faking Bad: 2 (raw) Random: 4 (raw)

The two reports generated are as follows:

First Report

The results indicate that this patient is a depressed, anxious, narcissistic individual who is feeling angry and hostile towards others. Her low tolerance for frustration indicates difficulty with impulse control, resulting in erratic and unpredictable aggressive outbursts. Because of her narcissism, any acting out tendencies will likely be geared towards others. Part of this anger is a result of feeling rejected by others and her ambivalent feelings towards nurturance and dependency needs. She sees her environment as hostile in that she tends to project her own negative connotations onto others. She is submissive towards authority figures, in particular males, although she is suspicious of their behavior. She seeks out affection with males, looking for someone to fulfill her nurturant needs. She is resentful of her own need for dependency, however, and reacts by avoiding or withdrawing from interpersonal relationships. The results further indicate that this patient is feeling inadequate, insecure, and has low ego strength. She tends to overreact to minor stress and is vulnerable to real and imagined threats. She is affectively labile and appears to be over-attending to her environment. This has resulted in a decompensation of reality testing. This has led to a fluidity of ego boundaries in that she is currently having difficulty differentiating herself from the environment. The patient tends to brood and ruminate about her problems. She tends to rationalize her behavior, and because of her projection of hostility and suspiciousness onto the environment, feels justified in acting out. She tries to control her behavior, however, through obsessive means, but such defenses are not adequately controlling her actions.

Second Report

Faking good attempts are about average. There is little suggestion of the presence of a response set to look bad or to fake anxiety symptoms deliberately. Indications are that she read the items carefully and clearly understood what was required. The random index is within normal limits. She is a highly impulsive, enthusiastic, immature, and fun-loving person who lacks restraint. She expresses such a high regard for the opinions of others, societal expectations, and conventional standards that others may see her as too rigid and overly concerned with appearances. She tends to displace and project angry feelings and does not get along with others in a close working situation. She is typically not well accepted by her peers. She operates at a very high level of guilt-proneness and superego-generated anxiety which makes her a chronic worrier. She is highly conservative and would tend not to be critical of her supervisors or peers. She appears to be suffering from an unusually high level of free-floating anxiety which may be interfering with her functioning efficiency. Her below average ego strength suggests the presence of much emotional instability and many neurotic conflicts with limited frustration tolerance and below average capacity for developing an effective network of ego defenses. She is a great deal more submissive and retiring than the average person, and this quality creates certain difficulties in the open expression of anger. She is relatively inexperienced with social groups and she tends to be too direct and forthright in her dealings with others. She shows high reliance on obsessive-compulsive defense mechanisms and is able to bind her anxiety.

Here, the first report was generated by the human clinician and the second by the computer. There are fairly striking similarities between them, even though the reports were generated on a completely different selection of tests and the battery was given after the patient was hospitalized.

Both reports imply depression—the first talks about depression and the second mentions guilt-proneness. Both mention the likelihood of aggressive acting out. Projection is singled out as an important defense mechanism in both reports. The first report suggests submissiveness toward males, the second a lack of criticalness toward supervisors and submissiveness. Low ego strength is a prominent feature of both reports.

At the same time, there are differences. The clinician's report suggests that the patient's obsessive defenses are not effective, while the automated report states the opposite. Further, both reports contain fairly blatant contradictions. The automated report notes at the beginning that the patient is impulsive and fun-loving and later talks about her guilt-proneness and anxiety. The clinician's report talks of aggressive outbursts and later says that the patient is submissive toward authority. Perhaps the human clinician's internal program is also not immune to contradictory statements!

Potential Barnum statements are fairly evident in both reports: everyone projects, has guilt feelings, and so on. But there seems to be a great deal of specificity in both reports, and both appear to be useful in the diagnostic process.

It is interesting to note that the report prepared by the human interpreter, based on far more information, is not particularly superior to that of the KCR. Of course we have almost no validity data on the case, so that, as often happens, it is difficult to make a proper evaluation.

Summary

Thus it is clear that the Karson Clinical Report remains a promising instrument. Validity data, although scant, is encouraging, and in the main the automated procedure appears to meet the applicable standards.

Where will computer-produced reports of this type find their largest use? We suspect that it will not be in the evaluation of a single case. It is likely that some practicing clinicians will continue to prefer administering and interpreting their own tests. It may well be that the future of automated interpretation lies in cases in which hundreds, perhaps thousands of people, say applicants for jobs, must be evaluated or screened at one time, and rapidly. Such a situation is ideally suited for the computer, which is tireless, objective, and clearly produces results much more quickly than any human evaluator.

REFERENCES

Allport, G. W., and Odbert, H. S. (1936). Trait-names: A psycholexical study. *Psychological Monographs*, 47, (211).

American Psychiatric Association. (1980). *Diagnostic and statistical manual of mental disorders* (3rd ed.). Washington, DC: Author.

American Psychological Association. (1985). *Standards for educational and psychological testing*. Washington, DC: Author.

American Psychological Association. (1986). *Guidelines for computer-based tests and interpretations*. Washington, DC: Author.

Butcher, J. N. (1978). Automated psychological assessment. In O. K. Buros (Ed.), *The eighth mental measurements yearbook* (pp. 942–945). Highland Park, NJ: Gryphon Press.

Cattell, R. B. (1946). *The description and measurement of personality*. Yonkers, NY: World Book Company.

Cattell, R. B. (1957). *Personality and motivation structure and measurement*. Yonkers, NY: World Book Company.

Cattell, R. B., Eber, H. W., and Tatsuoka, M. J. (1970). *Handbook for the 16 PF*. Champaign, IL: Institute for Personality and Ability Testing.

Cronbach, L. J. (1958). Review of Welsh, G. S., and Dahlstrom, W. G., *Basic readings on the MMPI in psychology and medicine*. *Psychometrika*, 23, 385–386.

Dana, R., Bolton, B., and West, V. (1983). Validation of eisegesis concepts in assessment reports using the 16 PF: A training method with examples. *Proceedings of the Third International Conference on the 16 PF Test* (pp. 20–29). Champaign, IL.: Institute for Personality and Ability Testing.

Fowler, R. D. (1969). Automated interpretation of personality test data. In J. N. Butcher (Ed.), *MMPI: Research developments and clinical applications* (pp. 105–125). New York: McGraw-Hill.

Gilberstadt, H., and Duker, J. (1965). *A handbook for clinical and actuarial MMPI interpretation*. Philadelphia: W. B. Saunders.

Green, C. J. (1982). The diagnostic accuracy and utility of MMPI and MCMI computer interpretive reports. *Journal of Personality Assessment*, 46, 359–365.

Hedlund, J. L., Morgan, D. W., and Master, F. D. (1972). The Mayo Clinic automated MMPI program: Cross validation with psychiatric patients in an army hospital. *Journal of Clinical Psychology*, 28, 505–510.

Institute for Personality and Ability Testing. (1979). *Karson Clinical Report Manual*. Champaign, IL: Author.

Karson, S., and O'Dell, J. W. (1975). A new automated interpretation system for the 16 PF. *Journal of Personality Assessment*, 39, 256–260.
Karson, S., and O'Dell, J. W. (1976). A *guide to the clinical use of the 16 PF*. Champaign, IL: Institute for Personality and Ability Testing.
Karson, S., and O'Dell, J. W. (in press). Personality profiles in the U.S. Foreign Service. In J. N. Butcher and C. D. Spielberger (Eds.), *Advances in personality assessment: Vol. 6*. Hillsdale, NJ: Lawrence Erlbaum.
Marks, P. A., and Seeman, W. (1963). *Actuarial description of abnormal personality*. Baltimore: Williams & Wilkins.
Marks, P. A., Seeman, W., and Haller, D. L. (1974). *Actuarial use of the MMPI with adolescents and adults*. Baltimore: Williams & Wilkins.
Meehl, P. E. (1954). *Clinical vs. Statistical Prediction*. Minneapolis, MN: University of Minnesota Press.
Meehl, P. E. (1956). Wanted—a good cookbook. *American Psychologist*, *11*, 262–272.
Norman, W. T. (1972). Psychometric considerations for a revision of the MMPI. In J. N. Butcher (Ed.), *Objective personality measurement* (pp. 59–83). New York: Academic Press.
O'Dell, J. W. (1972). P. T. Barnum explores the computer. *Journal of Consulting and Clinical Psychology*, 38, 270–273.
O'Dell, J. W., and Karson, S. (1969). Some relationships between the MMPI and 16 PF. *Journal of Clinical Psychology*, *25*, 279–283.
Pearson, J. S., and Swenson, W. M. (1967). A *user's guide to the Mayo Clinic automated MMPI program*. New York: Psychological Corporation.
Sherif, M. (1935). A study of some social factors in perception. *Archives of Psychology (New York)*, 27 (187).
Tallent, N. (1983). *Psychological report writing*. Englewood Cliffs, NJ: Prentice-Hall.
Webb, J. T. (1970). Validity and utility of computer produced MMPI reports with Veterans' Administration psychiatric populations. *Proceedings of the 78th Annual Convention of the American Psychological Association* (pp. 541–542). Washington, DC: American Psychological Association.
Webb, J. T., Miller, M. L., and Fowler, R. D. (1969). Validation of a computerized MMPI interpretation system. *Proceedings of the 77th Annual Convention of the American Psychological Association* (pp. 523–524). Washington, DC: American Psychological Association.

12

Computer Assistance in Rorschach Interpretation

John E. Exner, Jr.

Introduction

The idea of using computer technology to assist in Rorschach interpretation may seem incongruous to those with only superficial knowledge about the test. Unfortunately, many believe that the theoretical underpinings of Rorschach's original investigation focused on the symbolic translation of content. Nothing could be further from truth, nor is the richness of the test dependent on such an approach. Rorschach's postulate concerning the test was that the method of misidentifying inkblots evokes a variety of perceptual operations (1921). Drawing largely from the works of Mach, Lotze, and Helmholtz, he believed that the effectiveness of those operations is dependent on the accuracy of the apperceptive mass. His research, which lasted for little more than three years, seemed to support his contention, in that he was able to demonstrate that schizophrenic patients, as identified by his mentor Eugene Blueler, did indeed respond to the game of misidentifying inkblots (*Klexographie*) differently than did other patients, or nonpatients.

Rorschach was only casually concerned with the content of responses, and cautioned against suppositions that the verbal material of responses might yield some evidence about the unconscious workings of the mind. To the contrary, he believed that the *Klexen* (ink smudges) could be translated in any of a variety of ways (contents), but that each response would have some discrete characteristics of the perceptual operations that occurred in the formulation of the answer. In his judgment, which now appears to have been valid, people responding to the inkblots would be prone to use their "natural" psychological features—that is, habits, traits, coping styles—in the selection of what to call the inkblot when challenged to misidentify it. In the framework of that theory, Rorschach created a simple system for coding some of the basic characteristics of each answer. He used symbols to identify different kinds of location selections, others to denote whether form, color, or movement had been included as perceived characteristics in the answer, and a third set of symbols to signify the basic category into which the content of the answer would fall.

While testing his basic premise about the inkblot method—that is, that schizophrenics do misperceive the form characteristics of the blots—he also noted that nonschizophrenics tended to use some blot features more frequently than others and vice versa. It was this finding, based on work with 405 subjects, that led him to postulate that the "Form Perception Test," as he called it, might identify different components of the psychological functioning of people. If his premises are translated into the contemporary terminology of psychology, it seems reasonable to suggest that he was searching for evidence related to the variety of cognitive and affective operations and characteristics that mark the personality of the individual.

As mentioned, Rorschach believed that a format of scoring or coding different basic features of responses could provide frequency data from which information concerning the presence or absence of some features could be gleaned, and if some frequencies were elevated significantly, it might indicate the strength or valence of a given characteristic in the pattern of psychological operations. It was that notion that led many involved in the early development of the test to add to or attempt to refine the coding (scoring) format that Rorschach developed.* Unfortunately, coding or scoring formats differed considerably among these Rorschach pioneers, and as a result several Rorschach Systems evolved.

In 1968 the Rorschach Research Foundation was created for the purpose of studying the empirical sturdiness and clinical efficacy of each of the five basic Rorschach Systems. By 1970 the data yield made it obvious that each of the five approaches had considerable merit, but it was also obvious that each was flawed by the inclusion of some variables that could not withstand the tests of reliability and/or validity, or the omission of other variables for which the tests of reliability and validity proved positive. Those findings led to the decision to attempt to integrate the empirically defensible variables into a single format, which has come to be known as the Comprehensive System. What began as the simple integration of the hard-won wisdoms of the Rorschach pioneers has been expanded considerably by nearly twenty years of additional research. The Comprehensive System currently includes more than 130 scoring or coding variables, ratios, special indices, and percentages that are derived from the basic scoring or coding variables. These variables constitute the Structural Summary of the test. It is a complex compilation of data that is not interpreted simply. Single variables have little or no meaning, and if studied independently can often be very misleading in the interpretive process. Thus the variables must be reviewed in clusters that relate to various psychological operations or char-

* See Beck, 1944; Hertz, 1942; Klopfer and Kelley, 1942; Piotrowski, 1957; and Rapaport, Gill, and Schafer, 1946.

acteristics, such as capacities for control, tolerance for stress, coping preference, organizing and processing information, emotional responsiveness and control, self-concept, and the like.

Computer Technology and the Rorschach

Computer technology can provide considerable assistance in the interpretation of the structural data of the Rorschach in three ways. First, it can be used to create the Structural Summary. The entries and calculations that often take ten to fifteen minutes when done by hand can be completed in a minute or two by machine. Second, when programmed using appropriate guidelines—that is, empirically derived logic—a computer can sweep through the structural clusters in search of deviations and/or significant findings and signal the presence of positive findings. Third, the calculations and the sweep of the data are consistent—the possibilities of error by reason of fatigue, haste, or neglect are eliminated.

The first effort at using computer technology in Rorschach interpretation was made by Piotrowski. He completed a very elaborate computer program in 1963, using a Univac I mainframe. He revised it in 1968 using an IBM 360. Based on his own interpretive logic and designed to account for as many variables as possible, it included hundreds of parameters and rules. Unfortunately, it was far too advanced for most of the computer technology available at that time and consequently achieved far less acclaim than it should have. Beginning in the mid-1970s a project was undertaken at the Rorschach Research Foundation to increase computer utilization as an aid in interpreting the test. As a first step, a previously designed data storage program was upgraded so that it would calculate and produce the test's Structural Summary. Subsequently, drawing on data gleaned from a variety of intercorrelational and factorial studies, thirty-three semi-independent clusters were identified as related to a variety of psychological operations and characteristics. Logic rules were devised and a "sweep" segment was added by which the program searches all clusters and combinations of clusters for evidence of deviation or significant relationships. More than two hundred messages and modifiers are available in the program, which vary in length from one line to a brief paragraph. Thus, when a positive discovery occurs during the sweep, a message is "tagged" and printed calling attention to the psychological feature(s) usually associated with that finding.

This approach to computer use with the Rorschach has been labeled the Rorschach Interpretation Assistance Program (RIAP). It is not designed to interpret the full data of the Rorschach protocol, but instead can be useful in getting the first phase of interpretation under way. The programmed sweep of the structural data follows a progression very similar to that described in my book, *The Rorschach: A Comprehensive System. Vol. 1: Basic Foundations* (1986). Anyone familiar with the chapters in that work dealing with logical progression in Rorschach interpretation can probably detect the data sets that are involved in the selection of each message printed. Each message is numbered, and no effort has been made to attempt to create a narrative form of report. Any narrative based only on the structural data of the test would be, at best, incomplete and very possibly erroneous in many respects. Any competent Rorschacher is well aware that the full interpretation of the test must include a careful review of the Sequence of Scores as well as a thorough reading of the subject's responses, plus the Inquiry material that has been collected with regard to those answers.

In effect, the computer sweep is designed to approximate a review of the structural data in a progression similar to that commonly used by the human interpreter; however, there are substantial differences between the logical tactics of data review by a human as compared with a machine. First, the computer is unable to deviate from its assigned rounds. The human can stop and shift direction at any time. Second, the computer cannot think as it proceeds as directed. It cannot integrate data at a level higher than that for which it has been programmed. Third, the computer is limited to a review of data that has been entered. While some demographic material is entered in RIAP, much more information about the subject is available to the human interpreter. Thus, as stated earlier, the messages from the computer reflect an empirically based translation of the data available in the Structural Summary; but they may not always be stated in a way that best captures the idiographic functioning of a subject, and in some instances statements may be only partially correct, or even totally incorrect.

Each message or statement should be regarded as a hypothesis concerning some psychological characteristic of the subject. The Rorschacher can use those statements in either of two ways. One is as a check of his or her own interpretive conclusions. To do this, the interpreter would review the entire Structural Summary and write out some statements about the subject. Then he or she would review the interpretive statements that are generated from RIAP. This can be a good teaching and/or learning tactic, especially for the Rorschach novice who is still working to master the principles of interpretation. The second way in which the statements can be used is the one that will probably be of the greatest interest to those experienced in interpretation. Each message or statement is considered as a hypothesis to be fine-tuned and integrated in some way into the total interpretive picture. To do this, the interpreter should ask two questions about each statement: (1) Does the statement appear to be valid in light of other information that I know about the subject? and (2) How should this finding be integrated with other findings to create the most accurate picture of the subject?

In many instances the answers to either or both questions will require a review of data that are not in the Structural Summary. For instance, if the RIAP message indicates a high probability of schizophrenia, the interpreter will surely consider the history and the presenting complaint or cause for assessment, and probably read those responses in the record that contain M− answers and/or the six critical Special Scores before accepting or rejecting the hypothesis. Another illustration of the process can be derived using records in which the Lambda is elevated significantly. The printout message would "argue" that the subject tends to avoid and/or oversimplify his or her environment. Usually this means that the subject will have some history of confrontation with socially expected behaviors. Quite often, high Lambda subjects have histories that are marked by difficulties with the environment. If the history indicates that the subject is a "straightlaced" pillar of the community, the RIAP statement is at least partially incorrect. It may be that the subject does maintain a "neat and tidy" existence and does try to avoid complexity, especially when in new situations. But the structural data for a case such as this will probably also include a reasonably high X+% and a substantial number of Popular answers, both of which argue against the probability of environmental-social confrontations.

It is extremely important to emphasize again that any user of the RIAP program, or any similar program, be acutely aware that computer-generated statements are not etched in stone. Although empirically derived, they should always be regarded as subject to elaboration and/or challenge. Possibly the best way to illustrate the inductive and deductive steps that comprise this phase in the process of interpreting Rorschach data is through a case illustration. The verbal material of the protocol is not included as the focus of computer assistance is on the structural data.

A Sample Protocol

The subject is a thirty-five-year-old male inpatient who is married and a college graduate. He has been hospitalized for three months and is now being considered for discharge to a halfway house. His psychiatric history reveals two prior hospitalizations, one at age twenty during his third year at college for an acute anxiety attack and one at age twenty-four following a psychoticlike episode. The first time he was released after twelve days and continued as an outpatient through his fourth year in college. During that time he took anti-anxiety medication. He terminated treatment shortly after his graduation, obtaining a B.A. degree in sociology. After graduating he obtained employment as a social worker and shortly before his twenty-second birthday married a twenty-four-year-old woman who was a secretary. Their marriage lasted about two years and was quite stormy. He often accused her of being unfaithful and was physically abusive to her at least three times. The last abusive episode led to his second hospitalization. She filed for divorce, which he did not contest, while he was an inpatient, and they have had no contact since. His second hospitalization lasted about four months, during which time he was diagnosed as a Paranoid

Personality Disorder. After his discharge he continued in a day hospital program for about six months. He transferred to an outpatient group psychotherapy program after getting a job as a taxi driver. At age twenty-seven, he married a twenty-year-old woman, who he met in group psychotherapy. She had been treated for depression. They separated briefly after about one year and have separated and reunited four times during the past eight years. Each separation has lasted about four weeks and each has been provoked by his acts of physical violence against her. He has changed jobs four times since his second hospitalization and prior to his current hospitalization was working as a waiter. The current admission occurred when he became violent toward a customer, accusing the customer of stealing a tip from another table. The admission was involuntary but converted to voluntary status after five days. He now feels that he has improved, but has been cautioned about discontinuing treatment, and therefore is considering a halfway house. He is on antipsychotic medication. The assessment issues are: (1) Are his controls adequate to sustain him in a semi-independent setting? (2) Is the diagnosis of paranoid schizophrenia confirmed by the assessment data? and (3) Is he dangerous to himself or to others? The subject was somewhat reluctant but cooperative during the psychological evaluation and produced a Rorschach that yields the following Sequence of Scores:

```
RORSCHACH                                                          10

SEQUENCE OF SCORES: 35 YEAR OLD MALE
-------------------------------------------------------------------
   I    1. WO FDO A P 1.0
        2. DO4 FO A DR,PER

  II    3. DS+5 MA.FC'- H,CG 4.5 MOR,DR

 III    4. W+ MA.CFU 2 H,(A),CG P 5.5 FAB,MOR,DR,AG

  IV    5. DO6 FO 2 CG PER
        6. W+ FDO (H) P 4.0 DR,MOR

   V    7. DDO99 FO A
        8. WO mP- H 1.0 DR,MOR

  VI    9. DDO33 FU SX DR

 VII   10. W+ MPU 2 H,CG 2.5 DR
       11. WO F- AN 2.5 DR
       12. DO2 FVU FD

VIII   13. W+ MP.CF- (H),FI 4.5 ALOG,AG

  IX   14. WV C FI PER

   X   15. D+11 MA- SX 4.0
-------------------------------------------------------------------
```

These basic data constitute the input to RIAP. Obviously, the accuracy of this scoring or coding becomes a very critical linchpin in the interpretive process. To the extent that the coding is correct, the output, whether generated by human or machine, will be derived from valid data. Conversely, if the basic data of the test are incorrect, the error parameters are expanded, and in cases containing several scoring errors, the yield may well be disastrous for the subject. Unfortunately, some tend to use the Rorschach as a "rough and ready" technique that has sufficient sturdiness to withstand errors of neglect or ignorance. That is not the case, and those who adhere to that philosophy will do better for their clients by avoiding the use of the test. The Structural Summary and interpretive statements generated by RIAP for this case are depicted in figures 12.1 and 12.2.

```
SUBJECT NAME:SAMPLE                        AGE:35  SEX:M  RACE:W  MS:Mar  ED:16
================================================================================
                                STRUCTURAL SUMMARY
================================================================================
 R = 15     Zf =  9    ZSum = 29.5     P =  3     (2) =  3     Fr+rF =  0

LOCATION           DETERMINANTS              CONTENTS      S-CONSTELLATION
FEATURES        BLENDS          SINGLE                           (ADULT)
                                           H   =  4, 0  YES..FV+VF+V+FD>2
W    =  8       M.FC'           M  =  2    (H) =  2, 0   NO..Col-Shd Bl>0
 (Wv  =  1)     M.CF            FM =  0    Hd  =  0, 0  YES..Ego<.31,>.44
D    =  5       M.CF            m  =  1    (Hd)=  0, 0  YES..MOR > 3
Dd   =  2                       C  =  1    A   =  3, 0   NO..Zd > +- 3.5
S    =  1                       Cn =  0    (A) =  0, 1   NO..es > EA
                                CF =  0    Ad  =  0, 0  YES..CF+C+Cn > FC
   DQ                           FC =  0    (Ad)=  0, 0  YES..X+ < .70
.........(FQ-)                  C' =  0    Ab  =  0, 0   NO..S > 3
                                C'F=  0    Al  =  0, 0   NO..P < 3 or > 8
  +  =  6 ( 3)                  FC'=  0    An  =  1, 0   NO..Pure H < 2
v/+  =  0 ( 0)                  T  =  0    Art =  0, 0  YES..R < 17
  o  =  8 ( 2)                  TF =  0    Ay  =  0, 0      6.....TOTAL
  v  =  1 ( 0)                  FT =  0    Bl  =  0, 0
                                V  =  0    Bt  =  0, 0   SPECIAL SCORINGS
                                VF =  0    Cg  =  1, 3      DV     =  0
                                FV =  1    Cl  =  0, 0      INCOM  =  0
                                Y  =  0    Ex  =  0, 0      DR     =  8
                                YF =  0    Fi  =  1, 1      FABCOM =  1
          FORM QUALITY          FY =  0    Fd  =  1, 0      ALOG   =  1
                                rF =  0    Ge  =  0, 0      CONTAM =  0
   FQx        FQf      M Qual.  Fr =  0    Hh  =  0, 0       -- WSUM6 = 33
                                FD =  2    Ls  =  0, 0      AG     =  2
  +  =  0    + =  0   +  =  0   F  =  5    Na  =  0, 0      CONFAB =  0
  o  =  5    o =  3   o  =  0              Sc  =  0, 0      CP     =  0
  u  =  4    u =  1   u  =  2              Sx  =  2, 0      MOR    =  4
  -  =  5    - =  1   -  =  3              Xy  =  0, 0      PER    =  3
none=  1            none=  0               Idio=  0, 0      PSV    =  0
================================================================================

                   RATIOS, PERCENTAGES, AND DERIVATIONS

ZSum-Zest =  29.5 - 27.5         FC:CF+C   =  0: 3     W:M            =  8: 5
                                    (Pure C =  1)
Zd          =  +2.0                                    W:D            =  8: 5
                                 Afr         =  0.25
.------------------------.                             Isolate:R      =  0:15
:EB =  5: 3.5   EA =  8.5:       3r+(2)/R =  0.20
:                        >D= +2                        Ab+Art         =  0
:eb =  1:   2   es =  3  :       L           =  0.50
'------------------------'                             An+Xy          =  1
(FM= 0 : C'= 1 T= 0) (Adj D= +2) Blends:R =  3:15
(m = 1 : V = 1 Y= 0)                                   H(H):Hd(Hd)=   6: 0
                                 X+%         =  0.33     (Pure H =    4)
a:p           =  3: 3              (F+%      =  0.60)  (HHd):(AAd)=   2: 0
                                 X-%         =  0.33
Ma:Mp         =  3: 2                                  H+A:Hd+Ad   =  9: 0
--------------------------------------------------------------------------------
         SCZI = 5               DEPI = 3               S-CCN = 6
================================================================================
(c)1976,1985 by John E. Exner, Jr.
```

Figure 12.1. Rorschach structural summary.

SUBJECT NAME:SAMPLE AGE:35 SEX:M RACE:W MS:Mar ED:16

SEMANTIC INTERPRETATION OF THE RORSCHACH
PROTOCOL UTILIZING THE COMPREHENSIVE SYSTEM
(COPYRIGHT 1976, 1985 BY JOHN E. EXNER, JR.)

THE FOLLOWING COMPUTER-BASED INTERPRETATION IS DERIVED ** EXCLUSIVELY ** FROM THE STRUCTURAL DATA OF THE RECORD AND DOES NOT INCLUDE CONSIDERATION OF THE SEQUENCE OF SCORES OR THE VERBAL MATERIAL. IT IS INTENDED AS A GUIDE FROM WHICH THE INTERPRETER OF THE TOTAL PROTOCOL CAN PROCEED TO STUDY AND REFINE THE HYPOTHESES GENERATED FROM THESE ACTUARIAL FINDINGS.

* * * * *

1. THE RECORD APPEARS TO BE VALID AND INTERPRETIVELY USEFUL.

2. THIS PROTOCOL INDICATES A HIGH PROBABILITY OF SCHIZOPHRENIA.

3. THIS RECORD INDICATES A MARKED DEFICIT IN PERCEPTUAL ACCURACY SUCH AS OFTEN EXISTS WHEN REALITY TESTING IS IMPAIRED. IN OTHER WORDS, THE SUBJECT MISINTERPRETS AND/OR DISTORTS PERCEPTUAL INPUTS MUCH MORE THAN MOST PEOPLE.

4. THERE IS CLEAR EVIDENCE OF SIGNIFICANT COGNITIVE SLIPPAGE -- THAT IS, THE SUBJECT IS NOT PROCESSING, MEDIATING, OR RESPONDING TO STIMULI AT HIS/HER EXPECTED COGNITIVE ABILITY. THIS USUALLY INDICATES THE PRESENCE OF DISORDERED THINKING.

5. PLEASE BE CAUTIONED THAT RORSCHACH FEATURES COMMENSURATE WITH SCHIZOPHRENIA MAY ALSO APPEAR IN SOME CASES OF CHRONIC OR HEAVY DRUG USE. THIS IS ESPECIALLY LIKELY WHEN AMPHETEMINES HAVE BEEN USED EXTENSIVELY. A SCHIZOPHRENIC-LIKE PICTURE MAY ALSO OCCUR AMONG SOME OF THE LESS COMMON NEUROLOGICALLY RELATED DISEASES IN WHICH VISUAL AND/OR VISCERAL SYMPTOMS ARE PRESENT. CAREFUL EVALUATION OF THE HISTORY AND PRESENTING MEDICAL PICTURE ARE PREREQUISITE TO ANY FINAL DIAGNOSIS.

6. THIS SUBJECT HAS UNUSUALLY GOOD CAPACITIES FOR CONTROL. MANY MORE RESOURCES ARE READILY ACCESSIBLE FOR USE THAN ORDINARILY ARE REQUIRED. AS A RESULT, TOLERANCE FOR STRESS IS CONSIDERABLE AND THE SUBJECT IS READILY ABLE TO FORMULATE AND GIVE DIRECTION TO BEHAVIORS. THIS FEATURE TENDS TO ENHANCE STABILIZATION OF FUNCTIONING REGARDLESS OF GENERAL OR SPECIFIC ADAPTABILITY. THUS, NONPATIENTS WITH THIS CHARACTERISTIC ARE OFTEN PERCEIVED BY OTHERS AS PREDICTABLY STURDY. CONVERSELY, PATIENTS WITH THIS CHARACTERISTIC ARE OFTEN MORE DIFFICULT TO TREAT AS THE STABILIZATION IS PERVASIVE AND USUALLY WILL INCLUDE SYMPTOM PATTERNS EVEN THOUGH THEY MAY BE LESS ADAPTIVE OR EVEN MALADAPTIVE IN SOME SITUATIONS.

7. THERE IS EVIDENCE INDICATING THE PRESENCE OF CONSIDERABLE SUBJECTIVELY FELT DISTRESS.

==

Figure 12.2. Semantic interpretation of the Rorschach protocol utilizing the comprehensive system.

SUBJECT NAME:SAMPLE AGE:35 SEX:M RACE:W MS:Mar ED:16

PAGE -2-

8. THIS IS THE TYPE OF PERSON WHO TENDS TO VACILLATE BETWEEN "THINKING THROUGH" AND TRIAL-AND-ERROR BEHAVIORS WHEN PROBLEM SOLVING SITUATIONS ARISE. NEITHER FORMAT HAS BEEN VERY WELL DEVELOPED. THUS, SUCH PEOPLE TEND TO BE LESS PREDICTABLE AND LESS EFFICIENT THAN THOSE WITH BETTER ESTABLISHED APPROACHES TO PROBLEM SOLVING.

9. THIS SUBJECT DOES NOT MODULATE EMOTIONAL DISPLAYS AS MUCH AS MOST ADULTS AND, BECAUSE OF THIS, IS PRONE TO BECOME VERY INFLUENCED BY FEELINGS IN MOST THINKING, DECISIONS, AND BEHAVIORS.

10. THIS IS A PERSON WHO SEEMS TO BE WORKING HARD TO AVOID EMOTIONALLY TONED SITUATIONS. USUALLY PEOPLE WITH THIS TENDENCY HAVE A FEARFULNESS OF THOSE KINDS OF SITUATIONS OR OF THEIR OWN ABILITY TO RESPOND TO THEM. THIS MAY BE AN INDICATION OF SOME AWARENESS OF PROBLEMS IN EMOTION CONTROL AND REFLECTIVE OF AN EFFORT TO AVOID BEING DISRUPTED BY THOSE PROBLEMS.

11. THIS IS AN INDIVIDUAL WHO DOES NOT EXPERIENCE NEEDS FOR CLOSENESS IN WAYS THAT ARE COMMON TO MOST PEOPLE. AS A RESULT, THEY ARE TYPICALLY LESS COMFORTABLE IN INTERPERSONAL SITUATIONS, HAVE SOME DIFFICULTIES IN CREATING AND SUSTAINING DEEP RELATIONSHIPS, ARE MORE CONCERNED WITH ISSUES OF PERSONAL SPACE, AND MAY APPEAR MUCH MORE GUARDED AND/OR DISTANT TO OTHERS. IN SPITE OF THIS GUARDED INTERPERSONAL STANCE, SOME OF THE DATA SUGGEST A PREFERENCE FOR DEPENDENCY ON OTHERS WHICH WOULD SEEM TO CREATE A CONFLICT SITUATION. IN OTHER WORDS, THE SUBJECT WANTS TO TAKE FROM OTHERS WHILE REMAINING DISTANT FROM THEM.

12. THIS SUBJECT HAS AS MUCH INTEREST IN OTHERS AS DO MOST ADULTS AND CHILDREN.

13. THIS SUBJECT HAS MORE NEGATIVE SELF ESTEEM OR SELF VALUE THAN IS COMMON FOR EITHER ADULTS OR CHILDREN. IT IS THE PRODUCT OF MAKING COMPARISONS OF ONESELF TO OTHERS, USUALLY PEERS, AND CONCLUDING THAT THOSE EXTERNAL MODELS ARE MORE ADEQUATE. THIS CREATES A TENDENCY TO DISLIKE ONESELF AND CAN BECOME THE NUCLEUS FROM WHICH FEELINGS OF INFERIORITY AND/OR INADEQUACY EVOLVE. IN LIGHT OF THIS FINDING, IT IS VERY IMPORTANT TO REVIEW THE OVERALL RECORD CAREFULLY TO OBTAIN A SENSE OF THE SELF IMAGE.

14. THIS PERSON IS PRONE TO MUCH MORE INTROSPECTION THAN IS COMMON. WHEN THIS OCCURS, MUCH OF THE FOCUS CONCERNS NEGATIVE FEATURES PERCEIVED TO EXIST IN THE SELF IMAGE. THIS PROVOKES INTERNAL PAIN. SUCH A PROCESS IS OFTEN A PRECURSOR TO FEELINGS OF SADNESS, PESSIMISM, OR EVEN DEPRESSION.

15. THE SELF-IMAGE OR SELF-CONCEPT OF THE SUBJECT APPEARS TO HAVE MANY MORE NEGATIVE THAN POSITIVE FEATURES. IN OTHER WORDS, PERCEIVED LIABILITIES TEND TO OUTWEIGH ASSETS CONSIDERABLY. PEOPLE LIKE THIS OFTEN HAVE A SENSE OF BEING DAMAGED AND THIS HAS A CONSIDERABLE IMPACT ON BOTH THINKING AND ATTITUDES SO THAT A PESSIMISTIC AND/OR

and records such as this with an Adjusted D of +2, far fewer. It would seem that this subject has very good capacities for control and is apparently the type of person who will not lose control except under conditions of extreme and/or prolonged stress. If the D score was in the minus range, the RIAP printout would have warned about potential loss of control; the high D score raises some intriguing questions about the circumstances and nature of the subject's acts of violence in the past. Were they impulsivelike, out-of-control acts, or were they more deliberate and controlled? As noted earlier, RIAP cannot deviate from its pattern of search, and it cannot integrate findings to a level higher than that for which it has been designed. But the human interpreter can, and possibly some other statements generated by RIAP can add information related to this question.

Statements 9 and 10 afford some interesting findings concerning how the subject responds in emotional situations. The first indicates that he does not modulate emotional displays as much as most adults, and, as a consequence, emotions tend to become quite influential in his thinking and behaviors. The second indicates that he does not like to be around emotional stimuli. Assuming that the findings concerning control capabilities are valid, it would appear that he is a person who does not exert that capacity when discharging emotion. In other words, he is prone to passively give way to his feelings and permits them to be more intense than ordinarily would be desirable for an adult. That tendency to passively give way to feelings could easily lead to disruptive behaviors that are marked by intense affect, such as the violence noted in the history. Thus, while more data would be preferable, the RIAP findings to this point suggest that the subject is not very likely to exert controls over his feelings when they arise. In fact, statement 10 suggests that his solution to the problem is avoidance. In other words, even though he may have exceptionally good capacities for controlling and directing his behaviors, including his emotional behaviors, he apparently does not know how to use those capacities effectively other than to attempt to avoid provoking situations. Obviously, this finding relates directly to two of the three assessment questions posed, one concerning controls and the other concerning his potential for being dangerous to himself or others. The concern about his failure to modulate emotion very well might be afforded even more weight when considered in light of the RIAP statements 3 (perceptual problems) and 17 (not as oriented toward making socially acceptable responses even in situations when the conventional response is easily identified).

To this point then, it would appear that the subject is most likely to be schizophrenic, or at the very least tends to misinterpret stimulus inputs considerably and has strange thinking; that although he has capabilities for control (and consequently very good tolerance for stress), he usually does not exert those capabilities when emotions are involved, even though conventional responses are usually easily identified. Some added information concerning the issue of danger to himself or others may be derived from four other statements that have been generated from a sweep of the structural data by RIAP.

Statement 12 indicates that he is interested in people (the relatively brief


```
SUBJECT NAME:SAMPLE                    AGE:35  SEX:M  RACE:W  MS:Mar  ED:16

   PAGE -3-
==========================================================================
     NEGATIVISTIC FORM OF IDEATION IS COMMONPLACE.

16.  THIS SUBJECT APPEARS TO HAVE A MARKED SEXUAL PREOCCUPATION.

17.  THIS SUBJECT IS NOT AS ORIENTED AS MOST PEOPLE TO MAKING CONVENTIONAL
     AND/OR SOCIALLY ACCEPTABLE RESPONSES IN THOSE SITUATIONS WHERE THE
     CONVENTIONAL RESPONSE IS EASILY IDENTIFIED.

18.  THIS PERSON MAKES A MARKED EFFORT TO ORGANIZE STIMULI IN A MEANINGFUL
     AND INTEGRATED WAY.

19.  THIS PERSON IS WILLING TO INVEST MUCH MORE EFFORT IN PROBLEM-SOLVING
     SITUATIONS THAN MAY BE NECESSARY. THIS IS THE PRODUCT OF SUBSTANTIAL
     NEEDS TO ACHIEVE. IT IS NOT NECESSARILY A LIABILITY PROVIDED THAT THE
     INDIVIDUAL HAS GOOD CAPACITIES FOR IMPULSE CONTROL AND ORGANIZATIONAL
     ABILITIES THAT ARE RELATIVELY FREE FROM DISTORTION OR IMPAIRMENT.
     HOWEVER, WHEN THIS IS NOT THE CASE, THE FAILURE TO ECONOMIZE TENDS TO
     EXACERBATE OTHER EXISTING LIABILITIES.

20.  IN SPITE OF THE FACT THAT THE SUBJECT MAKES AN EFFORT TO ORGANIZE
     STIMULI, THIS PERSON IS SOMEWHAT CONSERVATIVE IN SETTING GOALS.
     USUALLY PEOPLE LIKE THIS WANT TO COMMIT THEMSELVES ONLY TO OBJECTIVES
     WHICH OFFER A SIGNIFICANT PROBABILITY OF SUCCESS.

                        * * *  END OF REPORT  * * *

==========================================================================
(c)1976, 1985 by John E. Exner, Jr.
```

Again, it is important to stress that the Structural Summary and the interpretive messages drawn from the structural data are derived from the input, that is, the scoring of the responses. If they are correct, the interpretive messages that are printed will have a high probability of being valid, or at least applicable to the overall picture of the subject. On the other hand, if the scores that have been entered for the responses are marked by several errors, the RIAP-generated statements are most likely to mislead the interpreter by suggesting the presence of operations and/or characteristics that, in fact, may not be applicable to the subject. Stated somewhat differently, persons relying on computer assistance must also have faith in their own scoring integrity.

Using the Interpretive Messages

The RIAP-generated statements begin with one indicating that the record appears to be valid and interpretively useful. There is little reason to question this. The Structural Summary shows that fifteen answers have been given and that the Lambda is not elevated. One might question whether the subject would have attempted to "look good" by his performance, but if that motive existed, a quick glance at the Schizophrenia Index (SCZI) suggests that it was not accomplished very effectively.

The next four RIAP statements are derived from the SCZI and those variables that contribute to it, and they should be the next focus of concern. The first indicates a high probability of schizophrenia (based on the SCZI value of 5). The second argues that marked deficits exist in perceptual accuracy (X−% is high and there are more minus than unusual answers). The third focuses on data suggesting problems in thinking (there are eleven of the six critical Special Scores, the weighted sum6 is very high, and the record contains three M− answers). The fourth statement in this series is a caution, and because the history is reasonably thorough it is probably the easiest to address first. The subject has no known history of drug abuse, and since he is an inpatient it seems reasonable to assume that physical-neurological examinations have been completed. Thus it seems appropriate to proceed to the other three statements with the assumption that the disarray indicated is neither drug or neurologically related. If the history included some evidence of significant drug abuse or unresolved medical problems, other data such as the results of drug screening or other biochemistry findings and/or other medical findings would be highly relevant to any final conclusions about the Rorschach data.

The question of whether the subject is schizophrenic cannot be resolved simply by reviewing other structural data. RIAP has already screened as much structural data as possible to get at this issue and has rendered empirically based conclusions. And the data are compelling. There is evidence of perceptual-mediational distortion and evidence for disordered thought. This is a combination of findings very common to schizophrenia and very uncommon to other conditions. Normative data indicate that the Rorschachs of more than 80 percent of schizophrenic patients, defined as such by other criteria, will contain evidence for both of these features. Conversely, only a very small percentage of inpatient affective disorders (approximately 5 percent) will have an SCZI of 5, and that percentage is lower for other groups. Thus the decision about whether to accept or reject the schizophrenia hypothesis requires more data from other sources. Some of those data exist in the protocol, but some must be gleaned from the history and other assessment sources.

In this case, the history seems at least partially supportive of the probability of schizophrenia. The subject has had two prior hospitalizations, has been abusive and violent, has an erratic work history, and appears to convey at least an unduly suspicious if not openly paranoid attitude toward others at times. Conversely, he has been able to sustain a marriage for approximately eight years and also has been able to maintain gainful employment during much of that time. The latter is more atypical for a schizophrenic who has required multiple hospitalizations. If the history had been much more favorable—that is, if it indicated that this was a first admission, that only one continuous marriage had existed over a ten- to thirteen-year period, and if the work history were more consistent—the likelihood of schizophrenia would be considerably less.

In most cases involving schizophrenia, confirming data will be foun careful evaluation of the protocol verbiage. Responses containing some of the six critical Special Scores will usually seem very strange or biza even the casual reader. For instance, the answer "Two dogs playing bal FABCOM, but it is not terribly strange, and in fact it is almost common in the records of very young children. On the other hand, the answer " women pulling the eyes out of a frog" is bizarre. It is also scored as a FABC but it rings out with pathology much more than the first. Similarly, a re of the M− answers in a record will typically yield considerably more evid of bizarreness in the case of schizophrenia than when some other conditi present. Thus in this record it would be quite important for the interprete consider carefully the verbal material as well as the history, before decidin accept or reject the schizophrenia hypothesis.

Regardless of whether the interpreter accepts or rejects that hypothesis, other two statements, regarding perceptual-mediational distortion and disorde thinking, are probably true. They are based on relatively "hard" data. T X−% is elevated; the number of minus answers is substantial in relation to number of unusual responses. In addition, the X+% is also quite low and th are only three Popular answers. It seems clear that the subject does not transl inputs in a very conventional way, and often does distort those inputs. T data concerning problems in thinking are equally compelling. There are elev critical Special Scores; and there are three M− answers. The large number critical Special Scores is magnified by the relative brevity of the record: the are only fifteen responses. Interestingly, although there are many more critic Special Scores than would be expected from a nonschizophrenic subject, th distribution of those scores has a characteristic that is atypical for most schizo phrenics. Nine of the eleven scores are DR. DR responses usually signal cir cumstantiality in thinking, but sometimes an answer that is appropriately score DR will not be circumstantial but will sound very peculiar or queer. The latte is more often the case among schizophrenics, especially those who are frequentl overwhelmed by delusional operations or well-systematized preoccupations. Again, it would behoove the interpreter to read the DR answers to distinguish what kind of cognitive slippage is represented. If the subject is a paranoid schizophrenic, it is likely that the answers will be marked by comments concerning magic, evil, guardedness, grandiosity, and the like rather than the circumstantial inability to bring closure to a response that is more typical of some maniclike subjects.

The sixth statement generated by RIAP is quite important in light of one of the assessment questions posed. Namely, does the subject have controls that are adequate to sustain him in a semi-independent environment? The question suggests that those around him tend to view the subject as having very fragile or limited controls, yet the structural data (EA es) support a very different position. The data concerning the stability of the Adjusted D score are substantial and indicate that it is unlikely to change much over lengthy intervals. Records showing an Adjusted D score of +1 are in the minority among nonpatients

record contains six human contents); however, statement 11 reveals that he does not experience as much need for being close to others as is common among adults. It reveals (by the absence of T) that he is less comfortable in interpersonal relations than most adults, but at the same time he would like to be dependent on others in some way (there is a food response in the record). Those statements suggest that he is likely to be more guarded and distant with people, a finding that does not necessarily signal a liability, except for the fact that he is married and many of his jobs have involved interpersonal contact (waiter, taxi driver, social worker). Moreover, RIAP statement 16 (derived from a content elevation) indicates that he has a marked sexual preoccupation, a finding that may relate to dependency need but could also derive from other issues. Statements 13 and 15 may be quite important in this respect. The first suggests that he tends to value himself more negatively than should be the case (the egocentricity index is quite low), while the second indicates that his self-image is marked by some very negative features (five MOR responses in the protocol), which, in turn, predisposes a sense of pessimism in his thinking and attitudes. Pessimism is an affective influence that, as the RIAP statement conveys, can breed very negativistic thinking. This feature is also noted in RIAP statement 14 (derived from the frequencies of vista and FD answers), suggesting that he is overly involved in self-inspection and that much of that activity centers on negative characteristics of his self-image. Although a large part of that tendency might be provoked by his extensive treatment, the fact that much of it has a negative and probably painful yield does not bode well. In fact, it may be that some of the subjectively felt distress signaled in RIAP statement 7 (derived from the data of the EB) is generated by this process.

Given that his thinking is disordered and that his translations of stimuli tend to be unusual and distorted; and given that he has good capacities for control but does not exert them when in situations when his feelings are stimulated; and given that he does not make many conventional responses, even in situations in which the conventional responses are rather obvious; and add to this the data related to his impoverished and negative self-image, low self-esteem, interest in but guardedness toward others, and logically ask the question, "What must this man's interpersonal world be like?" The answer, based only on RIAP's statements, must be one that raises concerns.

RIAP statement 8 (based on the data of the EB) indicates that he is not very efficient and/or predictable in coping situations. Instead, he vacillates and typically invests more energy than most people in problem-solving efforts. As such, he is prone toward more errors and the repetition of more errors than would be the case if he had developed a more consistent coping style. RIAP statements 18 (makes a marked effort to organize, Zf = 8 and DQ+ = 6), 21 (is willing to invest much more effort in problem solving than may be necessary—that is, the W:D is the reverse of that expected), and 20 (uses more time and energy than is necessary to organize a stimulus field, Zd = +4.5) suggest that he does work hard to be aware of what is going on around him. However, his problem in perceptual-mediational translation (statement 3) suggests that much of that effort goes awry, a factor that becomes even more of a liability when considered in relation to RIAP statement 19 (based on the DQ distribution), which indicates that much of his cognitive activity is less mature or sophisticated than might be expected for an adult, especially an adult who has graduated from college. Fortunately, as indicated by RIAP statement 22 (based on R and the W:M ratio), he is relatively conservative in setting goals, so that the likelihood of frustration being produced by failure to achieve is reduced.

In most instances, the description of the subject derived from the RIAP statements should be a good beginning. In this case, the composite of the RIAP statements plus some logical integration of their contents provides considerable information about the subject, and has also raised several questions that require further exploration.

At this point in the interpretive process, it appears as if the subject is burdened by some significant and severe psychological problems. It seems very likely that he is schizophrenic, although that issue requires further review. In any event, his thinking is disordered, his perceptual-mediational activities include far more distortion than is desirable, and he is not very oriented toward modulating the release of his emotions. In fact, it seems that there will be times when he is passively submissive to his feelings, and in those circumstances they will tend to become more intense and overly influential in his thinking, decisions, and behaviors than seems preferable for many day-to-day contacts with the environment and those in it.

The situation is made more complex by the fact that he has very substantial capacities for control and handling stress. Although at first glance that may seem like an asset, it is often more of a liability for the disturbed subject. The capacity to withstand stress easily does protect the subject from the intrusions of discomfort, but that often leads to a lower motivation for change or assistance; and if thinking and mediation are disturbed, the subject is less likely to accept or even consider the judgments and/or suggestions of others in formulating new behaviors. It is difficult to avoid the speculation that the subject's substantial capacity for control has, in some way, led those responsible for his treatment to assume that a halfway house situation might be desirable at this time. It also seems probable that his capacity for control permits him to engage in the avoidance behaviors that were noted in the RIAP printout concerning his responsiveness to emotional situations. It seems possible that, as an inpatient, he has been able to avoid provoking situations and in so doing has probably concealed, at least partially, his tendency to give way to feelings.

It also seems quite likely that his interests in people are marked by more unusual features than may readily meet the eye of the casual observer. Apparently he does not want to be emotionally close to others, but he would prefer some dependency relation; and he seems to have an unusually strong sexual preoccupation. It also seems obvious that he makes a substantial effort to process stimuli around him. Again, this may be an asset, especially in that he does not set very high goals for himself, but it may also signal something about his need to guard himself in the interpersonal world. At some level, probably not very apparent to others, he does not regard himself very favorably, and much of his thinking will contain pessimistic elements. He appears to be engaging in much more self-inspection than would be expected, but we are not privy to the specific yield of that process, except to note that some of it is creating distress for him. Although he seems to work hard at processing information, some of his cognition is less sophisticated than should be the case, and when added to the fact that some of his thinking is disordered, it seems likely that he will often be very misled by some of his own conclusions.

The preceding summary, based on the integration of RIAP statements and some history data, falls far short of the final interpretation. One of the assessment issues, that concerning control capability, appears to have been answered, but probably not in the context that might have been expected by whoever made the referral. The question of the diagnosis is still tentative, and the question about potential danger to himself or others has not been addressed. Several steps are required to complete the Rorschach interpretation, and others are needed before the interpreter will formulate a final report.

The interpreter should not naively assume that, because RIAP has printed a series of statements based on a sweep of the structural data, the Structural Summary can be set aside. To the contrary, RIAP has simply reviewed thirty-one clusters of data, using empirically derived parameters. Most experienced Rorschachers will be able to generate additional hypotheses from the structural data. To illustrate, the Structural Summary includes the following data, none of which were considered in the RIAP decisions because they do not meet set criteria in the program:

1. The S-CON is 7.
2. The DEPI is 3.
3. There are no FM responses.
4. There are two aggressive movement responses.
5. There are four clothing contents.

One of the referral questions concerns the possibility of danger to himself. While the S-CON value is not at the critical point of eight positive variables, seven is very close to that point, and in this instance it seems important to point out that if he had given one less Popular answer, the S-CON would be 8. Thus, while there is no firm empirical basis from which to caution about a self-destruction potential, it is realistic to note that the subject's record contains many features that are also found in protocols of people with that characteristic. Furthermore, the DEPI of 3 falls one less than the critical point at which the index would signal the presence of chronic depression or the features that give rise to frequent and intense experiences of depression. The value of 3 should not be regarded lightly. The subject does have some of those features, and if these non-RIAP findings are considered in light of his tendency to give way easily to feelings, it seems foolish to disregard the possibility of a controlled but emotionally based decision to self-injury.

In a similar context, the presence of the two AG answers in this relatively short record cannot be disregarded. Although technically it is not a substantial elevation, considered in proportion to R it may be. Elevations in AG suggest that the subject is prone to view interpersonal relationships as being marked by aggressiveness and also is prone to behave more aggressively in interpersonal relationships, either verbally or physically, than is commonplace among adults. He has a history of aggressiveness, which in itself is a good predictor of the future, and when that history is considered in conjunction with these data, the likelihood of future aggressive behavior seems possible (especially because, as noted in the RIAP statement, he is not a person very prone to be concerned with making socially expected responses, even though those responses may be somewhat obvious).

The absence of FM answers is quite intriguing. Most subjects, both children and adults, patients and nonpatients, will give at least two or three, and often as many as five. FM is apparently related to the psychological experience of need states. When a record is void of FM it seems illogical to assume that the subject has no needs. That is impossible. Although the data concerning these kinds of protocols are sparse, they do seem to indicate that people who give no FM are more likely to avoid delays in promoting need reduction. This does not mean that they act impulsively. Instead, they mobilize resources, no matter how sturdy or fragile the resources may be, to formulate action that is designed to bring about need reduction. If this is true, and if it is applicable to this case, it may be that the subject is the type of person who will not tolerate the aggravation of unmet needs for any lengthy time; that instead he will act to reduce their irritation. Quite possibly, a more detailed history may shed some light on this postulate.

Finally, the presence of many answers that include clothing contents in this brief record is also intriguing. The empirical data concerning clothing contents are also very sparse; however, logic suggests that clothing is a form of protection and/or concealment.

These added speculations derived from the structure have added slightly to the RIAP-derived summary. They have raised more questions and contributed some input to the third assessment question, concerning potential danger to himself or others.

If the interpretation were to end here, only one of the three assessment questions could be addressed with any degree of confidence. His controls are strong! He is probably schizophrenic, and he may well be a danger to either himself or others, but more clarification concerning those issues must come from other sources, the first of which is the remainder of the record. The next step is a careful review of the Sequence of Scores, searching for unusual clusterings of variables or unusual patterns. Then the responses should be read carefully with the objective of searching out projective material, capturing a clearer picture of the deviant material, and integrating those findings with the previously generated picture of this man.

Once the Rorschach has been fully reviewed, the yield can be integrated with other assessment data obtained from other tests, interviews, behavioral reports, and more casual observational data. If added history is available, it too will be helpful to the final objective of providing the most comprehensive description of the subject possible within the framework of contemporary procedures. Once that total package is in place, recommendations concerning treatment and placement can be generated from a solid base. Hopefully, computer programs such as RIAP can be used by many involved in the routines of personality assessment to facilitate this total assessment process.

A Look to the Future

It should be apparent to those knowledgable about computers and computer programming that any program designed to assist in test interpretation will not necessarily remain static. As new validation data relevant to interpretation become available, programs will be upgraded and new versions generated. This prospect is especially important to those who use the Rorschach, for it remains a test about which many issues are yet to be resolved. In spite of the fact that the test was devised more than sixty years ago and that the same ten Swiss inkblots continue to constitute the basic stimuli, the accumulated data fail to address satisfactorily the issue of what material is projected in responses. When that question is resolved the result will pose no small challenge to those interested in including such findings in a computer assistance package. Similarly, valid data continue to be very sparse relating to the interpretive importance of response sequencing. This is true not only concerning the sequence of location selections, but probably much more important concerning the sequence by which determinant features of the blots are reported. At the moment, these are issues that must be addressed more speculatively by the astute Rorschach interpreter; however, the ever-increasing sophistication in the technological capacities for complex data analysis of very large samples suggests that these are issues that will be resolved during the next decade. In turn, the result should be much more assistance to the Rorschach interpreter of the future than is now the case.

REFERENCES

Beck, S. J. (1944). *Rorschach's Test I: Basic processes*. New York: Grune & Stratton.

Exner, J. E. (1986). *The Rorschach: A comprehensive system: Vol. 1. Basic Foundations*. New York: Wiley.

Hertz, M. R. (1942). *Frequency tables for scoring Rorschach responses*. Cleveland, IL: Western Reserve University Press.

Klopfer, B., and Kelley, D. (1942). *The Rorschach technique*. Yonkers-on-Hudson, NY: World Book.

Piotrowski, Z. (1957). *Perceptanalysis*. New York: Macmillan.

Rapaport, D., Gill, M., and Schafer, R. (1946). *Diagnostic psychological testing, Vols. 1 and 2*. Chicago: Yearbook Publishers.

Rorschach, H. (1942). *Psychodiagnostik*. (Hans Huber Verlag, Trans.) Bern: Bircher. (Original work published 1921)

13

Computerized Psychological Assessment in Italy: State of the Art

Paolo Pancheri and Massimo Biondi

Computerized psychological assessment was introduced into Italy in 1970 when the first system of automated interpretation of the Minnesota Multiphasic Personality Inventory (MMPI) was designed by Pancheri and colleagues (1974) at the Institute of Psychiatry of the University of Rome (IPUR). Five years later the first and still only computerized interpretation system of the Rorschach available in Italy became operational at the same institute (Pancheri et al., 1979). In 1985 a second computerized MMPI interpretation system was presented by Mosticoni and Mosticoni (1986).

In addition to these three systems, which score the protocol and provide clinical interpretation of the case in the form of a narrative report, other scoring programs are available for the most common psychometric tests (Organizzazioni Speciali, 1986). The Institute of Psychology of the University of Padova has also designed a clinical assessment program for use in psychotherapeutic applications. This program furnishes a narrative report based on the scores obtained from a series of psychometric questionnaires (Sanavio et al., 1985).

All of these scoring and interpretation programs are available commercially, with the exception of the IPUR's interpretative programs for the MMPI and the Rorschach, which are available in the FORTRAN version at no charge to any public or private institution requesting them (see table 13.1).

This chapter describes the computerized interpretation systems for the MMPI, the most widely utilized psychometric test in Italy, and the Rorschach interpretation system, because this test is still widely used by clinicians.

TABLE 13.1

Computerized Systems for Psychological Assessment in Italy

Test	*Reference*	*Scoring*	*Narrative*	*Diagnostic*	*Stage of Development*	*Languages, Computers*	*Availability*
MMPI	IPUR system, Pancheri et al., 1974	yes	yes	yes, discriminant function analysis	15 years' experience in many psychiatric facilities	FORTRAN V	free
MMPI	IPUR system, Pancheri and Giusti, 1985	yes	yes	no	5 years' experience in many psychiatric facilities	BASIC: IBM PC, Apple II, Olivetti	commercial
MMPI	M-Two/2, Mosticoni and Mosticoni, 1986	yes	yes	yes, clinical criteria	early stages of use	BASIC: Apple II, IBM PC, Olivetti	commercial
Rorschach	PRALP, Pancheri et al., 1979	yes	yes	no	7 years of clinical application at the IPUR	FORTRAN V	free
Cognitive Behavioural Assessment[a]	CBA 2.0, Sanavio et al., 1985	yes	yes	no	early stage of use	BASIC: Apple II, IBM PC, Olivetti	commercial
PSY-SYSTEM[b]	Organizzazioni Speciali, 1986	yes	no	no	early stage of use	BASIC: IBM PC, Olivetti	commercial

[a]The CBA 2.0 battery includes Eysenck Personality Inventory, State and Trait Personality Inventory, Maudsley Obsessive Compulsive Questionnaire, and other self-rating scales.

[b]The PSY-SYSTEM battery includes the MMPI, Adjective Check List, Institute for Personality and Ability Testing CDQ (depression), IPAT ASQ (anxiety), Gordon Personal Profile, and attitudinal tests.

The IPUR–MMPI Interpretation System

RATIONALE

The IPUR-MMPI Interpretation System was designed to meet the need for a computerized scoring program; to serve as a narrative interpretative program to complement the traditional clinical interview in the assessment of psychiatric patients; and to provide a computerized diagnostic program based on empirical criteria to be used as an aid to clinical diagnosis.

GENERAL CHARACTERISTICS OF THE SYSTEM

The IPUR system was set up in 1971 by Pancheri and Morgana in order to give to the clinician, besides the results of a standard scoring, a narrative automated report and a diagnostic interpretation of the profile based on a comparative statistical analysis with reference to diagnostic groups.

It is made up of three different but complementary systems: the scoring program, the narrative program, and the diagnostic program.

THE SCORING PROGRAM

The program itself is basically similar in input-output configuration and structure to several scoring programs already available. In the IPUR scoring program, however, the authors tried to meet the need of both MMPI researchers and practicing clinical psychologists and psychiatrists. The input options are the true/false answers of the full-length or short-form questionnaire or the true/false answers typed by the patient in the self-administered version. The program gives the following output from the MMPI items:

1. Raw scores, K-corrected raw scores, and K-corrected T-scores for the ten clinical scales; raw scores for the *L*, *F*, *K* scales and "cannot say" scale scores. For the T-score computation, the official Italian norms (Nencini, 1958, 1965) were used.
2. Raw scores and T-scores for 142 special scales, listed in the printout separately under the basic scales. The T-scores for these scales were computed, as they were for the basic scales, with the usual formula (Dahlstrom, Welsh, and Dahlstrom, 1972) using means and standard deviations from a representative sample of Italian college students. This part of the printout is not expected to be used in the routine clinical evaluation of patients but rather by personality assessment researchers. Despite the low validity and reliability of many of the special scales, some information on them was provided to enable researchers to check directly the predictive value of the scales or to use them for research purpose.
3. Critical item lists. Despite its nonempirically derived structure, the Grayson Critical Item List (Grayson, 1951) was used in the scoring program because clinicians often use it in target-symptoms–directed interviews.
4. Graphic representation of the profile. The K-corrected T-scores are provided on the printout.

THE NARRATIVE PROGRAM

The narrative program was developed in the fall of 1972 as the final step in the IPUR-MMPI automated interpretative system (Pancheri, Girardi, Bernabei, and Morgana, 1974).

Decision Rules. The interpretative strategy followed in developing the narrative was to go through the profile by analyzing pairs of scales. The first stage involved selection of the combinations of groups and scales with which well-researched personality correlates were associated. To be consistent with clinical interpretation, it was decided not to focus only on high-point codes but to consider every possible combination of scores for all pairs of scales considered. The starting point for the bidimensional analysis was the Diamond scheme (1957), which seemed at least partially to fit the purpose of the research project. The interpretations were submitted for clinical examination to a group of experienced MMPI interpreters who suggested several modifications based on their clinical experience. Several new bidimensional patterns were added, others were modified, and still others were dropped because they were judged useless or clinically meaningless. The final list of scale combinations contained eleven items (see table 13.2), each of which was judged meaningful for the description of a clinically important personality trait.

In the second stage, a group of decision rules for each bidimensional combination was written. For every decision rule, four variables were taken into account: (1) type of scale combination (or group of scales); (2) highest scale (or group) in the combination considered; (3) T-score of the highest scale (or group) in the combination considered; (4) difference in T-scores between the highest and lowest scales (or groups). In most cases the score interval of 10 T-score was considered sufficient for a good discrimination; in some cases it was reduced to 5 T-score, according to clinical experience with the variables. Scores higher than T equals 90 and lower than T equals 30 were not taken into account. A total of 353 decision rules was thus obtained and used as a guide in writing the statement library.

Statement Library. For every decision rule thus established, a descriptive statement was written. To form the statement library, about eight hundred clinical cases, for which both the MMPI and a narrative mental status were available, were analyzed. The clinical cases were grouped by MMPI profiles according to the decision rules just described. The interpretative statements were based on the clinical description of patients with MMPI configurations grouped according to the same decision rule (or group of rules).

Thus for every decision rule a statement was written, obtaining a total of 353 statements. Each statement was limited to four lines of sixty characters to make the narrative report more compact and readable. The list of decision rules and related narrative statements was then rearranged and restructured according to sequential order to make the report more consistent and readable. By appropriately ordering the rules and statements, repetitions and contradictions were avoided.

Statements descriptive of the same behavioral and personality areas were

TABLE 13.2
Content Areas for Computer-Based Decision Rules

Sequential Order in the Program	*Scale Pattern*	*Personality Area*	*Number of Statements*
1	*L/K*	Test validity and control of self-image in social interactions.	40
2	*D/Ma*	Mood. Depression versus excitement.	47
3	*Pt/Pd*	Impulsiveness and control of aggressiveness.	44
4	*Si/Pd*	Activity-passivity in social interactions.	34
5	*D* + *Pt/Ma* + *Pd*	Self-esteem. Projection of aggressiveness versus self-aggressiveness.	32
6	*Hs/Hy*	Neurotic defenses. Tendency toward the use of somatic symptoms to get emotional rewards.	19
7	*Hy/Pa*	Social adaptability. Tendency to social compliance opposed to social hostility.	34
8	*Pa* + *Sc/Hy* + *Hs*	Contact with reality. Tendency to withdrawal and pathological fantasies opposed to socially finalized neurotic behavior.	28
9	*F/Sc*	Psychotic tendencies.	18
10	*Mf/Hs* + *Hy* *Mf/Ma* + *Pd*	Sexual problems and behavior.	24
11	*K/F*	Defenses: emotional control.	43

organized together in the list so that they would be printed in the same section of the narrative report. This was done to provide a better and more coherent description of the patient. The choice of the rules, the text of the statements, and their sequence is organized so that more statements describing the most relevant psychopathological traits are printed, and thus the descriptions of these traits are longer than the descriptions of other traits.

The Program. Once the decision rules and the statement library were established, a program was written in FORTRAN V. Because the interpretative philosophy was basically simple (a list of single decision rules with a corresponding list of statements), the program was structured to make possible further modifications without extensive rewriting or modification. The extensive use of the "logical" statement in FORTRAN makes it easy to modify one or more of the rules or descriptive statements by simply changing one statement in the program and avoiding any structural modification. The input of the program is in K-corrected T-scores, and the output is the narrative report, a translated version of which is given in figure 13.1. It is possible to enter the program either directly from the scoring program output or separately by teletype keyboard.

Internal Consistency Control. The first four hundred automated narrative reports were carefully examined by the group of experienced MMPI interpreters participating in the project. For each report all contradictions, inconsistencies, and redundancies were listed and discussed. Moreover, the consistency of every report was rated by the patient's attending psychiatrist, and this rating was

Institute of Psychiatry of the University of Rome
Psychological and Clinical Research Section
Automated MMPI Report

Identification #11058

In taking the test, the patient answered honestly and sincerely, but showed a slight tendency toward social nonconformity.

The patient is depressed and psychasthenic; lack of initiative and ideational uniformity are present; he responds with depression to unsatisfactory life situations; a picture of psychomotor retardation is observed.

There are very marked psychasthenic features: indecision, doubt, a tendency toward compulsive behaviors, as well as a very passive attitude. The patient shows alternating periods of extreme passivity and dependency toward others and periods when hostile and frankly aggressive behaviors are prominent.

The patient tends to avoid situations involving social interaction and finds it difficult to feel at ease in group situations. He shows a low level of self-esteem, self-depreciatory themes are evident, and he appears reluctant to take the initiative and abandon his passive role.

A tendency toward hypochondriacal somatization of anxiety is very evident: somatic disturbances without real objective bases tend to be utilized as a means of nonverbal communication. There are tendencies toward dependency and manipulation of relationships. Somatization is possible; one may see, however, interpretative trends characterized by the use of projection, aggressivity, and distrust as reactions to frustration.

There is also a pathological tendency toward isolation in an autistic and phantastic world with possible reduction of judgment and critical abilities.

The patient's emotional and behavioral disorders appear to be serious. Control and defense abilities are decisively reduced; personality disorganization is possible.

(Translated by Sergio Guglielmi)

Figure 13.1. Translated sample printout of a narrative report from the IPUR system.

analyzed. Clinical inconsistencies and lack of information in behavioral areas, important from a psychiatric standpoint, were taken into account and discussed. At the end of this phase, it was decided to modify about 30 percent of the decision-rule set and to change about 20 percent of the statement library. The current form of the IPUR system is the result of this revision.

THE DIAGNOSTIC PROGRAM

It is important for clinicians practicing in a psychiatric setting to obtain some kind of working diagnosis. The diagnostic program of the IPUR system provides a tentative diagnostic interpretation of MMPI profiles on the basis of a taxonomic classification system used at the Institute of Psychiatry of the University of Rome.

The Bayesian rule applied to discriminant functions derived from the thirteen basic MMPI variables was used in the diagnostic program to give an empirically derived measurement of the similarity of every new profile to groups of profiles constructed on the a priori criterion of the clinical diagnoses.

The discriminant-function method was used instead of a logical decision-tree procedure because it makes possible a diagnostic interpretation empirically derived from a well-defined sample of patients, thus avoiding any kind of theoretical inference about "typical configurations" related to clinical diagnoses. Another advantage of the discriminant-function method was the possibility of modifying the parameters of the "model" according to the new data available from clinical experience, to get a flexible and "learning" diagnostic system. On the other hand, the availability of a sufficiently large number of subjects for whom there was an MMPI profile and a clinical diagnosis fulfilled the basic requirements of the discriminant-function method.

Diagnostic Groups. The clinical records of patients admitted for treatment to the wards of the Institute of Psychiatry of the University of Rome between 1969 and 1971 were examined. Cases were selected for which there was an MMPI profile completed in the first four days of hospitalization before starting treatment and a clearly defined discharge diagnosis. The diagnostic classification system was the standard system used at that time at the IPUR (Giucci, Pancheri, and Pastena, 1968). Patients with organic brain disease or diagnoses that were infrequent or rare were excluded from the sample. From this preliminary selection, 835 cases were obtained: they were then divided into eleven groups according to clinical diagnosis. One group of normal subjects was included in the analysis as a reference group (see table 13.3).

It should be noted that because of the selection criteria followed, the final sample was representative of the psychiatric population admitted to the IPUR. The relative percentage for each diagnostic group reflects the structure of pathology in the general population.

Discriminant-Function Analysis. The discriminant-function computer program developed by Barker (1974) of the University of Alabama was used on the twelve groups and the thirteen MMPI variables. The scores on the eleven

TABLE 13.3
Subject Groups for the Diagnostic Model and Discriminant-Function Analysis

Diagnosis	*Sample size*
Hysterical neurosis	66
Anxiety neurosis	48
Depressive neurosis	69
Obsessive-compulsive neurosis	22
Acute schizophrenia	154
Chronic schizophrenia	92
Depressive psychosis	58
Manic psychosis	14
Psychopathy (sociopathic personality)	100
Epilepsy (behavioral disorders in epileptics)	23
Chronic alcoholism	62
Normality	127

orthogonal discriminant functions derived from the twelve original variables were used to reclassify every case of the sample on the basis of its discriminant score. Each profile can thus be described in the discriminant space by a point whose coordinates are the values scored by that profile for each discriminant variable, and each group can be described by a multivariate normal distribution characterized by that point and by the variance-covariance matrix. The probability that a particular score vector belongs to a given multivariate distribution depends on the distance of the individual's score vector from the mean vector in the multivariate distribution. The density of a multivariate normal distribution of a point identified by a score vector X is obtained, and the probability that an individual with a particular score pattern x belongs to the i(th) group is computed.

In this way the consistency of the diagnostic model used in the analysis can be checked by constructing classification tables on the basis of the pattern of discriminant scores computed for each case. Thus the highest probability of a given case belonging to one of the groups can be examined.

The reclassification of all cases on the basis of the criteria just described is given in table 13.4. The overall agreement of the discriminant-function clas-

TABLE 13.4
Classification of Cases According to the Discriminant-Function Model, Compared with Original Diagnosis

	Discriminant Function Classification											
Diagnosis	*1*	*2*	*3*	*4*	*5*	*6*	*7*	*8*	*9*	*10*	*11*	*12*
1. Anxiety neurosis	14[a]	2	3	5	2	5	0	4	4	4	1	4
2. Obsessive-compulsive neurosis	1	12	1	1	2	2	0	3	0	0	0	0
3. Hysterical neurosis	1	1	38	6	3	1	0	6	4	4	0	2
4. Depressive neurosis	4	5	6	31	3	6	0	2	5	1	0	6
5. Psychopathy	1	2	4	3	43	5	0	20	8	5	1	8
6. Depressive psychosis	2	3	0	4	1	32	0	12	1	2	1	0
7. Manic psychosis	0	0	0	0	1	0	13	0	0	0	0	0
8. Acute schizophrenia	3	4	4	8	14	7	0	90	8	7	2	7
9. Chronic schizophrenia	1	1	2	1	1	2	0	16	46	12	1	9
10. Chronic alcoholism	3	1	5	0	5	0	1	7	2	28	1	9
11. Epilepsy	0	1	0	1	1	1	0	5	1	2	11	0
12. Normality	1	1	2	3	3	0	0	4	2	3	0	108

[a]Underlined figures are the number of correct classifications for each group.

sification with the original clinical classification on an *a priori* basis is 55.35 percent. The chi-square statistic computed on the basis of the misclassified cases shows that the original groups are discriminated from each other at a satisfactory level of significance. The best agreement (92.85 percent) was obtained for the manic psychosis group, the worst (29.16 percent) for the anxiety neurosis group. It is worth noting that the highest agreements are found for diagnostic groups with the most clearly defined symptomatology and the lowest for groups for which there are no clearly defined symptoms. This confirms the results obtained in studies of interrater agreement on several kinds of psychopathological samples.

Validity of the Classification Model. The mean score for the eleven discriminant variables identifies every group in the discriminant space (centroids). The percentage of variance accounted for by the first two roots extracted contributed about 70 percent of the total. These first two discriminants can thus be used to plot the centroids in the discriminant space defined by them, with little loss of the total information. Figure 13.2 shows that the first variable discriminates along the normality/pathology axis and the second along the basic dimension neuroticism/psychoticism. All the neurotic centroids are thus plotted in the same discriminant space area, as are all the psychotic centroids, and groups with less clearly defined pathology are located between them. This is consistent with clinical observation and with what has been demonstrated in

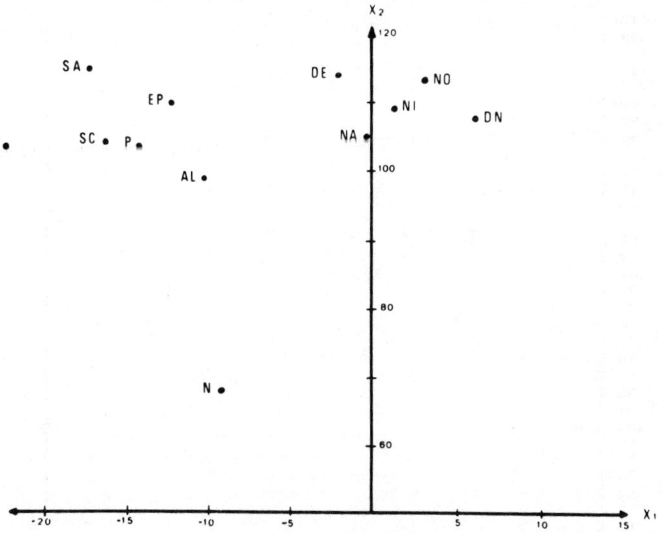

Figure 13.2. Plot of the first (normality/pathology) and second (neuroticism/psychoticism) discriminants.

EM—manic psychosis	EP—epilepsy	NA—anxiety neurosis
SA—acute schizophrenia	AL—alcoholism	NI—hysterical neurosis
SC—chronic schizophrenia	N—normality	NO—obsessive neurosis
P—psychopathy	DE—depression	DN—neurotic depression

several psychometric studies (pathology/normality and neuroticism/psychoticism dimensions).

Thirty-four code-type groups for which the mean profile in K-corrected T-scores was available were used to check the validity of the diagnostic model. Every mean profile was compared with the model, as if it were an individual case, and the classification results were compared with the code type. Most of the code-type groups analyzed were classified in the diagnostic group expected, according to the personality characteristics associated with the code type.

A total of 434 patients newly admitted to the IPUR during 1972–73 were used for the cross-validation of the original model. In 52.32 percent of the cases there was complete agreement between the diagnosis made by external clinical criteria and that made by the diagnostic model. The range of agreement reflected at a satisfactory level of significance the range found in the discriminant-function analysis of the original sample.

Classification of the Cases. A program was written to compute according to the Bayes probability rule the vector of discriminant scores for every new profile received by the system and the probability of its belonging to any of the twelve groups of the model. In the printout, these probabilities are ordered from highest to lowest (see figure 13.3). Before the list of probabilities, a few lines advise that the output is the result of a comparison with the IPUR diagnostic model.

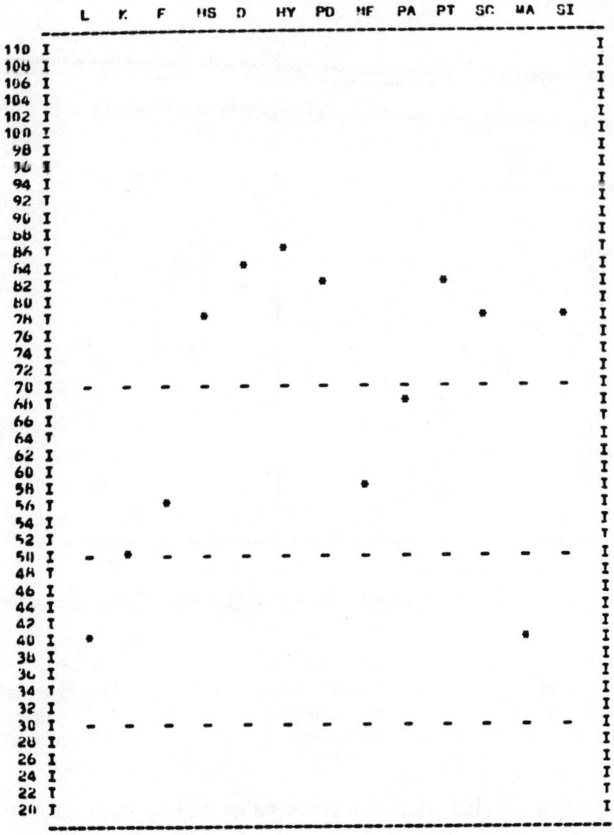

N. 37858

IL CONFRONTO DEL PROFILO MMPI DEL PAZIENTE CON
I PROFILI DI DODICI GRUPPI DIAGNOSTICI DI PAZIENTI
DELLO ISTITUTO DI PSICHIATRIA DELLA UNIVERSITA DI ROMA
HA DATO I SEGUENTI RISULTATI

GRUPPO DIAGNOSTICO	PROB. DI APPARTENENZA
NEVROSI D'ANSIA	.26
DEPRESSIONE NEVROTICA	.25
DEPRESSIONE	.13
SCHIZOFRENIA ACUTA	.12
PSICOPATIA	.11
NEVROSI OSSESSIVA	.07
SCHIZOFRENIA CRONICA	.04
NEVROSI ISTERICA	.01
NORMALITA'	.01
ALCOOLISMO CRONICO	.00
EPILESSIA	.00
ECCIT. MANIACALE	.00

INDICE DI PSICOPATOLOGIA = .99
>

Figure 13.3. Sample printout of the IPUR system: MMPI profile and discriminant-function classification.

FURTHER DEVELOPMENTS

From the experience of the first five hundred clinical cases processed and compared with the qualitative judgment of clinicians, it was soon evident that the narrative reports were satisfactory when profiles were of a pathological nature but that they were less precise in interpreting profiles within or approaching the normal range. This discrepancy was due to the fact that the IPUR program was developed for use in a psychiatric population, with patients displaying obvious psychopathological disorders, and not for use with normal subjects or those manifesting slight variations from the norm. Psychiatrists' evaluations of the narrative reports were basically positive, whereas psychologists' opinions were generally more critical, as might be expected given the greater frequency of nonclinical cases observed.

Based on this criticism, the original program was modified to make it more flexible in assessing subjects without severe psychopathological disorders. Fifty new statements and decision rules replaced those that previously had given an imprecise interpretation of profiles with standard scores below 70 T-score on the clinical scales. This change led to an increase in positive judgments by those using the program for screening purposes and the assessment of normal populations.

A second criticism of the IPUR-MMPI program emerged after its first years of use by clinicians who mainly treated subjects in extreme age ranges (adolescents and elderly subjects). The IPUR-MMPI system tended consistently to give psychopathological reports and diagnoses for these populations, even when the clinical interview did not reveal evident disorders. This tendency varied proportionally with the greater youth or age of the subject.

The issue of diagnostic precision with respect to age extremes has become more compelling in the last ten years, given the increasing number of elderly persons seeking help for various problems of emotional adjustment. The two possible solutions to the problem were to modify the decision rules as a function of age or to use the norms obtained from new age groups. The second more precise and empirical alternative was chosen. Normative values were obtained for the age ranges fourteen to eighteen years and sixty-five to seventy-five years, and the scoring program was then modified so as to calculate the T-scores based on age-group norms. The normative values of reference are now automatically selected on the basis of the subject's age, introduced with the initial data, and the scoring is calculated on them. The narrative report is based on the T-scores corrected for the age groups.

DIFFUSION OF THE IPUR-MMPI SYSTEM

The IPUR-MMPI system was diffused in Italy in two phases, the first phase occurring between 1970 and 1982. In this first period the only available version of the system, written in FORTRAN V, necessitated the use of mainframe computers, such as the Univac 1100. Consequently, system use was limited to terminals connected to central computer centers. This system is still operational today at the IPUR. About five thousand MMPI profiles have been processed to date.

This version of the program has been furnished free of charge to twenty university and hospital psychiatric facilities equipped with central computer processors and is routinely used in the assessment of psychiatric outpatients and inpatients.

The second phase covers the period from 1982 to 1986. Starting in 1982, the increasing availability of low-cost personal computers led to a growing request for a version of the program adapted to these computers. In response, the original scoring and narrative interpretation programs were translated into BASIC and made available on floppy disks for Apple computers (the most widely used in Italy). More recently, another version has been prepared for IBM-compatible personal computers.

In the personal computer version the input format allows the processing of the full-length and short-form MMPI, both in the self-administered and in the operator-introduced versions. The scoring program output was slightly changed: for example, scores on the special scales are no longer calculated since they were found to have little value in clinical practice, and the Italian norms available for these scales have rather low reliability. Moreover, due to memory limitations of most personal computers, the "personal" version does not yet include a diagnostic program based on discriminant-function analysis. Some new auxiliary formulas were calculated and the graphics of the profile were improved. Availability of the "personal" version has facilitated the dissemination of the system beyond the confines of large institutional centers. Beginning in 1983, the system spread rapidly to small local facilities and to the private offices of psychologists and psychiatrists. At present, the floppy disk with the program that allows one hundred interpretations sells for about $1,000. An automatic counter controls a subroutine that cancels the program when one hundred interpretations are completed. The program and the "killing" subroutine are protected against copying and manipulations. Even if the system is not completely safe, it allows reasonable protection against most abuse.

The M-Two/2 System

RATIONALE

The M-Two/2 interpretation system was designed to meet the need for computerized MMPI scoring and interpretation programs suited for use on normal as well as psychiatric populations, an interpretation program that takes into account the subject's age and sex; and a system adapted for use with different personal computers.

GENERAL CHARACTERISTICS OF THE SYSTEM

The M-Two/2 system, designed by Roberto and Stefano Mosticoni, was presented in 1985, and is the most recent Italian system for computerized interpretation of the MMPI (Mosticoni and Mosticoni, 1986). The M-Two/2 allows different input modes and gives a narrative report of two hundred to four hundred words with a probable diagnosis using clinical criteria based on a decision tree for a restricted number of diagnostic categories (see figure 13.4).

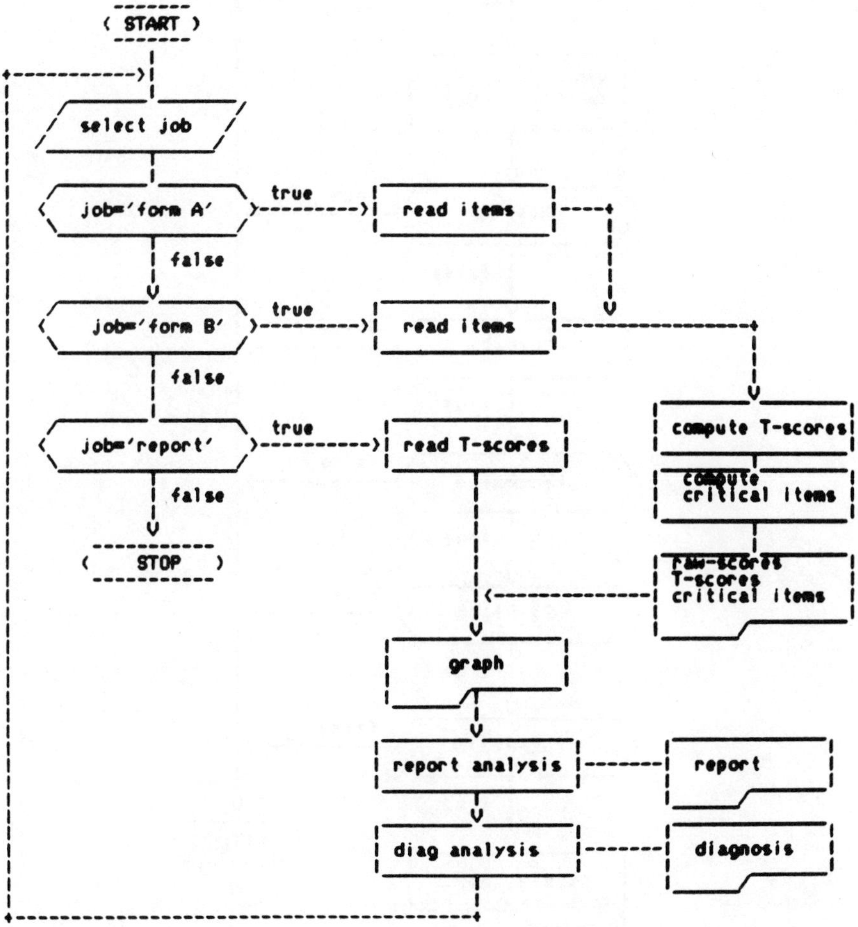

Figure 13.4. Flowchart of the narrative M-Two/2 system (input modality: Job Form A = the complete MMPI protocol; Job Form B = the short MMPI protocol; Job Report = T-scores).

THE SCORING PROGRAM

The input of the M-Two/2 system is organized in interactive form. The first step requires the introduction of subject's identifying data, age, sex, date of compilation, and the categorization of the subject as "normal" or "pathological." This information is based on the clinical or nonclinical purpose of assessment. The second step allows the user to choose among three input modes: the true/false responses of the full-length protocol; the true/false responses of the short form; or the T-scores of the thirteen basic scales (see figure 13.5).

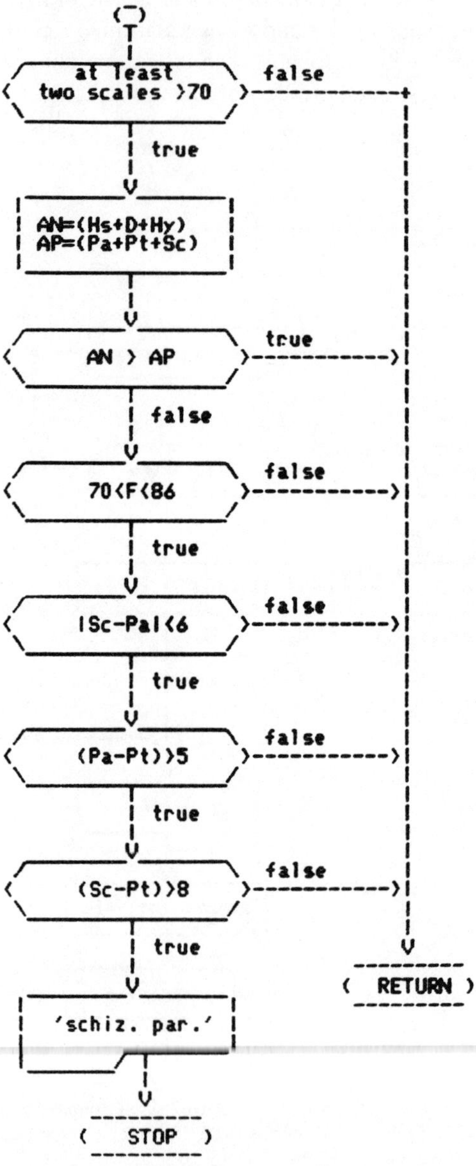

Figure 13.5. Sample flowchart of the "paranoid schizophrenia" diagnosis.

The system output gives a graphic MMPI profile, the Grayson list of critical items, and the raw scores and T-scores of the basic scales and of some selected scales. The T-scores are calculated according to Italian normative values using the Welsh formula (Nencini and Belcecchi, 1973).

THE NARRATIVE PROGRAM

As input for the narrative interpretation, the system requires data on age, sex, "normal" or "pathological" subject status, and T-scores of the thirteen basic scales. The report is then elaborated according to four interpretative criteria.

First a single high-point scale analysis of the profile is made; the scores on each scale are divided into ranges and evaluated as a function of age and sex. Based on these two variables, different interpretative statements may be selected within the same score range.

The system next interprets the profile using the combination of scale of the Diamond model (Diamond, 1957) divided into ranges, each associated with a specific descriptive statement from the statement library.

Next the system codifies the profile according to the Welsh method (Welsh, 1948). If the resulting code is compatible with the rules of inclusion in one of the thirteen code types identified for the Italian population (Mosticoni and Chiari, 1979), the system then provides the corresponding description.

Finally, by means of a decision tree, the system analyzes the configuration of the profile in a search for typical patterns. Validity scales and "neurotic" and "psychotic" patterns are checked, and conclusive statements are selected, thus completing the printout of the narrative report.

The rules, variables, and libraries used by the system are different as a function of the initial "psychiatric" or "nonpsychiatric" subject status chosen by the user. The same profile may therefore give rise to two different narrative reports based on the initial option selected. In any case, the system analyzes profile scores and evaluates profile congruency against operator choice, then reports its assessment in the narrative report. For example, if a subject has been assigned to the "nonpsychiatric" category but the profile is deviant, the narrative report suggests profile reevaluation. No validity or clinical acceptance studies are available at this time. A comparison study of the IPUR and the M-Two/2 system is in progress.

THE DIAGNOSTIC PROGRAM

Following profile analysis, the system indicates a probable diagnosis chosen from fifteen possible categories (see table 13.5). Criteria used in formulating the diagnosis are clinical, nonstatistical, and based on the correspondence of specific patterns and scale configurations with some more common diagnostic categories. An example of the criteria used in the diagnostic decision tree is given in table 13.6 and in the flowchart in figure 13.5.

Validity studies of the diagnostic interpretation are currently in progress, comparing the clinical interpretation of the M-Two/2 with the actuarial IPUR-MMPI interpretation and with clinical diagnoses.

TABLE 13.5
Diagnosis in the M-Two/2 System

Generalized anxiety disorder
Depressive neurosis
Obsessive compulsive neurosis
Phobic neurosis
Hypochondriacal neurosis
Hysterical neurosis
Schizophrenia
Paranoid schizophrenia
Schizoid personality disorder
Borderline personality disorder
Dependent personality disorder
Antisocial personality disorder
Schizoaffective disorder
Major depression
Manic excitement

TABLE 13.6
Examples of Diagnosis and Related Clinical Criteria in the M-Two/2 System

Paranoid schizophrenia	At least 2 scales >70
	Prevalence of psychotic scales
	F score
	Sc/Pa ratio
	Pa/Pt ratio
	Pt/Sc ratio
Hysterical neurosis	At least 2 scales >70
	Prevalence of neurotic scales
	F score
	Hs/Hy ratio
	Hs/D ratio
	D/Hy ratio
Phobic neurosis	At least 2 scales >70
	Prevalence of neurotic scales
	F score
	D/Pt ratio
	Pd score
	Sex
	Mf score
	Si score
Major depression	At least 2 scales >70
	Prevalence of psychotic scales
	F score
	Pt/Sc ratio
	Pa/Pt ratio
	Si score
	Age
	D score

SPECIFIC CHARACTERISTICS OF THE SYSTEM

The system consists of a software unit and six libraries. The M-Two/2 software unit includes a main program and six subroutines, automatically driven and controlled by the main program. The main program pilots the entire procedure and recalls the subroutines and the statements as necessary.

The M-Two/2 system was produced especially for clinical use with personal computers of the Apple series (II plus, IIe, IIc, and compatible), IBM PC (and compatible), and relative printers (eighty system columns) as the minimum basic hardware. M-Two/2 is contained in a single floppy disk; eleven minutes is required for protocol elaboration, five minutes for data entry ("operator" option), and six minutes for the analysis and printout of the narrative report.

Computerized Interpretation of the Rorschach: The PRALP System

RATIONALE

There were four reasons that led to the decision to design a computerized system for the Rorschach:

1. Projective techniques are still widely used in Europe in clinical settings, and the Rorschach is the most popular of these.
2. Notwithstanding its low reliability with respect to psychometric techniques, the Rorschach test may offer useful information in psychotherapeutic settings.
3. The scoring and interpretation of the Rorschach is generally time-consuming, and an automated procedure can notably reduce the cost of scoring the many protocols.
4. A standardized narrative interpretation may well reduce the wide variability of clinician's interpretations.

GENERAL CHARACTERISTICS OF THE SYSTEM

The computerized Rorschach interpretation system (PRALP) was constructed by Pancheri and associates (1979) at the Institute of Psychiatry of the University of Rome. The design of a computerized system to interpret a projective test presented greater difficulties than those encountered for psychometric techniques. The first step in planning the automated procedure was to evaluate the feasibility of automating the first scoring level (attribution of locations, determinants, and contents). This type of automatization, based on the comparison of protocol responses with a glossary of prescored responses (for example, using existing scoring manuals; Small, 1962), would have led to a glossary that was very rigid and highly error prone. Moreover, elements such as "shocks" and other particular phenomena can be assessed only by a human interpreter. For these reasons, in the final system the first scoring level was left to the clinician.

THE SCORING PROGRAM

In addition to demographic and test data, the input format requires entry of the total time of the test, the scoring variables for each following response, and, for each Rorschach card, the latency time in seconds, the number and type of shocks recorded, and the scoring of particular phenomena revealed. The usual scoring symbols are converted and codified into conventional, two-character symbols (see table 13.7). The scoring procedure is based on the computation of total responses, of absolute frequency and percentage of the different scoring variables, on the calculation of the type of thought pattern, and on the affective formulas (M:C) ratios. A list of "shocks" and particular phenomena are separately reported for each card.

TABLE 13.7
Scoring Symbols of the PRALP

Location		*Frequency*		*Determinants*		*Content*	
G	GL	Pop	VO	F+	F+	A	AA
D	DE	Orig+	O+	F−	F−	Ad	AD
Dd	DD	Orig−	O−	F±	F±	H	HU
		Dbl	DB			Hd	HD
						Anat	AN
						Sex	SX
						Blood	SG
						Food	AL
						Arch	AC
						Geo	GE
						Death	ME
						Obstet	OS
						Relig	RE
						Herald	HA
						Artist	AR
						Explos	EX
						Mask	MS
						Monster	MR
						Eyes	OC
						Skin	PE
						Scene	SA
						Anthrop	AP
						Clouds	NU
						Clothes	VE
						Abstract	AT
						Fire	FU
						Myth	MT
						Object	OB
						X-Ray	RX
						Other	AL

The output format reports demographic data and test date and scoring, which is divided into the absolute formulas and percentage of the scoring factors, the type of thought pattern, the affective formulas, a list of shock phenomena and relative cards, and a list of particular phenomena and relative cards.

THE NARRATIVE PROGRAM

The interpretative rules of the PRALP were constructed by a team of psychologists with many years of experience in the clinical interpretation of the Rorschach, and were drawn from a sample of 602 protocols (100 normal and 502 psychiatric subjects: 190 diagnosed as neurotic, 110 as schizophrenic, 70 as affective psychoses, 90 as personality disorder, 42 as organic brain syndrome). A clinical diagnosis, case history and psychopathological status, and Rorschach protocols and test interpretation were available for each of the 602 base samples. Analysis of the narrative reports as a function of the scoring factors together with an analysis of the ranges of variability of the scoring parameters enabled the construction of a list of rules on which to base the computer interpretation. The choice of the descriptive phrases making up the statement library and corresponding to the decision rules was made using international Rorschach terminology (Bohm, 1960, 1967; Loosli-Usteri, 1958; Rorschach, 1962; Small, 1962). Table 13.8 reports the interpretative variables, the meanings assigned to them, and the number of statements derived from them.

Some comments are necessary regarding the shock phenomena. The frequency and importance of shocks are evaluated by the human examiner and constitute an element of input. Shock phenomena were divided into three

TABLE 13.8
Variables Included in the Rorschach Interpretive Program

Interpretive Variable	*Significance*	*No. of Statements*
No. of responses	Ideational productivity	6
% of two most frequent contents	Variability of associations	8
% of A and Ad; % of Pop	Conformity with stereotyped social ideation	9
No. of Orig+ and Orig−; Total no. of Orig	Original or bizarre thought	11
% of G, D, and Dd locations	Mode of synthetic or analytic thought	11
% of F determinants	Capacity for rational control of emotions	5
% of F+, relative to F	Index of lability of associative connections	9
Ratio of M:C responses (affective formula); 14 patterns contrasted with 7 patterns of the secondary formula	Mode of control and expression of drives and emotions	98
Reciprocal relationships among FC, CF, and C determinants	Ego strength in the control of drives	11
Ratio of Dbl locations to some M:C (affective) patterns	Direction of aggressive valences	5
No. of H and Hd	Profound or superficial interest in interpersonal relationships	12
Relation between H and Monster contents	Tension and anxiety in interpersonal relationships	5
% of anatomy and X-ray contents with F+ determinants; % of some contents with F− determinants; % of contents with other determinants	Search for response quality; somatic preoccupation	8
No. of Sex responses; ratio of F+ to F−	Efficacy of censure mechanisms on emergence of sexual drives	10
12 different contents: Arch, Heraldry; Myth, Fire & Explos, Blood, Abstract, Mask, Death, Eyes, Obstet, Relig.	Various meanings for each of the different contents	36

grades according to their apparent intensity: third grade, refusal of the card; second grade, increase in latency time and/or abnormal verbalization; first grade, other abnormal behaviors observed during test administration. No significance was attributed to shocks on the first and fifth cards. Shocks on the second, third, fourth, sixth, and seventh cards were interpreted according to the classically evoked meaning of each (second: aggressivity; third: sex role; fourth: relation with the father figure; sixth: psychosexual problems; seventh: relation with the mother figure) and to the grade of shocks evoked. Shocks contemporaneously present on the second, fourth, sixth, and seventh cards were interpreted two by two. And the interpretation of shock on the third and sixth cards varies with the sex of the subject.

Given the importance of the shock phenomena in Rorschach interpretation, thirty-six statements were assigned to their description.

It should also be noted that the particular phenomena have been subdivided into three groups: (1) those indicating the presence of autistic and/or dissociative traits: color naming (CN), position responses (RP), self-references (AU), contaminated responses (CT), confabulated responses (CM), and symbolic responses (SI); (2) those interpreted as indexes of depressive traits: deteriorated responses (DZ) and devitalized responses (DV); and (3) those that indicate anxious reactivity to a cognitive task, such as may occur in patients with organic brain syndromes: incapacity (IC), insecurity (IN), verbal stereotypy (SV), quality irregularity (IQ), and perseveration (PR).

There are eighteen descriptive statements associated with the particular phenomena, and they conclude the automated narrative report in a sort of final clinical assessment.

The statement library was constructed using decision rules that considered, for each statement, the meaning attributed to the corresponding condition of variability in the 602 protocols examined. In the definition of the statement, the formal syntactic structure was modified to improve the flow of the narrative report, maintaining, whenever possible, the specific Rorschach terminology. The statement library consists of 288 statements, each one corresponding to a single condition of variability of the interpretative parameters. Table 13.9 presents some interpretative statements.

SPECIFIC CHARACTERISTICS OF THE PROGRAM

The system includes a main program and seven subroutines. The main program allows two input modes according to either the batch procedure or the demand procedure. It requires a prescoring of the protocol according to the standard PRALP input procedure.

The current version of the program is written in FORTRAN V for computers of medium to large size and is furnished free of charge upon request. A version for personal computers is under study.

TABLE 13.9
Interpretative Variables and Examples of Statement Printout of the PRALP

Variable	*Statement*
% W greater than 35, % D less than 40, % Dd greater than 20	"The subject tends to give a synthetic and generalized interpretation of reality, although a certain tendency to make a detailed and meticulous analysis of particular aspects is present"
Affective formula (M:C) 3:2; secondary formula 2:0	"The intratensive direction of the affective formula indicates that drives and emotional reactions are completely controlled at a behavioral level"
H content = 0; Hd content between 0 and 1	"The absence of H content indicates the presence of difficulty in interpersonal relationships in which the subject appears disinterested in any case"
Shock at the 4th card (1st grade)	"Signs of shock at the fourth card suggest the existence of problems in relationship with the father figure"
Score of 5 in the third group of particular phenomena	"The phenomena observed and the analysis of behavior during the trial suggest that the task provoked a marked anxiety reaction; it may be hypothesized that any request for intellectual performance, even in normal relational life, evokes a degree of anxiety"

FURTHER DEVELOPMENTS

The original version of the program underwent successive studies to test internal consistency and the validity of the narrative report. A group of clinicians expert in Rorschach interpretation were given 450 protocols and instructed to score them according to the Bohm method (Bohm, 1967) and to prepare a traditional clinical report. The scoring of these experts was used as input for the PRALP program, translating the traditional scoring codes into the program input codes. The two narrative reports derived from expert evaluation and from the computerized program were then presented to the patient's psychiatrist or psychotherapist, who then evaluated the descriptive fit of each version. The assessment was blind—the clinician could not distinguish the origin of the different versions. The clinician was also asked to indicate which part of the report was satisfactory and which was not.

Results of the first inquiry revealed that clinicians considered the computer report as "satisfactory" in 43 percent of cases (47 percent for the clinical report), "partially satisfactory" in 35 percent of cases (42 percent for clinical reports), and "unsatisfactory" in 13 percent of cases (11 percent for clinical reports).

Even though judgments regarding clinical reports were generally more favorable, the difference was not statistically significant. It should also be remembered that the relatively low concordance rate among clinicians regarding Rorschach interpretation is a phenomenon characteristic of all projective techniques.

The clinicians' qualitative evaluation of the computer-scored protocol was then used to modify some decision rules and statements of the library (for a total of twenty decision rules and thirty-three statements). The current version of the program (PRALP 2) has been modified based on the results of this study.

The PRALP 2 program is currently used, in combination with other tests, at the Institute of Psychiatry of the University of Rome in the assessment of all patients for whom psychotherapy is indicated. Clinicians desiring a deeper understanding of a patient's psychoaffective dimensions are also able to request use of the program. So far, 750 Rorschach protocols have been processed.

Concluding Comments

CLINICAL ACCEPTANCE OF COMPUTERIZED SYSTEMS

The acceptance and dissemination of computerized psychological assessment systems in Italy may be conveniently divided into two phases. The first or introductory phase, roughly covering the period 1970 to 1980, took place rather slowly. During this time some psychometric interpretation systems were designed and produced by university researchers, but the spread of these systems was limited to a few large institutional centers. This slow diffusion was partly due to the situation of psychiatry in Italy at the time; it was then dominated by sociopsychiatric tendencies, and "measurement" or "objectivization" of psychopathological traits was met with a certain diffidence (and sometimes hostility). Moreover, during this first phase the computerized interpretation of tests required the availability of large central computers, which were located exclusively in university centers and general hospitals.

The second phase, initiated in about 1980 after some legislative reforms of Italian psychiatry, saw an inverse tendency. Psychiatry in Italy turned progressively toward a reevaluation of the psychobiological aspects of mental disorders, and new importance was given to all assessment methods and objective measurements. This period coincided with the diffusion of the personal computer in all university psychiatric facilities, in many hospital psychiatric facilities, and among many private practitioners. These events led to progressively increasing requests for computerized interpretation systems of the most widely used psychological tests.

SCORING PROGRAMS

Automated scoring programs are today the most widely requested and used of the various programs available, and their diffusion is on the increase. Computerized scoring programs are now commercially available for most of the commonly used psychometric tests. It should be added, however, that given the ease of designing simple scoring programs for personal computers, many psychiatric facilities have produced their own scoring systems, thus avoiding the expense of buying them.

NARRATIVE INTERPRETATION PROGRAMS

Over the past three years there has been a clear increase in requests for narrative interpretation programs for psychiatric facilities. In 1985 about 60 percent of Italian university psychiatry clinics routinely used the narrative report program for the MMPI. This percentage may easily rise to nearly 80 percent within the next two years.

Usage of these programs in general hospital facilities is still relatively low. An estimate holds that only 10 percent of these centers use the systems now available. Based on the tendency of the last two years, however, this percentage is also expected to increase. No statistical data exist on the total number of computerized interpretations elaborated yearly in Italy. Around five hundred protocols per year are processed at the IPUR, and it may be expected that activity at other large facilities is similar to or only slightly less than at the IPUR.

DIAGNOSTIC INTERPRETATION PROGRAMS

As of this writing, there have been no extensive requests for diagnostic interpretation programs except by the university psychiatric facilities engaged in research activities. In fact, clinicians do not generally find a diagnostic assessment based exclusively on psychological tests particularly useful. Nevertheless, when the diagnostic evaluation is furnished together with the narrative report, as is routinely the case at the IPUR, clinicians find the information useful in confirming their diagnostic interpretation of the case. It should be added that only in the last few years have Italian psychiatrists begun to use standardized diagnostic references (DSM-III). This fact suggests the utility of constructing new computerized diagnostic systems based on the DSM-III classification and validated by statistical methods. Should these programs become available and be supported by adequate validity studies, it is likely that future demand for computerized diagnosis will rise.

REFERENCES

Barker, H. (1974). Behavioral sciences statistics program library (ANAL). Department of Psychology, University of Alabama.

Bohm, E. (1960). *Vademecum psicodiagnostico*. Firenze: Organizzazioni Speciali.

Bohm, E. (1967). *Lehrbuch der Rorschach-Psychodiagnostik* (3rd ed.). Bern: Hans Huber.

Butcher, J., and Pancheri, P. (1976). *A handbook of cross-national MMPI research*. Minneapolis, MN: University of Minnesota Press.

Dahlstrom, W. G., Welsh, G. S., and Dahlstrom, L. E. (1972). *An MMPI handbook: Vol. 1. Clinical Interpretation*. Minneapolis, MN: University of Minnesota Press.

Diamond, S. (1957). *Personality and temperament*. New York: Harper.

Giucci, D., Pancheri, P., and Pastena, L. (1968). Presentazione di una nuova scheda clinica per il rilevamento e l'elaborazione elettronica di dati in psichiatria [Presentation of a new clinical schedule for the collection and electronic elaboration of psychiatric data]. Technical Report ISS 68/30. Rome: Istituto Superiore di Sanità, 1968.

Grayson, H. M. (1951). A *psychological admission testing program and manual*. Los Angeles: Veterans Administration Center, Neuropsychiatric Hospital.

Loosli-Usteri, M. (1958). *Manuel pratique du test de Rorschach*. Paris: Herman.

Mosticoni, R., and Chiari, G. (1979). *Una descrizione obiettiva della personalità. Il Minnesota Multiphasic Personality Inventory* [*An objective assessment of personality. The MMPI*]. Florence: Organizzazioni Speciali.

Mosticoni, R., and Mosticoni, S. (1986). *Il sistema M-Two/2 per l'interpretazione automatica del MMPI. Manuale d'impiego* [*M-Two/2 system for automated MMPI interpretation. User's manual*]. Rome: M-Two Snc (via Nomentana 201, 00161 Rome, Italy).

Nencini, R. (1958, 1965). *Italian norms for the MMPI*. Unpublished data.

Nencini, R., and Belcecchi, M. V. (1973). Nuova taratura del MMPI [New norms for the MMPI]. *Bollettino di Psicologia Applicata, 118*, 89–99.

Organizzazioni Speciali (Ed.). (1986). *PSY-SYSTEM. Gestione di tests psicologici con l'ausilio del personal computer* [*Psychological testing with personal computers*]. Florence: Author.

Pancheri, P., Bernabei, A., Girardi, P., Mosticoni, R., and Tondo, L. (1979). P.R.A.L.P.: Un sistema per l'interpretazione del test di Rorschach [P.R.A.L.P.: An automated system for interpretation of Rorschach test]. *Bollettino di Psicologia Applicata, 150*, 113–122.

Pancheri, P., Girardi, P., Bernabei, A., and Morgana, A. (1974). A.P.A.P.: Metodo di interpretazione narrativa automatica del MMPI [A.P.A.P.: A method for narrative, automatic interpretation of MMPI]. In G. B. Cassano, P. Castrogiovanni, P. Pancheri, and M. Tansella (Eds.), *Tecniche di automazione in psichiatria*. Rome: Il Pensiero Scientifico.

Pancheri, P., and Giusti, A. (1985). *Un metodo di interpretazione narrativa automatica del MMPI per personal computers* [*A method for narrative automatic interpretation of MMPI on personal computers*]. Regione Lombardia "Progressi e prospettive dell'automazione in psicologia e psichiatria," Milan.

Pancheri, P., and Morgana, A. (1974). Sistema di scoring e di interpretazione diagnostica del MMPI completamente automatizzato "on line" [Scoring and diagnostic interpretation system of completely automated on-line MMPI]. In G. B. Cassano, P. Castrogiovanni, P. Pancheri, and M. Tansella (Eds.), *Tecniche di automazione in psichiatria* (pp. 164–185). Rome: Il Pensiero Scientifico.

Rorschach, H. (1962). *Psychodiagnostics*. Paris: Presses Universitaires de France.

Sanavio, E., Bertolotti, G., Michielin, P., Vidotto, G., and Zotti, A. M. (1985). C.B.A.: "*Cognitive Behavioural Assessment*." *Manuale C.B.A. 2.0, Scale Primarie*. Florence: Organizzazioni Speciali.

Small, L. (1962). *Manuale di localizzazione e siglatura del reattivo di Rorschach*. Florence: Organizzazioni Speciali.

Welsh, G. S. (1948). An extension of Hathaway's MMPI profile coding system. *Journal of Consulting Psychology, 12*, 343–346.

14

Automated Assessment of Child and Adolescent Personality: The Personality Inventory for Children (PIC)

David Lachar

The Personality Inventory for Children: An Overview

The Personality Inventory for Children (PIC; Lachar, 1982; Wirt, Lachar, Klinedinst, and Seat, 1984) was first published in 1977 and is, compared to other tests described in this volume, a relatively new psychometric instrument. Therefore, this chapter begins with an overview to familiarize the reader with the general characteristics and potential applications of the PIC. Approaches to the development of test interpretations characteristic of current PIC automated assessment and efforts under way to expand the diagnostic and descriptive potential of this test are then presented.

The PIC is an objective multidimensional measure of behavior, affect, ability, and family function that may be applied to the evaluation of children from preschool ages through adolescence. The PIC is completed by an adult informant (usually the mother of the referred child or adolescent), and scale scores are derived from that adult's responses to brief inventory items (for example, "My child has been difficult to manage"; "My child has many friends"; "My child worries about things that usually only adults worry about"; "My child can tell the time fairly well"). PIC items require a reading proficiency at the sixth- to seventh-grade level (Barad and Hughes, 1984; Harrington and Follet, 1984).

PIC informants respond "true" or "false" to the first 131, 280, or 420 items presented by computer monitor or by the Revised Format Administration Booklet. Responses are stored in a microcomputer (currently Apple and IBM versions are available) or are recorded on either optically scannable or hand-scoreable answer sheets. Responses are transformed to scale raw scores and T-scores (mean = 50, standard deviation = 10) by a microcomputer program, by the test publisher's (Western Psychological Services) mainframe computer, or through the application of hand-scoring templates and profile forms. Scale items are scored in a consistent manner so that increasing scale elevations reflect a greater likelihood of problems or pathology.

Interpretation options increase as additional inventory items are completed. When only the first 131 items (Part I) are completed, interpretations reflect elevation of the Lie scale, a measure of respondent defensiveness, and elevations on four factor-derived scales: I: Undisciplined/Poor Self-Control; II: Social Incompetence; III: Internalization/Somatic Symptoms; and IV: Cognitive Development (Lachar, 1982; Lachar, Gdowski, and Snyder, 1982).

Completion of the first 280 items (Parts I and II) provides the twenty scales of the Revised Format Profile Form: Four factor scales; three measures of informant response style; a general screening scale; and twelve scales that measure child ability, behavior, affect, and family status. Automated interpretation of Parts I and II also includes a presentation of the significant responses to a somewhat abbreviated critical item set. The relative efficiency of the 280-item format was obtained through item rearrangement and analysis in which fourteen of twenty scales were shortened by an average of 18 percent by removing items with poor correlation to scale total raw score. These shortened scales proved comparable to their full-length equivalents (Lachar, 1982). The suffix "-S" is often added to a scale's abbreviation to designate the shortened version.

Completion of the first 420 items (Parts I, II, and III) allows interpretation of all twenty scales in their full-length formats and presentation of all significant responses to an 162-item Critical Item List in which items are assigned to fourteen mutually exclusive categories: Depression and Poor Self-Concept; Worry and Anxiety; Reality Distortion; Peer Relations; Unsocialized Aggression; Conscience Development; Poor Judgment; Atypical Development; Distractibility, Activity Level, and Coordination; Speech and Language; Somatic Complaints/Current Health; School Adjustment; Family Discord; and Other. The final 180 items presented in the Revised Format Administration Booklet either appear on an "experimental" nonprofile scale or are not scored.

The dimensions represented by scales selected for the PIC profile do not reflect a specific theoretical perspective with regard to personality, psychopathology, or child development but rather reflect those dimensions routinely assessed by clinicians regardless of theoretical preference or bias (Achenbach and Edelbrock, 1978; Dreger, 1981). Scale construction methodology has also varied as a function of the characteristics to be measured and the variety of applications envisioned. Practical issues, such as the availability of appropriate criterion groups, also influenced choice of scale construction methodology.

Factor analysis, empirical keying, and rational/content methodologies have been applied to scale item selection in the construction of narrow- and broad-band scales. Characteristic of all the profile scales, however constructed, is their ability to successfully predict non-PIC measures of child adjustment and ability. It is this established actuarial character of the PIC that has formed the foundation for various interpretive strategies that are optimized through automation.

The PIC Profile Scales

INFORMANT RESPONSE STYLE

Lie Scale (L). This rationally developed scale was constructed to identify an informant's defensive response set demonstrated by his or her tendency to ascribe the most virtuous of behaviors and to deny minor, commonly occurring behavior problems in the referred child. Correlations with other PIC scales and ratings of the child suggest that L reflects the absence or denial of behavior problems, especially those classified as delinquent and asocial, as well as the absence or denial of family problems and psychological discomfort. L elevation increases when the respondent intentionally attempts to portray the child as having fewer problems than is actually the case (Daldin, 1985; McVaugh and Grow, 1983).

Frequency Scale (F). This scale consists of items that were seldom endorsed in the normative sample's scored direction (M = 5 percent) or in a sample of preadolescent boys evaluated at child guidance clinics (M = 14 percent). Item content was varied so that a single pattern of severe disturbance could not account for an extreme scale elevation. The F scale obtains extreme elevations (120*T*) for profiles when inventory items are completed without regard for item content (Wirt, Lachar, Klinedinst, and Seat, 1984). There is evidence that highly elevated F scores may reflect exaggeration of problems (Daldin, 1985; McVaugh and Grow, 1983), and it is possible that F elevation may be strongly influenced by parental perception of disturbance that need not be corroborated by systematic school or clinic observation (Lachar, Gdowski, and Snyder, 1984). On the other hand, 20 percent of a child guidance population obtain F elevations in excess of 99*T* (Lachar and Gdowski, 1979), and comparison of mean profiles for various criterion groups clearly supports the conclusion that F increases with severity of psychopathology (Wirt, Lachar, Klinedinst, and Seat, 1984).

Defensiveness Scale (DEF). This empirically constructed scale is composed of a heterogeneous set of inventory items that separated mothers judged to be high-defensive from those judged to be low-defensive based on a diagnostic interview about the referred child. Although a cutting score of greater than

59*T* correctly identified 93 percent of low-defensive and 88 percent of high-defensive scale construction protocols, a study under fake-good instructions demonstrated that DEF-S *T*-scores rose only from 35.6 to 54.1. The percentage of profiles with DEF greater than 59*T* rose from 0 percent to 40 percent, although DEF-S never exceeded 69*T* for these twenty-five profiles (Daldin, 1985). Lachar and Gdowski (1979) suggest that DEF be interpreted to reflect informant resistance and defensiveness starting at 70*T*, although only 4 percent of a heterogeneous child guidance sample obtained scores in this range. Indeed, only an additional 14 percent obtained scores of 60 to 69*T*.

GENERAL ADJUSTMENT

Adjustment Scale (ADJ). This empirically constructed scale identifies children in need of a psychological evaluation and is a general measure of poor psychological adjustment. Scale item content reflects both internalizing and externalizing characteristics. Application of a cutting score of greater than 59*T* correctly classified 86 percent of normal and 89 percent of clinic protocols. These classification rates have remained stable through subsequent analyses.

THE COGNITIVE TRIAD

The first three of the twelve substantive scales reflect the cognitive status of the referred child. Although clinicians may resist a procedure that evaluates a child's ability without directly assessing the child, the value of such measures on the profile is considerable. These scales may be applied to determine probable need for individual assessment of ability and achievement, and they play a central role in defining relatively homogeneous subgroups of disturbed children through classification of total profile configurations (Gdowski, Lachar, and Kline, 1985).

Achievement Scale (ACH). This empirically constructed scale identifies children whose academic achievement is significantly below age expectation regardless of intellectual capacity. A cutting score of greater than 59*T* correctly identified 97 percent of construction and 92 percent of cross-validation protocols (Wirt, Lachar, Klinedinst, and Seat, 1984). Factor analysis of scale items suggested that ACH measures not only limited academic abilities and poor achievement, but also a dimension of poor psychological adjustment characterized by impulsivity, limited concentration, over- or underassertiveness with peers, and disregard for parental expectations.

Intellectual Screening Scale (IS). This empirically keyed scale was constructed to identify children whose difficulties may be related to impaired intellectual functioning or specific cognitive deficits and for whom an individually administered intellectual assessment would be indicated. Items were identified by contrasting the protocols of retarded children with normal, nonretarded disturbed, and psychotic children.

Development Scale (DVL). These items, selected through the consensus of experts, primarily reflect retarded development in motor coordination, poor school performance, and lack of any special skill or abilities. Other factors reflect limited motivation to achieve in school, clumsiness and weakness, limited reading skills, and deficient pragmatic skills (for example, counting change).

Several investigators have established the relationship between ACH, IS, and DVL and a variety of ability and achievement measures as well as special education classification.* There is also evidence that a child's sex, age, and race do not moderate the relationship between scale T-score elevation and measured ability and achievement (Kline, Lachar, and Sprague, 1985).

OTHER CLINICAL SCALES

Somatic Concern Scale (SOM). This content scale is composed of items selected by judges to measure various health-related variables: frequency and seriousness of somatic complaints and illness, adjustment to illness, appetite and eating habits, sleep patterns, energy and strength, headaches and stomachaches, as well as the presence of a physical basis for symptoms. Study groups found to have a mean SOM elevation above 60*T* are boys exhibiting physical symptoms considered by a physician to be related to experienced stress (Stewart, 1971) and children with cancer (Armstrong, Wirt, Nesbit, and Martinson, 1982). Pipp (1979) found SOM significantly correlated with the Minnesota Multiphasic Personality Inventory (MMPI) Hypochondriasis scale for adolescents, and Kelly (1982) found SOM correlated with only one Child Behavior Checklist (CBCL) scale: Somatic Complaints.

Depression Scale (D). This content scale is composed of items judged by experienced clinicians to reflect childhood depression. Factor analysis of scale items yielded dimensions labeled Brooding/Moodiness, Social Isolation, Crying Spells, Lack of Energy, Pessimism/Anhedonia, Concern with Death and Separation, Serious Attitude, Sensitivity to Criticism, Indecisiveness/Poor Self-Concept, and Uncommunicativeness. Leon, Kendall, and Garber (1980) found D to correlate significantly with the Child Depression Inventory in a sample of elementary-school children. Children designated as "depressed" by their D T-scores attributed positive events to external causes significantly more often than did children not so identified. D has also significantly separated children independently labeled depressed according to DSM-III criteria obtained from maternal interview (M = 85*T*) from children who did not meet these criteria (M = 61*T*) (Lobovits and Handal, 1985).

Family Relations Scale (FAM). This content scale includes items selected to assess the following dimensions: parental role effectiveness, ability to cooperate in making family decisions, family involvement in community affairs, presence of feelings of love and happiness in the home, parental emotional adjustment,

* Bennett and Welsh, 1981; Clark, 1982; DeKrey and Ehly, 1985; DeMoor-Peal and Handal, 1983; Dollinger, Goh, and Cody, 1984; Durrant, 1983; Kelly, 1982; Lachar, Kline, and Boersma, 1986; and Schnel, 1982.

appropriateness of discipline, and concern for the rights of the child. FAM assists in determining the role that family and parental factors play in the development of child psychopathology and also evaluates the need for in-depth assessment of family and parental characteristics. Lachar and Sharp (1979) found that FAM was the only PIC profile scale that consistently correlated with a broad range of maternal MMPI scales. FAM elevations are higher for children from divorced than from nondivorced parents (Schreiber, 1982), and FAM obtained the highest mean scale elevation in profiles of children who had a parent in treatment for alcoholism (Anderson and Quast, 1983). Snyder and Gdowski (1980) compared the scores of the Marital Satisfaction Inventory (MSI; Snyder, 1981) obtained from parents when FAM was greater than 59*T* to the MSI scores when FAM was less than 46*T*. High FAM parents obtained significantly higher elevations on nine of the eleven MSI profile scales.

Delinquency Scale (DLQ). This empirically keyed scale is comprised of items that separated adjudicated from nonadjudicated adolescents. DLQ was designed to be a concurrent measure of the behavioral characteristics manifested by delinquents and a diagnostic aid in the identification of delinquent children. Factor analysis of scale items resulted in two substantial factors labeled Disregard for Limits/Interpersonal Insensitivity and Antisocial Tendencies, and several small factors labeled Irritability/Limited Tolerance, Sadness, Lack of Interest/Impulsivity, Interpersonal Hostility, and Disrespect for Parents. Pipp (1979) found DLQ to correlate significantly with the MMPI scales Psychopathic Deviate and Hypomania for both male and female adolescents. Kelly (1982) found that DLQ correlated the most highly with CBCL scales Delinquent and Aggressive. Lachar, Gdowski, and Snyder (1984) found DLQ to correlate significantly with parent, teacher, and clinician rating form dimensions of externalization, impulsivity, antisocial character, and hostility/emotional lability. Adjudicated delinquents obtained very high T-score elevations, with 58 percent obtaining DLQ scores greater than 99*T*. Because DLQ elevations between 70*T* and 100*T* are very frequent for children and adolescents seen at child guidance agencies (Lachar and Gdowski, 1979; 52 percent), it has been important to identify replicated external correlates of DLQ to guide the interpretation of this scale.

Withdrawal Scale (WDL). This content scale contains items nominated to measure withdrawal from social contact. Factor analysis of WDL items resulted in content dimensions labeled Social and Physical Isolation, Shyness/Fear of Strangers, Isolation from Peers/Uncommunicativeness, Emotional Distance, Intentional Withdrawal/Distrust, and Isolative Intellectual Pursuits. Psychotic children obtain mean WDL elevations above 69*T* (Wirt, Lachar, Klinedinst, and Seat, 1984). Kelly (1982) obtained significant correlations between WDL and CBCL scales Social Withdrawal, Uncommunicativeness, and Social. Pipp (1979) found that WDL correlated significantly with MMPI scale Social Introversion for both male and female adolescents.

Anxiety Scale (ANX). These items were nominated as measuring the various manifestations of anxiety. Factor analysis of scale items resulted in content dimensions labeled Brooding/Moodiness, Fearfulness, Worry, Fear of the Dark, Specific Fear/Crying Spells, Poor Self-Concept, Insecurity/Fearfulness, and Sensitivity to Criticism/Pessimism.

Psychosis Scale (PSY). This empirically keyed scale was constructed to discriminate children with psychotic symptomatology from normal, behaviorally disturbed nonpsychotic, and retarded children. Psychotic children obtain very high PSY elevations: 84 percent of the scale construction protocols scored above 99*T*. Pipp (1979) found that PSY correlated significantly with the MMPI scales Schizophrenia and Social Introversion for both male and female adolescents. PSY was the only PIC scale to correlate significantly with a clinician-rating dimension labeled Disorganization/Limited Reality Testing (Lachar, Gdowski, and Snyder, 1984).

Hyperactivity Scale (HPR). These scale items were empirically selected so as to separate children seen in guidance clinics who were described by their teachers as hyperactive (DSM-III: Attention Deficit Disorder with Hyperactivity) from children also evaluated at child guidance clinics who were not seen as hyperactive by their teachers. A cutting score of greater than 59*T* correctly classified 90 percent of hyperactive and 94 percent of maladjusted nonhyperactive samples. Breen and Barkley (1983) obtained similar classification rates, and Forbes (1985) found that HPR successfully differentiated between hyperactive and conduct-disordered children. Voelker, Lachar, and Gdowski (1983) found HPR elevation to be related to treatment with methylphenidate and favorable response to such treatment. Kelly (1982) obtained significant correlations between HPR and CBCL Hyperactive, Aggressive, and Delinquent scales. Clark, Wanous, and Pompa (1982) obtained a considerable number of significant correlations between HPR and teacher ratings of special education students on such rating scale items as "Does not conform to limits," "Easily distracted," "Poor achievement due to distractibility," and "Poor achievement due to impulsivity."

Social Skills Scale (SSK). This content scale includes items nominated to measure the various characteristics that reflect effective social relations in childhood. SSK item content dimensions reflected in factor groupings suggest that this scale measures both the lack of success in social activities (lack of friends, peer rejection, absence of club membership, adults as only social contacts) and the reasons for this lack of success (aggressive behavior with peers, absence of leadership qualities or social influence, social behavior suggesting poor sportsmanship, egocentrism, and obstinancy). SSK has been found to significantly relate to measures of moral judgment and cognitive perspective taking (Kurdek, 1980), a self-report measure of social competence (Kurdek and Krile, 1983), and a peer acceptance rating (Kurdek, 1982). SSK has been found to significantly correlate with the Peer Support scale of the self-report Children's Perception of Social Support Inventory as well as with parental and self-report measures of the quality of peer support (Schreiber, 1982).

THE FACTOR SCALES

Dimensions of child behavior derived through factor analysis have been characterized as either narrow-band or broad-band in character (Achenbach and Edelbrock, 1978). Narrow-band measures reflect limited dimensions of psychopathology, such as temper tantrums (Dreger, 1981). Broad-band measures, on the other hand, represent general patterns of behavioral disturbance, such as "internalizing" symptomatology (Achenbach, 1978) or "anxiety turned inward" (Dreger, 1981). Comparison of the relative utility of broad- versus narrow-band measures is a recurrent theme in the literature; in general, the broad-band measures are viewed as having favorable theoretical and research applications, while narrow-band measures with more behavioral specificity are seen as providing more clinical utility. The availability of validated broad- and narrow-band measures within the same instrument allows investigators and clinicians to pursue either or both approaches and facilitates the study of the relative utility of each approach.

The twelve PIC clinical scales (ACH through SSK), although not derived via factor analysis, can be classified as narrow-band measures in terms of both scale item content and correlate specificity. The 313 items of the twelve clinical scales were subjected to a series of factor analyses to identify item dimensions that would reflect a distillation of the variance measured by the PIC profile. Four item content dimensions, representing approximately half of the total variance of these 313 items, obtained sufficient discriminative item loadings to facilitate construction of inventory scales.

I. Undisciplined/Poor Self Control (I). Factor I items appear primarily on scales ADJ, DLQ, and HPR. A factor analysis of scale items resulted in content dimensions labeled Ineffective Discipline, Impulsivity, Problematic Anger, Poor Peer Relationships, Limited Conscience Development, and Poor School Behavior. Correlation with parent, teacher, and clinician ratings provides independent evidence that Factor I reflects hostility/emotional lability, impulsivity, and antisocial behavior (Lachar, Gdowski, and Snyder, 1984).

II. Social Incompetence (II). The majority of Factor II items are found on ADJ, D, WDL, ANX, PSY, and SSK scales. A factor analysis of scale items resulted in content dimensions labeled Sadness, Shyness, Peer Rejection, Lack of Leadership Qualities, Social Isolation, Lack of Friends, and Adjustment. Factor II correlates with teacher and clinician ratings of social withdrawal and a parent rating dimension labeled Depressive/Somatic Symptoms (Lachar, Gdowski, and Snyder, 1984). This relationship between dysphoric affect and deficient social skills and lack of positive peer relations in children and adolescents is not surprising (Costello, 1981)

III. Internalization/Somatic Symptoms (III). Factor III items appear primarily on SOM, D, and ANX scales. A factor analysis of scale items resulted in content dimensions labeled Worry/Poor Self-Concept, Somatization, Crying

Spells, Insecurity/Fearfulness, Vision Problems, Psychotic Behavior, and Body Temperature. Factor III significantly correlated with parent and clinician dimensions labeled Depressive/Somatic Symptoms (Lachar, Gdowski, and Snyder, 1984).

IV. *Cognitive Development (IV).* The majority of Factor IV items are also found on ACH, IS, DVL, and PSY scales. Factor IV significantly correlates with the parent rating dimensions Developmental Delay and Cognitive/Attentional Deficits, the teacher rating dimension Academic Delay, and the clinician rating dimension Language/Motor Deficits (Lachar, Gdowski, and Snyder, 1984). Factor IV has also been found to correlate −0.53 with the McCarthy General Cognitive Index and −0.63 with the Peabody Picture Vocabulary IQ (Durrant, 1983).

Selection of an Interpretive Strategy: Clinical Versus Actuarial

An automated interpretive program defines units of test performance and assigns meaning to them. In clinical assessment, these units of test performance and their meaning are defined by some measure of consensual or idiosyncratic clinical practice. That is, one or more "clinicians" (experts or novices with a given test) articulate a set of decision rules that assigns a meaning to each unit of test performance. A general goal of such a procedure is to have a computer duplicate the interpretive activity of a clinician. Fowler (see chapter 4) has outlined the variables involved in determining the quality of such a product. Certainly the "clinical" interpretation of an unreliable and unproven instrument cannot be more accurate than the test itself, although a computer-generated report might suggest a degree of unsubstantiated credibility. On the other hand, the utility of a clinical interpretation of a test with established validity, such as the MMPI, is determined by factors that include the compatibility of the test's data base with the necessary definition of explicit and objective test/interpretation relationships, the degree of professional consensus regarding clinical application of the test, and the interpretive skill of the author of the computer program.

This author has had the experience of developing an automated clinical interpretive program for the MMPI (Lachar, 1974a, 1974b). The process included surveying published interpretations of MMPI code types and other indices, developing consensual conservative interpretations of accepted units of test performance, and performing a variety of studies of the finished "automated clinician" product. Limitations in the extensive MMPI literature, however, eventually necessitated the empirical analysis of the utility of age-specific adolescent norms (Lachar, Klinge, and Grisell, 1976), and collection of data bases necessary to generate a comprehensive validated set of MMPI critical items (Lachar and Wrobel, 1979), interpretations for the Wiggins content scales (Lachar and Alexander, 1978), and an interpretation of the MacAndrew alcoholism scale (Lachar, Berman, Grisell, and Schooff, 1976). The alternative to data collection in these instances would have been to rely on the judgment of one individual—a position that was, and continues to be, unacceptable to this writer.

What options are available to a clinician who would like to develop an automated interpretation for the PIC? In 1975 and 1976 this author and a small number of students found ourselves in a unique situation. During the time when we were generating and organizing much of the technical data that would form the basis for scale descriptions in the PIC manual, PIC protocols were also regularly collected for the children being evaluated by our agency's child and adolescent inpatient and outpatient services. In spite of the availability of a good deal of favorable information regarding scale reliability and validity, it was disconcerting to discover how little of this technical information could be comfortably translated into predictions that would be found clinically useful. It became clear that the exercise of one's "clinical skill" frequently became a gymnastic feat of vaulting over gaps in knowledge and performing test interpretations based on general knowledge about childhood psychopathology and the performance dimensions of objective personality tests. (For example, what T-score ranges for each scale should be interpreted as clinically significant? Would these ranges differ for each scale or within various populations? How should a scale elevation be interpreted when it was obtained for a client who was not a member of the scale's construction criterion population?) Indeed, it was absolutely amazing to discover shortly after the test's publication in 1977 how quickly a "clinical lore" could develop to guide the interpretation of the PIC! In some cases psychologists who had used this inventory fewer than twelve times had developed working hypotheses totally inconsistent with the small growing body of PIC literature.

Without a considerable "clinical lore" and a history of test application that would accommodate the accumulation of empirical evidence concerning the performance of PIC scales, it was necessary to gather data that would both allow the development of an automated interpretive system and provide for the accurate clinical application of the data presented within individual profiles. (Fowler [see chapter 4] considers the concurrent development of test and interpretive system an "ideal" strategy, in that test development efforts enrich the evolving interpretation system.)

Efforts to develop a data base that would allow the development of empirically supported interpretive guidelines were initiated even before the PIC was published. Criterion collection forms (see Lachar and Gdowski, 1979, app. A) were accepted by the staff of an active teaching service as performing clinically meaningful functions: an application form gathered presenting complaints, developmental history, and facts concerning pregnancy and birth. A form mailed to the child's school recorded teacher observations, estimates of achievement, and judgments as to the etiology of observed problems as well as suggested solutions. A final form was completed by the psychiatry resident or psychology intern who conducted the initial evaluation of the child or adolescent and parents. This form allowed the collection of relatively sophisticated judgments through dichotomous ratings (present/absent) of a wide variety of potential descriptors arranged under the following headings: affect, cognitive functioning, interpersonal relations, physical development and health, other, family relations, and parent description. In addition, DSM and GAP diagnoses and ideal treatment recommendations were recorded.

Collection of data using these three forms resulted in an initial actuarial analysis of 431 children and adolescents who had participated in an evaluation between December 1975 and April 1977 (Lachar and Gdowski, 1979). A second effort identified scale correlates of the four factor scales using an enlarged sample of 691 children and adolescents (Lachar, 1982), while the most recent efforts to develop an interpretive strategy for a twelve-option profile typology have involved a sample that has grown to 786 children and 547 adolescents. Other sources of potential PIC test correlates have been systematically collected. One sample of 329 children and adolescents includes PIC protocols and scores from individually administered intelligence and achievement tests (Kline, Lachar, and Sprague, 1985). Another sample of 248 elementary-grade children was obtained from regular classrooms and from six different special education placements (Lachar, Kline, and Boersma, 1986). Yet another source of potential PIC correlates is the criteria obtained from review of the medical records of 327 children and adolescents within the three-form data base (LaCombe, 1984).

Construction of an Actuarial Interpretive System

Efforts to develop an automated interpretation system for the PIC first focused on the clinical meaning of each profile scale (Lachar, 1982; Lachar and Gdowski, 1979). The initial goal was to construct an interpretive system similar to that developed at the Mayo Clinic for the MMPI (see Marks and Seeman, 1963, app. E and F), in which each scale is individually interpreted within set ranges of T-scores. Comprehensive information was obtained for individual scales rather than correlates for total profiles classified through some nominal method, such as the MMPI code types. The individual scale approach would result in an interpretation for every PIC profile, while actuarial interpretive systems based on the profile code type have proved, in the case of the MMPI, to often be of limited value because a significant number of profiles may remain unclassified (see Lachar, 1974b, p. 30).

An actuarial data base that provided the content for interpretive paragraphs and paragraph assignment to individual profiles was generated in two phases. In the first phase, the 322 descriptive variables derived from the parent, teacher, and clinician forms were correlated with each of twenty profile scales to identify replicated scale correlates as well as scale descriptors that applied only to a subsample of the study group (for example, only children, only adolescent girls). In this manner, each PIC profile scale obtained an average of thirty-four correlates applicable in all evaluations; in addition, each PIC profile scale obtained an average of twelve correlates of more limited applicability.

In the second phase, each identified correlate (that is, non-PIC variable that significantly correlates with a PIC scale) was studied to determine the relationship between correlate presence and PIC scale T-score elevation. That is, correlate frequency was tabulated within a number of contiguous T-score ranges, usually ten points in width (50 to 59*T*, 60 to 69*T*, and so on). The goal of this process was to identify the lowest T-score to which a given descriptor should be applied (or the highest T-score, for those correlates of low scale elevations) as well as to obtain an estimate of the frequency of each correlate within the identified T-score ranges, subsequently labeled clinical elevations.

The final process of determining the T-score ranges predictive of each correlate reflected a mixture of the application of measurement theory, assessment art, and individual preference. Interpretive guidelines optimally reflect the purpose for which the interpretations are intended. If scale interpretations are to be limited to those that improve the accuracy of prediction over currently available information, or at least symptom base rates (Sechrest, 1963), the degree to which a scale can improve upon base rate prediction should be calculated. If the goal of scale interpretation is to provide accurate descriptive material, regardless of its uniqueness in the diagnostic process, correlate selection becomes the process of locating scale-score ranges most descriptive of each criterion. The goal of the 1979 and 1982 studies was to provide comprehensive and accurate information based on the PIC profile scales.

An approach that is based on maximizing correct predictions must assume the pervasive accuracy of the criteria data studied and the equal utility of correct (or incorrect) prediction of criterion presence and absence. In actuality, error is introduced at both ends of the predictive process, in both the test measurement and in the criterion rating. In addition, prediction of criteria with very high or very low base rates, even when the criterion-to-scale-score relationship is replicated and reasonably substantial, is unlikely to improve on base rate prediction (Meehl and Rosen, 1955). Total reliance on exact criterion frequencies would limit the application of the resulting scale interpretations to very similar populations and would exclude infrequent or pervasive personality characteristics that are seen as important diagnostically and that have been established as stable correlates. Other factors being equal, rules were established to lead to correlate classification rates similar to their base rates within the study sample. Decision rules became more stringent and were applicable to a more limited proportion of the sample for those criteria that reflected severe pathology. Appendixes in Lachar (1982) and Lachar and Gdowski (1979) detail the process of evaluating the relationship between correlate frequency and T-score elevation.

These analyses resulted in the establishment of two to five interpretive ranges for the T-score distribution of each PIC profile scale. An observation of equal importance for automated and individual interpretation of PIC scales was made on the basis of these analyses: no individual cutting score delineated the "clinical range" for all scales. Some scales became clinically meaningful at 60*T*, some at 70*T*, while for others, elevations under 80*T* did not appear to differ from base rate.

A subsequent effort integrated the correlates obtained from parent, teacher, and clinician for each interpretive range, added phrases that reflected the likelihood of each descriptor (for example, "may be present" versus "is likely"), and incorporated other information presented in the manual and other sources. Lachar (1982) and Lachar and Gdowski (1979) provide narrative paragraphs for forty-nine of these "clinical" T-score ranges. The current automated interpretation available from Western Psychological Services goes a step further in integrating interpretive material. A secondary analysis determined frequent patterns of elevated interpretive ranges and allowed the development of narrative paragraphs that reflected the elevation of two or more profile scales. This approach provided an improved simulation of a clinical report by limiting redundancies and allowing integration at the content, versus the scale, level. Narrative paragraphs were intentionally written in clear, direct prose. Professional jargon was avoided. The goal was to provide a descriptive report in the form of a series of hypotheses requiring further investigation. The audience for this report was envisioned to be a variety of professionals to whom parents turn for help (pediatricians, psychologists, educators, social workers, psychiatrists).

Examples of Automated Interpretation

The following section presents the automated reports for mothers of two children who completed the PIC for quite different reasons. In the first example, Sean's mother completed the PIC as an intake, or triage, procedure in an outpatient clinic of a pediatric hospital. In the second example, Bill's mother completed the PIC as one of several measures obtained concurrently as part of an evaluation completed during a psychiatric hospitalization.

OUTPATIENT INTAKE

Sean's mother completed the first 280 items of the PIC, allowing processing of the answer sheet to obtain both the 131-item and 280-item report. This six-year-old boy was referred for the first evaluation of his behavior management problems by a pediatric neurologist who was treating his seizure disorder. Sean's mother noted current problems to include a high activity level at home and school, poor concentration, drowsiness, expressive language problems, and irritability, especially when fatigued. School personnel were concerned about his performance in the first grade and had recently recommended a placement in a special class that would emphasize the development of speech and language skills.

The PIC report based on 280 responses classifies the child to be in need of a psychological evaluation, emphasizes the need for a thorough intellectual evaluation, and suggests the presence of problems in academic performance and the likelihood of an ADD-H syndrome (hyperactivity, distractibility, impulsivity, and so forth). This report reflects the limited profile scale elevations of ADJ-S = 73*T*, ACH-S = 60*T*, IS-S = 97*T*, and HPR-S = 70*T* (see figure 14.1). Such a report would guide a clinician to determine the most appropri-

PERSONALITY INVENTORY FOR CHILDREN (PIC)
INTERPRETATION
A WPS TEST REPORT by Western Psychological Services
12031 Wilshire Boulevard
Los Angeles, California 90025
Copyright (c) 1985 by Western Psychological Services
IBM VERSION 1.0, P1

Form: II (FACTOR AND SHORTENED SCALES)

Client: SEAN
ID Number: NOT PROVIDED — Race: CAUCASIAN
Sex: MALE — School Grade: FIRST GRADE
Age: 6 years, 7 months — Informant: MOTHER

* * * * * PIC INTERPRETATION * * * * * *

This PIC interpretation is based on the systematic analysis of data obtained in the evaluation of behaviorally disturbed children and adolescents. This report consists of a series of hypotheses that may serve to guide further investigation.

GENERAL ADJUSTMENT AND INFORMANT RESPONSE STYLE:

Number of items not answered: 0

Inventory responses do not suggest that this informant attempted to minimize or deny any problems that this child may have.

The description of this child's behavior suggests that a psychological/ psychiatric evaluation may assist in the remediation of current problems.

COGNITIVE DEVELOPMENT AND ACADEMIC PERFORMANCE:

Reported child behavior and development suggest the need for a thorough intellectual assessment. Limitations in verbal, social, and perceptual-motor skills are likely to be noticed by parents, teachers, and peers. Similar children act younger than their chronological age, may be unconcerned about personal appearance, often are rejected by peers, and may seek friends among younger children. Preadolescents are likely to display poor physical education skills. Adolescents may be troubled by nocturnal enuresis.

Inventory responses suggest the possibility of poor school performance and associated academic retardation. Teacher observation of limited concentration or difficulty in completion of classroom assignments may be associated with below-age-expectation performance in reading, mathematics, or spelling.

PERSONALITY AND FAMILY EVALUATION:

A history of problematic peer relations is suggested that may be characterized by poorly controlled expression of hostility, fighting, provocation and teasing, or poor sportsmanship. Current and/or past behavior

Figure 14.1 (abridged). Computer interpretation of 280-response PIC description of Sean.

may also suggest hyperactivity, distractibility, restlessness, or impulsivity. Similar children are often inattentive in class, do not complete homework assignments, and may require adult intervention to conform to stated limits. A limited frustration tolerance may be associated with temper tantrums, destruction of objects, projection of blame, direct expression or displacement of anger, or a lack of trust in others. Other problems may include excessive seeking of attention and approval, clumsiness, frequent accidents or fire setting.

NOTE: The studies that form the foundation for this PIC REPORT are presented in three publications published by Western Psychological Services: "Multidimensional Description of Child Personality: A Manual for the Personality Inventory for Children" (WPS Catalog No. W-152G), "Actuarial Assessment of Child and Adolescent Personality: An Interpretive Guide for the Personality Inventory for Children Profile" (W-305), and "Personality Inventory for Children Revised Format Manual Supplement" (W-152GS).

* * * * CRITICAL ITEMS * * * *

These Inventory items were answered by the informant in the direction indicated. Although too much interpretive value should not be placed on individual responses, they may suggest areas for further inquiry.

(Only those items scored on the shortened scales could appear.)

Relative frequency of item endorsement in male normative and clinic samples is indicated at the end of each statement by this notation: [normative % / clinic %].

--- WORRY AND ANXIETY ---

222. My child insists on keeping the light on while sleeping. (T) [9% / 11%]

--- REALITY DISTORTION ---

96. My child gets confused easily. (T) [6% / 39%]

228. Often my child will laugh for no apparent reason. (T) [7% / 20%]

244. Often my child will wander about aimlessly. (T) [5% / 27%]

--- PEER RELATIONS ---

158. Most of my child's friends are younger than he/she is. (T) [8% / 29%]

--- CONSCIENCE DEVELOPMENT ---

56. My child often disobeys me. (T) [17% / 50%]

122. Spanking doesn't seem to affect my child. (T) [5% / 41%]

--- POOR JUDGMENT ---

41. My child can be left home alone without danger. (F) [18% / 42%]

87. My child will do anything on a dare. (T) [7% / 26%]

--- DISTRACTIBILITY, ACTIVITY LEVEL, AND COORDINATION ---

71. My child can't seem to wait for things like other children do. (T) [17% / 49%]

86. My child seems more clumsy than other children his/her age. (T)
[6% / 27%]

--- SPEECH AND LANGUAGE ---

33. At one time my child had speech difficulties. (T)
[17% / 38%]

78. My child first talked before he/she was two years old. (F)
[8% / 24%]

--- SCHOOL ADJUSTMENT ---

64. My child is in a special class in school (for slow learners). (T)
[2% / 30%]

79. School teachers complain that my child can't sit still. (T)
[9% / 41%]

PERSONALITY INVENTORY FOR CHILDREN (PIC)

Client: SEAN
ID Number: NOT PROVIDED

```
                                                  T SCORES
          SCORES              20   30   40   50   60   70   80   90   100  110  120
           T      RAW         |++++|++++|++++|++++|++++|++++|++++|++++|++++|++++|
                              |              |         |                        |
Factor Scales                 |              |         |                        |
                              |              |         |                        |
    I           74    (16)    |              |         | X                      |
    II          42    ( 2)    |          X   |         |                        |
    III         43    ( 1)    |           X  |         |                        |
    IV          67    ( 8)    |              |        X|                        |
Validity Scales               |====|====|====|====|====|====|====|====|====|====|
    L           57    ( 7)    |              |  X      |                        |
    F-S         59    ( 4)    |              |   X     |                        |
    DEF-S       48    (10)    |             X|         |                        |
    ADJ-S       73    (27)    |              |         | X                      |
Shortened Clinical Scales     |====|====|====|====|====|====|====|====|====|====|
    ACH-S       60    (13)    |              |    X    |                        |
    IS-S        97    (21)    |              |         |            X           |
    DVL         55    ( 8)    |              | X       |                        |
    SOM-S       40    ( 1)    |         X    |         |                        |
    D-S         41    ( 2)    |          X   |         |                        |
    FAM-S       42    ( 1)    |          X   |         |                        |
    DLQ-S       74    (16)    |              |         | X                      |
    WDL-S       38    ( 0)    |        X     |         |                        |
    ANX-S       46    ( 3)    |            X |         |                        |
    PSY-S       52    ( 3)    |              |X        |                        |
    HPR-S       70    (17)    |              |         X                        |
    SSK-S       49    ( 8)    |              X         |                        |
                              |              |         |                        |
           T      RAW         |++++|++++|++++|++++|++++|++++|++++|++++|++++|++++|
             SCORES           20   30   40   50   60   70   80   90   100  110  120
                                                  T SCORES
```

```
NOTE: Abbreviations on the PIC profile refer to the following scales:

     Factor I:  Undisciplined/Poor Self-Control
     Factor II:  Social Incompetence
     Factor III:  Internalization/Somatic Symptoms
     Factor IV:  Cognitive Development

     L:  Lie
     F-S:  Frequency-S
     DEF-S:  Defensiveness-S
     ADJ-S:  Adjustment-S

     ACH-S:  Achievement-S
     IS-S:  Intellectual Screening-S
     DVL:  Development
     SOM-S:  Somatic Concern-S
     D-S:  Depression-S
     FAM-S:  Family Relations-S
     DLQ-S:  Delinquency-S
     WDL-S:  Withdrawal-S
     ANX-S:  Anxiety-S
     PSY-S:  Psychosis-S
     HPR-S:  Hyperactivity-S
     SSK-S:  Social Skills-S
```

ate source for a continued psychometric evaluation and would lead to the evaluation and recommendation of appropriate pharmacological and behavioral interventions.

When only the first 131 items are evaluated, the automated narrative reflects the performance of only five (versus twenty) scales (see figure 14.2). The only scale to reach the clinical level for a factor scale (greater than 69*T*) is Factor

```
              PERSONALITY INVENTORY FOR CHILDREN (PIC)
                          INTERPRETATION
        A WPS TEST REPORT by Western Psychological Services
                     12031 Wilshire Boulevard
                   Los Angeles, California  90025
        Copyright (c) 1985 by Western Psychological Services
                      IBM VERSION 1.0, P1

              Form:  I (FACTOR SCALES)

Client: SEAN
ID Number: NOT PROVIDED                  Race: CAUCASIAN
Sex: MALE                                School Grade: FIRST GRADE
Age:  6 years,  7 months                 Informant: MOTHER


              * * * * * PIC INTERPRETATION * * * * * *

     This PIC interpretation is based on the systematic analysis of data
obtained in the evaluation of behaviorally disturbed children and adolescents.
This report consists of a series of hypotheses that may serve to guide further
investigation.

     These symptoms, characteristics, and/or problem areas may be further
delineated through completion of additional Inventory items by using one
of the longer forms.

INFORMANT RESPONSE STYLE:

     Number of items not answered:   0

     Inventory responses do not suggest that this informant attempted to
minimize or deny any problems that this child may have.
```

Figure 14.2 (abridged). Computer interpretation of 131-response PIC description of Sean.

BROAD BAND FACTOR SCALES:

Parents and teachers are likely to find this child's behavior problematic. Impulsivity, distractibility, and an inability to conform to limits are frequently characteristic. Similar children often argue with and talk back to adults. They frequently disturb classmates by teasing, interrupting, provoking fights, and other attention-seeking maneuvers. These children are often frustrated and may have a history of destructive behavior.

NOTE: The studies that form the foundation for this PIC REPORT are presented in three publications published by Western Psychological Services: "Multidimensional Description of Child Personality: A Manual for the Personality Inventory for Children" (WPS Catalog No. W-152G), "Actuarial Assessment of Child and Adolescent Personality: An Interpretive Guide for the Personality Inventory for Children Profile" (W-305), and "Personality Inventory for Children Revised Format Manual Supplement" (W-152GS).

CRITICAL ITEMS: (Not printed for this Form.)

PERSONALITY INVENTORY FOR CHILDREN (PIC)

Client: SEAN
ID Number: NOT PROVIDED

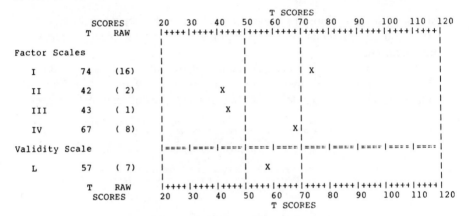

```
                                                   T SCORES
                 SCORES        20   30   40   50   60   70   80   90   100  110  120
                 T    RAW      |++++|++++|++++|++++|++++|++++|++++|++++|++++|++++|
                               |              |         |                        |
Factor Scales                  |              |         |                        |
                               |              |         |                        |
   I            74    (16)     |              |         | X                      |
                               |              |         |                        |
   II           42    ( 2)     |         X    |         |                        |
                               |              |         |                        |
   III          43    ( 1)     |          X   |         |                        |
                               |              |         |                        |
   IV           67    ( 8)     |              |        X|                        |
                               |              |         |                        |
Validity Scale                 |====|====|====|====|====|====|====|====|====|====|
                               |              |         |                        |
   L            57    ( 7)     |              |   X     |                        |
                               |              |         |                        |
                 T    RAW      |++++|++++|++++|++++|++++|++++|++++|++++|++++|++++|
                 SCORES        20   30   40   50   60   70   80   90   100  110  120
                                                   T SCORES
```

NOTE: Abbreviations on the PIC profile refer to the following scales:

Factor I: Undisciplined/Poor Self-Control
Factor II: Social Incompetence
Factor III: Internalization/Somatic Symptoms
Factor IV: Cognitive Development

L: Lie

Scale I, and the brief interpretive paragraph emphasizes externalizing behaviors without differentiating between hyperactivity and conduct disorder syndromes. In addition, Factor Scale IV (Cognitive Development) does not reach the minimum interpretable level (an increase in one raw scale point would have resulted in a T-score of 72 versus 67). This example suggests the relatively limited clinical value of a fifteen-minute questionnaire. Part I reports should be used for research and screening applications in only those cases where the mother cannot spend the thirty to forty-five minutes it takes to complete both parts.

INPATIENT EVALUATION

Bill's ten-year, ten-month history, which included reports of being expelled from a variety of preschool programs, suggested the presence of a chronic behavior disorder. This was his third psychological evaluation during a five-year period in which he had been treated with stimulant medication and had attended special classes for the emotionally/behaviorally impaired. This boy had always been described as a risk-taker, as noncompliant and difficult to manage. Recently he had become increasingly manipulative, disrespectful, had run away, had become preoccupied with morbid topics, including war and violence, and had begun to express suicidal ideation. This first hospitalization was precipitated by exclusion from school because of destruction of a time-out room and a subsequent bizarre shoplifting/trespass episode.

Bill's mother completed the first 420 items of the Revised Format Administration Booklet, allowing generation of reports based on 420, 280, and 131 items. The automated narratives based on 420 and 280 items were identical, except that the 420-item format resulted in twenty more Critical Items (fifty-three items) than the 280-item format (thirty-three items). These reports reflect

```
          PERSONALITY INVENTORY FOR CHILDREN (PIC)
                      INTERPRETATION
     A WPS TEST REPORT by Western Psychological Services
                  12031 Wilshire Boulevard
               Los Angeles, California  90025
     Copyright (c) 1985 by Western Psychological Services
                    IBM VERSION 1.0, P1


              Form:  II (FACTOR AND SHORTENED SCALES)

Client: BILL
ID Number: NOT PROVIDED               Race: CAUCASIAN
Sex: MALE                             School Grade: FIFTH GRADE
Age: 10 years,  0 month               Informant: MOTHER


             * * * * * PIC INTERPRETATION * * * * * *

     This PIC interpretation is based on the systematic analysis of data
obtained in the evaluation of behaviorally disturbed children and adolescents.
This report consists of a series of hypotheses that may serve to guide further
investigation.

GENERAL ADJUSTMENT AND INFORMANT RESPONSE STYLE:

     Number of items not answered:  11

     Inventory responses do not suggest that this informant attempted to
minimize or deny any problems that this child may have.

     The description of this child's behavior suggests that a psychological/
psychiatric evaluation may assist in the remediation of current problems.

PERSONALITY AND FAMILY EVALUATION:

     A history of poor peer relations may lead this child to expect criticism
and rejection from others.  Parents and teachers frequently observe that
```


Figure 14.3 (abridged). Computer interpretation of 280-response PIC description of Bill.

similar children have few, if any, friends. Poor social skills may be demonstrated by a failure to initiate relationships, with resulting isolation, or by conflict with peers that reflects poor sportsmanship and limited frustration tolerance.

This child's behavior is likely to be characterized by social isolation and emotional lability. Parents frequently describe similar children as "often confused or in a daze," and may note excessive daydreaming as well as other strange or peculiar behaviors.

This child's behavior is likely to reflect the presence of depression, anxiety, and social withdrawal. Presenting complaints may include problems with sleeping and eating, emotional lability, multiple fears, distrust of others, or excessive worry, self-blame, or self-criticism. Similar children are likely to be described as excessively shy by parents and teachers. They play alone, avoid group activities at school, and stay away from other family members at home. Preadolescents may be unresponsive to school surroundings and may evidence separation anxiety, while adolescents may display suicidal thought and behavior.

A disregard for rules and societal expectations is likely to be evidenced by behavior displayed at home and at school. Similar children dislike school and demonstrate a poor academic adjustment associated with hostility and defiance or apathy and disinterest. Current behavior is likely to reflect impulsivity, poor judgment, or unmodulated hostility. A character disorder may be suggested by symptoms such as lying, theft, problematic sexual behavior, group delinquent activities, or an established tendency to blame others for current problems.

Law enforcement agencies may be aware of delinquent child behavior such as truancy, running away from home, or alcohol/drug abuse. Mental health professionals are likely to be pessimistic about remediation of current problems and may feel that institutional treatment is indicated.

Current child behavior may reflect a poor social and academic adjustment that is associated with overactivity, distractibility, or provocation of peers. Similar children are frequently described as restless, fidgety, and inattentive in the classroom. They are excessively social in school and may require adult intervention to limit impulsive, disruptive, and annoying behaviors. Demonstrating limited frustration tolerance, such children frequently fight with and pick on other children, break things, displace anger, distrust others, or are described as poor losers. Poor gross-motor coordination or accident proneness may be present.

NOTE: The studies that form the foundation for this PIC REPORT are presented in three publications published by Western Psychological Services: "Multidimensional Description of Child Personality: A Manual for the Personality Inventory for Children" (WPS Catalog No. W-152G), "Actuarial Assessment of Child and Adolescent Personality: An Interpretive Guide for the Personality Inventory for Children Profile" (W-305), and "Personality Inventory for Children Revised Format Manual Supplement" (W-152GS).

* * * * CRITICAL ITEMS * * * *

These Inventory items were answered by the informant in the direction indicated. Although too much interpretive value should not be placed on individual responses, they may suggest areas for further inquiry.

(Only those items scored on the shortened scales could appear.)

Relative frequency of item endorsement in male normative and clinic samples is indicated at the end of each statement by this notation: [normative % / clinic %].

--- DEPRESSION AND POOR SELF-CONCEPT ---

13. My child has little self-confidence. (T) [18% / 54%]

132. My child tends to pity him/herself. (T) [26% / 38%]

179. My child doesn't seem to care for fun. (T) [2% / 8%]

185. Several times my child has threatened to kill him/herself. (T) [2% / 6%]

274. My child speaks of him/herself as stupid or dumb. (T) [7% / 22%]

--- WORRY AND ANXIETY ---

4. My child worries about things that usually only adults worry about. (T) [15% / 21%]

--- REALITY DISTORTION ---

96. My child gets confused easily. (T) [6% / 39%]

244. Often my child will wander about aimlessly. (T) [5% / 27%]

--- PEER RELATIONS ---

16. My child is usually rejected by other children. (T) [4% / 26%]

36. My child doesn't seem to care to be with others. (T) [4% / 18%]

47. My child really has no real friend. (T) [6% / 29%]

158. Most of my child's friends are younger than he/she is. (T) [8% / 29%]

160. My child never takes the lead in things. (T) [13% / 32%]

215. My child would rather be with adults than with children his/her own age. (T) [7% / 23%]

--- UNSOCIALIZED AGGRESSION ---

43. My child has been in trouble for attacking others. (T) [2% / 16%]

276. Several times my child has threatened to kill others. (T) [2% / 11%]

--- CONSCIENCE DEVELOPMENT ---

56. My child often disobeys me. (T) [17% / 50%]

122. Spanking doesn't seem to affect my child. (T) [5% / 41%]

202. Several times my child has been in trouble for stealing. (T) [2% / 29%]

208. My child has never been in trouble with the police. (F) [9% / 30%]

--- ATYPICAL DEVELOPMENT ---

100. My child was difficult to toilet train. (T) [16% / 34%]

116. My child could eat with a fork before age four years. (F) [7% / 21%]

156. My child has had convulsions. (T) [3% / 13%]

--- DISTRACTIBILITY, ACTIVITY LEVEL, AND COORDINATION ---

71. My child can't seem to wait for things like other children do. (T) [17% / 49%]

--- SOMATIC COMPLAINTS/CURRENT HEALTH ---

92. My child often has headaches. (T) [6% / 17%]

--- SCHOOL ADJUSTMENT ---

20. The school says my child needs help in getting along with other children. (T) [5% / 36%]

79. School teachers complain that my child can't sit still. (T) [9% / 41%]

204. My child has never failed a grade in school. (F) [12% / 44%]

250. My child has never been expelled from school. (F) [9% / 29%]

--- FAMILY DISCORD ---

188. My child seems unhappy about our home life. (T) [7% / 27%]

245. Several times my child has threatened to run away. (T) [10% / 28%]

275. There is a lot of tension in our home. (T) [17% / 39%]

--- OTHER ---

181. My child often stays in his/her rooms for hours. (T) [9% / 16%]

PERSONALITY INVENTORY FOR CHILDREN (PIC)

Client: BILL
ID Number: NOT PROVIDED

```
                                                 T SCORES
                      SCORES     20   30   40   50   60   70   80   90   100  110  120
                    T     RAW    |++++|++++|++++|++++|++++|++++|++++|++++|++++|++++|
                                 |              |         |                        |
Factor Scales                    |              |         |                        |
                                 |              |         |                        |
   I               82    (20)    |              |         |     X                  |
                                 |              |         |                        |
   II              86    (21)    |              |         |       X                |
                                 |              |         |                        |
   III             61    ( 6)    |              |    X    |                        |
                                 |              |         |                        |
   IV              62    ( 5)    |              |    X    |                        |
                                 |              |         |                        |
Validity Scales                  |====|====|====|====|====|====|====|====|====|====|
                                 |              |         |                        |
   L               34    ( 1)    |      X       |         |                        |
                                 |              |         |                        |
   F-S             96    (11)    |              |         |            X           |
                                 |              |         |                        |
   DEF-S           48    (10)    |             X|         |                        |
                                 |              |         |                        |
   ADJ-S          105    (43)    |              |         |                 X      |
                                 |              |         |                        |
Shortened Clinical Scales        |====|====|====|====|====|====|====|====|====|====|
                                 |              |         |                        |
   ACH-S           54    (11)    |              | X       |                        |
                                 |              |         |                        |
   IS-S            66    (13)    |              |       X |                        |
                                 |              |         |                        |
   DVL             55    ( 8)    |              |  X      |                        |
                                 |              |         |                        |
   SOM-S           57    ( 6)    |              |   X     |                        |
                                 |              |         |                        |
   D-S            100    (29)    |              |         |              X         |
                                 |              |         |                        |
   FAM-S           53    ( 6)    |              | X       |                        |
                                 |              |         |                        |
   DLQ-S          124    (32)    |              |         |                        *
                                 |              |         |                        |
   WDL-S           84    (11)    |              |         |      X                 |
                                 |              |         |                        |
   ANX-S           73    (11)    |              |         | X                      |
                                 |              |         |                        |
   PSY-S           92    (13)    |              |         |          X             |
                                 |              |         |                        |
   HPR-S           66    (16)    |              |       X |                        |
                                 |              |         |                        |
   SSK-S           91    (25)    |              |         |          X             |
                                 |              |         |                        |
                    T     RAW    |++++|++++|++++|++++|++++|++++|++++|++++|++++|++++|
                      SCORES     20   30   40   50   60   70   80   90   100  110  120
                                                 T SCORES
```

* Graph of T-score values below 20 and above 120 are truncated.

```
NOTE:  Abbreviations on the PIC profile refer to the following scales:

     Factor I:  Undisciplined/Poor Self-Control
     Factor II:  Social Incompetence
     Factor III:  Internalization/Somatic Symptoms
     Factor IV:  Cognitive Development

     L:  Lie
     F-S:  Frequency-S
     DEF-S:  Defensiveness-S
     ADJ-S:  Adjustment-S

     ACH-S:  Achievement-S
     IS-S:  Intellectual Screening-S
     DVL:  Development
     SOM-S:  Somatic Concern-S
     D-S:  Depression-S
     FAM-S:  Family Relations-S
     DLQ-S:  Delinquency-S
     WDL-S:  Withdrawal-S
     ANX-S:  Anxiety-S
     PSY-S:  Psychosis-S
     HPR-S:  Hyperactivity-S
     SSK-S:  Social Skills-S
```

the chronic and severe nature of this child's behavioral and emotional maladjustment; interpretive paragraphs reflect problematic peer relationships, noncompliance at home and school, problematic anger and hyperactivity, and psychological discomfort (see figure 14.3).

The paragraph added to the highest of DLQ elevations (T greater than 109) is more usually seen in reports of disturbed adolescents:

> Law enforcement agencies may be aware of delinquent child behavior such as truancy, running away from home, or alcohol/drug abuse. Mental health professionals are likely to be pessimistic about remediation of current problems, and may feel that institutional treatment is indicated.

However, this boy was known by law enforcement agencies because of his vandalism and running away from home, and thus the inclusion of this paragraph was deemed appropriate. It is interesting to note that his hospitalization in an acute treatment unit was followed by residential placement rather than return to home. PIC predictions of deficient social skills and emotional lability were substantiated through observation of his behavior during hospitalization. "Excessive daydreaming" and "strange or peculiar behaviors" were suggested by his behavior, as well as extensive bizarre responses to Thematic Apperception Test stimuli, which elaborated themes of violence and sex.

This report also provides an example of a narrative paragraph that reflects the correlates of a pattern of profile scales:

> This child's behavior is likely to reflect the presence of depression, anxiety, and social withdrawal. Presenting complaints may include problems with sleeping and eating, emotional lability, multiple fears, distrust of others, or excessive worry, self-blame, or self-criticism. Similar children are likely to be described as excessively shy by both parents and teachers. They play alone, avoid group activities at school, and stay away from other family members at home. Preadolescents may be unresponsive to school surroundings, and may evidence separation anxiety, while adolescents may display suicidal thought and behavior.

This paragraph reflects the integration of correlates placed at D greater than 79*T*, ANX 70 to 79*T*, and WDL greater than 79*T*.

The report generated from the first 131 items presents the interpretation of the moderate I: Undisciplined/Poor Self-Control and II: Social Incompetence scale T-score ranges (80 to 89T). Although providing evidence of both externalizing and internalizing psychopathology, this report does not serve as an adequate representation of the total profile variability and should be used clinically only when the 280-item version cannot be obtained (see figure 14.4).

PERSONALITY INVENTORY FOR CHILDREN (PIC)
INTERPRETATION
A WPS TEST REPORT by Western Psychological Services
12031 Wilshire Boulevard
Los Angeles, California 90025
Copyright (c) 1985 by Western Psychological Services
IBM VERSION 1.0, P1

Form: I (FACTOR SCALES)

Client: BILL
ID Number: NOT PROVIDED
Sex: MALE
Age: 10 years, 0 month

Race: CAUCASIAN
School Grade: FIFTH GRADE
Informant: MOTHER

* * * * * PIC INTERPRETATION * * * * * *

This PIC interpretation is based on the systematic analysis of data obtained in the evaluation of behaviorally disturbed children and adolescents. This report consists of a series of hypotheses that may serve to guide further investigation.

These symptoms, characteristics, and/or problem areas may be further delineated through completion of additional Inventory items by using one of the longer forms.

INFORMANT RESPONSE STYLE:

Number of items not answered: 0

Inventory responses do not suggest that this informant attempted to minimize or deny any problems that this child may have.

BROAD BAND FACTOR SCALES:

A disregard for rules and societal expectations at home and at school is very likely. Associated symptoms often include lying, stealing, labile affect, argumentativeness, irritability, limited frustration tolerance, and temper outbursts. Current behavior is likely to reflect impulsivity, poor judgment, and an impaired interpersonal adjustment that may be associated with complaints about the unfairness of others, destructiveness (including episodes of fire setting for boys), hostility, and defiance. Similar children may have difficulty achieving in school, which may be related to behavior suggestive of distractibility and overactivity. They may disturb classmates, other peers, and siblings by teasing, interrupting, and provoking and engaging in fights. Parents often describe them as untrustworthy and as poor sports and poor losers. For adolescents, delinquent behaviors such as school truancy and running away from home may have attracted the attention of law enforcement personnel.

Many of these children have few or no friends, avoid social interaction, and expect failure in activities and rejection from peers. An analysis of social skills may reveal patterns of interaction more characteristic of younger children. Teachers, especially of preadolescents, may also observe social isolation and associated psychological distress. These children are

Figure 14.4 (abridged). Computer interpretation of 131-response PIC description of Bill.

often described by parents as shy, sad, and afraid of many things. They may have difficulty falling asleep, fear going to school, and may be seen as unresponsive to their surroundings. In some children these characteristics are associated with thoughts of self-destruction.

NOTE: The studies that form the foundation for this PIC REPORT are presented in three publications published by Western Psychological Services: "Multidimensional Description of Child Personality: A Manual for the Personality Inventory for Children" (WPS Catalog No. W-152G), "Actuarial Assessment of Child and Adolescent Personality: An Interpretive Guide for the Personality Inventory for Children Profile" (W-305), and "Personality Inventory for Children Revised Format Manual Supplement" (W-152GS).

CRITICAL ITEMS: (Not printed for this Form.)

Client: BILL
ID Number: NOT PROVIDED

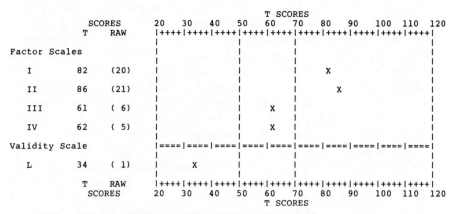

```
                                                T SCORES
            SCORES       20   30   40   50   60   70   80   90   100  110  120
            T    RAW     |++++|++++|++++|++++|++++|++++|++++|++++|++++|++++|
                         |              |         |                        |
Factor Scales            |              |         |                        |
                         |              |         |                        |
   I        82   (20)    |              |         |    X                   |
                         |              |         |                        |
   II       86   (21)    |              |         |      X                 |
                         |              |         |                        |
   III      61   ( 6)    |              |   X     |                        |
                         |              |         |                        |
   IV       62   ( 5)    |              |   X     |                        |
                         |              |         |                        |
Validity Scale           |====|====|====|====|====|====|====|====|====|====|
                         |              |         |                        |
   L        34   ( 1)    |      X       |         |                        |
                         |              |         |                        |
            T    RAW     |++++|++++|++++|++++|++++|++++|++++|++++|++++|++++|
            SCORES       20   30   40   50   60   70   80   90   100  110  120
                                                T SCORES
```

NOTE: Abbreviations on the PIC profile refer to the following scales:

Factor I: Undisciplined/Poor Self-Control
Factor II: Social Incompetence
Factor III: Internalization/Somatic Symptoms
Factor IV: Cognitive Development

L: Lie

New Developments in Computer Interpretation of the PIC

The current automated report for the PIC is not viewed as a permanent, static product. Rather it is intended as a method of providing state-of-the-art actuarial interpretation of PIC scales and other indices as they are developed. This goal requires continual review of the developing literature on the PIC (a regularly updated PIC bibliography is available from the author). Few studies focus on the effectiveness or meaning of PIC performance, which would add to the actuarial data base of the PIC, but rather apply the PIC in the study of child-focused phenomena.

Two current areas of study involve the writer and a small number of colleagues (see Gdowski, Lachar, and Kline, 1985; Lachar, Kline, and Boersma, 1986; LaCombe, 1984). One study explored the ability of PIC scales to predict likely classroom placement. The data base for these analyses has included an elementary-school sample with the following subgroups: (1) children placed in regular classrooms; children placed in self-contained classrooms for the (2) trainable retarded, (3) educable retarded, and (4) learning disabled; (5) learning disabled children placed in regular classrooms (mainstreamed) receiving learning resource center support; (6) emotionally impaired/handicapped children in self-contained classrooms or mainstreamed with special education support; and (7) children who did not meet standards to justify classification as emotionally impaired/handicapped, yet received formal counseling for emotional problems that had not interfered with the learning process. Replication samples have been made available through the efforts of Clark (1982), DeKrey (1983), and Schnel (1982), who had applied the PIC to various special education samples.

Two approaches have been applied with reasonable success to identify the need for various special education services. In one, a series of six discriminant-function equations were developed to allow an individual profile (280-item version) to be classified into one of seven alternatives. In a second approach to classification, an individual's revised-format profile is compared to seven mean profiles through the calculation of a multivariate similarity index comparable in form to a correlation coefficient. This approach is especially promising for clinical application because it does not assume that these seven education classifications are mutually exclusive. For example, one child's profile may be equally similar to learning disabled and emotionally impaired/handicapped samples, while another child's profile may be equally similar to regular classroom and counseled samples. The purpose of such an addition to the automated report would be to suggest most likely and most unlikely educational placements. In both approaches the computer provides statistical results that would be either tedious or almost impossible to compute with a hand-held calculator.

A second area of investigation that has direct implications for actuarial interpretation of the PIC is the identification of profile types. Initial efforts to classify profiles followed the two-point code-type approach that has been used with considerable success in the interpretation of the MMPI (DeHorn, Lachar, and Gdowski, 1979). Although this system demonstrated relative success in classifying members of homogeneous criterion groups, its application (using either absolute T-score elevations of ACH through SSK or a modified approach that incorporated established clinical ranges of these scales) resulted in the majority of cases being classified within a few code types (such as DLQ/PSY) while very few cases were grouped within numerous other code types.

Clinical and actuarial configural interpretive strategies for the MMPI were developed after systematic observation identified frequently repeated patterns that involved the entire profile or a subset of contiguous scales. Rather than wait patiently for such a process, the multivariate technique of cluster analysis has been applied to large representative samples of PIC profiles (in the form of T-score ranges of the twelve profile scales, ACH through SSK). The outcome of this process has been the identification of replicated profile types and the development of a set of classification rules that are applied to individual profiles through the use of a decision tree. The twelve possible alternatives have been found to classify over 90 percent of a very large heterogeneous clinical sample (N = 1,333).

Subsequent studies have identified replicated correlates of these twelve profile types in a manner similar to that applied to contemporary study of MMPI code types (for example, Gynther, Altman, and Sletten, 1973). These efforts have identified a considerable number of correlates: an average of ninety-seven per profile type from the three-form data base and an average of thirty-nine additional correlates through the process of review and coding of a sample of the medical records classified by PIC profile type. The first analysis sought to identify concurrent descriptive correlates, while the medical records analysis extended this review to determine if stable relationships between descriptive correlates and a developmental perspective could be incorporated into profile-type interpretations.

This actuarial data base now includes estimates of reason for referral, age at onset of difficulties, judged etiologies of problems, and the relative importance of manifest symptoms. Additional efforts have identified the psychometric (IQ, achievement) correlates of these profile types and have compared the predictive utility of these classifications to DSM groupings. Efforts are currently under way to organize these studies into a variety of publications as well as to translate the results into a series of profile-type interpretations. With an average of 136 significant correlates per profile type, the process of data integration and the more subjective assessment of the probable generalizability of each correlate is a formidable task!

It may be of some interest, however, to return to the cases of Sean and Bill and apply some of these emerging actuarial approaches to PIC profile interpretation. When the six discriminant rules are applied to suggest the single best educational placement, Sean's profile is classified as learning disabled/self-contained classroom, while Bill's profile is classified as emotionally impaired/handicapped. These results are quite encouraging, because Bill had attended a self-contained classroom for the emotionally impaired/handicapped prior to his hospitalization and the recommendation for Sean had been to evaluate his appropriateness for a learning-disabled program.

Sean's profile was classified as a Profile Type 6. The following excerpt provides an integrated interpretation of Profile Type 6 correlates:

> Children who obtain this classification are significantly younger than base rate. This group appears to represent a "pure" cognitive dysfunction group with correlates from all rating sources indicative of developmental delay, cognitive deficits, hyperactive behavior, poor school achievement, and immature social skills. Cerebral dysfunction is viewed as the primary problem, often due to pre- or perinatal central nervous system insult. Nevertheless, they usually function well within the context of their families (often viewed as supportive) and special education classrooms. Referral to a child guidance agency is often motivated by relatively minor conduct problems that reflect a limited ability to adjust well to environmental variations that would be classified as a mild stressor, such as a change in classroom teacher. Only two percent of children who obtain similar profile types are placed in regular classrooms. The majority (more than sixty percent) are in classrooms for the learning disabled, while

> almost twenty-five percent are in classrooms for the mentally retarded. About one-half of children who obtain this profile type score below 80 on standardized, individually administered tests of intelligence.

Bill's profile was classified as a Profile Type 7. Correlates of Profile Type 7 provide the basis for the following interpretation:

> Children who obtain this classification are often significantly older than base rate, with problems frequently first appearing in adolescence. Both conduct and emotional problems are in evidence: disobedience, stealing, aggression, school dislike, hyperactive behavior, drug and alcohol abuse, and police involvement, as well as sadness, sleep disturbance, mood lability, and previous suicide attempts. Family dysfunction and the child's feelings are often seen as causal. These children were typically overly active and difficult to manage from an early age which was often attributed to inconsistent parental childrearing and discipline techniques. They often became participants in parental conflict which caused them to feel angry and insecure. These feelings were often associated with the acting-out of anger and the development of depressive symptoms. Noted conduct problems usually had a self-punitive quality and/or were directed toward family members, rather than toward school staff or other authority figures who usually did not view them as difficult to manage. Depressive symptoms, such as poor self-esteem, sadness, anxiety, and a tendency to withdraw from others, also resulted from this conflict because these children typically felt rejected by their parents and often feared being abandoned by them. When these children receive special education services their placement most likely is a response to their emotional adjustment and behavior patterns that disrupt the educational process for them and their classmates.

Summary

This chapter has introduced the Personality Inventory for Children (PIC) and reviewed current automated interpretation strategies, as well as efforts to develop additional interpretive options. PIC test items are completed by a parent informant to allow scoring of scales that reflect child and adolescent behavior, affect, ability, and family function, and also provide estimates of profile validity by evaluation of a respondent's tendency to deny or exaggerate child problems and symptoms. Current automated interpretations draw from a considerable data base and are most accurately conceptualized as *actuarial* in nature, predicting non-PIC measures such as parent, teacher, and clinician ratings. Additional data sets have allowed the prediction of psychometric assessment of the child, special education class placement, and clinical case history information viewed from a developmental perspective. Current interpretations evaluate individual scale elevations and patterns consisting of two or three scales, while recent studies have sought to identify prototypic total profile patterns and to determine their clinical utility. The sample interpretations demonstrate PIC clinical application and provide examples of current and future automated assessment strategies.

REFERENCES

Achenbach, T. M. (1978). The Child Behavior Profile: I. Boys aged 6–11. *Journal of Consulting and Clinical Psychology*, *46*, 478–488.

Achenbach, T. M., and Edelbrock, C. S. (1978). The classification of child psychopathology: A review and analysis of empirical efforts. *Psychological Bulletin*, *85*, 1275–1301.

Anderson, E. E., and Quast, W. (1983). Young children in alcoholic families: A mental health needs–assessment and an intervention/prevention strategy. *Journal of Primary Prevention*, *3*, 174–187.

Armstrong, G. D., Wirt, R. D., Nesbit, M. E., and Martinson, I. M. (1982). Multidimensional assessment of psychological problems in children with cancer. *Research in Nursing and Health*, *5*, 205–211.

Barad, S. J., and Hughes, H. M. (1984). Readability of the Personality Inventory for Children. *Journal of Consulting and Clinical Psychology*, *52*, 906–907.

Bennett, T. S., and Welsh, M. C. (1981). Validity of a configural interpretation of the intellectual screening and achievement scales of the Personality Inventory for Children. *Educational and Psychological Measurement*, *41*, 863–868.

Breen, M. J., and Barkley, R. A. (1983). The Personality Inventory for Children (PIC): Its clinical utility with hyperactive children. *Journal of Pediatric Psychology*, *8*, 359–366.

Clark, E. (1982). Construct validity and diagnostic potential of the Personality Inventory for Children (PIC) with emotionally disturbed, learning disabled, and educable mentally retarded children. (Doctoral dissertation, Michigan State University, 1982). *Dissertation Abstracts International*, *43*(5A), 1473–1474.

Clark, E., Wanous, D. S., and Pompa, J. L. (1982, August). Construct validation of the Personality Inventory for Children (PIC). Paper presented at the 90th annual convention of the American Psychological Association, Washington, DC.

Costello, C. G. (1981). Childhood depression. In E. J. Mash and L. G. Terdal (Eds.), *Behavioral assessment of childhood disorders* (pp. 305–346). New York: Guilford Press.

Daldin, H. (1985). Faking good and faking bad on the Personality Inventory for Children-Revised, shortened format. *Journal of Consulting and Clinical Psychology*, *53*, 561–563.

DeHorn, A. B., Lachar, D., and Gdowski, C. L. (1979). Profile classification strategies for the Personality Inventory for Children. *Journal of Consulting and Clinical Psychology*, *47*, 874–881.

DeKrey, S. J. (1983). Construct validity and educational applications of the Personality Inventory for Children (PIC)—shortened form version. (Doctoral dissertation, University of Iowa, 1982). *Dissertation Abstracts International*, *43*(12A), 3844.

DeKrey, S. J., and Ehly, S. (1985). The Personality Inventory for Children: Differential diagnosis in school settings. *Journal of Psychoeducational Assessment*, *3*, 45–53.

DeMoor-Peal, R., and Handal, P. J. (1983). Validity of the Personality Inventory for Children with four-year-old males and females: A caution. *Journal of Pediatric Psychology*, *8*, 261–271.

Dollinger, S. J., Goh, D. S., and Cody, J. J. (1984). A note on the congruence of the WISC-R and the cognitive development scales of the Personality Inventory for Children. *Journal of Consulting and Clinical Psychology*, *52*, 315–316.

Dreger, R. M. (1981). First-, second-, and third-order factors for the Children's Behavioral Classification Project Instrument and an attempt at rapprochement. *Journal of Abnormal Psychology*, *90*, 242–260.

Durrant, J. E. (1983). *Concurrent validity of the narrow-band and broad-band intellectual scales of the Personality Inventory for Children within a preschool population*. Unpublished master's thesis, University of Windsor, Canada.

Forbes, G. B. (1985). The Personality Inventory for Children (PIC) and hyperactivity: Clinical utility and problems of generalizability. *Journal of Pediatric Psychology*, *10*, 141–149.

Gdowski, C. L., Lachar, D., and Kline, R. B. (1985). A PIC profile typology of children and adolescents: I. An empirically-derived alternative to traditional diagnosis. *Journal of Abnormal Psychology*, *94*, 346–361.

Gynther, M. D., Altman, H., and Sletten, I. W. (1973). Replicated correlates of MMPI two-point code types: The Missouri actuarial system. *Journal of Clinical Psychology Monographs*, *29*, 263–289.

Harrington, R. G., and Follett, G. M. (1984). The readability of child personality assessment instruments. *Journal of Psychoeducational Assessment*, 2, 37–48.

Kelly, G. T. (1982). A comparison of the Personality Inventory for Children (PIC) and the Child Behavior Checklist (CBCL) with an independent behavior checklist completed by clinicians. (Doctoral dissertation, Duke University, 1982). *Dissertation Abstracts International*, 43(4B), 1257.

Kline, R. B., Lachar, D., and Sprague, D. J. (1985). The Personality Inventory for Children (PIC): An unbiased predictor of cognitive and academic status. *Journal of Pediatric Psychology*, *10*, 461–477.

Kurdek, L. A. (1980). Developmental relations among children's perspective taking, moral judgment, and parent-rated behaviors. *Merril-Palmer Quarterly*, 26, 103–121.

Kurdek, L. A. (1982). Long-term predictive validity of children's social-cognitive assessments. *Merrill-Palmer Quarterly*, 28, 511–521.

Kurdek, L. A., and Krile, D. (1983). The relation between third- through eighth-grade children's social cognition and parents' ratings of social skills and general adjustment. *Journal of Genetic Psychology*, 143, 201–206.

Lachar, D. (1974a). Accuracy and generalizability of an automated MMPI interpretation system. *Journal of Consulting and Clinical Psychology*, 42, 267–273.

Lachar, D. (1974b). *The MMPI: Clinical assessment and automated interpretation*. Los Angeles: Western Psychological Services.

Lachar, D. (1982). *Personality Inventory for Children (PIC) revised format manual supplement*. Los Angeles: Western Psychological Services.

Lachar, D. (1986). *Bibliography for the Personality Inventory for Children*. Unpublished Manuscript. (Available from author: Institute of Behavioral Medicine, Good Samaritan Medical Center, 1111 E. McDowell Rd., P.O. Box 2989, Phoenix, AZ 85062.)

Lachar, D., and Alexander, R. S. (1978). Veridicality of self-report: Replicated correlates of the Wiggins MMPI content scales. *Journal of Consulting and Clinical Psychology*, 46, 1349–1356.

Lachar, D., Berman, W., Grisell, J. L., and Schooff, K. (1976). The MacAndrew Alcoholism Scale as a general measure of substance misuse. *Journal of Studies on Alcohol*, 37, 1609–1615.

Lachar, D., and Gdowski, C. L. (1979). *Actuarial assessment of child and adolescent personality: An interpretive guide for the Personality Inventory for Children profile*. Los Angeles: Western Psychological Services.

Lachar, D., Gdowski, C. L., and Snyder, D. K. (1982). Broad-band dimensions of psychopathology: Factor scales for the Personality Inventory for Children. *Journal of Consulting and Clinical Psychology*, 50, 634–642.

Lachar, D., Gdowski, C. L., and Snyder, D. K. (1984). External validation of the Personality Inventory for Children (PIC) profile and factor scales: Parent, teacher, and clinician ratings. *Journal of Consulting and Clinical Psychology*, 52, 155–164.

Lachar, D., Kline, R. B., and Boersma, D. C. (1986). The Personality Inventory for Children: Approaches to actuarial interpretation in clinic and school settings. In H. M. Knoff (Ed.), *The psychological assessment of child and adolescent personality* (pp. 273–308). New York: Guilford Press.

Lachar, D., Klinge, V., and Grisell, J. L. (1976). Relative accuracy of automated MMPI narrative generated from adult-norm and adolescent-norm profiles. *Journal of Consulting and Clinical Psychology*, 44, 20–24.

Lachar, D., and Sharp, J. R. (1979). Use of parents' MMPIs in the research and evaluation of children: A review of the literature and some new data. In J. N. Butcher (Ed.), *New developments in the use of the MMPI* (pp. 203–240). Minneapolis, MN: University of Minnesota Press.

Lachar, D., and Wrobel, T. A. (1979). Validating clinicians' hunches: Construction of a new MMPI critical item set. *Journal of Consulting and Clinical Psychology*, 47, 277–284.

LaCombe, J. A. (1984). *Development of a genotypic and phenotypic actuarial interpretive system for the Personality Inventory for Children*. Unpublished doctoral dissertation, Wayne State University, Detroit.

Leon, G. R., Kendall, P. C., and Garber, J. (1980). Depression in children: Parent, teacher, and child perspectives. *Journal of Abnormal Child Psychology*, 8, 221–235.

Lobovits, D. A., and Handal, P. J. (1985). Childhood depression: Prevalence using DSM-III criterion and validity of parent and child depression scales. *Journal of Pediatric Psychology, 10*, 45–54.

McVaugh, W. H., and Grow, R. T. (1983). Detection of faking on the Personality Inventory for Children. *Journal of Clinical Psychology, 39*, 567–573.

Marks, P. A., and Seeman, W. (1963). *The actuarial description of abnormal personality*. Baltimore, MD: Williams & Wilkins.

Meehl, P. E., and Rosen, A. (1955). Antecedent probability and the efficiency of psychometric signs, patterns, or cutting scores. *Psychological Bulletin, 52*, 194–216.

Pipp, F. D. (1979). *Actuarial analysis of adolescent personality: Self-report correlates for the Personality Inventory for Children profile scales*. Unpublished master's thesis, Wayne State University, Detroit.

Schnel, J. (1982). The utility of the Student Behavior Checklist and the Personality Inventory for Children to assess affective and academic needs of students with learning disabilities. (Doctoral dissertation, University of San Francisco, 1982). *Dissertation Abstracts International*, 43(7A), 2291.

Schreiber, M. D. (1982). The relationship between extra familial support networks and coping in children of divorced and non-divorced families. (Doctoral dissertation, Ohio State University, 1982). *Dissertation Abstracts International*, 43(11B), 3742.

Sechrest, L. (1963). Incremental validity: A recommendation. *Educational and Psychological Measurement, 23*, 153–158.

Snyder, D. K. (1981). *Marital Satisfaction Inventory (MSI) manual*. Los Angeles: Western Psychological Services.

Snyder, D. K., and Gdowski, C. L. (1980, October). *The relationship of marital dysfunction to psychiatric disturbance in children: An empirical analysis using the MSI and PIC*. Panel discussion: New developments in the actuarial assessment of marital and family interaction. Paper presented at the annual meeting of the National Council of Family Relations, Portland, OR.

Stewart, D. T. (1971). The construction of a somatizing scale for the Personality Inventory for Children. (Doctoral dissertation, University of Minnesota, 1970). *Dissertation Abstracts International*, 32(1B), 572.

Voelker, S., Lachar, D., and Gdowski, C. L. (1983). The Personality Inventory for Children and response to methylphenidate: Preliminary evidence for predictive utility. *Journal of Pediatric Psychology, 8*, 161–169.

Wirt, R. D., Lachar, D., Klinedinst, J. K., and Seat, P. D. (1984). *Multidimensional description of child personality: A manual for the Personality Inventory for Children* (Rev. by David Lachar). Los Angeles: Western Psychological Services.

15

Computer-Assisted Interpretation of the Strong Interest Inventory

Jo-Ida C. Hansen

Introduction

The Strong Interest Inventory has the longest history of all interest measures in the practitioner's repertoire. First published in 1927 by E. K. Strong, Jr., as the Strong Vocational Interest Blank (SVIB), the inventory has been thoroughly revised five times in the ensuing sixty years. With each revision, the profile has been expanded to measure the interests of people in an increasing number of occupations, and during the last fifteen years special attention has been paid to the inventory's sex fairness.

David P. Campbell, second author of the Strong Interest Inventory, revised it twice, each time adding scales that provided more parsimony for interpretation. The homogeneous Basic Interest Scales, developed by cluster analyzing the SVIB items, were added to the profile in the 1960s (Campbell et al., 1968), and in 1972 Campbell developed the General Occupational Themes (Campbell and Holland, 1972; Hansen and Johansson, 1972), based on John L. Holland's theory of vocational types, to formally integrate Strong's empiricism with theoretical constructs. At the same time, the earlier women's and men's forms were merged into the Strong-Campbell Interest Inventory of the Strong Vocational Interest Blank (SVIB-SCII) (Campbell, 1974).

The last two revisions (Campbell and Hansen, 1981; Hansen and Campbell,

1985) were directed at increasing the inventory's sex equity and expanding the occupations represented to cover a broader base, including nonprofessional and vocational/technical occupations as well as professional occupations. Thus the inventory has grown from the earliest version, which included ten Occupational Scales, to the 1985 version, which includes 264 scales: six General Occupational Themes (GOT) that measure Holland's vocational types, 23 homogeneous Basic Interest Scales (BIS), 207 Occupational Scales representing 106 occupations (101 occupations represented by both a female- and a male-normed scale, four represented by a female-normed scale only, and one represented by a male-normed scale only), two special scales to measure Academic Comfort (AC Scale) and Introversion-Extroversion (IE Scale), and 26 Administrative Indexes.

The large number of scales has increased profile complexity and has, of course, had an impact in a number of areas, including: the amount of information the inventory provides to a practitioner or client; the depth of sophistication needed by the practitioner to provide adequate interpretations; the amount of time spent examining the profile results; the way in which the inventory is integrated into career counseling and decision making; the technology needed to score the scales; and the predictive validity of the inventory for educational choices and occupational entry.

No inventory the size of the current Strong Interest Inventory could be scored by hand, and computer technology has made the expansion of the SVIB-SCII possible. Considering how labor intensive it is to score even a few Occupational Scales, which are about sixty to seventy items long, it is amazing that templates for hand scoring the SVIB were used occasionally up until the development of the 1974 version of the instrument.

Computers for Scoring the SVIB-SCII

The first scoring machine—not a computer—for the Strong Interest Inventory was developed in the 1930s (Campbell, 1974). The procedure used a Hollerith machine that provided 1,260 cards for the 420-item pool. The cards were manipulated manually by a technician and then run through a tabulator three times to produce scores on twenty-two scales. Five answer blanks could be scored in an hour.

True automation of SVIB scoring arrived in the 1940s when Elmer Hankes built a scoring-and-profiling machine that worked electronically (Campbell, 1974). And, finally, in the 1960s National Computer Sytems (NCS) in Minneapolis built an optical scanning machine, for reading the responses on SVIB answer sheets, that was integrated with a Control Data computer for scoring the scales.

Over the years improvements in the technology used to machine-score the answer sheets have reduced profile scale-score inaccuracies and have increased the consistency and reliability of profile reports (Hansen, 1977, 1982). Once the software for scoring the SVIB-SCII is developed and its accuracy is verified, scoring errors should be nonexistent and profile scores may be interpreted with confidence.

Computer-Assisted Interpretations of Interest Inventories

The ability to computer-score interest inventories made the development of a large number of empirical scales a realistic possibility. Profiles for inventories such as the SVIB-SCII and the Kuder Occupational Interest Survey (Kuder, 1966) were quickly expanded to include more occupations. With the increased number of scales came increased practitioner concern over how best to do interpretations, especially in situations with time-limited counseling such as high-school counseling offices.

The development of computer-assisted interpretive reports offered one mechanism for providing some assistance to the overburdened practitioner. The procedure still required that the individual complete the inventory in the traditional paper-and-pencil fashion, but the copy that was returned to the practitioner and client carried interpretive paragraphs that integrated the results from the entire profile and, also, provided recommended resources for learning more about occupations.

Once computers were capable of assisting in interpretation, it became possible to develop career exploration and career decision-making software for computers. The most recent *Guidance and Counseling Directory of Microcomputer Software* (Bellotto, 1985) has identified over fifty computer-assisted self-assessment, career, and educational guidance and counseling programs. The programs run the gamut from those that are limited to providing educational and career information to those that include an assessment of interests, abilities, and values as well as provide interpretation and career options. They all are designed to be self-administered with a minimum of human intervention other than that of the client.

Computerized Interest Inventory Administration

The next innovation in computer-assisted testing—computer administration of the inventory—became possible with the development of microprocessors and became practical when the prices for the computer hardware dropped low enough to allow individual practitioners to invest in it. The main advantage of computer administration of interest inventories is the efficiency with which the task can be completed. An individual can be seated at a terminal that has the capacity not only for recording item responses but also for immediately scoring the item responses. Testing results can be displayed on the monitor or printed as hard copy or both—within seconds.

One concern, however, about computer administration of any inventory or test is whether the computerized mode of administration, which represents a change in the standardized testing procedure, produces results equivalent to those obtained using the standard paper-and-pencil format. Because the nature of the test has changed, the reliability of the automated procedure must be established. If the automated form of the inventory performs as if it were a parallel form of the original version of the inventory, then the norms of the original version are applicable to the automated version.

COMPUTER ADMINISTRATION OF THE STRONG INVENTORY

Most research on computerized test administration has been conducted on measures of ability and personality (Biskin and Kolotkin, 1977; Elwood, 1972; Lushene, O'Neil, and Dunn, 1973) with encouraging results. Brown (1984) conducted one study that examined the validity and reliability of computerized administration of the Strong Interest Inventory.

Using four groups of participants, Brown examined the extent to which a computer-administered version of the Strong Interest Inventory, which was adapted from the paper-and-pencil-version, yielded results that were equivalent to those of the traditional mode. Each group was tested and then two weeks later retested with one of four different combinations of paper-and-pencil and computer modes of administration. Profile similarities between modes of testing were assessed at three levels of specificity: at the item-response level using an item-response disagreement index to indicate how consistently subjects chose identical, somewhat similar, or dissimilar response alternatives to each item on test and retest; at a general level using Euclidean distances; and at a more specific level that used multivariate repeated-measure computations on six-dimensional vectors of scale scores.

Brown used a sample of 116 female and 88 male college students ranging in age from seventeen to thirty-seven years with a mean age of nineteen years. Subjects were directed to interact with the computer by pressing the character on the attached keyboard that corresponded to their chosen alternative for each test item; for example, the key "L" for a like response, the key "I" for an indifferent response, and the key "D" for a dislike response. No time limit was placed on the administration but the computer was programmed to call the study director to offer assistance if one minute elapsed for any item.

Subjects were divided into four groups based on test administration mode: one group completed the paper-and-pencil form at test and retest; a second group completed the paper-and-pencil form at test and the computerized version at retest; a third group completed the computerized version at test and the paper-and-pencil mode at retest; and the fourth group completed the computerized version both times.

Brown found that in the paper-and-pencil test and retest mode, his college students had stability coefficients equal to those of the two-week test-retest stability coefficients reported in the *Manual for the SVIB-SCII* (Hansen and Campbell, 1985): a median of 0.91 for the General Occupational Themes, 0.92 for the Basic Interest Scales, and 0.92 for the Occupational Scales.

No significant differences were found in item test-retest responses between the mode-of-administration groups nor in the analyses of Euclidean distances between test-retest profiles. The multivariate analyses of six-dimensional vectors of test-retest mean scale scores found no significant differences between mode-of-administration groups, either for all groups or for homogeneous versus heterogeneous groups on the General Occupational Themes, the Basic Interest Scales, or the Occupational Scales. However, the retest vectors did tend to be slightly higher than the original test vectors. All of the mean retest vectors were elevated and, therefore, not attributable to the mode of test administration; the magnitude of the difference was too small to be of clinical or psychological significance even though the difference was statistically significant.

Development of the Interpretive Report for the SVIB-SCII

Computers now have the capacity to give interest inventories, compute scale scores, print results, and provide interpretive comments and diagnostic information. Computer systems have the potential to be self-contained, needing only a client who can read a video display and can type, or a clerk who can assist with these tasks.

Interest inventories are undoubtedly the easiest of all assessment instruments for which to develop interpretive reports. Unlike the Minnesota Multiphasic Personality Inventory (MMPI) or other personality measures that have a multitude of interpretive combinations and levels, the interpretation of an interest inventory is relatively straightforward. The primary purpose of an interpretive report for an interest inventory, therefore, is to synthesize a vast amount of information and data to allow the practitioner more time for more important interventions with the client. The synthesis helps to speed up the counseling process in those situations with time-limited intervention opportunities. And, of course, the interpretive reports are useful as memory refreshers for those practitioners who are only occasional users of the inventory. Research also has shown that interpretive reports for interest inventories can be developed for use by the client directly (Krivatsky and Magoon, 1976); some reports are designed for use without practitioner intervention if a qualified professional is available to answer questions and address client concerns.

Because the number of interpretive paragraphs and possible configurations within the report are far fewer than is the case with personality instruments, it is relatively simple to develop an interpretive report for an interest inventory. For example, the current *Interpretive Report* for the Strong Interest Inventory involves only three major branches (Hansen, 1985) and about two hundred interpretive paragraphs.

APPROACH TO THE SVIB-SCII INTERPRETIVE REPORT

The theory behind the development of the SVIB-SCII *Interpretive Report* was to provide a synthesis that simplifies the amount of information presented on the profile. A standard counselor-to-client interpretation of the inventory involves integrating the various sets of scales on the profile—the homogeneous General Occupational Themes, the Basic Interest Scales, and the empirical Occupational Scales. The more well integrated an individual's profile is—in other words, the more consistent scores are across the three sections of the profile—the more powerful the results and the interpretive information that can be gleaned from the profile.

Essentially the same integrative model used for counselor-to-client interpretations was followed in developing the *Interpretive Report*. It was designed to emphasize agreement between the homogeneous General Occupational Themes and the Basic Interest Scales and, then, to confirm related occupational interests from high scores on the empirical Occupational Scales.

In addition to measuring occupational interests, the Strong Interest Inventory also measures avocational interests; interest in environments such as living environments, leisure environments, or work environments; and interest in different types of people. In those instances where the agreement between the homogeneous and empirical sets of scales is not evident, the client is advised to introspect on other types of interests (for example, leisure) he or she may have that are reflected by the scores on the homogeneous scales.

HOLLAND'S THEORY AND THE SVIB-SCII

The importance of John Holland's theory of vocational types to the organization of the SVIB-SCII profile and the *Interpretive Report* cannot be overlooked. According to Holland (1985), most people can be categorized into six types—realistic (outdoors/mechancial/military), investigative (science), artistic (creative arts), social (social service), enterprising (business contact), or conventional (business detail)—or some combination, such as realistic-investigative or enterprising-social. Occupational or work environments also can be divided into the six types, and people will search for the environment that is appropriate for their interests, values, and abilities. The General Occupational Themes, developed to represent Holland's six types (Campbell and Holland, 1972; Hansen and Johansson, 1972), provide a structure for the SVIB-SCII that is useful in understanding the Basic Interest Scales and the Occupational Scales.

For example, the SVIB-SCII Basic Interest Scales have been assigned primary codes that identify them with one of Holland's six types. The Occupational Scales also have been assigned codes that reflect their relationship to the six types; for example, the Engineer Scale was coded "RI," indicating a primary interest in the realistic area and a secondary interest in the investigative area. Thus Holland's theory has been used to organize the entire profile and consequently plays an important role in the development of the interpretive paragraphs for the *Interpretive Report*.

SVIB-SCII REPORT MATERIALS

Each customer receives, from the scoring agency, two copies each of the *Interpretive Report* and the standard profile for the SVIB-SCII as illustrated in figures 15.1 to 15.11. One copy is for the person who completed the inventory; the other is for the institution's psychological service to use with the client and to retain on file. The two copies are identical in layout.

The Profile. The front side of the profile (figures 15.8 and 15.9) is divided into the six main groupings described earlier—realistic, investigative, artistic, social, enterprising, and conventional—beginning with the General Occupational Theme (GOT) for the type, then related Basic Interest Scales (BIS), and to their right, the related Occupational Scales. For all scales the respondent's standard scores are printed next to the scale name, and each score is plotted visually at the appropriate point along the scale range. For the GOT and the BIS, interpretive comments based on the level of the score compared to a norm group of the person's own sex are printed in the column to the left of the standard scores. For each scale, interpretive bars also are presented that illustrate the mean score and the range of scores for the norm samples—women in general represented by the open bars and men in general represented by the closed bars.

For the Occupational Scales, standard scores also are printed to the right of the scale name; scores on the female-normed scales appear in the column labeled "F" and scores for the male-normed scales under "M." Female- and male-normed scales with identical codes, which are based on their correlations with the GOT, appear on the same line on the profile. For those scales with dissimilar codes, the scale name appears twice on the profile—once in each appropriate General Occupational Theme area. For example, the first Occupational Scale on the profile—MARINE CORPS ENLISTED PERSONNEL—is coded "RC" for the male-normed scale and the scale name appears with other realistic Occupational Scales; the female-normed scale is coded "CRS" and, therefore, MARINE CORPS ENLISTED PERSONNEL also appears in the area reserved for conventional Occupational Scales (see figures 15.8 and 15.9).

An asterisk is plotted on the Occupational Scale graph at the point that

TITLE: STRONG INTERPRETIVE REPORT by Jo-Ida C. Hansen, Ph.D.

► NAME: **► ID:** **► SEX:** F **► DATE SCORED** 08/05/85

You responded to all 325 Strong items.

The following interpretive comments are based on scores obtained from your pattern of responses. The Strong results are indicators of vocational interests, not aptitudes, and they should be used to help identify overall patterns of interests rather than to focus on one or two high scores. The Strong may aid you in exploring educational and occupational options, increase your knowledge of the relationship of occupations to the world of work, and help you identify avocational or leisure interests. As a tool for vocational exploration, the Strong will assist you in increasing your occupational options.

The following narrative will explain your highest General Occupational Themes, which are scales that measure six vocational types. Your interests may be focused within one of six Themes, such as Realistic, Investigative, Artistic, Social, Enterprising, or Conventional; or they may be represented by some combination of the Themes, such as Realistic-Investigative or Enterprising-Social. The narrative also will explain your Basic Interest Scale and Occupational Scale scores that are high and that are related to your General Occupational Themes.

The Basic Interest Scales are sub-divisions of the General Occupational Themes and high scores may reflect several different types of interests. First, they may be reflecting your occupational or vocational interests; second, they may be indicating your leisure or recreational interests; third, they may be showing your preferences for the types of people who are your co-workers or friends; and fourth, they may be identifying your preferences for working, living, or recreational environments. Low scores on the Basic Interest Scales reflect a disinterest or aversion to a particular area.

In addition, there are 207 Occupational Scales (male or female) representing 106 occupations. Your scores on each Occupational Scale show how similar your interests are to the interests of people in that occupation. Your Strong profile organizes the Occupational Scales by their relationship to the General Occupational Themes. The diagram presented next displays the six General Occupational Themes, your standard score on each, and how high or low your scores are compared to Women-in-General.

CONSULTING PSYCHOLOGISTS PRESS, INC.

PUBLISHED BY CONSULTING PSYCHOLOGISTS PRESS, INC., 577 COLLEGE AVENUE, PALO ALTO, CA 94306

Figure 15.1. Page 1 of the SVIB-SCII *Interpretive Report*. Reprinted by permission (see p. 320 for copyright information).

TITLE: STRONG INTERPRETIVE REPORT by Jo-Ida C. Hansen, Ph.D.

▶ NAME: **▶ ID:** **▶ SEX:** F **▶ DATE SCORED** 08/05/85

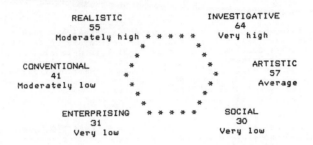

```
                   REALISTIC                          INVESTIGATIVE
                      55                                   64
                Moderately high * * * * *             Very high
                               *          *
                              *            *
     CONVENTIONAL            *              *              ARTISTIC
          41                *                *                57
     Moderately low          *              *              Average
                              *            *
                               *          *
                 ENTERPRISING   * * * * *           SOCIAL
                      31                              30
                   Very low                        Very low
```

These six Themes are arranged in a hexagon with the Themes most similar to each other falling next to each other, and those most dissimilar falling directly across the hexagon from each other. Types adjacent to one another on the hexagon, such as Realistic and Investigative, or Social and Enterprising, have more in common with one another than do types diametrically opposed to each other on the hexagon, such as Realistic and Social or Investigative and Enterprising.

Your highest General Occupational Theme: Investigative

You expressed preferences in Investigative areas, particularly mathematics, physical sciences, and medical and biological sciences. These areas include occupations in research; mathematics, statistical analysis, and measurement; sciences that study physical objects and the chemical composition of substances; medicine; and sciences that deal with living beings and life processes.

Investigative types tend to view themselves as persistent, self-controlled, analytical, scholarly, and achievement-oriented.

You often prefer to work independently on ambiguous and theoretical tasks.

You probably like to work with numbers, symbols, words, and ideas. You may already have computational and numerical skills. And, you may want to work in a medical setting.

Occupationally, your interests are like the following Investigative type(s):

Computer programmer	Systems analyst
Medical technologist	Research & Development manager
Geologist	Biologist
Chemist	Physicist

CONSULTING PSYCHOLOGISTS PRESS, INC. 4

PUBLISHED BY CONSULTING PSYCHOLOGISTS PRESS, INC., 577 COLLEGE AVENUE, PALO ALTO, CA 94306

Figure 15.2. Page 2 of the SVIB-SCII *Interpretive Report*.

TITLE: STRONG INTERPRETIVE REPORT by Jo-Ida C. Hansen, Ph.D.

▶ NAME: ▶ ID: ▶ SEX: F ▶ DATE SCORED 08/05/85

Veterinarian	Science teacher
Physical therapist	Respiratory therapist
Pharmacist	Dietitian
Optometrist	Dentist
Physician	Mathematician
Geographer	College professor
Psychologist	Sociologist

You probably enjoy spending your leisure time participating in complex activities that require learning many new facts, theories, and principles, such as astronomy, computer science, sailing, or skiing. Your approach to both your avocation and your vocation will be analytical.

Your second highest General Occupational Theme: Realistic

You indicated Realistic interests encompassing outdoor, nature, military, and mechanical activities. People with these interests like to work with machines and tools in activities that involve mechanical and motor skills, and enjoy field study of nature, gardening, and plant and animal husbandry. They choose occupations in horticulture, forestry, high technology, skilled trades, or law enforcement and protection.

You also may like the structure and organization of the military, or situations that have a well-defined hierarchy of authority.

Realistic types regard themselves as practical, rugged, persistent, and robust; they like concrete problems, activities that require physical exertion, and outdoor work.

Your Realistic interests resemble those of people in the following occupation(s):

Navy officer	Air Force officer
Bus driver	Horticultural worker
Forester	Athletic trainer
Carpenter	Electrician
Architect	Engineer

Your lowest General Occupational Theme: Enterprising

CONSULTING PSYCHOLOGISTS PRESS, INC.

PUBLISHED BY CONSULTING PSYCHOLOGISTS PRESS, INC., 577 COLLEGE AVENUE, PALO ALTO, CA 94306

Figure 15.3. Page 3 of the SVIB-SCII *Interpretive Report*.

TITLE: STRONG INTERPRETIVE REPORT by Jo-Ida C. Hansen, Ph.D.

▶ NAME: ▶ ID: ▶ SEX: F ▶ DATE SCORED 08/05/85

It is often helpful to compare your areas of highest interest with your areas of lowest interest, to consider the types of occupations or avocations that you would not likely find as enjoyable or satisfying.

Your score on the Enterprising Theme shows that you do not have many interests in common with Enterprising types. They have a strong drive to attain organizational goals or economic aims, are often suited to selling, dominating, and leading, and tend to avoid work situations requiring long periods of intellectual effort. You may view Enterprising people as status-conscious, aggressive, and materialistic.

Your preferences indicate an interest in athletics, which may refer to participation in sports as either a competitor or as a spectator or sports fan.

You have a response pattern that reflects a willingness to be involved in risky or adventuresome undertakings. This may be expressed as physical risk-taking, such as mountain climbing or skydiving; as financial risk-taking, for example, working strictly on a commission basis; or perhaps as a readiness to make changes. People who have the wanderlust, or like to travel, also have adventuresome response patterns.

The following are your strongest Basic Interest Area(s):

Nature	Adventure
Military activities	Mechanical activities
Science	Mathematics
Medical science	Music/dramatics
Athletics	

You may wish to think about your basic areas of interest to determine if the interests are related to vocational possibilities, or recreational and avocational activity.

You have interests similar to people in the following occupation(s):

Navy officer	Horticultural worker
Forester	Carpenter
Electrician	Architect
Engineer	Computer programmer
Systems analyst	Medical technologist
Research & Development manager	Geologist

CONSULTING PSYCHOLOGISTS PRESS, INC.

PUBLISHED BY CONSULTING PSYCHOLOGISTS PRESS, INC., 577 COLLEGE AVENUE, PALO ALTO, CA 94306

Figure 15.4. Page 4 of the SVIB-SCII *Interpretive Report*.

TITLE: STRONG INTERPRETIVE REPORT by Jo-Ida C. Hansen, Ph.D.

► NAME: ► ID: ► SEX: F ► DATE SCORED 08/05/85

Biologist	Chemist
Physicist	Veterinarian
Physical therapist	Pharmacist
Optometrist	Dentist
Physician	Mathematician
Geographer	College professor
Psychologist	Sociologist
Medical illustrator	Artist, fine
Artist, commercial	Photographer
Musician	Lawyer
Librarian	Marketing executive
Investments manager	Accountant

You have interests moderately similar to people in the following occupation(s):

Air Force officer	Bus driver
Athletic trainer	Science teacher
Respiratory therapist	Dietitian
Chef	

You have interests that are very dissimilar to people in the following occupation(s):

Art teacher	English teacher
Foreign language teacher	Minister
Guidance counselor	Special education teacher
Speech pathologist	Nurse, LPN
Home economics teacher	Personnel director
Elected public official	Life insurance agent
Chamber of Commerce executive	Store manager
Restaurant manager	Travel agent
Funeral director	Realtor
Buyer	Banker
Credit manager	Business education teacher
Nursing home administrator	Secretary

Your score on the College Professor scale suggests that you may want to work in an academic environment, teaching adults and associating with colleagues who have intellectual interests.

Of course, Occupational Scale scores only evaluate how similar your interests are to people already in the occupation. The scores give no indication of your ability or probability of success. Therefore, consider your abilities as well as your interests as you explore career possibilities.

CONSULTING PSYCHOLOGISTS PRESS, INC.

PUBLISHED BY CONSULTING PSYCHOLOGISTS PRESS, INC., 577 COLLEGE AVENUE, PALO ALTO, CA 94306

Figure 15.5. Page 5 of the SVIB-SCII *Interpretive Report*.

TITLE: STRONG INTERPRETIVE REPORT by Jo-Ida C. Hansen, Ph.D.

▶ NAME: ▶ ID: ▶ SEX: F ▶ DATE SCORED 08/05/85

Non-Occupational Scales: Academic Comfort and Introversion-Extroversion.

There are two non-occupational scales derived from your Strong responses that may give you additional insight into your interests and expectations:

The Academic Comfort Scale (AC Scale) differentiates between people who enjoy being in an academic setting and those who do not. High scores are associated with continuation into high academic degree programs. Remember, however, that the AC scale does not measure ability. About two-thirds of all people who take the Strong score in the range of 32 to 60.

People with low AC scores (below 40) often are inclined to view education as a means to an end -- in other words, as a necessary hurdle for entry into a career. People with high AC scores (above 50) typically seek out courses that allow them to explore theory and research in their chosen field.

Your score on this scale is 65.

You should consider how you are going to satisfy your academic interests in the future. Possibilities include enrolling in a college or university to seek an undergraduate, graduate, or professional degree; enrolling in community or continuing education programs to continue your learning; or entering a new job or position that requires the acquisition of new knowledge.

The Introversion-Extroversion Scale is associated with a preference for working with things or ideas as opposed to an interest in working with people. About two-thirds of all people who take the Strong score in the range of 38 to 62.

Your score on this scale is 72.

Your score is in the introverted direction. You probably prefer to work alone, to complete projects independently, and to work with ideas or things. When you do work with other people, you may find that you need to reserve some time to be alone to regenerate.

CONSULTING PSYCHOLOGISTS PRESS, INC.

PUBLISHED BY CONSULTING PSYCHOLOGISTS PRESS, INC., 577 COLLEGE AVENUE, PALO ALTO, CA 94306

Figure 15.6. Page 6 of the SVIB-SCII *Interpretive Report*.

TITLE: STRONG INTERPRETIVE REPORT by Jo-Ida C. Hansen, Ph.D.

▶ NAME: ▶ ID: ▶ SEX: F ▶ DATE SCORED 08/05/85

Additional Resources:

You have just had the opportunity to examine your interests in general areas of occupational activities and to compare them with interests of people in specific jobs. You can find out more about the occupations in which you have the most interest by talking to your counselor, reading about and talking to people employed in those jobs, and volunteering in work environments that you enjoy.

Career planning is a lifelong process. It is helpful to collect information from a variety of sources to make informed choices about possible career paths. The following resources are recommended to learn more about occupations and about yourself; the list on the left contains books that are typically found in the library, and the list on the right contains books that may be purchased from the publisher or a local bookstore.

Library Resources

Dictionary of Occupational Titles

Occupational Outlook Handbook

Exploring Careers

(The above books are published by the U.S. Department of Labor)

For Your Personal Library

What Color is Your Parachute?
by Richard Bolles

The Three Boxes of Life
by Richard Bolles

Who's Hiring Who
by Richard Lathrop

Career and Life Planning Guide
By John Loughary and Theresa Ripley

The Career Game
by Charles Guy Moore

The publisher of this report, Consulting Psychologists Press, distributes the books listed 'For Your Personal Library,' and may be contacted at: 577 College Avenue, Palo Alto, CA 94306.

CONSULTING PSYCHOLOGISTS PRESS, INC.

PUBLISHED BY CONSULTING PSYCHOLOGISTS PRESS, INC., 577 COLLEGE AVENUE, PALO ALTO, CA 94306

Figure 15.7. Page 7 of the SVIB-SCII *Interpretive Report*.

STRONG-CAMPBELL INTEREST INVENTORY OF THE
STRONG VOCATIONAL INTEREST BLANK

PAGE 1 **PROFILE REPORT FOR:** **DATE TESTED:** / /

ID: **DATE SCORED:** 08/06/85

AGE: **SEX:** F

SPECIAL SCALES: ACADEMIC COMFORT 65
INTROVERSION-EXTROVERSION 72

TOTAL RESPONSES: 325 **INFREQUENT RESPONSES:** 4

REALISTIC

GENERAL OCCUPATIONAL THEME - R 30 40 50 60 70 F M
Mod. High 55

BASIC INTEREST SCALES (STANDARD SCORE)

AGRICULTURE — Average 46
NATURE — Mod. High 58
ADVENTURE — Very High 63
MILITARY ACTIVITIES — High 60
MECHANICAL ACTIVITIES — High 58

INVESTIGATIVE

GENERAL OCCUPATIONAL THEME - I 30 40 50 60 70 F M
Very High 64

BASIC INTEREST SCALES (STANDARD SCORE)

SCIENCE — High 63
MATHEMATICS — Very High 65
MEDICAL SCIENCE — Mod. High 57
MEDICAL SERVICE — Mod. Low 41

ARTISTIC

GENERAL OCCUPATIONAL THEME - A 30 40 50 60 70 F M
Average 57

BASIC INTEREST SCALES (STANDARD SCORE)

MUSIC/DRAMATICS — Mod. High 62
ART — Average 54
WRITING — Average 49

CONSULTING PSYCHOLOGISTS PRESS
577 COLLEGE AVENUE
PALO ALTO, CA 94306

OCCUPATIONAL SCALES

F	M	Occupation	Standard Score F	Standard Score M	VERY DISSIMILAR (15)	DISSIMILAR (25)	MODERATELY DISSIMILAR (30)	MID-RANGE	MODERATELY SIMILAR (40)	SIMILAR (45)	VERY SIMILAR (55)
REALISTIC											
[CRS]	RC	Marine Corps enlisted personnel	(CRS)	23							
RC	RC	Navy enlisted personnel	38	23				*			
RC	RC	Army officer	34	25				*			
RI	RIC	Navy officer	46	39						*	
R	R	Air Force officer	42	35					*		
[C]	R	Air Force enlisted personnel	(C)	24							
R	R	Police officer	37	26				*			
R	R	Bus driver	43	33					*		
R	R	Horticultural worker	48	42						*	
RC	R	Farmer	21	26		*					
R	RCS	Vocational agriculture teacher	36	16				*			
RI	R	Forester	56	36							*
[IR]	RI	Veterinarian	(IR)	34							
RIS	[SR]	Athletic trainer	40	(SR)					*		
RS	R	Emergency medical technician	33	22				*			
RI	RI	Radiologic technologist	31	30				*			
RI	R	Carpenter	48	38						*	
RI	R	Electrician	51	28						*	
RIA	[ARI]	Architect	63	(ARI)							*
RI	RI	Engineer	58	47							*
INVESTIGATIVE											
IRC	IRC	Computer programmer	59	49							*
IRC	IRC	Systems analyst	61	50							*
IRC	IR	Medical technologist	60	46							*
IR	IR	R & D manager	66	53							*
IR	IR	Geologist	59	60							*
IR	[I]	Biologist	58	(I)							*
IR	IR	Chemist	60	57							*
IR	IR	Physicist	53	56						*	
IR	[RI]	Veterinarian	55	(RI)							*
IRS	IR	Science teacher	42	40					*		
IRS	IRS	Physical therapist	49	34						*	
IR	IRS	Respiratory therapist	44	38					*		
IC	IR	Medical technician	37	35				*			
IC	IE	Pharmacist	56	34							*
ISR	[CSE]	Dietitian	43	(CSE)					*		
[SI]	ISR	Nurse, RN	(SI)	29							
IR	I	Chiropractor	32	38				*			
IR	IR	Optometrist	58	61							*
IR	IR	Dentist	58	50							*
I	IA	Physician	55	58							*
[IR]	I	Biologist	(IR)	55							
I	I	Mathematician	55	46							*
IR	I	Geographer	62	58							*
I	I	College professor	56	49							*
IA	IA	Psychologist	57	61							*
IA	IA	Sociologist	45	39						*	
ARTISTIC											
AI	AI	Medical illustrator	53	39						*	
A	A	Art teacher	10	27	*						
A	A	Artist, fine	51	43						*	
A	A	Artist, commercial	45	46						*	
AE	A	Interior decorator	19	28		*					
[RIA]	ARI	Architect	(RIA)	55							
A	A	Photographer	53	53						*	
A	A	Musician	46	50						*	
AR	[EA]	Chef	40	(EA)					*		
[E]	AE	Beautician	(E)	30							
AE	A	Flight attendant	27	41			*				
A	A	Advertising executive	35	45				*			
A	A	Broadcaster	29	40			*				
A	A	Public relations director	23	16		*					
A	A	Lawyer	46	31						*	
A	AS	Public administrator	35	27				*			
A	A	Reporter	35	39				*			
A	A	Librarian	46	40						*	
AS	AS	English teacher	4	24	*						
[SA]	AS	Foreign language teacher	(SA)	27							

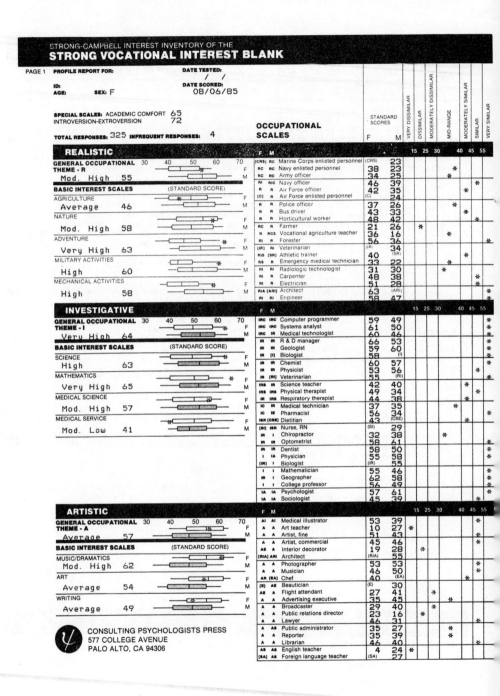

Figure 15.8. SVIB-SCII profile form, upper half.

STRONG-CAMPBELL INTEREST INVENTORY OF THE

STRONG VOCATIONAL INTEREST BLANK

PAGE 2 **PROFILE REPORT FOR:**

ID:

AGE: **SEX:** F

DATE TESTED: / /

DATE SCORED: 08/06/85

SOCIAL

GENERAL OCCUPATIONAL THEME - S (30 40 50 60 70)

Very Low 30

BASIC INTEREST SCALES (STANDARD SCORE)

TEACHING	Low	35
SOCIAL SERVICE	Very Low	35
ATHLETICS	High	58
DOMESTIC ARTS	Very Low	37
RELIGIOUS ACTIVITIES	Low	35

ENTERPRISING

GENERAL OCCUPATIONAL THEME - E (30 40 50 60 70)

Very Low 31

BASIC INTEREST SCALES (STANDARD SCORE)

PUBLIC SPEAKING	Very Low	33
LAW/POLITICS	Mod. Low	38
MERCHANDISING	Low	35
SALES	Very Low	36
BUSINESS MANAGEMENT	Low	34

CONVENTIONAL

GENERAL OCCUPATIONAL THEME - C (30 40 50 60 70)

Mod Low 41

BASIC INTEREST SCALES (STANDARD SCORE)

OFFICE PRACTICES	Very Low	36

OCCUPATIONAL SCALES

F	M	Occupation	Standard Score F	Standard Score M	Very Dissimilar (15)	Dissimilar (25)	Moderately Dissimilar (30)	Mid-Range	Moderately Similar (40)	Similar (45)	Very Similar (55)
SA	[AS]	Foreign language teacher	6	(AS)	*						
SA	SA	Minister	9	20	*						
SA	SA	Social worker	16	14		*					
S	S	Guidance counselor	10	14	*						
S	S	Social science teacher	16	14		*					
S	S	Elementary teacher	17	18		*					
S	S	Special education teacher	8	13	*						
SRI	SAR	Occupational therapist	34	29				*			
SIA	SAI	Speech pathologist	11	18	*						
SI	[ISR]	Nurse, RN	27	(ISR)			*				
SCI	N/A	Dental hygienist	32	N/A				*			
SC	SC	Nurse, LPN	14	15	*						
[RIS]	SR	Athletic trainer	(RIS)	23							
SR	SR	Physical education teacher	26	8			*				
SRE	SE	Recreation leader	39	28				*			
SE	SE	YWCA/YMCA director	20	16		*					
SEC	SCE	School administrator	15	16		*					
SCE	N/A	Home economics teacher	5	N/A	*						
E	ES	Personnel director	13	14	*						
ES	E	Elected public official	14	13	*						
ES	ES	Life insurance agent	11	5	*						
EC	E	Chamber of Commerce executive	6	5	*						
EC	EC	Store manager	11	11	*						
N/A	ECR	Agribusiness manager	N/A	7							
EC	EC	Purchasing agent	17	14		*					
EC	E	Restaurant manager	11	12	*						
[AR]	EA	Chef	(AR)	29							
EC	E	Travel agent	12	20	*						
ECS	E	Funeral director	14	14	*						
[CSE]	ESC	Nursing home administrator	(CSE)	11							
EC	ER	Optician	21	36		*					
E	E	Realtor	1	10	*						
E	[AE]	Beautician	26	(AE)			*				
E	E	Florist	25	24			*				
EC	E	Buyer	-3	11	*						
EI	EI	Marketing executive	52	50						*	
EIC	ECI	Investments manager	56	42							*
C	C	Accountant	47	28						*	
C	C	Banker	14	25	*						
CE	CE	IRS agent	37	15				*			
CES	CES	Credit manager	12	16	*						
CES	CES	Business education teacher	-5	-1	*						
[CS]	CES	Food service manager	(CS)	16							
[ISR]	CSE	Dietitian	(ISR)	24							
CSE	[ESC]	Nursing home administrator	12	(ESC)	*						
CSE	CSE	Executive housekeeper	18	22		*					
CS	[CES]	Food service manager	17	(CES)		*					
CS	N/A	Dental assistant	20	N/A		*					
C	N/A	Secretary	10	N/A	*						
C	[R]	Air Force enlisted personnel	22	(R)		*					
CRS	[RC]	Marine Corps enlisted personnel	26	(RC)			*				
CRS	CR	Army enlisted personnel	28	11			*				
CIR	CIR	Mathematics teacher	34	34				*			

ADMINISTRATIVE INDEXES (RESPONSE %)

OCCUPATIONS	27 L %	17 I %	56 D %
SCHOOL SUBJECTS	42 L %	14 I %	44 D %
ACTIVITIES	31 L %	10 I %	59 D %
LEISURE ACTIVITIES	54 L %	31 I %	15 D %
TYPES OF PEOPLE	38 L %	33 I %	29 D %
PREFERENCES	40 L %	40 = %	20 R %
CHARACTERISTICS	71 Y %	0 ? %	29 N %
ALL PARTS	37 %	20 %	44 %

CONSULTING PSYCHOLOGISTS PRESS
577 COLLEGE AVENUE
PALO ALTO, CA 94306

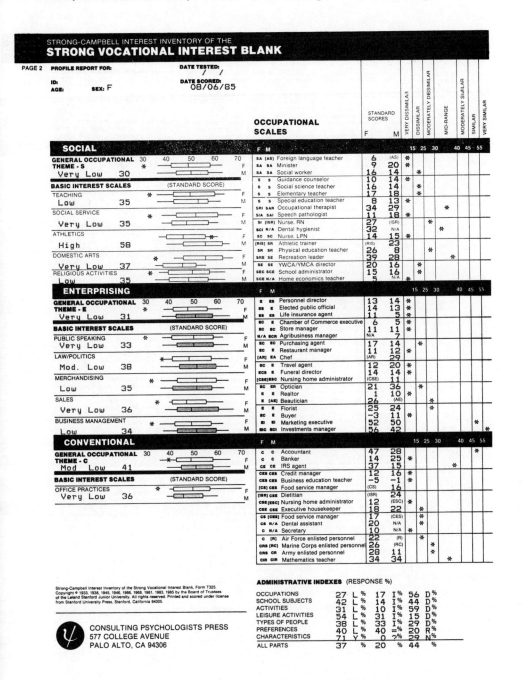

Figure 15.9. SVIB-SCII profile form, lower half.

Understanding Your Results on the Strong

Your answers to the test booklet were used to determine your scores; your results are based on what you said you liked or disliked. The results can give you some useful systematic information about yourself, but you should not expect miracles.

Please note that this test does not measure your abilities; it can tell you something about the patterns in your interests, and how these compare with those of successful people in many occupations, but the results are based on your *interests,* not your abilities. The results may tell you, for example, that you like the way engineers spend their day; they do *not* tell you whether you have an aptitude for the mathematics involved.

Although most of us know something of our own interests, we're not sure how we compare with people actively engaged in various occupations. We don't know "what it would be like" to be a writer, or receptionist, or scientist, for example. People using these results are frequently guided to considering occupations to which they had never given a thought before. In particular, this inventory may suggest occupations that you might find interesting but have not considered simply because you have not been exposed to them. Or the inventory may suggest occupations that you ignored because you thought they were open only to members of the opposite sex. Sexual barriers are now falling, and virtually all occupations are open to qualified people of either sex — so don't let imagined barriers rule out your consideration of any occupation.

Men and women, even those in the same occupation, tend to answer some items on the test differently. Research has shown that these differences should not be ignored — that separate scales for men and women provide more meaningful results. Generally, the scales for your sex — those marked in the "Standard Scores" column corresponding to your sex — are more likely to be better predictors for you than scales for the other sex would be.

Your answers have been analyzed in three main ways: first, under "General Occupational Themes," for similarity to six important overall patterns; second, under "Basic Interest Scales," for similarity to clusters of specific activities; third, under "Occupational Scales," for similarity to the interests of men and women in 106 occupations. The other two groups of data on the profile — labeled "Administrative Indexes" and "Special Scales" — are of interest mainly to your counselor. The first are checks to make certain that you made your marks on the sheet clearly and that your answers were processed correctly. The second are scales that have been developed for use in particular settings and require special interpretation; your counselor will discuss them with you.

The Six General Occupational Themes

Psychological research has shown that vocational interests can be described in a general way by six overall occupational-interest Themes. Your scores for these six Themes were calculated from the answers you gave to the test questions. The range of these scores is roughly from 30 to 70, with the average person scoring 50.

Men and women score somewhat differently on some of these Themes, and this is taken into account by the printed statement for each score; this statement, which might be, for example, "Very High," is based on a comparison between your score and the average score for your sex. Thus, you can compare your score either with the scores of a combined male-female sample, by noting your numerical score, or with the scores of only members of your own sex, by noting the phrasing of the printed comment.

The differences between the sexes on these Themes also are shown on the profile; the open bars indicate the middle 50 percent of female scores, the shaded bars show the middle 50 percent of male scores. The extending, thinner lines cover the middle 80 percent of the scores, and the mark in the middle is the average.

Following are descriptions of the "pure," or extreme, types for the six General Occupational Themes. These descriptions are only generalizations; none will fit any one person exactly. In fact, most people's interests combine several Themes to some degree or other.

R-Theme: People scoring high here usually are rugged, robust, practical, physically strong; they usually have good physical skills, but sometimes have trouble expressing themselves or in communicating their feelings to others. They like to work outdoors and to work with tools, especially large, powerful machines. They prefer to deal with things rather than with ideas or people. They enjoy creating things with their hands and prefer occupations such as mechanic, construction work, fish and wildlife management, radiologic technologist, some engineering specialties, some military jobs, agriculture, or the skilled trades. Although no single word can capture the broad meaning of the entire Theme, the word REALISTIC has been used here, thus the term R-Theme.

I-Theme: This Theme centers around science and scientific activities. Extremes of this type are task-oriented; they are not particularly interested in working around other people. They enjoy solving abstract problems, and they have a great need to understand the physical world. They prefer to think through problems rather than act them out. Such people enjoy ambiguous challenges and do not like highly structured situations with many rules. They frequently are original and creative, especially in scientific areas. They prefer occupations such as design engineer, biologist, social scientist, research laboratory worker, physicist, technical writer, or meteorologist. The word INVESTIGATIVE characterizes this Theme, thus I-Theme.

A-Theme: The extreme type here is artistically oriented, and likes to work in artistic settings that offer many opportunities for self-expression. Such people have little interest in problems that are highly structured or require gross physical strength, preferring those that can be solved through self-expression in artistic media. They resemble I-Theme types in preferring to work alone, but have a greater need for individualistic expression, and usually are less assertive about their own opinions and capabilities. They describe themselves as independent, original, unconventional, expressive, and intense. Vocational choices include artist, author, cartoonist, composer, singer, dramatic coach, poet, actor or actress, and symphony conductor. This is the ARTISTIC Theme, or A-Theme.

S-Theme: The pure type here is sociable, responsible, humanistic, and concerned with the welfare of others. These people usually express themselves well and get along well with others; they like attention and seek situations that allow them to be near the center of the group. They prefer to solve problems by discussions with others, or by arranging or rearranging relationships between others; they have little interest in situations requiring physical exertion or working with machinery. Such people describe themselves as cheerful, popular, and achieving, and as good leaders. They prefer occupations such as school superintendent, social worker, high school teacher, marriage counselor, playground director, speech therapist, or vocational counselor. This is the SOCIAL Theme, or S-Theme.

E-Theme: The extreme type of this Theme has a great facility with words, especially in selling, dominating, and leading; frequently these people are in sales work. They see themselves as energetic, enthusiastic, adventurous, self-confident, and dominant, and they prefer social tasks where they can assume leadership. They enjoy persuading others to their viewpoints. They are impatient with precise work or work involving long periods of intellectual effort. They like power, status, and material wealth, and enjoy working in expensive settings. Vocational preferences include business executive, buyer, hotel manager, industrial relations consultant, political campaigner, realtor, sales work, and sports promoter. The word ENTERPRISING summarizes this pattern, thus E-Theme.

(Continued on page 2 back)

Figure 15.10. SVIB-SCII profile form, reverse side, upper half.

Computer-Assisted Interpretation of the Strong Interest Inventory

(Continued from back of page 1)

C-Theme: Extremes of this type prefer the highly ordered activities, both verbal and numerical, that characterize office work. People scoring high fit well into large organizations but do not seek leadership; they respond to power and are comfortable working in a well-established chain of command. They dislike ambiguous situations, preferring to know precisely what is expected of them. Such people describe themselves as conventional, stable, well-controlled, and dependable. They have little interest in problems requiring physical skills or intense relationships with others, and are most effective at well-defined tasks. Like the E-Theme type, they value material possessions and status. Vocational preferences are mostly within the business world, and include bank examiner, bank teller, bookkeeper, some accounting jobs, mathematics teacher, computer operator, inventory controller, tax expert, credit manager, and traffic manager. The word CONVENTIONAL more or less summarizes the pattern, hence C-Theme.

These six Themes can be arranged in a hexagon with the types most similar to each other falling *next* to each other, and those most dissimilar falling directly *across* the hexagon from each other.

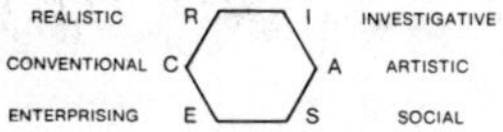

Few people are "pure" types, scoring high on one and only one Theme. Most score high on two, three, or even four, which means they share some characteristics with each of these; for their career planning, such people should look for an occupational setting that combines these patterns.

A few people score low on all six Themes; this probably means they have no consistent occupational orientation and would probably be equally comfortable in any of several working environments. Some young people score this way because they haven't had the opportunity to become familiar with a variety of occupational activities.

The Basic Interest Scales

These scales are intermediate between the General Occupational Themes and the Occupational Scales. Each is concerned with one specific area of activity. The 23 scales are arranged in groups corresponding to the strength of their relationship to the six General Themes.

On these scales, the average adult scores about 50, with most people scoring between 30 and 70. If your score is substantially higher than 50, then you have shown more consistent preferences for these activities than the average adult does, and you should look upon that area of activity as an important focus of your interests. The opposite is true for low scores. Your scores are given both numerically and graphically, and an interpretive comment, based on a comparison between your scores and the average score for your sex, also is provided.

Your scores on some of the Basic Interest Scales might appear to be inconsistent with scores on the corresponding Occupational Scales. You might, for example, score high on the Mathematics scale and low on the Mathematician scale. These scores are not errors; they are in fact a useful finding. What they usually mean is that although you have an interest in the subject matter of an occupation (mathematics), you share with people in that occupation (mathematicians) very few of their other likes or dislikes, and you probably would not enjoy the day-to-day life of their working world.

The Occupational Scales

Your score on an Occupational Scale shows how similar your interests are to the interests of people in that occupation. If you reported the same likes and dislikes as they do, your score will be high and you would probably enjoy working in that occupation or a closely related one. If your likes and dislikes are different from those of the people in the occupation, your score will be low and you might not be happy in that kind of work. Remember that the scales of your sex — marked in the "Standard Scores" column with the sex corresponding to yours — are more likely to be good predictors for you than scales for the other sex.

Your score for each scale is printed in numerals — for those scales normed for your sex — and also plotted graphically. Members of an occupation score about 50 on their own scale — that is, female dentists score about 50 on the Dentist F scale, male fine artists score about 50 on the Fine Artist M scale, and so forth. If you score high on a particular scale — say 45 or 50 — you have many interests in common with the workers in that occupation. The higher your score, the more common interests you have. *But note that on these scales your scores are being compared with those of people working in those occupations;* in the scoring of the General Themes and the Basic Interest Scales you were being compared with "people-in-general."

The Occupational Scales differ from the other scales also in considering your dislikes as well as your likes. If you share in the same *dislikes* with the workers in an occupation, you may score moderately high on their scale, even if you don't agree with their *likes*. But a higher score — 50 — reflects an agreement on likes *and* dislikes.

To the left of each Occupational Scale name are one to three letters indicating the General Themes characteristic of that occupation. These will help you to understand the interest patterns found among the workers in that occupation, and to focus on occupations that might be interesting to you. If you score high on two Themes, for example, you should scan the list of Occupational Scales and find any that have the same two Theme letters, in any order. If your scores there are also high — as they are likely to be — you should find out more about those occupations, and about related occupations not given on the profile. Your counselor can help you.

Academic Comfort and Introversion-Extroversion

There are two Special Scales derived from your Strong responses that may give you additional insight into your interests and expectations.

The Academic Comfort Scale differentiates between people who enjoy being in an academic setting and those who do not. Remember, however, that the Academic Comfort Scale *does not measure ability.* About 2/3rds of all people who take the Strong score in the range of 32 to 60. People with low scores (below 40) often are inclined to view education as a necessary hurdle for entry into a career. People with high scores (above 50) typically seek out courses that allow them to explore theory and research in their chosen field.

The Introversion-Extroversion Scale is associated with a preference for working with things or ideas (high scores, say, above 55) or with people (low scores, say, below 45). Scores between 45 and 55 indicate a combination of interests that include working with people and ideas or things in the same occupation.

Using Your Scores

Your scores can be used in two main ways: first, to help you understand how your likes and dislikes fit into the world of work; and second, to help you identify possible problems by pointing out areas where your interests differ substantially from those of people working in occupations that you might be considering. Suppose, for example, that you have selected some field of science, but the results show that you have only a moderate interest in the daily practice of the mathematical skills necessary to that setting. Although this is discouraging to learn, you at least are prepared for the choice among (1) abandoning that field of science as a career objective, (2) trying to increase your enthusiasm for mathematics, or (3) finding some branch of the field that requires less mathematics.

In the world of work there are many hundreds of specialties and professions. Using these results and your scores on other tests as guides, you should search out as much information as you can *about those occupational areas where your interests and aptitudes are focused.* Ask your librarian for information on these jobs and talk to people working in these fields. Talk with your counselor, who is trained to help you, about your results on this test and other tests, and about your future plans. Keep in mind that choosing an occupation is not a single decision, but a series of decisions that will go on for many years. Your scores on this inventory should help.

Figure 15.11. SVIB-SCII profile form, reverse side, lower half.

corresponds to the client's own-sex score to represent the similarity between the individual's score and those of people in that occupation.

The Special Scales for Academic Comfort and Introversion-Extroversion are presented at the top of the profile along with the respondent's name.

The reverse side of the profile (see figures 15.10 and 15.11) incorporates explanatory material that will help the client to understand his or her scores when considered along with the *Interpretive Report*.

The Interpretive Report. This report (described in detail in the following text) averages seven pages in length, is produced completely by computer, and provides interpretive statements expressly for the individual respondent. Although the *Interpretive Report* addresses the client directly, it is recommended that a practitioner guide the individual to a complete understanding of the scales and the scores.

The interpretive paragraphs for the Strong Interest Inventory *Interpretive Report* were drawn from existing data and publications that provide construct validity for the interpretations through a series of research studies (Campbell et al., 1968; Campbell and Holland, 1972; Hansen and Johansson, 1972; Hansen, 1984; Hansen and Campbell, 1985).

Subject 1, used to illustrate the most important features of the report, is a female psychologist on the faculty of a major university. Her primary professional and recreational activities include research, writing, serving as faculty representative for intercollegiate athletics, attending athletic events, skiing (water and snow), golfing, travel (business and pleasure), going to the theater, and raising roses and tomatoes.

Interpretive Report Introduction and Disclaimers. Most automated interpretations of inventories and tests begin with several orienting statements that include appropriate cautions and disclaimers; the SVIB-SCII *Interpretive Report* is no exception. As illustrated in figure 15.1, the report begins with a brief introduction that explains that the interpretive comments are based on the individual's responses to the inventory items, provides an overview of the interpretation, and reminds the individual and the practitioner that the Strong Interest Inventory is a measure of interests, not aptitudes.

GOT and BIS Interpretation. The first interpretive paragraphs for each individual integrate the highest General Occupational Theme scores with high scores of related BIS. The BIS are subclusters within each General Occupational Theme category; the clustering of the scales with the themes is based on the correlations between the two. So, for example (see table 15.1), the BIS Agriculture, Nature, Adventure, Military Activities, and Mechanical Activities each have their highest correlation with the General Occupational Theme Realistic. Thus the interpretive paragraphs for interests in the realistic area are built, first, on a high score on the Realistic General Occupational Theme (or R-Theme) and, then, are expanded to accommodate each additional related R-Theme Basic Interest Scale high score.

The highest General Occupational Theme score for subject 1 (see figure 15.2), for example, is on the Investigative Theme, with supporting high scores on three of the four I-Theme BIS—Science, Mathematics, and Medical Science.

All of these interests are referenced in the interpretive paragraph along with a general description of the interests of people with high scores in the investigative area.

GOT and BIS Cutting Scores. The cutting scores used to determine which interpretive paragraphs are included in an *Interpretive Report* are the same ones established for the SVIB-SCII profile; on the GOT and the BIS any score that is at the seventieth percentile or higher compared to either women or men in general is considered in the interpretable range. The women- and men-in-general samples are those groups used for the standardization of the GOT and BIS. They include subjects drawn from ninety-three different occupations, all of which are represented by Occupational Scales on the Strong Interest Inventory profile. The subjects used in the women- and men-in-general samples are matched on occupational title. For example, if the women-in-general sample includes one female carpenter, the male sample also includes one male carpenter; if the men-in-general sample contains two male beauticians, the women-in-general sample contains two female beauticians. This procedure was used in to ensure that any sex differences in interests that appear between the women and men in general are not simply artifacts of the two samples.

Post-hoc comparisons of the two in-general samples indicate that there are legitimate sex differences between the two groups that are substantial enough on many scales to warrant providing interpretive data based on an individual's own sex (Hansen and Campbell, 1985). For example, as reported in table 15.1, men in general have a mean score that is seven points higher than do women in general on the Mechanical Activities Scale. Thus a score at the seventieth percentile compared to men in general would be at the ninetieth percentile compared to women in general. On the other hand, women in general score, on the average, five points higher than do men in general on the Artistic General Occupational Theme. A score at the seventieth percentile compared to women in general would be at the eighty-fifth percentile compared to men in general.

Incorporation of the Occupational Scales. The second step in the integration of information within the main interpretive paragraphs is to identify the Occupational Scales that fall in the area of interest related to the dominant GOT. The Occupational Scales, like the BIS, are coded (based on Holland's theory of six types) according to their relationship to the GOT.

For subject 1 (see figures 15.2 and 15.3), whose strongest interests are in the investigative area, twenty-two Occupational Scales with scores that meet the cutting-score criterion (described in the next section) are listed in conjunction with the global Investigative General Occupational Theme and Basic Interest Scale interpretations.

Occupational Scale Cutting Scores. The cutting scores used to identify interpretable high scores for the Occupational Scales are those greater than or equal to one standard deviation below the mean of the Criterion Sample (occupational sample) used in the empirical scale construction and standardization of the scale.

The Occupational Scales of the SVIB-SCII are normed by scoring the original

TABLE 15.1

Means and Standard-Score Interpretive Boundaries of the General Occupational Themes and Basic Interest Scales for Women- and Men-in-General Samples (Each N = 300; numbers in parentheses are percentiles)

			Interpretive Boundaries						
Scale	*Sex*	*Mean*	*Very Low (0–6)*	*Low (7–15)*	*Mod. Low (16–30)*	*Average (31–69)*	*Mod. High (70–84)*	*High (85–93)*	*Very High (94–100)*
REALISTIC[a]	F	46	29–32	33–37	38–41	42–51	52–55	56–59	60–72
THEME	M	54	29–37	38–42	43–48	49–58	59–63	64–67	68–72
Agriculture	F	48	31–33	34–36	37–42	43–51	52–58	59–61	62–68
	M	52	31–36	37–39	40–45	46–58	59–61	62–64	65–68
Nature	F	51	21–34	35–38	39–44	45–57	58–61	62–63	64–66
	M	49	21–32	33–38	39–42	43–55	56–61	62–63	64–66
Adventure	F	47	30–33	34–37	38–41	42–52	53–58	59–62	63–71
	M	53	30–37	38–41	42–46	47–58	59–64	65–66	67–71
Military Activities	F	47	40–41	42–43	44–45	46–47	48–56	57–62	63–73
	M	53	40–41	42–43	44–45	46–59	60–66	67–71	72–73
Mechanical	F	47	32–34	35–36	37–40	41–50	51–56	57–64	65–70
Activities	M	53	32–36	37–41	42–47	48–59	60–63	64–66	67–70
INVESTIGATIVE[a]	F	49	22–33	34–37	38–42	43–55	56–69	60–62	63–69
THEME	M	51	22–35	36–40	41–46	47–56	57–61	62–64	65–69
Science	F	49	31–33	34–36	37–41	42–55	56–59	60–64	65–69
	M	51	31–35	36–39	40–44	45–58	59–62	63–64	65–69
Mathematics	F	49	32–33	34–35	36–43	44–55	56–59	60–62	63–67
	M	51	32–33	34–39	40–45	46–57	58–62	63–64	65–67
Medical Science	F	49	30–31	32–35	36–44	45–56	57–60	61–63	64–66
	M	51	30–33	34–40	41–44	45–56	57–60	61–63	64–66
Medical Service	F	50	34–35	36–38	39–42	43–54	55–61	62–68	69–76
	M	50	34–35	36–40	41–42	43–54	55–58	59–65	66–76
ARTISTIC[a]	F	53	24–37	38–41	42–48	49–58	59–62	63–64	65–66
THEME	M	47	24–31	32–35	36–41	42–53	54–58	59–62	63–66
Music/Dramatics	F	53	26–38	39–43	44–47	48–58	59–63	64–65	66–70
	M	47	26–30	31–35	36–39	40–52	53–57	58–61	62–70

Art	F	54	27–36	37–43	44–49	50–59	60–61	62–64	65–67
	M	46	27–30	31–35	36–40	41–51	52–57	58–61	62–67
Writing	F	52	27–35	36–42	43–48	49–58	59–60	61–63	64–66
	M	48	27–30	31–34	35–41	42–53	54–59	60–62	63–66
SOCIAL[a] THEME	F	50	21–33	34–39	40–43	44–56	57–61	62–66	67–74
	M	50	21–33	34–39	40–44	45–54	55–60	61–64	65–74
Teaching	F	50	26–32	33–37	38–44	45–55	56–60	61–65	66–68
	M	50	26–34	35–37	38–44	45–55	56–60	61–62	63–68
Social Service	F	52	26–36	37–40	41–44	45–57	58–63	64–67	68–72
	M	48	26–34	35–38	39–42	43–53	54–59	60–63	64–72
Athletics	F	47	29–33	34–37	38–39	40–52	53–57	58–61	62–70
	M	53	29–35	36–42	43–47	48–59	60–62	63–66	67–70
Domestic Activities	F	54	29–39	40–43	44–48	49–59	60–63	64–65	66–73
	M	46	29–32	33–34	35–41	42–50	51–54	55–59	60–73
Religious Activities	F	50	33–34	35–38	39–42	43–56	57–61	62–65	66–68
	M	50	33–34	35–38	39–42	43–54	55–61	62–65	66–68
ENTERPRISING[a]	F	49	27–35	36–38	39–43	44–54	55–59	60–64	65–77
THEME	M	51	27–33	34–38	39–44	45–55	56–61	62–66	67–77
Public Speaking	F	49	29–34	35–38	39–42	43–55	56–59	60–65	66–70
	M	51	29–34	35–38	39–44	45–55	56–61	62–65	66–70
Law/Politics	F	49	30–34	35–37	38–42	43–53	54–60	61–64	65–69
	M	51	30–35	36–39	40–45	46–56	57–61	62–64	65–69
Merchandising	F	51	28–34	35–38	39–45	46–56	57–61	62–64	65–70
	M	49	28–33	34–37	38–43	44–55	56–59	60–63	64–70
Sales	F	49	36–37	38–39	40–42	43–52	53–58	59–65	66–82
	M	51	36–37	38–39	40–44	45–56	57–61	62–69	70–82
Business	F	49	26–33	34–37	38–42	43–55	56–59	60–63	64–70
Management	M	51	26–34	35–39	40–45	46–56	57–61	62–66	67–70
CONVENTIONAL[a]	F	50	23–33	34–37	38–43	44–56	57–60	61–67	68–79
THEME	M	50	23–36	37–39	40–44	45–54	55–60	61–64	65–79
Office Practices	F	51	36–37	38–40	41–42	43–54	55–62	63–72	73–81
	M	49	36–37	38–39	40–42	43–52	53–58	59–63	64–81

NOTE: Reprinted by permission (see p. 320 for copyright information).
[a]General Occupational Themes.

Occupational Criterion Samples, used for scale construction, on their respective Occupational Scales (for example, the farmer Criterion Sample is scored on the Farmer Scale and the physicist Criterion Sample is scored on the Physicist Scale). The resulting raw score means and standard deviations are used in a linear standardization formula that converts all scores into distributions with standard-score means of 50 and standard deviations of 10. Thus respondents' scores on all of the Occupational Scales can be compared quickly on a common numerical measure that indicates how similar their interests are to those of the people composing the Criterion Sample, or, in other words, how similar their interests are to people in various occupations. Scores between 40 and 44 (one-half to one standard deviation below the mean of 50) are interpreted as representing interests that are moderately similar to the interests of the occupation, and scores of 45 or higher are in the similar interpretive category.

Predictive validity data for the hit rate for scores in the moderately similar or higher category indicate that 70 to 75 percent of college students score at that level on the SVIB-SCII Occupational Scale most related to their occupation or college major (Swanson, 1985).

Redoing the Sequence. Most people's interests are not limited to one pure Holland type, as measured by the GOT, but rather are a combination of two or more of the types (Holland, 1985). Therefore, the third step in the program is to return to the GOT and identify secondary interests. The individual's second-highest General Occupational Theme score, which meets the minimum cutting-score criterion, is identified along with related high BIS and Occupational Scales. This procedure is repeated up to three times if three General Occupational Theme scores are at, or exceed, the cutting-score criterion.

The profile illustrated in subject 1 (figure 15.3) has two General Occupational Theme scores that meet the seventieth percentile cut-off; thus, the second loop through the program picks up interpretation of the Realistic Theme and related BIS—Nature, Military Activities, and Mechanical Activities—and ten Occupational Scales with a Realistic primary code. Note that the Adventure Scale, although reaching the criterion cutting score, is not included in the interpretation at this point. As will be described later, Adventure, Athletics, and Domestic Activities BIS are treated as special cases.

At this point all GOT for subject 1 that meet the cutting-score criterion have been reported, and thus the majority of the salient high scores for this subject have been identified and interpreted. If, however, a respondent did have another General Occupational Theme score that met the cutting-score criterion, a third loop through the program would be performed.

Interpretation of Low Scores. One feature provided by the *Interpretive Report* but frequently neglected by many practitioners because of time constraints is reference to the individual's lowest scores in addition, of course, to the highest scores. This is done first at the General Occupational Theme and Basic Interest Scale level.

The *Interpretive Report* provides a description of the type with whom the individual has the least in common if he or she has a General Occupational

Theme score that is at the thirtieth percentile or lower compared to the appropriate in-general sample, and if the BIS related to that General Occupational Theme also have scores at the thirtieth percentile or lower for the appropriate sex in-general sample. All themes at that level or lower are identified. Most people will have at least one General Occupational Theme score at this percentile or lower. However, some people who have a wide variety of interests, and at least a tolerance for activities in all of the areas represented by the GOT, will not have a score sufficiently low to elicit an interpretive paragraph. In these instances, the respondent's dislikes are not a serious component in the interest exploration process and the report simply moves on to identify other areas of interest that have not been discussed yet.

As shown in figures 15.3 and 15.4, the interest for this subject that meets the criterion for inclusion in the interpretation is the Enterprising Theme. The subject's score here was below the thirtieth percentile as compared to women in general, and she had no E-Theme Basic Interest Scale scores above the thirtieth percentile.

BIS with Special Interpretations. Once the integrative paragraphs elicited by high scores on the GOT are generated, the program moves to interpretation of three special BIS. Because these scales have only modest correlations with a General Occupational Theme (in the 0.40 range rather than the 0.60 to 0.90 range exhibited between other GOT and BIS scales), they frequently appear as high scores without accompanying high scores on related BIS or GOT.

The three scales include Athletics, Adventure, and Domestic Activities. The Athletics Scale is composed of items representing a wide variety of activities related to sports such as athletic director, professional athlete, golf, boxing, and sports pages in the newspaper. In other words, the scale represents an all-consuming interest in athletics. People who score high on the scale may be avid fans who currently are not participating themselves as athletes although most have some previous athletic experience, especially in team sports (Hansen, 1984).

The Adventure scale is one of the most complicated on the Strong Interest Inventory to interpret because it has been shown to measure a variety of risk-taking behaviors that may be expressed in different ways for different people (Douce and Hansen, 1986; Hansen, 1984). For some people a high score expresses a willingness to take physical risks, such as mountain climbing, sky-diving, or auto racing. Other people express their risk-taking interest by taking financial risks: for example, people who work strictly on a commission basis or the high rollers in the stock market. Still others express their need for adventure through travel, which provides a socially acceptable mechanism for satisfying this interest.

The Domestic Activities Scale is composed of several subsets of items that may lead to above-average scores on the profile (Hansen, 1984). These subcategories include more than the routine housekeeping activities normally associated with the scale name. A person also may score high on the scale if he or she has interests in the following areas: cooking and social entertaining activities participated in by many amateur or professional gourmet cooks; sewing and craft activities; or teaching and care activities focused on young children.

These scales are described in the *Interpretive Report* if the individual scores at the seventieth percentile or higher, the same cutting-score criterion used for the other BIS. For subject 1 (see figure 15.4), two of the three scales—Athletics and Adventure—meet the criterion and are included in the report.

Basic Interest Scale Summary. Next, all of the BIS on which the person has scored at the seventieth percentile or higher are summarized. It is suggested that the individual consider whether the scores reflect an occupational interest or an avocational or leisure interest.

Occupational Scale Summary. The next step in the program (see figures 15.4 and 15.5 for subject 1) is to summarize all Occupational Scales with scores in the interpretable range; in other words, those scores within one standard deviation of the mean for the Criterion Sample on which the scale was developed. Most of these scales already have been mentioned in conjunction with the integrative paragraphs that included the GOT and BIS as well as related Occupational Scales. However, this is an opportunity to pick up any Occupational Scales that may not have been included previously. In addition to identifying the scales on which the person has interests moderately similar or similar to the Occupational Samples, those scales on which the person looks very dissimilar also are identified at this time. Any scales with scores that are three and one-half standard deviations or more below the mean for the Criterion Sample are included in this list.

Special Occupational Scales. Two Occupational Scales—College Professor and Army Officer—have been identified as having surplus meaning that goes beyond the interpretation suggested by the scale name and that can be useful in career exploration.

High scores on the College Professor Scale suggest a general interest in working in an academic environment. However, the occupation actually engaged in within that environment may not always be as a professor per se. For example, a person's primary occupational choice may be secretary, accountant, or lawyer but their choice of work environment—reflected in a high score on the College Professor Scale—may be an academic one (see subject 1, figure 15.5).

A high score on the Army Officer Scale generally indicates an interest in managerial activities and responsibilities that may be found in any field or discipline, not just the military. Therefore, the following brief interpretive paragraph is included to stress this point:

> Your score on the Army Officer Scale denotes managerial interests, which means that you like to be in charge of other people, to have supervisory responsibility, to participate in competitive activities, and to resolve personnel problems. These are interests similar to people, no matter what their field, who assume supervisory and administrative positions.

At this point, all high scores will have been discussed and the individual is admonished to consider his or her abilities as well as interests in the identified areas, since scores on the Strong Interest Inventory give no indication of ability or probability of success in an occupation.

Interpretation of the AC *and* IE *Scales.* The final interpretive paragraphs focus on two special scales—Academic Comfort and Introversion-Extroversion—of the SVIB-SCII.

The AC Scale differentiates between people who enjoy being in an academic setting and those who do not; consequently, high scores are associated with continuation in school (Swanson and Hansen, 1985). However, the AC Scale does not measure ability, and the individual is advised by the *Interpretive Report* to remember that important fact as he or she examines the AC score on the profile. Subject 1, for example, has an AC score of 65, which elicits an interpretive paragraph appropriate for high scores on this scale that advises the individual to consider how she is going to satisfy her academic interests in the future and suggests several alternative behaviors for her to consider (see figure 15.6).

People who score low on the AC Scale frequently view education as a means to an end or as a necessary hurdle to enter their career. People with scores in the lower range are advised by the *Interpretive Report* that if they do enter an academic program, they may wish to be involved in internship programs or to hold part-time jobs that will give them practical experience to complement their coursework.

The IE Scale originally was constructed by identifying Criterion Samples of introverts and extroverts using the MMPI's Social Introversion Scale. Translated into vocational behaviors, the Strong Interest Inventory's IE Scale identifies those individuals who prefer to work with ideas and things as opposed to those who prefer to work with people (Hansen, 1984). If the IE score is within ±0.5 standard deviation of the mean for most occupations, which is 50, the individual has indicated interests that involve a combination of introverted and extroverted activities. High scores, on the other hand, as illustrated by subject 1 (figure 15.6), are in the introverted direction and indicate an interest in working alone, completing projects independently, and working with ideas or things rather than with people. Persons who have low scores have interests in the extroverted direction, indicating that they prefer to work on group projects, like being in leadership positions, and rarely need time alone (Hansen, 1984).

Final Warnings and Suggestions. The *Interpretive Report* closes advising the individual that the next step in the exploration process is to obtain additional information about the occupations in which he or she has the greatest interest and a reminder that career planning is a lifelong process (see subject 1, figure 15.7).

Identifying Invalid Profiles. Most Strong Interest Inventory profiles are valid for interpretation but on rare occasions two exceptions can occur; the Total Responses Index and Infrequent Response Index flag these invalid profiles.

The Total Responses Index indicates the number of item responses read by the computer. If every item is answered, the number printed at the top of the profile and at the beginning of the *Interpretive Report* is 325. Occasionally, however, a person may fail to mark a few items or the computer does not pick up all responses. A few items can be omitted without invalidating the scale scores; however, if the Total Response Index falls below 305, the following narrative is printed and processing is discontinued:

> You responded to XXX of the 325 SCII items, an insufficient number of responses to provide a valid profile for interpretation. Thus, the answer sheet is being returned to you without profile scores or interpretive comments.

The Infrequent Response (IR) Index indicates, when the score is a *negative* number, that some confusion or problem has occurred during test administration. The IR Index is composed of response choices that are selected infrequently. Any respondent who selects a large number of uncommon response choices will receive a low IR Index score. When the number of unusual responses exceeds those given by the average person, the score becomes negative and the following paragraphs are printed.

> Compared to most people you responded atypically to several items.
>
> There may have been a problem with marking your answer sheet that needs to be corrected before a valid interpretation can be made. Please check with your counselor or test administrator.

The IR Index can indicate the presence of a potential problem but it cannot identify the specific problem; thus each case should be examined individually. Occasionally legitimate confusion has occurred during the test administration; sometimes an individual is trying to fool the system or sabotage the testing; and in some cases the respondent has unique interests and no problem exists. In any event, when the IR Index is negative, processing is discontinued to allow practitioner intervention and assistance.

Videodisc Technology: The Future for Computer-Assisted Interpretation

The *Interpretive Report* for the Strong Interest Inventory is amenable to integration into computer-assisted career exploration and decision-making programs that provide the user with detailed psychological assessment information along with career-related material necessary for informed decisions.

The recent development of videodisc technology combined with previously existing computer capabilities to administer, score, and interpret assessment results promises to be revolutionary, with important implications for computer-assisted decision making. When used in a career counseling setting, the new technology will expand the capabilities of earlier technologies, which were limited to whatever information could be put on a computer monitor, such as data, graphics, and printed words. The videodisc technology can incorporate all of the traditional materials and it can be supplemented with audio and visual—either motion picture or still-frame—material.

VIDEODISC TECHNOLOGY

Videodiscs store video and audio information on the surface of a laser disc that is similar to a phonograph record. The tremendous amount of information stored on the videodisc can be accessed randomly in both the video and audio formats. Format flexibility is one of the most attractive features of this technology for computer-assisted counseling. Each side of the videodisc can contain still-frame or motion-picture videotape information, and the two formats can be mixed within one program or presentation.

In addition to the motion and still pictures, two tracks of audio can be laid down. The soundtrack can be randomly accessed, which offers the benefit of providing different soundtracks for different audiences to facilitate, for example, multilingual programming.

An external microcomputer is used to drive the videodisc and to incorporate maintenance functions, such as branching criteria as well as the traditional testing, scoring, and interpretation functions of microcomputers.

An interdisciplinary team typically is required to produce a videodisc. Key players include experts on content or subject matter, instructional designers who know how to put together a meaningful curriculum, audio-visual people skilled in motion picture and television production, and computer programmers.

PATHFINDER for the SVIB-SCII. PATHFINDER, developed by Interactive Videostyems, Inc. (1985), is one of the first systems to integrate videodisc technology with computer-assisted career guidance. It is a four-step process designed for use with groups or individuals. The system incorporates the Strong Interest Inventory and a workbook to assist users to understand their unique pattern of measured interests; identify a wide variety of occupations that match their interests; select potential occupational choices based on criteria such as educational requirements, actual job duties, and long-term job potential; and develop the action steps needed to pursue the career plan (for example, training and education needs, résumé preparation, network development).

The SVIB-SCII used in PATHFINDER can be administered on the microcomputer that drives the laserdisc and scored on site for immediate turnaround or it can be administered using the traditional paper-and-pencil method. The system resembles other computer-assisted career exploration programs in that it leads users to a set of possible career choices that match their interests. However, it is unique because it uses an onscreen counselor to guide users through the program. The mixed format provides an effective presentation of the interpretive information and at the same time is paced at a rate that keeps users involved; is varied enough in content and format to prevent boredom; integrates and simplifies the information on the SVIB-SCII profile, as does the

Interpretive Report; and frees the practitioner to provide personal counseling as appropriate throughout the process. The entire program is built around the career exploration philosophy of first expanding potential choices and then reducing the options to a manageable number for in-depth exploration.

The videodisc technology has many of the same advantages that have made computer-assisted assessment popular with practitioners: it allows the practitioner to perform at a higher level of efficiency by freeing him or her for therapy, consultation, research, and other professional activities, and, at the same time, it saves time and is more economical.

In Conclusion

The *Interpretive Report* for the Strong Interest Inventory was not designed to replace the practitioner, but rather to enhance or facilitate the career exploration process. The report can be used with individual clients as well as in group settings to: provide an economical method for presenting test results; inform the practitioner, especially beginning professionals or those who use the Strong Interest Inventory only occasionally; and provide an efficient and accurate mechanism for giving clients an opportunity to review their results at a later time. The report also can be given to clients during career exploration but prior to the SVIB-SCII interpretive session, to orient them to the information that they will be discussing later with the practitioner.

Comparisons of methods of giving test feedback to individuals have shown that written or interpretive reports are as effective as individual interpretations of profiles in increasing an individual's accuracy of self-estimates of test scores (Folds and Gazda, 1966). And interpretive reports can be more effective than individual interpretations in increasing an individual's knowledge about vocational opportunities and requirements, in increasing skill in making educational-vocational decisions, and in setting up educational and vocational goals that are consistent with interests, personality characteristics, and abilities (Graff, Danish, and Austin, 1972). Clients do express a preference for individualized interpretations rather than group or self-administered ones; however, considerations such as cost, counselor availability, and interview time limits may make minimizing the amount of time spent with a counselor administratively attractive. Fortunately the data indicate that clients do not suffer under modified interpretive formats with reduced counselor contact.

REFERENCES

Bellotto, B. (1985). *Guidance and counseling directory of microcomputer software*. San Jose, CA: Department of Career/Vocational Education and Guidance Publications.

Biskin, B. H., and Kolotkin, R. L. (1977). Effects of computerized administration on scores of the MMPI. *Applied Psychological Measurement, 1*(4), 543–549.

Brown, J. M (1984). *Similarity of Strong-Campbell Interest Inventory scores and profiles from computerized versus paper-and-pencil administrations*. Unpublished doctoral dissertation, University of Minnesota.

Campbell, D. P. (1974). *Manual for the SVIB-SCII* (1st ed.). Stanford, CA: Stanford University Press.

Campbell, D. P., Borgen, F. H., Eastes, S., Johansson, C. B., and Peterson, R. A. (1968). A set of Basic Interest Scales for the Strong Vocational Interest Blank for Men. *Journal of Applied Psychology Monographs*, 52(6): 1–54.

Campbell, D. P., and Hansen, J. C. (1981). *Manual for the SVIB-SCII* (3rd ed.). Stanford, CA: Stanford University Press.

Campbell, D. P., and Holland, J. L. (1972). Applying Holland's theory to Strong's data. *Journal of Vocational Behavior*, 2, 353–376.

Douce, L., and Hansen, J. C. (1986). *Construct validation of the Adventure Scale*. Minneapolis, MN: Center for Interest Measurement Research.

Elwood, D. L. (1972). Automated WAIS testing correlated with face-to-face WAIS testing: A validity study. *International Journal of Man/Machine Studies*, 4, 129–137.

Folds, J. H., and Gazda, G. M. (1966). A comparison of the effectiveness and efficiency of three methods of test interpretation. *Journal of Counseling Psychology*, 13, 318–324.

Graff, R. W., Danish, S., and Austin, B. (1972). Reactions to three kinds of vocational-educational counseling. *Journal of Counseling Psychology*, 19, 224–228.

Hansen, J. C. (1977). Evaluation of accuracy and consistency of machine scoring the SCII. *Measurement and Evaluation in Guidance*, 10, 141–143.

Hansen, J. C. (1982). *Scale score accuracy of the 1981 SCII*. Minneapolis, MN: Center for Interest Measurement Research.

Hansen, J. C. (1984). *User's Guide to the SVIB-SCII*. Stanford, CA: Stanford University Press.

Hansen, J. C. (1985). *Interpretive report for the SVIB-SCII*. Palo Alto, CA: Consulting Psychologists Press.

Hansen, J. C., and Campbell, D. P. (1985). *Manual for the SVIB-SCII* (4th ed.). Stanford, CA: Stanford University Press.

Hansen, J. C., and Johansson, C. B. (1972). The application of Holland's model to the Strong Vocational Interest Blank for Women. *Journal of Vocational Behavior*, 2, 479–493.

Holland, J. L. (1985). *Making vocational choices* (2nd ed.). Englewood Cliffs, NJ: Prentice-Hall.

Interactive Video-Systems, Inc. (1985). *PATHFINDER: A career decision process*. Minneapolis, MN: Interactive Video Systems.

Krivatsy, S. E., and Magoon, T. M. (1976). Differential effects of three vocational counseling treatments. *Journal of Counseling Psychology*, 23, 112–118.

Kuder, G. F. (1966). *General manual: Occupational Interest Survey Form—DD*. Chicago: Science Research Associates.

Lushene, R. E., O'Neil, H. F., Jr., and Dunn, T. (1973). Equivalent validity of a completely computerized MMPI. *Journal of Personality Assessment*, 38(4), 353–361.

Strong, E. K., Jr. (1927). *Vocational Interest Blank*. Stanford, CA: Stanford University Press.

Swanson, J. L. (1985, August). *Predictive validity of the 1985 SVIB-SCII for College Majors*. Paper presented at the 93rd annual meeting of the American Psychological Association, Los Angeles.

Swanson, J. L., and Hansen, J. C. (1985). The relationship of the construct of academic comfort to educational level performance, aspiration, and prediction of college major choice. *Journal of Vocational Behavior*, 26, 1–12.

PART IV

COMPUTER INTERPRETATION OF COGNITIVE AND ABILITY MEASURES

16

Computerized Adaptive Testing for Measuring Abilities and Other Psychological Variables

David J. Weiss and C. David Vale

Introduction

Adaptive testing was first applied to the measurement of individual differences in abilities by Binet and Simon (see DuBois, 1970) in what later became known as the Binet IQ tests. In general, adaptive or tailored testing involves selecting for each examinee, during the process of test administration, a set of test items that best measures some psychological characteristic of that person.

Binet operationalized the adaptive process using a trained examiner. In the Binet test, the examiner first estimates an individual's ability level to determine the age level at which to begin the test. Each question is scored as it is answered. Once a block of items has been answered, the examiner decides whether the next block of questions should be easier or more difficult. This process is repeated until a ceiling level and a basal level have been established. These two levels—respectively, the mental ages at which the examinee answers all items incorrectly and all items correctly—define the range of effective measurement for that individual. Items below the basal level are too easy for the examinee and, therefore, are not administered. Items above the ceiling level are too difficult and, likewise, are not administered. Neither set of items would provide any information about that person. The resulting items between the basal and ceiling levels define an efficient set of items for measuring a particular individual.

Because the basal and ceiling levels may differ for different people, the resulting set of administered items represents an adaptive test in which the set of items administered is tailored or adapted to that examinee's ability level as it is estimated during the process of test administration.

Over half a century after Binet implemented this adaptive process of item selection, psychometric theory verified his method—a test measures best when it uses items for which the examinee has a 0.5 probability of answering correctly (Birnbaum, 1968, chap. 20). Binet's testing procedure and most good adaptive tests will result in a set of items with this optimal measurement property.

At about the same time Binet's method was verified, psychometricians became interested in further improving the process of adaptive testing. Early efforts (see Weiss and Betz, 1973) attempted to implement adaptive testing with paper-and-pencil tests or simple testing machines, in order to eliminate the need for a trained test administrator. Later, as interactive computers became available, computerized adaptive testing (CAT) was born.

Computerized Adaptive Testing

In CAT the interactive computer replaces Binet's test administrator. As in the Binet tests, the computer serves several functions: it presents the items to the examinee, receives and scores the item responses, chooses the next item to administer, and terminates the test when appropriate. In contrast to the Binet tests, a properly programmed CAT requires no human intervention. Like Binet's test administrator, a good CAT system can even write an interpretive report that summarizes the test administration and reports appropriate scores.

CAT is not simply computer-assisted testing, which may simply mean administering on a computer a conventional test in which everyone gets the same items. While this use of interactive computers for test administration can expedite the test-scoring and test-interpretation process, it provides neither the efficiency nor the psychometric advantages of a properly implemented CAT.

Research on CAT has identified its advantages over conventional tests. The essential measurement advantages can be summarized in two words: efficiency and precision. Control over measurement efficiency means that CAT can obtain measurement quality equivalent to that of a conventional test with fewer items (or better quality than that provided by a conventional test with the same number of items). A general finding is that CAT can reduce test length by an average of 50 percent, with individual test length reductions of up to 80 percent, without compromising measurement quality (Brown and Weiss, 1977; Kiely, Zara, and Weiss, 1983; McBride and Martin, 1983; Moreno, Wetzel, McBride, and Weiss, 1984). The time saved in administering tests by CAT can be used for additional testing of other abilities to increase the predictive validity of a test battery, or in an instructional setting the time can be used for additional instruction. Alternatively, if the number of items is kept the same, increases in precision may translate to higher levels of validity.

Control over measurement precision means that everyone can be measured with the same degree of precision (that is, the same standard error). A fixed-length conventional test cannot achieve equiprecise measurement without drastically reducing its overall precision; since everyone takes the same set of items, precision is maximized by matching the difficulty of the test to the average ability of the examinee population. People of near-average ability will be measured well, while those at the tails of the distribution will be measured poorly. CAT, on the other hand, tailors the test to the individual and is thus able to provide appropriate items for everyone. Furthermore, test length can be tailored so that testing terminates when each examinee's ability is estimated with a predetermined degree of precision.

Early approaches to CAT involved a number of different "strategies" for designing adaptive tests (Weiss, 1974). These strategies were different ways of implementing the three basic components of CAT—choosing the appropriate items, keeping score as the test progresses, and terminating the test when appropriate. These early approaches generally functioned by structuring the item pool by item difficulties in various ways and using this structure to select items as they were answered by an examinee. In one approach, the item pool is structured into subtests (or strata) like the items in a Binet-type test, and a subtest-to-subtest branching rule is used to select the next item to be administered. Weiss (1985) illustrates how even this simple CAT can increase testing efficiency over that possible with Binet's approach to adaptive testing.

As CAT research progressed, it became evident that item-response theory (IRT), which was maturing at about the same time, had much to offer. One major problem in early implementations of CAT was that no metric was available on which scores could be reported, since the number-correct score is not useful in CAT. A second problem was that there were no logical methods for terminating CAT administration beyond those originally proposed by Binet. The result was a number of CAT strategies that administered a fixed number of items, likely losing one of CAT's major advantages. Other problems with these early approaches to CAT involved the use of differential starting points for test administration and the selection and evaluation of the "best" of the prestructured CAT strategies.

IRT provided a coherent methodology for the solution of many of these CAT problems. The result of the marriage of IRT and CAT is a family of CAT approaches for solving a variety of measurement problems. These approaches to CAT result from variations in the way item pools are designed and the way CAT tests are begun and terminated for an individual.

Most approaches to CAT are designed to optimally measure individual differences on a trait (for example, ability, achievement, personality, attitude, or any unidimensional psychological variable) when there is a wide range of trait levels in a target population (Weiss, 1982). In a variation of this approach, such as might occur in a vocational counseling environment, the goal is to precisely and efficiently measure each individual on a number of scales in a test battery; to implement this goal the basic idea of CAT is extended to branching among subtests (Brown and Weiss, 1977; Vale, 1980).

Another variation of CAT (Kingsbury and Weiss, 1983) can be used to efficiently classify individuals into two or more groups, such as might be done in clinical diagnosis, employee selection, criterion-referenced testing, or assigning school grades. CAT can also be designed to measure short- or long-term change or growth (Kingsbury and Weiss, 1983), such as change in achievement levels due to instruction, developmental change, or change due to some environmental event. Each of these implementations of IRT-based CAT involves variations on the basic elements in the design of a CAT procedure.

IRT-based CAT

IRT is a family of mathematical models that can be used to describe and make inferences about the test performance of individuals (see, for example, Hambleton and Swaminathan, 1985). These mathematical models permit the description of test items in terms of their characteristics using, but redefining, the familiar concepts of item difficulty and item discrimination. For CAT purposes, IRT test-item parameters permit the creation of item banks designed for specific testing purposes, from which a CAT can draw its items for a given examinee.

At the individual level, IRT describes how an individual is likely to respond to a test item as a function of his or her trait level, assuming that the trait level or an estimate of it is available. At the same time, IRT mathematical models permit the estimation of an individual's trait level based on his or her observed responses to a set of test items with known characteristics. IRT also permits the determination of estimates of the error of measurement (or, conversely, the precision) of an individual's trait-level estimate.

CHOOSING APPROPRIATE ITEMS

In IRT the mathematical function that describes the probability of a correct response to a single test item as a function of (known) trait level is called the item-response function (IRF; it has also been referred to as the item-characteristic curve, or ICC, and the item-response curve, or IRC). IRFs are described by a mathematical equation, usually based on a logistic curve (see Lord, 1980, equation 2–1). The three parameters of the IRF are usually referred to as a, the item's discrimination or slope parameter; b, the item's difficulty or location parameter; and c, the item's guessing or lower asymptote parameter. Figure 16.1 shows IRFs for several items in which a, b, and c differ for each item.

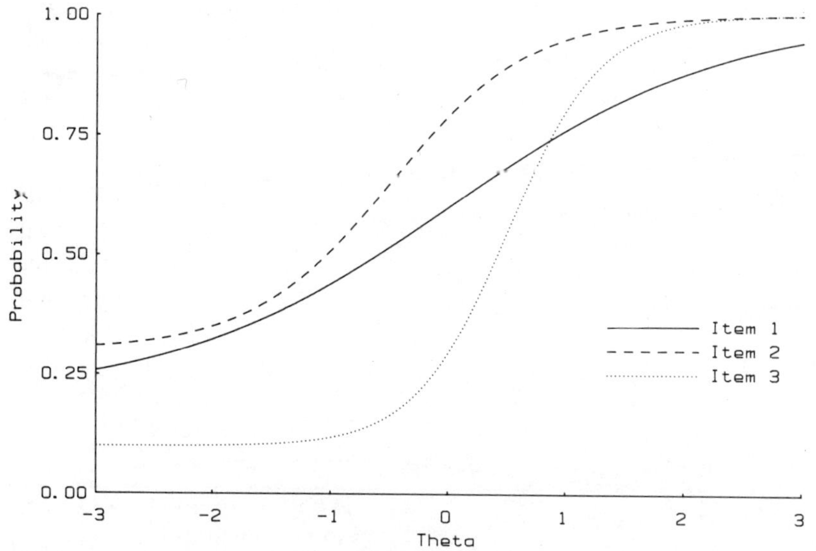

Figure 16.1. Item response functions for three items.

Some IRT models, such as the Rasch model (for example, Wright and Stone, 1979), describe items only in terms of the difficulty parameter (*b*), holding *a* constant across all items and assuming *c* to be zero.

An IRF for an item can be transformed into an item information function (IIF), which is more useful than the IRF for test design and for CAT. Information is interpretable as precision; the higher the information value, the more precisely that item measures at a given level of θ (theta, the symbol generally used in IRT to indicate the trait being measured by a given measuring instrument). The IIF is inversely proportional to the squared standard error with which ability could be estimated from the item. Figure 16.2 shows the IIFs for the items in figure 16.1. On the vertical axis of figure 16.2 is the value of item information; the horizontal axis is θ on a standard-score scale. In figure 16.2, item 1 measures most precisely for θ values around 0.3; item 2 measures people best if their θ levels are low, around -0.3; and item 3 measures best for people who have higher θ values, in the range of 0.6. At a θ level of 0.0, item 3 measures best (that is, provides the most information), item 2 is next best, and item 1 measures people most poorly. At a θ level of -1.0, item 2 measures best, item 1 is next, and item 3 measures most poorly. Thus the item that is best at $\theta = 0.0$ is poorest at $\theta = -1.0$.

IRT-based CAT uses IIFs to select items. Following Binet's example, an adaptive test starts with an estimate of the individual's ability (that is, θ) level; in the Binet tests this initial θ estimate is restricted to a fixed set of mental age levels. In CAT the initial θ estimate, usually derived from whatever information the examiner has about the individual, can be any value on a continuous scale from very high to very low. Using that initial "best guess" about the person's

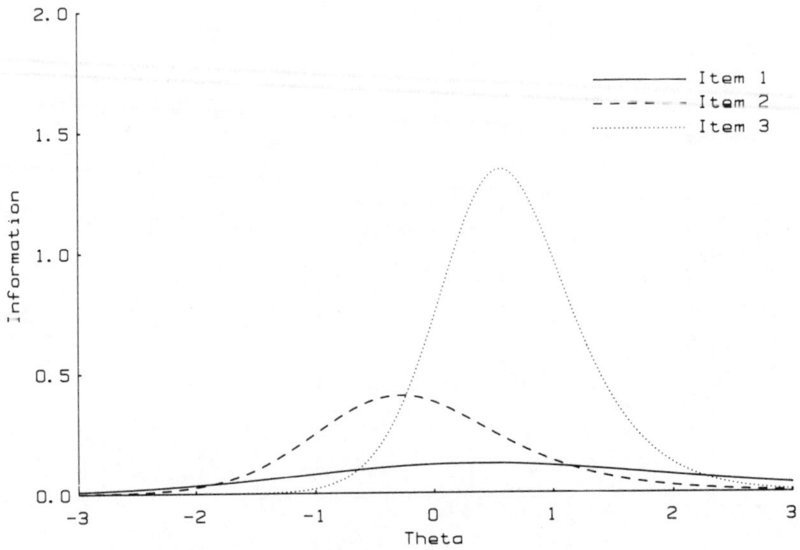

Figure 16.2. Information functions for three items.

θ level, IRT-based CAT then chooses the item that provides the most precise measurement for that individual, assuming that the initial estimate of the person's θ level was correct. The selected item is administered and scored as in the Binet test, except that the item is administered on a video display terminal and the examinee answers it by typing on the terminal keyboard or by using a light pen or touch screen.

Since the item-selection procedure in CAT requires an estimate of θ for selecting additional items (which are then used to refine the estimate of θ), a method is required to convert the scored (correct, incorrect) responses to test items into θ estimates. In IRT, this process involves combining the data in the IRFs with data on how an examinee responded to each of the items administered.

Figure 16.3 shows the IRF for item 1, the probability of a correct response to that item, and the complement (that is, one minus the IRF) of the IRF for item 2, or the probability of an incorrect response. These data can be used to estimate θ for an examinee who answered item 1 correctly and item 2 incorrectly. The figure also shows the multiplicative product of these two IRFs, which is called a likelihood function. The likelihood function describes the likelihood (that is, probability) of the response pattern (in this case a correct response to item 1 and an incorrect response to item 2) as a function of trait level. To infer an examinee's θ level that is most likely to provide that response pattern to that set of items, the θ level associated with the maximum of the likelihood function is determined (see Lord, 1980, for the mathematical procedures involved). In figure 16.3, the maximum of the likelihood function occurs at $\theta = -1.4$. Thus the maximum likelihood estimate of θ for the examinee who answered item 1 correctly and 2 incorrectly is -1.4. This maximum likelihood estimate of θ

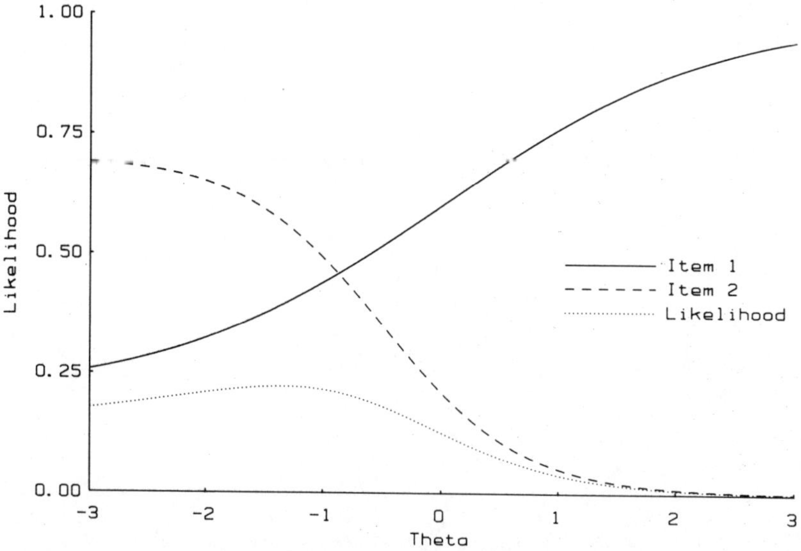

Figure 16.3. Individual and joint likelihoods for two-item responses.

incorporates the characteristics of all of the items administered (as they are reflected in their IRFs) and the correct/incorrect information obtained from the individual.

Maximum likelihood estimation of θ will usually work when an examinee has answered two or more items with at least one correct and one incorrect response. If an individual has answered only one item, has answered all the items correctly (or incorrectly), or if maximum likelihood estimation fails for numerical reasons (as it occasionally does), an alternative approach to estimating θ is necessary. One alternative approach, called Bayesian estimation (see Hambleton and Swaminathan, 1985, pp. 91–95), can be used as a temporary expedient in CAT or as a legitimate estimation procedure in its own right. In Bayesian estimation of θ an assumption is made about the shape and location of a distribution of θ (called a prior distribution), which is then combined with the observed IRF data and the response pattern. The result is a θ estimate similar to that derived from maximum likelihood estimation. It is influenced by the prior distribution, however, and does not give the unreasonable estimates that maximum likelihood estimation may (for example, an ability estimate of infinity if an examinee answers all of the items correctly).

In IRT-based CAT the θ estimate from previously administered items (or the initial estimate) is used in conjunction with the IIFs of all the items in the bank to choose the next item to administer. Each item is selected, immediately prior to its administration, because it is the unadministered item that has the highest IIF at the current estimate of θ. After each item is administered, the θ estimate is updated and another item is chosen. As the test continues, the item-selection procedure results in estimates of θ that converge on a value that is a

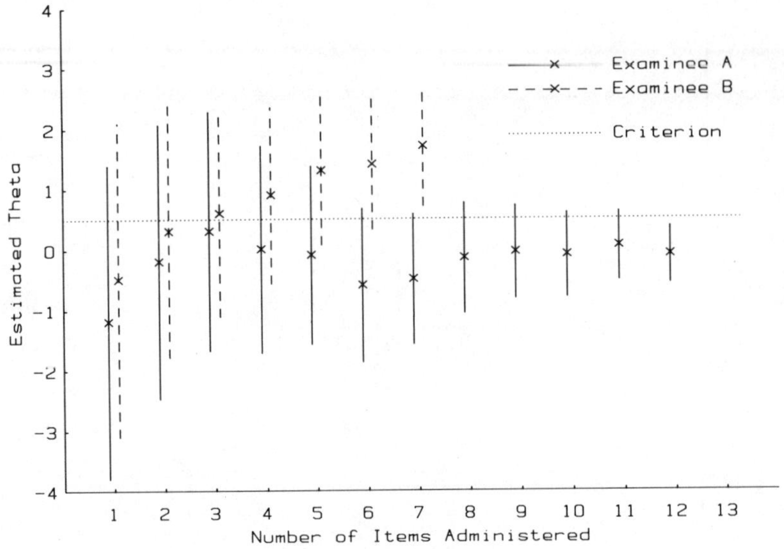

Figure 16.4. Convergence and classification in a computerized adaptive test.

good representation of an examinee's "true" trait level. Figure 16.4 shows an example of the convergence process that occurs in an IRT-based CAT.

ENDING THE ADAPTIVE TEST

In addition to providing a method for estimating θ levels from any set of test items for which parameter estimates are available, maximum likelihood (and Bayesian) estimation methods also result in standard errors associated with the θ estimates. Like the θ estimates, the standard errors are based only on the parameters of the items administered and the responses of an examinee to those items. Thus different individuals answering the same set of items in different ways may obtain both different θ estimates and different standard errors; conversely, different examinees answering different items may obtain similar θ estimates and similar standard errors. The availability of these standard errors from IRT trait-level estimation procedures makes it possible to develop from CAT individual standard errors of measurement, or confidence bands, for each examinee's θ estimate.

Examples of IRT-derived standard error bands are shown as the vertical lines around the θ estimates (Xs) in figure 16.4. This figure shows an important characteristic of the standard error in CAT: as the number of items administered increases, the standard error band around the θ estimates decreases at a decreasing rate. In conjunction with the convergence process that occurs for the θ estimates, as is indicated by the continuing decreases in the differences between successive θ estimates, these two characteristics indicate that with each item administered in CAT the θ estimates become better representations of an examinee's true θ level.

The standard error bands, in conjunction with the θ estimates, can be used to terminate CAT in several ways, depending on the purpose for which the test is being administered. When a test is administered for diagnostic purposes, such as in clinical evaluation of an individual, in vocational counseling, or in a placement situation, it is important to obtain an estimate of the examinee's trait level (perhaps on each of a number of different traits) that is as precise as possible. Furthermore, it may be important to be sure that examinees at various levels of the trait continuum are measured equally well. This translates into a requirement of equiprecise measurement (Weiss, 1982), which is difficult to achieve with fixed-length conventional tests.

In CAT, however, test length is free to vary. When combined with IRT's capability of estimating individualized standard errors of measurement, a CAT test termination rule emerges: continue testing until each examinee's estimates have a prespecified standard error. If sufficient items exist in the item pool for the appropriate θ levels, and if the examinees respond to the items in reasonable accordance with the IRT model, the result will be differences among examinees in test length but measurements with essentially equal precision.

A second purpose for which tests are administered is classification, or dividing individuals into two or more groups on the basis of test scores. In a clinical setting the decision may be to treat or not to treat, or to send home or keep in the hospital. In an employment or college admissions setting the decision may be to accept or reject. In a classroom setting the decision might be to assign a grade of A, B, or C. When tests are administered for classification purposes, equiprecise measurement is no longer relevant as a CAT termination criterion. What becomes important, instead, is classification accuracy around one or more cutting scores.

By adopting a different test-termination rule based on the individualized error of measurement, CAT can be used to efficiently classify individuals with respect to one or more cutting scores. In this case the test-termination rule is: continue testing until an examinee's θ estimate is at least a certain number of standard errors on one side or the other of a cutting score (after the cutting scores have been transformed to the θ metric; see Kingsbury and Weiss, 1983, for how this transformation can be made). Investigations of this CAT procedure (Kingsbury and Weiss, 1983; Weiss and Kingsbury, 1984) show that it results in a very efficient classification procedure, and one that provides classifications of greater accuracy under realistic testing conditions than do fixed-length conventional tests and sequential (but nonadaptive) classification testing procedures. As would be expected from the nature of this type of classification problem, the shortest test lengths from the variable-length CAT occur for individuals whose θ levels are distant from the cutting score—these examinees are clearly above or below the cutting score. Instead, testing time is concentrated on the examinees who need it—those whose θ levels are near the cutting score, for whom testing must continue until an accurate classification decision can be made.

Figure 16.4 illustrates this CAT-based classification procedure. The horizontal dashed line in the figure is a cutting score transformed to the θ metric. As the figure shows, the 1.65 standard error band (a 90 percent confidence interval) for examinee A's θ estimates overlapped the cutting score through item 11. At that point the error band was entirely below the cutting score, indicating a less than 0.05 probability that the examinee's θ estimate was above the cutting score of θ. On the other hand, the θ estimate of examinee B was further from the cutting score of 0.5. As a consequence, only seven items were needed before this individual's error band failed to encompass the cutting score.

Implementing CAT on a Microcomputer

There are a number of steps involved in implementing CAT in an operational testing environment. In addition to selecting the microcomputer on which the tests are to be administered, the following must be accomplished:

1. Items must be created and entered into a random-access item bank.
2. The items must be administered to a calibration group and the IRT item parameters estimated.
3. An adaptive testing item-selection strategy must be chosen and programmed into the computer.
4. Starting and termination rules consistent with the purposes for which the tests are being administered must be selected.
5. The testing strategy should be evaluated before it is administered, from characteristics of the item bank, to determine whether it will function adequately for the purposes for which it is intended (and the item pool further improved, if necessary).
6. The test has to be administered with software appropriate to present the items and to accept, check, process, score, and store the responses, and to report test scores.

The implementation of these steps is illustrated in the next sections using the MicroCAT* Testing System, which is designed for use on IBM Personal Computers and compatible units.

ITEM AUTHORING AND BANKING

An item-authoring facility should permit test developers to use items that have been developed in paper-and-pencil format as well as to create items that improve on that mode of administration. For the former type of item, high-

* MicroCAT is a trademark of Assessment Systems Corporation. Figures 16.5–16.9 reproduced by permission.

resolution text is necessary; for the latter, the use of color graphics is desirable to create items on the screen that have special impact.

An item-banking facility should be designed to permit easy access to items for test development purposes as well as random access so that the program controlling test administration can locate and present an item with minimal delay. In addition, complex items such as those including graphics may need to be preprocessed to speed up graphics presentation; examinees cannot be expected to watch a computer screen for more than a second or two while the computer draws a graphics image.

Figures 16.5 and 16.6 show an example of a graphics-based item prepared

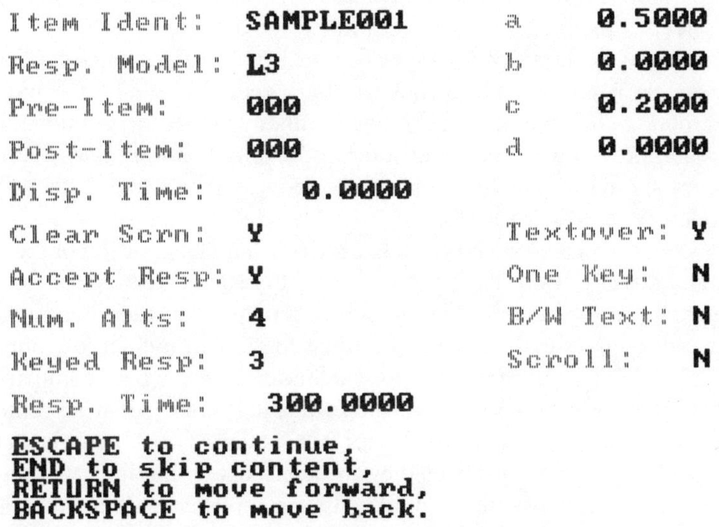

Figure 16.5. A MicroCAT item characteristics screen.

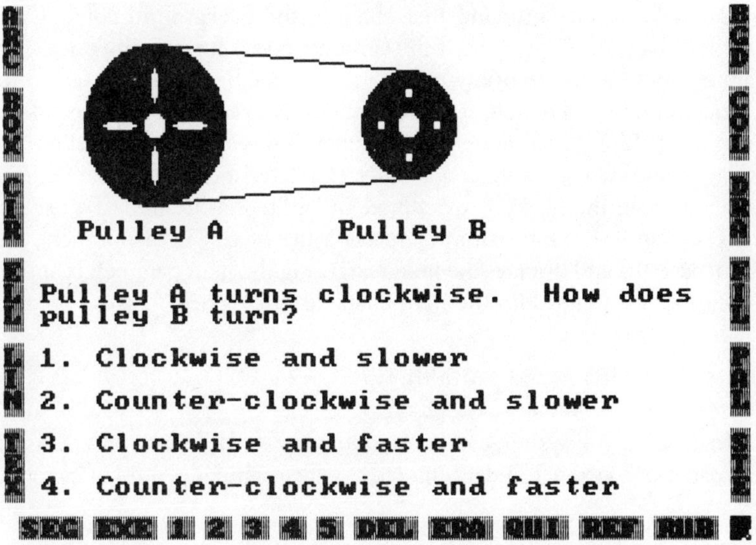

Figure 16.6. A MicroCAT Graphics Item Banker display.

by the MicroCAT system's Graphics Item Banker. Figure 16.5 displays the item characteristics screen, one of the two screens associated with each banked item. On this screen the user enters a unique item identifier (for example, verbal), which the system uses as an item number; IRT item parameters for the item, used in the item selection process, are entered alongside the *a*, *b*, and *c*; and the keyed (correct) response alternative is specified. The system also allows several display options; a preitem and postitem can be specified (by number)—these may be special instructions to the examinee for that item or may pertain to what to do next. The screen may be cleared before an item is administered, or left intact if the test developer wants to overlay this item on a previous item. A response may be accepted if the screen is a test item or rejected if the screen is an instruction to the examinee. Two timing options are available: the screen may be displayed for a specific time before the examinee can respond, or a maximum number of seconds can be specified in which the individual may respond. The "one-key" option determines whether the examinee will be required to press the "return" key after responding to an item or whether the computer should accept the response as soon as it is typed. Other options control other aspects of the display.

The item text screen is shown in figure 16.6. The text portion of the screen is entered directly from the keyboard, using the special text editor that is incorporated into the system. The graphics portion of the item is created with the special graphics commands that outline the screen (which, of course, are not displayed as part of the item during administration). These commands are initiated either with a mouse or using the keyboard. Primitive drawing commands include arcs (ARC), boxes (BOX), circles (CIR), ellipses (ELL), and lines (LIN). To initiate these commands once they are selected, the user indicates a starting and an ending point, and the graphics editor completes the specified drawing. Freehand drawing is also possible with the DRA command. Color can be specified by appropriate use of the palette (PAL) and color (COL) commands and the background (BGD) command that changes the background color. Complete graphics images can be created in segments (SEG) for repetitive use. The remaining commands are utility commands for deleting, erasing, and so forth.

Once an item is created, it can be randomly accessed by the test developer simply by entering its unique item number. The item characteristics screen is displayed and item parameters or other characteristics can be edited; the item text screen can then also be examined and edited, as desired. To use an item in a test, the test creator simply creates a file of test item numbers, and the system accesses and displays the item text, using the item parameters and control specifications entered into the item characteristics screen.

ESTIMATING IRT ITEM PARAMETERS

The MicroCAT system can be used to estimate IRT item parameters either from paper-and-pencil test data entered as a file or under control of an interactive test especially designed to collect data for item-calibration purposes. In the latter case, the procedure is simplified, resulting in less file manipulation for input to the item-calibration program. Classical test theory item analyses are also supported by the system.

IRT item parameters may be estimated using either the three-parameter logistic model (program ASCAL) or the one-parameter logistic (Rasch) model (program RASCAL). ASCAL uses a combined Bayesian and maximum likelihood method, applying prior distributions to the likelihood functions of both the item parameters and the examinee abilities. A normal prior distribution of ability is used in conjunction with beta prior distributions (see Lindgren, 1976) for the *a* (discrimination) and *c* (guessing) parameters. All three parameters are bounded to provide realistic ranges of parameter estimates. A Pearson chi-square goodness-of-fit test is provided for each item.

Data comparing ASCAL with LOGIST (Wingersky, Barton, and Lord, 1982) indicate that ASCAL's parameter estimates compare well with those produced by LOGIST (Vale and Gialluca, 1985). In their study, Vale and Gialluca compared ASCAL and LOGIST on three simulated examinations. They found that, when compared in terms of the quality-of-ability estimation that the parameter estimates allowed, ASCAL and LOGIST were essentially equivalent. On an IBM AT computer with a numeric coprocessor, ASCAL can estimate IRT parameters for the three-parameter model in under two hours, given a test containing fifty items administered to one thousand examinees.

IMPLEMENTING AN ADAPTIVE TESTING STRATEGY

The MicroCAT system includes a number of predefined adaptive testing strategies that are accessed by "templates" provided with the system. These templates allow the user to implement an adaptive test simply by answering a few questions.

Figure 16.7 is an example of the template provided for the maximum-information adaptive test using a minimum-standard-error termination criterion (that is, a test designed for equiprecise measurement). To implement this adaptive test, the user is asked to provide (1) a name by which the test is to be referenced for later use in test administration; (2) the minimum variance (squared standard error) test termination criterion; (3) a minimum number of items to be administered (if the test administrator desires to specify some minimum number); (4) a maximum number of items, in the event that the variance termination criterion is not reached in a reasonable number of items; and (5) a list of items from the item bank that constitute the item pool to be searched during test administration (the list can be a previously prepared file, in which case only the file name is provided).

Several additional templates are currently provided with the system. Three conventional (that is, nonadaptive) tests include a standard fixed-length conventional test, a fixed-length conventional test designed to output data for the

```
                    Template MAXINF

The maximum information test selects items to provide maximum
statistical information, as each item is administered.  Responses
are scored using the maximum likelihood algorithm.  To complete
this template, you will need to specify a test name, a level of error
variance for terminating the test, a minimum number of items to
administer, and a maximum number of items to administer.

Enter a name for the test (ten or fewer characters).

? DemoTest

At what variance should testing terminate?

? 0.1

What is the minimum number of items that should be administered
before testing is allowed to terminate?

? 10

What is the maximum number of items that should be administered
before stopping the test (even if the variance is not small enough)?

? 30

Now enter the items you want to include, one per line, when you
see the # sign.  When you have entered them all, press the return
key without entering an item.

#Demo1
#Demo2
#Demo3
#Demo4
#Demo5
#

That completes specification of the test.  Remember that you need
to COMPILE the test before it can be administered.
```

Figure 16.7. Specifying a test using a template.

item-calibration program, and a variable-length conventional test with Bayesian scoring. Additional adaptive tests include a Bayesian adaptive test and a stradaptive test (see Weiss, 1985).

For the sophisticated test developer, the system provides a complete test specification language, called MCATL. Using MCATL, various kinds of adaptive testing strategies can be designed by the user and saved as user-created templates; these can then be used by less-sophisticated test developers in the same manner as the standard templates. MCATL includes testing-oriented commands for selecting scoring methods (for example, number correct, Bayesian θ estimate, maximum-likelihood θ estimate, response time), terminating tests, saving scores, searching item pools using specified criteria, and other testing-oriented functions. These are combined with other standard logical and arithmetic operators to create a testing language that is powerful and easy to use. MCATL also provides the means for creating individualized interpreted score reports, using the clinician's own words and formatting them as desired.

Once a test is created, either through a template or MCATL, it is still one step from being ready to administer. The final step, compiling the test, ensures efficient and high-speed item presentation. In response to system menus, the user enters the command COMPILE, followed by the name of the test he or she wishes to compile. The compiler then processes the specification file. Errors are checked for, such as errors in MCATL specifications or items that do not exist. The compiler also draws and bit maps the graphics portion of each item so that the graphics will be displayed in a minimum amount of time. A successful compilation results in a test file that can be executed efficiently during test administration.

EVALUATING A TEST BEFORE IT IS ADMINISTERED

Tests designed for different purposes should have different psychometric characteristics. IRT allows the evaluation of test performance before a test is administered by the use of test information functions (Birnbaum, 1968), which are the sum of IIFs of all of the items in a test; or, in the case of CAT, subsets of items from the item pool that are optimal for a chosen level of ability. A test designed for equiprecise measurement should have a flat information function at a level that will provide the precision desired with a minimum number of items.

The MicroCAT Test Pre-Evaluation Program performs several analyses that permit evaluation of a test before it is administered. Using the IRT parameters entered on the item characteristics screen in conjunction with a test specification file, the program provides output of the type shown in figure 16.8. This includes the mean item parameters for the item file specified; estimated test reliability; expected information, the average amount of information that would be obtained in a population with a normal distribution of ability; average information (such as expected information but assuming a uniform distribution of ability); and plotted test information curves. Reliability and information are provided for the entire item pool and for adaptive tests that are one-fourth, one-half, and three-fourths as long as the full test, based on items providing maximum information at each level of θ. While a real CAT could not exactly match the performance of this ideal CAT, a good one will approximate these levels. Thus these data permit the test user to select appropriate test-length termination criteria for CAT, based on the inverse square-root relationship between test information and the standard error of the ability estimate.

ADMINISTERING THE ADAPTIVE TEST

After items have been created and calibrated, the testing strategy has been chosen, the test has been compiled, preevaluated, and any desired changes have been made, the test is ready for administration. The MicroCAT system is designed to administer a test or test battery to an individual. It includes a recovery facility to restart a test after an interruption (such as a power failure)

MicroCAT (tm) Pre-Evaluation Report for Test SAMPLE

Mean item parameters:
a = 1.286
b = 0.375
c = 0.178

Test characteristics:	Estimated Reliability	Expected Information	Average Information
All items (16 items)	0.791	4.050	3.342
Adaptive (12 items)	0.790	4.044	3.339
Adaptive (8 items)	0.786	3.927	3.255
Adaptive (4 items)	0.752	3.245	2.729

Test Information Curves
* All 16 items
o 12 item adaptive
+ 8 item adaptive
. 4 item adaptive

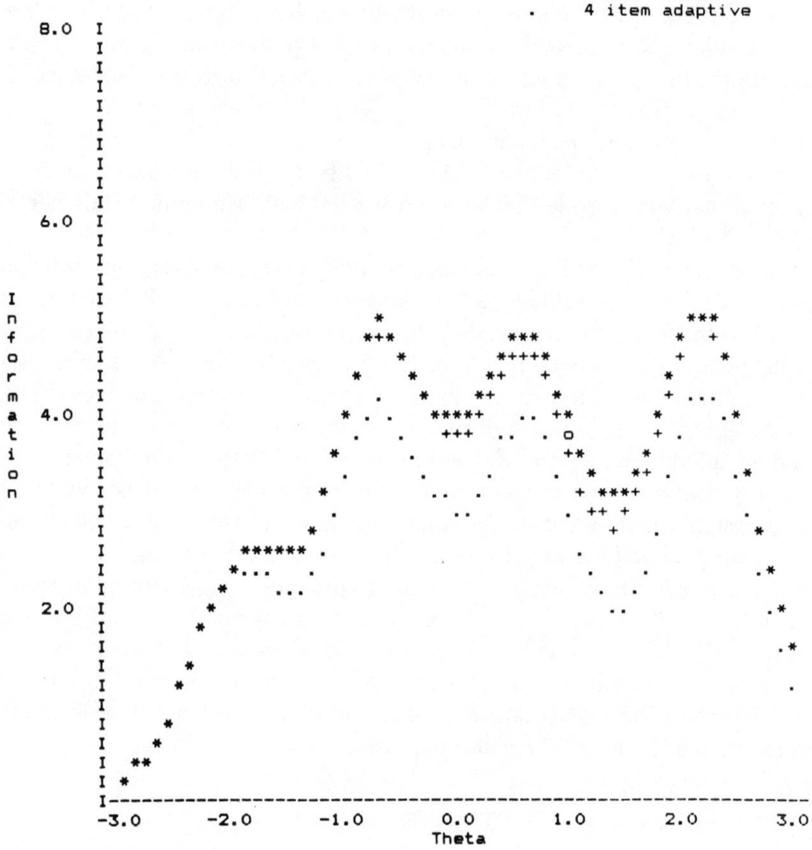

Figure 16.8. Output from the MicroCAT Test Pre-Evaluation Program.

without requiring the examinee to reanswer the items and allows proctored test administration using a local area network.

The test administration process is a nontrivial part of computerized testing. In a well-designed computerized test, examinees must learn how to use the keyboard to enter identification data, demographic data, and test responses. A good instructional sequence will permit examinees to practice entering various kinds of responses and will incorporate remedial sequences of screens for persons who are having problems. For examinees who continue to have problems, a proctor must be summoned.

The MicroCAT system includes a set of basic instructional screens designed to introduce the keyboard and to instruct examinees in communicating with the computer. These screens can be used as a sequence or can be interleaved with (or replaced by) any other screens that a test administrator wishes to design and use.

An important aspect of computerized test administration is its capability of checking responses to be sure that they are admissible. This results in a "clean" data file with no missing data or invalid responses. Response checking is automatic in the MicroCAT system; only responses within the range of specified alternatives are accepted. Response times are also kept and may be automatically recorded by the system when desired; response time limits can be imposed as specified for each item on the item characteristics screen.

An important advantage of computerized testing, of course, is that it is no longer necessary to enter item responses into a computer for data analyses—item responses and appropriate scores are recorded during the test administration process. By appropriate use of MCATL specifications, a formatted data file might include the responses chosen, the scored item response, response time, the IRT ability estimate, and the squared standard error of this estimate. These data files are produced in a format that allows their use directly in the test validation analysis program that is also a part of the MicroCAT system.

REPORTING AND INTERPRETING TEST SCORES

A major advantage of using microcomputers for test administration is the possibility of immediate scoring of tests and the capability of producing narrative reports for clinical use. In the MicroCAT system, tests are scored as they are administered. Consequently an examinee's test scores are accessible within seconds after a test or test battery is completed. To be useful to the practicing clinician, however, scores should be interpreted with respect to relevant norms and integrated into a clinical report that is easily understood and that highlights and integrates the results of each examinee's test performance. To be maximally useful, the clinician should be able to design the interpretive report to his or her specifications.

The MCATL test language provides the means for creating narrative reports of the type shown in figure 16.9. For producing interpretations, MCATL

Test interpretation for John Smith July 2, 1986

This examinee achieved a mathematical aptitude score of 2.235 on a standard score scale. This suggests that this examinee is quite capable in terms of mathematical aptitude and would probably excel in areas requiring mathematics (i.e., majors such as engineering, physics, mathematics).

The examinee's verbal aptitude score was only 0.120, however, an average score for people in the college norm group. This suggests that the examinee may have difficulty in a curriculum that requires great verbal facility (e.g., majors such as English literature and pre-law).

The overall score was 1.178, an above-average score for the college population. This suggests that the examinee has a good chance of succeeding with college coursework.

Figure 16.9. A sample test interpretation.

provides a logic-based language that permits the creation and implementation of statement libraries that can be integrated into a narrative report when specified test-score configurations are obtained. These statements can consist of sentences, paragraphs, or pages of text with locations specified for variable entries such as test-score values. The interpretive segments are selected by application of a series of logical rules implemented in MCATL (for example, "if Verbal is greater that 120, Performance less than 95, and Depression greater than 72 . . ."). The selected text segments are then concatenated and formatted for output to disk. Further editing may then be done before the interpreted report is printed. Use of the MCATL language to produce interpreted reports assures clinicians that the reports they prepare will be designed to be consistent with their approach to interpretation and use of psychological test data.

Conclusions

Adaptive testing has matured considerably since Alfred Binet first applied it to ability measurement. When combined with IRT and computer administration, adaptive testing provides a family of techniques that result in more efficient and effective solutions to a variety of measurement problems; it can be used to measure ability and achievement and other psychological variables in a variety of clinical, business, and educational environments. When implemented on a microcomputer, using software such as the MicroCAT testing system, CAT provides an increasingly cost-effective solution to a variety of testing functions. These include item banking, IRT item-parameter estimation, test preevaluation, test validation, test interpretation, and, of course, the efficient implementation of CAT for individual and group testing.

REFERENCES

Birnbaum, A. (1968). Some latent trait models and their use in inferring an examinee's ability. In F. M. Lord and M. R. Novick, *Statistical theories of mental test scores* (part 5, pp. 397–479). Reading, MA: Addison-Wesley.

Brown, J. M., and Weiss, D. J. (1977). *An adaptive testing strategy for achievement test batteries* (Research Report No. 77-6). Minneapolis, MN: University of Minnesota, Department of Psychology, Psychometric Methods Program.

DuBois, P. H. (1970). *A history of psychological testing*. Boston: Allyn & Bacon.

Hambleton, R. K., and Swaminathan, H. (1985). *Item response theory: Principles and applications*. Boston: Kluwer-Nijhoff.

Kiely, G. L., Zara, A. R., and Weiss, D. J. (1983, January). *Alternate forms reliability and concurrent validity of adaptive and conventional tests with military recruits*. Draft report submitted to Navy Personnel Research and Development Center, San Diego.

Kingsbury, G. G., and Weiss, D. J. (1983). A comparison of IRT-based adaptive mastery testing and a sequential mastery testing procedure. In D. J. Weiss (Ed.), *New horizons in testing: Latent trait test theory and computerized adaptive testing* (pp. 257–283). New York: Academic Press.

Lindgren, B. W. (1976). *Statistical theory*. New York: Macmillan.

Lord, F. M. (1980). *Applications of item response theory to practical testing problems*. Hillsdale, NJ: Lawrence Erlbaum.

McBride, J. R., and Martin, J. T. (1983). Reliability and validity of adaptive ability tests in a military setting. In D. J. Weiss (Ed.), *New horizons in testing: Latent trait test theory and computerized adaptive testing* (pp. 223–236). New York: Academic Press.

Moreno, K. E., Wetzel, C. D., McBride, J. R., and Weiss, D. J. (1984). Relationship between corresponding Armed Services Vocational Aptitude Battery (ASVAB) and computerized adaptive testing (CAT) subtests. *Applied Psychological Measurement*, 8, 155–163.

Vale, C. D. (1980). *Development and evaluation of an adaptive testing strategy for use in multidimensional interest assessment*. Unpublished doctoral dissertation, University of Minnesota, Minneapolis.

Vale, C. D., and Gialluca, K. A. (1985). *ASCAL: A microcomputer program for estimating logistic IRT item parameters* (ASC-85-4). St. Paul, MN: Assessment Systems Corporation.

Weiss, D. J. (1974). *Strategies of adaptive ability measurement* (Research Report No. 74-5). Minneapolis, MN: University of Minnesota, Department of Psychology, Psychometrics Methods Program.

Weiss, D. J. (1982). Improving measurement quality and efficiency with adaptive testing. *Applied Psychological Measurement*, 6, 473–492.

Weiss, D. J. (1985). Adaptive testing by computer. *Journal of Consulting and Clinical Psychology*, 53, 774–789.

Weiss, D. J., and Betz, N. E. (1973). *Ability measurement: Conventional or adaptive?* (Research Report 73-1). Minneapolis, MN: University of Minnesota, Department of Psychology, Psychometrics Methods Program.

Weiss, D. J., and Kingsbury, G. G. (1984). Application of computerized adaptive testing to educational problems. *Journal of Educational Measurement*, 21, 361–375.

Wingersky, M. S., Barton, M. A., and Lord, F. M. (1982). *LOGIST user's guide*. Princeton, NJ: Educational Testing Service.

Wright, B. D., and Stone, M. H. (1979). *Best test design: Rasch measurement*. Chicago: MESA Press.

17

Computers in Neuropsychology

Charles J. Golden

The use of computers in neuropsychology remains at present more of a promise than a reality. Thus while we can review some of the early work in this area, we must still talk more about what we are likely to be doing than what we have accomplished. Despite this, it is clear that computers will play an increasingly large role in the field over the next decade.

The areas that are most likely to benefit from computers fall into several categories: (1) test scoring, (2) test interpretation, (3) test administration, and (4) rehabilitation tasks. While there is some overlap among these categories, each shall be considered separately.

Test Scoring

Test scoring by computer is common in psychology, especially in complex true-false or multiple-choice tests such as the Strong Campbell or the Minnesota Multiphasic Personality Inventory (MMPI). However, there is considerably less use of such approaches in neuropsychology. There are a variety of reasons for this. First, most neuropsychological tests are quite simple to score. Few tests require anything other than simple counting skills. Few tests employ a multiple-choice or true-false format, formats that lend themselves to computer scoring. In most tests, scorers simply count a basic number of errors or correct responses or record a time. Computers are useless in such cases.

The scoring of many neuropsychological tests requires judgment, such as judging adequate answers in an expressive speech task or smoothness of performance in a motor task. Tests may require free recall of lists or generation of new words. In other cases scoring is simpler, but in most it is as easy for the examiner to do the scoring as it is to punch the information into a computer.

In most neuropsychological tests there are few corrections provided for such factors as age, education, IQ, social factors, response bias, lying, faking bad, or other dimensions in which corrections are made in other tests. This is not to say that such corrections are unnecessary in neuropsychology but rather that such corrections are available for only a small handful of tests. When they are available, again such corrections are generally simple and require little help from a computer. In contrast, other instruments, such as the Millon Personality tests, require complex weightings, computations, and corrections before base-rate scores can be determined.

When looking at tests designed primarily for neuropsychological use, there is one major exception to these ideas: the Luria-Nebraska Neuropsychological Battery, designed initially by this author and his associates (Golden et al., 1985). The LNNB, as it is commonly called, differs from the tests just described in that it uses a series of 279 item scores (which are scored by hand) that are combined into over fifty scale scores. Indeed, the test is set up so that a wide variety of scale scores can be derived from different combinations of the basic item set, much the same as with the MMPI. The scoring of this wide range of scales, along with basic corrections for age and education, can take up to two hours by hand.

A scoring version for the LNNB for microcomputers published by Western Psychological Services (WPS) can complete the scoring in less than thirty minutes. Users of the test may also send in to WPS optical scanning sheets with the basic answers from which the full-scale complement can be calculated. The computer program also provides calculations on which scales differ significantly from one another, the probability that there may be brain damage, and other basic statistical data that would take many additional hours of either calculation or table reference. Users of Form II of the LNNB are provided with regression-based data that allows them to compare directly to Form I test scores.

The future of computers in the scoring area is not yet clear. As noted, most popular tests simply do not need computer-assisted scoring at this time. Nor is it likely that these tests will need such help in the future. If more tests designed like the LNNB come along, then programs are likely to be needed for them, but I foresee no overwhelming trend in this direction.

However, another scoring area may indeed have a future if someone enterprising enough comes along and creates the data needed to develop the program. Help is needed in the comparison of scores across tests. For most people in neuropsychology today, it is generally accepted that an adequate patient evaluation consists of a series of tests that measure all the different aspects of neuropsychological performance, such as motor skills, auditory skills (verbal and nonverbal), visual skills (verbal and nonverbal), somatosensory skills, receptive and expressive language skills, reading, writing, arithmetic, memory (both verbal and nonverbal, long and short term, with and without interference), and intellectual skills in addition to noncognitive personality variables.

The difficulty with such massive evaluations is that they generally employ a wide range of tests normed on different populations, using different methods of reporting scores, having different intercorrelations and reliabilities, and generally presenting a plethora of statistical attributes. Despite these wide differences between the tests, it is the goal of neuropsychologists to compare the scores from different tests and to decide which tests are better, worse, comparable, severely apart, and so on. This is generally done more by ignoring the statistical issues than by confronting them. Decisions are made not on a scientific basis but rather on some intuitive basis unique to each clinician, a method by which even the basic statistical facts may contradict each other.

A properly researched and developed computer system could generate from the scoring system of each test a standard common score, compare those scores based on the known qualities of each test and their interactions, and present profiles and ranges of performance differences solidly grounded in the statistical facts known about a test. Such an approach would yield much more consistent evaluations across laboratories and clinicians and advance the use of this wide variety of tests in a more scientific manner.

There have been one or two small attempts in this direction. For example, in the early 1970s Russell, Neuringer, and Goldstein (1970) attempted to solve such problems in the group of tests called the Halstead-Reitan Battery. Although this test battery was designed to be given as a whole, the tests themselves used widely varying scoring systems and normative populations and there was little standardization in how scores could be compared with one another, save a classification of each score as brain-damaged or normal. This latter served basically as the one method for interpreting the pattern of test scores.

Russell, Neuringer, and Goldstein introduced a scoring program written by Carolyn Shelley that classified each score on the test as to degree of severity, ranging from a score of 0 (very normal) to 4 (very impaired). This introduced a new and more effective level of comparison of the test scores and has proven to be quite popular. This program marked the first use of score patterning in neuropsychological computer evaluation.

The program used norms based on clinical rather than statistical evidence to assign score severities, a fact that can be criticized by those wishing a more quantitative statistical approach. I do not know how closely a statistical approach would match the clinical severity scores yielded by the program. Nevertheless, the basic ideas behind the program offer a good beginning for future approaches.

At present, the type of program I envision could not be developed for all tests; yet a large number of tests could be compared. For example, there have been several studies comparing the Luria-Nebraska, Halstead-Reitan, and Wechsler Adult Intelligence Scale; a program could be designed to compare an individual's results on these tests. Since these are some of the most frequently used tests in clinical and forensic situations, such a program could prove very valuable as well as a prototype for future programs.

Test Interpretation

It has clearly been a dream of psychologists to develop a computer program that would be able to take raw data and generate psychological reports that would write themselves. (Why psychologists are so eager for such programs is not clear. If the tests could be interpreted by computers, it is obvious that there would be a much smaller need for psychologists.) Again, the first major attempt to do this was seen in the Shelley program presented by Russell, Neuringer, and Goldstein (1970). The original implementation of this program was for the huge mainframe machines of the early 1970s (written in FORTRAN). Over the years it has proven to be so popular that it has been adapted for a wide variety of mini- and microcomputers, including the Apple II series and the IBM 8088–compatible machines.

As mentioned, the Shelley program is essentially a modest one that attempts to classify patients as brain damaged or normal. If the patient is brain damaged, the program attempts to answer two questions: where is the location of the damage (left, right, or bilateral) and is the damage acute or chronic? The program does this by examining a series of decision rules that rate the likelihood of each of these possibilities. The program reports whatever possibility is seen as the most likely (with no estimate of the confidence in the decision), and reports the scale scores for each test (on a 0-to-4 score as described earlier) and the basic conclusions it has reached.

Heaton, Grant, Anthony, and Lehmen (1981) provided an experimental analysis of the Shelley program along with an analysis of several other programs developed to do the same thing with the Halstead-Reitan. These programs differed in the complexity and type of approach used to make the decisions, generally employing more complex regression techniques theoretically better suited for the simultaneous analysis of multiple variables. In general, the results were disappointing. While computer rules were reasonably able to predict the presence or absence of brain damage, the programs were unable to reach adequate levels of accuracy in answering the other questions. Similar results have been found with programs designed to predict such dimensions from other test batteries, such as the LNNB.

The question we are faced with is why these programs have been generally disappointing. There are several possible explanations, the most obvious being that the programs themselves are defective or based on inadequate data gathering. In my opinion, this probably is not the answer, however. Several of the programs are sophisticated and reasonable. It is unlikely that the current problems will be solved merely with better implementations of those approaches that have already been employed.

A more likely explanation lies in the very nature of what neuropsychology attempts to predict. Unlike programs aimed at personality interpretation, neuropsychology interpretation programs have concentrated on producing not descriptions of the patient's difficulties but rather predictions to extremely concrete and testable pieces of data, such as the location of a lesion. The problem is that so many variables influence test scores, including present age, age of onset, sex, prior learning, current learning, rehabilitation, nature of the injury, age of the injury, cultural background, education, personal interests, motivation to recover, personality (before and after), neurological recovery and treatment, status of the rest of the brain, the manner of testing, and other medical complications. With only a little effort this list could be greatly expanded.

What this means is that any program working with a limited number of test variables has very little chance of predicting the increasingly sophisticated physiological dimensions we are not able to measure by computerized tomography, positron emission tomography, magnetic imaging, regional cerebral blood flow, and the other new electrophysiological and neuroradiographic techniques. Does this mean that the use of computers in neuropsychological testing is unlikely to be worthwhile?

I do not believe that this is the case. However, there is a clear need for these programs to take a new direction. First, there should be an emphasis not on localizing brain lesions but rather on describing the problems the patients have. One concern in this alternate approach is that elevations on individual neuropsychological tests may be caused by a variety of factors. For example, a patient may do poorly on the Halstead Category Test because she has a frontal lesion, but also because she fails to comprehend or retain instructions or is so easily frustrated as to be unable to handle negative feedback. Visual problems can cause impairment in scores, as can problems with simple counting.

As a result, there is a need to interpret *patterns* of test scores rather than single test scores. Such patterns can be identified not only among tests but within items on the test as well. The patient with difficulties in the first sixty Category Test items is very different from the patient who breezes through these items but shows difficulty with the last twenty items. Intratest analysis can yield a wealth of data that is lost in current techniques focusing on total scores.

Qualitative observations also help intra- and intertest comparisons. Qualitative observations present data on why a patient performed in a certain way on a certain item. For example, on the Benton Visual Retention Test answers can be scored not only right or wrong but also for the type of error within a limited number of categories. Computers are well adapted to integrating this information.

Indeed, small lap computers can easily be used as data-gathering terminals as a test is in progress. Basic scores (right/wrong or time, as appropriate) could be typed in along with a limited number of qualitative observations as they occur. The computer could then integrate this information with the objective score. This combination of information could be used to generate much more sophisticated reports that combine clinical observations with objective scientific data. Moreover, such a technique would relieve the clinician of the need to take notes on or remember all the individual behaviors of the patient and the reliance on global impressions, which are easily biased by personal conclusions. Frequency data could be generated that would allow for a statistical analysis of the clinical qualitative data, moving things forward to a more scientific footing.

Such programs could employ combinations of rule-based interpretations along with statistical predictions based on more complex data relationships and an integration of the qualitative and quantitative data. The sophistication and preciseness of the results would depend mostly on the compulsiveness and accuracy of the programmer; refinements would bring about increasingly precise interpretations.

In addition to generating more complex descriptive data, computers could be used to suggest possible rehabilitation approaches and the likelihood of success. Programs could also approach the issue of "diagnosis." However, the field would benefit if most such statements were associated with clear statements that gave the relative probabilities of different outcomes given the data available, instead of giving a final answer. Further, demographic and personal variables could also be considered in discussing the likelihood of any conclusion.

At present no available software even approaches this level of sophistication. However, currently available software and hardware are sophisticated enough for such a project to be developed. What is missing at present is an adequate data base on which to base a program. Such attempts—whether successful or not—should have a profound effect on the development of the field.

Test Administration

Test administration represents another area whose potential has barely been touched. I should state at the outset that for several reasons I do not believe an adequate neuropsychological test will be developed that will be administered solely by computer. First, neuropsychological patients as a group have substantial problems with persisting in tasks and following directions. Unless such individuals are properly guided, their test results will not be comparable to those obtained in individual test administration.

Second, as suggested in the last section, qualitative observations are an important aspect of all scoring and interpretation. At this time such observations are not adequately made by computer. Computers are unable to tell different types of receptive and expressive language deficits by listening to patients, or to decide whether a patient has given a satisfactory explanation for a parable or a joke. Thus the area likely to show growth is not computer testing but rather computer-*assisted* testing.

The first major attempt at a computer-administered neuropsychological system was the various forms of the SAINT program put together by Swiercinsky (1983) for Compu-Psych, Inc., a company now owned by National Computer

Systems (NCS) in Minneapolis. The SAINT is a set of ten tests that are intended to form a comprehensive, computer-administered neuropsychological test battery. The SAINT shows some of the ways in which a computer can be adapted to do neuropsychological testing.

The first tests are a form of the Trail Making Test (which requires connecting numbered dots or connecting alternating numbered and lettered dots) where the test form is put on the computer screen and the drawing is done by use of a joystick rather than a pencil. The third test is a multiple-choice vocabulary test in which subjects type the identification of the chosen alternative. The fourth test is a finger-tapping device that plugs into the computer and measures tapping speed within ten-second intervals. The fifth test is a right-left orientation task in which subjects must say whether a pictured person holds an object in the right or left hand. Another test requires completion of sequences such as those found on the Shipley-Hartford Scale for Living. The next subtest uses the computer speaker to present pairs of beep sequences that must be compared as same or different. The symbol association subtest requires subjects to match a number to a nonsense figure, the opposite of the Digit Symbol Test where one must associate the shape to the number. In this case the number is typed in response to the symbol. At the end of the test, there is a recall section for incidental memory in which subjects must identify the nine figures used out of a sample of fifteen suggested figures.

The ninth subtest presents two stories by tape recorder. Subjects must then type in the answers to questions about the story asked by the computer. This is a variation of the free-style recall used by the Wechsler Memory Scale. The last subtest is a visual figural memory. Subjects are shown a series of eight two-dimensional figures. After each figure is presented, subjects must choose it from a group of figures that are shown after it.

Although the SAINT must be regarded as a milestone, much can be learned from its faults. First, it is written only for the Psychometer 300-A, a proprietary computer not in general use. In most cases today such programs are written for general-purpose computers, such as the Apple Macintosh or one of the IBM PCs. This is much more useful for the consumer since these computers can be used for other purposes and, as mass-market computers, are generally cheaper than dedicated machines that do not have a general market.

In addition, there is a great deal of compromise in the test. While subtests are similar to those found in the field, there have been substitutions: multiple choice for free recall, recognition instead of memory, joysticks instead of pencils, and so on. In the interpretive part of the program—and among test users I have run across in my work—there is an unfortunate tendency to regard these tests as generally equivalent to their paper-and-pencil counterparts. Such assumptions of equivalency are dangerous and very likely to be wrong. Tests must be studied thoroughly from a research perspective before any equivalency claims are made, and this generally is not done.

It would be much better if the tests were to have exact paper-and-pencil equivalences rather than approximate ones, both for research purposes as well as for instances when the computer version cannot be given either because of the logistics involved or because of computer malfunction. As these tests stand now, data on standardization, norms, validity, and reliability are clearly inadequate.

Finally, the SAINT currently does not have the scoring flexibility that the human scorer has. The biggest example of this can be seen in the verbal memory section, where subjects must answer questions from the computer. While acceptable misspellings and variations of answers have been programmed in, in actual practice patients can come up with many more variations that would be acceptable to a human examiner but not to the computer. While warnings for such circumstances can be included in the manual, users tend to ignore such things unless forced to attend to them.

One approach to handling such a problem would be to include as correct and incorrect answers as many examples as possible requiring not a perfect match but some high level of concurrence of characters or character strings. For example, if we ask who was the primary character in a story, the computer might look for a key word "Mary," "Mari," "Marie," "Merry," and so on. It would accept as accurate such sentences as "Mary was the primary character," "The primary character was Merry," "Mari," "The best character was Mary," and so on. Names of other characters in the story would be rejected as wrong, as would inclusion of more than one name from the story. All other responses would be referred to the examiner at the end of the test before any scoring was done, thus making it impossible for the psychologist to ignore the variations and ensuring a maximum amount of flexibility.

While today's artificial intelligence may not be intelligent, it has developed to the point where it can accept and analyze much more complex sentences and paragraphs, allowing patients much more free expression and providing a more sophisticated analysis of such material.

Thus, while the SAINT system was a landmark in its time, it can no longer be considered acceptable for use because of the lack of adequate data on accuracy and equivalence as well as its failure to take advantage of current computer programming techniques. This illustrates another pitfall in neuropsychology: a program that is written today must be consistently rewritten and updated to stay abreast of the latest advances, especially since many of our earlier compromises were based on computer limitations rather than the limitations of our needs and ideas.

Perhaps the most ambitious computer-aided testing program is the Nebraska Neuropsychological Examination (NENE) currently being developed (by the author and others). This test is an attempt to integrate the better aspects and advantages of the SAINT with more detailed tests and with the better computer equipment now available. The NENE is intended to be presented primarily by computer, with the computer controlling presentations of most materials, including timing and item sequence. Using the latest in graphics, storage, and memory processes, a computer can be used to quickly and efficiently present items of all kinds. The test consists of a wide range of items appropriate for ages three to ninety-nine. The computer selects a subset of the items based on an individual's performance so that all items need not be given to all patients. This allows for an examination that is comprehensive but is able to skip over areas in which detailed testing is not necessary due to either excellent or poor performance.

The computer is also capable of such functions as direct timing of motor tapping speed, measuring the speed of tapping on the keyboard while allowing the examiner's input of qualitative observations as they occur, as well as making a permanent record of the patient's performance. Screen graphics are used that allow material to be enlarged when necessary for patients with poor eyesight. Computers can produce a variety of sounds at different intensities without distortion, unlike tapes and tape recorders. With the computer ensuring that presentation order and time are controlled, the examiner will be able to focus on both objective and qualitative scoring rather than the mechanical details of the examination.

The computer can also examine trends in the patient's answers over time for fatigue effects. Examinations can be stopped at any point and then picked up at exactly that point or elsewhere as necessary. Parts of the exam can be repeated and compared when necessary, and complex scoring combinations of items will be generated immediately at the end of testing. Quick tabulation of qualitative results by area will be available, as will preliminary interpretation of the results by ability area. The program will ensure that all basic demographic information is filled in or at least considered. Because of the efficiency of the examination process, testing time should be reduced. Computer use also appears to encourage patient cooperation and interest, especially for children, where motivation is such a big issue. For patients who have a fear of the computer or other interfering processes, there will be a regular card version of the test as well.

Another advantage of computer administration is in the ability to collect data and have the computer keep track of the system's diagnostic effectiveness. By updating final diagnosis or outcomes as they become available, the system's efficiency can be monitored and statistics made available quickly. This will make it difficult to avoid research and should encourage clinicians to be more aware of what they are doing. Such chores as documentation, report writing, billing, and other functions can be made much easier.

This version of the NENE will not take advantage of several currently available computer applications. The addition of a drawing board could allow the computer to administer and score drawings very precisely. Other equipment could allow a wider range of motor abilities to be directly computer administered. Addition of some sensors could monitor eye movement, which gives insight to certain types of visual disorders, while monitoring could also be done of specific motor group responses. The possibilities are limited only by hardware and the degree to which workers wish to get involved.

Of all the categories discussed thus far, it is likely that test administration will be affected more than any other area. As the technology develops, eventually test administration should be revolutionized.

Rehabilitation

Rehabilitation programs have appeared in greater numbers than programs in the three other areas we have discussed. Unfortunately, such programs are much harder to judge. As a rule there is little or no data available on the efficacy of the programs other than anecdotal reports and what amount to personal endorsements. There have been no comparison studies between such programs and other techniques, nor have there been good outcome studies on whether these programs produce what they promise. Nonetheless such programs have proliferated in rehabilitation hospitals and private offices, with charges for sittingwith the computer often equaling or even exceeding the cost of a private therapist.

While there can be no doubt about the programs' economic success, their efficacy and in many cases their purpose can be questioned. On the most basic level, many programs are slow or carelessly written, containing bugs that are easily accessed by those of us skilled at messing up anything that doesn't work properly. Some rather expensive software simply refuses to work after a certain point (without starting over) and other software does not appear to do what it claims to do. One fascinating program takes patients over eight hours to get through, but the program does not allow you to stop and restart at the same place: you always have to go back to the start, a frustrating waste of the patient's time and money.

There are other concerns with what the programs really do: Are they teaching patients specific cognitive skills useful outside the hospital, or simply teaching patients to play computer games that have nothing to do with the outside world? Are they merely expensive baby-sitters for patients while they recover on their own? Do the programs improve rehabilitation by giving patients something fun and relatively nonjudgmental? Are they just teaching attention rather than specific cognitive skills?

Rehabilitation programs are unquestionably being misused. They are used in lieu of a trained neuropsychologist or by individuals with no real understanding of brain functions who feel the program makes them instant rehabilitation specialists. Strong ethical questions arise when patients are made to pay for essentially experimental techniques without being notified and told of alternative approaches available. (It can also be argued that no rehabilitation techniques are really proven, so that such an issue is really irrelevant.) A related concern is whether the allure and ease of the programs are denying patients both better evaluations and more realistic and useful experiences. The tendency toward use of personal endorsements also raises what could be serious ethical issues.

On the more positive side, computers do seem to increase motivation in a number of patients (though clearly not in all patients). Generally patients who are more intact initially seem to do better, but these are the patients who do better under any conditions. The computer also has the advantage of being tireless, willing to repeat a lesson long after a human therapist may have given up. (This, however, also raises the question of whether repetition simply promotes rote memorization of a specific task rather than the more general cognitive skill that is intended by most software claims.)

It is clear that this section has a largely negative tone. This may arise from the fact that computers in rehabilitation seem to have become more of a fad, like the latest psychotherapeutic techniques that are "in" one moment and "out" the next. Unlike the more careful introduction of neuropsychological software in the other areas already discussed, in the area of rehabilitation there has been more of an outpouring of unproven material that has been accepted for the most part uncritically by many user institutions and individuals. It is likely that only after a shakeout and the end of computer rehabilitation as fad will we be able to see if anything really new and useful has been created.

At present serious users must be cautioned to institute the use of the new techniques slowly, excercising discretion in their selection of patients. Patient progress and the reasons for it should be followed very carefully. The need for research is undeniable. While I have seen some research results in my position as an editor and reviewer, so far none has met basic standards of research and interpretability.

Conclusions

In neuropsychology, computerized material is clearly at a much more primitive state than it is in fields such as personality assessment. Given the complexity of the brain and of neuropsychological assessment and rehabilitation, the potential advantages of computers are many. However, they will be realized only when the programs for interpretation and assessment as well as the rehabilitation materials reflect an understanding and appreciation of this complexity. Work currently in progress is encouraging, and I expect that the next decade will see a quantum leap in the sophistication and usefulness of computerized material available in neuropsychology.

REFERENCES

Heaton, R. K., Grant, I., Anthony, W. Z., and Lehmen, R. A. (1981). A comparison of clinical and automatic interpretation of the Halstead-Reitan Battery. *Journal of Clinical Neuropsychology*, 3, 121–141.

Russell, E., Neuringer, C., and Goldstein, G. (1970). *Assessment of brain damage*. New York: Wiley.

Swiercinsky, D. P. (1983). *Users manual: SAINT-II system for the administration and interpretation of neuropsychological tests*. Liberty, MO: Compu-Psych.

18

Computerized Neuropsychological Assessment: Issues and Applications

Kenneth M. Adams and Robert K. Heaton

Introduction

This chapter provides an introduction to the current and potential uses of computers in the neuropsychological laboratory. Technical reviews are available for readers who seek more detailed information about the characteristics and performance of currently available computerized programs in neuropsychology (Adams and Heaton, 1985; Adams, Kvale, and Keegan, 1984). Four major types of computer applications are considered here: support of administrative functions in the running of a neuropsychological laboratory, test administration, intermediate analysis of test and clinical data, and diagnostic test interpretation. The discussion of these applications is followed by a brief presentation of some ethical issues and tentative guidelines for use of computers in this field.

Administrative Uses of the Computer

An important and currently practical use of computers in neuropsychology is in the management of patient services, communications, and data. Obvious examples involve word processing formats for various appointment and instruction letters, routine consent/request forms, master versions of test forms or norms for modification or reproduction, and stored/preset structures for the common elements of neuropsychological reports. Programs also exist for such functions as patient scheduling/follow-up, financial management, billing, supply management, and cost accounting.

Another readily attainable "administrative" role of computers in neuropsychological practices is in creating and maintaining an informational data base. This data base may include information concerning patient demographics, referral sources, historical data, criterion test results (for example, medical examinations or brain tests), neuropsychological results, and clinical outcome—as is shown in table 18.1. Such information can be of great value in documenting the sources of patients, their demographic and base-rate profiles, the relationship of neuropsychological tests to other results, and the impact of testing on patient outcome. Yet relatively few practitioners have used computers in this way.

Extra effort is often required to secure historical and collateral data points necessary to create such a patient data base. Outcome studies will also require

TABLE 18.1

A Simple Informational Data Base Record

Case #	*Date Referred*	*Referral Source Code*	*Address*	*Telephone*
	9-20-85	*36—Dr. Morton Neurology*	*18 Arrow Rd. Detroit, MI 48230*	*(666) 555-1423*
	Insurance Codes	Date Tested	Patient Birthdate	Patient Sex
	BC 43602215	10-2-85	1-1-49	Male
	Patient Age at Testing	Education in Years	Special Educational Codes	EEG Results
	36	12	None	Within normal limits
	CT Results	Drug Status	Sensory Loss	Date Admitted
	Within normal limits	No meds.	None	9-15-85
	Date Discharged	Patient Cooperation	Follow-up Plan	Outcome
	9-28-85	Good	Retest	Improved
	Global Impairment Rating	Date Rescheduled	Discharge Diagnosis 1	Discharge Diagnosis 2
	Peripheral Impairments	Neuropsychological Prognostic Rating	Employment Status at Disch.	Date Billed
	Billing Source	% Collected		

case research; for example, school grades or the results of a computed tomography study may have to be requested. It is also important that the data base include how long a patient remained in the hospital or how the testing was used in the care plan.

Such data are of importance in quality assurance, in evaluation research, and in demonstrating the positive contribution of the neuropsychological examination. External reviewers and third-party agencies are increasingly likely to ask that providers demonstrate the impact of examinations in terms of earlier diagnosis, reductions in hospital or clinic utilization, more appropriate care, and improved outcome. Computers can greatly facilitate the storage and retrieval of data relevant to such concerns.

For example, in the lab of one of the authors (KA), a retrospective study concerning the impact of neuropsychological testing on length of hospital stay in psychiatric and neurological services was completed using data that were routinely maintained in a computer data base. Sixty consecutive patients were selected from referral records from these services. In turn, these patients were matched for age, sex, education, and diagnosis with nonreferred consecutive patients who were utilizing these hospital services at the same time. Compared to the control cases, patients who were referred for neuropsychological assessment were hospitalized for an average of five fewer days ($p < 0.01$). Closer evaluation suggested that faster resolution of diagnostic questions and accurate identification of emotional concomitants of physical symptoms accounted for this finding.

No amount of professional insistence on freedom to practice will substitute for such data, given the current climate in health services delivery. Once this view is accepted, it follows that the optimal way to gain control of the quality and accuracy of such data is to implement one's own system to generate it.

In large institutions, the data base features illustrated in the table can be integrated with existing large-scale data systems for patient information. Indeed, some organizations are implementing fully automated patient tracking and medical record systems. Information can be requested from a centralized data base system and the practitioner's data added to create a regular report. These "standard" statistical reports can include such major variables as number of patients seen, their referral sources, diagnosis, and so forth. In practice, updated demographic and other data can be made available for administrative or research purposes under the neuropsychologist's quality-control direction. Finally, it should be noted that regular reports allow practitioners to identify trends emerging in their practices.

Even when organizational data base systems are not available or accessible, practitioners can still develop a data base capability. Microcomputers are relatively inexpensive and easy to use for such purposes. Moreover, an array of powerful relational data base programs are available for nearly every existing make of computer. These programs allow users to readily enter, transform, and retrieve patient data in a variety of ways. They may even allow practitioners more flexibility and control over data base implementation than is possible in larger organizational data bases.

A word of warning is in order here and will be repeated later in other contexts. The limiting factor in setting up microcomputer systems for practitioners is time. This may seem ironic, since one rationale for computer use is often thought to be time savings. In some laboratories, however, data base projects of the kind just described are undertaken without a realistic understanding of the time investment and discipline needed to make them successful. Psychologists creating their own data base systems should weigh the need for each data point in light of the time required to secure the information for each case and in terms of the general size and practical manageability of the completed system.

There are many possible variations on the administrative uses described earlier. Perhaps the best initial standards to apply in ways to improve neuropsychological lab administration with the computer are those suggested by the repetitiveness or reporting qualities inherent in a particular task. For example, typing the same patient appointment letter or generating the same patient contact statistics are perfect jobs for a computer.

Computerized Test Administration

Computerized administration of neuropsychological tests has been attempted with increasing frequency in recent years. Early schemes for automated testing in neuropsychology date back to the 1930s, when Ward Halstead (Halstead, Walker, and Bucy, 1940) devised a console for testing patients. Various devices were developed for cognitive, perceptual, and motor tests in the ensuing years, but their utility was constrained by the practical problems of mechanical reliability and capacity. In general, these types of electromechanical devices afford few practical advantages in the neuropsychology laboratory's human assessment tasks.

Despite the limited capabilities of early mechanized devices for neuropsychological test administration, the idea remained very much alive and was repeatedly revived and fostered as computers improved over the years. The reasons for continuing interest in computerized test administration—even in the face of less than full success—are important. Certain computer capabilities have been of obvious interest to those involved in neuropsychological assessment and remain so today. Three of these capabilities are particularly important: (1) The computer is able to select from a large library of stimuli, questions, tasks, and parameters, (2) the computer has extraordinary potential for measuring many small components of performance involving latency, force, and other qualities; and (3) the computer can reproduce patient responses, adaptively react to the rate and nature of patient responses, and introduce feedback.

COMPUTERS HAVE VAST STORAGE CAPACITY

Large numbers of items, tests, and problems can be stored for ready access on a computer disk, a fact that enables users to avoid the problem of storing a variety of physically separate test "kits" or materials in an office or testing suite. Thus replacement from loss occurs less frequently and financial savings may be realized.

In earlier technology, slides containing various questions and stimuli were stored on trays having potential "random access." Yet this setup was less than ideal, since slides tended to become lost and sometimes a person was needed to change slide trays during a test.

Today storage technology allows for complete retention and full reproduction of any conceivable stimulus in various modalities. This development, when coupled with truly rapid access from hard disks, makes any size ensemble of tasks, tests, or items feasible. Computers exceed the capacities of human examiners to learn a very wide range of test procedures and to retain such information and skills even if they are used infrequently. Also, computers may have an edge in the reliable adherence to standardized procedures for test administration and scoring.

COMPUTERS CAN MEASURE NUMEROUS COMPONENTS

With automation, measurement of response or reaction time is quite feasible. Moreover, microswitch systems can measure very short intervals (such as tapping alternations) not possible with manual instruments. Indeed, entire tests not feasible with manual administration (for example, continuous performance paradigms) can be deployed when computers are used. This rapidity of data acquisition becomes quite important in the study of phenomena where very short timing intervals (such as speed/accuracy trade-off measurement in reaction time experiments) or small mechanical force or consistency measurements (such as finger tapping force, motor steadiness) are desired.

COMPUTERS CAN REPRODUCE AND REACT TO RESPONSES

In some applications, it might be desirable to show the patient how "close" a verbal or visual-motor response might be to the ideal or desired result. With a verbal response, the patient's voice can be encoded via digital means and played back for comparison and even subsequent response and improvement. In a similar way, the computer can "show" the patient his or her drawings, pointings, or tracings with reference to an ideal. Feedback can be programmed in any number of ways.

The computer can directly monitor and change speed or timing of stimulus parameters of performance requirements. In the laboratory of one author (KA) the continuous performance paradigm in use is controlled by the computer so that the speed of stimuli presented "shadows" the patient's rate of responding over trials.

This computer monitoring and response is related to a more general strategy of "adaptive testing" being pursued by designers of computer assessment systems. In an adaptive testing mode, a computer selects and delivers tasks or tests to patients with emphasis on finding and challenging the patient's abilities in an efficient and flexible way. Computer programs, for example, seek correct basal and ceiling difficulty levels within given tests and even terminate testing when certain criteria are satisfied. In addition, these adaptive testing paradigms even select tests from a library to be used selectively to meet patient needs estimated from earlier test performance.

COMPUTER PERIPHERAL DEVICES CAN EXPAND TESTING POSSIBILITIES

More recently, the availability of microprocessors and microcomputers has spurred attempts to develop sophisticated neuropsychological measurement devices. In actuality, the many peripheral devices available "off the shelf" for microcomputers provide considerable potential for those seeking to automate their testing. Sophisticated graphics, voice synthesizers, graphics tablets, timers, and transducers of all types abound. These devices enhance data acquisition to extraordinary realms of precision and combine with software programs to constitute "automata" (Bavel, 1983).

Actually, "overacquisition" of data is becoming a real problem. The power of timers and transducers quickly leads psychologist-designers to try to capture everything. This can quickly lead to problems with storage of unmanageable numbers of data points and can slow analysis of the *essential* results.

On the other hand, the computer can simultaneously monitor patient responses in multiple dimensions when appropriate. A strategy long in use in electrophysiology has been to sample randomly and/or regularly some fraction or proportion of responses to get an estimate of the parameter being measured. For example, in studying finger tapping, the measurement of every fourth intertap interval might suffice if the patient is being asked to tap for a number of minutes in a muscle-fatigue study.

Potential Problems in the Patient–Machine Interface

The very ease with which computers can be obtained and placed in the assessment laboratory paradoxically poses a problem. Practitioners may assume that automating neuropsychological test procedures mainly involves obtaining correct computer instrumentation for test administration. Frequently, the practitioner's problem is not in the technology of the translation to automation but in the patient-machine interface. Several problems are ubiquitous:

1. Programs for testing currently do not make allowances for the patient with motor handicap, peripheral injury, sensory loss, or linguistic limitation. While each of these problems is potentially resolvable, the procedures required to adjust to such patient problems are bound to be very complex.
2. Programs for testing currently cannot adapt to the needs of the patient with fluctuating cooperation due to drug effects, variations in level of consciousness, fatigue, or resistance. Note carefully that this involves more than an occasional reminder on a screen that testing can be discontinued if the patient feels unwell. One test designer, happily not a psychologist, included a step to guard against such an event by having the question "Are you having a seizure?" appear on the screen.
3. Neuropsychological tests are difficult for some patients. Interpersonal support, structured encouragement, and the availability of human reassurance are vital. Patients being tested often become frustrated, and the management of this affect is a key task for the neuropsychological examiner (Heaton and Heaton, 1981). In some concept formation tasks, for example, patients have expressed the view that they are "being tricked."

   It is important to imagine how a patient is likely to receive a computer's video exhortations to WORK FASTER! or reassurances that THE CORRECT ANSWER IS ON THE SCREEN in the face of a recent unannounced conceptual shift.

We do not mean to suggest that automated test administration is not possible. Rather we maintain that it is unlikely that maximal rapport and maximal performance will be elicited by isolating the patient with a testing console—no matter how attractively designed. Since most neuropsychological inferences are based on the assumption that the patient's performance is a "best effort," no compromise in the patient's effort and compliance can be accepted. At present, technology for test administration has not yet met this need.

Despite these obstacles, computerized testing has a clear promise and allure for neuropsychologists. Only the hurried and unreflective deployment of automated procedures defeats the practitioner's objective and produces invalid results.

Intermediate (Nondiagnostic) Analysis of Clinical and Test Data by Computer

In neuropsychological applications, the analytic power of the computer has not been used to its potential. This potential includes detailed scoring, application of research scales or formulas, normative comparisons, and clinical pattern recognition.

Detailed scoring of neuropsychological tests is time-consuming. While some scoring or counting is often done by technical staff, many simple numerical and summary preparations can be done by the computer. Also, some higher-level evaluations (that is, scoring of drawings) could be done via computer if the original performance was done on a graphics tablet. The algorithms for scoring such patient work would probably use visual feature detection technology (Swets, Tanner, and Birdsall, 1961).

The computer's computational speed and power truly comes into play in the calculation of extra scoring steps, research scales, or special formulas. These calculations are cumbersome if not prohibitive when done manually by technical staff. Computer routines to do this extra scoring can produce for the clinician a "spreadsheet" of information that enhances interpretation and is impractical by manual means. In a recent review (Adams and Heaton, 1985), we have suggested that this informational spreadsheet represents the main contribution that automated neuropsychology test-interpretation programs make at this time.

An excellent example of how such scoring can work in practice can be seen in Delis's automated version of the California Verbal Learning Test (Delis, Kramer, Ober, and Kaplan, 1986). This program produces extensive information on a variety of aspects of memory performance. While some of these indices are held to be qualitative, their objectification is a step forward in demonstrating the validity of styles of patient performance in neuropsychological prediction.

In some areas of psychology the extra scoring of research or clinical indices is far more developed (for example, in the Minnesota Multiphasic Personality Inventory). In these applications, the computer can bring to bear in a practical way the great power of research on clinical problems. The only real risk in this kind of development is overabundance of information and spurious significance of small numbers of "deviant" findings amid huge numbers of possibilities.

Normative comparisons are among the most easy and valuable calculations possible for the computer. Comparison of patient data to previous testing results on the same patient, demographically similar patients, or diagnostically similar patients is possible and highly desirable.

In the future, the availability of improved normative information will make these comparisons a likely minimal standard for the use of neuropsychological tests. At the same time, it is important to note that exclusive reliance on "level of performance" in neuropsychological interpretation is not appropriate (Adams, 1986).

Finally, the comparison of a patient's data against a normative base can be paralleled by a pattern comparison of various normative bases against the patient's obtained data. That is, the computer can seek a "goodness of fit" between previously seen cases of various types and the obtained data for an individual patient currently under study.

This kind of search can be by cluster analysis–like algorithms, profile analysis (Knights, 1973), or simple multivariate goodness-of-fit procedures. To make such comparisons in a valid way, pattern-type searches should be constrained by demographics to encompass only appropriate parts of the total data base (for example, only adults or only those with less than twelve years of education).

Again, it would be wise to emphasize the just-noted cautions concerning overreliance on level-of-performance interpretations. The authoritative format of a computer program and the large amounts of data it can furnish have the potential to cloud the practitioner's perspective concerning the unidimensional nature and finite value of level-of-performance data.

Automated Interpretation

We have reviewed the theory, design, and performance of computer programs for neuropsychological test interpretation (Adams and Heaton, 1985). The "first generation" of such programs does not produce satisfactory results in clinical trials. While some of the programs show marginal superiority in one or another area of evaluation (Adams, Kvale, and Keegan, 1984), the overall conclusion is that the expert clinician is superior to these programs.

In an earlier debate on clinical versus statistical prediction, Meehl (1973) challenged expert clinicians who believed they could improve on rates of diagnostic accuracy achieved by formulas to "publish empirical studies filling in the score board with numbers more to their liking" (p. 173). In the initial work on neuropsychological interpretation, the results have provided an unintended, but powerful, demonstration of human superiority over computer algorithms.

It should be noted, though, that no available scheme for automated interpretation is truly actuarial, and further refinements in the first generation of programs may be possible and are certainly desirable. Progress may not be easy, because the tasks confronting designers of neuropsychological automata are complex and difficult. The problems to be solved involve more than the extraction of unidimensional diagnostic information from a profile to encompass a known taxonomy of psychological disorders (see Kleinmuntz, 1968). That is, the number of parameters to be weighed in defining the criteria for "brain damage" in such programs is large (see Adams and Heaton, 1985). These may include: (1) the presence or absence of neuropsychological dysfunction, (2) the localization or lateralization of such dysfunction, (3) the acuity or chronicity of brain-behavior problems, (4) a set of statements concerning possible etiologies of these problems, and (5) an estimate of prognosis for reversibility of impairment.

The prospects for future development of automated interpretation programs in neuropsychology are bright. The advent of "expert" system technology derived from the growing literature on artificial intelligence (AI) heralds what could be a new age of advances in creating computer programs. In addition, clinical neuropsychology as a discipline has grown sufficiently in recent years to have gained substantial information from which to fashion the knowledge base in which AI software can operate.

Ethics of Computerization

We have discussed the major applications of computer technology in neuropsychology. The alert practitioner cannot be unaware of the many specific ways in which computers stand to aid clinical neuropsychological assessment in these four areas.

At present, none of the technical areas of application (administration, scoring, numerical analysis, and interpretation) is fully functional. While clear ethical guidelines exist concerning security of patient data needed for use in the administrative realm, few computer testing guidelines are widely disseminated among practitioners. Standards for computerized tests and testing have been developed by the American Psychological Association (APA, 1986), and are reproduced in appendix B of this volume.

However, no guide or rulebook can prepare the practitioner for every situation, and some general suggestions might be of value in avoiding questionable practices:

1. Patients have an absolute right to refuse to be tested by machine or other proxy. Consent is needed and may be revoked at any time.
2. Patients must be made as comfortable as possible and must have reasonable control of the session in terms of breaks or rests.
3. Patients taking automated tests must be constantly and actively supervised and monitored. A qualified psychologist should be available at a moment's notice, if technical personnel are monitoring.
4. Automated tests, testing, and interpretation (reports) must be done under careful supervision and quality control of a qualified psychologist.
5. Portions of automated scoring reports may be integrated, in context, in a consultation report. However, no computer-printed report should go to an end user, referral source, or other consumer without full annotation and review by a qualified psychologist.
6. Use of automated tests, testing, or interpretation (reports) in practice must be supported by adequate evidence of validity and reliability. Results of automated procedures in research or pilot phases must be used with patient consent and must be kept conceptually and physically separate from clinical reports. As a general rule, research in automated procedures must encompass the usual principles of research practice in psychology (APA, 1982).

These suggestions are far from complete, but adherence to their spirit and letter is likely to aid the practitioner in avoiding problems of an ethical nature. In general, it is probably best to remember that using a computer for assessment tasks does not lessen the psychologist's responsibility for patients, data, and reporting.

In Closing

Neuropsychological assessment is a clinical enterprise requiring labor intensive investment in managing patient logistics as well as in data acquisition, data analysis, and reporting. Advances in computer technology have invited integration of the computer in every phase of practice. While initial efforts in these areas have not always met with complete success, there are reasons for optimism concerning the potential of further efforts to refine the interface between automation and neuropsychology.

REFERENCES

Adams, K. M. (1986). Concepts and methods in the design of automata for neuropsychological test interpretation. In S. B. Filskov and T. J. Boll, *Handbook of clinical neuropsychology, vol.* 2 (pp. 561–576). New York: Wiley-Interscience.

Adams, K. M., and Heaton, R. K. (1985). Automated interpretation of neuropsychological test data. *Journal of Consulting and Clinical Psychology*, 53, 790–802.

Adams, K. M., Kvale, V. I., and Keegan, J. F. (1984). Performance of three automated systems for neuropsychological interpretation based on two representative tasks. *Journal of Clinical Neuropsychology*, 6, 413–431.

American Psychological Association. (1982). *Ethical principles in the conduct of research with human participants*. Washington, DC: Author.

American Psychological Association. (1986). *Guidelines for computer-based tests and interpretations*. Washington, DC: Author.

Bavel, Z. (1983). *Introduction to the theory of automata*. Reston, VA: Reston Publishing.

Delis, D. C., Kramer, J., Ober, B. A., and Kaplan, E. (1986). *The California Verbal Learning Test*. New York: Psychological Corporation.

Halstead, W. C., Walker, A. E., and Bucy, P. C. (1940). Sparing and nonsparing of "macular" vision associated with occipital lobectomy in man. *Archives of Ophthalmology*, 24, 948–962.

Heaton, S., and Heaton, R. K. (1981). Testing the impaired patient. In S. B. Filskov and T. J. Boll (Eds.), *Handbook of clinical neuropsychology, vol.* 2 (pp. 526–544). New York: Wiley-Interscience.

Kleinmuntz, B. (Ed.). (1968). *Formal representation of human judgement*. New York: Wiley.

Knights, R. M. (1973). Problems in criteria in diagnosis: A profile similarity approach. *Annals of the New York Academy of Sciences*, 205, 124–131.

Meehl, P. E. (1973). *Psychodiagnosis: Selected papers*. Minneapolis, MN: University of Minnesota Press.

Swets, J. A., Tanner, W. P., and Birdsall, T. G. (1961). Decision processes in perception. *Psychological Review*, 68, 301–340.

Appendix A

Commercially Available Computerized Psychological Software and Services

This appendix contains an alphabetized listing of computer-based interpretation services and test-scoring and interpretation software. A wide range of products and services are described. Brief descriptions of the techniques are supplied along with addresses and phone numbers for obtaining further information.

The items listed represent a compilation of information from publishers and product advertisements. These products have *not* been evaluated, and no endorsement of their quality and coverage can be given. Further information about a particular technique can be found in the more comprehensive resource guide *Psychware: A Reference Guide to Computer-based Products for Behavioral Assessment in Psychology, Education, and Business* (Krug, 1984).

Activity Completion Technique—Computer Version
Type: Personality
Distributor: Multi-Health Systems, Inc.
10 Parfield Drive, Willowdale, Ontario M2J 1B9 Canada
(416)498-1200
Services: Microcomputer—IBM PC and Apple II and compatibles
Description: An administration and prompted-scoring program for the Activity Completion Technique, the revised form of the Sacks Sentence Completion Test.

Adjective Check List (ACL)
Type: Normal personality
Distributor: National Computer Systems
P.O. Box 1416, Minneapolis, MN 55440
(612)933-2800 and (800)328-6759
Services: Arion II teleprocessing, central scoring
Description: A standard tool used in assessing personal attributes through response to common adjectives as they are applied to self or others. It is helpful in identifying major personal needs and problems, setting therapy goals, and addressing issues of self-identity or identity within a group. The software provides a summary of adjectives endorsed.

Adjective Check List (ACL)
Type: Personality assessment and psychometric research
Distributor: Consulting Psychologists Press, Inc.
577 College Avenue, Palo Alto, CA 94306
(415)857-1444
Services: Mail-in scoring; microcomputer software
Description: Enables ACL users to administer, score, and report the results of the ACL on an IBM PC or PC-compatible. The ACL is a standardized 300-adjective list widely used in personality assessment and psychometric research. There is a per-use royalty fee for each administration. ACL Apple software is being developed.

Adult Career Concerns Inventory (ACCI)
Type: Measures Donald Super's theory of life stages
Distributor: Consulting Psychologists Press, Inc.
577 College Avenue, Palo Alto, CA 94306
(415)857-1444
Services: Microcomputer—IBM PC and compatibles (256K memory)
Description: Measures Super's theory of life stages. The stages are exploration, establishment, maintenance, disengagement, and a special scale on career change status. The ACCI is valuable in measuring the client's career stage and growth. Researchers may use it to see how an individual's life stages impact on productivity, creativity, turnover, and so on. The ACCI software administers, scores, and reports the results. There is a per-use royalty fee for each administration. ACCI Apple software is being developed.

Adult Diagnostic Screening Battery
Type: Interview
Distributor: Joseph Eisenberg, Ph.D.
204 East Joppa Road, Suite 10, Towson, MD 21204
(301)321-9101
Services: Microcomputer—Apple
Description: Designed to aid the clinician in arriving at a DSM-III diagnosis.

Patients and the clinician each fill out a questionnaire. Problem areas, as pointed out by clinician or patient, are noted on the printout.

Adult Personality Inventory (API)
Type: Personality
Distributor: Institute for Personality and Ability Testing, Inc.
P.O. Box 188, Champaign, IL 61820
(217)352-4739
Services: Mail-in; teleprocessing
Description: Measures individual differences in personality, interpersonal style, and career/lifestyle preferences. Designed to measure sixteen personality traits, the report transforms the psychometric profile into answers to the kinds of questions most frequently asked by personality test users: What is the person like? How does the person relate to others? What implications do these data hold for career decisions and life planning?

AIM (Aptitude Inventory Measurement)
Type: Vocational
Distributor: Intran Corporation
4555 West 77th Street, Minneapolis, MN 55435
(800)328-7930
Services: Mail-in
Description: The report combines information from the interest inventory and the GATB to help individuals learn about their abilities and career opportunities. Twelve interest areas related to career opportunities are included.

Alcohol Assessment and Treatment Profile (AATP)
Type: Intake
Distributor: Multi-Health Systems, Inc.
10 Parfield Drive, Willowdale, Ontario M2J 1B9 Canada
(416)498-1200
Services: Microcomputer—IBM PC and Apple II and compatibles
Description: A structured interview program that obtains comprehensive information about individuals with drinking problems.

Alcohol Troubled Person Questionnaire
Type: Interview
Distributor: Applied Innovations
South Kingston Office Park, Suite A-1, Wakefield, RI 02879
(800)272-2250
Services: Microcomputer—IBM PC and compatibles
Description: Assesses risk for alcohol problem behavior. Reports focus on several areas: emotional, social, financial, and physical.

Alcohol Use Questionnaire
Type: Interview
Distributor: Applied Innovations, Inc.
South Kingston Office Park, Suite A-1, Wakefield, RI 02879
(800)272-2250
Services: Microcomputer—IBM PC and compatibles
Description: This forty-item questionnaire addresses the extent of alcohol use. Medical and physical factors are included as well as current alcohol intake.

Aptitude Interest Measurement (AIM)
Type: Aptitude and interest
Distributor: National Computer Systems
P.O. Box 1416, Minneapolis, MN 55440
(612)933-2800 and (800)328-6759
Services: Mail-in scoring; profile and interpretive reports available
Description: Combines the GATB and the U.S. Employment Service Interest Inventory test results in a condensed, comprehensive, narrative report. Useful for vocational counseling, AIM provides an assessment describing occupations that match an individual's interests and skills.

Areas of Change Computer Program
Type: Assessment
Distributor: Multi-Health Systems, Inc.
10 Parfield Drive, Willowdale, Ontario M2J 1B9 Canada
(416)498-1200
Services: Microcomputer: IBM PC and Apple II and compatibles
Description: This computerized version of the Areas of Change Questionnaire was designed to assess the amount of change a couple desires to bring about in their relationship.

Assessment of Career Decision Making (ACDM)
Type: Career decision-making styles inventory
Distributor: Western Psychological Services (WPS TEST REPORT)
12031 Wilshire Boulevard, Los Angeles, CA 90025
(213)478-2061
Services: Scoring and interpretation report
Description: Scores are developed and plotted to assess a student's career decision-making style, satisfaction and adjustment to school, and progress in the selection of a major and in formulating occupational plans. An interpretive narrative explains the scores. Statistical analyses determine the probability that the student is representative of four kinds of theoretical decision-making styles and indicate unusual patterns of scores. Group results (for batches of scores) are presented.

Automated Manual DSM-III
Type: Diagnosis
Distributor: Multi-Health Systems, Inc.
10 Parfield Drive, Willowdale, Ontario M2J 1B9 Canada
(416)498-1200
Services: Microcomputer—IBM PC and Apple II and compatibles
Description: Aids in learning, teaching, and using the current system of psychiatric diagnosis (DSM-III), as described by Swartz in the *Journal of Clinical Psychiatry* (1981), 42, 359.

Automated Mental Health System (AMHS)
Type: Office Management
Distributor: Multi-Health Systems, Inc.
10 Parfield Drive, Willowdale, Ontario M2J 1B9 Canada
(416)498-1200
Services: Microcomputer—Apple II and compatibles
Description: A microcomputer-based office management system designed for mental health practitioners.

Barclay Classroom Assessment System (BCAS)
Type: Child personality using data from self, peers, teacher
Distributor: Western Psychological Services
12031 Wilshire Boulevard, Los Angeles, CA 90025
(213)478-2061
Services: Scoring and interpretation report
Description: Collects data from self, peers, and teacher and makes recommendations about general referrals, learning handicaps, gifted, problem areas (seven are discussed), classroom problems, vocational awareness, peer tutoring candidates, contracting candidates, temperament patterns, achievement problems, factor scores, comparison of total ratings, achievement summary, and recommendations.

Beck Depression Inventory Report
Type: Assessment
Distributor: Multi-Health Systems, Inc.
10 Parfield Drive, Willowdale, Ontario M2J 1B9 Canada
(416)498-1200
Services: Microcomputer—IBM PC and Apple II and compatibles
Description: Administers, scores, and interprets the Beck Depression Inventory.

Bender Report
Type: Assessment
Distributor: Multi-Health Systems, Inc.
10 Parfield Drive, Willowdale, Ontario M2J 1B9 Canada
(416)498-1200
Services: Microcomputer—IBM PC and Apple II and compatibles
Description: Facilitates scoring and furnishes a detailed interpretation of the Bender-Gestalt test for children and adults.

California Adaptive Behavior Scale
Type: Child Development
Distributor: Multi-Health Systems, Inc.
10 Parfield Drive, Willowdale, Ontario M2J 1B9 Canada
(416)498-1200
Services: Microcomputer—IBM PC and Apple II and compatibles
Description: Provides a comprehensive measure of child and adolescent development. The scale consists of 353 items yielding age equivalency scores across eleven domains and either twenty-four or thirty-two areas. The item age ranges from 0.3 to 19 years.

California Psychological Inventory (CPI)
Type: Normal personality
Distributor: National Computer Systems
P.O. Box 1416, Minneapolis, MN 55440
(612)933-2800 and (800)328-6759
Services: Arion II teleprocessing, central scoring
Description: The CPI Profile Report records and plots all scores on the twenty-four scales to facilitate interpretation and provides a narrative explanation on the special scales and indexes. It also has comments on deviant test-taking styles when appropriate.

California Psychological Inventory (CPI)
Type: Personality
Distributor: Applied Innovations, Inc.
South Kingston Office Park, Suite A-1, Wakefield, RI 02879
(800)272-2250
Services: Microcomputer—IBM PC and compatibles
Description: Provides scoring and interpretation of the CPI.

California Psychological Inventory (CPI)
Type: Personality assessment
Distributor: Consulting Psychologists Press, Inc.
577 College Avenue, Palo Alto, CA 94306
(415)857-1444

Services: Mail-in scoring; software (IBM PC and compatibles)
Description: Administers, scores, and reports the results of the California Psychological Inventory. The CPI is a 480-item true-false questionnaire used to assess personality and behavior of normal individuals. It provides eighteen scales measuring easily understood and socially desirable behavioral tendencies rather than pathological characteristics. There is a per-use royalty fee for each administration. CPI Apple software is being developed.

Career and Vocational Interest Inventory
Type: Vocational
Distributor: Integrated Professional Systems
5211 Mahoning Avenue, Suite 135, Youngstown, OH 44515
(216)799-3282
Services: Microcomputer—IBM PC and compatibles
Description: The six Holland themes are used to develop narrative reports for guiding high-school students in their career choice.

Career Assessment Inventory
Type: Career/vocational interest survey
Distributor: National Computer Systems
P.O. Box 1416, Minneapolis, MN 55440
(612)933-2800 and (800)328-6759
Services: Arion II teleprocessing, central scoring, MICROTEST assessment software (on-line administration and scanned scoring)
Description: A vocational interest assessment tool that compares a person's interests and preferences with those of individuals in specific careers. The inventory was designed for use with individuals planning to enter occupations requiring up to a four-year college degree. It can be used in high schools, colleges, and human resource development and vocational rehabilitation programs. Scores are reported on six general occupational themes, twenty-two basic interest scales (business and sales, arts/crafts, and so on), and ninety-one specific occupations. Two reports are available. The color-coded Profile Report graphically presents scores on each scale. The eight-page Narrative Report provides scale descriptions, score interpretations and comparisons, and additional reference information.

Career Decision Making Interpretive Report
Type: Vocational
Distributor: American Guidance Service
Publisher's Building, Circle Pines, MN 55014
(800)328-2560
Services: Mail-in; microcomputer—IBM PC and compatibles
Description: Based on the Harrington-O'Shea Career Decision-Making System, this report includes several factors: abilities, job values, future plans, subject preferences, and interests. The goal is to provide career decision information for the client.

Career Development Inventory (CDI)
Type: Assesses knowledge and attitudes about career choice
Distributor: Consulting Psychologists Press, Inc.
577 College Avenue, Palo Alto, CA 94306
(415)857-1444
Services: Mail-in; software (IBM PC and compatibles, 256K memory)
Description: Assesses knowledge and attitudes about career choice. The results are useful in determining the appropriate career guidance for individuals and in designing and evaluating career counseling programs. The CDI software administers, scores, and reports the results of the CDI. There is a per-use royalty fee for each administration. CDI Apple software is being developed.

Career Directions Inventory
Type: Vocational
Distributor: Research Psychologists Press
P.O. Box 984, Port Huron, MI 48061
(800)265-1285
Services: Mail-in
Description: This vocational inventory was developed to assist students with vocational choices. The report is based on scores for sixteen interest scales. These patterns are compared with individuals in a variety of occupations.

CareerWise
Type: Combined career interest, aptitude, and personality
Distributor: National Computer Systems
P.O. Box 1416, Minneapolis, MN 55440
(612)933-2800 and (800)328-6759
Services: Central scoring
Description: A comprehensive, cost-effective career guidance program that surveys interests, personality, and values. The program incorporates an individual's test results from the Career Assessment Inventory Word and Number Assessment Inventory and Temperament and Values Inventory. The Word and Number Assessment Inventory can be omitted if an aptitude measure is not needed. Vocational and career guidance counselors find CareerWise useful for a variety of group settings including high school, higher education, adults planning career changes, vocational rehabilitation, and outplacement counseling settings.

Childpace—Child Development Program
Type: Child development
Distributor: Multi Health Systems, Inc.
10 Parfield Drive, Willowdale, Ontario M2J 1B9 Canada
(416)498-1200

Services: Microcomputer—IBM PC and Apple II and compatibles
Description: Designed to help parents monitor their children's development between the ages of three months and five years. The program evaluates a child's gross and fine motor control, language, and personal/social skills.

Children's Personality Questionnaire (CPQ)
Type: Personality
Distributor: Institute for Personality and Ability Testing, Inc.
P.O. Box 188, Champaign, IL 61820
(217)352-4739
Services: Mail-in; teleprocessing
Description: Provides a complete narrative report for each child assessed with the CPQ. The report includes descriptions of all significant personality characteristics as well as the individual's projected levels of creativity and anticipated achievement in ten school-related areas. The CPQ itself is a broad-range normal personality test useful in predicting and evaluating personal, social, and academic development for children eight to eleven years old (third-grade reading level required).

Clinical Analysis Questionnaire (CAQ)
Type: Abnormal personality
Distributor: National Computer Systems
P.O. Box 1416, Minneapolis, MN 55440
(612)933-2800 and (800)328-6759
Services: Arion II teleprocessing, central scoring, MICROTEST assessment software (on-line administration and scanned scoring)
Description: Combines diagnostic assessment of deviant behavior with the measurement of a patient's normal coping skills. The CAQ helps the practitioner assess personality traits, measure psychopathology, develop and evaluate treatment strategies, and provide vocational guidance and rehabilitation.

Clinical Analysis Questionnaire (CAQ)
Type: Personality
Distributor: Psychological Assessment Resources, Inc.
P.O. Box 98, Odessa, FL 33556
(800)331-TEST
Services: Microcomputer—IBM PC and compatibles
Description: Administers, scores, and interprets the 16 PF. Sten scores are provided for sixteen scales and twelve dimensions.

Clinical Analysis Questionnaire (CAQ)
Type: Personality: normal/clinical
Distributor: Institute for Personality and Ability Testing, Inc.
P.O. Box 188, Champaign, IL 61820
(217)352-4739

Services: Mail-in; teleprocessing; local processing
Description: Intended for general clinical diagnosis and evaluating therapeutic progress, the CAQ was developed to meet the need of clinical psychologists for objective measurement of primary behavioral dimensions. A special feature of the test is that it measures sixteen normal personality dimensions (the 16 PF scales) as well as hypochondriasis, agitated depression, suicidal depression, anxious depression, guilt, energy level, boredom, and five other pathological dimensions.

Complex Attention Rehabilitation
Type: Cognitive ability
Distributor: Robert Sbordone, Ph.D., Inc.
8840 Warner Avenue, Suite 301, Fountain Valley, CA 92708
(714)841-6293
Services: Microcomputer—IBM PC and compatibles
Description: Provides training in attentional tasks by using a visual tracking system. It was designed for use with cognitively impaired individuals. The program monitors the patients' attentional behavior to determine when rest periods are needed.

Comprehensive Client History
Type: Interview
Distributor: Applied Innovations, Inc.
South Kingston Office Park, Suite A-1, Wakefield, RI 02879
(800)272-2250
Services: Microcomputer—IBM PC and compatibles
Description: This interactive computer interview was designed to provide an indication of the individual's past history regarding education, employment, family, social aspects, and psychological factors. The individual's responses are printed out after he or she has completed the interview.

Computerized Stress Inventory
Type: Personality
Distributor: Preventive Measures, Inc.
1115 West Campus Road, Lawrence, KS 66044
(913)842-5078
Services: Microcomputer—IBM PC and compatibles
Description: Samples individual's responses over twenty-five areas of life, including work, lifestyle, family relations, life changes, eating habits, worries, and frustrations. The report provides a stress and coping summary.

Conners Parent Rating Scale Computer Program, Conners Teachers Rating Scale Computer Program
Type: Child behavior

Distributor: Multi-Health Systems, Inc.
10 Parfield Drive, Willowdale, Ontario M2J 1B9 Canada
(416)498-1200
Services: Microcomputer—IBM PC and Apple II and compatibles
Description: Administer, score, and interpret the revised versions of these most widely used measures of child behavior.

Coping with Tests
Type: Assesses level of test anxiety
Distributor: Consulting Psychologists Press, Inc.
577 College Avenue, Palo Alto, CA 94306
(415)857-1444
Mail-in scoring; software (IBM PC or PC-compatible
Services: [256K memory]).
Description: Enables test-anxious students or adults to assess their level of text anxiety using Dr. C. Spielberger's Test Anxiety Inventory. Coping with Tests is designed to assist test-anxious individuals to reduce their test anxiety level through behavioral modification techniques. Apple software is being developed. There is a per-use royalty fee for each administration.

Developmental History Report
Type: Intake
Distributor: Multi-Health Systems, Inc.
10 Parfield Drive, Willowdale, Ontario M2J 1B9 Canada
(416)498-1200
Services: Microcomputer—IBM PC and Apple II and compatibles
Description: Presents an automated structured interview that gathers comprehensive developmental information and generates a written narrative.

Developmental Profile II
Type: Personality
Distributor: Psychological Assessment Resources
P.O. Box 98, Odessa, FL 33556
(813)977-3395
Services: Microcomputer—IBM PC and compatibles
Description: Assesses child development following the Alpern-Boll Developmental Profile. Several areas of development are evaluated: physical skills, self-help, socialization, communication skills, and academic areas. The profiles produced can help establish the child's developmental level.

Developmental Profile II (DP-II)
Type: Test of developmental age in five areas
Distributor: Western Psychological Services (WPS TEST REPORT)
12031 Wilshire Boulevard, Los Angeles, CA 90025
(213)478-2061

Services: Scoring and interpretation report
Description: Scores the five DP-II scales and plots the results. For each of the 186 behaviors in the DP-II, the program gives the current status (pass/fail), the percent of children at the same chronological age who pass or fail the item, the expected probability that the client child will pass or fail the item in six months, and the expected probability of a typical child of the same chronological age passing or failing the item in six months.

Diagnostic Interview for Children and Adolescents (DICA) Computer Program: (1) Parent Version (2) Child Version
Type: Diagnosis
Distributor: Multi-Health Systems, Inc.
10 Parfield Drive, Willowdale, Ontario M2J 1B9 Canada
(416)498-1200
Services: IBM PC and Apple II and compatibles
Description: Allows for direct administration of the DICA to the child's parent or to an adolescent. It automatically branches to the proper question and identifies the DSM-III categories met by the patient.

Digit-Digit Attention Test
Type: Cognitive
Distributor: Robert Sbordone, Ph.D., Inc.
8840 Warner Avenue, Suite 301, Fountain Valley, CA 92708
(714)841-6293
Services: Microcomputer—IBM PC and compatibles
Description: This on-line computer-administered attention test was devised to be used with brain-injured and intellectually impaired patients. Attention span is tested.

Dyadic Adjustment Scale
Type: Marital adjustment
Distributor: Psychological Assessment Resources
P.O. Box 98, Odessa, FL 33556
(813)977-3395
Services: Microcomputer—IBM PC and Apple II and compatibles
Description: This program was devised to interpret the Locke-Wallace Marital Adjustment Scale. The program allows for the scoring and interpretation of the inventory, providing scores on dyadic satisfaction, dyadic cohesion, dyadic consensus, and affective expression.

Dyadic Adjustment Scale: Computer Version
Type: Assessment
Distributor: Multi-Health Systems, Inc.
10 Parfield Drive, Willowdale, Ontario M2J 1B9 Canada
(416)498-1200

Services: Microcomputer—IBM PC and Apple II and compatibles
Description: A self-report measure of relationship adjustment developed by Graham Spanier that scores four factored subscales: dyadic satisfaction, dyadic cohesion, dyadic consensus, and affectional expression.

Eating Disorder Inventory
Type: Personality
Distributor: Psychological Assessment Resources
P.O. Box 98, Odessa, FL 33556
(813)977-3395
Services: Microcomputer—IBM PC and Apple II and compatibles
Description: Administers a sixty-four-item inventory covering a broad range of eating problems. The scoring and profile interpretation provide an assessment of the individual's psychopathology with respect to eating problems.

Eating Disorder Inventory: Computer Version
Type: Diagnosis
Distributor: Multi-Health Systems, Inc.
10 Parfield Drive, Willowdale, Ontario M2J 1B9 Canada
(416)498-1200
Services: Microcomputer—IBM PC and Apple II and compatibles
Description: This sixty-four-item, self-report inventory measures psychological and behavioral traits common in eating disorders. It was developed in association with Dr. David Garner, author of the Eating Disorder Inventory (EDI).

Edwards Personal Preference Schedule (EPPS)
Type: Personality
Distributor: Applied Innovations, Inc.
South Kingstown Office Park, Suite A-1, Wakefield, RI 02879
(800)272-2250
Services: Microcomputer—IBM PC and Apple II and compatibles
Description: The EPPS, a forced-choice personality schedule, is administered, scored, and interpreted. The program scores fifteen scales based on Murray's need patterns.

Executive Profile Survey (EPS)
Type: Personality
Distributor: Institute for Personality and Ability Testing, Inc.
P.O. Box 188, Champaign, IL 61820-0188
(217)352-4739
Services: Mail-in; teleprocessing
Description: Measures self-attitudes, values, and beliefs of individuals compared with over two thousand top-level executives. Developed from a ten-year study of the executive personality, the eleven profile dimensions assess

the individual's ambitious, assertive, enthusiastic, creative, spontaneous, self-focused, considerate, open-minded, relaxed, practical, and systematic traits. The report provides a concise, nontechnical description of those dimensions most important in business, management, and executive settings.

Executive Profile Survey (EPS)
Type: Personnel assessment
Distributor: National Computer Systems
P.O. Box 1416, Minneapolis, MN 55440
(612)933-2800 and (800)328-6759
Services: Mail-in scoring; teleprocessing scoring service
Description: Measures eleven dimensions, each a personality trait important to executive success. An individual's scores are then compared to a norm group of two thousand top-level corporate executives. Results are produced in a five-page narrative report.

Eysenck Personality Questionnaire (EPQ) (Adult Form)
Type: Personality
Distributor: EDITS
P.O. Box 7234, San Diego, CA 92107
(619)222-1666
Services: Microcomputer—IBM PC and compatibles
Description: Administers, scores, and interprets the EPQ. It provides scores on extraversion, neuroticism, and psychoticism. Scores can be printed out as well as stored for research.

Eysenck Personality Questionnaire (EPQ) (Junior)
Type: Personality
Distributor: EDITS
P.O. Box 7234, San Diego, CA 92107
(619)222-1666
Services: Microcomputer
Description: Administers the EPQ for children. The test dimensions (extraversion, neuroticism, and psychoticism) are provided. The scales are scored and printed out and can be stored for research purposes.

Fundamental Interpersonal Relations Orientation-Behavior (FIRO-B)
Type: Personality
Distributor: Psychological Assessment Resources, Inc.
P.O. Box 98, Odessa, FL 33556
(800)331-TEST
Services: Microcomputer—IBM PC and compatibles
Description: Administers, scores, and interprets the FIRO-B.

FIRO-B: Computer Version 2.0
Type: Assessment
Distributor: Multi-Health Systems, Inc.
10 Parfield Drive, Willowdale, Ontario M2J 1B9 Canada
(416)498-1200
Services: Microcomputer—IBM PC and Apple II and compatibles
Description: Administers, scores, and interprets the FIRO-B.

FIRO-B: Interpretive Report
Type: Assessment
Distributor: Multi-Health Systems, Inc.
10 Parfield Drive, Willowdale, Ontario M2J 1B9 Canada
(416)498-1200
Services: Microcomputer—IBM PC and Apple II and compatibles
Description: By entering the six scale scores for the FIRO-B, the user can obtain unlimited interpretive reports.

General Aptitude Test Battery (GATB)
Type: Aptitude test
Distributor: National Computer Systems
P.O. Box 1416, Minneapolis, MN 55440
(612)933-2800 and (800)328-6759
Services: Mail-in scoring, hand-scoring materials, microcomputer scoring
Description: The GATB measures an individual's aptitude in nine categories: general, verbal, numerical, spatial, form perception, clerical perception, motor coordination, finger dexterity, and manual dexterity. The GATB, a 434-question, twelve-part test, is useful in job placement and counseling settings.

Giannetti On-line Psychological History (GOLPH)
Type: Clinical assessment/structured interview
Distributor: National Computer Systems
P.O. Box 1416, Minneapolis, MN 55440
(612)933-2800 and (800)328-6759
Services: MICROTEST assessment software (on-line administration)
Description: Gathers essential information about ten different facets of an individual's background and current life circumstances through the use of a branching interactive computer program. Explores current living situation, family of origin, client development, educational history, marital history, present family, occupational history/current finances, legal history, symptom screening-psychological, and military history. Information on each of the ten facets is reported in narrative form to provide a comprehensive, personalized psychosocial history report.

GuidePak
Type: Vocational
Distributor: Behaviordyne, Inc.
599 College Avenue, Suite 1, Palo Alto, CA 94306
(415)857-0111
Services: Mail-in
Description: Includes a number of measures that focus on vocational guidance: California Psychological Inventory, the Strong-Campbell Vocational Inventory, and a planning inventory. The results can be valuable for career planning.

Guilford-Zimmerman Temperament Survey (GZTS)
Type: Normal personality
Distributor: National Computer Systems
P.O. Box 1416, Minneapolis, MN 55440
(612)933-2800 and (800)328-6759
Services: Arion II teleprocessing, central scoring, MICROTEST assessment software (on-line administration and scanned scoring)
Description: Designed to provide a comprehensive, nonclinical description of personality and temperament. It provides scores on the following personality traits: general activity level, ascendance/social boldness, emotional stability, friendliness, personal relations, restraint, sociability, objectivity, thoughtfulness, masculinity/femininity.

Halstead-Reitan Neuropsychological Battery
Type: Cognitive/ability
Distributor: Integrated Professional Systems
5211 Mahoning Avenue, Suite 135, Youngstown, OH 44515
(216)799-3282
Services: Microcomputer—IBM PC and compatibles
Description: The tests included in this battery were developed to provide information relevant to cognitive and neuropsychological functioning. The report was designed to summarize information from a number of measures.

Health Problems Checklist
Type: Health questionnaire
Distributor: Psychological Assessment Resources, Inc.
Box 98, Odessa, FL 33556
(800)331-TEST
Services: Microcomputer—IBM PC and compatibles
Description: Administers the checklist, allowing the subject to indicate whether the problem is current. The program calculates the number of endorsed problems and presents them in rank order.

Health Problems Checklist: Computer Version
Type: Intake
Distributor: Multi-Health Systems, Inc.
10 Parfield Drive, Willowdale, Ontario M2J 1B9 Canada
(416)498-1200
Services: Microcomputer—IBM PC and Apple II and compatibles
Description: Provides a comprehensive survey of a wide range of health problems as described by the client.

High School Personality Questionnaire (HSPQ)
Type: Personality
Distributor: Institute for Personality and Ability Testing, Inc.
P.O. Box 188, Champaign, IL 61820-0188
(217)352-4739
Services: Mail-in; teleprocessing
Description: This report is intended to guide counselors and school psychologists in working with students. The report is built around fourteen primary personality dimensions that include stability, tension, warmth, enthusiasm, and ten others. Scores for anxiety, extroversion, creativity, leadership, and other broad trait patterns are also calculated and reported.

Hogan Personality Inventory (HPI)
Type: Normal personality
Distributor: National Computer Systems
P.O. Box 1416, Minneapolis, MN 55440
(612)933-2800 and (800)328-6759
Services: Mail-in scoring, teleprocessing, and local scoring via NCS MICROTEST
Description: This self-reported personality inventory is designed to assess dimensions of personality important to effective personal and social interaction. It is intended for vocational counseling and assessment and personal and family counseling. Results include six primary scales: intellectance, adjustment, prudence, ambition, sociability, and likeability.

Hogan Personnel Selection System (HPSS)
Type: Personnel assessment/personality
Distributor: National Computer Systems
P.O. Box 1416, Minneapolis, MN 55440
(612)933-2800 and (800)328-6759
Services: Mail-in scoring, teleprocessing, and local scoring via NCS MICROTEST
Description: Includes four inventories useful for personnel selection and job placement: prospective employee, clerical, sales, and managerial tests. Designed to assess personality characteristics important to occupational success, the HPSS inventories match an individual's personality with the requirements of a given job.

Holland Occupational System
Type: Vocational
Distributor: Publisher's Test Service
2500 Garden Road, Monterey, CA 93940
(800)538-9547
Services: Microcomputer—IBM PC and compatibles
Description: This program was designed to automate the matching of the Holland codes to *Dictionary of Occupational Titles* (DOT) entries.

Human Resource Development Report for the 16 PF
Type: Personality
Distributor: Institute for Personality and Ability Testing, Inc.
P.O. Box 188, Champaign, IL 61820
(217)352-4739
Services: Mail-in; teleprocessing
Description: This computer-generated narrative report assesses an individual's management style by looking at his or her personality characteristics. Five main management skills are addressed: leadership, interaction with others, decision-making abilities, initiative, and personal adjustment. This report is designed for use in human resource development and/or management development programs.

Individualized Stress Management Program
Type: Training program/stress levels and personality
Distributor: Institute for Personality and Ability Testing, Inc.
P.O. Box 188, Champaign, IL 61820
(217)352-4739
Services: Mail-in
Description: This is a complete assessment and training package designed for those who conduct stress management training. Using their own customized book, individuals learn how to understand the stress they experience, recognize its sources, and develop ways to control or prevent it. Diagnostic data from the 16 PF and Stress Evaluation Inventory yield personality and lifestyle information that forms the basis for a personalized prescription plan for each individual.

Intake Evaluation Report
Type: Intake
Distributor: Multi-Health Systems, Inc.
10 Parfield Drive, Willowdale, Ontario M2J 1B9 Canada
(416)498-1200
Services: Microcomputer—IBM PC and Apple II and compatibles
Description: Designed to provide a computer-generated summary of the clinician's initial evaluation of the client.

Interpersonal Style Inventory (ISI)
Type: Personality inventory assessing social style
Distributor: Western Psychological Services (WPS TEST REPORT)
12031 Wilshire Boulevard, Los Angeles, CA 90025
(213)478-2061
Services: Scoring and interpretation report
Description: This program scores the fifteen ISI scales and plots the results. A narrative is generated based on patterns in the scale scores. A set of statistical tests probe the generality of the profile patterns and determine the probability that the client has a score profile representative of that of each of six major empirically identified groups.

Inwald Personality Inventory
Type: Personality
Distributor: Hilson Research, Inc.
82-28 Abingdon Road, Kew Gardens, NY 11415
(718)805-0063
Services: Mail-in; microcomputer—IBM PC and compatibles
Description: This personality inventory was developed for use in personnel selection. Scoring and narrative reports are provided.

IQ Test Interpretation
Type: Cognitive
Distributor: Precision People, Inc.
3452 North Ride Circle, S., Jacksonville, FL 32217
(904)262-1096
Services: Microcomputer—IBM PC and compatibles
Description: Designed to provide interpretations for the Wechsler Intelligence Scale for Children-Revised. The scores on the test are analyzed and interpreted and detailed recommendations for both clinical and educational uses are made.

Irrational Beliefs Report
Type: Personality-clinical
Distributor: Test Systems International
P.O. Box 18347, Wichita, KS 67218
(316)262-0102
Services: Mail-in
Description: This narrative reporting system is based on Ellis's rational emotive therapy.

Jackson Vocational Interest Survey
Type: Vocational
Distributor: Research Psychologists Press
P.O. Box 984, Port Huron, MI 48061
(800)265-1285
Services: Mail-in
Description: This 289-item inventory includes statements covering ten occupational themes, such as logical, expressive, inquiring, helping, enterprising, assertiveness, and so on. The inventory was designed for use in career planning for high-school and college groups.

Jenkins Activity Survey
Type: Personality
Distributor: Psychological Corporation
7500 Old Oak Boulevard, Cleveland, OH 44130
(216)234-5300
Services: Mail-in
Description: This fifty-two-item multiple-choice inventory measures Type A behavior. The test was designed for use with medical patients to assess risk for coronary disease. The four scales that are scored are job involvement, hard driving, competitive, and speed and impatience. The computer-interpreted report provides scores on all four scales.

Jesness Inventory
Type: Personality inventory for youth between eight and eighteen
Distributor: Consulting Psychologists Press, Inc.
577 College Avenue, Palo Alto, CA 94306
(415)857-1444
Services: Mail-in scoring
Description: A personality inventory specifically designed for youth between ages eight and eighteen, the Jesness Inventory is a brief (155-item) true-false questionnaire with easily comprehended, idiomatic items yielding ten trait scores and powerful index predictive of asocial tendencies. The scales are: social maladjustment, value orientation, immaturity, autism, alienation, manifest aggression, withdrawal, social anxiety, repression, denial, and the asocial index. Although the inventory is hand-scorable, the publisher also provides a scoring service.

Karson Clinical Report for the 16 PF
Type: Personality
Distributor: Institute for Personality and Ability Testing, Inc.
P.O. Box 188, Champaign, IL 61820-0188
(217)351-1739
Services: Mail-in; teleprocessing; local processing
Description: Provides psychologists, psychiatrists, psychiatric social workers,

and physicians with a report that features an in-depth analysis of underlying personality dynamics in clinical language. This report includes a concise narrative that provides a complete overview of personality and clinical patterns. Additional charts give a visual display of the scores in five significant areas: primary personality characteristics, clinical signs and syndromes, interpersonal patterns, cognitive factors, and need patterns.

Kaufman Assessment Battery for Children
Type: Cognitive
Distributor: American Guidance Service
Publisher's Building, Circle Pines, MN 55014
(800)328-2560
Services: Microcomputer—IBM PC and compatibles
Description: Provides standard scores and profile results for the Kaufman Assessment Battery. Subtests for sequential processing, simultaneous processing, and achievement are scored and interpreted.

Law Enforcement Assessment and Development Report (LEADR) (16 PF/CAQ)
Type: Personality: normal/clinical
Distributor: Institute for Personality and Ability Testing, Inc.
P.O. Box 188, Champaign, IL 61820-0188
(217)352-4739
Services: Mail-in; teleprocessing
Description: This five-page computer-based report identifies individuals who are most likely to become successful law enforcement officers. This report allows comparisons of applicants in terms of predicted overall performance as well as in four job-related areas: emotional maturity, integrity/control, intellectual efficiency, and interpersonal relationships as well as twelve clinical areas.

Louisville Behavior Checklist (LBC)
Type: Inventory of social and emotional behaviors indicative of childhood psychopathology
Distributor: Western Psychological Services (WPS TEST REPORT)
12031 Wilshire Boulevard, Los Angeles, CA 90025
(213)478-2061
Services: Scoring and interpretation report
Description: Scores up to twenty major scales for the appropriate age and plots the profile of scores. A narrative report is produced that yields major conclusions about the child's pattern of scores.

Luria-Nebraska Neuropsychological Battery (LNNB), Forms I and II
Type: Neuropsychological problem inventory
Distributor: Western Psychological Services (WPS TEST REPORT)
12031 Wilshire Boulevard, Los Angeles, CA 90025
(213)478-2061
Services: Scoring and statistical reports
Description: Detailed statistical summaries determine the relative strengths and weaknesses of the individual client.

Luria-Nebraska Scoring
Type: Cognitive
Distributor: Precision People, Inc.
3452 North Ride Circle So., Jacksonville, FL 32217
(904)262-1096
Services: Microcomputer—IBM PC and compatibles
Description: This software program was designed to organize and summarize scores for the Luria-Nebraska Battery.

McDermott Multidimensional Assessment of Children
Type: Vocational
Distributor: Psychological Corporation
7500 Old Oak Boulevard, Cleveland, OH 44130
(216)234-5300
Services: Microcomputer—IBM PC and compatibles
Description: Integrates information from tests, behavioral data, and demographic data to provide educational evaluations of children. The program provides a report of several educational tests and systematic classification decisions based on intellectual deficiencies and PL 94-142 guidelines.

Marital Satisfaction Inventory (MSI)
Type: Inventory of marital style and quality
Distributor: Western Psychological Services (WPS TEST REPORT)
12031 Wilshire Boulevard, Los Angeles, CA 90025
(213)478-2061
Services: Scoring report
Description: The MSI is scored for nine major scales, a total score, and a validity score. The results are compared to the norms and plotted on a profile.

Marriage Counseling Report for the 16 PF
Type: Personality
Distributor: Institute for Personality and Ability Testing, Inc.
P.O. Box 188, Champaign, IL 61820
(217)352-4739
Services: Mail-in; teleprocessing

Description: This seven-page computer-interpreted report of paired 16 PF profiles examines individual and joint strengths and weaknesses in the personality organization of the two individuals. Valuable in both premarital and troubled marriage situations, it identifies interpersonal patterns and differences that represent potential sources of conflict or rapport in the relationship.

Meyer-Kendall Assessment Survey (MKAS)
Type: Personality inventory related to work style
Distributor: Western Psychological Services (WPS TEST REPORT)
12031 Wilshire Boulevard, Los Angeles, CA 90025
(213)478-2061
Services: Microcomputer—IBM PC and compatibles
Description: Scores the twelve MKAS scales and plots the results. A narrative is generated based on patterns in the scale scores. A set of statistical tests probe the generality of the profile patterns and determine the probability that the client has a score profile representative of that of each of ten major empirically and theoretically identified groups.

Millon Adolescent Personality Inventory (MAPI) Clinical Interpretive Report
Type: Adolescent personality
Distributor: National Computer Systems
P.O. Box 1416, Minneapolis, MN 55440
(612)933-2800 and (800)328-6759
Services: Arion II teleprocessing, central scoring, MICROTEST assessment software (on-line administration and scanned scoring)
Description: Designed to assess the overall configuration of an adolescent's personality, including his or her coping styles, expressed concerns, and behavioral patterns. The Clinical Interpretive Report, providing statements coordinated with DSM-III, was developed in full consultation with clinical psychologists seeking a tool to aid them in describing emotional, psychological, and interpersonal difficulties. The inventory is especially useful to clinical psychologists and adolescent psychiatrists to predict, identify, and understand a wide range of relevant adolescent social functioning, including relationships with peers and family members, adjustment to the biological changes that occur during adolescence, self-esteem, impulse control, and social tolerance.

Millon Adolescent Personality Inventory (MAPI) Guidance Interpretive Report
Type: Adolescent personality
Distributor: National Computer Systems
P.O. Box 1416, Minneapolis, MN 55440
(612)933-2800 and (800)328-6759

Services: Arion II teleprocessing, central scoring, MICROTEST assessment software (on-line administration and scanned scoring)

Description: Designed to assess the overall configuration of an adolescent's personality, including his or her coping styles, expressed concerns, and behavioral patterns. The Guidance Interpretive Report, which was developed in consultation with school counselors, is useful for educational and vocational counseling purposes.

Millon Behavioral Health Inventory (MBHI)

Type: Behavioral health and medicine

Distributor: National Computer Systems
P.O. Box 1416, Minneapolis, MN 55440
(612)933-2800 and (800)328-6759

Services: Arion II teleprocessing, central scoring, MICROTEST assessment software (on-line administration and scanned scoring)

Description: Facilitates the formulation of a comprehensive treatment plan for adult medical patients. It provides psychologists and physicians with important information regarding a patient's style of relating to health care personnel, problematic psychosocial attitudes and stressors, and similarity to patients with psychosomatic complications or poor responses to either illness or treatment intervention.

Millon Clinical Multiaxial Inventory (MCMI) Clinical Interpretive Report

Type: Abnormal personality

Distributor: National Computer Systems
P.O. Box 1416, Minneapolis, MN 55440
(612)933-2800 and (800)328-6759

Services: Arion II teleprocessing, central scoring, MICROTEST assessment software (on-line administration and scanned scoring)

Description: Specifically designed to assess the DSM-III categories of personality disorders and clinical syndromes. Theory-derived constructs are quantitatively measured to suggest diagnoses and psychodynamics as well as testable hypotheses about patient history and current behavior. The Clinical Interpretive Report includes the profile (which plots raw and base rate scores on each of the twenty scales) and provides a detailed narrative explanation of psychodynamic relationships between the patient's personality patterns of behavior and feelings and the acute clinical symptoms he or she exhibits. Noteworthy responses record items that may alert the clinician to specific problem areas. Also provided is a discussion of the therapeutic implications of test results.

Millon Clinical Multiaxial Inventory (MCMI) Profile Report
Type: Abnormal personality
Distributor: National Computer Systems
P.O. Box 1416, Minneapolis, MN 55440
(612)933-2800 and (800)328-6759
Services: Arion II teleprocessing, central scoring, MICROTEST assessment software (on-line administration and scanned scoring)
Description: Specifically designed to assess the DSM-III categories of personality disorders and clinical syndromes. Theory-derived constructs are quantitatively measured to suggest diagnoses and psychodynamics as well as testable hypotheses about patient history and current behavior. The twenty clinical scales of the MCMI are divided into three categories to reflect the distinction between relatively enduring personality features and acute symptoms. Two validity indicators are also included. The Profile Report plots on an easy-to-read graph raw and base rate scores on each of the twenty scales.

Minnesota Multiphasic Personality Inventory (MMPI)
Type: Personality inventory to assess psychopathology
Distributor: Western Psychological Services (WPS TEST REPORT)
12031 Wilshire Boulevard, Los Angeles, CA 90025
(213)478-2061
Services: Scoring and interpretation report
Description: This report scores the MMPI for all standard scales and a number of "content" and "research" scales. Code types are generated, and the profile is plotted. A narrative report of approximately three pages interprets major features of the score profile using a set of empirically determined decision rules. Responses to the Lachar-Wrobel critical item set are printed.

Minnesota Multiphasic Personality Inventory
Type: Personality; psychopathology
Distributor: Western Psychological Services (WPS TEST REPORT)
12031 Wilshire Boulevard, Los Angeles, CA 90025
(213)478-2061
Services: MMPI Diagnostic and Classification Report (4 variations)
Description: This report accepts T-scores from an optical scan sheet and compares the profile of the individual client to more than forty empirically determined prototypic patterns. The result is a statistical classification analysis that gives probability estimates that the client is representative of each group. There are four variations of this report: Clinical Report, Health Problems Report, Prisoner Report, and Individual Clinician Report.

Minnesota Multiphasic Personality Inventory (MMPI) Basic Service Profile Report
Type: Abnormal personality

Distributor: National Computer Systems
P.O. Box 1416, Minneapolis, MN 55440
(612)933-2800 and (800)328-6759

Services: Arion II teleprocessing, central scoring, MICROTEST assessment software (on-line administration and scanned scoring)

Description: The MMPI is designed to assess major personality characteristics that reflect the social and personal adjustment of individuals and that are commonly indicative of disabling psychological abnormality. A core of ten clinical and four supplemental scales, plus four indicators of test validity, is included in the Basic Service Profile Report.

Minnesota Multiphasic Personality Inventory (MMPI) The Minnesota Report: Adult Clinical System Clinical Interpretive Report

Type: Abnormal personality

Distributor: National Computer Systems
P.O. Box 1416, Minneapolis, MN 55440
(612)933-2800 and (800)328-6759

Services: Arion II teleprocessing, central scoring, MICROTEST assessment software (on-line administration and scanned scoring)

Description: The MMPI is designed to assess major personality characteristics that reflect the social and personal adjustment of individuals and that are commonly indicative of disabling psychological abnormality. The report contains all of the materials in the Clinical Profile plus an interpretive narrative that employs code-type correlates and content as well as special indexes and demographic data to generate interpretive statements. The narrative assesses the individual's test-taking attitudes and such issues as interpersonal relationships and behavioral stability. Included are sections on DSM-III–compatible diagnostic and treatment considerations that can help the clinician draw appropriate conclusions about each case. When this report is used in correctional settings, the Megargee Typology is also included. A Critical Items listing provides the clinician with potentially significant "themes" that may be helpful in diagnosis.

Minnesota Multiphasic Personality Inventory (MMPI) The Minnesota Report: Adult Clinical System Clinical Profile Report

Type: Abnormal personality

Distributor: National Computer Systems
P.O. Box 1416, Minneapolis, MN 55440
(612)933-2800 and (800)328-6759

Services: Arion II teleprocessing, central scoring, MICROTEST assessment software (on-line administration and scanned scoring)

Description: The MMPI is designed to assess major personality characteristics that reflect the social and personal adjustment of individuals and that are commonly indicative of disabling psychological abnormality. The report contains the Clinical Profile of the MMPI validity and clinical scales contained in the Basic Service Profile Report: percentage of true responses; average clinical scale elevation; the Welsh code's F-K Dissimulation Index, and, when appropriate, the Goldberg Index and Henrichs Rules. A supplemental profile provides raw and T-scores for anxiety, repression, ego strength, and the Wiggins Content scales. The Extended Score Report provides raw and T-scores for other widely used special scales, including the MacAndrew Addiction scale and the Harris-Lingoes and Serkownek subscales.

Minnesota Multiphasic Personality Inventory (MMPI) The Minnesota Report: Personnel Selection System: The Interpretive Report

Type: Abnormal personality
Distributor: National Computer Systems
P.O. Box 1416, Minneapolis, MN 55440
(612)933-2800 and (800)328-6759
Services: Arion II teleprocessing, central scoring, MICROTEST assessment software (on-line administration and scanned scoring)
Description: The MMPI is designed to assess major personality characteristics that reflect the social and personal adjustment of individuals and that are commonly indicative of disabling, psychological abnormality. The Personnel Selection System is designed specifically to identify individuals emotionally unsuitable for high-risk, high-stress positions. Specialized reports are available for any of the following occupations: law enforcement officer, firefighter, airline or military (noncombat) flight crew member, air traffic controller, nuclear power plant operator, medical school and graduate mental health program applicant, and seminarian. The Personnel Interpretive Report contains all of the materials in the Screening Report, except for the rating scales, which are replaced by a detailed Narrative Report that focuses on the following characteristics of the individual: approach to taking the MMPI, level of personal adjustment, level of interpersonal relations, level of personal stability, and possible employment problems.

Minnesota Multiphasic Personality Inventory (MMPI) The Minnesota Report: Personnel Selection System: The Screening Report

Type: Abnormal personality
Distributor: National Computer Systems
P.O. Box 1416, Minneapolis, MN 55440
(612)933-2800 and (800)328-6759
Services: Arion II teleprocessing, central scoring, MICROTEST assessment software (on-line administration and scanned scoring)
Description: The MMPI is designed to assess major personality characteristics commonly indicative of disabling psychological abnormality. The Personnel Selection System is designed specifically to identify individuals emotionally unsuitable for high-risk, high-stress positions. Specialized reports are available for any of the following occupations: law enforcement officer, firefighter, airline or military (noncombat) flight crew member, air traffic con-

troller, nuclear power plant operator, medical school and graduate mental health applicant, and seminarian. The Personnel Screening Report contains rating scales that provide five ratings based on configurations of various MMPI scales designed to detect key potential problem areas: openness to evaluation, social facility, potential for addiction, stress tolerance, and overall adjustment. Also included is the Clinical Profile of the MMPI basic validity and clinical scales plus such additional indexes as the Welsh Code, F-K Dissimulation Index, average clinical scale elevation, and percentage of true responses. A supplemental profile plots scores on the sixteen selected special scales, including anxiety, repression, ego strength, and the Wiggins Content scales. An Extended Score lists other widely used special scales, including the MacAndrew Addiction scale and the Serkownek and Harris-Lingoes subscales. Significant content themes alert assessors to possible problem areas and provide a basis for further investigation.

MMPI Interpretive System
Type: Assessment
Distributor: Multi-Health Systems, Inc.
10 Parfield Drive, Willowdale, Ontario M2J 1B9 Canada
(416)498-1200
Services: Microcomputer—IBM PC and Apple II and compatibles
Description: Provides a comprehensive single-scale and configural interpretation of up to one hundred MMPI scales.

MMPI Interpretive System
Type: Personality
Distributor: Psychological Assessment Resources
P.O. Box 98, Odessa, FL 33556
(800)331-TEST
Services: Microcomputer—IBM PC and Apple II and compatibles
Description: Operates from T-score input and provides a profile and interpretive report based on the clinical scales and several frequently scored research scales.

MMPI Report
Type: Assessment
Distributor: Multi-Health Systems, Inc.
10 Parfield Drive, Willowdale, Ontario M2J 1B9 Canada
(416)498-1200
Services: Microcomputer—IBM PC and Apple II and compatibles
Description: Generates an automated interpretation of the MMPI based on T-score configurations.

Multidimensional Personality Questionnaire (MPQ) Clinical Interpretive Report
Type: Normal personality
Distributor: National Computer Systems
P.O. Box 1416, Minneapolis, MN 55440
(612)933-2800 and (800)328-6759
Services: Arion II teleprocessing, central scoring
Description: Assesses normal personality in college students and adults, yielding results that can be easily communicated to the client or patient.

Multidimensional Personality Questionnaire (MPQ) Guidance Interpretive Report
Type: Normal personality
Distributor: National Computer Systems
P.O. Box 1416, Minneapolis, MN 55440
(612)933-2800 and (800)328-6759
Services: Arion II teleprocessing, central scoring
Description: Assesses normal personality in college students and adults, yielding results that can be easily communicated to the client or patient.

Myers-Briggs Type Indicator (MBTI)
Type: Measures personality disposition and interests based on Jung's theory of types
Distributor: Consulting Psychologists Press, Inc.
577 College Avenue, Palo Alto, CA 94306
(415)857-1444
Services: Mail-in scoring and software (IBM PC with 256K memory)
Description: The MBTI Software package enables the MBTI user to administer, score, and report the results of the MBTI. MBTI Apple software is being developed. The MBTI Software Complete Program contains one hundred administrations of any combination of Forms F, G, or AV, plus user's guide and binder. There is a per-use royalty fee for each administration.

Myers-Briggs Type Indicator (MBTI)
Type: Normal personality
Distributor: National Computer Systems
P.O. Box 1416, Minneapolis, MN 55440
(612)933-2800 and (800)328-6759
Services: Arion II teleprocessing, central scoring
Description: A measure of personality dispositions and interests based on Carl Jung's theory of types. It characterizes individuals according to their style of gathering information, drawing conclusions, and relating to the world around them. The indicator facilitates decision making involving employment, education, and many areas of interpersonal relations.

Ohio Vocational Interest Survey
Type: Vocational
Distributor: Psychological Corporation
7500 Old Oak Boulevard, Cleveland, OH 44130
(216)234-5300
Services: Mail-in
Description: Provides a vocational/career assessment of individuals from seventh grade through college.

Peabody Individual Achievement Test-Diagnostic Report
Type: Cognitive
Distributor: Precision People, Inc.
3452 North Ridge Circle, S., Jacksonville, FL 32217
(904)262-1096
Services: Microcomputer—IBM PC and compatibles
Description: Provides a profiling and interpretation of the Peabody Individual Achievement Test.

Personal Career Development Profile for the 16 PF
Type: Personality
Distributor: Institute for Personality and Ability Testing, Inc.
P.O. Box 188, Champaign, IL 61820
(217)352-4739
Services: Mail-in; teleprocessing
Description: Offers a professionally developed computer interpretation of the 16 PF for career exploration and personal development purposes. The report organizes relevant information about individual strengths, behavioral attributes, and gratifications to accomplish personal career development objectives. The report helps individuals achieve deeper insights about their strengths and needs and provides administrators with a powerful tool for identifying hidden employee talent.

Personal Problems Checklist
Type: Personality
Distributor: Psychological Assessment Resources, Inc.
P.O. Box 98, Odessa, FL 33556
(800)331-TEST
Services: Microcomputer—IBM PC and Apple II and compatibles
Description: The program administers the checklist, allowing the individual to indicate the extent of the problem. The program calculates the number of problems and presents the most significant ones in rank order.

Personal Problems Checklist: Computer Version
Type: Intake
Distributor: Multi-Health Systems, Inc.
10 Parfield Drive, Willowdale, Ontario M2J 1B9 Canada
(416)498-1200
Services: Microcomputer—IBM PC and Apple II and compatibles
Description: An administration and reporting instrument designed to facilitate the rapid assessment of an individual's problems as seen from the person's point of view.

Personality Inventory for Children (PIC)
Type: Inventory of child personality as perceived by parent
Distributor: Western Psychological Services (WPS TEST REPORT)
12031 Wilshire Boulevard, Los Angeles, CA 90025
(213)478-2061
Services: Mail-in; microcomputer—IBM PC and compatibles
Description: Scores the PIC for all standard scales and a number of research scales. Code types are generated, and the profile is plotted. A narrative report interprets major features of the score profile using a set of empirically determined decision rules. Responses to critical items are printed.

Piers-Harris Children's Self Concept Scale (PHCSCS)
Type: Self-concept inventory for children
Distributor: Western Psychological Services (WPS TEST REPORT)
12031 Wilshire Boulevard, Los Angeles, CA 90025
(213)478-2061
Services: Mail-in; microcomputer—IBM PC and compatibles
Description: Scores the PHCSCS for six major subscales and plots the results. A narrative report interprets different patterns of profile scores. Critical item responses are printed. A group report is produced for sets of children processed at the same time.

Porch Index of Communicative Ability (PICA)
Type: Measures speech impairments
Distributor: Consulting Psychologists Press, Inc.
577 College Avenue, Palo Alto, CA 94306
(415)857-1444
Services: Mail-in scoring and software (48K Apple II Plus or IIe and at least one disk drive (DOS 3.3))
Description: PICA software ("PICAPAD") computes all ninety-eight values and percentiles for the PICA. Scores are entered into the computer, which calculates and displays the results. PICA converts the keyboard into an electronic keypad for entering scores. Subtests can be ranked by difficulty, individual subtests displayed for comparison and correction, and scores can be saved on the disk. PICAPAD software is available on an annual lease basis.

Problem Solving Rehabilitation: I
Type: Cognitive
Distributor: Robert J. Sbordone, Ph.D., Inc.
8840 Warner Avenue, Suite 301, Fountain Valley, CA 92708
(714)841-6293
Services: Microcomputer IBM PC and compatibles
Description: Monitors patient responses and provides computer-based training in visual-spatial problem-solving skills.

Problem Solving Rehabilitation: II
Type: Cognitive
Distributor: Robert J. Sbordone, Ph.D., Inc.
8840 Warner Avenue, Suite 301, Fountain Valley, CA 92708
(714)841-6293
Services: Microcomputer—IBM PC and compatibles
Description: Monitors patient responses and trains patients to plan and evaluate the consequences of their behavior. The program is designed to train cognitively impaired individuals to improve their problem-solving skills.

Projective Drawing Analysis
Type: Personality (projective)
Distributor: Joseph M. Eisenberg, Ph.D.
204 E. Joppa Road, Suite 10, Towson, MD 21204
(301)321-9101
Services: Mail-in; microcomputer—IBM PC and compatibles
Description: Designed to interpret the House-Tree-Person or the Human Figure Drawing Test. The data can be entered from paper-and-pencil scoring of the protocol or by an on-line scoring procedure. The program interprets the results and provides a report covering thirteen areas of personality and social functioning.

Psychological/Psychiatric Status Interview
Type: Intake
Distributor: Multi-Health Systems, Inc.
10 Parfield Drive, Willowdale, Ontario M2J 1B9 Canada
(416)498-1200
Services: Microcomputer—IBM PC and Apple II and compatibles
Description: Designed for on-line computer administration of an initial mental status exam and psychological-psychiatric interview.

Psychological Resources Reports
Type: Personality; vocational; interest and cognitive
Distributor: Psychological Resources, Inc.
74 14th Street NW, Atlanta, GA 30309
(404)892-3000

Services: Mail-in; teleprocessing; microcomputer—IBM PC and compatibles
Description: Provides an integrated psychological report based on several psychological tests. It was tailored for specific settings, such as correctional facilities.

Psychological/Social History Report
Type: Intake
Distributor: Multi-Health Systems, Inc.
10 Parfield Drive, Willowdale, Ontario M2J 1B9 Canada
(416)498-1200
Services: Microcomputer—IBM PC and Apple II and compatibles
Description: Conducts a structured psychological intake interview and generates a narrative report.

Psychological/Social History Report
Type: Personality
Distributor: Psychological Assessment Resources, Inc.
P.O. Box 98, Odessa, FL 33556
(800)331-TEST
Services: Microcomputer—IBM PC and Apple II and compatibles
Description: Presents an automated structured interview. Information related to the individual's personal history, developmental background, work and educational history, and current stressors are included. The program can be administered on the computer.

Report Writer: Adult's Intellectual Achievement, and Neuropsychological Screening Tests
Type: Intelligence
Distributor: Multi-Health Systems, Inc.
10 Parfield Drive, Willowdale, Ontario M2J 1B9 Canada
(416)498-1200
Services: Microcomputer—IBM PC and Apple II and compatibles
Description: This comprehensive interpretation system provides an interpretive report for the following tests: WAIS-R, Stanford-Binet Intelligence Test, WRAT, WRAT-R, Stroop Color and Word Test, Trail Making Test, Benton Visual Retention Test, Purdue Pegboard Test, Aphasia Screening Signs, and the Symbol Digit Modalities Test.

Report Writer: Children's Intellectual and Achievement Tests 1.1
Type: Intelligence; achievement
Distributor: Multi-Health Systems, Inc.
10 Parfield Drive, Willowdale, Ontario M2J 1B9 Canada
(416)498-1200
Services: Microcomputer—IBM PC and Apple II compatibles

Description: A powerful but very easy to use computer program that provides comprehensive psychoeducational interpretations of the K-ABC, the WISC-R, WPPSI, Stanford-Binet Intelligence Scales, PIAT, and WRAT.

Report Writer: Parent's Interpretive Program
Type: Intelligence; achievement
Distributor: Multi-Health Systems, Inc.
10 Parfield Drive, Willowdale, Ontario M2J 1B9 Canada
(416)498-1200
Services: Microcomputer—IBM PC and Apple II and compatibles
Description: The companion to Report Writer: Children's Intellectual and Achievement Tests, this program provides parents with a step-by-step explanation of the meaning of psychological test scores in general; their child's strengths and weaknesses when compared to group norms; and each test's scores, significant subtest differences, and educational relevance of the evaluation.

Rorschach System
Type: Personality
Distributor: Applied Innovations, Inc.
South Kingstown Office Park, Suite A-1, Wakefield, RI 02879
(800)272-2250
Services: Microcomputer—IBM PC and compatibles
Description: Prints out an interpretative report using statements based on a summary of ten Rorschach scores.

RSCORE (Exner's Scoring of the Rorschach)
Type: Personality (projective)
Distributor: Psychological Assessment Resources
P.O. Box 98, Odessa, FL 33556
(813)977-3395
Services: Microcomputer—IBM PC and Apple II and compatibles
Description: Accepts raw scores from the Exner Rorschach Scoring System and performs the structural summary operations and draws charts of the summary.

RSCORE: Version 2.0 Rorschach Scoring Program
Type: Personality (projective)
Distributor: Multi-Health Systems, Inc.
10 Parfield Drive, Willowdale, Ontario M2J 1B9 Canada
(416)498-1200
Services: Microcomputer—IBM PC and Apple II and compatible
Description: Handles data generated from the Rorschach Test according to Exner's Comprehensive System.

Sacks Sentence Completion Test-K
Type: Personality (projective)
Distributor: Psychological Assessment Resources
P.O. Box 98, Odessa, FL 33556
(813)977-3395
Services: Microcomputer
Description: Accepts typed-in responses from handwritten sentence completions or can be used on-line. The scoring program arranges the completed sentences in a systematic order according to content grouping.

Salience Inventory (SI)
Type: Assesses the relative importance of five major life roles
Distributor: Consulting Psychologists Press, Inc.
577 College Avenue, Palo Alto, CA 94306
(415)857-1444
Services: Software (IBM PC or PC-compatible [256K memory])
Description: Assesses the relative importance of five major life roles: student, worker, homemaker, leisurite, and citizen. The SI is a way to measure a client's orientation to life roles, readiness for career decisions, and exposure to work and occupations, in relation to Super's Life-Career Rainbow model. The SI software administers, scores, and reports the results of the SI. There is a per-use royalty fee for each administration. SI Apple software is being developed.

Sbordone-Hall Memory Battery
Type: Cognitive
Distributor: Robert J. Sbordone, Ph.D., Inc.
8840 Warner Avenue, Suite 301, Fountain Valley, CA 92708
(714)841-6293
Services: Microcomputer—IBM PC and compatibles
Description: Allows for the testing of normal or brain-impaired individuals through on-line administration. The battery of tests include eighteen different memory tasks that are administered by computer. A narrative report is generated after the subject has completed the test battery.

SCL-90-R
Type: Personality-clinical
Distributor: Applied Innovations, Inc.
South Kingstown Office Park, Suite A-1, Wakefield, RI 02879
(800)272-2250
Services: Microcomputer
Description: Administers the Symptom Check List (SCL-90) on-line. The program scores the items, calculates T-scores, compares the raw scores with relevant norms, and prints a report highlighting the major problem areas.

Self-Description Inventory (SDI)

Type: Normal personality

Distributor: National Computer Systems
P.O. Box 1416, Minneapolis, MN 55440
(612)933-2800 and (800)328-6759

Services: Central scoring

Description: Measures personality dimensions and vocationally oriented temperament dimensions of the general population. There are eleven bipolar personal description scales and the six general vocational scales based on the well-known dimensions—realistic, investigative, artistic, social, enterprising, and conventional. The short, easy-to-read Profile Report presents standard scores and a graphic display of all of the scales and indexes. The Self-Description Inventory is frequently used with other vocational interest inventories to provide insights into personal characteristics that influence the education and career planning process.

Session Summary

Type: Treatment Planning

Distributor: Multi-Health Systems, Inc.
10 Parfield Drive, Willowdale, Ontario M2J 1B9 Canada
(416)4988-1200

Services: Microcomputer—IBM PC and compatibles

Description: Designed to aid the clinician in the completion of case notes and documentation of treatment. The program allows the clinician to quickly and easily summarize the client's presentation and the significant events of each session, within the framework of the client's treatment goals.

Shipley Institute of Living Scale

Type: Cognitive

Distributor: Integrated Professional Systems
5211 Mahoning Avenue, Suite 135, Youngstown, OH 44515
(216)799-3282

Services: Microcomputer—IBM PC and compatibles

Description: Administers two subtests of the Shipley scale, Vocabulary and Abstract Reasoning. The program provides mental age scores for vocabulary, abstract reasoning, and a total level of functioning. An intellectual impairment index is computed.

Shipley Institute of Living Scale

Type: Intellectual screening

Distributor: Western Psychological Services (WPS TEST REPORT)
12031 Wilshire Boulevard, Los Angeles, CA 90025
(213)478-2061

Services: Scoring and interpretation report

Description: Computes age-adjusted WAIS-R and WAIS IQ scores as well as separate raw and T-scores for Vocabulary and Abstraction scales. Includes basic validity checks, brief narrative interpretation, and IQ estimation. Test takes a minimum of twenty minutes and may be given on-line or via standard paper-and-pencil administration. An updated and revised manual is to be published in 1987; it will link studies to computerized version.

SHRINK: Mental Health Office Management System
Type: Office management
Distributor: Multi-Health Systems, Inc.
10 Parfield Drive, Willowdale, Ontario M2J 1B9 Canada
(416)498-1200
Services: Microcomputer—IBM PC and Apple II and compatibles
Description: An office management and billing system designed specifically for mental health practitioners that automates the client-related business and accounting aspects of a practice, for example, income-producing activities, client history, service provision, expenses, and payments.

Sixteen Personality Factor Questionnaire (16 PF)
Type: Personality
Distributor: Institute for Personality and Ability Testing, Inc.
P.O. Box 188, Champaign, IL 61820-0188
(217)352-4739
Services: Mail-in; teleprocessing; local processing
Description: A general, all-purpose type of report that is very economical. Provides a complete report for each individual, including descriptions of all personality characteristics of significance as well as vocational and occupational comparisons of importance in counseling.

Sixteen Personality Factor Questionnaire (16 PF)
Type: Personality
Distributor: Integrated Professional Services
5211 Mahoning Avenue, Suite 135, Youngstown, OH 44515
(216)799-3282
Services: Microcomputer—IBM PC and compatibles
Description: Offers a profile of the 16 PF scores and an interpretative analysis.

Sixteen Personality Factor Questionnaire (16 PF/CL)
Type: Personality
Distributor: Precision People, Inc.
3452 North Ride Circle South, Jacksonville, FL 32217
(904)262-1096
Services: Microcomputer—IBM PC and Apple II and compatibles
Description: Provides a narrative clinical report for the 16 PF that incorporates personality descriptions, dynamics, psychological problems, and clinical prognosis along with occupational interests and possible medical problems.

Sixteen Personality Factor Questionnaire (16 PF)
Type: Normal personality
Distributor: National Computer Systems
P.O. Box 1416, Minneapolis, MN 55440
(612)933-2800 and (800)328-6759
Services: Arion II and teleprocessing, central scoring, MICROTEST assessment software (on-line administration and scanned scoring)
Description: Provides detailed information on sixteen primary personality traits to assist professionals in a wide range of clinical, human resource development, and counseling situations. It is useful to psychologists and other mental health professionals in individual, family, and marital counseling.

Sixteen Personality Factor Questionnaire (16 PF)
Type: Personality
Distributor: Applied Innovations, Inc.
South Kingstown Office Park, Suite A-1, Wakefield, RI 02879
(800)272-2250
Services: Microcomputer—IBM PC and compatibles
Description: Provides a profile of 16 PF scores and a narrative report covering personality description, psychopathology, personality dynamics, medical concerns, and occupational interests.

Sixteen Personality Factor Report (16 PF)
Type: Personality
Distributor: Multi-Health Systems, Inc.
10 Parfield Drive, Willowdale, Ontario M2J 1B9 Canada
(416)498-1200
Services: Microcomputer—IBM PC and Apple II and compatibles
Description: Generates an automated interpretation of the Sixteen Personality Factor Questionnaire based on Sten scores.

Sixteen Personality Factor Test (16 PF)
Type: Personality
Distributor: Psychological Assessment Resources
P.O. Box 98, Odessa, FL 33556
(813)977-3395
Services: Microcomputer—IBM PC and Apple II and compatibles
Description: Provides on-line administration, scoring, and interpretation of the 16 PF. The narrative report was written by Dr. Sam Karson.

Sixteen Personality Factor Test (16 PF) Karson Report
Type: Personality
Distributor: Psychological Assessment Resources, Inc.
P.O. Box 98, Odessa, FL 33556
(800)331-TEST
Services: Microcomputer—IBM PC and Apple II and compatibles
Description: Administers the test items, calculates the raw and T-scores for over forty-five different scales. The interpretive report provides a summary profile and a narrative summary.

Slosson Intelligence Test-Computer Report
Type: Cognitive
Distributor: Psychological Assessment Resources
P.O. Box 98, Odessa, FL 33556
(813)977-3395
Services: Microcomputer—IBM PC and Apple II and compatibles
Description: Provides the clinician with a profile of intellectual skills and serves as a screening decision as to whether to evaluate the patient's intellectual or academic problems further. The narrative report provides a comparison of achievement with ability.

Social History Questionnaire
Type: Interview
Distributor: Integrated Professional Systems
5211 Mahoning Avenue, Suite 135, Youngstown, OH 44515
(216)799-3282
Services: Microcomputer—IBM PC and compatibles
Description: Administers a series of interview questions then produces a narrative report dealing with the patient's early educational and military history, presenting problems, interpersonal relations, and a history of substance abuse.

Strong-Campbell Interest Inventory (SCII)
Type: Career interest inventory
Distributor: Consulting Psychologists Press, Inc.
577 College Avenue, Palo Alto, CA 94306
(415)857-1444
Services: Mail-in scoring and software (IBM and Apple [256K memory] compatible)
Description: The Strong Software System is designed to administer, score, and report the results of the SCII on an immediate, affordable basis at practitioners' own locations. Included in this system are the Software Set (diskettes, user's guide, and binder), System 180 Controller, CodeLock,™ Scoring Key, and an optical scanner program. The complete system is $800. There is a per-use royalty fee of $1.55 to $2.00 for each administration.

Strong-Campbell Interest Inventory (SCII)
Type: Career/vocational interest survey
Distributor: National Computer Systems
P.O. Box 1416, Minneapolis, MN 55440
(612)933-2800 and (800)328-6759
Services: Arion II teleprocessing, central scoring, MICROTEST assessment software (on-line administration and scanned scoring)
Description: A vocational interest assessment tool that compares a person's interests and preferences with those of individuals in specific careers. The inventory was designed to measure occupational interests in areas requiring advanced technical, college, or postgraduate training. It can be used in a wide range of counseling, educational, and business settings. Scores are reported on general occupational themes, 23 basic interest scales, and 162 occupational scales. The computerized Profile Report presents scores on all of the scales in an easy-to-read format. The detailed seven-page Narrative Report explains the scores on all scales and supplies references for further career information.

Temperament and Values Inventory (TVI)
Type: Normal personality
Distributor: National Computer Systems
P.O. Box 1416, Minneapolis, MN 55440
(612)933-2800 and (800)328-6759
Services: Arion II teleprocessing and central scoring
Description: Designed to measure work-related dimensions of temperament and reinforcers. It measures relatively stable temperament characteristics of individuals in the world of work such as mood quality, activity level, intensity of reaction, and persistence. The value dimensions measure the importance people place on work-related reinforcers such as leadership or social recognition. The short, easy-to-read profile report plots scores on the seven Personal Characteristics (temperament) scales and seven Reward Values scales. The TVI is used in educational settings for career planning, in business and industry for employee development programs, and in clinical practice to provide programs and clues to emotional difficulties that may be work-related.

Tennessee Self Concept Scale (TSCS)
Type: Inventory of self-concept tendencies
Distributor: Western Psychological Services (WPS TEST REPORT)
12031 Wilshire Boulevard, Los Angeles, CA 90025
(213)478-2061
Services: Diagnosis and classification report
Description: Accepts T-scores and compares the profile of the individual client to more that twenty empirically determined prototypic patterns from major diagnostic groups. The result is a statistical classification analysis that gives probability estimates that the client is representative of each group.

Termination/Discharge Summary
Type: Treatment planning
Distributor: Multi-Health Systems, Inc.
10 Parfield Drive, Willowdale, Ontario M2J 1B9 Canada
(416)498-1200
Services: Microcomputer—IBM PC and compatibles
Description: Assists the clinician in developing a comprehensive yet concise summary of the client and the course of evaluation and/or treatment.

TimeLine: Customized Time Management
Type: Training program/ability/personality
Distributor: Institute for Personality and Ability Testing, Inc.
P.O. Box 188, Champaign, IL 61820
(217)352-4739
Services: Mail-in
Description: Offers a unique approach to personal time management skills. Designed for use in on-the-job settings, it can be administered by specialists from the human resources, personnel, or staff development areas as a part of ongoing training and development programs. The program injects a personal uniqueness perspective into standard time-management training modes. Using a combination of personal insights and sound step-by-step exercises, participants learn how to improve their time-management skills effectively. The workbook format of the program is individually developed for each participant. This is made possible through computerized analysis of the 16 PF and a Skills Assessment Inventory.

Values Scale (VS)
Type: Measures intrinsic and extrinsic life-career values
Distributor: Consulting Psychologists Press, Inc.
577 College Avenue, Palo Alto, CA 94306
(415)857-1444
Services: Microcomputer—IBM PC and compatibles (256K memory)
Description: The VS is a measure of intrinsic and extrinsic life-career values, developed as part of the international Work Importance Study as an improvement on existing values scales. As such it also measures many cultural perspectives and lists international norms. The VS software administers, scores, and reports the results of the VS. There is a per-use royalty fee for each administration. VS Apple software is being developed.

Vineland Adaptive Behavior Scales-ASSIST
Type: Interview
Distributor: American Guidance Service
Publisher's Building, Circle Pines, MN 55014
(800)328-2560

Services: Microcomputer
Description: Scores the Vineland Adaptive Behavior Scales, which assess adaptive behavior in four areas: communication, daily living skills, socialization, and motor skills. The interview ratings are administered by booklet and later entered into the computer. The program provides the clinician with scoring and profiling.

Vocational Information Profile
Type: Aptitude and interest measure
Distributor: National Computer Systems
P.O. Box 1416, Minneapolis, MN 55440
(612)933-2800 and (800)328-6759
Services: Local scoring via NCS MICROTEST
Description: Combines the General Aptitude Test Battery and the U.S. Employment Service Interest Inventory, and relates an individual's interest patterns to clusters of work groups called Occupational Aptitude Patterns (OAP). Results are produced in a narrative report summarizing interest and aptitude results and referencing page numbers to the Guide for Occupational Exploration. This program is used largely in vocational counseling settings.

Vocational Interest Inventory (VII)
Type: Assesses interest in eight major types of occupational areas
Distributor: Western Psychological Services (WPS TEST REPORT)
12031 Wilshire Boulevard, Los Angeles, CA 90025
(213)478-2061
Services: Mail-in
Description: Computer scored by WPS TEST REPORT, which provides a five- to six-page personalized narrative report that is easily understood by the student. The report includes a profile of scores by percentile, a score summary giving the percentiles and T-scores for each scale, an analysis and discussion of all scores at or above the seventy-fifth percentile, and a college majors profile that shows how the individual's scores compared to the mean scores of graduating college majors who took the VII when they were high-school juniors.

Vocational Interest Profile Report
Type: Vocational assessment
Distributor: Multi-Health Systems, Inc.
10 Parfield Drive, Willowdale, Ontario M2J 1B9 Canada
(416)498-1200
Services: Microcomputer—IBM PC and Apple II and compatibles
Description: Administers, scores, and interprets the Interest Check List developed by the United States Department of Labor.

Vocational Preference Inventory
Type: Vocational/personality
Distributor: Integrated Professional Systems
5211 Mahoning Avenue, Suite 135, Youngstown, OH 44515
(216)799-3282
Services: Microcomputer—IBM PC and compatibles
Description: Measures vocational and career interests through personality inventory–type questions. Items dealing with interpersonal relationships, personal attitudes, masculine-feminine interests, self-control, and so forth, are included in the inventory. The program provides a profile and an interpretive report.

WAIS-R (Holliman Report)
Type: Intelligence
Distributor: Psych Lab
1714 Tenth Street, Wichita Falls, TX 76301
(817)723-0012
Services: Mail-in; microcomputer—IBM PC and compatibles
Description: Accepts calculated scores and provides a narrative interpretation of the behavior observations and the Wechsler Adult Intelligence Scale-Revised scores.

WAIS-R Report
Type: Cognitive
Distributor: Psychologistics, Inc.
P.O. Box 3896, Indialantic, FL 32903
(305)259-7811
Services: Microcomputer—IBM PC and compatibles
Description: Accepts WAIS-R raw scores and provides a standard score profile, the IQ classification range, and an interpretive report. The report provides a description of behavioral observations and of the intelligence quotient difference, and a scale-by-scale analysis of the WAIS-R subtests.

WAIS-R Report
Type: Intellectual assessment
Distributor: Multi-Health Systems, Inc.
10 Parfield Drive, Willowdale, Ontario M2J 1B9 Canada
(416)498-1200
Services: Microcomputer—IBM PC, Apple II and compatibles, and Macintosh
Description: Provides automated interpretation of the WAIS-R based on behavioral observations and scale scores.

Wechsler Interpretation System
Type: Intelligence
Distributor: Applied Innovations, Inc.
South Kingstown Office Park, Suite A-1, Wakefield, RI 02879
(800)872-2250
Services: Microcomputer—IBM PC and compatibles
Description: Several programs are available to provide narrative reports on the WAIS-R and the WISC-R tests. The raw scores are entered and a profile and a narrative report are produced.

Wechsler Memory Scale Report
Type: Assessment
Distributor: Multi-Health Systems, Inc.
10 Parfield Drive, Willowdale, Ontario M2J 1B9 Canada
(416)498-1200
Services: Microcomputer—IBM PC and Apple II and compatibles
Description: Interprets and graphs the results of the Wechsler Memory Scale.

WISC-R (Holliman Report)
Type: Intelligence
Distributor: Psych Lab
1714 Tenth Street, Wichita Falls, TX 76301
(817)723-0012
Services: Mail-in; microcomputer—IBM PC and compatibles
Description: Prints out a profile and a narrative report of the Wechsler Intelligence Scale for Children-Revised scores.

WISC-R Report
Type: Intellectual Assessment
Distributor: Multi-Health Systems, Inc.
10 Parfield Drive, Willowdale, Ontario M2J 1B9 Canada
(416)498-1200
Services: Microcomputer—IBM PC, Apple II and compatibles, and Macintosh
Description: Provides an automated interpretation of the WISC-R based on behavioral observations and scaled scores.

WISC-R Report
Type: Intelligence
Distributor: Psychological Assessment Resources
P.O. Box 98, Odessa, FL 33556
(813)977-3395
Services: Microcomputer—IBM PC and Apple II and compatibles
Description: A computer version of the Whitworth and Sutton compilation

editor. Intellectual deficiencies and remedial objectives are included in the report.

WISC-R Report
Type: Intelligence
Distributor: Psychologistics, Inc.
P.O. Box 3896, Indialantic, FL 32903
(305)259-7811
Services: Microcomputer
Description: Accepts raw scores of the WISC-R and provides a profile and a narrative report that summarizes demographic information and the child's performance on the subtests.

Woodcock Reading Mastery Test (ASSIST)
Type: Cognitive
Distributor: American Guidance Service
Publisher's Building, Circle Pines, MN 55014
(800)328-2560
Services: Mail-in; microcomputer—IBM PC and compatibles
Description: Provides the diagnostician with an evaluation of reading achievement and educational disability.

Word and Number Assessment Inventory (WNAI)
Type: Aptitude test
Distributor: National Computer Systems
P.O. Box 1416, Minneapolis, MN 55440
(612)933-2800 and (800)328-6759
Services: Arion II teleprocessing and central scoring
Description: Measures verbal and numerical aptitudes usually acquired by the time of high-school graduation. The inventory is used to help direct individuals toward careers and provide advice on improving skills. Both the Word Section Score and the Number Section Score are compared with those of persons with different educational backgrounds. The Narrative Report explains individuals' scores in terms of educational level and occupational examples. It also suggests support materials that may be used to improve skills.

WPPSI Report
Type: Intellectual assessment
Distributor: Multi-Health Systems, Inc.
10 Parfield Drive, Willowdale, Ontario M2J 1B9 Canada
(416)498-1200
Services: Microcomputer—IBM PC and Apple II and compatibles
Description: Provides automated interpretation of the Wechsler Preschool and Primary Scale of Intelligence based on behavioral observations and scaled scores.

WPPSI Report
Type: Cognitive
Distributor: Psychologistics, Inc.
P.O. Box 3896, Indialantic, FL 32903
(305)259-7811
Services: Microcomputer—IBM PC and compatibles
Description: Accepts raw scores and provides a profile and narrative report of intellectual functioning. The narrative report consists of a summary of demographic information, a description of the child's behavior, a discussion of assessed strengths and weaknesses, and a summary of achievement potential.

Appendix B

American Psychological Association Guidelines for Computer-Based Tests and Interpretations

Committee on Professional Standards (COPS) and Committee on Psychological Tests and Assessment (CPTA)

Introduction

The use of computers in psychological testing and assessment is not a recent development. With the introduction of user-friendly microcomputers and software within the economic grasp of the individual practitioner, however, the variety of such uses has increased at a hitherto unequaled rate. These uses include computer administration of psychological tests, computerized test scoring, and computer-generated interpretations of test results and related information. The rapid increase in the availability and use of these applications of computer technology has served as the impetus for the writing of this document.

In addition, the market is swiftly expanding for automated test scoring services, computerized test interpretations, computer-administered tests, and software to perform these functions. It is essential that the users, developers, and distributors of computer-based tests, scoring services, and interpretation services apply to these technological innovations the same ethical, professional, and technical standards that govern the development and use of traditional means of performing these functions.

The American Psychological Association (APA) first adopted interim standards on "Automated Test Scoring and Interpretation Practices" many years ago (Newman, 1966, p. 1141). The 1974 *Standards for Educational and Psychological Tests* (APA) included several references to computerized assessment. The 1985 *Standards for Educational and Psychological Testing* (Standards, 1985) contains even more. The guidelines that follow are a special application of the revised *Testing Standards* and relate specifically to the use of computer administration, scoring, and interpretation of psychological tests. These guidelines are advisory in nature and are intended to provide a frame of reference for addressing relevant issues arising from the use of computer technology in testing.

PURPOSE

In January 1984 the APA Board of Directors instructed the Committee on Professional Standards (a committee of the Board of Professional Affairs) and the Committee on Psychological Tests and Assessment (a committee of the Board of Scientific Affairs) to develop guidelines for computer-based test administration, scoring, and interpretation. During the development of these Guidelines the Committee on Professional Standards has consisted of Susan R. Berger, William Chestnut, LaMaurice H. Gardner, Jo-Ida Hansen, Carrie Miller, Marlene Muse, Lyle F. Schoenfeldt, William Schofield (chair), and Barbara Wand. The Committee on Psychological Tests and Assessment has consisted of Wayne F. Cascio, Fritz Drasgow, Richard Duran, Bert F. Green (chair, 1984), Lenore Harmon, Asa Hilliard, Douglas N. Jackson (chair, 1985), Trevor Sewell, and Hilda Wing. Central Office staff assistance was provided by Debra Boltas and Rizalina Mendiola.

These Guidelines were written to assist professionals in applying computer-based assessments competently and in the best interests of their clients. The Guidelines were designed also to guide test developers in establishing and maintaining the quality of new products.

Specific reference is made to existing APA standards of particular relevance to computerized testing, which are abbreviated as follows: the *Ethical Principles of Psychologists* (*Ethical Principles*; APA, 1981); the *Standards for Educational and Psychological Testing* (*Testing Standards*; APA, 1985); and the *Standards for Providers of Psychological Services* (*Provider Standards*; APA, 1977). In addition, use has been made of selected sections of *Standards for the Administration and Interpretation of Computerized Psychological Testing* (Hofer & Bersoff, 1983).

The general purpose of these Guidelines is to interpret the *Testing Standards* as they relate to computer-based testing and test interpretation. They are intended to indicate the nature of the professional's responsibilities rather than to provide extensive technical advice, although some technical material of particular relevance to computer-based assessment has been included. The *Testing Standards* provide complete technical standards for testing. Technical guidance in computerized adaptive cognitive testing can be found in Green, Bock, Humphreys, Linn, and Reckase (1982, 1984).

When the circumstances of computer testing are essentially equivalent to those of conventional tests, it is presumed here that the issue is covered in the *Testing Standards*. For example, test security is essential to the integrity and meaning of scores on any test, whether the test is administered conventionally or by computer. Users should guard computer software for a test as diligently as they would booklets of a conventional test, so no special mention was deemed necessary.

The Guidelines are deliberately slanted toward personality assessment and the migration of conventional tests to the computer form of presentation. Many new tests are now being developed specifically for computer presentation, including many tests requiring novel responses. In general, the *Testing Standards* provides pertinent guidance for the development of such tests and should be considered to take precedence over these Guidelines.

In preparing these Guidelines, the Committee on Professional Standards (COPS) and the Committee on Psychological Tests and Assessment (CPTA) were aware that the sale and use of computerized test scoring and interpretive services extends beyond the membership of APA and that the guidelines may be of some relevance to others. Nevertheless, as an APA document, it has been appropriate to refer to APA documents throughout, even though they are binding only on APA members.

The Committees were further aware that APA standards refer to the obligations of individual members, whereas computerized testing services are usually the products of incorporated companies. The purpose of these Guidelines is to offer guidance to APA members as professional psychologists when they use, develop, or participate in the promotion or sale of computerized test scoring or interpretive services, either alone or as an agent or director of a company. The Guidelines apply particularly to the administration and use of tests for individual decision making. However, the Guidelines also are relevant when the test results are to be used in research or in general group evaluation. In all cases, it is expected that professional judgment will determine the relevance of a particular guideline to a particular situation.

PARTICIPANTS IN THE TESTING PROCESS

TEST DEVELOPER

The *Testing Standards* identifies the test developer as an individual or agency who develops, publishes, and markets a test. For purposes of this document it is useful to distinguish among the following: (a) the *test author*, who originally develops a test; (b) the *software author*, who develops the algorithm that administers the test, scores the test and, in some cases, provides interpretive statements; and (c) the *test or software publisher*, who markets the computer software and accompanying documentation for the test.

TEST USER

The professional who requires the test results for some decision-making purpose. In some cases the test user provides the scores or an interpretation of the results to some separate decision maker, such as a probation officer or a director of college admissions. In that case, both parties bear responsibility for proper test use.

TEST TAKER

The individual who takes the test. In some cases, such as in a self-directed guidance system, the test taker may be the ultimate consumer and is in this sense both test taker and test user. When the test taker is the ultimate consumer, special care is needed in providing an appropriate context for understanding the test results.

TEST ADMINISTRATOR

The individual who actually supervises and has professional responsibility for administering the test. In cases where the test administrator delegates the proctoring of test administration to another person, the administrator retains responsibility for adherence to sound professional practice.

Responsible actions of these various parties all contribute to the effective delivery of services to clients. Many of these responsibilities have been set forth in the *Ethical Principles* and *Provider Standards*. Reference is made here to these documents even though it is recognized that the parties might not be psychologists in all cases. Although binding only on psychologists, these documents provide sound advice for any person responsible for developing and offering computer-based administration, scoring, and interpretation of psychological tests.

The User's Responsibilities

Some aspects of testing can be carried out advantageously by a computer. Conditions of administration of some tests can be better standardized and more accurately timed and controlled when the test is administered by a computer. Test scoring can be done more efficiently and accurately by a computer than it can by hand. Test score interpretation based on complex decision rules can be generated quickly and accurately by a computer. However, none of these applications of computer technology is any better than the decision rules or algorithm upon which they are based. The judgment required to make appropriate decisions based on information provided by a computer is the responsibility of the user.

The test user should be a qualified professional with (a) knowledge of psychological measurement; (b) background in the history of the tests or inventories being used; (c) experience in the use and familiarity with the research on the tests or inventories, including gender, age, and cultural differences if applicable; and (d) knowledge of the area of intended application. For example, in the case of personality inventories, the user should have knowledge of psychopathology or personality theory.

The responsibilities of users are expressed by the following clauses from the *Ethical Principles* and *Provider Standards*.

ETHICAL PRINCIPLE 1: RESPONSIBILITY

In providing services, psychologists maintain the highest standards of their profession. They accept responsibility for the consequences of their acts and make every effort to ensure that their services are used appropriately.

Interpretation. Professionals accept personal responsibility for any use they make of a computer-administered test or a computer-generated test interpretation. It follows that they should be aware of the method used in generating the scores and interpretation and be sufficiently familiar with the test in order to be able to evaluate its applicability to the purpose for which it will be used.

ETHICAL PRINCIPLE 2: COMPETENCE

Psychologists recognize the boundaries of their competence and the limitations of their techniques. They only provide services and only use techniques for which they are qualified by training and experience. They maintain knowledge of current scientific and professional information related to the services they render.

2e. Psychologists responsible for decisions involving individuals or policies based on test results have an understanding of psychological or educational measurement, validation problems, and test research.

Provider Standards 1.5 and 1.6 further underscore the nature of the professional's responsibility.

PROVIDER STANDARD 1: PROVIDERS

1.5 Psychologists shall maintain current knowledge of scientific and professional developments that are directly related to the services they render.

1.6 Psychologists shall limit their practice to their demonstrated areas of professional competence.

Interpretation. Professionals will limit their use of computerized testing to techniques with which they are familiar and competent to use.

ETHICAL PRINCIPLE 6: WELFARE OF THE CONSUMER

Psychologists fully inform consumers as to the purpose and nature of an evaluative . . . procedure.

ETHICAL PRINCIPLE 8: ASSESSMENT TECHNIQUES

8a. In using assessment techniques, psychologists respect the right of clients to have full explanations of the nature and purpose of the techniques in language the clients can understand, unless an explicit exception to this right has been agreed upon in advance. When the explanations are to be provided by others, psychologists establish procedures for ensuring the adequacy of these explanations.

8c. In reporting assessment results, psychologists indicate any reservations that exist regarding validity or reliability because of the circumstances of the assessment or the inappropriateness of the norms for the person tested. Psychologists strive to ensure that the results of assessments and their interpretations are not misused by others.

Interpretation. The direct implication of Principles 8a and 8c for the user of computer-based tests and interpretations is that the user is responsible for communicating the test findings in a fashion understandable to the test taker. The user should outline to the test taker any shortcomings or lack of relevance the report may have in the given context.

Guidelines for Users of Computer-Based Tests and Interpretations

The previous references to the *Ethical Principles*, *Provider Standards*, and *Testing Standards* provide the foundation for the following specific guidelines for computer-based tests and interpretations.

ADMINISTRATION

Standardized conditions are basic to psychological testing. Administrative procedures for tests are discussed in Chapters 15 and 16 of the 1985 *Testing Standards*. The main technical concern is standardization of procedures so that everyone takes the test under essentially similar conditions. Test administrators bear the responsibility for providing conditions equivalent to those in which normative, reliability, and validity data were obtained. The following guidelines are of particular relevance to the computerized environment.

1. Influences on test scores due to computer administration that are irrelevant to the purposes of assessment should be eliminated or taken into account in the interpretation of scores.

2. Any departure from the standard equipment, conditions, or procedures, as described in the test manual or administrative instructions, should be demonstrated not to affect test scores appreciably. Otherwise, appropriate calibration should be undertaken and documented (see Guideline 16).

Comment. A special problem with computerized administration may arise with the use of different equipment by different professionals or use of equipment different from that for which the system originally was intended. Where equipment differences are minor it may be determined on the basis of professional judgment that test scores are unlikely to be affected. In other cases, users should demonstrate empirically that the use of different equipment has no appreciable effects on test scores.

3. The environment in which the testing terminal is located should be quiet, comfortable, and free from distractions.

Comment. The overall aim is to make the environment conducive to optimal test performance for all test takers. Ideally, a separate cubicle for each terminal is recommended. If this is not possible, at a minimum, terminals should be located in a comfortable, quiet room that minimizes distractions. Users should be prepared to show that differences in testing environments have no appreciable effect on performance.

The test administrator should be careful to ensure that the test taker is free from distraction while taking the test and has adequate privacy, especially for tests or inventories involving personal or confidential issues. The environment should be quiet, free of extraneous conversation, and only the test administrator and test taker should be in a position to see either the test items or the responses. In addition to maintaining consistency in the testing environment, this helps to prevent inadvertent item disclosure.

4. Test items presented on the display screen should be legible and free from noticeable glare.

Comment. (See *Testing Standards*, 1985, 15.2) The placement of the equipment can introduce irrelevant factors that may influence test performance. Proper design and position of the display screen will avoid reduction in the legibility of the test materials by reflections from windows, ceiling lights, or table lamps.

5. Equipment should be checked routinely and should be maintained in proper working condition. No test should be administered on faulty equipment. All or part of the test may have to be readministered if the equipment fails while the test is being administered.

Comment. Proper equipment design and optimum conditions do not ensure against malfunctioning equipment. To prevent disruptions such as sticky keys or dirty screens that may adversely affect test performance, there should be a schedule of regular and frequent maintenance, and the equipment should be checked for each test taker prior to its use.

6. Test performance should be monitored, and assistance to the test taker should be provided, as is needed and appropriate. If technically feasible, the proctor should be signaled automatically when irregularities occur.

Comment. Monitoring test performance is important so that the user can remedy any problem that might affect the psychometric soundness of the eventual score or interpretation. For users who test a few individuals, this can be done by simply looking in on the test taker; users who regularly test large numbers of people may wish to monitor automatically. This can be done by using computer programs that notify the test proctor if a test taker is responding too quickly or slowly or outside the range of response options. Peculiar responses might generate a warning to the proctor that the test taker does not understand the test directions, is not cooperating, or that the terminal is malfunctioning. In most cases, help should be immediately available to the test taker. In the case of self-administered tests for guidance and instruction, help may not be urgently needed, but some provision should always be made for assisting the test taker.

7. Test takers should be trained on proper use of the computer equipment, and procedures should be established to eliminate any possible effect on test scores due to the test taker's lack of familiarity with the equipment.

Comment. It is important to ensure that test takers are so familiar with the equipment and procedures that they can devote their full attention to the substance of the test items. Adequate training should be given to those who need it. This may require an ample store of sample items. It is very likely that such practice will reduce anxiety, increase confidence, and improve the reliability and validity of test results.

8. Reasonable accommodations must be made for individuals who may be at an unfair disadvantage in a computer testing situation. In cases where a disadvantage cannot be fully accommodated, scores obtained must be interpreted with appropriate caution.

Comment. Computerized testing may facilitate testing persons with some physical disabilities by providing especially large type or especially simple response mechanisms. In other cases, the computer may place persons who have certain handicapping conditions at a disadvantage. Chapter 14 of the 1985 *Testing Standards* addresses the testing of persons who have handicapping conditions.

Although tests have been successfully administered by computer to large numbers of both younger and older adults, some older people may need special reassurance and extended practice with the equipment and can be expected to respond more slowly than younger test takers. Of course, no accommodation is appropriate when the disadvantage is what is being tested. A person with poor eyesight is at a disadvantage in a test of visual acuity; it is precisely that disadvantage that is being assessed.

INTERPRETATION

9. Computer-generated interpretive reports should be used only in conjunction with professional judgment. The user should judge for each test taker the validity of the computerized test report based on the user's professional knowledge of the total context of testing and the test taker's performance and characteristics.

Comment. A major concern about computer-generated reports is that they may not be as individualized as those generated in the conventional manner. Some information, such as demographic characteristics of the test taker, can be included in interpretation programs so that the computer will use more appropriate norms or base rates, if they exist, and qualify interpretations to take into account the particular test taker's characteristics. But no assessment system, whether computer based or conventional, can, at this time, consider all the unique relevant attributes of each individual.

A test user should consider the total context of testing in interpreting an obtained score before making any decision (including the decision to accept the score). Furthermore, a test user should examine the differences between characteristics of the person tested and those of the population for whom the test was developed and normed. This responsibility includes deciding whether the differences are so great that the test should not be used for the person (*Testing Standards*, 1985, 7.6). These, as well as other judgments (e.g., whether conditions are present that could invalidate test results), may be ones that only a professional observing the testing situation can make. Thus, it is imperative that the final decision be made by a qualified professional who takes responsibility for overseeing both the process of testing and judging the applicability of the interpretive report for individual test takers, consistent with legal, ethical, and professional requirements. In some circumstances, professional providers may need to edit or amend the computer report to take into account their own observations and judgments and to ensure that the report is comprehensible, free of jargon, and true to the person evaluated.

A long history of research on statistical and clinical prediction has established that a well-designed statistical treatment of test results and ancillary information will yield more valid assessments than will an individual professional using the same information. Only when the professional uses more information than the statistical system will the professional be in a position to improve the system's results. Therefore, if the system has a statistical, actuarial base, the professional should be wary of altering the system's interpretation. Likewise, if the system represents the judgments and conclusions of one or more skilled clinicians, the professional must recognize that changing the computerized interpretation means substituting his or her judgment for that of the expert. The final decision must be that of a qualified provider with sensitivity for nuances of test administration and interpretation. Altering the interpretation should not be done routinely, but only for good and compelling reasons.

The Developer's Responsibilities

Developers of computerized test administration, scoring, and interpretation services are referred to the *Testing Standards* (1985), which provides standards for test development. The following general principles from the *Ethical Principles* and the *Provider Standards* also are relevant.

ETHICAL PRINCIPLE 8: ASSESSMENT TECHNIQUES

8b. Psychologists responsible for the development and standardization of psychological tests and other assessment techniques utilize established scientific procedures and observe the relevant APA standards.

8d. Psychologists recognize that assessment results may become obsolete. They make every effort to avoid and prevent the misuse of obsolete measures.

8e. Psychologists offering scoring and interpretation services are able to produce appropriate evidence for the validity of the programs and procedures used in arriving at interpretations. The public offering of an automated interpretation service is considered a professional-to-professional consultation. Psychologists make every effort to avoid misuse of assessment reports.

8f. Psychologists do not encourage or promote the use of psychological assessment techniques by inappropriately trained or otherwise unqualified persons.

PROVIDER STANDARD 1: PROVIDERS

1.5 Psychologists shall maintain current knowledge of scientific and professional development that are directly related to the services they render.

PROVIDER STANDARD 3: ACCOUNTABILITY

3.4 Psychologists are accountable for all aspects of the services they provide and shall be responsive to those concerned with these services.

When advertising and selling computer-based testing services, the following are relevant.

ETHICAL PRINCIPLE 4: PUBLIC STATEMENTS

Public statements, announcements of services, advertising, and promotional activities of psychologists serve the purpose of helping the public make informed judgments and choices. Psychologists represent accurately and objectively their professional qualifications, affiliations, and functions, as well as those of the institutions or organizations with which they or the statements may be associated. In public statements providing psychological information or professional opinions or providing information about the availability of psychological products, publications, and services, psychologists base their statements on scientifically acceptable psychological findings and techniques with full recognition of the limits and uncertainties of such evidence.

4b. Public statements include, but are not limited to, communication by means of periodical, book list, directory, television, radio, or motion picture. They do not contain (i) a false, fraudulent, misleading, deceptive, or unfair statement; (ii) a misinterpretation of fact or a statement likely to mislead or deceive because in context it makes only a partial disclosure of relevant facts; (iii) a testimonial from a patient regarding the quality of a psychologist's services or products; (iv) a statement intended or likely to create false or unjustified expectations of favorable results; (v) a statement implying unusual, unique, or one-of-a-kind abilities; (vi) a statement intended or likely to appeal to a client's fears, anxieties, or emotions concerning the possible results of failure to obtain the offered services; (vii) a statement concerning the comparative desirability of offered services; (viii) a statement of direct solicitation of individual clients.

4e. Psychologists associated with the development or promotion of psychological devices, books, or other products offered for commercial sale make reasonable efforts to ensure that announcements and advertisements are presented in a professional, scientifically acceptable, and factually informative manner.

4g. Psychologists present the science of psychology and offer their services, products, and publications fairly and accurately, avoiding misrepresentation through sensationalism, exaggeration, or superficiality. Psychologists are guided by the primary obligation to aid the public in developing informed judgments, opinions, and choices.

4j. A psychologist accepts the obligation to correct others who represent the psychologist's professional qualifications, or associations with products or services, in a manner incompatible with these guidelines.

4k. Individual diagnostic and therapeutic services are provided only in the context of a professional psychological relationship. When personal advice is given by means of public lectures or demonstrations, newspaper or magazine articles, radio or television programs, mail, or similar media, the psychologist utilizes the most current relevant data and exercises the highest level of professional judgment.

PROVIDER STANDARD 2: PROGRAMS

2.3.1 Where appropriate, each psychological service unit shall be guided by a set of procedural guidelines for the delivery of psychological services. If appropriate to the setting, these guidelines shall be in written form.

Guidelines for the Developers of Computer-Based Test Services

The *Testing Standards* (1985) and the previous cited sections of the *Ethical Principles* and *Provider Standards* provide the foundation for the following specific guidelines for the developers of computer-based test services.

HUMAN FACTORS

10. Computerized administration normally should provide test takers with at least the same degree of feedback and editorial control regarding their responses that they would experience in traditional testing formats.

Comment. For tests that involve a discrete set of response alternatives, test takers should be able to verify the answer they have selected and should normally be given the opportunity to change it if they wish. Tests that require constructed responses (e.g., sentence completion tasks) typically require more extensive editing facilities to permit test takers to enter and modify their answers comfortably. Tests that involve continuous recording of responses (e.g., tracking tasks) can make use of a variety of visual, auditory, or tactile feedback sources to maximize performance and minimize examinee frustration.

11. Test takers should be clearly informed of all performance factors that are relevant to the test result.

Comment. Instructions should provide clear guidance regarding how the test taker is to respond and the relative importance of such factors as speed and accuracy. If changes are permitted, directions should explain how and when this is to be done. Before the actual test begins, the testing system itself or the proctor should check that these instructions are understood and that the examinee is comfortable with the response device.

The availability of screen prompts, an on-line help facility, or a clock display (in the case of timed performances) may be used advantageously to guide the examinee through the test instructions, test practice, and possibly the test itself. If used during the test, such devices become a part of the test itself, and cannot be changed without recalibrating the test.

12. The computer testing system should present the test and record responses without causing unnecessary frustration or handicapping the performance of test takers.

Comment. Advances in hardware and software design have provided a wide range of ways to transmit information to the computer. Computer test design should explore ways that are most comfortable for test takers and allow them to perform at their best. For example, a touch-sensitive screen, light pen, and mouse may all be perceived as being significantly less confusing than a standard computer keyboard. When a standard keyboard is used, it may be appropriate to mask (physically or through software control) all irrelevant keys to reduce the potential for error.

The type of test and test item may create special design problems. Speed tests must have especially quick and uniform time delays between items to minimize frustration. Tests that require reading of long passages or that have complicated directions to which test takers may want to refer occasionally require procedures that allow display changes and recall. Diagrams with fine detail require displays with greater resolution capacity than normal. If such modifications are not possible, the test takers should be provided with the diagrams or instructions in booklet form.

13. The computer testing system should be designed for easy maintenance and system verification.

Comment. When teleprocessing is involved, reasonable efforts should be made to eliminate transmission errors that could affect test scores. Software design should permit ways of checking that scoring and interpretive parameters recorded on a disk, for example, remain intact and accurate.

14. The equipment, procedure, and conditions under which the normative, reliability, and validity data were obtained for the computer test should be described clearly enough to permit replication of these conditions.

15. Appropriate procedures must be established by computerized testing services to ensure the confidentiality of the information and the privacy of the test taker.

Comment. Several services that provide computerized administration of clinical instruments maintain confidentiality by avoiding any use of test takers' names. (See Chapter 16 of the 1985 *Testing Standards*.)

PSYCHOMETRIC PROPERTIES

16. When interpreting scores from the computerized versions of conventional tests, the equivalence of scores from computerized versions should be established and documented before using norms or cutting scores obtained from conventional tests. Scores from conventional and computer administrations may be considered equivalent when (a) the rank orders of scores of individuals tested in alternative modes closely approximate each other, and (b) the means, dispersions, and shapes of the score distributions are approximately the same, or have been made approximately the same by rescaling the scores from the computer mode.

Comment. If individuals obtain equivalent scores from both conventional and computer administration, computer-specific factors will have been shown to have no appreciable effect, and the computer version may legitimately be used in place of the conventional test. If condition (a) is not met, the tests cannot be claimed to be measuring the same construct and should not be used interchangeably. If (a) is met but (b) is not, then one set of scores can be rescaled to be comparable with scores from the other test. If conventional norms are being used, then the computer test scores should be rescaled. If condition (b) is met but (a) is not, then scaling will produce similar distributions, but test equivalence has not been demonstrated. If the tests are not equivalent, new norms should be established. Chapter 4 of the *Testing Standards* (1985) concerns norming and score comparability. Testing Standard 4.6 states that data on form equivalence should be made available, together with detailed information on the method of achieving equivalence. (See also the comment on Standard 2.11, pp. 22–23.)

A number of research designs can be used to study equivalence. Differences in the means, dispersions, or shapes of computer and conventionally obtained test score distributions all indicate a lack of strict equivalence when equivalent groups are tested. Although perfect equivalence may be unattainable (and unnecessary), the following condition should be satisfied if one wishes to use norms from a conventionally developed test to interpret scores from a computerized test. Computer-obtained test scores should preserve, within the acceptable limits of reliability, the ranking of test takers. If ranking is maintained, then scale values can be transformed through such procedures as linear or equipercentile equating so that test takers receive the same score as they would have obtained through conventional administration. In this way, cutting scores, validity estimates, norms, and other data generated from the conventional scale can be applied to the computer-obtained scores. The same considerations would apply (with the obvious changes) to a test developed entirely in the computer medium that was later printed in paper-and pencil format. The equivalence of the forms should be established before norms developed for the computer version are used in interpreting the derivative paper-and-pencil format.

The present Guidelines are conservative in suggesting empirical information about equivalence for each test that is rendered in a different presentation mode. At present some tests in some situations show differences; others do not. As the literature expands, generalizations presumably will permit accurate expectations of the effect of presentation mode.

17. The validity of the computer version of a test should be established by those developing the test.

Comment. Procedures for determining validity are the same for tests administered conventionally and by computer (see Chapter 1 of the 1985 *Testing Standards*). A new computer test should be validated in the same way as any other test. If equivalence has been established between the conventional and computer-administered forms of a test, then the validity of the computer version can be generalized from the validity of the conventional version. If equivalence has not been established, the validity and meaning of the computer version should be established afresh. At present, there is no extensive evidence about the validities of computerized versions of conventional tests. Until such evidence accumulates, it will be better to obtain new evidence of predictive and construct validity.

18. Test services should alert test users to the potential problems of non-equivalence when scores on one version of a test are not equivalent to the scores on the version for which norms are provided.

Comment. This will most often be a problem when comparing a computer version of a test with a conventional paper-and-pencil version, but it can also be a problem when comparing tests presented on two different computer systems. Screens of very different size, or special responding devices such as a light pen, could in some circumstances affect test norms. This is especially an issue with timed responses, which are known to vary in speed for different types of required responses. Until enough information accumulates to permit generalization about the relevance of equipment variation, caution is prudent. When a test is offered on different equipment the offerer should provide assurance of comparability of results, and the accompanying manual should reflect the different equipment.

19. The test developer should report comparison studies of computerized and conventional testing to establish the relative reliability of computerized administration.

20. The accuracy of computerized scoring and interpretation cannot be assumed. Providers of computerized test services should actively check and control the quality of the hardware and software, including the scoring, algorithms, and other procedures described in the manual.

21. Computer testing services should provide a manual reporting the rationale and evidence in support of computer-based interpretation of test scores.

Comment. The developer is responsible for providing sufficient information in the manual so that users may judge whether the interpretive or classification systems are suited to their needs. Chapter 5 of the 1985 *Testing Standards* summarizes the information that should be presented in the manual.

CLASSIFICATION

Certain classification systems depend on the determination of optimal cutting scores. The determination of the cutting score is, in turn, dependent on a number of statistical and practical variables including (a) the base rate of the characteristic to be inferred, (b) the error of measurement at various points along the test score scales, (c) the validity of the tests for the inference to be made, and (d) the costs of errors of classification. Balancing all these considerations is as difficult in making computerized test interpretations as it is in making clinical interpretations.

22. The classification system used to develop interpretive reports should be sufficiently consistent for its intended purpose (see Chapter 2 of the 1985 *Testing Standards*). For example, in some cases it is important that most test takers would be placed in the same groups if retested (assuming the behavior in question did not change).

Comment. There is a trade-off between consistency and precision. The more classification decisions the test is asked to make, the less consistent will such assignments be. Making too few classifications may lead test users to ignore meaningful differences among test takers; too many may lead test users to overestimate the precision of the test.

Classification systems should be sufficiently consistent so that most test takers would be placed in the same groups and given the same interpretations if retested, and sufficiently precise to identify relevant differences among test takers. Consistency depends upon both the reliability of the test and the size of the score intervals in each class. Precision requires that the test be capable of discriminating meaningfully among test takers. Cutting scores and decision rules should take into account the discriminability of the test at different points of the measurement scale and the purposes for which the interpretations will be used. At a minimum, classification categories must represent rational decisions made in the light of the goals users have in mind. The more important the consequences for the test taker, the more assurance there should be that the interpretation and ultimate decisions are fair and accurate. Developers of interpretive systems should exercise discretion in deciding how many and what kinds of classifications will be useful.

23. Information should be provided to the users of computerized interpretation services concerning the consistency of classifications, including, for example, the number of classifications and the interpretive significance of changes from one classification to adjacent ones.

VALIDITY OF COMPUTER INTERPRETATIONS

24. The original scores used in developing interpretive statements should be given to test users. The matrix of original responses should be provided or should be available to test users on request, with appropriate consideration for test security and the privacy of test takers.

25. The manual or, in some cases, interpretive report, should describe how the interpretive statements are derived from the original scores.

Comment. Professionals who provide assessment services bear the ultimate responsibility for providing accurate judgments about the clients they evaluate. It should be possible to fulfill these ethical demands without infringing on the testing service's proprietary rights. To evaluate a computer-based interpretation, the test user should know at least two facts: (a) the nature of the relationship of the interpretations to the test responses and related data, and (b) the test taker's score or scores on the relevant measures. (In addition, raw data or item responses often will be very useful.) For example, the test developer could describe the organization of interpretive statements according to the scale on which they are based, otherwise provide references for statements in the report, or provide in the manual all the interpretive statements in the program library and the scales and research on which they are based. Each test taker's test and scale profile can be printed along with the narrative interpretations, together with the original set of responses where appropriate.

26. Interpretive reports should include information about the consistency of interpretations and warnings related to common errors of interpretation.

Comment. Test developers should provide information that users need to make correct judgments. Interpretive reports should contain warning statements to preclude overreliance on computerized interpretations. Unusual patterns of item responses can lead to seemingly inconsistent statements within a single report ("the respondent shows normal affect"; "the respondent may have suicidal tendencies"). Either the manual or the introductory comments on the interpretation might indicate that inconsistent statements result from inconsistent test responses, which may indicate that the result is not valid.

27. The extent to which statements in an interpretive report are based on quantitative research versus expert clinical opinion should be delineated.

28. When statements in an interpretive report are based on expert clinical opinion, users should be provided with information that will allow them to weigh the credibility of such opinion.

Comment. Some interpretations describe or predict objective behavior, whereas others describe states of mind or internal conflicts. Some interpretations are quite specific, others very general. Some make statements about the test taker's present condition; others make predictions about the future. Some make use of well-established, consensually understood constructs, others use terms drawn from ordinary language. The type of interpretation determines the nature of the evidence that should be provided to the user.

29. When predictions of particular outcomes or specific recommendations are based on quantitative research, information should be provided showing the empirical relationship between the classification and the probability of criterion behavior in the validation group.

Comment. Computerized interpretation systems usually divide test takers into classes. It is desirable to present the relationship among classes and the probability of a particular outcome (e.g., through an expectancy table) as well as validity coefficients between test scores and criteria.

30. Computer testing services should ensure that reports for either users or test takers are comprehensible and properly delimit the bounds within which accurate conclusions can be drawn by considering variables such as age or sex that moderate interpretations.

Comment. Some reports, especially in the area of school and vocational counseling, are meant to be given to the test taker. In many cases, this may be done with limited professional review of the appropriateness of the report. In such cases, developers bear a special burden to ensure that the report is comprehensible. The reports should contain sufficient information to aid the test taker to understand properly the results and sufficient warnings about possible misinterpretations. Supplemental material may be necessary.

REVIEW

31. Adequate information about the system and reasonable access to the system for evaluating responses should be provided to qualified professionals engaged in a scholarly review of the interpretive service. When it is deemed necessary to provide trade secrets, a written agreement of nondisclosure should be made.

Comment. Arrangements should be made for the professional review of computer-based test interpretation systems by persons designated as reviewers by scholarly journals and by other test review organizations, including the Buros-Nebraska Institute of Mental Measurement. Such reviewers need more information than a regular consumer could absorb, but generally will not need access to the computer code or the entire array of statements from which interpretations are fashioned. At present, there is no established style for reviewing a CBTI system, and different reviewers may want different information. At a minimum, a reviewer should be able to communicate freely with technically qualified, knowledgeable persons associated with the test developer, who can answer questions about the system. Access to the system should be provided for trying actual or simulated test responses and for exercising the offered components of the system.

In some cases it may be necessary to impart trade secrets to the reviewer, in which case a written agreement should state the nature of the secret information and the procedures to be used to protect the proprietary interests of the test author, the software author, and the test publisher. As a rule, however, it is advisable to make readily available enough information for a reviewer to evaluate the system. This would include the general structure of the algorithms and the basis for transforming test responses into interpretive reports, but it might not extend to the entire library of interpretive statements or to the specific numerical values of the cutting point and other configural definitions. The general size of the statement library or equivalent process of generating interpretations should be provided, along with information about its source. The algorithms can usually be explained in reasonable detail without disclosing trade secrets.

REFERENCES

American Psychological Association. (1981). Ethical principles of psychologists. *American Psychologist, 36(6)*, 633–638.

American Psychological Association. (1977). *Standards for providers of psychological services*. Washington, DC: Author.

American Psychological Association, American Educational Research Association, and National Council on Measurement in Education. (1974). *Standards for educational and psychological tests*. Washington, DC: American Psychological Association.

Green, B. F., Bock, R. D., Humphreys, L. G., Linn, R. B., and Reckase, M. D. (1982). Evaluation plan for the computerized Adaptive Vocational Aptitude Battery. Baltimore, MD: Johns Hopkins University, Department of Psychology.

Green, B. F., Bock, R. D., Humphreys, L. G., Linn, R. B., and Reckase, M. D. (1984). Technical guidelines for assessing computerized adaptive tests. *Journal of Educational Measurement*, 347–360.

Hofer, P. J. and Bersoff, D. N. (1983). *Standards for the administration and interpretation of computerized psychological testing*. (Available from D. N. Bersoff, APA, Suite 511, 1200 Seventeenth St, N.W., Washington, DC 20036)

Newman, E. B. (1966). Proceedings of the American Psychological Association, Incorporated, for the year 1966. *American Psychologist, 21(12)*, 1125–1153.

Standards for educational and psychological testing. (1985). Washington, DC: American Psychological Association.

INDEX

Index